Lecture Notes in Artificial Intelligence   9427

Subseries of Lecture Notes in Computer Science

More information about this series at http://www.springer.com/series/1244

Maosong Sun · Zhiyuan Liu
Min Zhang · Yang Liu (Eds.)

Chinese Computational Linguistics and Natural Language Processing Based on Naturally Annotated Big Data

14th China National Conference, CCL 2015 and
Third International Symposium, NLP-NABD 2015
Guangzhou, China, November 13–14, 2015
Proceedings

 Springer

Editors
Maosong Sun
Tsinghua University
Beijing
China

Zhiyuan Liu
Tsinghua University
Beijing
China

Min Zhang
Soochow University
Suzhou, Jiangsu
China

Yang Liu
Tsinghua University
Beijing
China

ISSN 0302-9743   ISSN 1611-3349   (electronic)
Lecture Notes in Artificial Intelligence
ISBN 978-3-319-25815-7   ISBN 978-3-319-25816-4   (eBook)
DOI 10.1007/978-3-319-25816-4

Library of Congress Control Number: 2015952054

LNCS Sublibrary: SL7 – Artificial Intelligence

Printed on acid-free paper

Springer International Publishing AG Switzerland is part of Springer Science+Business Media
(www.springer.com)

Preface

Welcome to the proceedings of the 14th China National Conference on Computational Linguistics (14th CCL) and the Third International Symposium on Natural Language Processing Based on Naturally Annotated Big Data (3rd NLP-NABD). The conference was hosted by Guangdong University of Foreign Studies.

CCL is an annual conference (bi-annual before 2013) that started in 1991. It is the flagship conference of the Chinese Information Processing Society (CIPS), which is the largest NLP scholar and expert community in China. CCL is a premier nation-wide forum for disseminating new scholarly and technological work in computational linguistics, with a major emphasis on computer processing of the languages in China such as Mandarin, Tibetan, Mongolian, and Uyghur.

Affiliated with the 14th CCL, the Third International Symposium on Natural Language Processing Based on Naturally Annotated Big Data (NLP-NABD) covered all the NLP topics, with particular focus on methodologies and techniques relating to naturally annotated big data. In contrast to manually annotated data such as treebanks that are constructed for specific NLP tasks, naturally annotated data come into existence through users' normal activities, such as writing, conversation, and interactions on the Web. Although the original purposes of these data typically were unrelated to NLP, they can nonetheless be purposefully exploited by computational linguists to acquire linguistic knowledge. For example, punctuation marks in Chinese text can help word boundaries identification, social tags in social media can provide signals for keyword extraction, and categories listed in Wikipedia can benefit text classification. The natural annotation can be explicit, as in the aforementioned examples, or implicit, as in Hearst patterns (e.g., "Beijing and other cities" implies "Beijing is a city"). This symposium focuses on numerous research challenges ranging from very-large-scale unsupervised/semi-supervised machine leaning (deep learning, for instance) of naturally annotated big data to integration of the learned resources and models with existing handcrafted "core" resources and "core" language computing models. NLP-NABD 2015 was supported by the National Key Basic Research Program of China (i.e., "973" Program) "Theory and Methods for Cyber-Physical-Human Space-Oriented Web Chinese Information Processing" under grant no. 2014CB340500.

The Program Committee selected 115 papers (81 Chinese papers and 34 English papers) out of 283 submissions from China, Hong Kong (region), Singapore, and the USA for publication. The 34 English papers cover the following topics:

- Lexical semantics and ontologies (4)
- Semantics (4)
- Sentiment analysis, opinion mining and text classification (2)
- Machine translation (3)
- Multilinguality in NLP (4)
- Machine learning method for NLP (3)
- Knowledge graph and information extraction (3)

- Discourse, coreference, and pragmatics (1)
- Information retrieval and question answering (3)
- Social computing (2)
- NLP applications (5)

The final program for the 14th CCL and the Third NLP-NABD was the result of a great deal of work by many dedicated colleagues. We want to thank, first of all, the authors who submitted their papers, and thus contributed to the creation of the high-quality program that allowed us to look forward to an exciting joint conference. We are deeply indebted to all the Program Committee members for providing high-quality and insightful reviews under a tight schedule. We are extremely grateful to the sponsors of the conference. Finally, we extend a special word of thanks to all the colleagues of the Organizing Committee and secretariat for their hard work in organizing the conference, and to Springer for their assistance in publishing the proceedings in due time.

We thank the Program and Organizing Committees for helping make the conference successful and we hope the participants enjoy a memorable visit to Guangzhou.

November 2015   *CCL Program Committee Chairs:*
                                                        Maosong Sun
                                                         Keh-Yih Su
                                    CCL Program Committee Co-Chairs:
                                                          Jun Zhao
                                                         Min Zhang
                                                           Heng Ji
                            NLP-NABD Program Committee Chairs:
                                                        Maosong Sun
                                                        Randy Goebel
                                                          Ting Liu

Organization

General Chairs

Bo Zhang   Tsinghua University, China
Ming Li   University of Waterloo, Canada

Program Committee

14th CCL Program Chair

Maosong Sun   Tsinghua University, China
Keh-Yih Su   Academia Sinica

14th CCL Program Co-chairs

Jun Zhao   Institute of Automation, CAS, China
Min Zhang   Soochow University, China
Heng Ji   Rensselaer Polytechnic Institute, USA

14th CCL Area Co-chairs

Linguistics and Cognitive Science

Weidong Zhan   Peking University, China
Hongyin Tao   University of California, Los Angeles, USA

Fundamental Theory and Methods of Computational Linguistics

Wanxiang Che   Harbin Institute of Technology, China
Chunyu Kit   City University of Hong Kong, SAR China

Information Retrieval and Question Answering

Xuanjing Huang   Fudan University, China
Bin Wang   Institute of Information Engineering, CAS, China

Text Classification and Summarization

Tingting He   Central China Normal University, China
Sujian Li   Peking University, China

Knowledge Graph and Information Extraction

Juanzi Li	Tsinghua University, China
Jing Jiang	Singapore Management University, Singapore

Machine Translation

Qun Liu	Dublin City University, Ireland; Institute of Computing Technology, CAS, China
Hao Zhang	Google, USA

Machine Learning Method for NLP

Jun Zhu	Tsinghua University, China
Ming Li	Nanjing University, China

Minority Language Information Processing

Xiaobing Zhao	Minzu University of China, China
Jian-Yun Nie	University of Montreal, Canada

Language Resource and Evaluation

Erhong Yang	Beijing Language and Culture University, China
Qin Lu	The Hong Kong Polytechnic University, SAR China

Social Computing and Sentiment Analysis

Hongfei Lin	Dalian University of Technology, China
Yulan He	Aston University, UK

NLP Applications

Xiaojie Wang	Beijing University of Posts and Telecommunications, China
Hui Zhang	Facebook, USA

14th CCL Technical Committee Members

Rangjia Cai	Qinghai Normal University, China
Dongfeng Cai	Shenyang Aerospace University, China
Baobao Chang	Peking University, China
Qunxiu Chen	Tsinghua University, China
Xiaohe Chen	Nanjing Normal University, China
Xueqi Cheng	Institute of Computing Technology, CAS, China
Key-Sun Choi	KAIST, Korea
Li Deng	Microsoft Research, USA
Alexander Gelbukh	National Polytechnic Institute, Mexico
Josef van Genabith	Dublin City University, Ireland
Randy Goebel	University of Alberta, Canada

Tingting He	Central China Normal University, China
Isahara Hitoshi	Toyohashi University of Technology, Japan
Heyan Huang	Beijing Polytechnic University, China
Xuanjing Huang	Fudan University, China
Donghong Ji	Wuhan University, China
Turgen Ibrahim	Xinjiang University, China
Shiyong Kang	Ludong University, China
Sadao Kurohashi	Kyoto University, Japan
Kiong Lee	ISO TC37, Korea
Hang Li	Huawei, Hong Kong, SAR China
Ru Li	Shanxi University, China
Dekang Lin	Google, USA
Qun Liu	Dublin City University, Ireland; Institute of Computing Technology, CAS, China
Shaoming Liu	Fuji Xerox, Japan
Qin Lu	Polytechnic University of Hong Kong, SAR China
Wolfgang Menzel	University of Hamburg, Germany
Jian-Yun Nie	University of Montreal, Canada
Yanqiu Shao	Beijing Language and Culture University, China
Xiaodong Shi	Xiamen University, China
Rou Song	Beijing Language and Culture University, China
Jian Su	Institute for Infocomm Research, Singapore
Benjamin Ka Yin Tsou	The Hong Kong Institute of Education, SAR China
Haifeng Wang	Baidu, China
Fei Xia	University of Washington, USA
Feiyu Xu	DFKI, Germany
Nianwen Xue	Brandeis University, USA
Erhong Yang	Beijing Language and Culture University, China
Tianfang Yao	Shanghai Jiaotong University, China
Shiwen Yu	Peking University, China
Quan Zhang	Institute of Acoustics, CAS, China
Jun Zhao	Institute of Automation, CAS, China
Guodong Zhou	Soochow University, China
Ming Zhou	Microsoft Research Asia, China
Jingbo Zhu	Northeast University, China
Ping Xue	Research & Technology, the Boeing Company, USA

Third NLP-NABD Program Chairs

Maosong Sun	Tsinghua University, China
Randy Goebel	University of Alberta, USA
Ting Liu	Harbin Institute of Technology, China

Third NLP-NABD Technical Committee Members

Key-Sun Choi	KAIST, Korea
Li Deng	Microsoft Research, USA
Alexander Gelbukh	National Polytechnic Institute, Mexico
Josef van Genabith	Dublin City University, Ireland
Randy Goebel	University of Alberta, Canada
Isahara Hitoshi	Toyohashi University of Technology, Japan
Xuanjing Huang	Fudan University, China
Donghong Ji	Wuhan University, China
Sadao Kurohashi	Kyoto University, Japan
Kiong Lee	ISO TC37, Korea
Hang Li	Huawei, Hong Kong, SAR China
Hongfei Lin	Dalian Polytechnic University, China
Qun Liu	Dublin City University, Ireland; Institute of Computing Technology, CAS, China
Shaoming Liu	Fuji Xerox, Japan
Ting Liu	Harbin Institute of Technology, China
Yang Liu	Tsinghua University, China
Qin Lu	Polytechnic University of Hong Kong, SAR China
Wolfgang Menzel	University of Hamburg, Germany
Hwee Tou Ng	National University of Singapore, Singapore
Jian-Yun Nie	University of Montreal, Canada
Jian Su	Institute for Infocomm Research, Singapore
Zhifang Sui	Peking University, China
Le Sun	Institute of Software, CAS, China
Benjamin Ka Yin Tsou	The Hong Kong Institute of Education, SAR China
Fei Xia	University of Washington, USA
Feiyu Xu	DFKI, Germany
Nianwen Xue	Brandeis University, USA
Jun Zhao	Institute of Automation, CAS, China
Guodong Zhou	Soochow University, China
Ming Zhou	Microsoft Research Asia, China
Ping Xue	Research & Technology, the Boeing Company, USA

14th CCL and Third NLP-NABD Local Arrangements Chair

Shengyi Jiang	Guangdong University of Foreign Studies, China

14th CCL and Third NLP-NABD Local Arrangements Co-chair

Xiaohua Ke	Guangdong University of Foreign Studies, China

14th CCL and Third NLP-NABD System Demonstration Chairs

Jingbo Zhu   Northeast University, China
Ting Liu   Harbin Institute of Technology, China

14th CCL and Third NLP-NABD Publications Chairs

Zhiyuan Liu   Tsinghua University, China
Xin Zhao   Renmin University of China, China

14th CCL and Third NLP-NABD Publicity Chairs

Kang Liu   Institute of Automation, CAS, China
Xianpei Han   Institute of Software, CAS, China

14th CCL and Third NLP-NABD Sponsorship Chair

Yang Liu   Tsinghua University, China

Contents

Machine Translation

Multilinguality in NLP

Machine Learning Method for NLP

Knowledge Graph and Information Extraction

Discourse, Coreference and Pragmatics

Information Retrieval and Question Answering

Social Computing

NLP Applications

Lexical Semantics and Ontologies

Building a Collation Element Table for a Large Chinese Character Set in YES

Xiaoheng Zhang[1(✉)] and Xiaotong Li[2]

[1] Department of Chinese and Bilingual Studies,
Hong Kong Polytechnic University, Hong Kong, China
ctxzhang@polyu.edu.hk
[2] College of International Exchange,
Shenzhen University, Shenzhen, China
sharklxt@aliyun.com

Abstract. YES is a simplified stroke-based method for sorting Chinese characters. It is free from stroke counting and grouping, and thus much faster and more accurate than the traditional method. This paper presents a collation element table built in YES for a large joint Chinese character set covering (a) all 20,902 characters of Unicode CJK Unified Ideographs, (b) all 11,408 characters in the Complete List of Chinese Characters Used by the Media in 2013, (c) all 13,000 plus characters in the latest versions of Xinhua Dictionary(v11) and Contemporary Chinese Dictionary(v6). Of the 20,902 Chinese characters in Unicode, 97.23% have one-to-one relationship with their stroke order codes in YES, comparing with 90.69% of the traditional method. Enhanced with the secondary and tertiary sorting levels of stroke layout and Unicode value, there is a guarantee of one-to-one relationship between the characters and collation elements. The collation element table has been successfully applied to sorting CC-CEDICT, a Chinese-English dictionary of over 112,000 word entries.

Keywords: Chinese characters · Collation · Unicode · YES

1 Introduction

Collation, or determining the sorting order of strings of characters, is a key function in computer systems and a basic need of the human society. Whenever a list of texts—such as the records of a database and the entries of a dictionary—is presented to users, they are likely to want it in a sorted order so that they can easily and reliably find their target words. Collation is so important to computational linguistics that a special standard, i.e. *Unicode Technical Standard #10: Unicode Collation Algorithm* [1], has been developed to support automatic sorting. At the center of the standard is a default collation element table, which usually needs to be customized for different natural languages before real life application.

There are tens of thousands of different characters in the Chinese writing system. Collation of Chinese has been a long time challenge for lexicography. Search for a word in a Chinese dictionary is notoriously time consuming and sometimes frustrating [14, p. 243, 5]. Even a small dictionary may be difficult to use, especially if one does

© Springer International Publishing Switzerland 2015
M. Sun et al. (Eds.): CCL and NLP-NABD 2015, LNAI 9427, pp. 3–14, 2015.
DOI: 10.1007/978-3-319-25816-4_1

not know the exact pronunciation of the target Chinese character and have to rely on the radical method, as evidenced by the following quotation from section How to Use the Dictionary in *Oxford Chinese Mini Dictionary* [18 px]. After a lengthy introduction of the radical collation method, the editors say:

> "… If you have trouble finding the character in the Character Index, first check above or below in the list under that radical, **in case your stroke count was incorrect**. It is best to write the character down as you count, being sure to write it using the proper strokes and stroke order. If you still cannot find it, the character is probably listed under a different radical, and **you will need to start again from the beginning of the process described above, looking under a different radical**. Beginners sometimes find this process **frustrating**, but if you keep trying, it will become easier."

Obviously there is an urgent need for improvement of Chinese collation. The dominant sorting methods for Chinese are Radical (部首法), Pinyin (拼音法), Four-corners (四角号码法) and Stroke-based (笔画法) [14, p. 189–207, 13, p. 67–69). The stroke-based approach is employed by all the other methods: to sort characters of the same pronunciation (homophones) in the phonetic method, to sort the radical list and the characters belonging to a common radical in the radical method, and to sort characters sharing the same code in the four-corner method. That means the stroke-based method is the simplest and most fundamental among them. Improvement of Chinese collation should first consider stroke-based sorting.

YES (or 一二三 in Chinese) is a simplified stroke-based sorting method with better performance than the traditional method. In the following sections, we will introduce YES and its application to the design and implementation of a collation element table of a large Chinese character set.

2   Stroke-Based Collation

The early stroke-based arrangement of Chinese dictionaries merely relies on stroke numbers, and was used as an auxiliary method for the radical system. In the 20th century, it was developed into an independent method by adding stroke order as a second level of sorting [15, p. 107, 17, p. 357).

Strokes (笔画, bǐhuà) are the most basic unit of Chinese writing. A Chinese character is written stroke by stroke in a certain order. For example the standard stroke order of character 福 (good fortune, happiness) is "丶 乛 丨 丶 一 丨 乛一 丨 乛一 丨 一". If we regard it as a sequence of letters, then it can be ordered alphabetically as an English word, provided we have a stroke "alphabet" defining the sequence of different strokes.

Most dictionaries in China classify strokes into 5 categories or groups, each represented by a primary stroke. There are two popular sequences: "丶,一, 丨, 丿, 乛" in Hong Kong and Taiwan, and "一 , 丨, 丿, 丶, 乛" which is the official standard of the Mainland, as shown in Table 1.

Contemporary Chinese Dictionary (现代汉语词典) [4], *Oxford Chinese Dictionary* [2] and many other dictionaries follow the standards by the National Language Commission of China [8, 9]. The basic rules are:

Table 1. The standard 5-categories stroke list

Primary Stroke	Secondary strokes	Name of group
一	╱	Héng 横 (horizontal)
丨	亅	Shù 竖 (vertical)
丿		Piě 撇 (left falling)
丶	╲	Diǎn 点 (dot)
→	乛, ㄴ, 〈, ...	Zhé 折 (bending)

(1) Sort the characters by their number of strokes in ascending order, i.e. all the characters of one stroke are put before two-stroke characters, followed by three-stroke characters, and so on.

(2) Characters of the same number of strokes are arranged by their first stroke categories in the order of Table 1. If they belong to the same category, then check the second strokes, and so on.

3 The YES Collation Method

Briefly speaking, the YES Chinese character collation method is formed by eliminating stroke counting and grouping from the traditional stroke-based method. Arranging Chinese in YES order is similar to arranging English in alphabetic order, if we consider the stroke sequence of a Chinese character as the letter sequence of an English word.

Two Chinese characters are sorted by their first stroke positions in the YES stroke alphabet (Table 2). If the first strokes are the same, then compare the second strokes, and so on. For example, the different characters in "一二三排检法|一二三排檢法" (the YES Sorting Method) are sorted as:

一 (一)
二 (一一)
三 (一一一)
檢 (一丨丿丶丿╲一丨乛一丨乛一丿丶丿丶)
检 (一丨丿丶丿╲一丶丶丿一)
排 (一丿╱丨一一一丨一一一)
法 (丶丶╱一丨一╱丶)

In the rare cases of more than one glyph or stroke order for a Chinese character, YES follows the standards of the National Language Commission of China [7, 8, 11].

Words of multiple characters are sorted by their first characters in YES order. If the first characters are the same, then check the second characters, and so on. Non-Chinese characters appear after Chinese characters in alphabetical/Unicode order. For example,

覺
覺醒
觉
觉醒
觉悟
B超
T恤

Table 2. The YES stroke alphabet

Stroke	Stroke Name	Example Characters
㇐	横	十/七
㇕	横折竖	口 达 贯/敢 為
㇅	横折竖折横	凹 卍
㇎	横折竖折横折竖	凸 㠯
㇡	横折竖折横折竖钩	乃/杨
㇋	横折竖折横折撇	及 延
㇊	横折竖折提	计 颓 鸠
㇍	横折竖弯横	朵 投
㇈ (乙)	横折竖弯横钩	几 九/艺 亿
㇆	横折竖钩	同 却 母 仓 羽/也
㇇ (乛)	横折撇	又 之/令 了/买 宝
㇌	横折撇折撇钩	阳 部
㇠	横折捺钩	飞 风 执
㇀	提	堆 打/江
㇑	竖	中/五
㇗	竖折横	山/母 乐/发 降/车
㇞	竖折横折竖	鼎 卐 亞 吳
㇉	竖折横折竖钩	马 与 钙/号 弓
ㄣ	竖折横折撇	专/奊/矢
㇙	竖折提	长 鼠 以 瓦 收 岭
㇄	竖弯横	四 西 朮
㇟	竖弯横钩	己 匕 电 心 乱
㇚	竖钩	小 水 了
㇒	撇	千/人/月
㇜	撇折提	公 离 红 乡 亥
㇛	撇折点	女 巡
㇁ (㇢)	撇钩	犹 家/乄
㇔ (ˊ)	点	主 丸/火 刃 然
㇏ (○)	捺	八边/○
㇂	捺钩	代 我

The YES stroke alphabet is based on the standards of the Standard Bending Strokes of GB13000.1 Character Set [10] and the Unicode CJK Strokes [16]. There are totally 30 strokes, sorted by the standard basic strokes sequence of "横 (一) 提 (㇀) 竖 (丨) 撇 (丿) 点 (丶) 捺 (㇏)" and bending points sequence of "折 弯 钩" [21].

The Chinese name of the sorting method, i.e. "一二三", are the first three characters in YES order. The English name "YES" is the abbreviation of the Chinese name's Pinyin (Yī Èr Sān).

Table 3 presents the "code:characters" distribution of the 20,902 Chinese characters of GB13000.1 (the same character set as the Unicode CJK Unified Ideographs primary character set) in the traditional stroke-based method and in YES. YES performs much better than the traditional method. 97.23% of the characters (or 20,324 out of 20,902) have one-to-one relationship with their stroke order codes in YES, much higher than the 90.69% of the traditional method. The maximum number of characters sharing one code is 9 in the traditional method, and 4 in YES. In the traditional method the nine characters of "夕久夂夊么勺凡丸及" share the five-category stroke order of 354 [9, p. 8]. In YES, they are further classified into 6 groups: 及/凡丸/勺/夕/夊夂久/么.

Details of the YES collation can be found in [20].

Table 3. Code:characters distribution of GB13000.1 characters in traditional and YES sorting

	1:1	1:2	1:3	1:4	1:5	1:6	1:7	1:8	1:9	Total
Codes (Traditional)	18956	756	85	25	9	3	1	0	1	19836
Characters (Traditional)	18956	1512	255	100	45	18	7	0	9	20902
Percentage (Traditional)	90.69%	7.23%	1.22%	0.48%	0.22%	0.09%	0.03%	0.00%	0.04%	100%
Codes (YES)	20324	258	14	5						20601
Characters (YES)	20324	516	42	20						20902
Percentage (YES)	97.23%	2.47%	0.20%	0.10%	0.00%	0.00%	0.00%	0.00%	0.00%	100%

4 Further Improvement of YES

There still exists a handful of stroke orders shared by two or more Chinese characters. For example, 犬 (dog) and 太 (too (much)) have the same stroke order of "一 丿 乀 丶". Among the 20,902 characters of the GB13000.1 character set, 578 or 2.77% do not have their unique stroke orders. The maximum number of characters sharing one stroke order is 4, totally 5 groups of them, as shown in Table 4.

Table 4. Five groups of 4 characters sharing a stroke order in GB13000.1

Characters	Stroke order
甲甲叶申	丨 一 一 丨
另另叨叻	丨 一 一 丿
叭叺央史	丨 一 一 丿 乀
父从父爻	丿 丶 丿 乀
八人乂入	丿 乀

Even if the four characters are randomly sorted in the group, we can still easily find a character in a one-tier search. However, an ideal collation method should be "total" (not partial), or be capable to arrange all characters into a reasonable order in which every character has its one and only one position.

When two characters have the same stroke order, their difference is in the appearance and layout of strokes in the 2-dimentional block area of a Chinese character, including each stroke's position, size and orientation. For example, the difference between character 犬 and 太 is in the position of their last stroke 乀, the difference between 口 and 囗 are in their sizes, and the 丿 strokes in 千人 have difference in orientation. In other words, when the position, size and orientation of each stroke in the Chinese character are decided, the form of the whole character is decided. And these factors can be accurately defined by the positions of the starting point and ending point of a stroke. Though the absolute positions of the points can be detected by the computer easily, it is unlikely to be totally feasible for human's eyes. Hence it seems preferable to focus on the character distinguishing differences easily recognizable by the reader. For example, the distinguishing difference between character 犬 and 太 is in the position of their last stroke 乀, higher in 犬 than in 太. According to the rule of "top-to-down", 犬 is put before 太. If the two strokes are at the same height, than consider the difference in horizontal positions. For example, characters 人入八乂 share the stroke order of "丿 乀". The starting point of " 丿 " in 入 is distinguishingly lower than the others, thus 入 is put at the end. 人八乂 are sorted according to the horizontal positions of the starting points of their first strokes (丿) in a left-to-right order, resulting in the reasonable order of 八人乂入.

On the other hand, the computer can be over accurate. For example, the computer can easily detect a difference in height of the 一 (horizontal) stroke in 犬太, but moving stoke 一 in 犬 up to the height of its counterpart in 太 does not change the character's meaning. However, if we move the dot down to the position of its counterpart in 太, then 犬 becomes 太. Hence, the difference in the position of the dot strokes is character distinguishing between 犬 and 太, while the difference in the positions of stroke 一 is not character distinguishing and not easily recognizable by human's eyes.

Therefore, we add a second-level sorting rule to YES as follows:

If two Chinese characters are of the same stroke order, then find their first (according to the stroke order) pair of character distinguishing strokes and put the character with a higher or lefter stroke before the other character. More accurately, If the starting points of the two corresponding strokes are in different height, then put the character with a higher stroke starting point before the other character, else if the ending points are in different height, then put the character with a higher stroke ending point before the other character, else if the starting points are in different horizontal positions, then put the character with a comparatively left stroke starting point before the other character, else put the character with a left stroke ending point before the other character.

For example, 圡 and 坴 have the same stroke order of "一 | 一". The first strokes (the upper 一) in both characters are of similar height, but horizontally the stroke starting point is comparatively more left in 坴 than in 圡, as shown in Fig. 1. Hence, 坴 is put before 圡.

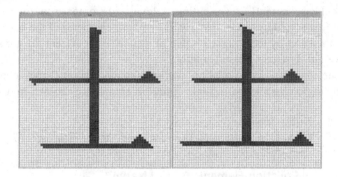

Fig. 1. Two characters in font SimSun

An advantage of considering the vertical position of the ending points before the horizontal positions of the starting points is two-fold: easier to operate and putting the character in up-down (畐) structure before the character in left-right (田) structure. For example 炎炏 (丶 丿 丿 丶 丶 丿 丿 乀), the starting point of the first stroke 丶 is lower in 炏 than in 炎, hence 炏 is put after 炎. In characters 甼町 (| ㄱ一 | 一一 丿), the starting points of the first stroke | are of similar height, if we compare the horizontal positions of the starting points first, it is more left in 町 than in 甼, and 町 is put before 甼. The sorting result is

炎炏, 町甼

In the first pair, the character in up-down (畐) structure is before the character in left-right (田) structure. In the second pair, the character in up-down (畐) structure is after the character in left-right (田) structure.

If we compare the vertical positions of the ending points right after the vertical positions of the starting points, the sorting is

炎炊, 甼町.

In both cases, the character in up-down (⊟) structure is before the character in left-right (⊞) structure, which is a more consistent result.

Even when the top stroke is heng2 (⼀) in both characters, it is still reasonable to put the character in up-down (⊟) structure before the character in left-right (⊞) structure. Because the top point is the top of the triangle (Fig. 1) at the end of stroke ⼀ (we use the standard font of SimSun 宋体), when the upper component of the character is stretched downward, the starting point of stroke héng 横 (一) becomes proportionally lower. And there is space around the character, which will also make the left component lower than the upper component, for instance 泵砕 (一 丿 丨 乛一 丿 フ 丿 乀).

5 Design of the Collation Element Table

5.1 The Unicode Default Collation Element Table

The Unicode default collation element table is Latin letters oriented [1]. A typical collation element consists of 3 weight values in hexadecimal, in the format of "[.base character.accent.case/variant]" representing 3 levels of comparison for sorting. The characters are first sorted by the weight 1 value of base character, if the base characters are the same, then sort by the weight 2 value of accent, if the accent are the same, then sort by the weight 3 value of case/variant.

Most of the mappings in a collation element table are simple: they consist of the mapping of a single character to a single collation element, as shown in Table 5.

Table 5. A collation element table with simple mapping

Character	Collation Element	Name
0300 " ` "	[.0000.0021.0002]	COMBINING GRAVE ACCENT
0061 "a"	[.06D9.0020.0002]	LATIN SMALL LETTER A
0062 "b"	[.06EE.0020.0002]	LATIN SMALL LETTER B
0063 "c"	[.0706.0020.0002]	LATIN SMALL LETTER C
0043 "C"	[.0706.0020.0008]	LATIN CAPITAL LETTER C

The default collation element values for Chinese characters are generated from the Unicode code point. The Unicode code point order is realized by dividing the CJK characters into several charts, each roughly sorted by the Kangxi Radical order. Hence, very cumbersome for human usage.

Collation is not code point (binary) order. The only way to get the linguistically-correct order is to use a language-sensitive collation, not a binary ordering [1] (Section 1.8). Hence we need a collation element table tailored-made for the Chinese language.

5.2   Design of the Chinese Collation Element Table

Our design of a Chinese collation element table is in similar format of the Unicode default table, as shown in Table 6.

Table 6. A Chinese collation element table in YES

Character	Collation Element	Stroke Order
臧	[.177E.1.81E7]	一 丿 乚 一 丿 一 丨 フ 一 丨 乚 乀 丿 丶
鳴	[.177F.1.9D04]	一 丿 乚 乚 丿 丨 フ 一 一 一 フ 丶 丶 丶 丶
兀	[.1780.1.5140]	一 丿 乚
兀	[.1780.1.FA0C]	一 丿 乚
尢	[.1780.2.5C22]	一 丿 乚

Where a collation element consists of a primary weight of stroke order, followed by a second weight of stroke layout, followed by a third weight of Unicode.

The characters are first sorted by the primary weight of stroke orders according to the YES stroke alphabet, putting 臧 before 鳴 before 兀兀尢. Characters 兀兀尢 share the stoke order of 一 丿 乚, and are arranged by the secondary weight of stroke layout. The first stroke 一 in 兀兀 is higher than in 尢, hence兀兀 come before 尢.

There are some duplicate characters in Unicode [19]. To make sure that every Unicode character can be sorted properly on the computer, we have added Unicode code point as the third-level weight. For example, 兀 (5140) and 兀 (FA0C) are in the same form, and are sorted by their Unicode values, resulting in 兀 (5140) before 兀 (FA0C). Such a design guarantees a strict one-to-one relationship between characters and collation elements.

6   Experiment Results and Analysis

We have built a collation element table for a large joint Chinese character set covering:

- All of the 20,902 characters in Unicode CJK Unified Ideographs (same as the national standard GB13000.1 Character Set);
- All 11,408 characters in the Complete List of Chinese Characters Used by the Media in 2013 (2013年度媒体用字总表) [12];
- All 13,000-plus characters in the latest version of the Xinhua Chinese Characters Dictionary [3];
- All 13,000-plus characters in the latest version of the Contemporary Chinese Dictionary [4].

There are totally 21,976 Chinese characters in the joint character set, among which

- 21,335 characters have distinctive stroke orders from others
- 612 characters have similar stroke orders as one or more other characters but in different shapes
- 29 characters are of the same shapes (or forms) as one or more other characters but have different Unicode code points.

Table 7 presents the first 21 characters with similar stroke orders in the collection elements table.

Table 7. The first 21 characters with similar stroke orders

Character	Collation Element	Stroke Order
王	[.60.1.738B]	一 一 丨 一
㞷	[.60.2.9FB6]	一 一 丨 一
㺩	[.A4.1.738A]	一 一 丨 一 丶
玉	[.A4.2.7389]	一 一 丨 一 丶
珈	[.11E.1.73C8]	一 一 丨 丿 フ 丿 丨 フ 一
㧟	[.11E.2.73BF]	一 一 丨 丿 フ 丿 丨 フ 一
㺾	[.13A.1.73BE]	一 一 丨 丿 丨 フ 一 一 丨
珅	[.13A.2.73C5]	一 一 丨 丿 丨 フ 一 一 丨
末	[.217.1.672B]	一 一 丨 丿 丶
未	[.217.2.672A]	一 一 丨 丿 丶
亐	[.21C.1.4E90]	一 一 乚
亏	[.21C.2.4E8F]	一 一 乚
于	[.21F.1.4E8E]	一 一 丨
亍	[.21F.2.4E8D]	一 一 丨
开	[.228.1.5F00]	一 一 丿 丨
亓	[.228.2.4E93]	一 一 丿 丨
井	[.228.3.4E95]	一 一 丿 丨
无	[.23B.1.65E0]	一 一 丿 乚
元	[.23B.2.5143]	一 一 丿 乚
天	[.255.1.5929]	一 一 丿 丶
夫	[.255.2.592B]	一 一 丿 丶

There is a one-to-one relationship between the characters and collation elements in the collation table, i.e., each character has one and only one distinctive collation element.

7   Conclusion and Further Development

Chinese collation has been a long-time challenge to lexicography and natural language processing. This paper introduces the YES stroke-based collation method and its application to the design and implementation of a user-friendly collation element table to support automatic Chinese sorting. The new method is significantly simpler and more accurate than the traditional approaches. According to our experiment on 20,902 Chinese characters in Unicode, 97.23% of the characters have one-to-one relationship with their stroke order codes in YES, comparing with 90.69% of the traditional method. The maximum number of characters sharing one code is 9 in the traditional method, and 4 in YES.

The collation element table is based on the Unicode Standard and covers a large number of 21,976 Chinese characters. With the three sorting levels of stroke order, stroke layout and Unicode value, there is a guarantee of one-to-one relationship between the characters and collation elements.

The collation table has been successfully employed to sort all 112,178 word entries in CC-CEDICT, a large Chinese-English dictionary downloadable from the Web [6]. A trial version YES-CEDICT Chinese Dictionary is also on the Web for free download [22, 23]. And it is our intention to further develop the collation element table to cover all the 70,000 plus Chinese characters in Unicode.

However there are a number of tricky issues. For example, 鞄鞄, 坦坦 and 旦且. A close look will find the heights of first stroke | shu5 in the components of 旦 and 且 are not consistent: higher in 鞄 than in 鞄, lower in 坦 than in 坦, and similar in 旦 and 且. Another example, the starting point of the left stroke in 八 is slightly lower than the right stroke. But the difference is usually ignored linguistically. Moving the left stroke up to the level of the right stroke does not change the character into another one. A more interesting case. The first stroke | in 吅吕 (NSimSun 12p) are of similar height. When we down size the characters to 吅吕 (NSimSun 10p), the first stroke is clearly lower in 吅. The situation in 旱旰 and 旱旰 is similar. These inconsistencies have brought inconvenience to language processing, however YES can consistently put the top-down structure character before the left-right structure character in all cases.

On the whole, the glyphs need to be more consistent. And there is a need for an optimal balance between the glyph, the computer and people. Fortunately, the above-mentioned tricky issues only involve the secondary sorting level of stroke layout, hence unlikely to bring serious inconvenience to the application of YES.

Acknowledgements. The project has been partially supported by a University research fund (Account Code: 4-ZZEW). The authors are also very grateful to the three anonymous reviewers, whose valuable comments played an important role in the revision of the paper.

References

1. Davis, M. Whistler, K., Scherer, M.: Unicode Technical Standard #10: Unicode Collation Algorithm, version 8.0 (2015). http://www.unicode.org/reports/tr10/
2. Kleeman, J., Yu, H. (eds.): The Oxford Chinese Dictionary. Oxford University Press, Oxford (2010)

3. Linguistic Institute of the Chinese Academy of Social Sciences: Xinhua Dictionary (Xinhua Zidian, 新华字典), 11th edn. The Commercial Press, Beijing (2011)
4. Linguistic Institute of the Chinese Academy of Social Sciences: Contemporary Chinese Dictionary (Xiandai Hanyu Cidian, 现代汉语词典), 6th edn. The Commercial Press, Beijing (2012)
5. Mair, V.H.: The need for an alphabetically arranged general usage dictionary of Mandarin Chinese: a review article of some recent dictionaries and current lexicographical projects. Sino-Platonic Papers **1**, 1–31 (1986)
6. MDBG: CC-CEDICT Chinese to English Dictionary (2015). http://www.mdbg.net/chindict/chindict.php?page=cedict (Downloaded on 31 January 2015)
7. National Language Commission of China (国家语委): Standard Stroke Order of Commonly-Used Characters of Modern Chinese (现代汉语通用字笔顺规范). Language & Culture Press (语文出版社), Beijing (1997)
8. National Language Commission of China (国家语委): The Standard Stroke Order of the GB13000.1 Character Set (GB13000.1 字符集汉字笔顺规范). Shanghai Education Press (上海教育出版社), Shanghai (1999)
9. National Language Commission of China (国家语委): The Standard (Stroke-Based) Order of the GB13000.1 Character Set (GB13000.1字符集汉字字序(笔画序)规范). Shanghai Education Press, Shanghai (2000)
10. National Language Commission of China (国家语委): The Standard Bending Strokes of GB13000.1 Character Set (GB13000.1字符集汉字折笔规范). Language & Culture Press, Beijing (2001)
11. National Language Commission of China (国家语委): Standard List of Commonly-Used Chinese Characters (通用规范汉字表). Language & Culture Press, Beijing (2013)
12. National Language Commission of China (国家语委): Language Situation in China: 2014. (中国语言生活状况报告(2014)). Commercial Press, Beijing (2014)
13. Norman, J.: Chinese. Cambridge University Press, Cambridge (1988)
14. Su, P.: Essentials of Modern Chinese Characters (现代汉字学刚要), 3rd edn. Commercial Press, Beijing (2014)
15. Sun, C.: Chinese: A Linguistic Introduction. Cambridge University Press, Cambridge (2006). (Ch. 5 Chinese writing)
16. The Unicode Consortium: The Unicode Standard, Version 8.0. The Unicode Consortium, Mountain View, CA (2015). (http://www.unicode.org/versions/Unicode8.0.0/)
17. Yong, H., Luo, Z., Zhang, X.: Chinese Dictionaries: Three Millennia. Shanghai Foreign Language Education Press, Shanghai (2010)
18. Yuan, B., Church, S.K.: Oxford Chinese Mini Dictionary, 2nd edn. Oxford University Press, New York (2008)
19. Zhang, X.: Duplicate encoding of Chinese characters (中文的同形异码字问题). J. Chin. Inf. Process. **4**(29), 233–240 (2015)
20. Zhang, X., Li, X.: Handbook of the YES Stroke-Based Sorting Method for Chinese Characters (一二三笔顺检字手册). Language & Culture Press, Beijing (2013)
21. Zhang, X., Li, X.: Integration and optimization of standard Chinese stroke lists (标准笔形表的整合与优化). In: Li, X., Jia, Y., Xu, J. (eds.) Digital Teaching of Chinese Language 2014 (数字化汉语教学 2014), pp. 200–208. Tsinghua University Press, Beijing (2014)
22. Zhang, X., Li, X., Lun, C.: The YES-CEDICT Chinese Dictionary (一二三汉英大词典, Trial Edition, Sorted by Simplified Chinese). J. Mod. Chin. Lang. Edu. (中文教学现代化学报), **4**(1) June 2015. (http://xuebao.eblcu.com/)
23. Zhang, X., Li, X., Lun, C.: The YES-CEDICT Chinese Dictionary (一二三漢英大詞典, Trial Edition, Sorted by Traditional Chinese). J. Mod. Chin. Lang. Edu. (中文教学现代化学报), **4**(1) June 2015. (http://xuebao.eblcu.com/)

Improved Learning of Chinese Word Embeddings with Semantic Knowledge

Liner Yang[1]([✉]) and Maosong Sun[1,2]

[1] Department of Computer Science and Technology,
State Key Lab on Intelligent Technology and Systems,
National Lab for Information Science and Technology,
Tsinghua University, Beijing 100084, China
lineryang@gmail.com
[2] Jiangsu Collaborative Innovation Center for Language Ability,
Jiangsu Normal University, Xuzhou 221009, China
sms@tsinghua.edu.cn

Abstract. While previous studies show that modeling the minimum meaning-bearing units (characters or morphemes) benefits learning vector representations of words, they ignore the semantic dependencies across these units when deriving word vectors. In this work, we propose to improve the learning of Chinese word embeddings by exploiting semantic knowledge. The basic idea is to take the semantic knowledge about words and their component characters into account when designing composition functions. Experiments show that our approach outperforms two strong baselines on word similarity, word analogy, and document classification tasks.

Keywords: Word embeddings · CBOW · Semantic knowledge

1 Introduction

Distributed word representations, also known as word embeddings, have proven to be effective in capturing both semantic and syntactic regularities in language [1,6,13,14,16]. These word embeddings have benefited a range of natural language processing (NLP) tasks, including named-entity recognition [5], word sense disambiguation [3], syntactic parsing [17] and sentiment analysis [18].

While early approaches treat words as the basic unit for learning distributed representations from unlabeled data (e.g., [13,19]), a number of researchers have demonstrated the usefulness of exploiting the internal structure of words and modeling the minimum meaning-bearing units, such as morphemes in English or characters in Chinese [2,4,10]. Luong et al. [10] propose a recursive neural network (RNN) model to encode morphological structure of words. Botha and Blunsom [2] introduce a log-bilinear model which uses addition as composition function to derive word vectors from morpheme vectors. Chen et al. [4] extend their idea and present a character-enhanced word embedding (CWE) model.

© Springer International Publishing Switzerland 2015
M. Sun et al. (Eds.): CCL and NLP-NABD 2015, LNAI 9427, pp. 15–25, 2015.
DOI: 10.1007/978-3-319-25816-4_2

These morpheme- and character-based models significantly outperform the original word-based models in a variety of tasks.

We believe there is still a room to improve word embeddings by considering the intricate dependencies between the minimum meaning-bearing units rather than simply taking addition as composition function when deriving word vectors. For example, the ways how characters interact to determine the meaning of a word are significantly different between two words "远眺 (overlook)" and "村落 (villages)". Instead of simply adding the vectors of two characters, our intuition is that the semantic relations between characters should be modeled to better learn distributed representations of Chinese words. In this work, we propose to exploit semantic knowledge to improve the learning of distributed representations of Chinese words. Based on semantic categories and relations derived from Tongyi Cilin, a Chinese semantic thesaurus, we design new composition functions to compute word vectors from character vectors. Experiments on word similarity, word analogy, and documentation classification tasks show that our approach significantly outperforms the state-of-the-art baseline methods.

2   Background

2.1   The CBOW Model

The continuous bag-of-words (CBOW) model [12] is a recently proposed framework for learning continuous word representations based on the distributional hypothesis. In the model, each word $w \in W$ is associated with vector $v_w \in \mathbb{R}^d$, where W is the word vocabulary and d is the vector dimension. The entries in the vectors are treated as parameters to be learned. Specifically, we learn these parameters values so as to maximize the log likelihood of each token given its context:

$$L(\theta) = \frac{1}{N} \sum_{i=1}^{N} \log p(w_i | w_{i-k}^{i+k})$$ (1)

where N is the size of corpus and w_{i-k}^{i+k} is the set of words in the window of size k centered at w_i (w_i excluded). The CBOW model formulates the probability $p(w_i | w_{i-k}^{i+k})$ using a softmax function as follows:

$$p(w_i | w_{i-k}^{i+k}) = \frac{\exp\left(v_{w_i}' \cdot \sum_{-k \leq j \leq k, j \neq 0} v_{w_{i+j}}\right)}{\sum_{w \in W} \exp\left(v_w' \cdot \sum_{-k \leq j \leq k, j \neq 0} v_{w_{i+j}}\right)}$$ (2)

where v_w and v_w' represent the input and output vectors of the word w respectively. In order to learn model efficiently, the techniques of hierarchical softmax and negative sampling are used [13]. One key limitation of the CBOW model is that it treats each word as the basic unit and fails to capture the internal structure of words. Therefore, some morphological-based methods have been proposed, for example Chen et al. [4].

2.2   The CWE Model

To the best of our knowledge, the closest work to ours for learning Chinese word embeddings is character-enhanced word embedding (CWE) model [4], which learns character and word embeddings jointly. The key idea of the model is to represent the word with its surface form itself and its component characters as follows:

$$v_{w_i} = v_{w_i}^f + \frac{1}{n_i} \sum_{j=1}^{n_i} v_{c_j^i}^f \qquad (3)$$

where $v_{w_i}^f$ is the surface form word vectors, $v_{c_j^i}^f$ is the character vector, n_i is the number of characters in word w_i and c_j^i is the j-th character in word w_i. They use the addition operation for simplicity. This is a principled way of handling new words, we can get the vector of a new word by adding vectors of its component characters. Our work does not simply add vectors of characters, but rather combines them using more linguistically-motivated composition functions.

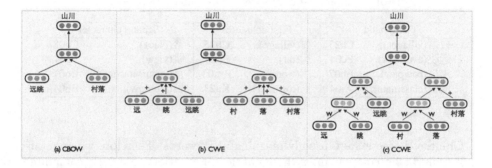

Fig. 1. The architectures of (a) continuous bag-of-words (CBOW) model, (b) character-enhanced word embeddings (CWE) model and (c) compositional Chinese word embeddings (CCWE) model. Here "远眺 (overlook) 山川 (mountains) 村落 (villages)" is a word sequence. The word "远眺 (overlook)" is composed of characters "远 (far)" and "眺 (view)", and the word "村落 (villages)" is composed of characters "村 (village)" and "落 (place)".

3   Our Models

The way how characters are composed to form the meaning of a word is far more intricate than addition. Thus, we propose to learn different compositional functions for different semantic relations of words and their characters. In this paper, we use a semantic formation corpus to identify the semantic relation of words and propose two novel models for learning compositional functions as well as word representations.

In this section, we first describe the semantic formation corpus as they serve as the basis of our model. We then introduce a compositional Chinese word embeddings (CCWE) using semantic category and semantic relations to learn word embeddings and compositional functions. Figure 1(c) shows the overview of our proposed model. Finally, we provide complexity analysis about our model and some baseline models.

3.1 Semantic Formation Lexicon

The Tongyici Cilin [11], a Chinese thesaurus, is adopted in this paper that contains 12 main categories labeled "A-L", 96 middle categories labeled with lower case letters and 1,506 subcategories labeled with numbers. Each small category consists of a group of synonyms that have the same or similar meaning. For example, under the major category "B", the middle category "Bh" groups all words that refer to "plant". Under the middle category "Bh", the subcategory "Bh02" groups all words that refer to flower, e.g., "兰花 (orchid)".

Table 1. Examples of annotated disyllabic compounds.

Compound		First character		Second character	
村落(villages),	Cb25	村(village),	Cb25	落(place),	Cb08
远眺(overlook),	Fc04	远(far),	Eb21	眺(view),	Fc04
木瓜(pawpaw),	Bh07	木(wood),	Bm03	瓜(cucurbitaceae),	Bh07
同窗(classmate),	Aj04	同(together),	Ka23	窗(window),	Bn04

Chinese characters are usually meaningful in words. Therefore we annotate 52,362 disyllabic compounds with semantic information, in which compound and component characters are appended with semantic categories, as shown in Table 1. In Table 1, "Cb25" is the semantic category of compound "村落 (villages)" which is composed of character "村 (village)" with semantic category "Cb25" and character "落 (place)" with semantic category "Cb08". Although Chinese characters are highly ambiguous, i.e. having more than one semantic category, the semantic category of the character in a word is determined.

3.2 The CCWE Model

As illustrated in Fig. 1(c), the word vectors are derived from their component character vectors. The word vector v_{w_i} is constructed by character vector $v_{c_j^i}^f$ and the surface form word vector $v_{w_i}^f$ as follows:

$$v_{w_i} = v_{w_i}^f + \frac{1}{n_i} \sum_{j=1}^{n_i} h_j^t \odot v_{c_j^i}^f \tag{4}$$

where $h_j^t \in \mathbb{R}^{d \times 1}$ are tag-specific weight vectors[1] and $\odot$ denotes element-wise multiplication. This forms the basis of our CCWE model with $\theta = \{h_j^t, v_{w_i}^f, v_{c_j^i}^f\}$ being parameters to be learned.

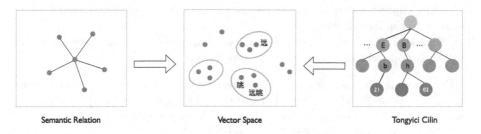

Semantic Relation   Vector Space   Tongyici Cilin

Fig. 2. Overview of our models which leverage semantic category and semantic relation information to improve the quality of word representations.

It is very important to define tag c which we will use to incorporate semantic knowledge. In this paper, we propose two different tags, i.e. categorical tags and relational tags.

Category-Based Model. According to the right part of Fig. 2, semantic category knowledge encodes the semantic properties of words, from which we can group similar words according to their attributes. Then we may require the representations of words that belong to the same semantic category to be close to each other. Therefore, we give the definition of tag $t \triangleq (s, p)$, where $s \in S$, S is the semantic category sets and $p \subset \{B, E\}$, B, E corresponding to the position of character in a word, i.e. Begin and End.

Therefore, we replace tag t in Eq. (4) with (s, p). This gives the new representation of the word w:

$$e_{w_i} = e_{w_i}^f + \frac{1}{n_i} \sum_{j=1}^{n_i} h_j^{(s,p)} \odot e_{c_j^i}^f \tag{5}$$

We call this model category-based model and denote this category-based model as C-CCWE for ease of reference.

Relation-based Model. We first give the definition of semantic relation knowledge.

Definition 1 (Semantic Relation). *Semantic relation r indicates which character's meanings is closer to word meanings, where $r \in R$, R is the set of semantic relationships.*

---

[1] We use tag-specific weight vectors rather than weight matrices, as the vLBL model [14] does, for significantly faster training. This has been discussed by Mnih and Teh [15].

Since we only take disyllabic compounds into consideration, we divide r into three main types:

1. Beginning character biased, which means that the meaning of first character is closer to the meaning of word.
2. Ending character biased, which means that the meaning of last character is closer to the meaning of word.
3. Unbiased, which means that either of two characters semantic distance to the word is approximate or the word is non-compositional.

For example, the meaning of "远眺 (overlook)" should be closer to character "眺 (view)" than "远 (far)", we label the (r, p) of "远眺 (overlook)" as "ending character biased", where p is also position of character in a word.

Similarly, we replace tag t in Eq. (4) with (r, p):

$$e_{w_i} = e_{w_i}^f + \frac{1}{n_i} \sum_{j=1}^{n_i} h_j^{(r,p)} \odot e_{c_j^i}^f \tag{6}$$

We call this model relation-based model and denote this relation-based model as R-CCWE for ease of reference.

3.3   Optimization

In this paper, the proposed compositional Chinese word embeddings (CCWE) are learned using stochastic gradient descent (SGD) algorithm.

3.4   Complexity Analysis

We now analyze model complexities of the CBOW, CWE, C-CCWE and R-CCWE models.

Table 2 shows the complexity of model parameters of various models. In the table, the dimension of vector is d, the word vocabulary size is $|W|$, the character vocabulary size is $|C|$, the semantic category set size is $|S|$ and the semantic relation size is $|R|$. The CBOW window size is $2k$, the corpus size is N, the average number of characters of each word is n, and the computational complexity of negative sampling and hierarchical softmax for each target word is f.

Table 2. Model complexities.

Model	Model parameters	Computational complexity
CBOW	$|W|d$	$2kNf$
CWE	$(|W| + |C|)d$	$2kN(f + n)$
C-CCWE	$(|W| + |C| + |S|)d$	$2kN(f + n)$
R-CCWE	$(|W| + |C| + |R|)d$	$2kN(f + n)$

From the complexity analysis, we can observe that, compared with CWE, the computational complexity of CCWE does not increase and the CCWE only requires a little more parameters for saving weight vectors (note that $|S| \ll |W|$). In our experiment, we set $|S| = 1000$ and $|R| = 3$.

4 Experiments

In this section, we first describe our experimental settings, including the datasets and baseline methods. Then we compare our models with baseline methods on three tasks, *i.e.*, word similarity, word analogy, and document classification.

4.1 Experimental Settings

We use a text corpus with news articles from *The People's Daily* for learning word embeddings, which is also used by Chen et al. [4]. The corpus in total has about 31 million words. The word vocabulary size is 105 thousand and the character vocabulary size is 6 thousand.

Following the parameter settings in Chen et al. [4], the context window size is 5 and the dimension of word vector is 200. For training model we use hierarchical softmax and also adopt the same linear learning rate strategy described in [13], where the initial learning rate is 0.05.

4.2 Word Similarity

In this task, each model is required to compute semantic relatedness of given word pairs. The correlations between results of models and human judgements are reported as the model performance.

In this paper, we evaluate the word vectors with semantic similarity dataset provided by organizers of SemEval-2012 Task 4 [7]. This dataset contains 296 Chinese word pairs with similarity scores estimated by humans and the words in 60 word pairs have appeared less than 100 times. We compute the Spearman correlation between relatedness scores from a model and the human judgements for comparison. The relatedness score of two words are computed via cosine similarity of word vectors.

Table 3. Evaluation results on wordsim-296 ($\rho \times 100$).

Method	wordsim-296	
	60 pairs	296 pairs
CBOW	55.24	60.89
CWE	60.07	62.13
C-CCWE	62.30	63.46
R-CCWE	**63.03**	**65.17**

The evaluation results of CCWE and baseline methods on wordsim-296 are shown in Table 3. From the evaluation results, we observe that: CCWE and its extensions all significantly outperform baseline methods on both 60 word pairs and 296 word pairs.

4.3 Word Analogy

The word analogy task is introduced by [12] to quantitatively evaluate the linguistic regularities between pairs of word representations. The task consists of question like "男人 (man) is to 女人 (woman) as 父亲 (father) to as ___ ", where as ___ is missing and must be predicted from the entire vocabulary. To answer such question, we need to find a word x such that its vector x is close to vec(女人 − vec(男人) + vec(父亲) according to the cosine similarity. The question is judged as correctly answered only if x is exactly the answer in the evaluation set. The evaluation metric for this task is the percentage of questions answered correctly.

We use Chinese analogy dataset from [4]. The dataset contains 1,124 analogies and 3 analogy types: (1) capitals of countries (687 groups); (2) states/provinces of cities (175 groups); and (3) family words (240 groups).

Table 4 shows the results of word analogy. The R-CCWE method outperforms C-CCWE methods and performs significantly better than all baseline methods.

Table 4. Evaluation accuracies (%) on word analogy.

Model	Total	Capital	State	Family
CBOW	45.15	36.34	55.43	62.50
CWE	56.04	52.58	69.71	55.83
C-CCWE	58.88	53.47	77.14	60.83
R-CCWE	61.63	55.24	69.71	73.75

4.4 Document Classification

Another way to evaluating the quality of the word embeddings is using the word vectors to compute document representation, which can be evaluated with document classification tasks. To obtain document vectors, we choose a very simple approach that takes the average of the word vector representations in that document. This is because we aim to compare the word embeddings with different approaches instead of finding the best method for document embeddings.

In this paper, we run experiments on the dataset Chinese Encyclopedia, which is from the electronic version of the Chinese Encyclopedia. This dataset was also used by Li and Sun [8]. This dataset contains 55 categories and about 70,000 documents and is split into training set and test set with 9:1. Each document belongs to only one category. All document vectors are used to train classifier using the LibLinear package[2]. We report the classification metrics Micro-F1 and Macro-F1. The results are averaged over 10 different runs.

---

[2] http://www.csie.ntu.edu.tw/~cjlin/liblinear/

Table 5. Results on document classification. "*": significantly better than CBOW ($p < 0.05$). "+": significantly better than CWE ($p < 0.05$).

Method	Micro-F1	Macro-F1
CBOW	75.93	74.23
CWE	77.01	75.76
C-CCWE	77.65*	76.00*
R-CCWE	77.97*+	76.45*+

Table 5 shows the results of document classification. Similar conclusion can be made as in the word analogy task. The R-CCWE method outperforms C-CCWE methods and performs significantly better than all baseline methods.

4.5 Qualitative Analysis

In order to demonstrate the characteristics of CCWE model, we select two example words and use R-CCWE model to find the most similar words of these words. For comparison, we also used CBOW model and CWE model to find similar words of these example words. In Table 6, we can observe that, the most similar words returned by the CBOW model are syntactically related words. The most similar words returned by the CWE model tend to share at least one character with the given word, for example: "他 途 (other way)", "牛蒡 (great burdock, which is a species of plants)". The most similar words found by the R-CCWE model are a mixture of syntactically and semantically related words.

Table 6. Target words and their most similar words under different word representations.

Words	CBOW	CWE	CCWE
仕途 (official career)	失意 (frustrated) 功名 (scholarly honour) 官场 (official circle) 穷愁 (depressed) 闻达 (illustrious)	仕宦 (be an official) 仕 (be an official) 宦途 (official career) 失意 (frustrated) 他途 (other way)	仕宦 (be an official) 功名 (scholarly honour) 中举 (pass imperial exams) 宦途 (official career) 书生 (intellectual)
种牛 (stud bull)	蛋鸡 (laying hen) 肉牛 (beef cattle) 出栏 (of livestock) 存栏 (livestock) 鸡场 (chicken farm)	种羊 (stud sheep) 种畜 (breeding stock) 肉牛 (beef cattle) 种羊场 (stud sheep farm) 牛蒡 (great burdock)	肉牛 (beef cattle) 奶牛 (milking cow) 黄牛 (ox) 养牛 (cowboying) 种羊 (stud sheep)

5 Related Work

This work is inspired by two lines of research: (1) compositional semantic models and (2) exploiting word internal structure.

Compositional Semantic Models. More recently, a number of authors have paid some efforts to learn compositional semantic models. Luong et al. [10] proposed a neural language model to learn morphologically-aware word representations by combining recursive neural network and neural language model. Botha and Blunsom [2] introduced the additive log-bilinear model (LBL++) which learns separated vectors for each component morpheme of a word and derves word vector from these vectors.

Finally, most similar to our model, Chen et al. [4] presented a general framework to integrate the character knowledge and context knowledge to learn word embeddings and also provides an efficient solution to character ambiguity. We solve this issue through annotating the sense of each component character in words.

Exploiting Word Internal Structure. Exploiting word internal structure to improve Chinese word segmentation and parsing has gained increasing popularity recently. Zhao [21] investigate character-level dependencies for Chinese word segmentation task in a dependency parsing framework. Their results show that annotated word dependencies can be useful for Chinese word segmentation. Li [9] annotate morphological-level word structures and proposed a unified generative model to parse the Chinese morphological and phrase structures. Zhang et al. [20] annotate character-level word structures which cover entire words in CTB and present a unified framework for segmentation, POS tagging and phrase structure parsing. Compared to their work, we annotate internal word structures from semantic view and use the knowledge to improve word embeddings. To the best of our knowledge, it is the first work in this direction.

6   Conclusion

We have presented a compositional neural language models that incorporates semantic category and semantic relation knowledge in resources to improve word embeddings. Compared to existing word representation models, CCWE is very efficient and can capture semantic relation between words and their component characters, which are crucial for semantic similarity tasks. We have demonstrated improvements on word similarity, word analogy, and document classification tasks. In summary, our contributions include:

1. We annotated the internal semantic structures of Chinese words, which are potentially useful to character-based studies of Chinese NLP.
2. We proposed a novel compositional Chinese word embeddings and investigated the effectiveness of our model in three tasks.

For future work, we plan to extend our models to learn word embeddings and semantic category of words jointly.

Acknowledgments. The authors thank Yang Liu, Xinxiong Chen, Lei Xu, Yu Zhao and Zhiyuan Liu for helpful discussions and three anonymous reviewers for the valuable comments. This research is supported by the Key Project of National Social Science Foundation of China under Grant No. 13&ZD190 and the Project of National Natural Science Foundation of China under Grant No. 61170196.

References

1. Bengio, Y., Ducharme, R., Vincent, P., Janvin, C.: A neural probabilistic language model. JMLR **3**, 1137–1155 (2003)
2. Botha, J.A., Blunsom, P.: Compositional morphology for word representations and language modelling. In: Proceedings of ICML (2014)
3. Chen, X., Liu, Z., Sun, M.: A unified model for word sense representation and disambiguation. In: Proceedings of EMNLP (2014)
4. Chen, X., Xu, L., Liu, Z., Sun, M., Luan, H.: Joint learning of character and word embeddings. In: Proceedings of IJCAI (2015)
5. Collobert, R., Weston, J., Bottou, L., Karlen, M., Kavukcuoglu, K., Kuksa, P.: Natural language processing (almost) from scratch. JMLR **12**, 2493–2537 (2011)
6. Faruqui, M., Dodge, J., Jauhar, S.K., Dyer, C., Hovy, E., Smith, N.A.: Retrofitting word vectors to semantic lexicons. In: Proceedings of NAACL (2015)
7. Jin, P., Wu, Y.: Semeval-2012 task 4: evaluating chinese word similarity. In: Proceedings of SemEval (2012)
8. Li, J., Sun, M.: Scalable term selection for text categorization. In: Proceedings of EMNLP (2007)
9. Li, Z.: Parsing the internal structure of words: a new paradigm for chinese word segmentation. In: Proceedings of ACL (2011)
10. Luong, T., Socher, R., Manning, C.D.: Better word representations with recursive neural networks for morphology. In: Proceedings of CoNLL (2013)
11. Mei, J., Zhu, Y., Gao, Y., Yin, H.: TongYiCi CiLin. Shanghai Cishu Publisher, Shanghai (1983)
12. Mikolov, T., Chen, K., Corrado, G., Dean, J.: Efficient estimation of word representations in vector space. In: Proceedings of Workshop at ICLR (2013)
13. Mikolov, T., Sutskever, I., Chen, K., Corrado, G.S., Dean, J.: Distributed representations of words and phrases and their compositionality. In: Proceedings of NIPS (2013)
14. Mnih, A., Kavukcuoglu, K.: Learning word embeddings efficiently with noise-contrastive estimation. In: Proceedings of NIPS (2013)
15. Mnih, A., Teh, Y.W.: A fast and simple algorithm for training neural probabilistic language models. In: Proceedings of ICML (2012)
16. Pennington, J., Socher, R., Manning, C.D.: Glove: global vectors for word representation. In: Proceedings of EMNLP (2014)
17. Socher, R., Lin, C.C., Ng, A.Y., Manning, C.D.: Parsing natural scenes and natural language with recursive neural networks. In: Proceedings of ICML (2011)
18. Socher, R., Perelygin, A., Wu, J., Chuang, J., Manning, C.D., Ng, A., Potts, C.: Recursive deep models for semantic compositionality over a sentiment treebank. In: Proceedings of EMNLP (2013)
19. Yu, M., Dredze, M.: Improving lexical embeddings with semantic knowledge. In: Proceedings of ACL (2014)
20. Zhang, M., Zhang, Y., Che, W., Liu, T.: Chinese parsing exploiting characters. In: Proceedings of ACL (2013)
21. Zhao, H.: Character-level dependencies in chinese: usefulness and learning. In: Proceedings of EACL (2009)

Incorporating Word Clustering into Complex Noun Phrase Identification

Lihua Xue[✉], Guiping Zhang, Qiaoli Zhou, and Na Ye

Knowledge Engineering Research Center,
Shenyang Aerospace University, Shenyang 110136, China
375618003@qq.com, zgp@ge-soft.com,
zhou_qiao_li@hotmail.com, yena_l@126.com

Abstract. Since the professional technical literature include amounts of complex noun phrases, identifying those phrases has an important practical value for such tasks as machine translation. Through analysis of those phrases in Chinese-English bilingual sentence pairs from the aircraft technical publications, we present an annotation specification based on the existing specification to label those phrases and a method for the complex noun phrase identification. In addition to the basic features including the word and the part-of-speech, we incorporate the word clustering features trained by Brown clustering model and Word Vector Class (WVC) model on a large unlabeled data into the machine learning model. Experimental results indicate that the combination of different word clustering features and basic features can leverage system performance, and improve the F-score by 1.83 % in contrast with the method only adding the basic features.

Keywords: Complex noun phrase · Word clustering · Brown clustering model · Word vector class model

1 Introduction

With the development of the aviation industry, translation for aircraft technical publications [1] becomes a significant problem to be solved. Because the sentence structures are simple and the descriptions are mostly on aircraft parts in technical publications, the translation quality of the terminology will affect the translation quality of the whole sentence. Thus, it is necessary to automatically indentify the terminology before acquiring their translations.

Instead of terminology, we use the concept of complex noun phrase with a certain structure to achieve the desired effect. The complex noun phrases should meet some requirements as follows: (1) formed by two or more words according to certain relationship; (2) cannot be included by other noun phrase; (3) not including "的". There are two reasons for the definition. First, through analysis on the terminology in technical

---

This work is supported by Humanities and Social Sciences Foundation for the Youth Scholars of Ministry of Education of China (№-14YJC740126) and National Natural Science Foundation of China (№-61402299).

M. Sun et al. (Eds.): CCL and NLP-NABD 2015, LNAI 9427, pp. 26–37, 2015.
DOI: 10.1007/978-3-319-25816-4_3

publications, there are high similarities in grammar structures among the large number of terminologies, such as "前 货舱" (the fwd cargo compartment) and "后 货舱" (the aft cargo compartment) in which "前" and "后" are nouns of location. Second, with the rapid development of aviation industry, a considerable number of new terms are created on a regular basis, but the new terms are always consistent in the structure with the old ones. Therefore, considering the structure of the term, we use complex noun phrase, not terminology. For labeling the complex noun phrases, we present a specification based on the bilingual corpus and the existing annotation scheme [2].

To automatically identify complex noun phrases, many supervised learning methods are applied. These methods require sufficient labeled data to achieve state-of-the-art performance. Although supervised learning methods can rapidly develop a robust phrase recognition system, the requirement of substantial amounts of training data is still an impediment to the quick deployment of phrase recognition in new languages or domains. However, it is often the case that developing sizable training data is considerably time-consuming whereas the amount of raw data is rapidly increasing. To further exploit the effects of unlabeled data, several studies investigated on how to incorporate raw data. Koo et al. [3] demonstrated excellent performance on dependency parsing in the use of word clustering feature. Word clustering is a technique for partitioning sets of words into subsets of semantically similar words. For example, "前" in "前 货舱" and "后" in "后 货舱" are similar under this definition, whereas "切断" (cut off) and "开关" (switch), although semantically related, are not. Intuitively, in a good clustering, the words in the same cluster should be similar. And word clustering is increasingly becoming a major technique used in a number of NLP tasks ranging from word sense or structural disambiguation to information retrieval and filtering. So unlike previous work, besides the word and part-of-speech (POS) tags as features for recognizing phrases, we incorporate word clustering [4] feature. We adopt Semi-supervised Learning (SSL) [5, 6] techniques to incorporate word cluster into ML model for phrase recognition. SSL is an ML approach that typically uses a large amount of unlabeled data and a small amount of labeled data to build a more accurate classification model than the models using only labeled data. In this paper, besides the word and POS features, we apply word cluster features, trained by Brown clustering [7] model and Word Vector Class (WVC) model on a large amount of unlabeled data, into Conditional Random Fields (CRF) [8].

2   Related Work

The noun phrase identification problem can be considered as a sequence labeling problem, whose task is that under the condition of a given observation training x, estimate the conditional probability of sequence. And researchers have done a lot of work on sequence labeling problems like chunk recognition, named entity recognition, word segmentation and part-of-speech tagging and so on.

Work on Chinese sequence labeling problem includes: Sun Ruina [9] combines the statistics-based and rule-based method, first performing base noun phrase boundary prediction through the mutual information between the words, and then adjusting the boundary prediction for base noun phrase identification according to the constitutive rules of base noun phrases. But this method can't identify the low-frequency phrases in case of sparse corpus. Wang Meng [10] et al. adopted a method for automatic acquisition of Chinese compound noun phrases based on corpus, making use of the statistical indexes to get the typical, frequent compound noun phrases as training data and extracting the various features from the training set to help find the infrequent ones. But the method viewed the compound noun phrase acquisition as a static problem and did not use the context information of "Noun-Noun" sequence. Li Guochen [11] et al. present a base chunk identification model based on deep neural network models, which takes Chinese characters as tagging unit and original input layer. The results show that the method is useful. But they did not integrate more abundant features of characters like POS, collocation information into the system. Zhang Kaixu [12] adopted a method for a joint Chinese word segmentation and POS tagging task. First, extract high-dimensional distributional lexical information from a large scale unlabeled corpus, then perform unsupervised dimension reduction for the low-dimensional lexicon features by an auto-encoder. Results show that the additional lexicon features improve the performance and are better than those features learned by using the principal component analysis and the k-means algorithm for phrase recognition.

Work on sequence labeling problem of other languages includes: Tsendsuren Munkhdalai [13] et al. adopt Semi-Supervised Learning techniques to incorporate domain knowledge into the Chemical and biomedical Named Entity Recognition model, and the results show the method leverage overall system performance. Yu-Chieh Wu [14] presents a cluster-based method to fuse labeled training and unlabeled raw data. They derive the term groups from the unlabeled data and take them as new features for the supervised learners in order to improve the coverage of lexical information. LING ZHU [15] et al. present a noun phrase chunking model based on Selection Base Classifiers on Bagging (SBCB) ensemble learning algorithm. The algorithm employs multiple learners and integrates their prediction capabilities to achieve a more accurate classification outcome instead of assembling all classifiers candidates. Results show that the proposed approach is able to achieve a remarkably better performance, which is superior to several comparable state-of-the-art chunking algorithms that apply SVM, HMM, and CRF as well. Michal Konkol et al. [16] propose new features for Named Entity Recognition (NER) based on latent semantics and experimented with two sources of semantic information: LDA and semantic spaces. Results show that the newly created NER system is fully language-independent thanks to the unsupervised nature of the proposed features and it achieves the same or even better results than state-of-the-art language-dependent systems.

From the work above, we can see that Semi-Supervised Learning (SSL) techniques have been applied to many NLP tasks such as phrase recognition, word segmentation and POS tagging. And many studies have proved that the features extracted from a large-scale corpus can better reflect the syntactic and semantic features of words. Thus we incorporate word clustering features trained by Brown clustering model and Word Vector Class (WVC) model on a large amount of unlabeled data respectively.

3 Annotation Specification

Considering the characteristics of complex noun phrases in the Chinese-English bilingual sentence pairs of aircraft technical publications, we refer to the annotation scheme for Chinese Treebank [2, 17] and change some rules of the annotation scheme to identify complex noun phrase. The rules modified are shown in Table 1.

Table 1. Comparison of Tinghua annotation specification and the proposed annotation specification

Phrase structure	Tsinghua	The proposed
np+s	[sp 青尼罗河/n 上游/s]	[np 青尼罗河/n 上游/s]
vp+att-c	进行/v 了/ uA [vp 实地/d 调查/v]	进行/v 了/uA [np 实地/d 调查/v]

np: the nominal phrase; s: the locative word; att-c: Attributive-centered structure

In the following subsections we will introduce the detail descriptions of the rules above.

3.1 np + s

Through analysis of the phrases in bilingual corpus, when s in "np+s" is the words like "上游", "顶部", "底部", "左后侧" et al., its corresponding translation is noun. Thus "np+s" is labeled as complex noun phrase. Some examples about "np+s" Chinese-English annotation and its phrase alignment are shown in Table 2.

Table 2. np+s Chinese-English annotation and its phrase alignment

位于 CNP[后设备舱 左后侧]

be on CNP[the left rear side of the aft equipment compartment]

从 CNP[APU 引气阀 上游]

from CNP[the upstream of the APU]

安装 在 CNP[机身 顶部、底部]

Installed on CNP[the top and the bottom of the fuselage]

3.2 vp+att-c

att-c is a phrase structure called attributive-centered structure as a linguistic form of attributives modifying the headword, and it plays an important role [18] both in Chinese and English. Particularly unusual is that the headword is verb acting as noun and the attribute modifying the headword may be adjectives, verbs or nouns. Some examples about "vp + att-c" Chinese-English annotation and its phrase alignment are shown in Table 3.

Table 3. "vp + att-c" Chinese-English annotation and its phrase alignment

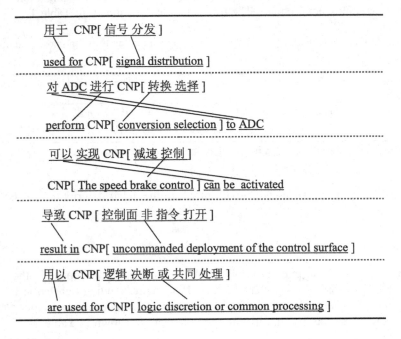

4 Method Description

Our complex noun phrase recognition system design is shown in Fig. 1. First, we perform preprocessing on aircraft technical publications and then extract two different feature sets, a base feature set and a word clustering feature set, in the feature processing phase. The unlabeled data is fed to build word classes. Finally, we apply the CRF sequence-labeling method to the extracted feature vectors to train complex noun phrase recognition model. These steps will be described in subsequent sections.

4.1 Preprocessing

Preprocessing mainly includes labeling 10 thousand sentences from aircraft technical publications according to the annotation specification modified in Sect. 3. Then the 10 thousand labeled sentences are used as training set for complex noun phrase recognition. Meanwhile, all raw corpora are tokenized by a tokenization tool and used as the input corpus to achieve the word clustering features.

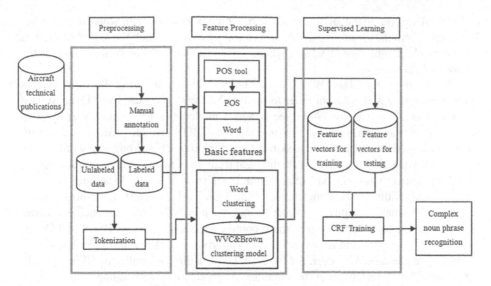

Fig. 1. System design for complex noun phrase recognition

4.2 Feature Processing

We extract features from the preprocessed text to represent each token as a feature vector, and then apply them to an ML algorithm for building a model for complex noun phrase recognition.

The proposed method includes extraction of baseline and the word clustering feature sets. The baseline feature set is essential in phrase recognition, but is poor at representing the word clustering feature. In this paper, we achieve the word clustering features by training on a large amount of unlabeled data.

We found that with the increase of window sizes, the performance of recognition becomes better. But due to the limitation of tool for modeling, the window sizes can only be increased to 4. Therefore, when choosing feature templates, we not only consider the current word and its part-of-speech tag, but also consider the long-distance associated words in the previous context, so as to add the richer information mentioned above. The baseline feature set is summarized in Table 4.

Table 4. The baseline features

Features	Feature description
W	The current word
P	POS of W
X	The fifth word before W
P	The sixth word before W

For word clustering features, we train Brown clustering models and word vector class (WVC) models on a large amount unlabeled data. Brown clustering is a bottom-up agglomerative word clustering algorithm to derive a hierarchical clustering of words. The input to the algorithm is a text, which is a sequence of word $W_1, \ldots, W_n$. The output from the clustering algorithm is a binary tree, in which the leaves of the tree are the words. It runs time $O(V*K^2)$, where V is the size of the vocabulary and K is the number of clusters.

The Word Vector Class (WVC) model is induced via clustering the word vectors using a clustering algorithm. In order to build WVC model, we used word2vec to train word vectors of each word. Word2vec is a tool implemented by Mikolov et al. [19], which contains two distinct models, namely the CBOW which predicts the current word based on the context, and the Skip-gram which predicts surrounding words given the current word. Each model has two different training methods (with/without negative sampling) and other variations (e.g. hierarchical softmax), which amount to small "space" of algorithms. About the choice of the Training Parameters, [20] shows that in the case of a smaller corpus, a simpler model, such as Skip-gram, can achieve better results, whereas for a larger corpus, more complex models, such as CBOW and Order, are typically superior. And for the semantic property tasks, larger dimensions will lead to better performance. However, for the NLP tasks, a dimensionality of 50 is typically sufficient. Therefore, in order to generate a good word embedding, the training parameters are set as follows: 35 iterations, 250-dimension, window size is 5 and Skip-gram and hierarchical softmax are used. Then the word vectors are clustered using a K-means algorithm to drive a Word Vector Class (WVC) model.

4.3   Supervised Learning

Conditional Random Fields (CRFs) is a probabilistic undirected graphical model which has been used successfully in many sequence tasks. Since CRFs have good description ability on the long-distance correlation that avoids the labeling paranoid problem, we apply the CRF tools to build the complex noun phrase recognition model.

5   Experiments

5.1   Dataset

For the word clustering features, we prepared 1.2 million Chinese sentences from aircraft technical publications. Ten thousand Chinese sentences extracted from the aircraft technical publications are tokenized manually and then labeled according to the annotation specification in Sect. 3 and then divided into two by the proportion of 8:2, one as training corpus, the other as testing corpus.

5.2   Evaluation Measure

The metrics for evaluating complex noun phrase recognition models include precision rate, recall rate and their harmonic mean F score.

Precision measures the percentage of labeled complex noun phrases that are correct. Here "correct" means both the boundary of complex noun phrase and the label are correct. And the precision is therefore defined as:

$$\text{Precision} = \frac{\#\text{correct proposed tagged word}}{\#\text{correct complex noun phrase tags}} \tag{1}$$

Recall measures the percentage of complex noun phrase presented in the input sentences that are correctly identified by the system. Recall is defined as follows:

$$\text{Recall} = \frac{\#\text{correct proposed complex noun phrase tags}}{\#\text{current complex noun phrase tags}} \tag{2}$$

The F-measure illustrates a way to combine the previous two measures into one metric. The formula of F-score s is defined as:

$$F = \frac{\#\left(\beta^2 + 1\right) \times \text{Recall} \times \text{Precision}}{\#\beta^2 \times \text{Recall} + \text{Precision}}, \beta = 1 \tag{3}$$

5.3   Experimental Results

Besides the basic features, we incorporate the word clustering features trained by Brown clustering model and WVC model. The range of the number of word clustering is from 100 to 1700, and the step is 100. We started conducting a run with a basic feature setting, and gradually increased the complexity of the feature space for further runs. In general, clustering is an optimization procedure based on a specific clustering criterion, so clustering combination can be regarded as a technique that constructs and processes multiple clustering criteria rather than a single criterion [21]. So we assume that the combination of different word cluster features may work better than one word clustering feature. In order to verify our assumption, during the experiments, we not only use a single word clustering feature, but also the combination of different word cluster features. The experimental results are shown in Table 5.

1. When adding the single word clustering feature, we found that the performances of Brown model and the WVC model increased by 1.27 % and 0.91 % F-measure than baseline, respectively. This shows that besides the basic features, adding the word clustering feature can improve the recognition performance.
2. Besides the basic features and one word clustering feature, we add a word clustering feature again. For example, for the baseline +Brown 300, we add the Brown 700 and WVC 1100, respectively. The results show that the system with the baseline +Brown 300 + Brown 700 and the baseline +Brown 300 + WVC 1100 performed higher than the baseline +Brown 300 by 0.43 % and 0.48 %, respectively. Obviously, the combination of two word clustering features performed better than the combination of one word clustering feature. In addition, the combination of the

Table 5. Results of different runs with varied features

Features			Pre/%	Rec/%	F-scr/%
baseline			89.10	89.08	89.09
baseline +Brown 300			90.40	90.33	90.36
baseline +Brown 300	+Brown 700		90.65	90.93	90.79
baseline +Brown 300	+Brown 700	+Brown 1000	90.85	90.93	90.89
baseline +Brown 300	+Brown 700	+WVC 1500	90.79	91.03	**90.91**
baseline +Brown 300	+WVC 1100		90.60	91.07	90.84
baseline +Brown 300	+WVC 1100	+Brown 300	90.68	91.11	**90.90**
baseline +Brown 300	+WVC 1100	+WVC 1000	90.74	91.11	**90.92**
baseline + WVC 1600			89.95	90.06	90.00
baseline + WVC 1600	+Brown 200		90.58	91.01	90.79
baseline + WVC 1600	+Brown 200	+Brown 800	90.61	91.15	**90.88**
baseline + WVC 1600	+Brown 200	+WVC 500	90.50	91.13	**90.81**
baseline + WVC 1600	+ WVC 900		90.27	90.70	90.48
baseline + WVC 1600	+ WVC 900	+Brown 1100	90.53	90.93	**90.73**
baseline + WVC 1600	+ WVC 900	+WVC 1000	90.41	90.84	90.63

Feature groups are separated by (+). The parameters following Brown and WVC
are the number of classes induced in each model. Pre: Precision; Rec: Recall;
F-scr: F-score

Brown clustering model and the WVC model performed better than the combination of the Brown clustering model or the WVC model. The results also verify that our assumption is correct.

3. Based on the features above, we continue to add a word clustering feature, namely the combination of the basic features and three word clustering features. For example, for baseline +Brown 300 + Brown 700, we add the Brown 1000 and WVC 1500, respectively. Results show that the system with the baseline +Brown 300 + Brown 700 + Brown 1000 and the baseline +Brown 300 + Brown 700 + WVC 1500 performed higher than the baseline +Brown 300 + Brown 700 by 0.1 % and 0.12 %, respectively. Obviously, the combination of three word clustering features tended to obtain higher F-score than the combination of two word clustering features. Although the increment is slight, the results are consistent with our assumption. Among the features, the combination of basic features and three word clustering features, namely the baseline + Brown 300 + WVC 1100 + WVC 1000, achieved 90.92 % F-score, which is 1.83 % higher than the baseline.

6   Error Analysis

Carrying on analysis on the complex noun phrases wrongly identified by the system, we observed that the following four types have a large proportion of all wrong examples.

1. A sentence containing "与" or "和" has accounted for about 8 % of all wrong examples.

   Wrong result: CNP[侧/NN 撑杆/JJ 上端/NN 与/C 机身/NN] 相连/VV
   Correct result:CNP[侧/NN 撑杆/NN 上端/ NN] 与/P 机身/NN 相连/VV
   English: CNP [The upper end of the side] stay connects to fuselage

2. The left border or the first word before the left border is verb, accounting for 17.7 % of all wrong complex noun phrase identified by the system.

   Wrong result: CNP[打开/VV 厨房/NN 区域/NN 天花板/NN]
   Correct result: 打开/VV CNP[厨房/NN 区域/NN 天花板/NN]
   English: open CNP [the ceiling in the galley area]

3. The right border or the first word after the right border is verb, accounting for 16.3 % of all wrong complex noun phrases identified by the system.

   Wrong result: … `导致/VV CNP[控制面/NN 非指令/NN] 打开/VV
   Correct result: … 导致/VV CNP[控制面/NN 非指令/NN 打开/VV]
   English: … result in CNP[an inadvertent deployment]

4. Some gerunds are not labeled, accounting for 10.3 % of all wrong complex noun phrases identified by the system.

   Wrong result: 在运输活体过程中，对于/P 过热/NN 保护/NN, …
   Correct result: 在运输活体过程中，对于/P [过热/NN 保护/NN], …
   English: during animal transportation for CNP[overheat protection], …

From the above analysis, the solutions for the problems are: (1) improve the accuracy of the POS tagging, for instance revising the POS manually; (2) mine the semantic knowledge by other ways.

7   Conclusion and Future Work

Due to the large amount of complex noun phrases in the technical publications, we propose a method for complex noun phrase recognition. Through analysis on the complex noun phrases in Chinese-English bilingual corpus from aircraft technical publications, we present an annotation specification to label the complex noun phrases in Chinese sentences based on the existing annotation specification. However, the annotation rules summarized in Sect. 3 are not complete because of the limitation of the scale of corpus, some cases may not occur in our corpus.

For the complex phrase identification, we incorporate the word clustering features into the machine learning besides the word and POS features. Experimental results show that the combination of two word clustering features tended to achieve higher F-score than the combination of one word clustering feature, and the combination of three word clustering features tended to achieve higher F-score than the combination of two word clustering features. In addition, the combination of word clustering features trained by the WVC model and word clustering trained by the Brown clustering model performed better than the combination of word clustering trained by the WVC model or the Brown model. Among the features, the system with the combination of three word clustering features (the baseline +Brown 300 + WVC 1100 + WVC 1000), achieved 90.92 % F-score, which is 1.83 % higher than the baseline.

In the future, we would like to continue to explore other methods for feature combination and try to find new features for the complex noun phrase identification.

A Appendix

The Table 6.

Table 6. Feature selection

Type	Feature
Atomic templates	W_{-4}, W_{-3}, W_{-2}, W_{-1}, W_0, W_1, W_2, W_3, W_4, P_{-3}, P_{-2}, P_{-1}, P_0, P_1, P_2, P_3, B_0^{300}, B_0^{1600}, B_1^{300}, B_1^{1600}, B_{-1}^{300}, B_{-1}^{1600}
Composite templates	$W_{-4}W_{-3}$, $W_{-3}W_{-2}$, $W_{-2}W_{-1}$, $W_{-1}W_0$, W_0W_1, W_1W_2, W_2W_3, W_3W_4, $W_0W_{-1}W_{-2}$, $W_{-1}W_0W_2$, $W_0W_1W_2$, $P_{-3}P_{-2}$, $P_{-2}P_{-1}$, $P_{-1}P_0$, P_0P_1, P_1P_2, P_2P_3, $P_0P_{-1}P_{-2}$, $P_{-1}P_0P_2$, $P_0P_1P_2$, $W_{-1}P_{-1}$, W_0P_{-1}, W_0P_0, W_0P_1, W_1P_1, X, Y, $W_{-4}X$, W_4X, XY, $W_0 B_0^{300}$, $W_{-1}B_{-1}^{300}$, $W_1B_1^{300}$, $W_0B_0^{1600}$, $W_{-1}B_{-1}^{1600}$, $W_1B_1^{1600}$, $W_0B_0^{300}B_0^{1600}$, $W_{-1} B_{-1}^{300}B_{-1}^{1600}$, $W_1B_1^{300}B_1^{1600}$, $P_0B_0^{300}$, $P_{-1}B_{-1}^{300}$, $P_1B_1^{300}$, $P_0B_0^{1600}$, $P_{-1}B_{-1}^{1600}$, $P_1B_1^{1600}$, $P_0B_0^{300}B_0^{1600}$, $P_{-1}B_{-1}^{300}B_{-1}^{1600}$, $P_1B_1^{300}B_1^{1600}$

W: word; P: pos; W_i: the current word; B^{300}: 300 Brown clustering, B^{1600}: 1600 Brown clustering; X: the fifth word before W_i; Y: the sixth word before W_i; W_{i-1}: the first word before W_i; W_{i+1}: the first word after W_i; B_i^{300}: 300 Brown clustering of W_i; B_i^{1600}: 1600 Brown clustering of W_i, and so on.

References

1. Xu, H.: Application of commercial aircraft technical publication specifications. J. Aviat. Maint. Eng. **6**, 91–93 (2012)
2. Zhou, Q.: Annotation scheme for Chinese treebank. J. Chin. Inf. **18**(4), 1–8 (2004)
3. Koo, T., Carreras, X., Collins, M.: Simple semi-supervised dependency parsing. In: Proceedings of 46th Annual Meetings of the Association for Computational Linguistics (ACL), pp. 595–603 (2008)
4. Candito, M., Crabbé, B.: Improving generative statistical parsing with semi-supervised word clustering. In: Proceedings of the 11th International Conference on Parsing Technologies. Association for Computational Linguistics, pp. 138–141 (2009)
5. Liang, P.: Semi-supervised learning for natural language. Massachusetts Institute of Technology (2005)
6. Zhu, X., Goldberg, A.B.: Introduction to semi-supervised learning. J. Synth. Lect. Artif. Intell. Mach. Learn. **3**(1), 1–130 (2009)
7. Brown, P.F., deSouza, P.V., Mercer, R.L., Pietra, V.J.D., Lai, J.C.: Class-based n-gram models of natural language. Comput. Linguist. **18**, 467–497 (1992)

8. Lafferty, J., McCallum, A., Pereira, F.C.N.: Conditional random fields: probabilistic models for segmenting and labeling sequence data, pp. 139–141 (2001)
9. Sun, R., Liu, Q.: Chinese base noun phrase identification based on mutual information. J. Chin. Comput. Commun. **11**, 71–72 (2012)
10. Meng, W., Zhu, H., Xu, Y.: A study of automatic acquisition of Chinese compound noun phrases based on corpus. J. Leshan Teach. **12**, 57–61 (2014)
11. Guochen, L., Jianbing, D., et al.: Chinese base-chunk identification based on distributed character representation. J. Chin. Inf. **28**(6), 18–25 (2014)
12. Kaixu, Z., Changle, Z.: Unsupervised feature learning for Chinese lexicon based on auto-encoder. J. Chin. Inf. **27**(5), 1–7 (2013)
13. Munkhdalai, T., Li, M., Batsuren, K., et al.: Incorporating domain knowledge in chemical and biomedical named entity recognition with word representations. J. Cheminf. **7**, s9 (2015)
14. Wu, Y.-C.: A top-down information theoretic word clustering algorithm for phrase recognition. J. Inf. Sci. **275**, 213–225 (2014)
15. Zhu, L., Chao, L.S., Wong, D.F., et al.: A noun-phrase chunking model based on SBCB ensemble learning algorithm. In: International Conference on Machine Learning and Cybernetics (ICMLC). IEEE, pp. 11–16 (2012)
16. Konkol, M., Brychcín, T., Konopík, M.: Latent semantics in named entity recognition. J. Expert Syst. Appl. **42**, 3470–3479 (2015)
17. Yu, S., Huiming, D., Xuefeng, Z.: The basic processing of contemporary Chinese corpus at Peking university. J. Chin. Inf. Process. **16**(5), 49–64 (2002)
18. Wang, Z.: A contrastive study between English and Chinese of attributive-centered structure. Liaoning Normal University (2012)
19. Mikolov, T., Chen, K., Corrado, G., Dean, J.: Efficient estimation of word representations in vector space. In: Proceedings of Workshop at ICLR (2013)
20. Lai, S., Liu, k., Xu, L., Zhao, J.: How to Generate a Good Word Embedding? arXiv preprint (2015). arXiv:1507.05523
21. Qian, Y., Suen, C.Y.: Clustering combination method. In: 15th International Conference on IEEE, vol. 2, pp. 732–735 (2000)

A Three-Layered Collocation Extraction Tool and Its Application in China English Studies

Jingxiang Cao[1], Dan Li[1(✉)], and Degen Huang[2]

[1] School of Foreign Languages, Dalian University of Technology,
Dalian 116024, Liaoning, China
caojx@dlut.edu.cn, linda_2013@mail.dlut.edu.cn
[2] School of Computer Science and Technology,
Dalian University of Technology, Dalian 116024, Liaoning, China
huangdg@dlut.edu.cn

Abstract. We design a three-layered collocation extraction tool by integrating syntactic and semantic knowledge and apply it in China English studies. The tool first extracts peripheral collocations in the frequency layer from dependency triples, then extracts semi-peripheral collocations in the syntactic layer by association measures, and last extracts core collocations in the semantic layer with a similar word thesaurus. The syntactic constraints filter out much noise from surface co-occurrences, and the semantic constraints are effective in identifying the very "core" collocations. The tool is applied to automatically extract collocations from a large corpus of China English we compile to explore how China English as a variety of English is nativilized. Then we analyze similarities and differences of the typical China English collocations of a group of verbs. The tool and results can be applied in the compilation of language resources for Chinese-English translation and corpus-based China studies.

Keywords: Collocation extraction · Dependency relation · China English

1 Introduction

Collocation is pervasive in all languages. *Collins COBUILD English Collocations* includes about 140,000 collocations of 10,000 headwords of English core vocabulary. Collocation is of great importance in Natural Language Processing (NLP) as well as in Linguistics and Applied Linguistics.

Various methods of automatic collocation identification and extraction have been proposed. The common procedure mainly consists of two phases: extracting collocation candidates and assigning association score for ranking [1]. Collocation candidates can be extracted based on surface co-occurrence, textual co-occurrence and syntactic co-occurrence [2], among which the syntactic co-occurrence contains the most linguistic information and is suitable for collocation analysis in the perspective of linguistic properties. The association score can be calculated through different association measures (AMs). Frequency method simply takes the collocation as a whole whereas mean and variance method [3], hypothesis test (including z-test, t-test, chi-square test, log-likelihood ratio) and information theory (MI^k) [2, 4] also consider the components,

© Springer International Publishing Switzerland 2015
M. Sun et al. (Eds.): CCL and NLP-NABD 2015, LNAI 9427, pp. 38–49, 2015.
DOI: 10.1007/978-3-319-25816-4_4

thus getting better performance; other methods using non-compositionality [5] and paradigmatic modifiability [6] further consider the substitutes of the collocation components, which works well for non-compositional phrases or domain-specific n-gram terms. Smadja's X-tract [3] starts from surface co-occurrence, extracts bigrams, n-grams with window-based method and extends them into syntactic co-occurrence with syntactic parser. Reference [7] constructs a tool for NOUN + VERB collocation extraction as well as morpho-syntactic preference detection (active or passive voice).

Those methods and tools are mainly designed and applied in NLP tasks like semantic disambiguation, text generation or machine translation, rarely oriented towards linguists other than computational scientists. But modern linguists have always been in need of appropriate tools. WordSmith [8] may be the popular corpus assistant software mostly used by linguistics with three modules: Concord, Keywords and WordList, among which the Concord can compute collocates of a given word through window-based method, far from enough for collocation studies.

Inspired by the various extraction methods and linguistic properties of collocation, we design a hierarchical collocation extraction tool based on the three-layered linguistic properties of collocation [9]. It considers different linguistic properties of collocation, which agrees more with the human intuitive conceptualization of collocation.

We also apply our collocation extraction tool in the China English studies. China English is a performance variety of English, which observes the norm of standard Englishes (e.g. British English, American English) but is inevitably featured by Chinese phonology, lexis, syntax and pragmatics [10]. Previous studies on China English have ranged from macro aspects, such as the attitudes towards China English [10, 11], the history of English in China [12, 13], the use of English in China [14] and the pedagogic models of English in China, to micro aspects which focus on specific linguistic levels including phonology, morphology, lexis, syntax, discourses, stylistics etc. [15–18]. Among those linguistic features, lexical innovation, which is argued to be more likely to get social acceptance compared with grammatical deviations [19], is usually the most active during the nativization of English. Collocations are "social institutions" or "conventional labels", which means the entailed concept is culturally recognized within a specific society. Therefore it is innately appropriate to study the nativization of English which focuses on the process to create a localized linguistic and cultural identity of a variety [20].

Due to the limit of applicable tools, lexical studies on China English are limited, either in the small manually-collected data, or in the rough analysis methods such as frequency, proportion comparison and examples relying on researchers' acute observation or introspection. In-depth empirical studies based on large corpus or latest methods from NLP are therefore needed. Moreover, the lack of effective methods to extract long-distance patterns forces most linguists to study consecutive collocations like noun phrase [15] or adjective phrase [17]. Verb phrase as a significant research object in language is downplayed.

In this paper, we build a large corpus of China English by crawling the last-five-year webpages of four mainstream newspapers in mainland China, and automatically extract all the collocations in the corpus. Then we collect 52 high-keyness verbs with the help of WordSmith Tools 5.0 and analyze similarities and differences of the typical China English collocations of a group of verbs.

2 The Three-Layered Collocation Extraction Tool

2.1 Three-Layered Collocation Definition

Collocation is often regarded as the bridge between free word combination and idiom [21–24]. It has broad definition as "a pair of words that appear together more often than expected" [25, 26], and narrow one as "recurrent co-occurrence of at least two lexical items in a direct syntactic relation" [1, 6], or further restricted one as "recurrent co-occurrence with both syntactic and semantic constraints" [5]. The definitions are gradually narrowed from frequency layer, syntactic layer down to semantic layer.

Based on the three layers, Collocates of a Base [23] are classified into core collocates, semi-peripheral collocates and peripheral collocates. Given a base, a word is a core collocate iff it satisfies all the constraints A, B and C, a semi-peripheral collocate iff it satisfies constraints A and B, and a peripheral collocate iff it only satisfies constraint A.

Three defining constraints are

(A) Frequency constraint: the frequency over a specific threshold
(B) Syntactic constraint: direct syntactic relation
(C) Semantic constraint: not substitutable without affecting the meaning of the word sequence

2.2 Collocation Extraction Architecture

The first step is to extract peripheral collocation. The texts are segmented into sentences with a punctuation package adapted from Kiss and Struct [27] in NLTK [28], and parsed with Stanford Parser [29] to extract syntactically related co-occurrences with no limit on their distances. Then the dependency triples are extracted from parsed texts and lemmatized with WordNet lemmatizer [30] in NLTK [28] in order to reduce data sparsity. We discard triples with "root" relations or stop word components and selected those with no less than 3 occurrences as peripheral collocations, also candidates of semi-peripheral collocation.

The second step employs an integrated association measure (AM) to extract semi-peripheral collocations. The three AMs are designed for different purposes: LLR (log-likelihood ratio) [4] answers "how unlikely is the null hypothesis that the words are independent?" [2], MI^K (revised MI of Lin [6]) answers "how much does observed co-occurrence frequency exceed expected frequency?" [2], and PMS [5] measures the substitutability of the components in a dependency triple.

For any word pair (u, v) adapted from dependency triple (u, rel, v), we have the contingency table as follows (Table 1):

$\bar{v}$ means the absence of v. a, b, c, d are the counts of word pairs (u, v), $(u, \bar{v})$, $(\bar{u}, v)$, $(\bar{u}, \bar{v})$. Obviously, $a + b + c + d$ is the sample size N. LLR is represented as follows:

Table 1. Contingency table of word pair (u, v)

	v	$\bar{v}$
u	a	b
$\bar{u}$	c	d

$$\begin{aligned} \text{LLR} = 2(a\log a + b\log b + c\log c + d\log d - (a+b)\log(a+b) \\ - (a+c)\log(a+c) - (b+d)\log(b+d) - (c+d)\log(c+d) \\ + (a+b+c+d)\log(a+b+c+d)) \end{aligned} \quad (1)$$

The three-variable $\text{MI}^k(u, rel, v)$ here is under the assumption that u and v are conditionally independent given dependency relation rel. As is known that MI biases to low frequency word, we add k-th power to the numerator in order to eliminate the effect.

$$\begin{aligned} \text{MI}^k(u, rel, v) &= log\left(\frac{p(u, rel, v)^k}{p(u|rel)p(rel)p(v|rel)}\right) \\ &= log\left(\frac{(|u, rel, v| - b)^k|rel|}{|u, rel||rel, v|N^{(k-1)}}\right) \end{aligned} \quad (2)$$

u and v are the component words in a dependency triple, rel is the dependency type, p(#) is the frequency of #, |#| is the count of #, $b(= 0.95$ in our experiments) is an adjustment parameter, and N is the sample size.

$$PMS(u, rel, v) = \frac{|u, rel, v|^6}{|u||rel||v||u, rel||rel, v||u, v|} \quad (3)$$

In order to take advantage of the three AMs, we normalize their values in interval [0,1] and integrate them using geometric mean. The integrated measure (LMP^k) is defined as follows:

$$\text{LMP}^k(u, rel, v) = \sqrt[3]{\text{LLR}'(u, v) * \text{MI}^{k'}(u, rel, v) * \text{PMS}'(u, rel, v)} \quad (4)$$

$'$ means the normalized AM.

The triples with LMP^k higher than a specified threshold are regarded as semi-peripheral collocations, and the rest of the candidates are peripheral collocations.

The third step filters out the semi-peripheral collocations to reserve the core collocations by assigning semantic constraints, i.e. to compute the probability of substituting the component words without affecting the meaning of the original collocation.

We adopt Lin [31] to measure the probability. First, we compile a thesaurus by taking all the collocations of a word as its features, computing the similarity between any two words, and selecting the top 10 most similar words for each entry. Based on the thesaurus we reserve the collocation whose MI^k is significantly different from its substitutive collocations at the 5 % level.

Given a word w_1, we calculate $Simi(w_1, w_2)$ to rank its similar words.

$$Simi(w_1, w_2) = \frac{2Info(F(w_1) \cap F(w_2))}{Info(F(w_1) + Info(F(w_2))} \tag{5}$$

$$Info(F(w)) = -\sum_{f \in F} \frac{p(f)}{p(POS(w))} \tag{6}$$

$F(w)$ is the feature set of w, $Info(F)$ is the amount of information of feature set F, $POS(w)$ is the POS of w, $p()$ is the frequency. For example, for the base *promote*, we extract (promote, dobj, exchange) and (promote, advmod, actively), and thus (dobj, exchange) and (advmod, actively) belong to the feature set of *promote*, F(*promote*).

Then we employ z-test to extract core collocations. A dependency triple X is not a core collocation if:

(a) There is a triple Y obtained by substituting the component with its similar word;

(b) $MI^k(Y) \in [log\left(\left(|u, rel, v| - b - Z_\alpha\sqrt{|u, rel, v|}\right)^k * \frac{|rel|}{|u, rel| * |rel, v| * N^{(k-1)}}\right),$
$log\left(\left(|u, rel, v| - b + Z_\alpha\sqrt{|u, rel, v|}\right)^k * \frac{|rel|}{|u, rel| * |rel, v| * N^{(k=1)}}\right)] \ (\alpha = 5\%).$

2.3 Comparison with Other Tools

We compare our tool with the window-based method and WordNet[1] [30] to test the performance of different steps in our tool.

As our collocation candidates are directly from dependency triples with syntactic constraints, we want to see how it differs from the traditional window-based method. Window-based method is a standard method in collocation extraction before mature syntactic parsers came out. It is broadly adopted but lack of interpretability due to

---

[1] http://wordnet.princeton.edu/.

mixing "true" and "false" instances as well as distance-different instances identified in the source text [1].

The first experiment is to verify the validity of syntactic co-occurrences in the first step compared with surface co-occurrences. The surface co-occurrences are generated with 5-word window size and the syntactic co-occurrences are generated from the dependency triples. We systemically sampled 100 measure points (by one percent interval) in the respective ranking list of surface co-occurrences and syntactic co-occurrences, extracted semi-peripheral collocations in the second step by LLR, and computed the precisions and recalls which are shown in Table 2.

Table 2. Comparison of surface and syntactic co-occurrences

Percentage	Window-based (%)			Syntax-based (%)		
	P	R	F	P	R	F
10	13.9843	28.5363	**18.7702**	32.7715	21.5252	25.9837
20	10.7229	38.1304	16.7387	28.7933	29.6433	29.2121
30	08.7080	45.2645	14.6061	25.7732	36.9004	**30.3490**
40	07.5996	53.5055	13.3089	22.3979	41.8204	29.1720
50	06.6740	59.9016	12.0099	20.0832	47.4785	28.2267
60	05.8837	63.8376	10.7743	18.3206	53.1365	27.2469
70	05.2647	67.4047	09.7665	15.9734	56.2116	24.8775
80	04.7825	70.6027	08.9583	14.0320	59.2866	22.6930
90	04.4079	72.2017	08.3086	12.5244	63.2226	20.9071
100	04.1159	**73.5547**	07.7956	11.2586	**66.7897**	19.2690

We find that the syntactic co-occurrences perform much better than the surface co-occurrences. The highest F1 of the surface co-occurrences is 18.77 %, and that of the syntactic co-occurrences is 30.35 %. However, the surface co-occurrences get higher recall, which indicates that, although the surface co-occurrences bring more potential candidates, they introduce massive noise. The lower recall of the syntactic co-occurrences is due to that the same surface co-occurrence can derive different syntactic co-occurrences which consist of the dependency relation and the original word pair in the surface co-occurrence, making the data sparser.

We also compare our thesaurus with WordNet, to see whether such world knowledge base can help to improve the performance of the tool. We adopt the precision for the evaluation. Our gold standard from *Oxford Collocation Dictionary* adopts a broad concept of collocation and contains many semi-peripheral collocations according to our definition (e.g. *great effort*), but our tool may filter out some semi-peripheral collocations in the gold standard (e.g. *great effort*). The recall decreases and thus is not appropriate for evaluation.

WordNet is a well-organized knowledge base which contains 117, 000 synsets "interlinked by means of conceptual-semantic and lexical relations", while our thesaurus only consists of 31,118 entries, with each attached with 10 similar words. Surprisingly, the result in Fig. 1 shows that our thesaurus performs better than WordNet before the top 38 %, and becomes worse after 38 %. Actually WordNet didn't filter

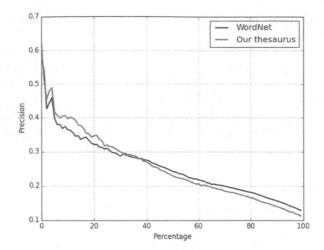

Fig. 1. Comparison of WordNet and our thesaurus

many semi-peripheral collocations out. Instead, it is relatively conservative because many substitutions of the collocation candidate which are composed of the synonym and the original base don't appear in our corpus at all, which means the condition (a) in the third step is not satisfied let alone condition (b), thus misleading the tool to regard the candidate as core collocation. It indicates that the word distribution difference between the created corpus and WordNet should be considered if we want to utilize the semantic information.

We list some collocations of the following 6 bases (3 (POS type)*2 (keyness type)) in the gold standard set: *effort, promote, mutual, deal, pursue,* and *gorgeous*. We set the threshold of four phases (or methods) as 8 %, 2 %, 42 % and 64 %, where the F value of the respective collocation ranking list gets the highest value (Table 3).

For example, as shown in Table 2, the window-based method can extract most collocations (e.g. *make effort, promote harmony, mutual benefit*) that our tool extract except some collocations (e.g. *mutual suspicion, under-the-table deal*).The collocations in our tool are narrowing down from the peripheral to the core. For example, the base *effort* has collocates *make, spare, put, extra* in Peripheral, has collocates *make, spare, put* in Semi-peripheral, and only has collocates *make* and *spare* in Core. The collocates of *gorgeous* are not extracted because of the absence of its collocates in our test corpus, and null is filled in that raw.

3 Application

3.1 Similarity

We employ Dice Coefficient to evaluate the similarity of two words. Taking each collocate of a word as one of its features, the more common features between two words, the more similar they are.

Table 3. Extracted collocation examples in different phases

Base	Window-based	Peripheral	Semi-peripheral	Core
Effort	make effort spare effort put effort strenuous effort tireless effort	make effort spare effort put effort extra effort	make effort spare effort put effort	make effort spare effort
Promote	promote harmony promote cooperation promote understanding	promote harmony promote cooperation promote benefit	promote harmony promote cooperation	promote harmony
Mutual	mutual benefit mutual cooperation **mutual suspicion**	mutual benefit mutual cooperation	mutual benefit mutual cooperation mutual dependence	mutual benefit
Deal	sign deal lucrative deal **under-the-table deal**	sigh deal good deal	sign deal announce deal	sign deal
Pursue	pursue dream pursue innovation	pursue dream pursue goal pursue education	pursue dream pursue goal	pursue dream
Gorgeous	null	null	null	null

$$\mathrm{Dice}(v1, v2) = \frac{2|coll(v1) \cap coll(v1)|}{|coll(v1)| + |coll(v2)|} \tag{7}$$

v is the head word, *coll* is the set of collocates of v.

3.2   Corpus

We build a Corpus of China English (CCE). The corpus size is 126 MB, 24 million words and 0.9 million sentences. The texts are crawled by Scrapy[2], a popular crawling framework in Python community, from the official webpages of China Daily[3], Xinhua News[4], the State Council of the People's Republic of China[5], and the Ministry of

---

[2] http://scrapy.org.

[3] http://www.chinadaily.cn.

[4] http://www.news.cn/english/.

[5] http://english.gov.cn/.

Foreign Affairs of the People's Republic of China[6]. China Daily and Xinhua News are mainstream comprehensive media that have international influence and publication. The rest two are mainly about politics, economics and diplomacy.

3.3   Test Set

Based on the keyword list made from the wordlists of CCE and British National Corpus (BNC) with WordSmith Tool 5.0 (the wordlist of BNC is cited from Scott [8]), we collected 52 verbs from the top 1,000 highest-keyness words. For each verb we extracted 100 collocations (if there exit so many) with our extraction tool, with a total of 5125 collocations. A high-keyness word is defined as one that occurs at least 3 times in CCE and its relative frequency in CCE is statistically significantly larger than in BNC (p-value is 0.05), meaning it is strongly preferred by the editors of the four newspapers.

3.4   Collocations of Similar Verb in China English

Now that most verbs in our list are positive or neutral, we also wonder, for example in the positive group, whether and to what extent the verbs are similar to each other. We calculated Dice Coefficient of the verbs. As shown in Fig. 2, the red points represent verbs, the orange edges represent similarity between two verbs. The thicker the line is, the more similar the two verbs are to each other.

We can see clearly that verbs such as *promote, strengthen, enhance, deepen, improve, expand, boost, push, accelerate, facilitate,* and *develop* are strongly connected with several other verbs, usually expressing a positive meaning. We made pairwise comparison of the 11 verbs, and their different collocates are given in Table 4. All the collocations are obviously loan translation rendered from Chinese conventional expressions.

These collocations in China English reflect conventional expressions of Chinese, especially "various forms of officialese and fixed formulations peculiar to the Chinese political tradition" [33]. In Chinese context our ears are uninterruptedly poured with such expressions, "极大促进", "积极扩大", "大力促进", or "坚定不移地推进". Yet when referring to the *Oxford Collocation Dictionary*, we find varied collocates, like (aggressively, likely) *promote*, (aggressively, playfully, carefully, slowly, blindly) *push*, (radically, exponentially) *expand*, (artificially) *boost*.

These VERB + ADV phrase in China English describe a strong feeling of individual intention and these collocation expressions originate in Chinese expressions appearing extensively in television or newspaper. Due to the quite abstract and opaque meanings of so similar collocations, Chinese people inevitably become confused when they encounter the lexicon selection problem even in Chinese, let alone in English. The collocation comparison may provide a pedagogical reference for China English.

---

[6] http://www.fmprc.gov.cn/mfa_eng/.

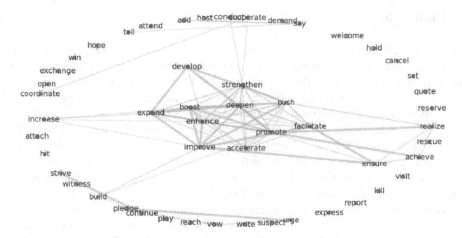

Fig. 2. Verb net based on collocation similarity

Table 4. Examples of extracted collocaitons of the 11 connected verbs

Base verb	Noun collocates	ADV collocates
Promote	development, peace, prosperity, growth, stability, integration	actively, vigorously, jointly
Strengthen	coordination, communication, supervision, dialogue, trust, management	within ~ framework, ~ on ~ issue
Enhance	trust, coordination, communication, capability, competitiveness	
Deepen	trust, relationship	constantly, continuously, third, ~ in area, within ~ framework
Improve	livelihood, quality, efficiency, system, mechanism, environment	constantly
Expand	scope, scale, business, demand	at pace, rapidly, continuously
Boost	confidence, demand, economy, consumption, vitality, sales, employment	significantly
Push	price	forward, up, ahead, for unceasing ~, to brink, for progress, to limit, along track
Accelerate	transformation, pace, negotiation, modernization, restructure	to ~ percent
Facilitate	clearance, transformation, flow, interflow, travel, implementation	
Develop	economy, industry, country, weapon	rapidly, smoothly, soundly

4 Conclusion

The hierarchical collocation extraction tool we propose corresponds the output of each phase to the structured definitions. The performance is comparable with the state-of-art extraction methods [2, 26]. By emphasizing broadness in the first two steps and accuracy in the last step, it may offer EFL learners and linguists more choices.

In its application experiment, we built a large corpus of Chinese English and extracted long-distance collocations as well as consecutive ones automatically. We explored how China English is nativilized in terms of verb collocation. Verbs are connected in a network to show their similarity in a collocation perspective instead of traditional semantic perspective. The collocation comparison of similar verbs provides a useful pedagogical reference for China English.

Most of the salient verb collocations are loan translation rendered from Chinese conventional officialeses. They are inevitably influenced by Chinese culture, Chinese linguistic features, and political traditions. We see that China English is exporting Chinese culture and a soft power to expand Chinese influence in the world.

Till now the model is monolingual, not multilingual. As collocation tends to be the one that can't be translated literally between two languages [33], we plan to add inter-lingual features so as to utilize multilingual resources such as aligned phrases and so on.

References

1. Seretan, V.: Syntax-based collocation extraction. Text, Speech and Language Technology Series. Springer, Netherlands (2011)
2. Evert, S.: Corpora and collocations. In: Lüdeling, A., Kytö, M. (eds.) Corpus Linguistics. An International Handbook, pp. 1112–1248. Mouton de Gruyter, Berlin (2008)
3. Smadja, F.: Retrieving collocations from text: Xtract. Comput. Linguist. **19**(1), 143–177 (1993)
4. Dunning, T.: Accurate methods for the statistics of surprise and coincidence. Comput. Linguist. **19**(1), 61–74 (1993)
5. Wermter, J., Hahn, U.: Paradigmatic modifiability statistics for the extraction of complex multi-word terms. In: Proceedings of the Conference on Human Language Technology and Empirical Methods in Natural Language Processing, pp. 843–850. Association for Computational Linguistics (2005)
6. Lin, D.: Extracting collocations from text corpora. In: Proceedings of the First Workshop on Computational Terminology, Montreal, Canada, pp. 57–63 (1998)
7. Heid, U., Weller, M.: Tools for collocation extraction: preferences for active vs. passive. In: Sixth International Conference on Language Resources & Evaluation LREC, vol. 24, pp. 1266–1272 (2008)
8. Scott, M.: WordSmith Tools Version 5.0. Lexical Analysis Software, Liverpool (2008)
9. Li, D., Cao, J., Huang D.: A hierarchical collocation extraction tool. In: The 5th IEEE International Conference on Big Data and Cloud Computing (BDCloud 2015), pp. 51–55, Dalian, China, 26–29 August 2015
10. He, D., Li, D.C.S.: Language attitudes and linguistic features in the "China English" debate. World Englishes **28**(1), 70–89 (2009)

11. Kirkpatrick, A., Zhichang, X.U.: Chinese pragmatic norms and 'China English'. World Englishes **21**(2), 269–279 (2002)
12. Wei, Y., Jia, F.: Using english in China. Engl. Today **19**(4), 42–47 (2003)
13. Du, R., Jiang, Y.: China English in the past 20 years. 33(1), 37–41 (2001)
14. Bolton, K., Graddol, D.: English in china today. Engl. Today **28**(03), 3–9 (2012)
15. Yang, J.: Lexical innovations in China English. World Engl. **24**(4), 425–436 (2005)
16. Zhang, H.: Bilingual creativity in Chinese English: Ha Jin's in the pond. World Engl. **21**(2), 305–315 (2002)
17. Yu, X., Wen, Q.: The nativilized characteristics of evaluative adjective collocational patterns in China's english-language newspapers. Foreign Lang. Teach. **5**, 23–28 (2010)
18. Ai, H., You, X.: The grammatical features of english in a chinese internet discussion forum. World Engl. **34**(2), 211–230 (2015)
19. Hamid, M.B., Baldauf, Jr., R.B.: Second language errors and features of world Englishes. World Engl. 32(4), 476–494 (2013)
20. Kachru, B.B.: World Englishes: approaches, issues and resources. Lang. Teach. **25**(1), 1–14 (1992)
21. Bahns, J.: Lexical collocations: a contrastive view. ELT J. **47**(1), 56–63 (1993)
22. Benson, M., Benson, I., Robert, E.: The BBI combinatory dictionary of English: a guide to word combinations, pp. x–xxiii. Benjamins John, New York (1986)
23. Sinclair, J.: Corpus, Concordance. Collocation. Shanghai Foreign Language Education Press, Shanghai (2000)
24. Mckeown, K.R., Ravd, D.R.: Collocations. In: Dale, R., Moils, H., Somers, H. (eds.) Handbook of Natural Language Processing, pp. 1–19. CRC Press (2000)
25. Firth, J.R.: A synopsis of linguistic theory, 1903–1955. In: Studies in Linguistic Analysis (Special volume of the Philological Society), pp. 1–15 (1962)
26. Bartsch, S., Evert, S.: Towards a firthian notion of collocation. Online publication Arbeiten zui Linguistik. **2**, 48–60 (2014)
27. Kiss, T., Strunk, J.: Unsupervised multilingual sentence boundary detection. Comput. Linguist. **32**, 485–525 (2006)
28. Bird, S., Loper, E.: NLTK: the natural language toolkit. In: Proceedings of the ACL Workshop on Effective Tools and Methodologies for Teaching Natural Language Processing and Computational Linguistics. Association for Computational Linguistics, Philadelphia (2002)
29. Klein, D., Manning, C.D.: Accurate unlexicalized parsing. In: Proceedings of the 41st Meeting of the Association for Computational Linguistics, pp. 423–430 (2003)
30. Miller, G.A.: Wordnet: a lexical database for English. Commun. ACM **38**(11), 39–41 (1995)
31. Lin, D.: Automatic identification of non-compositional phrases. In: Proceedings of ACL 1999, pp. 317–324. University of Maryland, Maryland (1999)
32. Alvaro, J.J.: Analyzing China's english-language media. World Engl. **34**(2), 260–277 (2015)
33. Pereira, L., Strafella, E., Duh, K., Matsumoto, Y.: Identifying collocations using cross-lingual association measures. In: ACL 2014 14th Conference of the European Chapter of the Association for Computational Linguistics Proceedings of the 10th Workshop on Multiword Expressions (MWE 2014), pp. 26–27 (2014)

Semantics

The Designing and Construction
of Domain-oriented
Vietnamese-English-Chinese FrameNet

Li Lin[1(✉)], Huihui Chen[2], and Yude Bi[1]

[1] Luoyang University of Foreign Languages,
Luoyang 471003, Henan, China
lamle@163.com, biyude@gmail.com
[2] Luoyang Institute of Science and Technology,
Luoyang 471003, Henan, China
ddchh@163.com

Abstract. Frame Semantics and the FrameNet are known as an example of a semantic theory model supporting large engineering projects of knowledge representation and maintaining a long-term vitality. At the same time, the initial goal of FrameNet is to build a large online computational dictionary, so the semantic frames are lacking in systematicness and hierarchy from the whole, and did not distinguish between the two concepts "semantic domain" and "topic domain". These problems make it difficult to unify the concrete goal, the domains, the frame structure, the annotation method and the overall scale of the non-English FrameNet construction and have created some obstacles for multi-language FrameNets to the applications of NLP. As a result, we propose some ideas on Domain-oriented Multilingual Frame Semantic Representation (DOMLFSR). The construction of Domain-oriented Vietnamese-English-Chinese FrameNet(DOV-E-CFN) is a concrete practice of DOMLFSR. On the basis of DOV-E-CFN, we gave a preliminary analysis of event extrction application based on kernel dependency graph(KDG).

Keywords: Domain-oriented · Frame semantics · Vietnamese · Knowledge representation · Event extraction

1 Introduction

Frame Semantics and the FrameNet are known as an example of a semantic theory model supporting large engineering projects of knowledge representation and maintaining a long-term vitality [1]. Frame semantics has a complete system, is an effective knowledge representation with empirical semantic properties against the background of cognitive mechanism, and directly oriented to the application. FrameNet is characterized as an organic unification of theoretical guidance and empirical induction, with outstanding multi-language expandability and domain extensibility [2].

The initial goal of FrameNet is to build a large online computational dictionary, so the semantic frames are lacking in systematicness and hierarchy from the whole [3]. In recent years, FrameNet began to pay attention to the understanding of domain corpus

M. Sun et al. (Eds.): CCL and NLP-NABD 2015, LNAI 9427, pp. 53–65, 2015.
DOI: 10.1007/978-3-319-25816-4_5

text [4], but still did not distinguish between the two concepts "semantic domain" and "topic domain". Although the construction of non-English FrameNets has developed rapidly [5–7], they also have the similar problems. These problems make it difficult to unify the concrete goal, the domains, the frame structure, the annotation method and the overall scale of the non-English FrameNet construction and have created some obstacles for multi-language FrameNets to the applications of NLP. As a result, we propose some ideas on Domain-oriented Multilingual Frame Semantic Representation (DOMFSR).

Vietnamese is an Austroasiatic language and has many similarities with Chinese. On the other hand, Vietnamese is spoken by about 82 million people, the Internet development enabled Vietnam to rank among the countries which enjoy the fastest growth in the number of Internet users in the world. This provides a great convenience for us to build a Domain-oriented Vietnamese-English-Chinese FrameNet (DOV-E-CFN). The construction of DOV-E-CFN is a concrete practice of DOMLFSR.

We chose "vietnamnet.vn" and "xaluan.com" as the Vietnam News corpus source. Currently, the news texts categories with reference to "http://vietnamnet.vn/vn/chinh-tri/" and divided into five topics: Foreign News (Đối Ngoại), Congress News (Thời Sự Quốc Hội), Constitutional amendments News (Sửa Hiến Pháp), Anti-Corruption News (Chống Tham Nhũng), Salary reform News (Cải Cách Lương). We focuses on Foreign News (Đối Ngoại) in this paper. Correspondingly, the main corpus source in English and Chinese includes the following websites: "ifeng.com", "huanqiu.com", "bbc.co.uk", "inquirer.net". The size of corpus has been obtained is more than 5000 texts, about 30 M.

The rest of the paper is structured as follows. Section 2 provides a brief overview of the DOMFSR designing, including the overall architecture, the Frame element hierarchical system and the Frame semantic construction expression system; Sect. 3 describes the specific process of DOV-E-CFN construction, including designing and developing news corpus extraction software to build domain corpus of Vietnamese, English and Chinese; exploring the building methods of lexical unit(LU) database and semi-automatic mapping method of frame database; designing and implementing assistive tools to build DOV-E-CFN, especially to annotate example sentences; Sect. 4 gives a preliminary analysis of event extrction application based on kernel dependency graph. Finally, Sect. 5 concludes and provides an outlook on future research.

2   The DOMFSR Designing

2.1   DOMLFSR Overall Architecture

After the comparative analysis of the construction methods and characteristics of the main non-English FrameNets, we present DOMLFSR mode as a theoretical model of domain-oriented multilingual FrameNet construction.

Because there is a relative lack of previous studies in Vietnamese [8], in order to make the research more targeted, in the process of frame element hierarchical system (FEHS) and frame semantic construction expression system(FSCES) construction, we put more attention on the analysis and consolidation of related Vietnamese language phenomena, summarizing the characteristics of the type of language to facilitate a future expansion to other similar language.

Specifically, we set up a relatively fixed three-tier hierarchical frame element system of 35 frame elements, and the frame elements of fourth-tier are expandable according to the specific needs identified in the domain-oriented multilingual FrameNet construction.

DOMLFSR overall architecture is shown in the following Fig. 1.

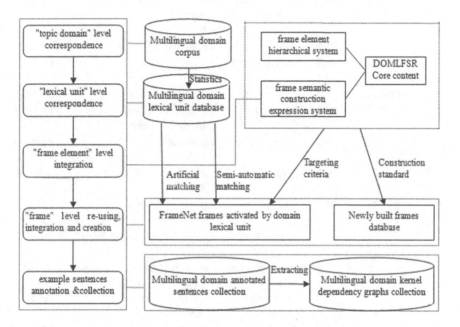

Fig. 1. DOMLFSR overall architecture

2.2   Frame Element Hierarchical System

Multilingual integration is more important than multi-language expandation in DOMLFSR, that is to say, cross-linguistic "multilinguality" will be realized in a same frame. we will build a relatively unified "frame element hierarchical system", making a primary reference for name, definition and annotation color of frame element, some adjustment will be made according to actual demand (Table 1).

FEHS has the following characteristics: the hierarchical system is corresponding to the verbal semantic classification; the system includes a hierarchical set of markup symbols, frame element HEX color code and the corresponding background color. In addition, it ensures that the same color will not use repeatly in the same FrameNet, while ensuring the a frame elements consistent with the same background color in different FrameNet [9]. It is of great importance to frame construction, sentence annotation and the valence patterns statistics of lexical unit, providing precondition for DOMLFSR.

Table 1. The core frames element of DOMLFSR

Tier 1	Tier 2	Tier 3				
		Chinese	English	Vietamese	Vietamese frame element kasus (FK)	HEX code
Core Frame Element	Subjects	施事	agent, Agt	vai tác thể	bị, được, do, bởi	FF0000
		当事	essive, Ess	vai thực thể	bị, được	FFFF00
		感事	expierencer, Exp	vai nghiệm thể	bị, được, vì	DC143C
		致事	causer, Cau	vai gây sự	bị, được	008080
		领事	possessor, Pos	vai chủ sở hữu	của	FF00FF
	Objects	受事	patient, Pat	vai bị thể	vào	00008B
		客事	entity, Ent	vai đối tượng	đối với, đến, ở, vào, cho	FF1493
		役事	causee, Cae	vai bị bắt buộc		6495ED
		成事	product, Prod	vai sản vật	thành, ra	00FF7F
	Relevances	与事	dative, Dat	vai tiếp thể	cho	FFE4C4
		协事	companion, Comp	vai đối chiếu	với, cùng, bằng	00FF7F
		类事	classification, Clas	vai tương ứng	như, trừ, làm, trở thành, trở nên	FF7F50
		属事	belongings, Belo	vài thuộc thể	của	7FFFAA
		位事	destination, Dest	vai đích thể	ở	F5DEB3

2.3   Frame Semantic Construction Expression System

To meet the needs of positioning domain frame hierarchical relationship accurately, we will build "frame semantic construction expression system"(FSCES) as a relatively complete hierarchical system of "semantic domain" [10], then mapping with Chinese Thesaurus -Tongyici Cilin (Extended Edition) (Table 2).

The "frame semantic construction expression system" is a hierarchical system of theoretical deduction on the collocation pattern between target lexical unit and core frame element. As the main emphasis of DOMLFSR, it can provide a basis for the analysis and annotation of sentential semantic structure.

We argues that based on the study of native language researchers, it should build a "frame semantic construction expression system" as a theoretical hierarchical system for deducting the collocation between target lexical unit and core frame element, providing the basis for semantic structure analysis and annotation of example sentences. At this

Table 2. Chinese and Vietanamese FSCES (Excerpts)

Semantic Classification				Frame Semantic Construction Expression System (FSCES)			
Tier 1	Tier 2	Semantic Features	Valency	Chinese basic FSCES		Vietnamese basic FSCES	
Action/ Behavior	Independent action	[Action] [Control]	Monovalent	ca	施事+Vp	va	Np_Agt+Vp
				cb	Vp+施事	vb	Vp +Np_Agt
				cc	领事+Vp +施事		
	Dominate	[Action] [Control] [Transitive]	Divalent	ca	施事+Vp +受事	va	Np_Agt +Vp +Np_Pat
				cb	施事+把/将 +受事 +Vp	vb	Np_Pat +bị +(Np_Agt)+Vp
				cc	受+被/由/ 归+(施 事)+Vp	vc	Np_Pat + bị+Vp +do+Np_Agt
	Manufacture	[Action] [Control] [result]	Divalent	ca	施事+Vp +成事	va	Np_Agt +Vp +Np_Prod
				cb	施事+把 +成事 +Vp	vb	Np_Prod +bị +Np_Agt +Vp
				cc	成事+被 +施事 +Vp	vc	Np_Prod +(Np_Agt)+Vp
				cd	成事+(施 事)+Vp		
	Displacement	[Action] [Control] [Direction]	Divalent	ca	施事+Vp +(介词) +位事	va	Np_Agt+Vp+K +Np_Dest
				cb	施事+位事 +Vp	vb	Np_Agt+Np_Dest +Vp
				cc	位事+Vp +施事	vc	Np_Dest+Vp +Np_Agt
	Placement	[Action] [Control] [Existence]	Trivalent	ca	施事+位事 +Vp+受 事	va	Np_Agt +Vp+ Np_Pat + Np_Dest
				cb	施事+Vp +受事 +位事	vb	Np_Pat + (được/bị) Np_Agt +Vp+ Np_Dest
				cc	施事+(把) 受事+Vp +位事	vc	Np_Dest + Np_Agt +Vp+ Np_Pat
				cd	受事+(被) 施事+Vp +位事	vd	Np_Agt +Vp+ Np_Dest + Np_Pat

(Continued)

Table 2. (*Continued*)

Semantic Classification				Frame Semantic Construction Expression System (FSCES)			
				ce	位事+施事 +Vp+受 事	ve	Np_Dest +Vp+ Np_Pat
				cf	施事+Vp +位事 +受事		
				cg	位事+Vp +受事(施 事隐含)		

stage, Chinese and Vietanamese FSCES is the focus of the study, English lexical unit semantic description of Berkeley FrameNet will be integrated in the next step.

3 The DOV-E-CFN Construction

The DOV-E-CFN is driven by NLP tasks, and has implemented an organic collocation and combination of three languages in the same semantic frame.

A concrete integration realized in three levels:

– The DOV-E-CFN corpus preparation: corresponding in the "topic domain" level;
– Domain lexical unit Collection and classification: integration in the "semantic domain" level;
– Frame System and its relationship description: reusing, integration and newly built.

Corpus preparation has been introduced earlier in Introduction. The following descriptions are about the second and third points.

3.1 Domain Lexical Unit Collection and Classification

After the word segmentation, POS tagging and word frequency statistics, we obtained the following data:

– There are 445 high-frequency words in English news corpus (1783 articles), which frequency of occurrence is more than 200 times, including 60 verbs, accounting for a lower proportion of 13.48%.
– There are 1064 high-frequency words in Chinese news corpus (2296 articles), which frequency of occurrence is more than 200 times, including 229 verbs, accounting for a proportion of 21.52%.
– There are 1433 high-frequency words in Vietnamese news corpus (2500 articles), which frequency of occurrence is more than 200 times, including 344 verbs, accounting for a proportion of 24.01%.

Table 3. Semantic classification of high frequency verbs of DOV-E-CFN (Excerpts)

Vietnamese LU	English LU	Chinese LU	Chinese LU Valency	Tongyici Cilin classification code
đề cập	mention	提及	Trivalent	Hi12A51#
kể	tell, relate	讲述	Trivalent	Hi13D01
lên tiếng	claim	声明	Trivalent	Hi13D08
báo cáo	report	报告	Trivalent	Hi15A01
đối phó	deal	应对	Divalent	Hi18B01
chấp nhận	accept, admit	承认	Trivalent	Hi22A01
can thiệp	intervene, interfere	干涉	Divalent	Hi23A01
bàn giao	transfer	移交	Trivalent	Hi27A08@
đối thoại	dialogue	对话	Divalent	Hi31A01
thỏa thuận	consent	协商,商定	Trivalent	Hi31A01

The synonymous Vietnamese-English-Chinese lexical units will be put into the same semantic frame to to retrieve the example sentences from respective news corpus.

3.2 Frame System and the Frame-Frame Relationship Description

The corresponding frames in Berkeley FrameNet can be evoked by domain English lexical units in Table 3. We reuse and integrate applicative frames of FrameNet primarily. After semi-automatic mapping, we chose 22 frames as an initial frame system of DOV-E-CFN (Table 4).

Table 4. The initial frame system of DOV-E-CFN

No	English frame name	Chinese frame name	Vietnamese frame name
1.	(Statement)	声明	Tuyên bố
2.	(Cause_change_of_position_on_a_scale)	造成位置变化	Gây ra thay đổi vị trí
3.	(Intentionally_create)	有意识创造	Cố ý tạo nên
4.	(Taking_sides)	偏袒	Đứng về phe
5.	(Giving)	给	Cho
6.	(Perception_experience)	认知体验	Kinh nghiệm nhận thức
7.	(Cause_to_perceive)	引起感知	Gây ra cảm nhận
8.	(Supply)	供应	Cung cấp
9.	(Impact)	影响	Tác động
10.	(Posture)	姿态	Tư thế
11.	(Grant_permission)	授予权限	Cấp phép

(Continued)

Table 4. (*Continued*)

No	English frame name	Chinese frame name	Vietnamese frame name
12.	(Awareness)	意识	Nhận thức
13.	(Possession)	拥有	Sở hữu
14.	(Compliance)	遵从	Tuân thủ
15.	(Request)	要求	Yêu cầu
16.	(Change_posture)	变化姿势	Thay đổi tư thế
17.	(Becoming_aware)	知悉	Trở thành nhận thức
18.	(Manufacturing)	制造	Chế tạo
19.	(Compatibility)	相容	Khả năng tương thích
20.	(Cause_motion)	引起运动	Gây ra chuyển động
21.	(Placing)	放置	Đặt
22.	(Bringing)	带来	Đưa

According to the FEHS, some frame elements in original frames of Berkeley FrameNet have been adjusted to meet the new requirements of DOV-E-CFN. Figure 2 shows the adjustment to core frame element of frame "Bringing".

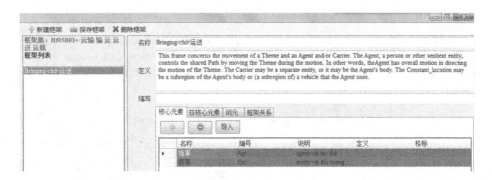

Fig. 2. The adjustment to core frame element of frame "Bringing"

In fact, there is no absolute boundaries between adjusting, integrating existing frames and builting new frames. According to investigation and the situation of other objective factors, we found that 18 domain lexical units have no corresponding frame in Berkeley FrameNet and need to newly built. The source and proportion of DOV-E-CFN frames shows in Fig. 3.

Because of smaller number, it is difficult to describe the frame-frame relations in a domain FrameNet according to the Berkeley FrameNet model. We proposed that in the frame system of domain-oriented multilingual FrameNet, the positioning of reused and newly built frames depends on the semantic classification of FSCES and Chinese Thesaurus -Tongyici Cilin (Extended Edition).

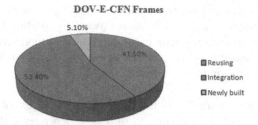

DOV-E-CFN Frames

- Reusing
- Integration
- Newly built

Fig. 3. The source and proportion of DOV-E-CFN frames

3.3 Example Sentence Annotation

Lexical unit and sentence annotation database construction are based on data statistics from Vietnamese-English-Chinese domain Foreign News corpus. The annotation format of example sentence is:

$$\{ <FE - PT - GF - (other) - (NE)\square w > \} o^n <tgt - PT - GF\square w >$$
$$\{ <FE - PT - GF - (other) - (NE)\square w > \} o^n$$

The target lexical unit is identified as "tgt"; "w" is to identify the specific text content; other symbols as "FE", "PT", "GF", "NE" are referring to frame element, phrase type, grammatical function and named entity. The tagset we used in annotating divided into two kinds of English and Chinese. The specific annotating results are shown as follows.

Example sentence (1):

(1) chúng tôi/P sẽ/R giải quyết/V các/L thách thức/N trong/E tương lai/N.

(We will resolve the challenges of the future.)

Annotating results in English tagset:

<Agt-NP-sub chúng tôi/P><ADP-adva sẽ/R><tgt-VP-pre giải quyết><Prob-NP-obj các/L thách thức/N><Time-PP-adva trong/E tương lai/N>

Annotating results in Chinese tagset:

<施事-名词短语-主语 chúng tôi/P><副词短语-状语 sẽ/R><词元-动词短语-谓语中心语 giải quyết><问题-名词短语-宾语 các/L thách thức/N><时间-介词短语-状语 trong/E tương lai/N>

In specific annotation aspect, the characteristics of Vietnamese phrase type and the grammatical functions is deserving more attention in order to make up for the inadequacy of Vietnamese vocabulary semantic resources to some extent. All the Vietnamese-English-Chinese annotated sentences constituted a frame semantic annotation database.

4   Application Exploration

Event extraction, an important research direction in the field of information extraction, has broad application prospects in automatic summarization, automatic question answering and information retrieval etc. Mapping the structure and meaning of language has been considered as one of the basic principles of reearches in Computational Linguistics and Language Information Processing, starting from the bottom of the language law, the pattern-matching event extraction method has important significance for domain-oriented multi-language news events extraction. So, the application of frame semantic annotation in event extraction is another major research topic of the paper.

Kernel dependency graph(KDG) includes small packages of information that associate the lexical head (governor) of a set of related dependents, the lexical heads of the constituents that are dependent on that governor, and the frame-specific semantic relations by which the dependent elements are related to the governor [11]. KDGs derived from a large corpus will provide a database offering reliable information about frequencies and collocations in the kind of corpus being used, and KDGs recognized in specific documents can be read off as indications of the subject matter and basic claims of given passages in the documents [12].

We built a DOV-E-CFN to explore the specific application of this method based on the kernel dependency graph(KDG). The method is based on semantic structure extraction, the main contents include KDG semantic analysis model; KGD automatic generation and event templates extraction based on KDG. It can be represented more intuitive by KDG when there is conflict between semantic and syntactic structure expression, such as support verb, transparent nouns, null instantiation and frame element fusion etc.

The KDG of example sentence (2) shows the analysis process of null instantiation.

(2) Sát thủ săn ngầm P-8A Poseidon của Hải quân Mỹ, dự kiến sẽ thay thế cho máy bay P-3C.

(Submarine P-8A Poseidon of US Navy which is called Hunter killer, is expected to replace the P-3C aircraft.)

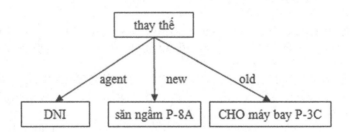

Fig. 4. Null Instantiated FEs of Vietnamese sentence

By analyzing the main process of FrameNet semantic analysis and the event extraction, we have made a feasibility demonstration that frame semantic annotation can be applied in event extraction and proposed a conversion method to generate kernel dependency graphs (KDG) and event template from annotated sentences (Fig. 4).

In order to extract event informations not only on the whole but also on parts, we tried to design and use the specific methods based on KDG to extract event informations of the Foreign News in Vietnamese, English and Chinese, especially in complex long sentences of news texts.

Example sentence (3) is comprising a plurality of target lexical untis. Its KDG generation and event model extraction process is as follows.

(3) Để phục vụ mục tiêu này, Chính phủ Mỹ cần sớm bỏ hoàn toàn lệnh cấm bán vũ khí cho Việt Nam và đóng góp tích cực hơn nữa trong việc giải quyết hậu quả chiến tranh.

(To achieve this goal, the US government must abandon completely the ban on arms sales to Vietnam as soon as possible, and make more positive contribution in solving the the legacy of war.)

Step 1, identify the target lexical units in sen-tence, determine the semantic frames they belongs to.

Step 2, determine annotation range. (3)' shows all the currently-annotated target lexical units in uppercase: PHỤC VỤ(achieve), BỎ(abandon), BÁN(sale), LỆNH CẤM(ban), ĐÓNG GÓP(contribute), GIẢI QUYẾT(solve); and followed by the names of their frames in boldface. This includes a number of nouns such as LỆNH CẤM in the Prohibiting frame whose frames are relatively simple, and so will not be discussed further.

(3)' Để PHỤC VỤ Function mục tiêu này, Chính phủ Mỹ cần sớm BỎ Activity_stop hoàn toàn LỆNH CẤM Deny_permission BÁN Commerce_sell vũ khí cho Việt Nam và ĐÓNG GÓP Giving tích cực hơn nữa trong việc GIẢI QUYẾT Resolve_problem hậu quả chiến tranh.

Because the current annotation range is the target lexical units in main clause, so we do not pay attention to PHỤC VỤ(achieve) in the adverbial.

Step 3, generate the corresponding KDG. Theoretically, all of the information shown in this graph was extracted algorithmically from the XML format of the FrameNet annotations [13]. But at the present stage, only simple sentence which contains only one target lexical unit can be extracted automatically based on the annotated format. The KDG of example sentence (3) shows in Fig. 5 is manually generated.

In Fig. 5, target lexical units are represented as nodes with their FEs as their dependents; the text of the node itself is <Frame name>,<LU name>.<POS>. The arrows to the dependents are labeled with the FE name. Named entity are highlighted in rose red.

Step 4, According to the KDG, we can Get extraction rules as an event template. Event template of example sentence (3):

1. { Type=目的: < Purpose >;Type=施事: < Agent >;Type=当事: < Theme > }< Purpose >< Agent >< tgt= bỏ >< Theme >;
2. { Type=目的: < Purpose >;Type=施事: < Agent >;Type=当事: < Theme > }< Purpose >< Agent >< tgt= đóng góp >< Theme >;
3. { Type=权威方: < Authority >;Type=行为: < Action >;(Type=当事方: < Protagonist >)}< Authority >< tgt= lệnh cấm >< Action >(< Protagonist >);
4. { (Type=卖方: < Seller >);Type=商品: < Goods >;Type=买方: < Buyer > }(< Seller >) < tgt= bán >< Goods > cho < Buyer >;
5. { Type=施事: < Agent >;Type=问题: < Problem > }< Agent ><tgt= giải quyết >< Problem >.

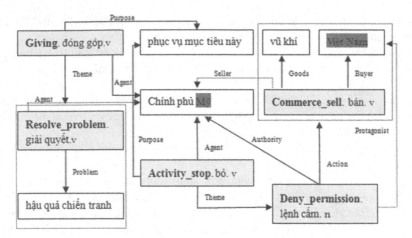

Fig. 5. KDG of example sentence (3)

5   Conclusion

This paper elucidates that our Domain-oriented Multilingual Frame Semantic Representation Model can take advantage of existing virtues from different FrameNets, highlighting the systematicness and hierarchy of semantic frames. On this basis, we built a Domain-oriented Vietnamese-English-Chinese FrameNet, implemented an organic collocation and combination of three languages in the same semantic frame.

Currently, 30 frames, 400 lexical units, and 210 annotated sentences are obtained as a result of DOV-E-CFN. The scale of DOV-E-CFN is not big enough to support the event extraction application, but the feasibility demonstration that frame semantic annotation can be applied in event extraction has been fully demonstrated [14].

Further research will concern expanding the number of annotated example sentences, exploring the automatic generation of KDG for complex sentences in news corpus. In addition, we will transfer above research productions to other suitable oriental languages like Malay, Thai, Japanese, and so on.

References

1. Fillmore, C.J.: A frames approach to semantic analysis. In: Heine, B., Narrog, H. (eds.) The Oxford Handbook of Linguistic Analysis, pp. 313–340, Oxford University Press (2009)
2. Fillmore, C.J., Lee-Goldman, R.R., Rhodes, R.-S.: The framenet constructicon. In: Boas, H. C., Sag, I.A. (eds.) Sign-based Construction Grammar. CSLI Publications, Stanford (2011)
3. Boas, H.C. (ed.): Multilingual FrameNets in Computational Lexicography: Methods and Applications. Mouton de Gruyter, Berlin (2009)

4. Behrang, M., Narayanan, S.: Semantic ex-traction with wide-coverage lexical resources. In: Proceedings of the 2003 Conference of the North American Chapter of the Association for Computational Linguistics on Human Language Technology: Companion Volume of the Proceedings of HLT-NAACL 2003–short papers, vol. 2. Association for Computational Linguistics, pp. 64–66 (2003)
5. Kaiying, L.I.U.: Reseach on chinese framenet con-struction and application technologies. J. Chin. Inf. Process. **6**, 47 (2011)
6. Ohara, K.H.: Toward constructicon building for japanese in japanese framenet. In: Veredas On-Line - Frame Semantics and its tech-nological applications **17**(1), PPG LINGUISTICA/UFJF-JUIZ DE FORA. 13 (2013)
7. Dhanon, L., et al.: Manifesting thai concep-tual scenarios through thai framenet. In: 7th International Conference on Natural Language Pro-cessing and Knowledge Engineering, NLPKE 2011, Tokushima, Japan, November 27–29, pp. 27–29 (2011)
8. Li, L.I.N., Yude, B.I.: A frame semantics analysis of the giving-type verbs in vietnamese. J. PLA Univ. Foreign Lang. **2**, 42–46 (2012)
9. Kuerban, A., Kuerban, W., Fang, D.: Conceptual design of uyghur framenet. J. Chin. Inf. Process. (2), 41–46 (2013)
10. Liping, Y., Tao, L., Kaiying, L.I.U.: Research on the chinese framenet. In: ConstructionNationality Language and Characters Information Research Technology—Proceedings in Eleventh National Information Academic Symposium on Nationality Language and Characters, pp. 453–461 (2007)
11. Fillmore, C.J., Baker, C.F., Hiroaki, S.: Seeing arguments through transparent struc-turcs. In: Proceedings of the Third International Conference on Languag Resources and Evaluation vol. III. Las Palmas: LREC, pp. 787–791 (2002)
12. Fillmore, C.J., Ruppenhofer, J., Baker, C.F.: FrameNet and representing the link between semantic and syntactic relations computational linguistics and beyond. In: Huang, C.-R., Lenders, W. (eds.) Language and Linguistics Monographs Series B. Taipei: Institute of Linguistics, Academia Sinica, pp. 19–62 (2004)
13. Fillmore, C.J., Narayanan, S., Baker, C.F.: What can linguistics contribute to event ex-traction. In: Proceedings of the 2006 AAAI Workshop on Event Extraction and Synthesis, pp. 18–23 (2006)
14. Li, L.I.N.: A study on vietnamese frame semantic annotation based on the news corpus. J. Chin. Inf. Process. **6**, 201–208 (2013)

Semantic Role Labeling Using Recursive Neural Network

Tianshi Li[1,2] and Baobao Chang[1(✉)]

[1] Key Laboratory of Computational Linguistics, Ministry of Education,
School of Electronics Engineering and Computer Science, Peking University,
Beijing 100871, China
lts_417@hotmail.com, chbb@pku.edu.cn
[2] Collaborative Innovation Center for Language Ability, Xuzhou 221009, China

Abstract. Semantic role labeling (SRL) is an important NLP task for understanding the semantic of sentences in real-world. SRL is a task which assigns semantic roles to different phrases in a sentence for a given word. We design a recursive neural network model for SRL. On the one hand, comparing to traditional shallow models, our model does not dependent on lots of rich hand-designed features. On the other hand, different from early deep models, our model is able to add many shallow features. Further more, our model uses global structure information of parse trees. In our experiment, we evaluate using the CoNLL-2005 data and reach a competitive performance with fewer features.

1 Introduction

Semantic analysis of natural language is a basic task in natural language processing (NLP) that makes computer understand the semantic of the language automatically and always plays an important role in most NLP works. Semantic role labeling (SRL) is a sub-task of semantic analysis. Given a predicate of a sentence, the goal of SRL is to assign sematic roles to the constituents of the sentence with respect to the predicate.

Given a sentence s and a predicate (or a verb) in the sentence, the goal of SRL task is to find out all the phrases in the sentence which have semantic roles respect to the predicate. For example, consider the following sentence: *Jack opened the window*. In this sentence, *Jack* is the agent of the verb *opened*, and *the window* is the patient of the verb *opened*. Here agent and patient are two semantic roles to the verb *opened*. Attention that one phrase in the sentence could only have at most one semantic role to the given predicate. The earliest and most popular SRL annotation corpus is PropBank built by Martha Palmer et al. [1]. In PropBank, the semantic roles are divided into two classes: core arguments and adjunctive arguments. Core arguments are consist of five subclasses: ARG0,...,ARG4. As the example sentence shown above, *Jack* is ARG0 and *the window* is ARG1. In recent years, the shared task of SRL as CoNLL-2005 usually gives the sentence and the predicate, the only goal is predicting the semantic roles of the given predicate.

SRL is a well-defined task explored by researchers over ten years. In the past decade, most researchers have been focusing on the SRL task mainly using shallow models. They extracted a lot of hand-designed features from the sentence and the parse

© Springer International Publishing Switzerland 2015
M. Sun et al. (Eds.): CCL and NLP-NABD 2015, LNAI 9427, pp. 66–76, 2015.
DOI: 10.1007/978-3-319-25816-4_6

tree of the sentence, and then put these features into a classifier. The researchers in previous works always used a two-step strategy [2]. The first step is to judge whether the constituent of the sentence is a semantic role of the predicate. The second step is distinguishing the different roles among the constituents which are classified as semantic role in the first step. Various machine learning method have been used in different SRL systems as SVM [3], decision tree [4], and log-linear model [5]. One of drawbacks of these traditional models is that they need a lot of hand-designed features and rich resources to reach high performance.

In recent years, deep learning is becoming more and more popular in NLP. Compare with traditional model, one significant advantage of deep learning is that deep neural model doesn't need too many manual features. The network can learn this feature itself during training. Some researchers have already tried some deep learning method in SRL. Collobert et al. [6] used convolutional neural network instead of traditional model. They model SRL task using Time Delay neural networks and got competitive performance compared to the state-of-art traditional model. However, they did not model the structure information during model training.

This paper builds a novel recursive deep neural network model for SRL. SRL is a task based on a lot of syntax knowledge, especially parsed syntax tree. Previous works usually use this knowledge as features. We hope to excavate more information than previous works. By the convenience of deep neural network, we can directly use the parsed tree as our network. We expect that our model can learn more syntax knowledge during the network propagating on the parsed tree. For this reason, The recursive neural network is appropriate to our work. Our model is a global structure model which is different with Collobert. In their work, their model handled each word in the sentence one by one independently. In our model, when considering whether a phrase has semantic role, we use global structure information in the parse tree. Different from two-step method, our model directly gives whether a constituent is semantic role and which the role type. Although using a few features in out experiment, our model is still extendible that it can also add more traditional hand-designed features and gets a competitive performance.

Section 2 talks about our model's architecture and how does our model work. Section 3 shows the experiment and the result. Section 4 shows some related works. Section 5 is the conclusion.

2 Recursive Neural Model

2.1 Basic Recursive Model

Our basic model is shown as Fig. 1. Each non-leaf node in the RNN tree has two children. Given a sentence s consist of words $t_1 t_2 \ldots t_n$, x_i is the word embedding of t_i. Here $x_i \in \mathbb{R}^n$, where n is the dimension of the embedding.

First, we focus on the network of the parse tree. Let x_p be the embedding of a parent tree node, x_l be the embedding of the left sub tree node, x_r be the embedding of the right sub tree node. So x_p can be computed as follows:

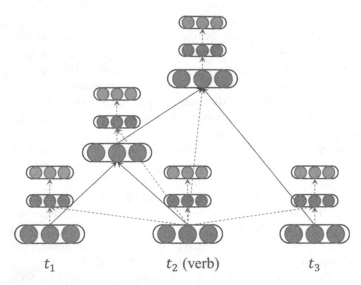

Fig. 1. Our basic recursive model for sentence s. The blue nodes are the parse tree nodes. Suppose t_2 is the verb.

$$x_p = f(W[x_l; x_r] + b) \qquad (1)$$

where $W \in \mathbb{R}^{n \times 2n}$, $[c_1; c_2] \in \mathbb{R}^{2n \times 1}$, b is the bias vector and $b \in \mathbb{R}^n$. f is the activation function, $f = tanh(\cdot)$.

Second, considering that our model predict each node whether it has a semantic role, each tree node has an output layer. Consider the expandability of the network, we also add a hidden layer below output layer. Because each sentence has a given predicate, we add the predicate information into our hidden layer. The network is shown in Fig. 2. Let x_i be the embedding of node i, $h_i \in \mathbb{R}^m$ be the hidden layer of node i, $o_i \in \mathbb{R}^d$ be the output layer of node i, x_{verb} be the embedding of the predicate node in the tree. Where m is the dimension of the hidden vector, d is the dimension of the output layer (d is also the number of semantic role types). h_i and o_i are computed as follows:

$$h_i = f(W_{hid}[x_i; x_{verb}] + b_{hid}) \qquad (2)$$

where $W_{hid} \in \mathbb{R}^{m \times 2n}$, $[x_i; x_{verb}] \in \mathbb{R}^{2n}$ and $b_{hid} \in \mathbb{R}^m$.

$$o_i = f(W_{out}h_i + b_{out}) \qquad (3)$$

where $W_{out} \in \mathbb{R}^{d \times m}$ and $b_{out} \in \mathbb{R}^d$.

Given the sentence s and semantic roles set y, $score(s, y, \theta)$ denotes the score of y in node i. Where θ is the parameter in the network. We directly use o_i as $score(s, y, \theta)$. We regard the role whose value is the max value among the dimension as the semantic role in this node. It is an intuitive way to predict all semantic roles in a sentence.

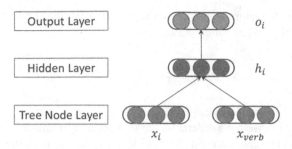

Fig. 2. The network of one tree node i. The blue ones are the tree nodes, the red one is the hidden node, the green one is the output node. x_i is the embedding of tree node i, x_{verb} is the embedding of the predicate node, h_i is the embedding of the hidden layer of node i, o_i is the embedding of the output layer of node i (Color figure online).

2.2 Pruning Strategy

A sentence may contain several clauses, the roles of a given predicate are always in the same clause as the predicate is. So we need not take too much attention on the roles of other clauses. We use a pruning strategy similar as Xue and Palmer [5].

Pruning Strategy
Step 1: Designate the predicate as the current node and collect its sisters (constituents attached at the same level as the predicate). If a sister is a PP, also collect its immediate children.
Step 2: Reset the current node to its parent and repeat Step 1 till it reaches the top level node.

Our strategy do not really discard the nodes which are cut off, we reserve their node embeddings computed as Eq. (2). But only the nodes which are not cut off have the hidden layer and output layer after out pruning strategy. In this way, our model can not only filter redundancy information and accelerate the train speed but also use the whole parse tree information.

2.3 Add Parse Tree Feature

The baseline RNN model can predict correct role in each tree node. However, there is drawback in it. Consider the following case: given a sentence s and the predicate v. t is a word that appears twice in s. To distinguish these two same word, we set them t_1 and t_2. In this sentence, suppose t_1 has a semantic role but t_2 hasn't. When using our baseline model to predict the role of t_1 and t_2, the model use the same weight. Because t_1 and t_2 are the same word, they have same word embedding. According to Eqs. (3) and (4), t_1 and t_2 will finally have the same output after forward propagation. So our baseline model will predict them either the same semantic role or none role. To solve this problem, our baseline model add extra feature from the parse tree.

- Top node feature: Top node is the nearest common parent between the current tree node and the predict node. Top node feature is the embedding of the top node.

We add top node feature in the hidden layer. After adding the feature, the hidden layer vector is computed as following equation:

$$h_i = f(W_{hid}[x_i; x_{verb}; x_{top}] + b_{hid})$$ (4)

where $W_{hid} \in \mathbb{R}^{m \times 3n}$, $[x_i; x_{verb}; x_{top}] \in \mathbb{R}^{3n}$.

Using this feature, we have different input in hidden layer and output layer between t_1 and t_2 in previous case. So our RNN model can distinguish the semantic roles between them now. Figure 3 shows the network after adding two features.

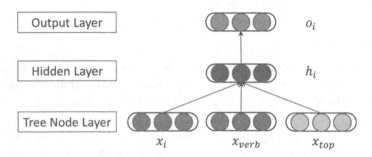

Fig. 3. The network after adding top feature. The yellow one is the feature embedding. x_{top} is the top node feature (Color figure online).

2.4   Distinguish Weight by POS Tag and Node Position

To improve basic model, we add more syntactic features in our RNN model. In this section, we distinguish the weights of the network by POS tag and node position.

POS Tag. In our baseline model, when the network is propagating, the weight W on the parse tree is a sharing parameter. Although the purpose of sharing weight is that the network can learning some general features from each recursive substructure, our goal is predict different semantic roles in one sentence. So our model not only needs the global features but local features as well. Achieving this goal, weight of the parse tree is tied by POS tag. We write it in equation as follows:

$$x_p = f(W^{T_l} x_l + W^{T_r} x_r + b^{T_l} + b^{T_r})$$ (5)

where $W^{T_l}, W^{T_r} \in \mathbb{R}^n$ are weight matrices depend on POS tag T_l and T_r. Here T_l is the POS tag of left sub-node and T_r is the POS tag of right sub-node. In this way, our model can learn global information by sharing weight in the same POS tag and learn local information using different weight between different POS tags.

Node Position. Like the way handling weight W, hidden layer weight W_{hid} is tied by node position. Node position is a feature which represents whether the tree node is in the left, right or middle of the predicate node. Here let all predicate's ancestor nodes (include itself) be the middle of predicate node. For other node in the tree, if it is in the left subtree of any predicate's ancestor nodes, we set it is in the left of the predicate node; if it is in the right subtree of any predicate's ancestor nodes, we set it is in the right of the predicate node. Here the hidden layer equation is updated as follows:

$$h_i = f(W_{hid}^P [x_i; x_{verb}; x_{top}] + b_{hid}^P) \qquad (6)$$

where $W_{hid}^P \in \mathbb{R}^{m \times 3n}$, P is the node position of x_i.

2.5 Decoding

When finding the optimal output of the whole tree, there is a problem: if a tree node is a real semantic role, its subtree node could never be any semantic roles. If we ignore this problem, considering the optimal output of each tree node independently, our model will make many wrong decisions. Algorithm 1 shows the decoding method. Consider there is a binary parse tree, we design two decode scores for each tree node. *decode score 1* is the sum of the score of the current node which is a semantic role (argument) and the score of its all subtree nodes are not arguments; *decode score 2* is the sum of the score that the current node which is not an argument and the score of its children node which chose their most likely assignments. So, the most likely assignment for a node is the one that corresponds to the maximum of these two decode scores. The most

---

Algorithm 1. GLOBALDECODING

```
Input: The root of the parse tree t for sentence s
Output: The most likely assignments for s
begin
    Let input regard as current node i
    Let l be the left son of i, r be the right son of i
    GLOBALDECODING(l)
    GLOBALDECODING(r)
    Compute decode score 1 and decode score 2
    if i is the root
        Return the assignment of max{decode score 1, de-
            code score 2}
    end
end
```

---

likely assignments for the whole tree are the ones that correspond to the maximum of the two decode scores of the root. We call this a global decoding algorithm because it decodes on whole parsed tree using some rules instead of decoding on each tree node independently.

2.6   Training the RNN Model

We use the Max-Margin criterion to train our model following Pei et al. [7]. Given a sentence x_i, let $T(x_i)$ denote the tree node set of x_i and the correct semantic role set is y_i. For given node $p \in T(x_i)$, the correct semantic role for p is $y_{i,p}$. The parameter of out model is $\theta = \{a\ set\ of\ W,\ a\ set\ of\ b,\ a\ set\ of\ W_{wid},\ a\ set\ of\ b_{wid},\ W_{out},\ b_{out}\}$. We first define a structured margin loss $\Delta(y_i, \hat{y})$ for predicting a semantic role set (contains none semantic role) $\hat{y}$ for a given correct semantic role set y_i in a tree:

$$\Delta(y_i, \hat{y}) = \sum_p^{|T(x_i)|} \kappa 1\{y_{i,p} \neq \widehat{y_p}\} \tag{7}$$

where $|T(x_i)|$ is the number of tree node in x_i and κ is a discount parameter.

The loss is proportional to the number of nodes with an incorrect role in the proposed role set, which increases the more incorrect the proposed role set is. We use $Y(x_i)$ to denote the set of all possible semantic role sets for the sentence x_i. For a given training instance (x_i, y_i), we search for the semantic role set with the highest score:

$$y^* = \arg\max_{\hat{y} \in Y(x_i)} S(x_i, \hat{y}, \theta) \tag{8}$$

where $S(x_i, \hat{y}, \theta)$ is computed as follows:

$$S(x_i, \hat{y}, \theta) = \sum_{p \in T(x_i)} Score(x_i, \widehat{y_p}, \theta) \tag{9}$$

where $score(\cdot)$ is designed in Sect. 2.1.

The object of Max-Margin training is that the highest scoring role set is the correct one: $y^* = y_i$ and its score will be larger up to a margin to other possible role set $\hat{y} \in Y(x_i)$:

$$S(x_i, y_i, \theta) \geq S(x_i, \hat{y}, \theta) + \Delta(y_i, \hat{y}) \tag{10}$$

This leads to the objective function with regularized term for m training samples:

$$J(\theta) = \frac{1}{m} \sum_{i=1}^m \max_{\hat{y} \in Y(x_i)} \left(S(x_i, \hat{y}, \theta) + \Delta(y_i, \hat{y}) - S(x_i, y_i, \theta) \right) + \frac{\lambda}{2} \| \theta \|^2 \tag{11}$$

By minimizing this object, the score of the correct role set y_i is increased and score of the highest score incorrect role set $\hat{y}$ is decreased.

There are many gradient based optimization methods to minimize the objective function. We chose Adaptive Sub-gradient Optimization [8] with minibatches. The parameter updates for the i-th parameter $\theta_{t,i}$ at time step t is as follows:

$$\theta_{t,i} = \theta_{t-1,i} - \frac{\alpha}{\sqrt{\sum_{\tau=1}^{t} g_{\tau,i}^2}} g_{t,i} \qquad (12)$$

where α is the initial learning rate and $g_\tau \in \mathbb{R}^{|\theta_i|}$ is the sub-gradient at time step τ for parameter θ_i.

3 Experiment

3.1 Experiment Settings

We use the CoNLL-2005 data for training and evaluating out model. The data consists of sections of the Wall Street Journal part of the Penn TreeBank, with information predicate-argument structures extracted from the PropBank corpus. There are 64 different semantic roles in the data. CoNLL-2005 data takes Sects. 2–21 of WSJ data as training set, Sect. 23 as testing set and Sect. 24 as validation set. In addition, the test set of the shared task includes three sections of the Brown corpus (namely, ck01-03). CoNLL-2005 data uses Charniak parser to generate POS tags and full parses automatically. We used English Giga word corpus [9] for word embedding pre-training. To make the experiment result more comparable, we use auto-parsed syntax trees as input, just like other researchers do. Because the parsed syntax trees given in data set are multiway trees and our RNN model needs binary tree, we change the multiway tree to binary tree in a heuristic method. For each tree node n in the multiway tree, we simply stay its left child the same in the new tree as the multiway tree and make a new tree node r as n's right child. Then let right sons of n in multiway tree become the son of r. We apply this method recursively in whole multiway tree from top to bottom. By this heuristic method, we reserve the structure and the span of the original multiway tree as much as possible.

There are many hyper-parameters in our model need be set before training our recursive neural network: the tree node embedding size $d = 50$, the hidden layer size $d_{hid} = 80$, the initial learning rate $\alpha = 0.08$, the discount parameter $\kappa = 0.1$, the regularized term parameter $\lambda = 0.0001$, the initial weight range of the whole network in $[-0.001, 0.001]$ and mini-batch size is 20.

3.2 Results and Analysis

Table 1 shows the final result of our experiment. Our RNN system reaches 71.53 F1 score in test set without pruning and 72.27 F1 score with pruning. Koomen et al. [10] get best performance in CoNLL-2005 and they reach 77.92 F1 score in test set. However, their best performance system uses six parse trees generated by Charniak parser. They also report the performance using only one Charniak parse tree. It is more comparable to

Table 1. Experiment result in for the CoNLL-2005 test set.

Approach	F1
Koomen et al. (six parse trees)	**77.92**
Koomen et al. (top Charniak parse tree only)	74.76
CNN	70.99
CNN + LM	74.15
Our RNN	71.53
Our RNN + pruning	72.27

our system. To rich a high level performance, they uses lots of syntactic and parse tree features. But our RNN system only use three simple parse tree features. CNN is another deep network model presented by Collobert et al.. They reach 74.15 F1 score in test set, lower than Koomen et al. as well. LM is the language model they use for word embedding initialization. Their embedding dictionary contains 130,000 words trained by Wikipedia and Reuters corpus. Although our model also use pre-training word embedding, our embedding dictionary only contains 18,551 words trained by Giga word. Their system uses much more extra resources for pre-training than our system. They also report the performance without LM (70.99), is lower than our performance.

Because our network is based on the parsed syntax trees, the result is more dependent on the accuracies of the parser than other systems. It is one of the reason our result don't exceed the state of the art. Although our RNN model's performance is lower than Koomen et al. and CNN, our model use less features and extra resource and learn the global structure information by the RNN network itself to reach a competitive performance.

Our RNN system is faster than other two systems. Comparing to Koomen et al., our systems uses a simple architecture and fewer features. And our system does not rely on the output of other existing NLP system as well. Comparing to CNN system, our system has fewer network layers. CNN system has at least five layers and our system only have three layers including tree node layer, hidden layer and output layer. Although our system is a recursive network based on parse tree, an average parse tree level is about ten and the length of sentence is about fifteen, the cost of computing on the recursive parse tree is similar with the cost of convolution layer in CNN. There is one more important point that our system directly use the output of the network as the score to predict semantic roles. We do not need waste time using softmax layer the compute the possibility of each semantic role. Table 2 shows the runtime between our system and other systems.

Table 2. Runtime speed comparison between our system and other systems. We give the runtime in seconds for running on testing sets.

SRL system	Time (s.)
Koomen et al.	6253
CNN	51
Our RNN	**3**

4 Related Work

Recent years, many NLP researches achieve competitive performance using neural network. Collobert et al. [6] propose a unified neural network architecture and learning algorithm that can be applied to various natural language processing tasks including: part-of-speech tagging, chunking, named entity recognition, and semantic role labeling. Socher et al. [11] build Recursive Auto-encoder to learn the vector representation of the phrase. They also use recursive deep models for sentiment analysis [12]. Hashimoto et al. [13] use an averaged RNN model for semantic relation classification. Zhang et al. [14] use a RNN-based translation model for minimizing the sematic gap in embedding space.

Our research also use a recursive model as Socher and other researchers do. Different from other researchers' work, we use recursive model into a new task and our model is extendible for traditional features. Compare to Collobert et al., our word use a recursive model to handle SRL task and capture structure information of parse tree by global decoding.

5 Conclusion

In this paper, we used a novel recursive neural network model for SRL. Compare to traditional model, our model uses fewer features. Our model is also extensible for add more features and resources as talked in Sect. 3. Unlike other deep neural network models for SRL, our model import more global structure information from parse tree by our global decoding algorithm. We did an exploration on structure deep learning for SRL and got a competitive performance.

Acknowledgments. This work is supported by National Key Basic Research Program of China (2014CB340504) and National Natural Science Foundation of China (61273318).

References

1. Martha, P., Dan, G., Paul, K.: The proposition bank: a corpus annotated with semantic roles. Comput. Linguist. J. **31**, 1 (2005)
2. Pradhan, S., Hacioglu, K., Krugler, V., Ward, W., Martin, J.H., Jurafsky, D.: Support vector learning for semantic argument classification. Mach. Learn. **60**(1–3), 11–39 (2005)
3. Pradhan, S.S., Ward, W., Hacioglu, K., Martin, J.H., Jurafsky, D.: Shallow semantic parsing using support vector machines. In: HLT-NAACL, pp. 233–240, May 2004
4. Surdeanu, M., Harabagiu, S., Williams, J., Aarseth, P.: Using predicate-argument structures for information extraction. In: Proceedings of the 41st Annual Meeting on Association for Computational Linguistics, vol. 1, pp. 8–15. Association for Computational Linguistics, July 2003
5. Xue, N., Palmer, M.: Calibrating features for semantic role labeling. In: EMNLP, pp. 88–94, July 2004

6. Collobert, R., Weston, J., Bottou, L., Karlen, M., Kavukcuoglu, K., Kuksa, P.: Natural language processing (almost) from scratch. J. Mach. Learn. Res. **12**, 2493–2537 (2011)
7. Pei, W., Ge, T., Baobao, C.: Maxmargin tensor neural network for chinese word segmentation. In: Proceedings of ACL (2014)
8. Duchi, J., Hazan, E., Singer, Y.: Adaptive subgradient methods for online learning and stochastic optimization. J. Mach. Learn. Res. **12**, 2121–2159 (2011)
9. Graff, D., Chen, K.: Chinese gigaword. LDC (2005). Catalog No.: LDC2003T09, ISBN: 1-58563-58230
10. Koomen, P., Punyakanok, V., Roth, D., Yih, W.T.: Generalized inference with multiple semantic role labeling systems. In: Proceedings of the Ninth Conference on Computational Natural Language Learning, pp. 181–184. Association for Computational Linguistics, June 2005
11. Socher, R., Huang, E.H., Pennin, J., Manning, C.D., Ng, A.Y.: Dynamic pooling and unfolding recursive autoencoders for paraphrase detection. In: Advances in Neural Information Processing Systems, pp. 801–809 (2011)
12. Socher, R., Perelygin, A., Wu, J.Y., Chuang, J., Manning, C.D., Ng, A.Y., Potts, C.: Recursive deep models for semantic compositionality over a sentiment treebank. In: Proceedings of the conference on empirical methods in natural language processing (EMNLP), vol. 1631, p. 1642, October 2013
13. Hashimoto, K., Miwa, M., Tsuruoka, Y., Chikayama, T.: Simple customization of recursive neural networks for semantic relation classification. In: EMNLP, pp. 1372–1376 (2013)
14. Zhang, J., Liu, S., Li, M., Zhou, M., Zong, C.: Mind the gap: machine translation by minimizing the semantic gap in embedding space. In: Association for the Advancement of Artificial Intelligence (2014)

A Comparative Analysis of Chinese Simile and Metaphor Based on a Large Scale Chinese Corpus

Zhimin Wang[1(✉)], Yuxiang Jia[2], and Pierangelo Lacasella[1]

[1] Beijing Language and Culture University, Beijing 100083, China
wangzm000@qq.com, pierolaca@hotmail.com
[2] Zhengzhou University, Zhengzhou 450052, China
yxjia@pku.edu.cn

Abstract. This paper puts forward the mapping inheritance hypothesis which states that the ultimate goal of mapping is to inherit the attributes of source domains by comparing structures 'as A as Y'(像Y一样A) and 'n n/n + n'. Furthermore, we have built a knowledge base for simile and explored the distribution of source domain and its attribute hierarchy. The study shows that the number of S domain words in Chinese simile is different from metaphor, they only have in common 155 S domain words. Although simile and metaphor both tend to choose the semantic category B_object as their source domain, simile expressions are more likely to choose plants and animals, metaphorical expressions are more likely to choose inanimate objects.

Keywords: Metaphor mapping · Attribute inheritance · *TongYiCi CiLin* · Semantic distribution

1 Introduction

In Chinese structures 'as A as Y'(像Y一样A) and 'n of n/n + n' contain two typical forms of simile and metaphor. For example.

(1) She is as naive as a child.
(2) The guy was as sly as a fox.
(3) Her flowers of life are more beautiful.
(4) The man was screened by the tide of era.

The difference between simile and metaphor is that the Topic, the Vehicle and the Ground are closely connected by the simile mark 'as…as'. There is neither an obvious mark, nor a Ground in the form of 'n + n', but it is directly connected between the Topic and Vehicle by 'of'. There are metaphor, such as flowers of life, tide of era, in which the 'of' can be omitted as in the examples below.

(5) She smelled the fragrance of life flowers.
(6) He writes a group of little people who up and down in the era tide.
(7) The company has long suffered heavy losses in that financial storm.

© Springer International Publishing Switzerland 2015
M. Sun et al. (Eds.): CCL and NLP-NABD 2015, LNAI 9427, pp. 77–88, 2015.
DOI: 10.1007/978-3-319-25816-4_7

In the traditional rhetoric, simile and metaphor are two parallel patterns. According to the modern theory of metaphor, the simile is considered as a kind of generalized metaphor, and its differences from the metaphor has been discussed by many scholars. (Aristotle 1954; Wangdao Chen 1964; Dingfang Su 2000).

Besides the structural differences between simile and metaphor, it's also very important to study whether in the simile structure 'as A as Y'(像Y一样A) the Vehicle Y has limited grouping and what is the mapping features between Topic and Vehicle. Veale Tony (2007) introduced a method of their collection of similes, Yuxiang Jia (2009) collected many Chinese similes and made detailed analysis with semantic classes. Bin Li (2012) collected Chinese similes and construct a large database of "noun-adjective" items in English and Chinese. The above collection of similes offers beneficial reference for similar project.

Therefore, this paper selects the construction 'as A as Y'(像Y一样A) from comprehensive modern Chinese BCC online corpus, which is a language corpus with 1 billion tokens. We summarize the principle of mapping differences of 'as A as Y'(像Y一样A) and 'n of n/n + n' based on Chinese TongYiCi CiLin (CiLin)classification system.

The remainder of the paper is organized as follows. We first describe the mapping inheritance nature of the simile and metaphor, then present a method of the simile mapping analysis of source domain. In Sect. 4, we get a comparison of the results of the semantic distribution based on CiLin. Finally, we conclude with a discussion for the future work.

2 Mapping Inheritance Nature of the Simile and Metaphor

The Aristotelian view of understanding metaphor is a process of finding the shared Ground between Topic and Vehicle through implicit comparison (Black 1962). Theories of metaphor interpretation have used the idea of interaction or comparison of attributes of Topic and Vehicle (Richards 1965; Lynne Cameron 1999). Later Lakoff and other scholars (Lakoff 1980) provided the Conceptual Metaphor theory, according to which metaphor can be understood as a cross domain mapping in the conceptual system. The mapping can be expressed as LOVE IS JOURNEY. According to the CM theory, both 'as A as Y'(像Y一样A) and 'n of n/n + n' patterns can describe a mapping between the source domain and the target domain such as the above expressions child-> people(she), fox-> guy, flower-> life, tide-> era, storm-> finance. The mapping of the source domain and the target domain is based on a similarity relation.

Conceptual metaphor theory, compared with the traditional studies of rhetoric, consider the nature or mapping based more on similarity, it sets up a relationship between the conceptual and syntactic layer, also expands the study of metaphor from the conceptual layer to the syntactic surface of mappings. In this sense, simile is a kind of metaphorical simile. Therefore, this paper uses terms of the Source and Target domain instead of the Topic and Vehicle.

Besides its mapping, metaphor has also an important pragmatic function. The reason why people use metaphor is that it is an instrument to describe the reality, from concrete to abstract, from simple to complex objects, it helps people understand deeply the world they live in. During the process of mapping, the abstract and complex things inherit partial attributes of other simple things. Therefore, in addition to the mapping of metaphor, there is also the inheritance of attributes. The ultimate goal of the mapping is to inherit the attributes of the source domains.

In addition, it can be noticed from the order of words in both simile and metaphor that the target domain is generally preceded by the source domain in the structure of 'as A as Y'(像Y一样A) and 'n of n/n + n', where the target domain is first determined to realize the purpose of inheritance. For example.

(8)   His practice is as lovely as a child.
(9)   His heart is as hard as stone.
(10)   Travel in the ocean of knowledge.

Speakers want to express ideas of 'practice - > lovely, heart- > hard, knowledge- > broad'. Here, 'practice, heart, knowledge' are targets that people first think about. 'lovely, hard and broad' are the attributes that speaker want to perform, by searching for people's collective unconscious to activate these attributes of the words in the S domain.

Therefore speakers choose a known S domains such as 'children, stone, the sea' for analogy and they make concepts 'practice, stone, knowledge' inherit some attributes of S domains, like 'lovely, hard, broad'. In this sense, the direction of metaphor should be the mapping of T - > S domains and the T domain inherits the similar attributes from the S domain words. So the generalized metaphor essentially can be seen as the inheritance of the target domain to the source domain, which is closely related to the function of a language.

3   The Simile Mapping Analysis of Source Domain Attribute

All the things in the world can be explained using metaphors when they are not easy to understand. Therefore, all familiar, unfamiliar things can act as X. Here X may be a specific or abstract while Y is often more specific than X. Y often is a familiar thing for speakers and listeners. Only in this way can the basis of communication be realized. What the speaker wants to express depends entirely on the attributes of Y. So Y plays a key role in 'as A as Y'(像Y一样A) and what attributes X inherited is determined by Y. Therefore, this paper mainly explores the structure and semantic classification of Y, based on the comprehensive modern Chinese BCC online, covers all the works from modern writers. We retrieved the pattern 'as A as Y'(像Y一样A) to manual and excluded other expressions. For example:

(11)   All the wild sea birds are like a moth to the flame quickly.
(12)   Looking at the problem is as sharp as your sword technology.

The expression of simile involves more complex source domain concepts which we do not examine in this study.

There are 1573 total S domain words, among which the words with two characters form the majority, with 1258 words that correspond to the 80 % of the total. The words with a single character are 182, with the proportion of 12 %. Words with three characters are a little bit less, only 123 of the total, and cover the proportion of 8 %. In the end we have the words with 4 characters, which cover only the 1 % percentage of the S domains (Fig. 1).

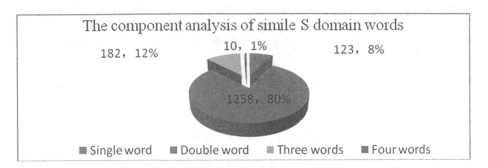

Fig. 1. The component analysis of S domain words for simile

We have discovered that there are many different properties from the same source domain.

When people make metaphorical mappings, according to the actual communication needs, the target domain generally only inherits one attribute of source domain. Therefore, S domain 'child' in 'as A as Y'(像Y一样A) has mapping expressions of 43 times. Target domain inherited 43 attributes such as 'excited, poor, happy, naive, naughty, gay and innocent and simple, quiet, grievances, kind, cheerful, curious, happy, clean, low, high, sorry, smart, fragile, Triumph, and naughty, shy, lively, firm and vigilant, stubborn, stubborn, lovely, happy, enthusiastic, gentle, modest, honest, obedient, helpless, careful, slender, careful, impatient, happiness, attachment and anxious'. The mapping of N target domains to 1 source domain is created.

In this study, we obtained 1573 concepts used in source domains that later we used to built a knowledge base for simile. The source domain words constitute the core of the simile knowledge base. We set the attribute fields such as [mark word], [T word], [S word], [Mapping] and [Mapping attribute] for simile 'as A as Y'(像Y一样A). In order to describe the mapping more clearly, the layer investigation is made as shown in the table below (Table 1):

Table 1. Distribution of the S domain words for Simile

SD Level	SD Word	Num. of SD Mapping	Toatal Num. of SD Mapping	Rate
>15	11	319	3317	9.62 %
>10	31	572	3317	17.24 %
>5	94	1036	3317	31.23 %
between 2 and 5	453	1255	3317	37.84 %
1	1026	1026	3317	30.93 %

At present, there are 3317 mapping expressions in knowledge base, and we set up 5 levels of statistics for the source domain. In the mapping of the source and target domains, we find that there are three important boundary points, that is, the source domain frequency equal 1, between 2 and 5, exceed 5, with each for about a third.

The top mapping is between 2 to 5, which is 453 with the proportion of 37.84 %. That means that the mapping of target domain to source domain, will activated between 2 to 5 attributes of S domain words. There are many literature similes, created with author's idea in order to be different, based on the similarity between the T domain and S domain. So only the S domain words with 1 times reached 1026, accounted for 30.93 % of all similes.

In order to better describe the corresponding relationship between the source domain and the attributes, the paper lists all the source domains, mapped more than 10 times (Table 2).

Table 2. The S domain words with Top 31

SD_word	Mapping Num.	SD_word	Mapping Num.	SD_word	Mapping Num.
People	66	Bird	14	Rabbit	12
Children	43	The wind	14	Mouse	12
Water	36	Cattle	14	Father	12
Dog	32	Kid	14	Fire	11
Cat	24	The sky	14	Lion	11
Woman	24	Ice	14	fille	11
Wolf	21	Girl	14	Angel	11
Stone	20	Snake	14	Sea	11
Ant	19	Pig	13	Mother	11
Child	18	Mountain	13		
Baby	16	The sun	13		

The table above shows that the top 31 S domain words that above 10, among them, the S domain for person contains 11 words such as 'people, children, women, and child, girl, father, fille, angel, mother, kid and baby'; the source domain for animal contains 11 words such as 'dog, cat, cow, wolf, ant, bird, snake, pig, rabbit, mice and lion'; the S domain for natural contains 9 words such as 'water, stone, wind, sky, ice, fire, sea, mountain and sun'.

The use of the S domain words for simile reflects completely the Chinese people thought, which gets inspiration by observing first the human body to describe the universe. A person which uses his body as a point of observation, would generally use 'a person' as source domain, then would refer to the beginning of life using words as 'infant, 'child', and words as 'mother', 'father' to express something that generates life. In similes, people often choose to use 'children, child, baby, and angel' as S domain words and for similes that concern the aspects sex, they use concepts of 'women, maiden, mother' is more than concepts of men. In the top 31 S domain words, the S domain words for male have only one like 'father'.

A source domain we selected housed animals such as 'dog, cat, cow, pig, rabbit', are familiar with us. First, there are 66 different mapping patterns from source domain of person. The second includes 43 patterns from 'child' domain. The third includes 36 patterns from 'water' domain.

Compared with S domain words, the attribute A also has a one-to-many mapping that the target domain and the source domain achieves the multi relationship, but they only have one attribute of S domain. For example:

(13)   Eye is as sharp as a blade.
(14)   Two front paws of strange insect are as sharp as a steel hook.
(15)   The situation is just as sharp as a knife, when it is sweeping the Quartet.

Here T domain words 'eyes, insect, situation' is mapping to the source domain 'blade, hook, knife', the selection of the inherited attribute A is 'sharp'. The statistics of A based on simile knowledge base are as follows (Table 3):

Table 3. The mapping distribution of attribute A in Simile

A Level	A Word	Num. of SD Mapping	Toatal of Mapping	Rate
>15	28	674	3317	20.32 %
>10	57	1044	3317	31.47 %
>5	162	1790	3317	53.96 %
between 2 and 5	395	1139	3317	34.34 %
1	388	388	3317	11.70 %

This paper also set the attribute A for 5 levels and finds that the selection of attributes A has shorter ranges than S domain words. That case is totally different from the above source domain. Firstly, the top A level has 162, covering the simile patterns of 1790, accounted for all forms of simile 53.96 %, in the highest proportion of all levels of the hierarchy. Secondly, the mapping frequency of A between 2 to 5, is covering 1139 simile expressions, accounted for the total of 34.34 %. Finally, the mapping frequency of A with only 1 times contains the total of 388, accounted for the simile rate of 11.70 %. Therefore, we conceive that original A is limited and people usually focus on the commonly used A.

4   The Comparative Analysis of the Source Domain of 'as A as Y'(像Y一样A) and 'n of n/n + n'

Wang Zhimin (2010) investigated the metaphorical expression of 'n of n/n + n' in the Grammatical Knowledge-base (GKB) of Contemporary Chinese, examined that whether words can be entered into the above expressions. The reference materials are mainly from the modern Chinese online corpus of the center for Chinese linguistics research, Peking University.

We investigated the 35198 words of GKB, and finally got Chinese metaphorical list of more than 700 S domain words. It indicates that when people use nouns as metaphorical mapping, the metaphorical domains selected are conditional, and are also limited, which accords with the universal law of human recognition. It is the limited source domain that constitutes the system of Chinese noun metaphor.

In order to know whether S domain words between 'as A as Y' (像Y一样A) and 'n of n/n + n' have same semantic features, we make a further inspection and put above S domain words into the classification of Cilin. The S words of two kinds of knowledge base are analyzed and compared as the following (Table 4).

Table 4. Semantic categories of SD words for simile and metaphor

Simile:as A as Y			Meta: N + N		
CiLin	Mapping	Rate	CiLin	Mapping	Rate
B_object	929	52.99 %	B_ object	373	49.67 %
A_person	316	18.03 %	D_ abstract things	208	27.70 %
D_abstract things	170	9.70 %	A_ person	85	11.32 %
OOV_unknown words	117	6.67 %	C_ time and space	48	6.39 %
C_time and space	29	1.65 %	OOV_unknown words	18	2.40 %
H_ activity	8	0.46 %	E_ features	9	1.20 %
E_ features	4	0.23 %	I_phenomenon and state	6	0.80 %
			H_ activity	4	0.53 %

There are 21 semantic categories for CiLin, labeled by A, B ...L. S domain words have obvious preference for the semantic category, which only projected onto 7 kinds of semantic categories such as B_object, A_person, D_abstract things, C_time and space, E_ features, H_ activity and I_phenomenon. That shows that no matter simile or metaphor, their S domain words produce regular projection as follows:

The top three highest projection categories are B_object, A_person, D_abstract things, among which category B_object, contains 929 S domain words in simile, accounted for 52.99 % of all source domains. The highest metaphorical projection is also category B_object, D_ abstract things and A_ person, where category B_object, contains 373 S domain words, covering nearly half of the total source domain. The ranking of the two or three place has changed, the number of A_ person drops sharply and it is reduced to the third, while the second is D_abstract thing.

It is worth notice that two structures of unknown words shows great differences, in similes there are 117 words that doesn't appear into Cilin dictionary, and among metaphors there are only 18 unregistered words. What kind of semantic category do the unknown words belong to? It will help to understand the case of S words comprehensively. We process all the unknown words and classified them into the corresponding semantic classification. After that, we made a new statistic of all the similes. The results are shown in the following (Table 5).

Table 5. Semantic categories of SD words with unknown words for simile and metaphor

Simile: as A as Y			Meta: N + N		
CiLin	Mapping Pat	Rate	CiLin	Mapping Pat	Rate
B_object	1007	57.44 %	B_ object	384	51.13 %
A_person	340	19.40 %	D_abstract things	212	28.23 %
D_abstract things	185	10.55 %	A_ person	86	11.45 %
C_time and space	29	1.65 %	C_ time and space	48	6.39 %
H_ activity	8	0.46 %	E_ features	11	1.46 %
E_ features	4	0.23 %	I_phenomenon and state	6	0.80 %
			H_ features	4	0.53 %

From the above table, we can see that the order of the semantic category has not changed. The top three categories B_object, A_person, D_abstract things in simile, have increased in different numbers due to the unknown words' tagging, among which the majority of unknown S domain words are classified as B_ semantic categories, second as the A_ people. There is more proof that the majority of the S domain words are concrete objects that are familiar with us.

But for n + n metaphorical expressions, there is only 1 source domain word that is classified to A_person. We see category A_people for metaphor still ranks third, but the total number of category A_person only have 86, which is less than a quarter of the total of simile of A_person.

Besides the semantic classes, this paper also investigated the distribution of two kinds of S domain words in the sub-category of Cilin. There are 18 semantic sub-categories of B in Cilin, where simile is covering all the type of categories of Cilin and it projects the most widely distributed sub-categories like Bi_ animals, Bp_ supplies, Bh_ plant, Bo_ equipment and Bm_ materials, accounted for approximately 60 % (Table 6).

Here the source domains of Bi_animals and Bh_plant have 159 and 112 respectively, ranked first and third, While the metaphor Bi_ animal, Bh_ plant only have 17 and 14 cases, ranking the ninth and tenth.

The distribution of the most source domains is five sub-categories such as Bp_-supplies, Bg_natural objects, Bo_implement, Be_landform and Bn_buildings for metaphor constructions 'as A as Y'(像Y一样A) and 'n of n/n + n'.

Here S domain words for metaphor that covering Bg_natural; objects, Be_landform and Bn_buildings, ranked in the forefront, but S domain words for simile are ranked at 6, 11, 10, the gap is very obvious.

From the top 5 category of metaphorical ranking, the metaphor is more inclined to choose inanimate objects, and similes tend to choose plants and animals.

There are 14 semantic sub-categories of people in Cilin, which S domain words for similes is covering all types of A semantic, but S domain words for metaphor are covering some categories, among them, Ad_membership, Ak_character, Ai_generation

Table 6. Semantic sub-categories of SD words for Cat_B

像Y一样A				'N的N/N + N'		
B_ object	Num. of S words	Rate		B_ object	Num. of S words	Rate
Bi animal	159	15.79 %		Bp supplies	52	13.54 %
Bp supplies	115	11.42 %		Bg natural objects	50	13.02 %
Bh plant	112	11.12 %		Bo implement	45	11.72 %
Bo implement	107	10.63 %		Be landform	43	11.20 %
Bm material	72	7.15 %		Bn buildings	38	9.90 %
Bg natural objects	67	6.65 %		Bj microorganism	29	7.55 %
Bk whole body	62	6.16 %		Bf Meteorology	29	7.55 %
Bf Meteorology	55	5.46 %		Ba generic terms	18	4.69 %
Br food and drug	54	5.36 %		Bh plant	17	4.43 %
Bn buildings	47	4.67 %		Bi animal	14	3.65 %
Be landform	39	3.87 %		Br food and drug	12	3.13 %
Ba generic terms	30	2.98 %		Bm material	10	2.60 %
Bq clothing	25	2.48 %		Bd celestial bodies	8	2.08 %
Bc part of an object	21	2.09 %		Bc part of an object	7	1.82 %
Bd celestial bodies	19	1.89 %		Bb pseudo object	6	1.56 %
Bb pseudo object	12	1.19 %		Bq clothing	5	1.30 %
Bl secretion	10	0.99 %		Bk whole body	1	0.26 %
Bj microorganism	1	0.10 %				
Total	1007	100.00 %		Total	384	100.00 %

are excluded. The S domain words for similes is covering Al_ability and insight, Ak_character, Ae_occupations, Ag_status and An_evil person widely, which reflects the tendency of selecting the source domain of similes and metaphors (Table 7).

Of course, in addition to the differences of the semantic classification of the source domain, this paper also found some common S words between them. As shown in the table below (Fig. 2):

The common S domain words of two knowledge bases are only 155, accounted for 7.23 % of the total number of similes and metaphor source domains. According to the previous thinking, this paper also projected the 155 common S domain words to the classification system of Cilin, as shown in the following Table 8:

Table 7. Semantic sub-categories of SD words for Cat_A

Simile: As...AS Y				Meta: N + N		
A_person	Num. of S words	Rate		A_person	Num. of S words	Rate
Ab People of all ages and both sexes	64	18.82 %		Al ability and insight	17	19.77 %
Ah family dependents	61	17.94 %		Ak character	14	16.28 %
Ae occupation	53	15.59 %		Ae occupation	10	11.63 %
Af identity	28	8.24 %		Ag status	9	10.47 %
Aj relationship	25	7.35 %		An evil person	8	9.30 %
Ad membership	22	6.47 %		Ah family dependents	8	9.30 %
Ak character	19	5.59 %		Af identity	8	9.30 %
An evil person	12	3.53 %		Aj relationship	6	6.98 %
Am belief	11	3.24 %		Ab People of all ages and both sexes	3	3.49 %
Aa general term	11	3.24 %		Ac posture	2	2.33 %
Al ability and insight	10	2.94 %		Am belief	1	1.16 %
Ai generation	9	2.65 %				
Ag status	9	2.65 %				
Ac posture	6	1.76 %				
Total	340	100.00 %		Total	86	100.00 %

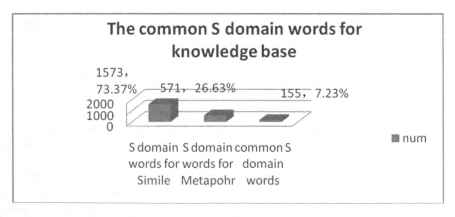

Fig. 2. The common S domain words for knowledge base

Table 8. Semantic sub-categories of common SD words

CiLin	Mapping Pat	Commen SD words	Rate
B_ object	113	155	72.90 %
D_ abstract things	25	155	16.13 %
A_person	14	155	9.03 %
H_ activity	2	155	1.29 %
C_time and space	1	155	0.65 %

The distribution of common S domain is changed from 6 classes to 5 classes. Meanwhile, the ranking of the 5 categories has also changed, the source domain of the second place A_ people sharply declined, containing only 14 words and ranked third, while the number of D_ abstract things arranged in second place.

The category C_ time and space, H_ activity also occurred to change, ranked in the last two. Whether there is a same Ground mapping for common S domain words in the constructions simile and metaphor deserves deep study. So we select category B_ species of public domain sources the word 'ocean' for example, In BCC online corpus ocean simile used for example:

(16)   A person's mind as deep as the ocean
(17)   Wisdom is as deep as the sea. Dong Daren
(18)   Jis sky is as deep as the ocean

Target domains are often expressed abstractly. For example: 'mind, wisdom, and sky', through the mapping from target to source domain to activate the attribute 'deep and profound'. That is totally different from the metaphor 'n ocean'. For example:

(19)   Three seemed caught up in a sea of flowers.
(20)   Let the car into a sea of laughter.
(21)   The city has become a sea of buildings.

The target domain such as 'flowers, laughter, building' is mapping into the ocean of the source domain, and activate the ground of ocean like 'much and large' and there is no sense 'deep'. In simile and metaphor, the source domain 'ocean' highlights the different attribute tendency, simile tendency to choose the attribute of 'deep', metaphor to choose the attribute of 'wide'. Meanwhile, distinction between simile and metaphor is that T domain words for simile select abstract words such as 'mind, wisdom, and heaven', while T domain words for metaphor choose specific things such as 'flowers, laughter, building'. T domain words are also the important key for the difference between two structural mappings. In the future, we will further study the semantic distribution of T domain words and their tendency to inherit the source domain.

5   Conclusion

This paper presents a mapping inheritance hypothesis which states that the ultimate goal of mapping is to transfer the attributes of source domains by comparative structures 'As… As'(像Y一样A) and 'n n/n + n'. We analyzed the distribution of the source domain in Chinese simile and the hierarchy of its attributes, processing the attributes in the source domain through a Chinese simile knowledge base. The study shows that S domain words for simile are distinguished from the change quantity of metaphors just because there are only 155 common words between them. The study shows that the number of S domain words for Chinese simile is different from the number of S domain words used in Chinese metaphors, similes and metaphors share only 155 common words. There is also a great difference between the semantic categories chosen from Chinese similes and metaphors. Simile generally expresses its comparison using concepts of plants and animals, but metaphor more commonly uses inanimate objects as words domain.

Acknowledgment. The work was supported by the National Science Foundation of China (No. 61170163, 61402419), the support program of young and middle-aged backbone teachers for Beijing Language and Culture University.

References

Aristotle, : Rhetoric and Poetics. The Modern Library, New York (1954)

Black, M.: Models and Metaphors. Cornell University Press, Ithaca (1962)

Eilts, C., Lönneke, B.: The Hamburg Metaphor Database [EB] (2002). http://www.metaphorik. de/03/eiltsloenneker.pdf

Li, B., Kuang, H., Zhang, Y., Chen, J., Tang, X.: Using similes to extract basic sentiments across languages. In: Wang, F.L., Lei, J., Gong, Z., Luo, X. (eds.) WISM 2012. LNCS, vol. 7529, pp. 536–542. Springer, Heidelberg (2012)

Su, D.: Studies in Metaphor. Shanghai Foreign Language Education Press, Shanghai (2000)

Lakoff, G., Johnson, M.: Metaphors We Live By. University of Chicago Press, Chicago (1980)

Lakoff, G., Turner, M.: More than Cool Reason—A Field Guide to Poetic Metaphor. The University of Chicago Press, Chicago (1989)

Cameron, L., Low, G.: Researching and Applying Metaphor. Cambridge University Press, Cambridge (1999)

Martin, J.H.: Metabank: a knowledge-base of metaphoric language convention. Comput. Intell. **10**(2), 134–139 (1994)

Wang, Q.: A General Survey of Chinese Rhetoric Studies. Central University of Science and Technology University Press (1995)

Richards, I.A.: The Philosophy of Rhetoric. Oxford University Press, NewYork (1965)

Veale, T.: Metaphor, Memory and Meaning: Symbolic and Connectionist Issues in Metaphor Interpretation. Trinity College, Dublin (1995)

Veale, T., Hao, Y.: Learning to understand figurative language: from similes to metaphors to irony. In: Proceedings of CogSci 2007, Nashville, USA (2007)

Chen, W.: An Introduction to Rhetoric. Shanghai Education Press, Shanghai (1964)

Yuxiang, J., Shiwen, Yu.: Instance-based metaphor comprehension and generation. Comput. Sci. **36**(3), 138–141 (2009)

Wang, Z., Yu, S., Sui, Z.: The Chinese noun metaphors knowledge base and its use in the recognition of metaphors. In: Workshop on 3rd Natural Language Processing and Ontology Engineering in Conjunction with The 2010 IEEE/WIC/ACM International Conference on Web Intelligence (WI-2010) (2010)

Chinese Textual Entailment Recognition Enhanced with Word Embedding

Zhichang Zhang, Dongren Yao[(✉)], Yali Pang, and Xiaoyong Lu

School of Computer Science and Engineering,
Northwest Normal University, Lanzhou, China
{zzc,pyl,luxy}@nwnu.edu.cn,
wade330628704@163.com

Abstract. Textual entailment has been proposed as a unifying generic framework for modeling language variability and semantic inference in different Natural Language Processing (NLP) tasks. By evaluating on NTCIR-11 RITE3 Simplified Chinese subtask data set, this paper firstly demonstrates and compares the performance of Chinese textual entailment recognition models that combine different lexical, syntactic, and semantic features. Then a word embedding based lexical entailment module is added to enhance classification ability of our system further. The experimental results show that the word embedding for lexical semantic relation reasoning is effective and efficient in Chinese textual entailment.

Keywords: Chinese textual entailment · RITE · Lexical entailment · Word embedding

1 Introduction

The Recognizing Textual Entailment (RTE) challenge focuses on detecting the directional entailment relationship between pairs of text expressions, denoted by T (the entailing "Text") and H (the entailed "Hypothesis"). We say that T entails H if human reading T would typically infer that H is most likely true [1]. A wide range of natural language applications which demand semantic inference need RTE to fulfill their tasks. For example, given the question *"Which team won the NBA championship in* 2013–2014?*"*, a question answering system needs to identify whether the text *"Popvich led Spurs to their fifth straight title on June* 16, 2014*"* entails a hypothesized answer form *"San Antonio Spurs win the championship in* 2013–2014*"* or not.

Many approaches have been proposed to solve this problem. Logic-based [2, 3] and decoding-based [4, 7] approaches require large-scale inference rules provided ahead to make entailment decision. However, it is a time consuming and labor intensive process to build enough number of entailment rules.

Machine Learning based recognition approaches [5, 6] therefore are used more widely where the task to detect whether a text T entails a hypothesis H is taken as a binary classification problem, and classification models can be trained automatically on a labeled textual entailment dataset. While this type of approach is easy to implement, the features demanded by the classification models should be carefully designed in

© Springer International Publishing Switzerland 2015
M. Sun et al. (Eds.): CCL and NLP-NABD 2015, LNAI 9427, pp. 89–100, 2015.
DOI: 10.1007/978-3-319-25816-4_8

order to achieving state-of-the-art recognition performance. Many features covering from lexical to semantic layer are studied and compared in existing research. But for Chinese textual entailment recognition, the analysis of different feature's contribution to recognition performance improvement is still not sufficient.

Based on our machine learning based textual entailment recognition system which took part in NTCIR-11 RITE-3 Chinese textual entailment Binary-class task, this paper presents the features used by the system and their effort to recognition performance. Particularly, a word embedding based lexical entailment module is added into the system and the system performance improved further.

The rest of the paper is organized as follows: Sect. 2 describes the features and algorithm employed in our system at NTCIR-11 evaluation. Section 3 details a word embedding based lexical entailment module added to improve our system's inference ability. In Sect. 4 we show the experimental results on the test data and give some analysis. Finally, we summarize our work and outline some ideas for future research.

2   System Description

Our system that based on machine learning takes the Chinese textual entailment recognition task as a binary classification problem. The system uses the different matching similarities between T and H as important features for this task, on the understanding that a Hypothesis H with "similar" content to the Text T is more likely to be entailed by that Text T than one with "less similar" content. The system contains four main modules including pre-processing, feature extraction, classification, and amending module. Figure 1 shows more details in our system.

The preprocessing module uses several different NLP resources and tools for basic processing like word segment, POS, and NE recognition. We use LTP[1] tool for word segment, POS tagging and dependency syntactic parsing and Stanford classifier for named entity recognition.

2.1   Features Extraction

2.1.1   Lexical Features
Existing researches show that lexical features are easy to obtain and effective for textual entailment recognition. We take over some traditional lexical features, and also supplement several new features according to the characteristic of Chinese textual relation. These lexical features can help our system solve some problems such as:

<t> 《罗马假期》是1953年拍摄的浪漫爱情片。("Roman Holiday" is a romantic love drama shot in 1953.) </t>

<h> 《罗马假期》是浪漫爱情片,于1953年拍摄。("Roman   holiday"   is   a romantic love story, which is shot in 1953.) </h>

With a very high lexical similarity, our system will classify them as "entailment", which is the right semantic relation between two texts.

---

[1] http://www.ltp-cloud.com/demo/.

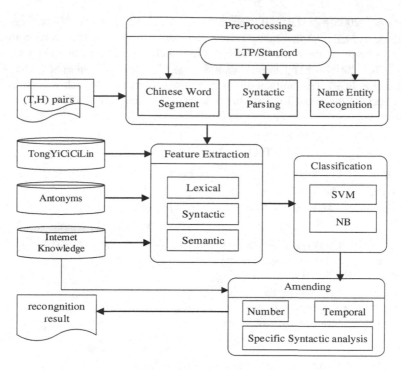

Fig. 1. System architecture

Following Table 1 illustrates the lexical features used in our system, where the symbol *T* stands for the text in text pair and *H* for the hypothesis.

These lexical features cannot capture the syntactic structures of two texts and view a text as a bag of words. But for some text pairs, their entailment relation could not be correctly detected if their syntactic structure is not considered and compared. Using the lexical features as a base, more complex features from syntactic to semantic aspects should be checked too.

2.1.2 Syntactic Features

As we discussed above, lexical features can't capture the text syntactic information. For example:

<pair id = "30">
    <t> 《瀛台泣血记》为清朝宫廷女官裕德龄所撰写的一本有关光绪皇帝一生的故事。(*Son of heaven* that talks about Guangxu emperor's whole life is written by DeLing yu who is a female official in Qing dynasty) </t>
    <h> 《瀛台泣血记》为清朝宫廷女官裕光绪所撰写的一本有关德龄皇帝一生的故事。(*Son of heaven* that talks about DeLing emperor's whole life is written by Guangxu yu who is a female official in Qing dynasty) </h>
    </pair>
<pair id = "237">

<t>日本于2005年发行上映的动画电影《蒸汽男孩》,其故事背景以英国1851年万国博览会为主。(An animated movie in Japan, *Steamboy*, which was on in 2005 shows a background about the World Exhibition held by England in 1851.) </t>

<h>日本于2005年发行上映的动画电影《蒸汽男孩》,其故事背景以1851年英国万国博览会为主。(An animated movie in Japan, *Steamboy*, which was on in 2005 shows a background about England held the World Exhibition in 1851.) </h>

</pair>

Table 1. Lexical features

Feature name	Comment	Formula
Word overlap	The overlap of words between two texts	$E_1 = \|T \wedge H\| / \|H\|$ $E_2 = \|T \wedge H\| / \|T\|$ $E = (2 * E_1 * E_2)/(E_1 + E_2)$
Length difference	Using text length to distinguish entailment direction	$Lt(T, H) = \|Len(T) - Len(H)\|$
Cosine similarity	Representing the text pair as vectors, then calculating their cosine similarity	$Sim_{cos}(T, H) = \dfrac{\sum\limits_{i=1}^{n} t_i * h_i}{\sqrt{\sum\limits_{i=1}^{n} t_i *}\sqrt{\sum\limits_{i=1}^{n} h_i}}$ n is vector dimensions
Tongyicicilin semantic similarity [8]	Using Tongyicicilin to calculate the similarity between different words	$f_{CilinSim} =$ $\dfrac{1}{2}(\dfrac{1}{m}\sum\limits_{i=1}^{m} \max\{sim_w(w_{1i}, w_{2j})\|1 \leq j \leq n\} +$ $\dfrac{1}{n}\sum\limits_{j=1}^{n} \max\{sim_w(w_{1i}, w_{2j})\|1 \leq i \leq m\})$
Number of antonyms	Using the Web resource to count the number of antonyms	$f_a = (\#w_T - \#w_H) \bmod 2$
Number of negative words	Combining the number of antonyms to assist decision	$f_n = (\#w_T - \#w_H) \bmod 2$
Overlap of named entity	Named entities can show the text topics in a way	$T_{NE} = \|T \wedge H\| / \|H\|$ $H_{NE} = \|T \wedge H\| / \|T\|$ $L_{NE} = (2 * T_{NE} * H_{NE})/(T_{NE} + H_{NE})$

Due to 100 % percent character similarity, machine learning algorithm predicates both of them as "entailment" if just utilizing lexical features. Apparently, we can see that in the text pair with id being "30", T don't entail H, T and H are contradicted on mentioned entities. When the most of words in the text T occur in hypothesis H, the order or syntactic structure of these words will determine semantic relation between two texts.

From this view, we put forward the method "Minimum syntactic trees" [12] to incorporate some import syntactic features into our system. The main idea of

"Minimum syntactic trees" is that two minimum trees which are generated by clipping the complete syntactic structure trees, and without useless nodes (no effect on entailment) can provide semantic features in the simplest way.

2.2 Classifier

Two machine learning methods are achieved to predicate the entailment relation, and the open source tool scikit-learn [10] is employed for classification in this system. SVM which is regarded as the best supervised learning method in general text classification didn't obtain the best result during the training phase, but got the best score on testing set. The Naïve Bayes method based on Gaussian distribution achieved the best performance on training set, but didn't do as good as SVM during the testing phases.

2.3 Amending Module

Numbers occurs in different forms (Arabic numerals, Chinese numerals, or numbers combing with Chinese character) among the sentences. For one thing, we need to transfer different number form into the same format. For another, some basis operation between these numbers should be taken into consideration. Such as:

<pair id = "311">
    <t>火地群岛总面积73，753平方公里。(The total area of Tierra del Fuego is 73,753 square kilometers.) </t>
    <h>火地群岛总面积超过六万平方公里。(The total area of Tierra del Fuego is over than sixty thousand square kilometers.) </h>
</pair>

Our system need to understand the word "超过(over)" and the fact that 73,753 is larger than "六万(sixty thousand)" to make a correct decision.

Furthermore, temporal recognition also faces the similar situation. So far, we made some rules solve this reasoning problem. Although these rules can improve our performance, they only work in a very limited circumstance.

3 Lexical Entailment Module

After participating NTCIR-11 RITE-3 evaluation, we added a lexical entailment module into our system to enhance the ability of reasoning on lexical level, and corresponding lexical knowledge were considered and used as follow.

3.1 Lexical Entailment vs. Semantic Relationship

When some researchers have applied semantic relation classification to lexical entailment, we think that semantic relation is different with lexical entailment in many respects. Lexical entailment is not just a superset of other known semantic relations, it is rather designed to select those sub-cases of other lexical relations that are needed for applied entailment inference [17]. Turney and Mohammad provide some further exploratory point of view and formulate a hypothesis [13]:

Semantic Relation Subcategories Hypothesis: Lexical entailment is not a superset of high-level categories of semantic relations, but it's a superset of lower-level subcategories of semantic relations.

When many methods have been proposed to solve word semantic relation problem, we utilize word embedding method to reveal the entailment relationship between words in this paper.

3.2   Word Embedding Training

Mikolov et al. [14] proposed two log-linear models, namely the Skip-gram and CBOW model, to efficiently induce word embeddings. These two models can be trained on a large scale corpus. We employ the Skip-gram model for estimating word embeddings in identifying lexical entailment relationship. The Skip-gram model adopts log-linear classifiers to predict context words given the current word $w(t)$ as input, and $w(t)$ is projected to its embedding. Then, log-linear classifiers takes the embedding as input and predict $w(t)$'s context words within a certain range. After maximizing the log-likelihood over the entire dataset with stochastic gradient descent (SGD), the embeddings are learned.

3.3   Lexical Entailment Relationship Learning

Word embedding preserve interesting linguistic regularities like $v(king) - v(queen) \approx v(man) - v(woman)$. It indicates that the embedding offsets indeed represent the shared semantic relation between two word pairs. Fu's work [15] shows that word embedding can measure semantic relationship effectively. When we deal with lexical entailment, this method should also be considered.

So our newly added module is based on a similarity difference hypothesis with word embedding:

Similarity Difference Hypothesis with Word Embedding: The tendency of a entails b based on their word embedding is correlated with the difference in their similarities $\text{sim}(a, r_i)\text{-sim}(b, r_j)$, referring to a set of entailment relation pairs $(r_i, r_j) \in$ R.

According to this hypothesis, we provide some reference pairs (r_1, r_2) which have kinds of entailment relationships to recognize whether two words (a, b) appearing in Text (T) and Hypothesis (H) have the same relationship as r_1 and r_2.

For brevity, we write a for both a word and its associated vector $< a_1, ..., a_n >$, and b, r_1, r_2 are in same way. The symbols **v** and **v**$'$ are used to denote the vector calculation results $r_1 - r_2 + a$ and $r_2 - r_1 + b$ respectively.

Define the function $\mathbf{sim}_{w2v}$ to represent the following procedure:

(a) Based on word embedding vectors, search three words w_1, w_2, w_3 from all words in corpus, which have the largest cosine similarities with $\mathbf{v}$, and search also three words w_1', w_2', w_3' for $\mathbf{v}'$ in similar way. We also use w_1, w_2, w_3 to represent the associated word embedding vectors of these words for convenience.

(b) Compose the matrix $\mathbf{M}$ for $\mathbf{v}$ taking the word vectors $\mathbf{w_1}$, $\mathbf{w_2}$, $\mathbf{w_3}$ as rows in the matrix, or $\mathbf{M} = (\mathbf{w_1}, \mathbf{w_2}, \mathbf{w_3})^T$. Similarly, compose the matrix $\mathbf{M}'$ for $\mathbf{v}'$ and $\mathbf{M}' = (w_1', w_2', w_3')^T$.

Define the following model to show this procedure:

$$\mathbf{M} = \mathrm{sim}_{w2v}(r_1 - r_2 + a)$$
$$\mathbf{M}' = \mathrm{sim}_{w2v}(r_2 - r_1 + b) \tag{1}$$

So 3×300 matrix $\mathbf{M}$ contains three word vectors associating to the most possible three words that exist the relationship with a as which exists between r_1 and r_2, and 3×300 matrix $\mathbf{M}'$ also contains three vectors corresponding to the most possible three words that exist the relationship with b as which exists between r_2 and r_1. Define a measure Thr_k as following:

$$Thr_k = \frac{\mathrm{Max}(\mathrm{sim}_{\cos}(\boldsymbol{w}_i, \boldsymbol{b})) + \mathrm{Max}(\mathrm{sim}_{\cos}(\boldsymbol{w}_j', \boldsymbol{a}))}{2} \tag{2}$$

Where $i, j = (1, 2, 3)$, $k = (1, 2, 3, 4, 5)$, and $\mathbf{sim}_{\cos}$ is just cosine similarity function. Different k represents different lexical entailment relationship which will be considered.

For a word pair (a, b), if the Thr_k value between them is larger than 0.80, we think that lexical entailment relationship k exists between a and b. For example, given a reference pair like ($r_1 = $ "中国(China)", $r_2 = $ "北京(Beijing)") and a word pair $a = $ "日本(Japan)" and $b = $ "东京(Tokyo)", use Eq. (1) to obtain $\mathbf{M} = $ ["东京(Tokyo)", "横滨(Yokohama)", "名古屋(Nagoya)"](use the word instead of their vectors to make the example easier to understand) and $\mathbf{M}' = $ ["日本(Japan)", "韩国(Korea)", "关西地区(Kansai region)"]. After filtering each matrix with Thr_k score using Eq. 2, we will treat $a = $ "日本(Japan)" and $b = $ "东京(Tokyo)" as entailment lexical pair.

Five relationships will be taken into considered (object-component, synonymy, contradictory, set-member, agent-recipient). These relationships are only based on experience and convenience. Consider cases of object-component instances "机翼(aerofoil)","飞机(plane)", "轮胎(tyre)", after simple operations (**add** and **minus**) on 300 dimensional word embedding vectors trained in Skip-gram model, the result is the same word "汽车(car)" which we wish. Although the relationships of synonymy and contradictory have been used as lexical features, we still keep these relationships. Another case about set-member also gets a good performance. Make "森林(-forest)","树木(tree)", "湖泊(lakes)" as input,and the outcome is "河水(river water)". And agent-recipient relationship inputs as "医生(doctor)", "患者(patient)", "商户

(merchant)", the result is "顾客(custom)". So we store some word-pairs having these relationship we told before. After calculation, some lexical entailment relationship can be reasoned. The experimental result shows that this kind of lexical entailment recognition increase the performance of textual entailment classification apparently.

4 Experimental Result and Analysis

4.1 Data and Evaluation Measures

Our textual entailment recognition system will be tested on NTCIR-11 RITE3 Simplified Chinese binary-class subtask data [9, 11], which consists of 1200 text pairs. The evaluation of the system is performed by applying it on recognizing entailment relation of test text pairs. The topics of these text pairs cover many domains including history, political, geography, sports etc. Many linguistic phenomena such as inference, paraphrase, and clause are contained in the evaluation data.

The performance of the system is evaluated using *precision*, *recall*, *F-score* and their variations as measures. *Precision* is defined as the ratio of the number of correctly made decisions to the total number of decisions, while *recall* is the number of pairs classified correctly over the total number of pairs. *F-score* is the harmonic mean of *precision* and *recall*.

There are other variations of *precision*, *recall* and *F-score*, concerning the focus on entailment (denote by Y) or not (denote by N). Let $C = (c_{ij})_{2\times2}$ be a 2×2 confusion matrix, where c_{ij} represents the real category i and classified category j (hence $i, j \in \{Y, N\}$),

$$C = \begin{pmatrix} c_{YY} & c_{YN} \\ c_{NY} & c_{NN} \end{pmatrix}$$

Then all variations of *precision*, *recall* and *F-score* are defined as follows:

$$Pre_Y = \frac{c_{YY}}{c_{YY} + c_{NY}} \quad Pre_N = \frac{c_{NN}}{c_{NN} + c_{YN}} \tag{3}$$

$$Rec_Y = \frac{c_{YY}}{c_{YY} + c_{YN}} \quad Rec_N = \frac{c_{NN}}{c_{NN} + c_{NY}} \tag{4}$$

$$F_Y = \frac{2 \times Rec_Y \times Pre_Y}{Rec_Y + Pre_Y} \quad F_N = \frac{2 \times Rec_N \times Pre_N}{Rec_N + Pre_N} \tag{5}$$

Furthermore, NTCIR-11 RITE3 competition used *Macro-F* and *Pre* as the two most important evaluation criteria, which are define as:

$$Macro - F = \frac{F_Y + F_N}{2} \quad Pre = \frac{Pre_Y + Pre_N}{2} \tag{6}$$

4.2   Experimental Result and Analysis

We firstly compare the contributions to system performance by different features. Figure 2 demonstrates the effect of different features in SVM decision model. Overall, the performance of the system improves gradually when the number of features increasing. We can also see that the lexical entailment feature can improve the performance of the system from *Macro-F* 59.03 to 62.75, which demonstrates that word embedding is effective in textual entailment recognition.

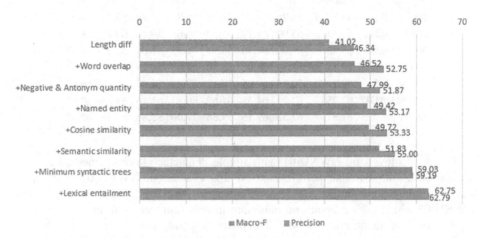

Fig. 2. System performance with different feature combinations

We also compare the performance of our system with other participators in NTCIR-11 RITE3 Simplified Chinese subtask. The formal run results of all systems on binary-class subtask are shown in Table 2. Our system **NWNW** achieves a second best result on all evaluation measures except F_y [11].

Table 2. The formula run result of all participated systems on BC

Participants	Macro-F	Pre	F_Y	F_N
BUPT	61.51	62.33	67.15	55.86
NWNU	59.71	59.75	60.95	58.47
III&CYUT	56.75	56.75	57.07	56.42
WHUTE	53.48	54.58	60.65	51.49
Yamraj	49.24	49.25	48.69	49.79
ASNLP	44.95	51.50	63.94	25.95
IMTKU	42.80	53.25	67.25	18.34
JAVN	42.32	51.17	64.91	19.73
WUST	39.14	52.25	67.39	10.89

We also analyze the effect of every module in our system to the overall performance of the system in terms of all evaluation measure when different classification algorithm is used. We got six run results shown in Table 3 in different ways, and compare them with those values achieved by the best system **BUPT** on NTCIR-11 RITE3 Simplified Chinese subtask.

Table 3. The formal run result of the system NWNU

System	Macro-F	Pre	F_Y	Pre_Y	Rec_Y	F_N	Pre_N	Rec_N
NWNU-01	45.82	51.75	63.74	51.05	84.83	27.90	55.17	18.67
NWNU-02	51.83	55.00	64.19	53.30	80.67	39.46	60.27	29.33
NWNU-03	58.03	59.00	64.40	56.91	74.17	51.67	62.92	43.83
NWNU-04	58.83	58.83	58.90	58.80	59.00	58.76	58.86	58.67
NWNU-05	59.71	59.75	60.95	59.18	62.83	58.47	60.39	56.67
NWNU-ADD	62.75	62.79	64.33	61.69	66.83	61.16	63.88	58.67
BUPT	**61.51**	**62.33**	**67.15**	**59.54**	**77.00**	**55.86**	**67.45**	**47.67**

Results achieved by NWNU-01 with simple character matching method can be considered as the baseline performance on this evaluation. NWNU-02 with more lexical features gain almost 6 % improvement in *Macro-F* measure. The system NWNU-03 which taking "syntactic minimum information tree" into consideration to capture some syntactic information still improve 6 % *Macro-F*. Both NWNU-04 and NWNU-05 employ an amending module to deal with some special situation.

Concerning Naïve Bayesian (NB) model has the best performance on RITE-1 and RITE-2 English textual entailment evaluations, all systems from NWNU-01 to NWNU-04 use it as classifier, but NWNU-05 uses SVM model to classify the text pair instead of NB, and this system shows the best performance among these five systems according to the final evaluation results.

Based on the system NWNU-05, a word embedding based lexical entailment module is appended into it and the new version of this system is then called as NWNU-ADD. The experiment result show that the newly added module works very well in recognizing those pairs with real entailment relationship, and the performance of the system enhanced with word embedding outperforms the best system BUPT on NTCIR-11 RITE3 Simplified Chinese subtask. This demonstrates again that word embedding is valuable for recognizing Chinese textual entailment.

The confusion matrices is Fig. 3 presents the numbers of text pairs classified by NWNU-05 and NWNU-ADD. We can see that the lexical entailment model gives an effective supplement to NWNU-05.

$$\begin{pmatrix} 377 & 223 \\ 260 & 340 \end{pmatrix}_{\text{NWNU-05}} \qquad \begin{pmatrix} 401 & 199 \\ 248 & 352 \end{pmatrix}_{\text{NWNU-ADD}}$$

Fig. 3. Classified text pair number confusion matrices

We believe that there is much room left to improve in our system. For one thing, the lexical entailment reasoning ability is still very limited, and more general approach should be proposed to deal with more complex lexical entailment phenomena. For another, more powerful neural network models such as recursive autoencoder [16] can be employed and explored against traditional classifiers or linguistic features.

5 Conclusion

Recognizing textual entailment is an important subtask in many natural language processing applications, and the statistical learning approaches gradually become the mainstream on this task. Using our Chinese textual entailment recognition system that participated in NTCIR-11 RITE-3 task, this paper evaluated the contribution of different linguistic feature types to the quality of the supervised Chinese textual entailment recognition models. Especially, we analyzed the impact of a word embedding based lexical entailment module on system performance. Experimental result shows that word embedding can enhance effectively the ability of the system.

Our future work is two-fold. We should find new features or new methods to express entailment relationship better. Meanwhile we also need to focus on the recognizing multi-directional Chinese textual entailment relation, and this challenge requires entailment system developed in a more robust and reasonable way.

Acknowledgements.   This work is supported by grants from National Natural Science Foundation of China (No. 61163039, No. 61163036, No. 61363058) and the Young Teacher Research Ability Enhancement Project of Northwest Normal University of China (NWNU-LKQN-10-2, NWNU-LKQN-13-23).

References

1. Dagan, I., Glickman, O.: Probabilistic textual entailment: generic applied modeling of language variability. In: PASCAL Workshop on Learning Methods for Text Understanding and Mining, Grenoble, France (2004)
2. Tatu, M., Moldovan, D.: COGEX at RTE 3. In: Proceedings of the ACL-PASCAL Workshop on Textual Entailment and Paraphrasing, Prague, Czech Republic, pp. 22–27 (2007)
3. Bos, J.: Is there a place for logic in recognizing textual entailment? Linguist. Issues Lang. Technol. **9**, 1–18 (2013)
4. Harmeling, S.: Inferring textual entailment with a probabilistically sound calculus. Nat. Lang. Eng. **15**(4), 459–477 (2009)
5. Quinonero Candela, J., Dagan, I., Magnini, B., et al.: MLCW 2005. LNCS, vol. 3944. Springer, Heidelberg (2006)
6. Burrows, S., Potthast, M., Stein, B.: Paraphrase acquisition via crowdsourcing and machine learning. ACM Trans. Intell. Syst. Technol. (TIST) **4**(3), 43 (2013)

7. Bar-Haim, R., Berant, J., Dagan, I.: A compact forest for scalable inference over entailment and paraphrase rules. In: Proceedings of the 2009 Conference on Empirical Methods in Natural Language Processing, vol. 3. Association for Computational Linguistics, pp. 1056–1065 (2009)

8. Tian, J.-L., Zhao, W.: Words similarity algorithm based on tongyici CiLin in semantic web adaptive learning system. J. Jilin Univ. **28**(6), 602–608 (2010)

9. Liu, M., Li, Y., Ji, D.: Event semantic feature based chinese textual entailment recognition. J. Chin. Inf. Process. **27**(5), 129–136 (2013)

10. Pedregosa, F., et al.: Scikit-learn: machine learning in python. JMLR **12**, 2825–2830 (2011)

11. Matsuyoshi, S., Miyao, Y., Shibata, T., Lin, C.-J., Shih, C.-W., Watanabe, Y., Mitamura, T.: Overview of the NTCIR-11 recognizing inference in TExt and validation (RITE-VAL) task. In: Proceedings of the 11th NTCIR Conference, Tokyo, Japan (2014)

12. Zhang, Z., Yao, D., Chen, S., Ma, H.: Chinese textual entailment recognition based on syntactic tree clipping. In: Sun, M., Liu, Y., Zhao, J. (eds.) CCL and NLP-NABD 2014. LNCS, vol. 8801, pp. 83–94. Springer, Heidelberg (2014)

13. Turney, P.D., Mohammad, S.M.: Experiments with three approaches to recognizing lexical entailment. Nat. Lang. Eng. 1–40 (2013)

14. Mikolov, T., Chen, K., Corrado, G., et al.: Efficient estimation of word representations in vector space. arXiv preprint arXiv:1301.3781 (2013)

15. Fu, R., Guo, J., Qin, B., et al.: Learning semantic hierarchies via word embeddings. In: Proceedings of the 52th Annual Meeting of the Association for Computational Linguistics: Long Papers, vol. 1 (2014)

16. Socher, R., Huang, E.H., Pennin, J., et al.: Dynamic pooling and unfolding recursive autoencoders for paraphrase detection. In: Advances in Neural Information Processing Systems, pp. 801–809 (2011)

17. Zhitomirsky-Geffet, M., Dagan, I.: Bootstrapping distributional feature vector quality. Comput. Linguist. **35**(3), 435–461 (2009)

Sentiment Analysis, Opinion Mining and Text Classification

Negative Emotion Recognition in Spoken Dialogs

Xiaodong Zhang[1]([⊠]), Houfeng Wang[1], Li Li[1], Maoxiang Zhao[2], and Quanzhong Li[2]

[1] Key Laboratory of Computational Linguistics (Peking University), Ministry of Education, Beijing, China
zxddavy@gmail.com, {wanghf,li.l}@pku.edu.cn
[2] Pachira Technology, Inc., Sunnyvale, USA
zmxiangde_88@163.com, quanzhong@hotmail.com

Abstract. Increasing attention has been directed to the study of the automatic emotion recognition in human speech recently. This paper presents an approach for recognizing negative emotions in spoken dialogs at the utterance level. Our approach mainly includes two parts. First, in addition to the traditional acoustic features, linguistic features based on distributed representation are extracted from the text transcribed by an automatic speech recognition (ASR) system. Second, we propose a novel deep learning model, multi-feature stacked denoising autoencoders (MSDA), which can fuse the high-level representations of the acoustic and linguistic features along with contexts to classify emotions. Experimental results demonstrate that our proposed method yields an absolute improvement over the traditional method by 5.2 %.

Keywords: Emotion recognition · Spoken dialogs · MSDA

1 Introduction

Emotion recognition of speech signals aims to identify the emotional or physical states of a person by analyzing his or her voice [25]. The automatic recognition of emotions in human speech has drawn increasing attention over the past few years, mainly because of the growing number of applications that may benefit from this research field, e.g. call center, man-machine interaction system, and speech recognition, etc. Take call center as an example. By analyzing emotions in spoken dialogs between customers and agents, the managers can find problems in the customer service so as to reduce customer losses. Besides, it can serve as evidences for agent performance evaluation.

Emotion recognition of spoken dialogs is a challenging and cross-disciplinary research area. A variety of acoustic features have been explored by previous work [4,5,24]. However, these works have neglected linguistic features. Emotion in an utterance is expressed by not only how it is being said, but also what is being said. Recently, more attention has been paid to the integration of acoustic

© Springer International Publishing Switzerland 2015
M. Sun et al. (Eds.): CCL and NLP-NABD 2015, LNAI 9427, pp. 103–115, 2015.
DOI: 10.1007/978-3-319-25816-4_9

and linguistic information. For linguistic feature representation, the mainstream is the bag-of-words (BoW) and n-grams model [12,18,19]. In previous works, the different kinds of features are combined at input level [12,18,21] or at decision level [11,16]. Both ways have drawbacks. How to represent and combine linguistic information for emotion recognition is worthy of further exploration.

In the past few years, a variety of deep neutral networks for emotion recognition have been studied [22,27] and have achieved good performance. The deep learning method can learn abstract representation from the raw feature space, and can tolerate noises, making it suitable for spoken language processing.

According to Ayadi's survey on speech emotion recognition [2], most of the previous studies employed speech data recorded from actors who were asked to express the prescribed emotions. Besides, these utterances were produced in isolation without any conversational context. In this work, we focus on recognizing emotions in Chinese spoken dialogs recorded in a call center that serves actual customers. The emotion recognition is at the utterance level. We only consider two categories, i.e. *negative* and *non-negative*, rather than a large variety of emotions, which may be unnecessary for our application. The negative emotion can be used as a strategy to improve the quality of service.

Here we give a brief introduction of our proposed method. First, we extracted some classical acoustic features mentioned in the previous work. Then the speech was transcribed to text automatically by an ASR engine. We employed the distributed representation (embeddings) as linguistic features. Therefore, for each utterance, there are two kinds of features. The contextual information is based on the surrounding utterances. A novel deep learning model, referred to as MSDA, was proposed to fuse the high-level abstractions of acoustic and linguistic features to a unified representation and classify the utterances into two categories.

The rest of the paper is organized as follows. The related work is surveyed in Sect. 2. The proposed approach is presented in Sect. 3. The experimental results are detailed in Sect. 4. Lastly conclusions are given in Sect. 5.

2   Related Work

The early works on speech emotion recognition have been focused on acoustic features. Various frame-level descriptors have been explored. Banse examined vocal parameters for emotion expression using actors' portrayals of 14 emotions [3]. Pitch, energy, speech rate, and spectral information were used. McGilloway studied 22 different acoustic features for the classification of five emotion states [14]. However, using only acoustic features cannot guarantee a good result because it is just one side of the problem.

Recently, more attentions have been paid to combining acoustic features with other information, especially linguistic information. The BoW and n-grams representation are often used as linguistic features [12,18,19]. Raaijmakers compared n-grams at different level (word, character, and phoneme) and concluded that character-level features outperform other two levels [19]. Lee proposed emotional salience to measure how much information a word provides towards a certain emotion [11] and Metze extended it to include bi-grams and tri-grams [16].

Some of the previous works were based on manual transcripts [11,12], while other studies relied on ASR [16,21]. In real-word application, only the ASR approach is feasible. Some studies concluded that the recognition errors brought by ASR were consistent enough that it had little influence on the results [13,16]. However, Rozgi demonstrated that the results based on ASR were much worse than the results based on manual transcription [21]. We believe the opposite conclusions are due to the different dataset and ASR system.

Some researchers employed discourse information for emotion recognition in human-computer interactive system and achieved good results [11,12]. However, the discourse feature was manually labeled so that it is not feasible for real-world applications. Liscombe augmented standard lexical and prosodic features with contextual features [12]. The contextual features were defined on the difference between present utterance and previous two utterances. In our method, the previous and following utterances are both taken into consideration, and the relation is learned by the neural network, rather than the predefined difference.

For feature combination method, two ways are mainly employed in previous works. One way is to train separated classifiers for different kinds of features and then combine the results of these classifier to make the final classification [11,16]. However, this way cannot learn the correlation of the different kinds of features and take full advantage of the complementation of them. The other way is to combine the different kinds of features at input level and train a unified classifier [12,18,21]. The acoustic and linguistic features generally have distinct statistical characteristics and the correlations between them are nonlinear. Consequently, joining the two kinds of features at low-level representation, e.g. the input layer, may not generate a good unified representation. Besides, this way may suffer from the dimensionality issues. Recently, Kiela proposed a multimodal representation method [10], which concatenated a skip-gram linguistic representation vector with a visual concept representation vector computed using a deep convolutional neural network. However, the different abstractions are just concatenated without learning their correlation. Our approach first learns the high-level abstraction of the acoustic and linguistic features separately and then fuses them to learn a unified high-level representation so that it can overcomes the shortcomings of the above methods.

3 The Proposed Approach

3.1 Features

Acoustic Features. The acoustic features were automatically extracted from the speech signal of each utterance by the open source toolkit openSMILE[1]. At first, we computed 26 acoustic features (including MFCC, LSP, F0, Intensity, and MZCR) for each frame (25 ms) with their respective first derivatives. The F0 features contain F0, F0's slope, and the prior probability of voice frames. The

---

[1] http://www.audeering.com/research/opensmile

intensity features contain the absolute and relative amplitudes in time domain. MFCC and LSP contain the information about the formant and audio coding.

Based on these per-frame features, we computed the statistical features over a whole utterance using the statistics listed in Table 1. Hence, each utterance is represented as a 988-dimensional feature vector: $(1+\Delta) \times (12 \text{ MFCC} + 8 \text{ LSP} + 3 \text{ F0} + 2 \text{ intensity} + 1 \text{ MZCR}) \times (4 \text{ regressions} + 6 \text{ percentiles} + 3 \text{ moments} + 6 \text{ extremes})$. Without performing feature selection, we directly use all extracted features as input, because our model has inherent capability of dimensionality reduction.

Table 1. The statistics for global features

Statistics	Number	Detail
Regressions	4	two linear regression coefficients, absolute mean and variance of error
Percentiles	6	25 %, 50 %, 75 %, 50 %–25 %, 75 %–50 %, 75 %–25 %
Moments	3	variance, skewness, kurtosis
Extremes	6	max, min, max-min, max position, min position, mean

Linguistic Features. To extract linguistic features, we first transcribed the audio data into text via an ASR engine. Our ASR system is mainly composed of five components: feature extraction, acoustic model, language model, lexicon, and decoder. We used log filter-banks [6] with 40 dimensions as acoustic features. The acoustic model, language model, and lexicon were combined into a single weighted finite state transducers (WFST) as in [1]. The ASR system was measured on a dataset containing 40 hours of phone dialogs and the character error rate (CER) is 16 %.

Word segmentation is the first step for Chinese text processing. The ICT-CLAS[2] was utilized to segment our transcribed text into words. We did not remove any stop words on the consideration that some function words, especially tone words, can contribute to the emotion recognition.

We represented the text of each utterance by the distributed representation rather than the traditional BoW. First, word embeddings were trained by word2vec[3] on the combination of three corpus, namely Chinese Gigaword[4], Chinese Wikipedia[5], and SougouCA[6]. Next, we composed word embeddings to get the distributed representation of the utterance text. Due to the bad performance of a parser on text with ASR errors, composition methods based on a parser [23]

---

[2] http://ictclas.nlpir.org/
[3] https://code.google.com/p/word2vec/
[4] https://catalog.ldc.upenn.edu/LDC2011T13
[5] http://download.wikipedia.com/zhwiki/
[6] http://www.sogou.com/labs/dl/ca.html

are not suitable for our work. Following Hermann's work [8], we represent the text of an utterance by the average of its word embeddings. Formally,

$$f(x) = \sum_{i=1}^{n} x_i \Big/ n \qquad (1)$$

where x_i is the embedding of the i-th word in the utterance text x and $f(x)$ is the utterance text vector. As the variance of the length of our text is large, we used the averaged vectors of words or pairs rather than the sum to alleviate the influence of text length. The utterance text vectors served as the linguistic features.

For completely out of vocabulary utterance, the averaged vector of all utterances in the training set serve as the linguistic features. In this case, the classification mainly depends on the acoustic features.

Contextual Information. Contextual information in dialogs is useful for emotion recognition. It is natural to use the surrounding utterances as additional evidence to help the emotion recognition of the present utterance.

The acoustic context is defined as the ordered concatenation of the acoustic feature vectors of utterances in a window. Formally,

$$w(t) = [x(t - s), ..., x(t), ..., x(t + s)] \qquad (2)$$

where $x(t)$ is the acoustic features of t-th utterance, $w(t)$ is the acoustic features with context of t-th utterance, and the window size is $2 \times s + 1$.

The linguistic context is defined in the same way.

3.2 Emotion Classification

We propose a novel classification model, referred to as multi-feature stacked denoising autoencoder (MSDA). Here, the multi-feature means several kinds of features with different statistical characteristics and non-linear correlation. Figure 1 demonstrates the framework of the model, which mainly includes two parts. In the bottom part, the acoustic features and linguistic features with their respective contexts are employed as inputs to train two stacked denoising autoencoders (SDA) to learn the high-level abstractions independently. Subsequently, in the top part, the two high-level abstractions are fused to generate a unified high-level feature representation by another SDA. Finally, the unified representation serve as the input to a classifier to make the prediction. Next, we introduce the details of MSDA.

The basic building block for MSDA is the denoising autoencoder (DAE) [26], which is an extension of the classical autoencoder. The DAE is trained to reconstruct the input from a partially destroyed version of it, so as to force the hidden layer to discover more robust features. It can be stacked for building deep networks, i.e. the stack denoising autoencoders (SDA).

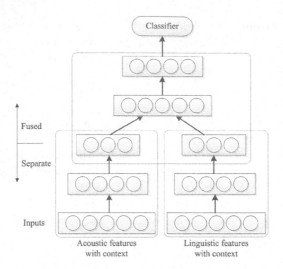

Fig. 1. The framework of MSDA

The unsupervised pretraining of MSDA is performed one layer at a time. Each layer is trained as a denoising autoencoder by minimizing the reconstruction of its input, which is the output of the previous layer. First, in the bottom part, the two SDAs are pretrained layer-wise from bottom to top. Then the outputs of the top layers of the two SDAs are joined together as the input of the top part. The top part is also pretrained layer-wise from bottom to top.

After pretraining, the MSDA are fine-tuned using labeled data. A classifier is put on the top of the network so as to be trained with the unified high-level representation. In our experiments, the logistic regression (LR) classifier was used. In our dataset, the number of non-negative utterances is far more than the negative utterances. The LR classifier does not perform well on imbalanced datasets. The most common solution of imbalanced learning is sampling [7], however this solution is not applicable to our approach because contextual information is used. Thinking differently, we made a modification on the loss function of LR.

$$J(\theta) = -\frac{1}{m} \left[\sum_{i=1}^{m} y^{(i)} \log h_\theta(x^{(i)}) + \alpha(1 - y^{(i)}) \log(1 - h_\theta(x^{(i)})) \right] \qquad (3)$$

$$h_\theta(x) = \frac{1}{1 + \exp(-\theta^T x)} \qquad (4)$$

where $x^{(i)}$ is the input, $y^{(i)} \in \{0, 1\}$ is the label (1 for negative and 0 for non-negative), and θ are model parameters. Note that the second term of Eq. 3 is multiplied by $\alpha \in (0, 1]$, which is a penalty factor of non-negative data to alleviate the imbalanced learning problem.

Next we introduce the advantages of MSDA. In the previous work, the different kinds of features were fused at the input layer [12, 18, 21], which may not generate a good unified representation because of distinct statistical characteristics, or after the independent prediction [11,16], which cannot take full advantage of the complementation of different features. Our approach fuses the acoustic and linguistic features at high-level abstraction and overcomes the shortcomings of the above two methods. It can be regarded as the trade-off of the two methods.

The utterance text was transcribed automatically by an ASR engine. In our dataset, some speakers use dialects and the Chinese dialects are diverse. Besides, the quality of our telephone recordings is not very good. Therefore, the transcription errors must be taken into account. In our model, the denoising autoencoders can discover robust features for classification so as to alleviate this problem.

It should be noted that although our model is introduced with two kinds of features, it can be easily extended to support more kinds of features. What needs to be done is to add more SDAs for more kinds of features and take the outputs of the SDAs as the input of the fused SDA.

4   Experiments and Results

4.1   Dataset and Evaluation Metrics

We collected 254 dialogs (8 kHz, 16 bit WAVE) from a call center, where actual customers are engaged in spoken dialog with human agents over the telephone. The dialogs were then segmented into utterances by a speaker diarization algorithm. The goal of speaker diarization is to segment an audio signal into several acoustic classes, each of which only contains the acoustic data from a single speaker [20]. The speaker diarization in our work mainly includes two processes: detecting speaker change points and unsupervised clustering [15]. To avoid overlong turns, each turn was segmented into one or several utterances based on the lengths of silences. Our speaker diarization algorithm was evaluated on a dataset containing 40 hours of phone dialogs and the diarization error rate (DER) was 7 %. We got 34416 utterances after applying speaker diarization on the 254 dialogs.

Three annotators independently labeled each utterance as negative or non-negative. In our study, the negative emotion represents anger and discontent, etc., whereas the non-negative emotion represents the complement, i.e., neutral or positive emotions such as happiness or satisfaction, etc. The annotation was done after listening to the audio corresponding to an utterance. The majority label of the three annotators was taken as the label of an utterance when there were disagreements. After annotation, we got 2437 negative utterances and 31979 non-negative utterances. The constructed dataset is referred to as Emotional Utterances in Chinese Spoken Dialogs (EUCSD).

Most of the previous work is evaluated on a balanced dataset. For comparison, we sampled non-negative utterances from the EUCSD to acquire a subset having a comparable amount to the negative utterances. This balanced dataset is referred to as EUCSD-B. Note that EUCSD-B is just used for comparison experiments, and the results on EUCSD are the final results. For both datasets, we used 70 % of the data for training and 30 % for testing. The statistics of the two datasets are shown in Table 2.

Table 2. The statistics of the two datasets

Dataset	Negative	Non-negative	Training	Testing	Total
EUCSD	2437	31979	23993	10423	34416
EUCSD-B	2437	2664	3701	1400	5101

Since we focused on the recognition of the negative emotion, the precision, recall and F1 score for the negative emotion class were employed as the evaluation metrics.

4.2 Comparison Between Feature Combination Methods

In the first set of experiments, we compare our proposed approach with some baseline methods. Because the features used in the previous work are diverse, for simplicity we focus on the feature combination methods. Our acoustic and linguistic features are used for all of the following methods.

RG: We use random guess to describe the different difficulties of the two dataset. The results are calculated theoretically, not experimentally. The recall is 0.5, and the precision is the proportion of the negative emotion category.

SVM-A: An SVM classifier using only the acoustic features.

SVM-L: An SVM classifier using only the linguistic features.

SVM-AL-O: Two SVM classifiers are learned from the acoustic and linguistic features separately. The final prediction is combined at the decision level by taking the prediction with the larger posterior probability. This combination method has been employed in [11,16].

SVM-AL-I: The acoustic and linguistic features are concatenated to unified features as the input of an SVM classifier. This feature combination method has been employed in [12,18,21].

MSDA-AL: Our proposed MSDA model is employed for classification but the contextual information is not used.

SVM-CRF: A two-stage SVM/CRF sequence classifier [9]. First, an SVM is trained to predict each individual sequence element. Second, a CRF is trained to predict the whole sequences using the prediction from the previously trained SVM as its input.

MSDA-ALC: Our proposed MSDA model is employed for classification and the contextual information is used. The contextual window size is 3.

In this paper, LIBSVM[7] and CRF++[8] are used for SVM and CRF implementation respectively, and MSDA is implemented using Theano[9]. As there are no unlabeled data in our datasets, we used the labeled data in the training set

---

[7] https://github.com/cjlin1/libsvm
[8] http://taku910.github.io/crfpp/
[9] http://deeplearning.net/software/thcano/

for unsupervised pretraining. In the pretraining and fine-tuning process, model parameters were optimized based on minibatch stochastic gradient descent and the batch size was 50. For experiments on EUCSD, the penalty factor of non-negative data was 0.2 for both the SVM and LR classifiers, while for experiments on EUCSD-B, the penalty factor was 1, i.e. no penalty. The destruction proportion of denoising autoencoders was 0.5.

The comparison results are shown in Table 3. The contextual information is not involved in Method 1–6, but considered in Method 7 and 8. Due to the destruction of contexts caused by the sampling, Method 7 and 8 are not applicable on EUCSD-B. The results on EUCSD are much worse than the results on EUCSD-B, because it is harder to learn a classifier on an imbalanced dataset than a balanced one, especially for the data with lots of ASR errors.

Table 3. Comparison results of feature combination methods

#	Methods	EUCSD-B			EUCSD		
		precision	recall	F1	precision	recall	F1
1	RG	0.478	0.500	0.489	0.071	0.500	0.124
2	SVM-A	0.721	0.767	0.743	0.337	0.439	0.381
3	SVM-L	0.652	0.868	0.745	0.262	0.467	0.335
4	SVM-AL-O	0.717	0.853	0.779	0.390	0.396	0.393
5	SVM-AL-I	0.726	0.851	0.784	0.326	0.518	0.400
6	MSDA-AL	0.713	0.896	**0.794**	0.398	0.461	0.428
7	SVM-CRF	N/A	N/A	N/A	0.421	0.112	0.177
8	MSDA-ALC	N/A	N/A	N/A	0.396	0.478	**0.433**

First, we analyze the experimental results on EUCSD-B. The F1 scores of SVM-A and SVM-L are close, showing that the linguistic feature cannot improve the performance individually. However, SVM-AL-O, which makes the prediction based on two classifier, achieves a 3.6 % higher F1 score than SVM-A. It demonstrates that the two kinds of features are complementary and the joint use can improve the emotion recognition. Furthermore, SVM-AL-I outperforms SVM-AL-O by 0.5 %, which demonstrates that combing features at input level is better than at decision level. This is because the correlation of acoustic and linguistic features can be learned. MSDA-AL outperforms SVM-AL-I by 1.0 % and SVM-A by 5.1 %. The improvements are due to the high-level representation fusion and robust features extracted by denoising autoencoders.

For EUCSD, similar conclusions can be drawn. The only exception is that SVM-L performs much worse than SVM-A, because the introduction of more ASR errors does harm to the classification. Nevertheless, the combination of the acoustic and linguistic features can still help emotion recognition, with SVM-AL-O and SVM-AL-I outperforming SVM-A by 1.2 % and 1.9 % respectively.

Furthermore, MSDA-AL outperforms SVM-AL-I by 2.8 % and SVM-A by 4.7 %. Next are two experiments with contexts taken into account. SVM-CRF modeled the task by sequence labeling model, however this method performs badly and may be because the CRF model needs a large number of data to learn the model parameters and the imbalanced learning problem is not concerned. This is why our proposed approach employs contextual information as input features rather than sequence labeling. One potential concern of our method is the curse of dimensionality, but it can be solved by the dimensionality reduction of DAE in our model. With contextual information, MSDA-ALC outperforms MSDA-AL by 0.5 % and SVM-A by 5.2 %. The absolute improvements on both datasets are highly consistent, demonstrating the effectiveness and reliability of the proposed approach.

4.3 Comparison Between Models for Linguistic Features

We compare our linguistic feature model with some baseline models. We only employ linguistic features for emotion classification and the experimental settings are as follows:

SVM-BOW: The inputs are the BoW representations and the classifier is SVM.
ES: The emotional salience [11] is used for emotion classification.
SVM-EMB: The inputs are the distributed representations and the classifier is SVM.

The dimensionality of the BoW representation is the vocabulary size, i.e. 13469 in our dataset, while the dimensionality of the distributed representation is 200, much lower and denser than BoW.

The EUCSD-B is used as the experimental dataset and the results are shown in Table 4. The F1 score of SVM-BoW is 0.728. The result of ES is even worse than SVM-BoW. This is because the classification method of emotional salience is simple. The SVM-EMB outperforms SVM-BoW, which demonstrates that the distributed representation is better than the traditional BoW representation.

Table 4. Comparison results of linguistic feature models

#	Methods	Precision	Recall	F1
1	SVM-BoW	0.740	0.718	0.728
2	ES	0.565	0.886	0.690
3	SVM-EMB	0.652	0.868	0.745

4.4 Comparisons Between MSDA and SDA

We also compare the proposed MSDA with SDA. The experimental settings are as follows:

SDA-AL: The acoustic and linguistic features are concatenated to generate a unified feature representation, which is the input to an SDA.

MSDA-AL: The same as described in Sect. 4.2.

SDA-ALB: The same as SDA-AL except that the BoW representation is used as linguistic features.

MSDA-ALB: The same as MSDA-AL except that the BoW representation is used as linguistic features.

Table 5 shows the results of the above methods on EUCSD-B. Although MSDA-AL outperforms SDA-AL, the improvement is small, only 0.4 %. This is because the linguistic feature is distributed representation and the same normalization methods are employed for the two kinds of features so that the statistical characteristics of acoustic and linguistic features are similar. The premise that the correlation of acoustic and linguistic features is non-linear does not hold. To prove the effectiveness of MSDA, two more experiments were conducted, in which the BoW representation was used as the linguistic feature. In this case, the correlation of acoustic and linguistic features is believed to be non-linear and MSDA-ALB outperforms SDA-ALB by 1.9 %. Therefore, for the cases that there are different kinds of features with non-linear correlation, the MSDA is a good choice. Furthermore, before fusing different features, MSDA has fewer model parameters than SDA, because the two kinds of features are separated in low layers.

Table 5. Comparison between MSDA and SDA

#	Methods	Precision	Recall	F1
1	SDA-AL	0.717	0.879	0.790
2	MSDA-AL	0.713	0.896	0.794
3	SDA-ALB	0.688	0.844	0.758
4	MSDA-ALB	0.714	0.853	0.777

5   Conclusion and Future Work

In this paper, we propose a novel approach for emotion recognition in spoken dialogs. The utterances are transcribed to text by an ASR engine and then the distributed representations of the text are employed as linguistic features. The acoustic and linguistic features along with contextual information are provided to MSDA to learn the high-level representation, which are then fused to a unified feature representation for emotion classification. To evaluate the effectiveness of the proposed approach, we constructed a dataset based on dialogs from a call center. The experimental results demonstrate that our proposed approach outperforms other comparative methods.

As to future work, we plan to study other approaches for leveraging contextual information. Additionally, we will explore our MSDA model to other tasks.

Acknowledgments. Our work is supported by National High Technology Research and Development Program of China (863 Program) (No. 2015AA015402), National Natural Science Foundation of China (No. 61370117 & No. 61433015) and Major National Social Science Fund of China (No. 12&ZD227).

References

1. Allauzen, C., Mohri, M., Riley, M., Roark, B.: A generalized construction of integrated speech recognition transducers. In: ICASSP, vol. 1, pp. 761–764 (2004)
2. Ayadi, M.E., Kamel, M.S., Karray, F.: Survey on speech emotion recognition: features, classification schemes, and databases. Pattern Recogn. **44**(3), 572–587 (2011)
3. Banse, R., Scherer, K.R.: Acoustic profiles in vocal emotion expression. J. Personal. Soc. Psychol. **70**(3), 614–636 (1996)
4. Bitouk, D., Verma, R., Nenkova, A.: Class-level spectral features for emotion recognition. Speech Commun. **52**(7), 613–625 (2010)
5. Dellaert, F., Polzin, T., Waibel, A.: Recognizing emotion in speech. In: ICSLP, vol. 3, pp. 1970–1973 (1996)
6. Deng, L., Li, J., Huang, J.T., Yao, K., Yu, D., Seide, F., Seltzer, M.L., Zweig, G., He, X., Williams, J., Gong, Y., Acero, A.: Recent advances in deep learning for speech research at Microsoft. In: ICASSP, pp. 8604–8608 (2013)
7. He, H., Garcia, E.A.: Learning from imbalanced data. TKDE **21**(9), 1263–1284 (2009)
8. Hermann, K.M., Blunsom, P.: Multilingual models for compositional distributed semantics. In: ACL (2014)
9. Hoefel, G., Elkan, C.: Learning a two-stage SVM/CRF sequence classifier. In: CIKM, pp. 271–278 (2008)
10. Kiela, D., Bottou, L.: Learning image embeddings using convolutional neural networks for improved multi-modal semantics. In: EMNLP, pp. 36–45 (2008)
11. Lee, C.M., Narayanan, S.S.: Toward detecting emotions in spoken dialogs. IEEE Trans. Speech Audio Process. **13**(2), 293–303 (2005)
12. Liscombe, J., Riccardi, G., Hakkani-Tür, D.: Using context to improve emotion detection in spoken dialog systems. In: Eurospeech (2005)
13. Litman, D.J., Forbes-Riley, K.: Predicting student emotions in computer-human tutoring dialogues. In: ACL (2004)
14. McGilloway, S., Cowie, R., Douglas-Cowie, E., Gielen, S., Westerdijk, M., Stroeve, S.: Approaching automatic recognition of emotion from voice: a rough benchmark. In: ITRW (2000)
15. Meignier, S., Moraru, D., Fredouille, C., Bonastre, J.F., Besacier, L.: Step-by-step and integrated approaches in broadcast news speaker diarization. Comput. Speech Lang. **20**(2), 303–330 (2006)
16. Metze, F., Polzehl, T., Wagner, M.: Fusion of acoustic and linguistic features for emotion detection. In: ICSC, pp. 153–160 (2009)
17. Morrison, D., Wang, R., De Silva, L.C.: Ensemble methods for spoken emotion recognition in call-centres. Speech commun. **49**(2), 98–112 (2007)
18. Pérez-Rosas, V., Mihalcea, R., Morency, L.P.: Utterance-level multimodal sentiment analysis. In: ACL, pp. 973–982 (2013)
19. Raaijmakers, S., Truong, K., Wilson, T.: Multimodal subjectivity analysis of multiparty conversation. In: EMNLP, pp. 466–474 (2008)
20. Reynolds, D.A., Torres-Carrasquillo, P.: Approaches and applications of audio diarization. In: ICASSP, vol. 5, pp. 953–956 (2005)

21. Rozgić, V., Ananthakrishnan, S., Saleem, S., Kumar, R., Vembu, A.N., Prasad, R.: Emotion recognition using acoustic and lexical features. In: Interspeech (2012)
22. Sánchez-Gutiérrez, M.E., Albornoz, E.M., Martinez-Licona, F., Rufiner, H.L., Goddard, J.: Deep learning for emotional speech recognition. In: Martínez-Trinidad, J.F., Carrasco-Ochoa, J.A., Olvera-Lopez, J.A., Salas-Rodríguez, J., Suen, C.Y. (eds.) MCPR 2014. LNCS, vol. 8495, pp. 311–320. Springer, Heidelberg (2014)
23. Socher, R., Perelygin, A., Wu, J.Y., Chuang, J., Manning, C.D., Ng, A.Y., Potts, C.: Recursive deep models for semantic compositionality over a sentiment treebank. In: EMNLP (2013)
24. Tato, R., Santos, R., Kompe, R., Pardo, J.M.: Emotional space improves emotion recognition. In: Interspeech (2002)
25. Ververidis, D., Kotropoulos, C.: Emotional speech recognition: resources, features, and methods. Speech commun. **48**(9), 1162–1181 (2006)
26. Vincent, P., Larochelle, H., Bengio, Y., Manzagol, P.A.: Extracting and composing robust features with denoising autoencoders. In: ICML, pp. 1096–1103 (2008)
27. Zhou, G., He, T., Zhao, J.: Bridging the language gap: learning distributed semantics for cross-lingual sentiment classification. In: Zong, C., Nie, J.-Y., Zhao, D., Feng, Y. (eds.) NLPCC 2014. CCIS, vol. 496, pp. 138–149. Springer, Heidelberg (2014)

Incorporating Sample Filtering
into Subject-Based Ensemble Model
for Cross-Domain Sentiment Classification

Liang Yang, Shaowu Zhang, Hongfei Lin[⊠], and Xianhui Wei

School of Computer Science and Technology,
Dalian University of Technology, Dalian 116024, China
yangliang@mail.dlut.edu.cn,
{zhangsw,hflin}@dlut.edu.cn

Abstract. Recently, cross-domain sentiment classification is becoming popular owing to its potential applications, such as marketing et al. It seeks to generalize a model, which is trained on a source domain and using it to label samples in the target domain. However, the source and target distributions differ substantially in many cases. To address this issue, we propose a comprehensive model, which takes sample filtering and labeling adaptation into account simultaneously, named joint Sample Filtering with Subject-based Ensemble Model (**SF-SE**). Firstly, a sentence level Latent Dirichlet Allocation (LDA) model, which incorporates topic and sentiment together (SS-LDA) is introduced. Under this model, a high-quality training dataset is constructed in an unsupervised way. Secondly, inspired by the distribution variance of domain-independent and domain-specific features related to the subject of a sentence, we introduce a Subject-based Ensemble model to efficiently improve the classification performance. Experimental results show that the proposed model is effective for cross-domain sentiment classification.

Keywords: Cross-domain · SS-LDA · Sentiment analysis

1 Introduction

Web 2.0 presents an online forum for people to express their feelings on anything freely. Under this situation, as a special task of text classification, sentiment classification (Pang et al. 2002; Pang and Lee 2008) has become attractive because of its potential commercial applications (Liu et al. 2007; Yu et al. 2012). However, sentiment classification is domain-specific due to the divergent distributions. Traditional supervised classification methods usually perform poorly when the training and test data belong to completely different domains. This is largely because the sentiment polarities depend on the domain or the topic where they are expressed to a large degree. Some opinion words, which convey positive sentiment in one domain may express little or opposite meaning in another domain. For example, in book reviews, the high-frequency word *"superficial"* often indicates negative sentimental orientation. But it hardly appears in electronics reviews. Similarly, the word *"smoothly"* may be positive in electronics reviews, but it bears little semantic orientation when talking about books.

© Springer International Publishing Switzerland 2015
M. Sun et al. (Eds.): CCL and NLP-NABD 2015, LNAI 9427, pp. 116–127, 2015.
DOI: 10.1007/978-3-319-25816-4_10

Furthermore, with the rise of new areas, collecting annotated data is time-consuming and expensive. So, how to effectively transfer a classifier trained on source domain to the target domain is challenging and significant.

In this paper, we propose a two-stage model, which takes sample filtering and labeling adaptation in account for cross-domain sentiment classification. During experimental procedure, each training review (sample) is segmented into a sentence set. In the first stage, we introduce a novel topic model that incorporates topic and sentiment simultaneous on sentence level (SS-LDA) for constructing a reliable training dataset. In the second stage, considering the subject of a sentence, a view mining method combining heuristic rules and machine learning algorithm will be proposed to classify each sentence into corresponding views, namely personal and object view for distinguishing. The experimental results demonstrate that our method is effective for cross-domain sentiment classification.

Organization of the rest paper is as follows. Section 2 will introduce the related works of domain adaptation in sentiment classification. In Sect. 3, we present SS-LDA model for sample filtering. Section 3.3 will discuss the Subject-based ensemble model for cross-domain sentiment classification. Then experimental results and analysis will be shown in Sect. 4. At last, Sect. 5 draws our conclusions and outlines directions for future work.

2   Related Work

Exiting works for domain adaptation in sentiment classification mostly belong to feature-based transfer methods (Blitzer et al. 2006; Blitzer et al. 2007; Pan et al. 2010; He et al. 2011; Duan and Xu 2012), such as the Structural Corresponding Learning (SCL) (Blitzer et al. 2007), the Spectral Feature Alignment (SFA) (Pan et al. 2010). The key idea of SCL is to detect a shared latent space by modeling the correlations between pivot features and non-pivot features for transfer learning. In SFA, spectral clustering algorithm is employed to co-cluster the domain-dependent and domain-independent features into a common latent space. In addition, Duan et al. (Duan and Xu 2012) augment the heterogeneous features from the source and target domains by using two newly proposed feature mapping functions respectively. The representative example of instance-based transfer method is instance weighting for domain adaptation proposed by Jiang et al. (Jiang and Zhai 2007).

There also exits some works belonging to parameter-based transfer method (Xia and Zong 2011; Samdani and Yih 2011; Gao et al. 2011; Yoshida et al. 2011), such as POS-based ensemble model introduced by Xia et al. (Xia and Zong 2011). In addition, Gao et al. (Gao et al. 2008) propose a locally weighted ensemble framework to combine multiple models for transfer learning. Our model also belongs to parameter-based transfer approaches, but different from above-mentioned works, we add a procedure for training sample filtering. During training sample filtering, we raise a topic model which incorporates topic and sentiment simultaneously based on sentence level. Distinguishing form Joint Sentiment/Topic model (*JST*) (Lin and He 2009) which adds a sentiment layer between the document and the topic, SS-LDA puts an additional sentiment layer between the topic and the word layer. Moreover, SS-LDA bases on sentence level while *JST* depends on document level.

The most closely related work to ours is Feature Ensemble plus Sample Selection model (**SS-FE**) (Xia and Zong 2013) proposed by Xia et al. But there are still several intrinsical differences between **SS-FE** and **SF-SE**. Firstly, **SF-SE** implements the sample filtering procedure on sentence level by topic model whereas **SS-FE** processes on document level relying on Principal Component Analysis (**PCA**). Secondly, the view division strategy of **SF-SE** is inspired by the distribution variance of domain-independent and domain-specific features related to the subject of a sentence. However, **SS-FE** considers that the features with different type of POS tags may have distinct change across domains. Overall, there are several limitations in **SS-FE**.

3   Methodology

3.1   SS-LDA

The Latent Dirichlet Allocation (LDA) (Blei et al. 2003) model is a well-known topic model based on the assumption that documents are mixture of topics. It has been widely used in the field of NLP (such as Lu et al. 2011). In order to mining the sentence sentiment polarities, we propose an expansion of LDA model, jointing sentiment with topic based on sentence level, named SS-LDA. The motivation is that sentiment polarities usually depend on topics. For example, in electronics reviews, the adjective "complex" may bear negative orientation while talking about cell phone operations. However, it also has positive orientation when describing the novel plot in books reviews. The SS-LDA model has four layers where a sentiment layer is added between the topic layer and the word layer, as shown in Fig. 1. In SS-LDA, the sentiment layer is associated with the topics while the words are associated with both the topic and sentiment layers. Figure 1 shows the framework of SS-LDA.

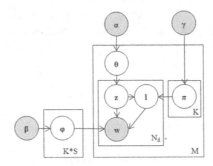

Fig. 1. The framework of SS-LDA

Assume that there is a dataset with a collection of M review sentences, denoted by $C = \{d_1, d_2,..., d_m\}$. Each sentence is a sequence of N_d words denoted by $d = \{w_1, w_2, ..., w_n\}$. And each word in sentence is an feature from a vocabulary index with

V distinct terms denoted by $V = \{1, 2,..., V\}$. K refers the total number of topics and S is the number of sentiment labels. More detailed notations are presented in Table 1.

Table 1. The notations of SS-LDA

Notations	Meanings
M/K/S/N_d	The number of sentences/topics/sentiments/words
z	Topic label
l	Sentimental label:(positive/negative/neutral)
θ	Multinomial distribution over topics
π	Multinomial distribution over sentiments
φ	Multinomial distribution over words
α/β/γ	The hyper parameters

In this paper, S is set to 3, that is to say, for a sentiment variable l, if $l = 1$, the corresponding sentiment is positive; "−1" indicates negative orientation; the value of "0" implies neutral sentiment. The formal definition of the generative process of SS-LDA model is as follows:

1. For each sentence d, choose a distribution θ from $Dir\,(\alpha)$
2. For each topic z, under sentence d, choose a distribution $\pi_{d,z}$ from $Dir\,(\gamma)$
3. For each word w_i in sentence d

   (1) Choose a topic z_i from θ_d
   (2) Choose a sentiment label l_i from π_{d,z_i}
   (3) Choose a word w_i from the distribution over words defined by topic z_i and sentiment label l_i, $\varphi_{z_i l_i}$

In order to inference the algorithm, we utilize Gibbs Sampling for estimating the latent variable θ, φ, π. Firstly, conditional probability $P\,(z_i = z,\ l_i = l|\ z_{-i},\ l_{-i},\ w)$, where z_{-i} and l_{-i} are vectors of assignments of topics and sentiment for all the words in collection exception the considered word at position i in a given sentence should be calculated.

$$P(z_i = z, l_i = l|z_{-i}, l_{-i}, w)$$

$$\propto \frac{\{n_m^{(z)}\}_{-i} + \alpha}{\{n_m\}_{-i} + K\alpha} * \frac{\{n_m^{(z,l)}\}_{-i} + \gamma_l}{\{n_m^{(z)}\}_{-i} + \sum_{l=1}^{S} \gamma_l} * \frac{\{n_{z,l}^{(t)}\}_{-i} + \beta}{\{n_{z,l}\}_{-i} + V\beta} \tag{1}$$

Where, n_m^z is the number of times words assigned to topic z in sentence m; n_m is the total number of words in sentence m; $n_m^{(z,l)}$ is the number of times words assigned to topic z and sentiment l in sentence m; $n_{(z,l)}^t$ is the number of times word i appeared in topic z with sentiment l; $n_{z,l}$ is the total number of times words assigned to topic z and sentiment l; the subscript$-i$ denotes a quantity that excludes data from the position i.

$$\theta_m^{(z)} = \frac{n_m^{(z)} + \alpha}{n_m + K\alpha} \tag{2}$$

The approximate probability of topic z for sentiment l in sentence m is:

$$\pi_m^{(z,l)} = \frac{n_m^{(z,l)} + \gamma_l}{n_m^{(z)} + \sum_{l=1}^{S} \gamma_l} \tag{3}$$

In addition, the approximated predictive distribution of word i for sentiment l and topic z is:

$$\varphi_{z,l}^{(t)} = \frac{n_{z,l}^{(t)} + \beta}{n_{z,l} + V\beta} \tag{4}$$

3.2   Sample Filtering

Due to varieties of topics, customers mostly express mixture sentiments in a product feedback review. The following provides two reviews in electronic domain. By observing the samples, the first one has overall positive sentimental orientation, while the second one bears negative orientation generally. Take the first review for example, the first three sentences are consistent with the overall sentiment polarity whereas the last sentence reveals opposite orientation on sentiment. Hence, assigning an accurate sentiment label to a given review may be uncertain when annotated. That is to say, the manual labeled training dataset may be unreliable actually. So how to construct a reliable training dataset for building a precise model is indispensable. Assuming that, a high quality training sample is supposed to be consistent for its included sentences on sentimental orientations (Table 2).

Table 2. Reviews with mixture sentiment

Reviews	Review sentences	Overall sentimental polarity
Case 1	The design for this headset is ingenious. The audio quality is pretty good. I'm also very satisfied with the reasonable price. *But the earpieces are uncomfortable for my ears*	positive
Case 2	*I bought this DVDs player eight months ago and was quite satisfied.*	negative
	But it constantly gives "Bad Disc" errors and skips since the last week.	
	I am really disappointed for its bad quality.	

Based on the above analysis, we propose a training sample filtering procedure on sentence level. In detail, we firstly split every sample into a sentence set. For a given training sample, we move the sentences whose sentiment orientations opposites to that of the sample. In order to mining the sentiment polarity of every sentence, SS-LDA is adapted for orientation prediction. Particularly, clustering is implemented for the sentence collection by SS-LDA. Furthermore, prior knowledge that obtained from sentiment lexicons is utilized during the initialization for Gibbs Sampling. After modeling the parameters, we can use the following equations to calculate the sentiment polarity for the sentence m.

$$p(s = l|d = m) = \sum_{z=1}^{K} \theta_m^{(z)} * \pi_m^{(z,l)} \tag{5}$$

$$y_m = \arg\max_l p(s = l|d = m) \tag{6}$$

Where the variable y denotes the sentiment label of sentence m. Given a training sample r that consists of n sentences denoted as $\{d_1, d_2,..., d_n\}$, we assume that its manual annotated overall sentiment label refers as l_r. We will remove the sentence d_i which satisfies the following criteria:

$$d_i \in \{d_i|l_r = Oppo(y_{d_i}) \wedge p(s = y_{d_i}|d_i) > \delta \wedge i \in [1, n]\} \tag{7}$$

Where the function $Oppo(y_m)$ denotes the opposite sentiment label from y_m. And δ is a posteriori probability confidence threshold value. From the description above, we can see that only the sentence associated with strong opposite sentiment polarity to the belonging sample will be filtered. We regard the samples which consist of the remaining sentence as high quality training dataset. These training samples are expected to build a more precise classification model for the remaining works due to its purity on sentimental orientation.

3.3   Subject-Based Ensemble Model

The task of sentiment classification is domain-specific. Classifiers trained on the source domain usually perform poorly in the target domain owing to the changing of feature distribution. So how to eliminate the differences between the source and target domain are significant for transfer learning.

The dataset is divided into two views based on the subject of the sentence, personal and object views in this paper. The intuition is that when domain changes, the vocabulary implying sentimental orientation in personal view usually changes slightly. In object view, however, it changes obviously. Based on this observation, we can conclude that the majority of words with semantic opinion orientation in personal view are domain-independent while domain-specific in object view. A motivating example will be shown in Table 3:

Table 3. An example on personal/object view

Domain	Personal view	Object view
Books	I *dislike* the cover style of this book.	The bestseller is really *informative*.
DVDs	My friends were *disappointed* to the sound.	It *broke down* several times in the past weeks.
Electronics	Do not *waste* your time and money	This flash disk is very *smart* and *portable*!
Kitchen appliances	Highly *recommend*.	Works *intermittently*.

Considering the reviews in Table 3, we find that words in personal view, such as *"disappointed"* and *"recommend"*, usually act domain-independent across domains. More specifically, they express similar sentimental orientation across domains. However, in object view, some opinion words like *"superficial"* and *"portable"* often behave domain-specific. In other words, they often appear in a particular domain. Apparently, the personal view changes rarely between domains. On the contrary, the object view varies sharply across domains. So, we infer that the performance of cross-domain sentiment classification might benefit more from personal view.

Holding this belief, we observe the Jensen-Shannon divergence (*JSD*) (Lin 1991) between source and target domains. The Jensen-Shannon divergence is widely used to measure the variance between two probability distributions. It is asymmetry and smoothed version of the Kullback-Leibler (*KL*) divergence. More specifically, the *JSD* divergence between distribution P and Q can be measured as follows:

$$JSD(P\,||\,Q) = \frac{1}{2}KL(P\,||\,M) + \frac{1}{2}KL(Q\,||\,M) \tag{8}$$

Where $M = 1/2\,(P + Q)$ and $KL(*\,||\,*)$ is the Kullback-Leibler divergence between two distributions. So, the less *JSD* of two domains is, the more similar their distributions act. That indicates that people often express their opinions using similar vocabularies in these domain reviews. Intuitively, domain-independent words appear frequently in similar domains.

4   Experiments and Analysis

4.1   Dataset Description

Our experiments are carried out on the Multi-Domain Sentiment Dataset collected by Blitzer et al. It has been widely used in the field of cross-domain sentiment classification. The dataset consists of product reviews from four domains: books, DVDs, electronics and kitchen appliances, B, D, E and K for short in this paper. Each domain contains 1000 positive, 1000 negative reviews besides hundreds of unlabeled reviews. Table 4 shows the scale of dataset. We can see that the review in domain books and DVDs is relatively longer than that in domain electronics and kitchen appliances. After observation, we find that people often discuss the story of books and films in these domain reviews. Owing to this reason, the review is usually larger.

Table 4. Scale of the dataset

Domain	Average number of sentences	Average length of review
Books	8.5	175.6
DVDs	9.6	194.6
Electronics	6.7	116.7
Kitchen appliances	5.8	98.6

4.2 Experiment Setting

For each domain, we randomly sample 800 positive reviews and 800 negative reviews from labeled dataset as training instances while the remaining is used for testing. During sentiment classification, 5-fold validation is applied to evaluate the performance. Following majority of previous works, we use accuracy to evaluate the classification performance in this paper.

In the stage of data preprocessing, Stanford Core NLP Parser is applied to stemming and segment all the reviews into sentences. Sentence subject detection is also carried out by parsing for the sake of view division in the following stage. Following pervious work (Xia and Zong 2011), in order to reduce the dimensionality, we only use features including unigrams and bigrams that appear at least 4 times in a particular task. Additionally, we remove the stop words and punctuations for sake of less noisy. Further, feature weight is measured via standard tf-idf algorithm.

With respect to the training sample filtering procedure, we implement SS-LDA model based on JGibbs LDA package. The number of topics is set ranging from 20 to 60. In the latter section, we will discuss the effect of topic number on the experimental performance. During Gibbs Sampling, we set the number of iterations to 1000 times because the distributions have been relatively stable after 1000 iterations. Besides, in order to improving the sentiment detection, prior knowledge is incorporated during the initialization of Gibbs Sampling. The sentiment prior knowledge is mainly obtained from the sentiment lexicon MPQA. At last, we set the confidence threshold δ to 0.8.

In the stage of Subject-based ensemble, the sentences are divided into personal/object views respectively. Then base classifiers are built according to corresponding dataset. Furthermore, Stochastic Gradient Descent (*SGD*) that optimizes the Minimal Classification Error (*MCE*) is exploited to obtain the best parameter settings for combination. For simplicity, we use "X_Y" to denote the task transferring from domain X to Y for sentiment classification. In our experiment, support vector machine (SVM) is implemented as classification algorithm with the help of Lib-SVM tools. And linear kernel function is adopted besides default parameter setting.

4.3   Baselines

For illustrating the effectiveness of our method **SF-SE**, we present several methods for comparison including some state-of-the-art cross-domain classification methods in this sub-section. All these algorithms are described as follows:

NoTrans: This baseline means that the classifier trained on all the source domain dataset only and applied to target domain samples for classification directly using SVM.

SF: SF (Sample Filtering) which refers the first stage of our model is similar to NoTrans. The only difference is that the classifier is trained on the high quality training data after SS-LDA filtering.

SCL: SCL, short for structural correspondence learning, is proposed by Blitzer et al. in 2006. We follow the details described in Blitzer's thesis to implement SCL.

SFA: SFA is well-known domain adaptation algorithm proposed by Pan et al. (Pan et al. 2010). It can discover the shared latent space via fully exploiting the features relationship with the aid of spectral clustering algorithm.

SS-FE: SS-FE (Feature Ensemble plus Sample Selection) is the most closely related work to ours. The basic idea of SS-FE is utilizing features ensemble according to Part-of-Speech (POS) after training sample selection procedure by PCA.

4.4   Experimental Results and Analysis

Considering the complex expression, we firstly employ SS-LDA to cluster the training dataset for detecting sentimental orientation on sentence level. The motivation is that the sentences deriving from a specific review might belong to different topics. Hence, people might convey completely different sentimental orientations. In summary, filtering the sentences whose polarities opposite to the overall orientation is significant for constructing a high quality training set.

Figure 2 shows the performance of **SF** when topics ranging from 20 to 60. The symbol "X_*" refers the tasks transferring from domain X to other domains. Noting that, the performance of **SF** is sensitive to the number of topics. Generally speaking,

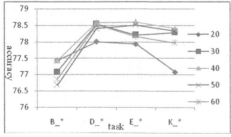

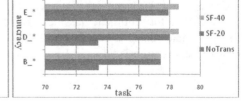

Fig. 2. Performance of SF   **Fig. 3.** Comparison between NoTrans and SF

best performance is obtained when the number of cluster topics is set to 40, whereas worst on 20 topics.

Figure 3 reveals the comparison between **NoTrans** and **SF** when best and worst performances obtained. Simply, we use the symbol "SF-topicNum" denoting the classification accuracy when topic number is set to "topicNum".

Observing the result above, we can conclude that the performance of **SF** gets significant improvement compared with **NoTrans** which using all the sentences in source domain. Particularly, when the cluster topic is set to 40, it gets the best performance, approximately 3.4 % improvement compared with **NoTrans** on average classification accuracy. As mentioned above, mixture sentimental polarities are usually conveyed owing to various topics talked in a review. This phenomenon leads to uncertainty when label the training samples. That is to say, the classification model might not accurate when applying these samples for training directly. By SS-LDA filtering, we move the sentences whose sentimental polarity strongly opposites the overall orientation. This procedure can enhance the reliability of the training set to a certain extent. Therefore the classification performance will be improved due to the more precise model built.

Figure 4 presents the classification performance of different base classifiers, where "personal" denotes the task using the personal view for training, the similar definition for "object" respectively. Note that the classifier based on personal view performs better than object classifier completely, 1.32 % in average. In particular, the task "E_D" achieves the largest improvement by 2.05 %. The experimental results are coincident with our assumption. More specifically, the personal view contributes more than object view in cross-domain sentiment classification because most domain-independent opinion words are from personal view.

To demonstrating the effectiveness of our model, we compare it with several state-of-the-art cross-domain classification methods mentioned in Baseline. Figure 5 shows these comparisons.

Compared with **SS-FE**, **SF-SE** shows its superiority in almost all the tasks, approximately 4.3 % in average. This justifies the effectiveness of our model again. Firstly, different from **SS-FE** which conducting filtration on sample level, **SF-SE** only

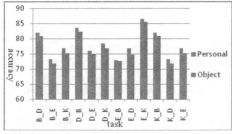

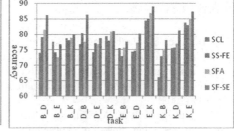

Fig. 4. Performance of personal/object view   **Fig. 5.** Performance of different algorithms

filters the sentences whose sentimental orientation opposite to that of the belonging sample. Obviously, we can fully exploit the training dataset. Furthermore, our subject-based view division strategy is more coincident with the distribution of domain-independent/domain-specific words compared with POS-based view division. In detail, thousands of domain-independent opinion words such as "like", "hate" are verbs. On the contrary, the subject-based model ignores the POS tags of vocabulary, mainly focusing on the distribution of domain-independent/domain-specific words. Still, compared with **SCL** and **SFA**, **SF-SE** gains relatively advantages by 5.2 %, 3.2 % in average accuracy.

5   Conclusions and Future Work

With the explosive expansion of online subjective data, cross-domain sentiment classification has attracted more attention in NLP and data mining field. In this paper, we propose a **SF-SE** model for cross-domain sentiment classification. During sample filtering, an extended LDA that incorporates sentiment on sentence level, named SS-LDA is adapted. Additionally, a Subject-based ensemble model is introduced, motivating that the opinion words in personal view are usually domain-independent while domain-specific in object view. Therefore, an efficient ensemble of them could leverage distinct strengths and improve the classification performance. Finally, experiments demonstrate that the proposed is effective for cross-domain sentiment classification.

In the future, subjectivity summarization strategy (Pang and Lee 2004) will be integrated to help reducing noisy objective sentences. Because objective sentences usually contains little semantic orientation. Moreover, we should improve our view mining algorithm for more accurate view division.

Acknowledgements. This work is partially supported by grant from the Natural Science Foundation of China (No. 61277370, 61402075), Natural Science Foundation of Liaoning Province, China (No. 201202031, 2014020003), State Education Ministry and The Research Fund for the Doctoral Program of Higher Education (No. 20090041110002), the Fundamental Research Funds for the Central Universities.

References

Pang, B., Lee, L., Vaithyanathan, S.: Thumbs up?: Sentiment classification using machine learning techniques. In: Proceedings of the ACL-2002 Conference on Empirical Methods in Natural Language Processing, pp. 79–86 (2002)

Pang, B., Lee, L.: Opinion mining and sentiment analysis. J. Found. Trends Inf. Retrieval **2**, 1–135 (2008)

Liu, Y., Huang, X., An, A., Yu, X.: ARSA: a sentiment-aware model for predicting sales performance using blogs. In: Proceedings of the 30th Annual International ACM SIGIR Conference on Research and Development in Information Retrieval, pp. 607–614 (2007)

Yu, X., Liu, Y., Huang, X., An, A.: Mining online reviews for predicting sales performance: a case study in the movie domain. IEEE Trans. J. Knowl. Data Eng. **24**, 720–734 (2012)

Pan, S.J., Yang, Q.: A survey on transfer learning. IEEE Trans. J. Knowl. Data Eng. **22**, 1345–1359 (2010)

Blitzer, J., McDonald, R., Pereira, F.: Domain adaptation with structural correspondence learning. In: Proceedings of the 2006 Conference on Empirical Methods in Natural Language Processing, pp. 120–128 (2006)

Blitzer J., Dredze M., Pereira, F.: Biographies, bollywood, boom-boxes and blenders: domain adaptation for sentiment classification. In: Proceedings of the 45th Annual Meeting of the Association of Computational Linguistics, vol. 7, pp. 440–447 (2007)

Pan, S. J., Ni, X., Sun, J., Yang, Q., Chen, Z.: Cross-domain sentiment classification via spectral feature alignment. In: Proceedings of the 19th International Conference on World Wide Web, pp. 751–760 (2010)

He, Y., Lin, C., Alani, H.: Automatically extracting polarity-bearing topics for cross-domain sentiment classification. In: Proceedings of the 49th Annual Meeting of the Association for Computational Linguistics: Human Language Technologies, vol. 1, pp. 123–131 (2011)

Duan, L., Xu, D., Tsang, I.: Learning with augmented features for heterogeneous domain adaptation. J. arXiv preprint (2012). arXiv:1206.4660

Jiang, J., Zhai, C.: Instance weighting for domain adaptation in NLP. In: Proceedings of the 45th Annual Meeting of the Association of Computational Linguistics, vol. 7, pp. 264–271 (2007)

Xia, R., Zong, C.: A POS-based ensemble model for cross-domain sentiment classification. In: Proceedings of the 5th International Joint Conference on Natural Language Processing, pp. 614–622. Citeseer (2011)

Samdani, R., Yih, W.: Domain adaptation with ensemble of feature groups. In: Proceedings-International Joint Conference on Artificial Intelligence, vol. 22, p. 1458 (2011)

Gao, J., Fan, W., Jiang, J., Han, J.: Knowledge transfer via multiple model local structure mapping. In: Proceedings of the 14th ACM SIGKDD International Conference on Knowledge Discovery and Data Mining, pp. 283–291 (2008)

Yoshida, Y., Hirao, T., Iwata, T., Nagata, M., Matsumoto, Y.: Twenty-Fifth AAAI Conference on Artificial Intelligence (2011)

Lin, C., He, Y.: Joint sentiment/topic model for sentiment analysis. In: Proceedings of the 18th ACM Conference on Information and Knowledge Management, pp. 375–384 (2009)

Xia, R., Zong, C., Hu, X., Cambria, E.: Feature ensemble plus sample selection: domain adaptation for sentiment classification. J. Intell. Syst. **28**, 10–18 (2013)

Blei, D.M., Ng, A.Y., Jordan, M.I.: Latent dirichlet allocation. J. Mach. Learn. Res. **3**, 993–1022 (2003)

Lu, B., Ott, M., Cardie, C., Tsou, B.K.: Multi-aspect sentiment analysis with topic models. In: IEEE 11th International Conference on Data Mining Workshops (ICDMW), pp. 81–88 (2011)

Lin, J.: Divergence measures based on the Shannon entropy. IEEE Trans. J. Inf. Theo. **37**, 145–151 (1991)

Fumera, G., Roli, F.: A theoretical and experimental analysis of linear combiners for multiple classifier systems. IEEE Trans. J. Pattern Analy. Mach. Intell. **27**, 942–956 (2005)

Juang, B.H., Katagiri, S.: Discriminative learning for minimum error classification. IEEE Trans. J. Signal Process. **40**, 3043–3054 (1992)

Pang, B., Lee, L.: A sentimental education: sentiment analysis using subjectivity summarization based on minimum cuts. In: Proceedings of the 42nd Annual Meeting on Association for Computational Linguistics, p. 271 (2004)

Machine Translation

Insight into Multiple References in an MT Evaluation Metric

Ying Qin[1]([✉]) and Lucia Specia[2]([✉])

[1] Beijing Foreign Studies University, Beijing 100089, China
qinying@bfsu.edu.cn
[2] University of Sheffield, Sheffield S10 2TN, UK
l.specia@sheffield.ac.uk

Abstract. Current evaluation metrics in machine translation (MT) make poor use of multiple reference translations. In this paper we focus on the METEOR metric to gain in-depth insights into how best multiple references can be exploited. Results on five score selection strategies reveal that it is not always wise to choose the best (closest to MT) reference to generate the candidate score. We also propose two weighting approaches by taking into account the recurring information among references. The modified METEOR scores significantly increase the correlation with human judgments on accuracy and fluency evaluation at system level.

Keywords: Machine translation evaluation · METEOR metric · Multiple references

1 Introduction

Human translations are essential to reference-based MT evaluation metrics such as BLEU [10], NIST [7] and METEOR [1]. Generally there are a number of valid translations for a given source, varying in style, word order and word choice, but conveying similar meaning. As many as possible references substantially improve the reliability of n-gram based metrics as demonstrated by HyTER, which employs an exponential number of reference translations for a given target [8]. Although most metrics can take advantage of multiple references, the scheme is fairly simple by choosing the highest score out of pairwise comparison between the candidate and the reference. Using the highest score to estimate translation quality actually implies that the matching approach always underestimates the real quality of the candidate: the more matching, the closer estimation to the real quality. Nevertheless there is neither full argument nor empirical data to underpin this assumption.

Furthermore, since they originate from the same source segment, multiple references are expected to share words and expressions, but this kind of information is usually under-explored in reference-based metrics. For example:

© Springer International Publishing Switzerland 2015
M. Sun et al. (Eds.): CCL and NLP-NABD 2015, LNAI 9427, pp. 131–140, 2015.
DOI: 10.1007/978-3-319-25816-4_11

Ref₁: *The report also shows that the US personal income rose 0.4 % last December.*

Ref₂: *The report also indicated that U.S. personal income increased by 0.4 percent in December last year.*

Ref₃: *The report also shows that Americans' incomes rose by 0.4 % last December.*

Ref₄: *The report also shows that the income of US individuals increased 0.4 % last December.*

Sys: *The report also showed that in December last year the US personal income rose by 0.4 %.*

In the above, some words like *report, shows, income, 0.4 %* appear frequently in references and convey the core meaning of the source sentence. However the recurring information is ignored by the current metrics. As a consequence, the score of this system translation according to these metrics can not reflect its quality (METEOR score for it is 0.403).

We suggest that common information in multiple references should appear in a good quality translation and therefore should be considered more relevant than non-recurring information by evaluation metrics. In our previous work, common information of multiple references is attempted to improve BLEU and NIST metrics [11]. As a further study, among a wide range of non-exact n-gram matching metrics we pick METEOR, which is reported to perform well in WMT evaluation task [2], and can be equally applied to segment and system-level evaluation. We thus propose a modification of METEOR to truly explore multiple references. First we provide an analysis comparing several approaches to handle scores produced by different references. Second we investigate how to make better use of common information in multiple references.

In the section follows we briefly review the METEOR metric. In Sect. 3 we discuss different ways of taking into account scores from multiple references and our proposal of two weighting strategies for METEOR to make better use of recurring information. Experiments with two into-English datasets are presented in Sect. 4.

2 METEOR Review

Based on word to word alignment of the candidate and the reference, METEOR calculates precision (P), recall (R) and final score (F). P is the ratio of the number of unigrams matched to the total number of unigrams in candidate. And R is computed as the number of unigrams matched divided by the total unigrams in reference. In addition to exact matching of words, METEOR allows for morphological variants and synonym matching to capture more similarities between candidate and references. A penalty is applied to favor the long chunks(sequential matches) over short ones. F_{mean}, the harmonic mean of precision and recall, combined with the penalty factor is used as the final score [1].

Recent improvements on METEOR include the matching of paraphrases for phrases [4], adjusting weights of content words versus function words, and a parameterized penalty [5]. The latest version of METEOR (v1.5) uses automatic extraction of language sources (including paraphrases and function words) and universal parameters in score formula to cope with specific translations [6]. The components F_{mean} and $Penalty$, as well as the final METEOR F_{score} are given in Eqs. 1–3 [6].

$$F_{mean} = \frac{PR}{\alpha P + (1 - \alpha)R} \tag{1}$$

$$Penalty = \gamma(\frac{ch}{m})^{\beta} \tag{2}$$

$$F_{score} = F_{mean} * (1 - Penalty) \tag{3}$$

where, α, γ and β are parameters tuned on corpora to maximize the correlation with human judgments. Equation 2 is used to favor longer matches by considering the number of chunks matched ch and the number of unigrams matched m.

When multiple references are available, METEOR picks the one with the highest score, i.e. the closest reference to the MT output. The intuition behind this choice is one of the questions we put forward in this paper.

3   Multiple References in METEOR

3.1   Handling Multiple Scores

In what follows we compare five options on the use of the final METEOR scores generated under the circumstance of multiple references: the highest score (current choice in METEOR), the lowest score and the arithmetic mean (AM), geometric mean (GM) and harmonic mean (HM) of all scores, as shown in Eqs. 4–6, where n is the number of references.

$$AM = \frac{1}{n}\sum_i x_i \tag{4}$$

$$GM = (\prod_i x_i)^{\frac{1}{n}} \tag{5}$$

$$HM = \frac{n}{\sum_i x_i^{-1}} \tag{6}$$

The highest score from multiple references is the one that results in the best quality score for the candidate. We believe that this leads to the quality of candidate being overestimated by METEOR.

3.2   Recurring Information in Multiple References

In the work of [6], several preferences are found in human judgments of translation quality:

- Precision is preferred over recall
- Correct word choice is preferred over correct word order
- Correct choice of content words is preferred over correct choice of function words
- Exact matching over matching of paraphrases

The repeated words in different references are expected relevant to correct word choice and content of translations which will in turn benefit accuracy evaluation. We thus propose two weighting strategies to make better use of the information and implement modification on standard METEOR metric.

The first weighting strategy is shown as Eq. 7. We define the ratio of the number of times a word recurs in references to the number of references as the degree of commonality of the word. We add this ratio in a logarithm function as the weight of the matching word. In order to avoid zero counts, a plus-one smoothing approach is applied.

$$X = log(1 + m/refno) \tag{7}$$

In Eq. 7, m denotes the number of times the word recurs. Notice that repeated words in single reference are not counted, so the ratio is never greater than 1. For the example above, the weight of *report*, which is covered by four references, is 0.69, heavier than *by* 0.41, which occurs twice.

Alternatively, we apply Zipf'law to lessen the impact of non-content words which may appear more often than content words, as defined in Eq. 8.

$$X' = log(1 + f \times r/refno) \tag{8}$$

where f is the frequency of word in references and r is the ranking order of the word by frequency. For the example above, the weight of *the*, which has the most frequency, is 0.92, comparing with 1.18 of the third-ranking word *income*. The most frequent non-content words can be neutralized.

Precision and recall are updated with the weighting of matching words accordingly. Since we cannot estimate the weight of unmatched words in candidate and references, we keep them unchanged. Precision and recall are updated as in Eqs. 9–10.

$$P = \frac{\sum x_i w_i}{\#UnmatchedWordsInSys + \sum x_i w_i} \tag{9}$$

$$R = \frac{\sum x_i w_i}{\#UnmatchedWordsInRef + \sum x_i w_i} \tag{10}$$

where x_i is the weight of word w_i according to Eq. 7 or 8. Obviously w_i is always 1 in normal METEOR. For simplicity, we use a fixed penalty as in earlier versions of METEOR. Accordingly, penalty is normalized by the sum of matching weights. Therefore the equations for F_{mean} and final score F remain the same as in standard METEOR.

4 Experiments

METEOR 0.4.3[1] (Perl version) is used in the experiment to test our two ideas. We also compare the performance against the latest version of the metrics, METEOR 1.5[2].

4.1 Datasets

The experiments require datasets with multiple references, which are rare. Two into-English translation datasets are used: the Multiple-Translation Chinese Part 2 (MTC-P2) (LDC2003T17) and the Multiple-Translation Chinese Part 4 (MTC-P4) (LDC2006T04), both including 4 sets of human translations for a single set of Mandarin Chinese source materials, totally 200 stories, 1797 segments. Altogether, the two datasets have nine system translations P2–05, P2–09, P2–14, P4–09, P4–11, P4–12, P4–14, P4–15 and P4–22, judged by 2-3 human annotators on fluency and accuracy. We use these judgments as ground truth to compare metrics. Notice that the Cohen's Kappa coefficient [3] of human judgments on segment level is only fair: 0.227 on fluency and 0.172 on accuracy annotation.

We investigate the variation among references in terms of TER (Translation Error Rate)[3] [12]. The average pairwise TER values of references for the two datasets are 0.72 and 0.67, indicating remarkable differences among the four references.

4.2 Multiple Score Selections

In order to examine the impact of synonym mapping, we run METEOR with two types of modules for alignment: exact matching and stemming module ($AS1$), versus added synonym matching ($AS2$).

The general relationship between the five score selections from references is as below.

$$HS \geq AMS \geq GMS \geq HMS \geq LS \tag{11}$$

where HS, AMS, GMS, HMS and LS denote the highest score, arithmetic mean, geometric mean, harmonic mean and the lowest score respectively.

Performances of METEOR based on different score selections on fluency and accuracy with and without synonym matching at system-level in terms of Pearson correlation are shown in Tables 1-2. The introduction of synonym alignment

---

[1] http://www.cs.cmu.edu/~banerjee/MT/METEOR/
[2] http://www.cs.cmu.edu/~alavie/METEOR/
[3] http://www.cs.umd.edu/~snover/tercom/

in METEOR significantly improves the correlation with human judgments on accuracy evaluation. However, it does not increase the performance on fluency evaluation.

Regardless of the type of alignment (with or without synonym matching) and the evaluation criteria (fluency or accuracy), the highest correlation with human judgment is always achieved when the reference with the *lowest* matching score is selected. Intuitively, the closer to the reference, the better quality the translation should have. Therefore, these results are somewhat puzzling and against the general practice in the use of METEOR with multiple references: that of choosing the closest matching reference.

Table 1. Correlation at system level with module $AS1$

		HS	AMS	GMS	HMS	LS
Flu	P	0.693	0.695	0.696	**0.699**	0.695
	R	0.354	0.367	0.371	0.376	**0.394**
	F	0.470	0.500	0.504	0.509	**0.545**
Acc	P	**0.741**	0.740	0.739	0.734	0.736
	R	0.863	0.869	0.870	0.872	**0.882**
	F	0.899	0.905	0.905	0.906	**0.913**

Table 2. Correlation at system level with module $AS2$

		HS	AMS	GMS	HMS	LS
Flu	P	0.729	0.729	0.730	0.731	**0.738**
	R	0.321	0.338	0.342	0.344	**0.365**
	F	0.447	0.486	0.490	0.494	**0.542**
Acc	P	**0.773**	0.766	0.765	0.764	0.758
	R	0.858	0.866	0.868	0.869	**0.878**
	F	0.909	0.919	0.920	0.921	**0.931**

In the remaining experiments, we use alignment module $AS2$, as the trend observed for score selection options with and without synonym matching is consistent.

In Tables 3-4 we compare the five score selection approaches at segment level. On fluency evaluation, the best score is obtained with the reference with the highest (HS) score in most cases. However, for accuracy evaluation, it seems better to choose the arithmetic mean of scores (AMS), as the arithmetic mean scores outperform in more than half system translations.

Table 3. Fluency evaluation correlation at segment level

System	HS	AMS	GMS	HMS	LS
p2-05	**0.213**	0.186	0.173	0.161	0.116
p2-09	**0.106**	0.100	0.085	0.083	0.075
p2-14	**0.218**	0.203	0.206	0.198	0.149
p4-09	**0.217**	0.200	0.194	0.190	0.173
p4-11	**0.164**	0.163	0.160	0.158	0.144
p4-12	**0.061**	0.049	0.046	0.041	0.017
p4-14	**0.155**	0.133	0.126	0.120	0.080
p4-15	0.196	**0.197**	0.190	0.185	0.162
p4-22	0.171	**0.172**	0.166	0.166	0.144

Table 4. Accuracy evaluation correlation at segment level

System	HS	AMS	GMS	HMS	LS
p2-05	0.281	**0.284**	0.275	0.265	0.221
p2-09	0.143	**0.156**	0.149	0.146	0.123
p2-14	**0.245**	0.231	0.222	0.214	0.175
p4-09	**0.293**	0.279	0.276	0.272	0.247
p4-11	0.208	**0.216**	0.213	0.209	0.188
p4-12	**0.199**	0.182	0.174	0.166	0.125
p4-14	**0.194**	0.172	0.171	0.164	0.131
p4-15	0.250	**0.256**	0.251	0.246	0.219
p4-22	0.190	**0.202**	0.188	0.192	0.184

4.3   Recurring Word Weighting

The best correlations are usually achieved using either the highest or the lowest score out of multiple references. We thus focus on these score selection comparisons for the weighting strategies proposed here to improve METEOR.

System Level Evaluation Using X and X′. Figuers 1 and 2 illustrate the performance of the modified METEOR after weighting the matching words by using recurring information in references at system level. The performance increases consistently when the weighting strategy is applied, regardless of whether the highest or the lowest scores are used (O denotes the original approach). The strategy using Zipf'law ($X′$) is weaker than the alternative strategy proposed (X). The possible reason is that Zipf'law does not work well on small scale of corpus.

From v1.3 on, METEOR discriminates content words and function words [5] by weighting differently. All parameters of METEOR v1.5 run in the experiment are set as the default values for English translation evaluation. While in

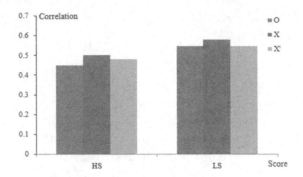

Fig. 1. Modified METEOR at system level on fluency

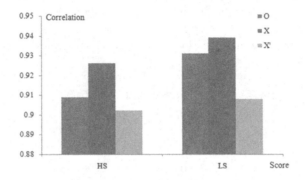

Fig. 2. Modified METEOR at system level on accuracy

METEOR v0.4.3, all matching words are equally weighted. By using common information of multiple references, we modify METEOR v0.4.3 (denoted as v0.4.3+) and compare it against the latest version v1.5 at system level using the highest score out of references.

This comparison is shown in Table 5. v0.4.3+ outperforms v1.5 in terms of accuracy, but it falls behind v1.5 in fluency evaluation. Nevertheless, the improvement with respect to v0.4.3 w.r.t fluency is evident. This confirms our intuition that taking recurring information of references into account is a sound strategy for MT evaluation.

Table 5. Comparison of METEOR versions at system level

	v1.5	v0.4.3	v0.4.3+
Flu	**0.619**	0.447	0.497
Acc	0.907	0.909	**0.926**

Segment Level Evaluation Using X. The proposed modification at segment level does not work well as at system level. Table 6 shows there is a slight drop of correlation with human judgment by introducing weighting strategy X (marked with $+$), as compared to the original METEOR on both fluency and accuracy evaluation.

Table 6. Segment level correlation comparison

System	Flu	Flu+	Acc	Acc+
p2-05	**0.213**	0.207	0.281	**0.284**
p2-09	**0.106**	0.102	**0.143**	0.140
p2-14	**0.218**	0.214	**0.245**	0.233
p4-09	**0.217**	0.204	**0.293**	0.279
p4-11	**0.164**	0.156	0.208	0.208
p4-12	**0.061**	0.051	**0.199**	0.179
p4-14	**0.155**	0.152	**0.194**	0.181
p4-15	**0.196**	0.179	**0.250**	0.113
p4-22	0.171	**0.176**	**0.190**	0.188

Due to the large TER values among the references, the data sparsity is severe at segment level. Therefore the most common words among references might not always be the content words especially for short sentences. For the example above, *would* is undesirably assigned more heavily than *American*. Data sparsity might be the main cause of performance drop at segment level. In addition, the low inter-agreements in human assessments pose challenges on the improvement of quality evaluation at segment level [9].

5   Conclusion and Future Work

We compared five score selection strategies for METEOR to handle multiple references and proposed to weight differently matching words by taking recurring information of these words in references into account. Results show that it is not always wise to select the reference with the highest matching score, especially at system level evaluation. It seemed we overestimated the translation quality by mean of alignment with candidate and references, contrary to the intuitive assumption in current reference-based evaluation metrics. Generally, the recurring information in references proved helpful to translation quality evaluation.

In future work, we will explore more common features of multiple references like POS and syntactic structures and integrate them into MT evaluation metrics.

Acknowledgments. Ying Qin's work is supported by a Beijing Social Science Funding Project (No. 15WYA006) and National Research Center for Foreign Language Education, BFSU.

References

1. Banerjee, S., Lavie, A.: Meteor: an automatic metric for MT evaluation with improved correlation with human judgments. In: Proceedings of the ACL Workshop on Intrinsic and Extrinsic Evaluation Measures for Machine Translation and/or Summarization, pp. 65–72 (2005)
2. Bojar, O., Buck, C., Federmann, C., et al.: Findings of the 2014 workshop on statistical machine translation. In: Proceedings of the Ninth Workshop on Statistical Machine Translation, pp. 12–58 (2014)
3. Cohen, J.: A coefficient of agreement for nominal scales. Educ. Psychol. Measur. **20**, 37–46 (1960)
4. Denkowski, M., Lavie, A.: Extending the meteor machine translation evaluation metric to the phrase level. In: Human Language Technologies: The 2010 Annual Conference of the North American Chapter of the Association for Computational Linguistics, pp. 250–253. Association for Computational Linguistics (2010)
5. Denkowski, M., Lavie, A.: Meteor 1.3: automatic metric for reliable optimization and evaluation of machine translation systems. In: Proceedings of the Sixth Workshop on Statistical Machine Translation, pp. 85–91. Association for Computational Linguistics (2011)
6. Denkowski, M., Lavie, A.: Meteor universal: language specific translation evaluation for any target language. In: Proceedings of the EACL 2014 Workshop on Statistical Machine Translation, vol. 6 (2014)
7. Doddington, G.: Automatic evaluation of machine translation quality using n-gram co-occurrence statistics. In: Proceedings of the Second International Conference on Human Language Technology Research, pp. 138–145 (2002)
8. Dreyer, M., Marcu, D.: Hyter: meaning-equivalent semantics for translation evaluation. In: 2012 Conference of the North American Chapter of the ACL: Human Language Technologies, pp. 162–171 (2012)
9. Graham, Y., Mathur, N., Baldwin, T.: Accurate evaluation of segment-level machine translation metrics. In: Human Language Technologies: The 2015 Annual Conference of the North American Chapter of the ACL, pp. 1183–1191 (2015)
10. Papineni, K., Roukos, S., Ward, T., et al.: Bleu: a method for automatic evaluation of machine translation. In: Proceedings of the 40th Annual Meeting on Association for Computational Linguistics, pp. 311–318. ACL (2002)
11. Qin Y., Specia, L.: Truly exploring multiple references for machine translation evaluation. In: Proceedings of European Association for Machine Translation (EAMT), pp. 113–120 (2015)
12. Snover, M., Dorr, B., Schwartz, R., Micciulla, L., Makhoul, J.: A study of translation edit rate with targeted human annotation. In: Proceedings of Association for Machine Translation in the Americas, pp. 223–231 (2006)

A Hybrid Sentence Splitting Method by Comma Insertion for Machine Translation with CRF

Shuli Yang, Chong Feng[✉], and Heyan Huang

Beijing Engineering Research Center of High Volume Language Information
Processing and Cloud Computing Application,
Beijing Institute of Technology, Beijing, China
{ysl2007,fengchong,hhy63}@bit.edu.cn

Abstract. When writing formal articles many English writers often use long sentences with few punctuation marks. Since long sentences bring difficulty to machine translation systems, many researchers try to split them using punctuation marks before translation. But dealing with sentences with few punctuation marks is still intractable. In this paper we use a log linear model to insert commas into proper positions to split long sentence, trying to shorten the length of sub-sentence and benefit to machine translation. Experiment results show that our method can reasonably segment long sentences, and improve the quality of machine translation.

1 Introduction

In writing English, especially in formal articles, authors often use long sentences with very complicated syntactic structure to enhance the coherence and fluency. But as the length of a sentence increases, the quality of machine translation fails dramatically. For example:

Source: Reconstruction and repair have been put on hold in some instances due to workers' fears that the spirits of the dead who passed away a year ago will bring them bad luck if they continue.

Reference: 某些重建和修复工作被暂时搁置，因为工人害怕如果继续下去，一年前的亡灵会给他们带来厄运。

Translation: 重建和修理已经被在一些实例里推迟进行，由于工人的恐惧即一年前消失的死者的情绪将给他们带来坏运如果他们继续。

As the example shows, the translation of the source sentence is quite messy because of the long length and complicated structure. The rule-based systems have difficulties in covering all possible language phenomena; the statistical systems often generate syntactically strange outputs.

Thus, lots of methods on sentence splitting have been explored. But we notice that most works on sentence segmentation try to use the punctuation marks that already exist in the sentences, so if the sentence to be split has few punctuation

M. Sun et al. (Eds.): CCL and NLP-NABD 2015, LNAI 9427, pp. 141–152, 2015.
DOI: 10.1007/978-3-319-25816-4_12

marks, these methods won't get improved results at all. In this paper we use a log-linear model together with a rule-based method to automatically insert commas into a sentence, in order to recover the omitted commas, reduce the length of each sub-sentence and improve the machine translation result. We tested our method on both rule-based and statistical machine translation systems. The results show that our method is quite helpful for improving the quality of translation.

2   Related Work

Lots of works have been done trying to split or simplify the sentences before translation or conducting other NLP tasks. Some works are rule-based. [2] proposed a multi-strategy method to analyze long sentences. The algorithm is mainly based on pattern match combined with rule analysis. [12] proposed a top-down analysis method to split long sentences. The author used regular expressions to match several sentence structures, and analyzed and split the matched sentences by rules. Despite the efficiency of these rule-based methods, the main problem of them is that the handcrafted rules cannot cover enough language phenomena, and cannot process sentences that contain more complicated components such as multiple nested clauses.

Some other works try to mine the information in the punctuation marks or conjunctions. [13] tried to use punctuation marks and conjunctions such as "and" and "or" to find split points in Chinese long sentences, and dealt with the two situations individually. [11] believed that in Chinese some commas could be "replaced" by periods because the contents on both sides of the comma did not have strong connection, so these commas could be treated as splitting position. They used a max-entropy classifier to find these commas. [10] also believed that some commas could be used to split Chinese long sentences and the authors used an algorithm based on syntactic parsing to find these commas. But these methods can only tackle with the commas already exist in the sentence, and cannot deal with more complicated syntactic structures.

We also notice that sentence splitting for English-Chinese machine translation is less researched in recent years.

In this paper we try to split sentences by finding proper positions and adding commas in them. A hybrid method is proposed considering that the rule-based algorithm can deal with simple situations, and the machine learning method can be better at covering more language phenomena. In this way we effectively shorten the length of sub-sentences and improve the quality of machine translation while keeping the original meaning of sentences.

3   Analysis on English Long Sentence

3.1   Standard of Long Sentence

In this paper we mainly deal with English long sentences with few punctuation marks. In fact there is no clear definition of long sentence. To decide the scope of the length of "long sentence", we extracted four groups of bilingual texts by different length(word count) from the news part of UM-Corpus [8], which is an English-Chinese sentence-aligned corpus. The four groups of sentences cover different sentence length and each group contains 2,000 sentences. We evaluated the BLEU score to analyze the influence of sentence length. The detailed information and results are listed in Table 1.

Table 1. Machine translation results on different groups by sentence length.

Group	Sentence length	BLEU
1	0 − 10	17.68
2	10 − 20	17.12
3	20 − 30	15.85
4	>30	15.11

From the table it can be clearly seen that when the sentence length is over 20 words, the BLEU score obviously drops. Also, some experts on linguistics also claims that 20 words per sentence is a desirable average length of a sentence [5]. So This paper defines "long sentences" as the sentences contain more than 20 words, and all the long sentence data sets used in this paper are extracted and built by this standard.

3.2 Difference in Processing Long Sentence in English and Chinese

In Chinese long sentences are usually made up of several short and comma-delimited sub-sentences, so we can easily dig information from these commas for splitting. In English, many writers often use long sentences especially in formal materials, and even worse they omit commas in some situations where there could have been one. In the example below, "Source" is the source sentence and the bracketed commas are the suggested splitting place where can we insert commas. "Trans-1" and "Trans-2" are respectively the machine translations before and after splitting.

Source: Colleges and universities are a community (,) and everyone within that community needs to be treated with dignity (,) and that means paying them a wage they can live on for their work.

reference: 高校是一个社区，社区内的每个人都需要有尊严的待遇，这意味着给他们发放的工资必须能让他们维持基本生活。

Trans-1: 大专院校一社区和每个人在那社区内需要用尊严处理并且那的意思是付款给他们能适合他们工作继续活着的一工资他们。

Trans-2: 大专院校是一个社区，并且在那个社区内的每个人需要被用尊严处理，并且那表明付款给他们他们能为他们的工作生活的一份工资。

As we can see, the source sentence has only one sub-sentence, while the corresponding Chinese translation is made up of three sub-sentences separated by commas. In fact the source sentence is concatenated by three simple sentence, but three simple sentences adding together will bring trouble to MT system. If we can find out the splitting points and divide the sentence into three, the source sentence will be closer to the target reference and achieve better translation quality.

This phenomenon of English brings two problems. First, it confuses the syntactic parser and leads to wrong parsing results, which is of great importance to RBMT systems. Second, it deviates the expressing pattern of the sentence from the target language. Previous study has found that when syntactic parsing fails to work, MT systems, especially RBMT systems, tend to conduct word-by-word translation [6]. At this time the similarity between the source and target sentence will greatly affect the translation results [7]. So we consider if we can add commas at positions where there could have been one, we can make the English sentence closer to the target language, and shorten the length of each sub-sentence to make parsing easier.

4   The Hybrid Model of Comma Insertion

4.1   Strategy of Choosing Splitting Point

The procedure of our model is shown in Fig. 1. The two methods works in parallel. A rule-based algorithm is designed to deal with several specific kinds of phrases or clauses while CRF is used to cover more complicated situations.

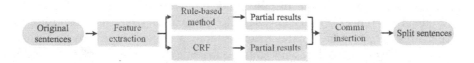

Fig. 1. The overview of our hybrid model.

4.2   Pattern Match Based on Dependency Structure

After analyzing many long sentences we conclude some situations that are easy to recognized by rules-based algorithm. We list them in Table 2. As is shown, sentences that contain adverbial clauses or prepositional phrases are very common, and sometimes these constituents can be very long. We find these sentences are easy to find out with dependency structure.

These constituents can be easily recognized by dependency structure. First we try to find the head word and then locate the boundary. The head words of prepositional phrases can be easily found by dependency label "prep"; the

Table 2. Splitting places easily recognized by rules.

Type	Example
Prepositional phrases	According to the most up to date marriage data from the Office for National Statistics (,) the number of marriages in the winter months has increased by around seven percent in two years
Adverbial clauses	When Bradley Wiggins goes for gold tomorrow afternoon in the men 's cycling time trial (,) the Tour de France champion could be forgiven for checking the crowd nervously for the face of the prime minister, who is starting to get a reputation as a bit of a jinx

leading word of an adverbial clauses is always labeled "advmob" and the word depended by the leading word should be labeled "advcl". After the head word is located, an algorithm is designed to find the boundary. The dependency structure of these components have a common characteristic which is the core of our algorithm: all words except the head word depend on words that are in the component. Figure 2 shows an simple example, the whole prepositional phrase can be easily recognized.

Algorithm 1. our rule-based algorithm

```
program findSplitPoint:
if advcl:
  leftList = [headWord, headWord.dep]
if prep:
  leftList = [headWord]
rightList = []
for word in sentence:
  if word.dep in leftList:
    leftList.add(word)
    do
      for word in rightList:
        if word.dep in leftList:
          leftList.add(word)
    while (rightList changed)
  else:
    rightList.add(word)
splitWord = maxIndex(leftWord)
```

Algorithm 1 is the python-like pseudo code of our rule-based splitting algorithm. In the pseudo code `headWord` represents the leading word of phrase or clause; `word.dep` represents the dependent of the governor, i.e., the current word. The algorithm maintains two lists to find the splitting point. the `leftList` contains words within the phrase or clause, and `rightList` contains words in other places.

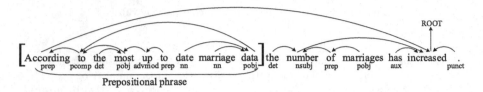

Fig. 2. The dependency structure of a prepositional phrase. All words except the head word depend on words that are in the prepositional phrase.

The splitting points are before and after the phrase or clause. Note that we only segment prepositional phrases longer than five words.

4.3   Comma Insertion Using CRF

Table 3 lists other complex situations which simple handcrafted rules cannot deal with, so we use CRF to solve them.

Table 3. Other complex situations for splitting.

Type	Example
Adjective and object clauses	The son of wartime emperor Hirohito said (,) he had been in a good health in a year (,) in which he marked 20 years on the Chrysanthemum Throne and 50 years of marriage to Empress Michiko
Coordinative components	Colleges and universities are a community (,) and everyone within that community needs to be treated with dignity (,) and that means paying them a wage they can live on for their work

Since what we need to do is to find the proper place to insert a comma, we cast this task into a sequence labeling problem by tagging the word before insertion place with a label of "COM" and other words "NUL". Sequence labelling tasks can be solved by conditional random field [4], which tries to find the global best solution and avoids the labeling bias problem.

Given a word sequence $w_1, w_2, ..., w_L$, the CRF tries to find a best label sequence $y_1, y_2, ..., y_L$ to make probability $p(y_1y_2...y_L|w_1w_2...w_L)$ maximal. According to the theory of CRF, it can be formulated and finally represented as:

$$Y^* = \underset{y_1y_2...y_L}{\mathrm{argmax}}\, p(y_1y_2...y_L|w_1w_2...w_L)$$

Using CRF needs careful consideration about feature selection. Since many factors might take part in finding the split points in a long sentence, we decide to utilize the following features.

- Words in sentence. We use this feature to recognize some fixed collocations.
- Dependency structure. This is the main feature we use. Dependency structure not only shows the constituent of each word in a sentence, but also conveys the dependent relationship between words.
- POS tag of words. POS tag can recognize the different usage of a word in different part-of-speech.

Besides the syntactic labels and POS tags of individual words we also need context information to find the proper positions for splitting. So we add a lot of context features on the basis of the above single features. Table 4 shows the actual feature template we use. The feature template seems very complicated. In fact we tested different number of context features and the template we present here is actually the best.

Table 4. Feature template we use.

ID	Feature	Comments
$1-5$	$w_{i-2}, w_{i-1}, w_i, w_{i+1}, w_{i+2}$	Words in sentence
$16-9$	$w_{i-2}\&w_{i-1}, w_{i-1}\&w_i,$ $w_i\&w_{i+1}, w_{i+1}\&w_{i+2}$	Context of words
$10-14$	$p_{i-2}, p_{i-1}, p_i, p_{i+1}, p_{i+2}$	POS tags
$15-18$	$p_{i-2}\&p_{i-1}, p_{i-1}\&p_i,$ $p_i\&p_{i+1}, p_{i+1}\&p_{i+2}$	Context of POS tag
$19-21$	$p_{i-2}\&p_{i-1}\&p_i,$ $p_{i-1}\&p_i\&p_{i+1},$ $p_i\&p_{i+1}\&p_{i+2}$	Context of POS tag
$22-30$	$d_{i-4}, ..., d_i, ..., d_{i+4}$	Dependency tag
$31-38$	$d_{i-4}\&d_{i-3}, d_{i-3}\&d_{i-2},$ $...,$ $d_{i+2}\&d_{i+3}, d_{i+3}\&d_{i+4}$	Context of dependency tag
$39-43$	$d_{i-3}\&d_{i-2}\&d_{i-1},$ $...,$ $d_{i+1}\&d_{i+2}\&d_{i+3}$	Context of dependency tag

5 Experiments

5.1 Data Sets

Training Corpus. The WMT workshop released large quantity of free corpora for researchers to train MT systems. We used "News Crawl (articles from 2007)" part of "monolingual language model training data" as our training data. This is a large and high-quality monolingual English news corpora for training language models, which can be downloaded freely on the WMT2013's web site[1].

---

[1] http://www.statmt.org/wmt13/translation-task.html.

We extracted about 450,000 long sentences and did preprocessing on them, such as removing the news source header and deleting special marks. Then we used the syntactic parser [1] and POS tagger [9] from Stanford University to conduct typed dependency parsing and POS tagging.

Test Corpus. To evaluate the effectiveness and rationality of comma insertion method we extracted 2,000 sentences which have at least two commas from the WMT corpora as Testset 1. Note that we didn't consider the length and these sentences are not included in the training data.

To evaluate the influence of our method on machine translation, a sentence-aligned bilingual corpora provided by HuaJian company was used. We extracted 2,027 long sentences from the corpora as Testset 2 to do our experiments, which has no more than one comma and are longer than 20 words.

Table 5 shows the detailed description of our data sets. The column of "Long sentence" stands for whether the data set is a corpus of long sentence.

Table 5. Detailed description of data sets.

Data set	Size	Long sentence	Comma limitation
Training set	About 450,000	Yes	At least 1
Testset 1	2000	Not limited	At least 2
Testset 2	2027	Yes	At most 1

5.2 Experiments on Effectiveness of Comma Insertion

Experiment Setup. First we tested the effectiveness and rationality of our method. For effectiveness we deleted all the commas in Testset 1, hoping that the method could recover the original commas as many as possible. For rationality we mean that the places which the algorithm find to insert commas are all reasonable, i.e., not to split the sentences at wrong places.

We first conducted feature extraction and then deleted all the commas in Testset 1. Both methods of CRF and CRF+rule were used to find where the original commas were. Precision, recall and the number of recovered commas were calculated and size of training corpus were considered. We gradually enlarged the size of the training corpus. The results are shown in Table 6 and Fig. 3 respectively. More concretely we listed several examples in Table 7.

Results. From Table 6 we see that the ability of recovering commas of our method is quite promising. the precision of CRF only reaches 77.2 % and the recall reaches 85.7 %. By adding rule-based method we gain the recall by 0.5 % at the cost of 0.1 % precision, and can also add more commas.

Table 6. Effectiveness experiment results on Testset 1.

	Precision	Recall	Count	Count of insert
CRF only	77.2	85.7	3850	154
CRF + rule	77.0	86.2	3910	214

We notice that the recall is much larger than the precision, which accords with our expectation. we expected that the positions found by the algorithm should cover most of the original ones which we deleted from the sentences, thus the recall would be relatively high while the precision wouldn't. The results proved our asumption.

Besides, this experiment is designed to test the ability to find the correct comma positions of our method. When building the data set we did'nt consider the sentence length, which resulted that many short sentences presented in the data set. There was not much room for new positions for splitting. As a result, the number of newly added commas is quite small.

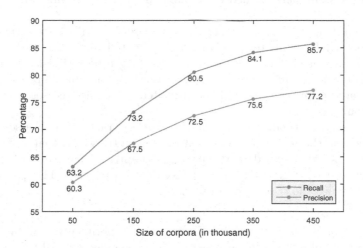

Fig. 3. Influence of training corpora size.

From Fig. 3 we can see that the precision and recall all increases as the size of corpus enlarges. Because the monolingual long sentences are very easy to obtain, we deliberately chose larger corpus to train the CRF model. Of course larger corpus means larger memory to consume and longer time to run CRF, so we have to trade off between performance and resource.

5.3   Experiments on Translation Results

Experiment Setup. Both RBMT and SMT systems were used to test whether our method was helpful for machine translation. We utilized HJTrans and Moses [3]

Table 7. Examples of Testset 1. The bracketed commas are recovered from the original sentence, and the underlined commas are inserted by the algorithm.

Before splitting	After splitting
The team had not won since their last trip to suburban Washington , starting the season 0–2 and having lost 9 of 11 games , dating to November	The team had not won since their last trip to suburban Washington (,) starting the season 0-2 , and having lost 9 of 11 games (,) dating to November
By law , Cubans can not sell their homes and because the state controls almost all property moves must be approved	By law (,) Cubans can not sell their homes , and because the state controls almost all property , moves must be approved
The fires have torched 1,790 homes but more than a dozen had been surrounded and nine others were 40 to 97 percent contained	The fires have torched 1,790 homes , but more than a dozen had been surrounded , and nine others were 40 to 97 percent contained

to conduct this part of experiment. HJTrans is a mature rule-based machine translation system with high quality and good robustness; Moses is a widely used statistical machine translation system. Both are very suitable for our experiment. The Moses system were trained on a bilingual corpus contains about 200,000 sentences.

We also set up a baseline system which is described in [10] to segment Testset 2, and used HJTrans to translate the segmented sentences. Since we used a web interface of HJTrans and couldn't generate n-best translation lists, we didn't follow the original paper's "sub translation combining" procedure. We just translated each segment, and concatenated the translated segments in the order of source sentence.

For our own method, we conducted feature extraction on Testset 2, used CRF to decode the features, and added commas after words that were labeled as "COM", as we designed in the previous chapter. Then we translated the segmented sentences by HJTrans, and used test script `mteval13a.pl` released by NIST to score the translation results.

Results. Table 8 shows the results of translation experiments. The table shows the number of split sentences, number of total commas, and BLEU and NIST metric scores of Moses and HJTrans respectively. The baseline method doesn't add new commas into sentences so the number of commas is the same as the original corpus.

From the table we see that the CRF-only method segmented more than 1,400 sentences, and combining the two methods we could split more sentences in the test set. The baseline system did not achieve good performance, we think that it is because the sentences we chose to build Testset 2 are all too long and have too few punctuation marks. Also, the baseline method is mainly designed to process Chinese long sentences. As we analyzed in the previous chapters, Chinese and English language have two very different patterns of using long sentences, these differences also deteriorate the performance of the baseline method.

Table 8. Results of translation experiments.

		#of split	#of commas	BLEU	NIST
Moses	Before split	0	1384	10.61	3.6431
	Baseline	577	1384	10.65	3.6642
	Rule	1198	2971	10.62	3.6873
	CRF	1481	3463	10.72	3.6971
	CRF+Rule	1575	3621	**10.81**	**3.7023**
HJTrans	Before split	0	1384	18.08	6.1152
	Baseline	577	1384	18.20	6.1384
	Rule	1198	2971	18.29	6.1462
	CRF	1481	3463	18.52	6.2820
	CRF+Rule	1575	3621	**18.60**	**6.3915**

The translation quality is also becoming better as the number of segmentations increases. After segmentation we obtain a gain of about 2.5 % of the BLEU score on the rule-based system, and a gain of about 1 % on the statistical Moses system. Although to maintain the original meaning of sentences we only split the sentences and didn't conduct further reordering or rewriting, such little changes to sentences still gets encouraging results.

6 Conclusion and Future Work

In this paper we try to add commas into sentences at proper positions. In this way we split long sentences improve the translation result. We use a rule-based algorithm to deal with some simple situations, and process complex situations by CRF. The experiments show that the precision of adding commas is quite high, and our method can reasonably insert commas into sentences and improves the translation quality.

Future work may focus on feature extraction and better template choosing, or developing better algorithms. Because in a sentence the potential split places not only depend on words or syntactic structure, but also and maybe more on semantic information, so we think add more semantic features may help improve the performance.

Acknowledgements. The work of this paper was supported by the National Basic Research Program of China (973 Program, Grant No. 2013CB329303) and National Natural Science Foundation of China (Grant No. 61201351, 61132009).

References

1. De Marneffe, M.C., MacCartney, B., Manning, C.D.: Generating typed dependency parses from phrase structure parses. In: Proceedings of LREC, vol. 6, pp. 449–454 (2006)

2. Huang, H., Chen, Z.: Tlie hybrid strategy processing approach of complex long sentence. J. Chin. Inf. Process. **16**(3), 1–7 (2002)
3. Koehn, P., Hoang, H., Birch, A., Callison-Burch, C., Federico, M., Bertoldi, N., Cowan, B., Shen, W., Moran, C., Zens, R., et al.: Moses: open source toolkit for statistical machine translation. In: Proceedings of the 45th Annual Meeting of the ACL on Interactive Poster and Demonstration Sessions, pp. 177–180. Association for Computational Linguistics (2007)
4. Lafferty, J., McCallum, A., Pereira, F.C.: Conditional random fields: probabilistic models for segmenting and labeling sequence data (2001)
5. Mudrak, B.: When two parts of a sentence should go their separate ways, April 2013. http://expertedge.aje.com/2013/04/16/editing-tip-of-the-week-when-two-parts-of-a-sentence-should-go-their-separate-ways/
6. Somers, H.: Round-trip translation: what is it good for. In: Proceedings of the Australasian Language Technology Workshop, pp. 127–133 (2005)
7. Sun, Y., O'Brien, S., O'Hagan, M., Hollowood, F.: A novel statistical pre-processing model for rule-based machine translation system. In: Proceedings of EAMT, p. 8 (2010)
8. Tian, L., Wong, D.F., Chao, L.S., Quaresma, P., Oliveira, F., Yi, L.: Um-corpus: a large english-chinese parallel corpus for statistical machine translation. In: Proceedings of the Ninth International Conference on Language Resources and Evaluation (LREC 2014). European Language Resources Association (ELRA) (2014)
9. Toutanova, K., Klein, D., Manning, C.D., Singer, Y.: Feature-rich part-of-speech tagging with a cyclic dependency network. In: Proceedings of the 2003 Conference of the North American Chapter of the Association for Computational Linguistics on Human Language Technology, vol. 1, pp. 173–180. Association for Computational Linguistics (2003)
10. Xiong, H., Xu, W., Mi, H., Liu, Y., Liu, Q.: Sub-sentence division for tree-based machine translation. In: Proceedings of the ACL-IJCNLP 2009 Conference Short Papers, pp. 137–140. Association for Computational Linguistics (2009)
11. Xue, N., Yang, Y.: Chinese sentence segmentation as comma classification. In: Proceedings of the 49th Annual Meeting of the Association for Computational Linguistics: Human Language Technologies: short papers, vol. 2, pp. 631–635. Association for Computational Linguistics (2011)
12. Yin, B., Zuo, J., Ye, N.: Long sentence partitioning using top-down analysis for machine translation. In: 2012 IEEE 2nd International Conference on Cloud Computing and Intelligent Systems (CCIS), vol. 3, pp. 1425–1429. IEEE (2012)
13. Yin, D., Ren, F., Jiang, P., Kuroiwa, S.: Chinese complex long sentences processing method for chinese-japanese machine translation. In: International Conference on Natural Language Processing and Knowledge Engineering. NLP-KE 2007, pp. 170–175. IEEE (2007)

Domain Adaptation for SMT
Using Sentence Weight

Xinpeng Zhou, Hailong Cao, and Tiejun Zhao[⊠]

Harbin Institute of Technology, Harbin, China
{zhouxinpeng, hailong, tjzhao}@mtlab.hit.edu.cn

Abstract. We describe a sentence-level domain adaptation translation system, which trained with the sentence-weight model. Our system can take advantage of the domain information in each sentence rather than in the corpus. It is a fine-grained method for domain adaptation. By adding weights which reflect the preference of target domain to the sentences in the training set, we can improve the domain adaptation ability of a translation system. We set up the sentence-weight model depending on the similarity between sentences in the training set and the target domain text. In our method, the similarity is measured by the word frequency distribution. Our experiments on a large-scale Chinese-to-English translation task in news domain validate the effectiveness of our sentence-weight-based adaptation approach, with gains of up to 0.75 BLEU over a non-adapted baseline system.

Keywords: Domain adaptation · Sentence weight · Statistical machine translation

1 Introduction

Statistical Machine Translation (SMT) systems are trained on a large parallel corpus. In general, the sentences in a parallel training set usually come from multiple domains, such as news, laws, conference proceedings and so on. However, a translation system trained on a mix-domain corpus can't take into account the difference in translation between different domains for the same word. When fulfilling the translation tasks from all domains with such a system, the results are usually poor. Therefore, domain adaptation is crucial for SMT systems. We distinguish the domain information of the sentences in training set by adding weights, which can improve the translation quality. Recently, there are many studies about domain adaptation for SMT systems. Some researchers use a mixture model for multi-domain model adaptation (Foster and Kuhn, 2007; Koehn and Schroeder, 2007; Finch and Sumita, 2008). It is a coarse-grained approach for domain adaptation. The mixture models are composed by several language models and translate models. This method can achieve a good performance, but it can't make full use of the domain information in the training set. Some other researchers propose a new approach for domain adaptation by filtering the out-domain data (Eck et al. 2004; Foster et al. 2010; Axelrod et al. 2011). By using the in-domain data the translation quality can be improved. In this method, only a part of the training

© Springer International Publishing Switzerland 2015
M. Sun et al. (Eds.): CCL and NLP-NABD 2015, LNAI 9427, pp. 153–163, 2015.
DOI: 10.1007/978-3-319-25816-4_13

sentences are used and they may filter out the sentences which belong to out-domain data but is helpful to improve the translation.

We describe a novel sentence-level weight method for domain adaptation in this paper. We assign weights which depend on the word distribution to each sentence pair in the training corpus. Then, we generate our domain adaptation translation system by using the sentence weights in the training process. Our method is a fine-grained approach, and we use all the sentences in the training set to train our translation system. Experimental results have shown that our method can significantly improve the translation quality on multiple domains translation task over a standard phrase-based SMT system (Koehn et al. 2003).

The rest of this paper is organized as follows: Related work on domain adaptation is presented in Sect. 2. The proposed approach is explained in Sect. 3. Experiment and results are presented in Sect. 4. Section 5 concludes the paper and suggests future research directions.

2 Related Work

Domain adaptation is an active topic in statistical machine translation. Many researchers focused on this area. Foster and Kuhn (2007) investigated the mixture model which is consists of multiple language models and translation models by liner or non-liner interpolation. This approach can improve the translating quality, but it can't make full use of the domain information in corpus. Lü et al. (2007) used the weight of the training sentences to get an in-domain subset according to the similarity with the test data by using information retrieval models. Matsoukas et al. (2009) used a discriminative training method to estimate weights for sentences in corpus. A translation system trained with sentence weights can improve the performance. However, their method may potentially lead to over-fitting, as the characteristic function is complex and the number of parameter is large. Moore and Lewis (2010) tried to select the training data by cross-entropy. This method is helpful to improve the translation quality, but it may filter out the out-domain data which also can improve the performance. Sennrich et al. (2012) invested the translation model perplexity minimization to set model weights in mixture modeling. Banerjee et al. (2013) explored a quality estimation-guided data selection method using the target-domain data which is poorly translated. This method can improve the quality of training set, however it may also filter out the data which contribute to the performance.

In this paper, we describe a sentence weight-based domain adaptation method. Applying the sentence weights which depend on the word distribution to the training process, we can get our domain adaptation system. Our approach has the following advantages over previously mentioned techniques:

1. It is a fine-grained method and can utilize the information in the corpus flexibly compared to the mixture modeling approach.
2. Unlike the filtering data method, our system is trained on the entire training set in which each sentence has a weight. We can change the influence of each sentence in translation model by the weights.

3. We build sentence weights model by word distribution which make the calculation efficient and simple.

3 Sentence Weight Domain Adaptation System

In this section we describe our domain adaptation translation system. We get our translation system by training the translation model with the sentence weights. In our method, the weights of training sentences are crucial to improve the performance. In our model, we use the maximum likelihood estimation to learn the weights. Our sentence-weight model is established on the monolingual corpus and we use the source language sentences in our model. The steps to calculate weights are as follows:

1. The establishment of sentence weights model. First, we assign a weight variable to each sentence. With these variables we calculate our words distribution. The frequency values are the non-linear function of weight variables. After that, we generate our model by calculating likelihood function of weights on target-domain text.
2. Model solution. The weights that we need in translation model are the values of variables when the likelihood function gains the maximum.

Our weights rely on target domain text, and they give preference to target domain. During rule extracting, we can improve the adaptation of rule by weighting training sentences. Training with the weights can both increase the adaptation of translation model and incorporate the domain information into the translation system. Our domain adaptation system is based on a phrase-based translation system and we improve the performance by training it with the sentence weights. The detailed description of the proposed approach is as follows:

First, we will introduce the variables and symbols used in this paper. We formalize the parallel training corpus like this:

$$C_{Train} = \{(f_1, e_1), (f_2, e_2), \ldots, (f_n, e_n)\}$$

where the (f_i, e_i) denotes the *ith* sentence pair in parallel training set, the f_i and the e_i represent the source language sentence and its translation, respectively. The subscript n is the number of the sentence pairs in the training corpus.

The target-domain text is formalized as follows:

$$C_{tar} = \{s_1, s_2, \ldots, s_m\}$$

where the s_i denotes the *ith* sentence in the target domain text. And the subscript m is the number of sentences in target domain corpus.

3.1 The Sentence-Weight Model

Our sentence-weight model is established on the training corpus and target-domain text according to domain characteristics. The goal of our sentence-weight model is to make the training corpus similar to the target domain text. We estimate the weight by the similarity between the training sentences and the target-domain text. Many features can be found in a text for calculating the similarity, such as the word alignment, the lengths of sentences, and the words distribution. In our method, we find that the words distributions of different texts are similar when the texts belong to the same domains. Therefore, we use the words distribution to calculate the similarity between the training corpus and the target domain text.

First, we assign a variable to each sentence pair in the training corpus. We formalize the sentence weights as follows:

$$\lambda = \{\lambda_1, \lambda_2, \ldots \lambda_i, \ldots, \lambda_n\}$$

where the λ_i references the weight assigned to ith sentence in corpus. The subscript n represents the dimensionality of the weight vector, which also is the number of parallel sentences in the training corpus.

The set of words in the training corpus is formalized as follows:

$$\mathbf{W} = \{w_1, w_2, \ldots w_i, \ldots, w_k\}$$

where w_i is the ith word in the words set, and the subscript k is the number of words in the corpus. The frequency of a word is calculated with all the weights. Formula 1 shows how we get our words frequency.

$$p(w_i) = \frac{\sum_{j=1}^{n} \sigma(w_i, f_j)\lambda_j}{\sum_w \sum_{j=1}^{n} \sigma(w_i, f_j)\lambda_j} \tag{1}$$

where the $\sigma(w_i, f_j)$ is a function to count the number of the word w_i in the sentence f_j. When the word w_i does not occur in the sentence f_j, the value of $\sigma(w_i, f_j)$ is zero. We obtain the word distribution by formula 1. For every word in training corpus, the frequency is a non-line function of the sentence weights.

As the weights we need are related to the target domain, we calculate the likelihood estimation of weights on the target domain text. Our likelihood estimation of weights shows as formula 2.

$$L(\lambda) = \prod_{j=1}^{m} P(s_j)$$
$$= \prod_{j=1}^{m} \prod_{i=1}^{l_i} p(w'_{ji}) \tag{2}$$

where the s_j represents the jth sentences in target domain text, and the $P(s_j)$ is its probability. In our model, the sentence probability is the multiplication of words' frequencies in the sentence. The symbol w'_{ji} represents the ith word in the sentence s_j, and the $p(w'_{ji})$ is the frequency of it.

In order to use the domain information, we set up it between the training corpus and target domain text. We can get weights for every domain by using the different target domain text.

3.2   The Optimal Weights

In this section we will introduce the method to get the best weights depending on the model generated in Sect. 3.1. The weights we need in our domain-adaptation system are the values on which the sentence-weight model takes the maximum. As the number of variable is too large to calculate, we use the log-likelihood function of weights to optimize the calculation. The optimized model shows as the formula 3.

$$\log L(\lambda) = \sum_{j=1}^{m} \sum_{i=1}^{l_j} \log p(w'_{ji}) \tag{3}$$

So, the weight values we need are like this:

$$\tilde{\lambda} = \arg \max_{\lambda} \sum_{j=1}^{m} \sum_{i=1}^{l_j} \log p(w'_{ji})$$

$$= \arg \max_{\lambda} \sum_{j=1}^{m} \sum_{i=1}^{l_j} \log \frac{\sum_{l=1}^{n} \sigma(w'_{ji}, f_l) \lambda_l}{\sum_{w} \sum_{l=1}^{n} \sigma(w'_{ji}, f_l) \lambda_l} \tag{4}$$

In a SMT system, the number of sentences in the training corpus usually is huge. So we should deal with a large number of variables in our model. It is a hard task to get the best values when the problem has a lot of variables. In our method, we use the L-BFGS algorithm (Sennrich, 2012) to deal with the sentence-weight model. We can get an approximate optimal solution by the L-BFGS algorithm.

3.3   Domain Adaptation Translation System

The domain adaptation translation system is based on a phrase-based machine translation system. By altering the phrase translation table, the performance of a translation system can be improved. We apply the weights in the training process to calculate the translation probability of a phrase pair. In a phrase-based translation model, the translation probability of the phrase pair (f', e') is defined as follows:

$$\phi(f'|e') = \frac{count(f', e')}{\sum_{f'} count(f', e')} \tag{5}$$

where the $count(f', e')$ is the occurrence number of phrase pair (f', e'). The phrase pairs are extracted form a sentence pair with the word alignment. In our domain adaptation system, we use the weights to calculate the translation probability of a phrase pair. Our method is like this:

$$\phi(f'|e') = \frac{\sum_{i=1}^{n} \Phi(f', e'|f_i, e_i) \lambda_i}{\sum_{f'} \sum_{i=1}^{n} \Phi(f', e'|f_i, e_i) \lambda_i} \tag{6}$$

where $\Phi(f', e' | f_i, e_i)$ is the occurrence number of phrase pair (f', e') in sentence pair (f_i, e_i), and λ_i is the weight of this sentence pair.

4   Experiments and Result Analysis

4.1   Data

We evaluate our domain adaptation approach on Chinese-to-English machine translation task. The training corpus in our experiment is a mixture corpus consisting of sentences from several domains such as news, laws, conference proceedings and so on. The target domain is the news in our experiment. The language model is training on the target side of FBIS and Gigaword. The Chinese-English parallel corpus that we use in our experiment is released by LDC[1]. The detail of corpus we used is shown in Table 1.

Table 1. The corpus. In the *role* column: train=train set, dev = development set, test=test set, tar=target-domain set; In the *genres* column: cp= conference proceedings, nw= newswire.

Role	Corpus	Genres	Sent
training	LDC-Hong Kong Hansards	cp	1,297 k
	LDC-Hong Kong Laws	laws	400 K
	LDC-Hong Kong News	nw	702 k
	FBIS+ Gigaword	nw	12,701 k
dev	NIST 2002 OpenMT Evaluation	nw	878
test	NIST 2005 OpenMT Evaluation	nw	1082
tar	LDC-Chinese news	nw	11,795 k

In our experiment, the training data consist of two parts: the monolingual data (FBIS+ Gigaword) and the bilingual data (Hong Kong Hansards, Hong Kong Laws, Hong Kong News). The monolingual data is used to train the language model, and the bilingual data is used to train the translation model. The target domain text is a monolingual data set, and it is used in the sentence-weight model. The number of Chinese-English parallel sentences is about 3.37 million and the number of sentences in Chinese News is about 1.7 million. The language training data contains about 12.7 million newswire sentences.

4.2   System Description

Our baseline is a standard phrase-based SMT system. Given a source sentence, it can find the most likely translation according to the phrase translation table and the Viterbi approximation. Our domain adaptation system consists of two components, the sentence-weight model and the domain adaptation translation system.

---

[1] LDC2003T05, LDC2004T08, LDC2005T06, LDC2010T10, LDC2010T14, LDC2011S01.

In the sentence-weight model, we generate the likelihood estimation of weights by calculating the probabilities of the target domain sentences. During this process, we use the Laplace smoothing (Field, 1988) to deal with the unknown words, and we also remove the stop words whose frequency is in the top 100 of words distribution. We use the L-BFGS algorithm (1989) to get the optimal value. In this algorithm, the initial values of all weights are 1.0.

Our translation model are trained on the bilingual data. We use the GIZA++(Och and Ney, 2003) to align the words in the bilingual sentence pair in both directions. Our 4-gram language model are trained on a in-domain monolingual corpuswith modifiedKneser-Ney smoothing(Kneser and Ney, 1995) through the SRILM language modeling toolkit(Stolcke, 2002). The evaluation metric we used for the translation quality is the BLEU4 (Papineni et al. 2002).

4.3   Result

The performance of our domain adaptation trainalation system is shown in Table 2. In the experiment, the target domian is news, we test our system on the same multiple domains corpus as the baseline system. As a comparison, we also trained a phrase-based translation system only with the news domain training data.

Table 2. The weight-based translation system result. In the *weight* column: PBMT = the baseline system, PBMT+W = sentence-weight-based domian adaptation translnation system, PBMT+D= the phrase-based translation system trained with in-domain training data.

System	BLEU
PBMT	26.90
PBMT+W	27.65
PBMT+D	27.73

Table 2 shows that for the same translation task from the news test set, the baseline system get a score of 26.90, and the score of the in-domain translation systemand is 27.73. The score of our domian adaptation translation system is 27.65, the gain is 0.75 according to the baseline. Through the Table 2 we can see that our system trained with the sentence weights can get a better performance over the baseline.

4.4   Analysis

In the experiment we random sample five values from the weights vector to check the performance of our sentence-weight model. Table 3 list several target domain sentences and five training sentences with their corresponding weights. In the Table 3, according to the content of the sentences we can know that the fifth sentence in train-ing sample set has the most number of the same words with the target sentences. Therefore, in our method the fifth sentence has the greatest similarity among the five training sentences. And the next two are the first sentence and the fourth sentence in order of the similarity

Table 3. The sentence weights sample result.

Role	Weight	Sentence
Target	–	国际足联规定, 从今年7月1日 开始, 球员的背心上不 得书写任何文字 。
	–	香港居民在沪申请设立个体工商户将享受绿色通道.
	–	民政部处罚中国地区开发促进会:停止活动3个月。
	–	按国家艾滋病统计数据,北京市艾滋病病毒感染者的报告数,在全国排名第8位。
Training	0.9864	当局亦已答应优先检讨亲父鉴定诉讼条例,以减少根据该条例规定提出申请的母亲的不便。
	0.9684	现在付诸表决,赞成的请举手。
	0.8658	(1)除第(2)款另有规定外,任何人的申索如已被根据第113条不准予或只局部准予。
	0.9765	民政事务总署现已在各区开放共十四个临时避寒中心,供有需要的市民避寒。
	1.074	他说,在香港有三人获证实死于该病毒,另有两名患有重病的病人,其死因可能亦与该病毒有关。

with the target sentences. In the weight column, the values of weights are, in order, the fifth, the first, the fourth, the second and the third.

The data in the Table 3 shows that the weight of sentence with greater similarity has a larger value. From Table 3 we can know that our sentence-weight model can increase the weight value of sentence with high similarity to the target domain text and reduce the weight value of sentence with low similarity.

In our domain adaptation translation system, we improve the performance by increasing the adaptation of translation model through the sentence weights. During the experiment we sample the phrase translation rules in our translation system, the baseline system and the news domain translation system. Table 4 lists some difference between our system and other translation systems in the phrase translation rules.

Table 4 shows the difference in the translation rules between our system and compared system. The phrases in the *rules* column in Table 4 are the translations for the phrases in the *source* column. For the phrase "成为重要", the probability of translation rules which translate the source phrase to "become an important" and "a leading" are all 0.6 in baseline, while we change the probabilities of rules by the sentence weights. Our system improves the probability of the translation rule which translate to "become an important" to 0.633204 and reduce the probability of the other one to 0.598505. In decoding step, the best translation to the phrase "成为重要" is "become an important" in our system, while the baseline choose the phrase "a leading". For the phrase "促进社会稳定", our system also change the probability of translation rules by weights, and when decode for this phrase, the result "the promoting social stability" is the best translation, while the baseline translate it to "foster social stability". From he Table 4 we can know that the translation rules of our domain adatptation system are more similar to that of the news domain translation system. So, by using our sentence weights we can change the probability of the translation rules and decoding result, which will lead to the improvement of the ability of domain adaptation.

Table 4. The difference in phrase translation rules between our system and other systems. In the *PBMT*, the *PBMT+W* and the *PBMT+D* column, the values are the probabilities of translation rules in the baseline system, our translation system, and the news domain system, respectively. The superscript "*" are the marks which means the translation rule is the best rule in decoding for the source phrase in the system.

Source	Rule	PBMT	PBMT+W	PBMT+D
成为重要	become an important	0.600000	0.633204^*	0.628895^*
	a leading	0.600000^*	0.598505	0.600000
	an important	0.600000	0.600064	0.600000
	as an important commercial	0.200000	0.191113	0.200000
促进社会稳定	promoting social stability	0.600000	0.616564^*	0.633168^*
	foster social stability	0.428571^*	0.395946	0.389746
	our society can be made stable	0.600000	0.608138	0.630000
	as to foster social stability	0.200000	0.197310	0.621658

The experiment result shows that our domain adaptation can improve the system performance. We sample several sentences whose translate results are different between our system and the baseline to check the translation quality. Table 5 show the translate results for the same sentences translated by our system, the baseline system and the domain adaptation system.

Table 5. The difference between the translation result. In system column: task = translation task, PBMT =baseline, PBMT+W=our domian adaptation system, PBMT+D=news domain adaptation system, ref = reference translation. In the result, we use shift characters to represent the spical character, " ' " = " ' ", " "" =" " ".

Role	Sentences
task	1. 明年日本经济成长速度可能放缓. 2. 世界各国领袖陆续走访斯里兰卡视察灾情.
PBMT	1. next year, the economic growth is likely to slow the pace of japan. 2. the world leaders continue to inspect the disaster to visit sri lanka.
PBMT+W	1. the speed of economic growth next year might be slow-down in japan. 2. world leaders have visited sri lanka to inspect the disaster.
PBMT+D	1. japan 's economic growth next year is likely to slow speed. 2. the world leaders to inspect the disaster will visit sri lanka.
ref	1. japan 's economy may slow down next year. 2. world leaders tour sri lanka to assess tsunami damage.

There are two translation instances in the Table 5, we list out the source sentences, the results translated by baseline system, our domain adaptation system and the news domain translation system, and the reference translation. For the instance 1, the difference between our system and the baseline is the target to slow down, in our system the target is the economic growth, while in the baseline system the target is the japan. And the meaning of the translation of our system is the same to that of the news domain translation system. In the sentence 1, the meaning of source sentence is that the economic growth may slow down, so, the translation of baseline is wrong and ours is accurately. When translate the instance 2, the difference in results is the translation of phrase "走访斯里兰卡视察灾情", our system translate it exact, while the translation of the baseline is wrong, as it turn over the order of "inspect the disaster" and "visited sri lanka". In the two instances, the meaning of our system translation result is the same as that of the news domain translation system. Through the two instances we can know that by applying the sentence weights, we can improve the performance of a translation system in the target domain.

5   Conclusion

In this paper, we describe a method to estimate the sentence weights to enhance the ability of domain adaptation and improve the performance of the translation system. Firstly, we build our sentence-weight model by using the word frequency distribution. And we use the L-BFGS algorithm to get the sentence weights according to target domain text in the model. Then, we train our translation model with sentence weights and get the domain adaptation translation system. Experiment results show that our approach brings a better performance in target domain over the phrase-based translation system (Koehn et al. 2003).

Our method is a fine-grained and sentence-level domain adaptation method in machine translation. And it is also a general domain adaptation approach. Our sentence-weight model depends on the word frequency distribution, we may also generate it by other features. In future work, we will try to use other characteristics to generate the sentence-weight model to improve the translation result.

References

Foster, G., Kuhn, R.: Mixture-model adaptation for SMT. In: Workshop on Statistical Machine Translation Association for Computational Linguistics (2007)

Koehn, P., Schroeder, J.: Experiments in domain adaptation for statistical machine translation. In: Proceedings of the Second Workshop on Statistical Machine Translation. Association for Computational Linguistics, pp. 224–227 (2007)

Finch, A., Sumita, E.: Dynamic model interpolation for statistical machine translation. In: Proceedings of the Third Workshop on Statistical Machine Translation. Association for Computational Linguistics, pp. 208–215 (2008)

Zhao, B., Eck, M., Vogel, S.: Language model adaptation for statistical machine translation with structured query models. In: Proceedings of the 20th International Conference on Computational Linguistics. Association for Computational Linguistics, pp. 411 (2004)

Foster, G., Goutte, C., Kuhn, R.: Discriminative instance weighting for domain adaptation in statistical machine translation. In: Proceedings of the 2010 Conference on Empirical Methods in Natural Language Processing. Association for Computational Linguistics, pp. 451–459 (2010)

Axelrod, A., He, X., Gao, J.: Domain adaptation via pseudo in-domain data selection. In: Proceedings of the Conference on Empirical Methods in Natural Language Processing. Association for Computational Linguistics, pp. 355–362 (2011)

Koehn, P., Och, F.J., Marcu, D.: Statistical phrase-based translation. In: Proceedings of the 2003 Conference of the North American Chapter of the Association for Computational Linguistics on Human Language Technology-vol. 1. Association for Computational Linguistics, pp. 48–54 (2003)

Lü, Y., Huang, J., Liu, Q.: Improving Statistical Machine Translation Performance by Training Data Selection and Optimization. In: EMNLP-CoNLL, pp. 343–350 (2007)

Matsoukas, S., Rosti, A.V.I., Zhang, B.: Discriminative corpus weight estimation for machine translation. In: Proceedings of the 2009 Conference on Empirical Methods in Natural Language Processing: vol. 2. Association for Computational Linguistics, pp. 708–717 (2009)

Moore, R.C., Lewis, W.: Intelligent selection of language model training data. In: Proceedings of the ACL 2010 Conference Short Papers. Association for Computational Linguistics, pp. 220–224 (2010)

Sennrich, R.: Perplexity minimization for translation model domain adaptation in statistical machine tra- nslation. In: Proceedings of the 13th Conference of the European Chapter of the Association for Computational Linguistics. Association for Computational Linguistics, pp. 539–549 (2012)

Bancrjee, P., Rubino, R., Roturier, J., et al.: Quality estimation-guided data selection for doma-in adaptation of smt. MT Summit XIV: Proc. Fourteenth Mach. Trans. Summit, 101–108 (2013)

Liu, D.C., Nocedal, J.: On the limited memory BFGS method for large scale optimization. Math. Program. **45**(1–3), 503–528 (1989)

Field, D.A.: Laplacian smoothing and Delaunay triangulations. Commun. Appl. Numer. Methods **4**(6), 709–712 (1988)

Och, F.J., Ney, H.: A systematic comparison of var- ious statistical alignment models. Comput. linguist. **29**(1), 19–51 (2003)

Kneser, R., Ney, H.: Improved backing-off for m-gram language modeling. In: 1995 International Conference on Acoustics, Speech, and Signal Processing, 1995. ICASSP-95., vol. 1, pp. 181–184. IEEE (1995)

Stolcke, A.: SRILM-an extensible language modeling toolkit. In: INTERSPEECH (2002)

Papineni, K., Roukos, S., Ward, T., et al.: BLEU: a method for automatic evaluation of mach- ine translation. In: Proceedings of the 40th Annual Meeting on Association for Computational Linguistics. Association for Computational Linguistics, pp. 311–318 (2002)

Multilinguality in NLP

Types and Constructions of Exocentric Adjectives in Tibetan

Di Jiang[✉]

Lab of Phonetics and Computational Linguistics,
Chinese Academy of Social Sciences,
Building 6, 27 Zhongguancun Southern Street, Beijing 100081, China
jiangdi@cass.org.cn

Abstract. The construction [N_R+V/ADJ_R+SUF] in Tibetan may be analyzed as nominal phrases or as adjectives of exocentric construction with different meanings. How to segment, tag and auto-translate the two constructions will be a problem in Tibetan natural processing. This paper describes the constructions, types, variants in given situations and the ways of production of the exocentric constructions, which will give enlightenments to relative researches.

Keywords: Nominal phrase · Compound adjective with derived suffixes · Constructional homonymity · Exocentric construction

1 Exocentric Construction of Adjectives in Tibetan

There are a number of compound adjectives, homomorphic with conventional modifier-head noun phrases. Both of them show great disparities in grammatical analysis and semantic understanding, which leads to whether word segment, syntactic tagging and machine translation is correct. Therefore, the design of distinctive segmenting and tagging strategies is to deal with such a problem. For example, ཚོང«་པོ *ngo nag po* as a noun phrase *ngo/N nag po/ADJ* means "black face", and as an adjective *ngo nag po/ADJ* means "sullen"; ཚོ་མཚར་པོ *ngo/N mtshar po/ADJ* as a phrase with the meaning "a fair face", *ngo mtshar po/ADJ* as an adjective "good-looking". སྐད་ཆ་གསང་པོ *skad cha/N gsang po/ADJ* as a phrase "blunt words", *skad cha gsang po/ADJ* as an adjective "lucid-spoken"; རྩལ་ལག་དོད་པོ *rtsal lag/N dod po/ADJ* as a phrase "prominent skill", *rtsal lag dod po/ADJ* as an adjective "proficiently-skilled". Figure 1 shows a lexicalization process by adjectivization of a metonymy in such a case of ཚོ་ནག་པོ *ngo nag po* in ཚོང་པ་ཚོ་ནག་པོ *tshong pa ngo nag po* [1, 2].

This class of adjectives may be named as compound adjectives with derived suffixes. In view of no more discussions on such a kind of adjectives, some concepts are firstly to be illustrated. Such a sort of words are called adjectives with exocentric construction [3].

For the purpose of a comprehensive understanding of compound adjective with derived suffixes, it is necessary to analyze the overall status and inner construction of Tibetan adjectives. The basic formation of them is a monosyllabic adjective/verbal root + adjective suffixes, called derived adjective, namely, ADJ/V_{ROOT}+po$_{SUF}$ (པོ *po* is a typical adjective suffix, and others like མོ *mo*, བ *ba*, པ *pa* etc.). For instance, ཚ་པོ *tsha po* "hot", གྲང་མོ *grang mo* "cold", ཆེན་པོ *chen po* "big", ཡག་པོ *yag po* "nice". In addition,

© Springer International Publishing Switzerland 2015
M. Sun et al. (Eds.): CCL and NLP-NABD 2015, LNAI 9427, pp. 167–179, 2015.
DOI: 10.1007/978-3-319-25816-4_14

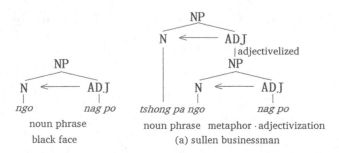

Fig. 1. Comparison of a homomorphic structure with different meanings

the reduplication of Tibetan roots form such reduplicated adjectives as ཆུང་ཆུང་ *chung chung* "small", ནར་ནར་ *nar nar* "banded", འཁྱོར་འཁྱོར་ *vkhyor vkhyor* "swaying". Disyllabic reduplicated adjective is another basic form, some of which have no corresponding form: a root with a suffix. Trisyllabic adjectives (including derived suffixes) in Tibetan are rare in number, such as སྙིང་རྗེ་པོ་ *snying rje po* "adorable", ཁྱད་མཚར་པོ་ *khyad mtshar po* "weird". This sort of antique multisyllabic adjectives emerge etymologically by lexicalization with no apparent inner meaning, nevertheless, distinctively different from adjectives discussed in the following sections.

Compared with basic adjectives, compound adjectives are obviously in a novel category. Originally, they are formed through the lexicalization of nominal-adjective phrases, such as ཞགས་པ་རིང་པོ་ *zhags pa ring po* "a long rope", རིང་པོ་ *ring po* "long", a modifier of ཞགས་པ་ *zhags pa* "rope". However, the ingenuity of Tibetan logic is that རིང་པོ་*ring po* as such is void of property to represent the length of an object, as a result, unable to modify directly nouns involving no items of length, such as སྦུག་ *sbug* original meaning "valley bottom,depth", no form སྦུག་རིང་པོ་ *sbug ring po*. In another case, མཛད་པ་ *mdzad pa* "career" cannot be modified by ཆེ་བ་ *che ba* "big", སྡུག་པ་ *sdug pa* "severe" cannot be used to modify བྱད་ *byad* "appearance". In this connection, Tibetan utilizes conventional nouns and adjectives to constitute NP+AP phrase, and then make them adjectivized as $[N_R+ADJ_R+SUF]_{ADJ}$, i.e. compound adjectives with derived suffixes by means of semantic generalization and metonymy. For example, in ཐག་རིང་པོ་ *thag ring po* "distant", ཐག་ *thag* "cordage", entailing the property of length, can be modified by རིང་པོ་ *ring po*. When this construction is further combined with a noun, such as ལམ་ཐག་རིང་པོ་ (ལམ་ *lam* "way", ཐག་རིང་པོ་ *thag ring po*) "a long way", སྡུག་ཐག་རིང་པོ་(སྡུག་ *sdug* "bottom", ཐག་རིང་པོ་ *thag ring po*) "deep valley", the modification of nouns with no length property is consequently realized. In accordance with qualia construction of Generative Lexicon Theory, the meaning of an item itself is generally stable, however, the combination of items together gives rise to integrated meaning [2, 4]. Among them are type coercion and type selection governing the combination. In construction $[N_R+ADJ_R+SUF]_{ADJ}$, ADJ_R is short of arguments matching adjectives [5], mandatorily converting nouns into consistent properties, which serve as certain role in qualia construction (including formal role, constitutive role, telic role and agentive role) [4]. Such a psychological process allows the meanings of N_R to experience generalization, metonymy, and even transformation of concept domain. Thereby, the construction $[N_R+ADJ_R+ SUF]_{ADJ}$ and its meaning are gradually solidified, converting into an adjective.

[N$_R$+ADJ$_R$+SUF]$_{ADJ}$ is a typical lexical form of exocentric construction. Its inner construction conforms with attributive-centered construction. However, N$_R$ is a property value of ADJ$_R$ semantically and functionally, utterly converse with conventional attributive-centered construction. Thus, its allomeric function is embodied as an adjective.

Another property worth the whistle is that this sort of adjectives which should be analyzed as [N$_R$+[ADJ$_R$+po$_{SUF}$]] construction, i.e. noun + adjective with suffix, however, in practice, are reanalyzed cognitively as [[N$_R$+ADJ$_R$]+po$_{SUF}$] construction. From the glossary of dictionaries, there are some [N$_R$+ADJ$_R$] constructions, such as ཁྱད་མཚར་ *khyad mtshar*, "curiosity, miracle" as a metonymy, and as a nominal phrase with its meaning "distinctive difference" if we use [[khyad] "difference" N [mtshar po] "distinctive"ADJ] to analyze, without any transferred meanging, inconsistent with its original meaning, therefore, it is estimated that ཁྱད་མཚར་ *khyad mtshar* is constructed with disyllabic nouns + affixes. Similiar adjectives are གྲ་རྒྱས་པོ་ [[gra rgyas]"abundance",N po] "abundant", གྲ་འགྲིག་པོ་ [[gra vgrig] "completeness" +po]"thoughtful, detailed", ཞིབ་ཚགས་པོ་ [[zhib] "meticulosity" N [tshags] "compactness" N] "thoroughness" N po] "careful". However, some of words have no [N$_R$+ADJ$_R$]construction and directly are constructed with N$_R$+[ADJ$_R$+po$_{SUF}$], such as ཁ་འབལ་པོ་ [[kha]$_N$ "mouth" [vbal po]$_{ADJ}$ "plentiful"] "talkative". If this approach is adopted, two maladies then come about. It is known to us that [[N$_R$+ADJ$_R$]+ po$_{SUF}$] construction originates etymologically from the lexicalization of phrases, although so far brought about by analogy of an abundance of lexicon, while originally its lexical form and lexical generalization are closely related to metonymy, without which, it is yet a conventional nominal-adjective phrase. On the other hand, Tibetan nouns, verbs and adjectives show distinctive form disparities, which can create intensive psychological traces on native speakers, accepting canonical adjective construction as root +affix (པོ *po-* as a model). Therefore, even though compound affixes are put to use, it is acknowledged that only by adding affixes can a valid adjective be constructed. This is the reason why this sort of constructions are named compound adjectives with derived suffixes.

Exocentric construction adjectives can be grouped into four categories according to inner morphemic meanings. (1) category refers to an estimation on objective description of shape, dimension, Materials and methods; (2) category refers to an estimation on concepts derived from our body or on relevant abstract concepts, such as "soul, attitude, skill and habit"etc; (3) category refers to the description and estimation of metaphor and metonymy of our body parts; (4) category refers to the description and estimation of hyperbole or metonymy of actions.

1: ཐག *thag* "distance", རྒྱ *rgya* "acreage", གཏིང *gting* "depth", ཐབས *thabs* "method", གོང *gong* "value".

2: སེམས *sems* "soul", ཐུགས *thugs* "spirit", ངང *ngang* "nature", རུས་པ *rus pa* "lineage", ཁུངས *khungs* "sourse", སྟོབས *stobs* "power", རིག་པ *rig pa* "wisdom", རྣམ་པ *rnam pa* "appearance", ཉམས *nyams* "posture", ཡིད་ཆེས *yid ches* "mood", སྣང་པ *snang pa* "perception", གཤིས་ཀ *gshis ka* "property", རྩལ *rtsal* "skill", སྐད *skad* "sound", ལབ་རྗེས *lab rjes* "promise".

3: (five sense organs) ཁ *kha* "mouth", ལྕེ *lce* "tongue", རྣ *rna* "ear", སྣ *sna* "nose", མིག *mig* "eye", གདོང/ གདོང་ཁ *gdong/ gdong kha* "face".

(limbs) ལག་པ *lag pa* "hand", རྐུབ *rkub* "hip", རྐང་པ *rkang pa* "foot", མཇིང་པ *mjing pa* "neck", ཕྲག་པ *phrag pa* "shoulder", གཟུགས་པོ *gzugs po* "body", ཤ *sha* "fresh", སྐད་ཆ *skad cha* "throat".

4: འཁྲབ *vkhrab* "performance", བཞོན *bzhon* "ride", ཁོབ་ཤ *khob sha* "stupidity", གྲུང་ཤ *grung sha* "cleverness".

Sentence 1 is an example of metonymy in category 3 relating to limbs. More instances are shown in Sect. 2.

1. ཁ་བདེ་པོ་   མེད་   ན་   ལས་ཀ་   གཚོད་   བྱས་   ཀྱང་   མི་ཡིས་   མཐོང་ཆུང་བྱེད་   ཀྱི་རེད།

kha-bde-po med na las-ka ga-tshod byas kyang mi-yis mthong-chung-byed kyi red

good-talk not-be if work how-much done also others look-down-upon   ASP

If you are not good at words, no matter how much work you do, you will also be looked down upon by others.

2 Construction and Syntactic Function of Exocentric Adjectives

Exocentric construction adjectives can serve as various components in a sentence, mainly including adjective predicate and postpositive attributive. By adding different markers, they serve as prepositive attributive, adverbials and complements.

Predicate: An adjective + a predicate sentence-final marker constitutes an adjective predicate sentence, of which the primary component is an aspect marker [6]. Generally speaking, adjectives of property manifests static state, the result of describing properties of an object, thus labeled with aspect markers ཡོད་ *yod*, འདུག *vdug*, ཡོག་རེད་ *yog red*. These three markers are relevant to evidentiality, denoting self-knowing evidentials, visual evidentials, information-newly-found evidentials, hearsay or inferential evidentials, pertaining to the subject's person of and the narrator's cognitive state of [7]. (ASP=aspect, AG=agentive, GEN=genitive, NEG=negative, NMZ=nominalized, -LY=adverbial, LOC=locative, CONJ=conjunction, OBJ= objective, ALA=allative, ABL=ablative, TOP=topic marker)

2. ལུང་པ་   འདིའི་   སྦུག་   ཐག་རིང་པོ་   ཡོག་མ་རེད།

lung-pa vdi-vi   sbug   thag-ring-po   yog-ma-red.

place this-GEN valley (distance)deep ASP-NEG

This valley is not deep.(adjective predicate sentence with a compound adjective)

3. རུས་   དེ་   ཞིད་   གངས་   ཁྲོད་   ཀྱི་   ཕ་བོང་   དེའི་   སྟེང་   དུ་   དམིགས་བསལ་

rus de zhod gangs khrod kyi pha-bong devi   steng du   dmigs-bsal

bone this big snow in GEN rock   that-GEN on LOC special

ཀྱི་   ལམ་རྟགས་   ལྟར་   ཧ་ཅང་   མངོན་གསལ་དོད་པོ་   འདུག

gyi lam-rtags ltar ha-cang mngon-gsal-dod-po vdug.

GEN landmark like very   obvious   ASP

The bone on the rock in the snow is like a landmark, becoming very obvious. (a predicate)

The root of adjective without an affix as a predicate may use continuous aspect, perfect aspect, like གི་རེད་ *gi red*, གིས་མ་རེད་ *gi ma red*, པ་རེད་ *pa red*, གི་འདུག *pa ma red*, གི་འདུག *gi vdug*, གི་མི་འདུག *gi mi vdug*, ཤག *shag* etc., because of the usual embodiment of its dynamics. In specific cases, judgment verbs ཡིན་ *yin*, རེད་ *red* are employed as aspect marker.

4. གལ་ཏེ་ གློག་བརྙན་བལྟས་   ན་ པ་སེ་ འདི་ ཐག་ཉེ་ དྲགས་ ཤག།

gal-te glog-brnyan-bltas na pa-se vdi thag-nye drags shag.

If   film-watch   if ticket this near   too ASP
If we watch a film, this ticket is(distance) too near.

5. ཁོ་རང་ རྐང་པ་ཡང་པོ་   ཡིན་ པས་   དེ་རིང་ ཚུར་ འཁོར་ ཐུབས།

kho-rang rkang-pa-yang-po yin-pas   de-ring tshur vkhor thubs.

he   (action)nimble   ASP-CONJ today   come back   can
He is nimble in his action, so he can come back today. (dictionary)

Attribute: Adjectives of exocentric construction, like any other common adjectives, serve as postposed modifiers, a few of which can be added with possessive case marker གི་ *gi* (variants: གྱི་ *gyi*, ཀྱི་ *kyi*, bound form འི་ *-vi*) as preposed modifier.

6. གཅུང་པོ། འདི་ ནས་ ཡུལ་ ཚང་ཀྲུ་བ་ར་   རྒྱང་ ཐག་རིང་པོ་ མེད།

gcung-po. vdi ' nas yul tshang-kravu-ba-r   rgyang thag-ring-po med.
brother   this ABL place tshang-kravu-ALA   distance far   NEG-ASP
Brother, this place is not far from tshang-kravu-ba. (Existential sentence with a compound derived adjective as postposed modifier)

7. སྒེག་ཉམས་དོད་པའི་   བྱད་བཞིན་ ལས་   དངོས་གནས་ མོ་ ལ་

sgeg-nyams-dod-pavi   byad-bzhin las   dngos-gnas mo la
charming-and-delicate-GEN appearance besides really   she POS

རེ་འདོད་བྱེད་   མཁན་   མི་ཉུང་བ་   ཡོད།

re-vdod-byed mkhan   mi-nyung-ba yod.

expectation   NMZ-person   not a few   have
Besides charming and delicate appearance, she really has not a few expectations.

Under exceptional circumtances, it is possible that adjectives are not followed by a marker as a preposed modifier. For example, an adjective phrase and a verbal phrase together in Sentence 8 in juxtapostion, modifies མཁན་ *mkhan*, acting as both a nominalization marker and a person's name affix denoting "a person".

8. གཞུང་དྲང་པོ་   དང་ གུས་བཀུར་བྱེད་   མཁན་   གཅིག་ ཡིན།

gzhung-drang-po dang gus-bkur-byed mkhan gcig yin.
simple-and-honest and respectful-being person   a   is
(He) is a (character) simple, honest and respectful person. (གཞུང་ *gzhung* "character", དྲང་པོ་ *drang po* "honest")

Adverbial: Adjectives in Tibetan, when acting as adverbials, are added with an adverbial marker, such as བྱས་ནས་ *byas nas*, ནས་ *nas*, སེ་ *se*, དེ་ *de*, ལ་/-ར་ *la/-r*, དུ་ *du* etc..

9. ཁོང་ གིས་ ང་ ལ་ ངང་རྒྱུད་རིང་པོ་   བྱས་ནས་ རོགས་རམ་བྱེད་ ཀྱི་འདུག

khong gis nga la   ngang-rgyud-ring-po byas-nas rogs-ram-byed kyi-vdug.
he   AG me OBJ patient   -LY   help   ASP

He help me patiently. (བྱས་ནས་ *byas-nas* follows after an adjective to convert it into an adverb)

10. གཙོ་དོན་ མངོན་གསལ་དོད་པོ་ར་   བརྗོད་པ།

gtso-don mngon-gsal-dod-po-r   brjod pa.
main   significance-highlighted-LY state

State the main significance highlightedly. (ར་ -*r* is adhesive to the last syllable of adjective པོ་ *po*, modifying predicate)

Complement: Complements come before predicates. The adjectives, acting as complements, for the most part are followed by structural particles of supplement ལ་ *la* or ར་ -*r*. However, structural particles in a few cases are omitted.

11.་ཕུན་ཚོགས་   འཕྲལ་   སེམས་   ཚབས་པོ་   གྱུར་   ཏེ་   ན་རེ……
    phun-tshogs vphral   sems tshabs-po gyur   te   na re ......
    phuntshogs immediately (heart) anxious   become-PST hence say
    Phuntshogs becomes anxious and says immediately……

12. ང་ ལ་ སྡང་པོ་   དེ་འདྲ་   བྱེད་པ་ ཅི་ཡིན་ ནམ་   བསམ་ བཞིན་ ཡུད་ཚམ་   ཡིད་མུག་པོ་ར་ གྱུར་
    nga-la sdang-po de-vdra byed-pa ci-yin nam.   bsam bzhin yud-tsam yid mug-po-r gyur.
    I-OBJ vicious so   do   what MOOD think face immediately vexed-FAT be

I immediately become vexed for the reason why do you treat me so viciously. (ཡིད་མུག་པོ་ *yid mug po* = ཡིད་རྨུག་པ་ *yid rmug pa* "blurred mind")

Here describes the adjectives in [N$_R$+ADJ$_R$+SUF]$_{ADJ}$ construction discussed in Sect. 1. In practice, exocentric construction adjectives have other forms made up from verbs. The most veteran is རླུང་ལང་པོ་ *rlung lang po* "bad-tempered, irritable". It stems from a verbal phrase རླུང་ལང(ས)་ *rlung lang(s)* "irritate, enrage" by adding a suffix so that it will be lexicalized to a exocentric construction adjective. Such a schema in Tibetan, generally speaking, is a finite. Among them are ངོ་ཚ་པོ་ *ngo tsha po* "bashful" (< ངོ་ཚ་ *ngo tsa* "abash" V), དོགས་པ་ཟ་པོ་ *dogs pa za po* "suspicious" (< དོགས་པ་ཟ་ *dogs pa za* "suspect" V). As is known to us, disyllabic verbs are attached with a suffix པོ་ -*po* to constitute an adjective, which is not productive, and its construction is [[N$_{R/PHR}$+V$_R$]+SUF]$_{ADJ}$. The followings are examples in the same construction, but from other forms.

བག་ཡངས་ *bag yangs*$_{(fearless, carefree ADJ)}$ > བག་ཡངས་པོ་ *bag yangs po*$_{(careless ADJ)}$

གཤིབ་འདོད་ *gshib vdod*$_{(to get accessible to· verbal phrase)}$ > གཤིབ་འདོད་པོ་ *gshib vdod po*$_{(easy- going, ADJ)}$

ངོ་སོ་ *ngo so*$_{(face· delight N)}$ ཐོན་ *thon*$_{(to appear V)}$ > ངོ་སོ་ཐོན་པོ་ *ngo so thon po*$_{(honorable, ADJ)}$

བསྟུན་མཁས་ *bstun mkhas*$_{(conformity, adaption N)}$ > བསྟུན་མཁས་པོ་ *bstun mkhas po*$_{(circulating, ADJ)}$/(see བསྟུན་མཁས་བྱེད་ *bstun mkhas byed* $_{tocontactV}$)

Zhou Jiwen et al. argued that བཟོ་དོད་པོ་ *bzo dod po* indicates actions are specially fine in manner, posture or bearing (see Sentences 3, 10), and that བྱང་ལང་པོ་ *byang lang po* followed after a verb in present tense constitutes an adjective [8]. For example:

འགྲོ་བཟོ་དོད་པོ་ *vgro bzo dod po*, walking with good posture (འགྲོ་ *vgro* "to walk"V)

ངུ་བྱང་ལང་པོ་ *ngu byang lang(s) po*, easy-crying (ངུ་ *ngu* "to cry" V)

However, we note that the initial syllable of a part of words can constitute with བཟོ་ *bzo* a compound noun. For example, བྱེད་བཟོ་དོད་པོ་ *byed bzo dod po* "dissolute, ostentatious", བྱེད་ *byed,* with its dependent verb meaning "make" and independent verb meaning "become", can constitute a compound noun བྱེད་བཟོ་ *byed bzo* "appearance, shape and gesture". Therefore, the composite construction is analyzed བྱེད་བཟོ་དོད་པོ་ [[byed bzo] "posture" dod po "appear"]$_{NA}$. Furthermore, we find that initial syllables are not necessarily all verbs, such as ཁ་བཟོ་དོད་པོ་ *kha bzo dod po* "butter-tonsiled"(*kha* "mouth"), its construction [[kha bzo] "statement" dod po]. It's no doubt that not all of initial syllables can constitute new words with བཟོ་ *bzo*. However, no matter if V/N+*bzo* is an independent word, it will be taken in NP+ADJ construction as a compound noun and analyzed as [[V/N+bzo] [dod po]]$_{ADJ}$ for benefit. For example, ལྟ་བཟོ *lta bzo* "good-looking/handsome" N དོད་པོ *dod po* "niffy, handsome", *lta bzo*$_{(N)}$ a word included in dictionary; འཁྲབ་བཟོ *vkhrab bzo* "dancing" དོད་པོ *dod po* "skillful". Although the word འཁྲབ་བཟོ *vkhrab bzo* is excluded from dictionary, its inner meaning "the way of dancing" is apparent, and thus can be deduced from lexicalization.

Will བྱང་ལང་པོ *byang lang po* possess the same property if བཟོ་དོད་པོ *bzo dod po* is analyzed as the combination attached to a verb? In བྱང *byang*$_{<V>}$ "to master" (< future tense of the independent verb འབྱང *vbyang*), the root + the affix constitutes བྱང་ཆ *byang cha*$_{<N>}$ "proficiency", བྱང་པོ/བྱང་བ/བྱང་མ *byang po/pa/ma*$_{<ADJ>}$ "skillful, sophisticated". According to its meaning, "to master" is a mode of behavior, and thus can be extended to refer to a habit (habitual behavior). In such a way, the verb is converted to a noun denoting abstracts. It will be illustrated with some specific instances.

Based on the analysis of inner structure, ངུ་བྱང་ལངས་པོ *ngu byang lang(s) po* is analyzed in three approaches:

a. [ངུ་[བྱང་ན་ལངས་ν་པོ]]$_{ADJ}$ [ngu $_V$+[byang $_N$+lang $_V$+ po]] $_{ADJ}$ [8]

b. [[ངུ་+བྱང་ν]$_{NMZ}$+[ལངས་པོ]$_{ADJ}$]$_{ADJ}$ [[ngu $_V$+byang $_N$]$_{NMZ}$+[lang$_V$ po]$_{ADJ}$]$_{ADJ}$

c. [[[ངུ་+བྱང་ν]$_{NMZ}$+ལངས་ν]ν+པོ་]$_{ADJ}$ [[[ngu $_V$+byang $_N$]$_{NMZ}$+lang$_V$]$_V$+po]$_{ADJ}$

Approach a. takes བྱང་ལང་པོ *byang lang po* as a whole without further analysis of inner structure, called, in Zhou's view, movable word ending. The point of Approach b. is that ལང་པོ *lang po* is considered as an adjective used to modify the nominalization of ངུ་བྱང *ngu byang*, but not coincidental with the original meaning of the phrase. Approach c. is merely adopted, in which ངུ་བྱང *ngu byang*, together with lang after it, constituting a verb or verbal phrase, possesses the property of a noun. When combined with a verb, the meaning of བྱང *byang* is generalized, not particularly referring to the mastery or proficiency a person has in certain aspect, but to a sort of behavioral habit. Therefore, the combination of བྱང *byang* and a verb makes for nominalized phrases in grammar. Furthermore, ལང *lang* combined with the phrase brings about a compound verb ངུ་བྱང་ལང *ngu byang lang*. Due to *lang* being a dependent verb, it shows the autonomous representation of an event. Thus, it generates the meaning of repeated actions by means of being combined with the noun V+*byang* indicating habitual actions. For example:

13. ང་ ནི་ དགུན་ཁ་   རན་པ་ དང་ ཆམ་པ་བརྒྱབ་བྱང་ལང་པོ་   ཡོད་ །
nga-ni dgun-kha ran-pa dang cham-pa-brgyab-byang-lang-po yod .
I-TOP winter   come and have a cold   ASP
When winter comes, I always have a cold.

14. རྨོ་བོ་ལགས་   ཁྱེད་རང་ གློག་བརྙན་བལྟ་   དུས་ གཉིད་ཚོག་བརྒྱབ་བྱང་ལང་པོ་   འདུག་གང་ །
rmovo-lags khyed-rang glog-brnyan-blta dus gnyid-cog-brgyab-byang-lang-po vdug gang.
old lady   you   watch-film   time doze(always represent)   ASP
The old lady dozes while seeing a film.

15. དཔལ་འབྱོར་   ནི་ འཛིན་གྲྭ་གྲོལ་བ་   དང་ གཞས་བཏང་ བྱང་ལང་པོ་   འདུག །
dpal-vbyor ni vdzin-grwa-grol-pa dang gzhas-btang byang-lang-po vdug.
dpal-vbyor TOP class-finish-NMZ   and sing(always represent)   ASP
Dpal vbyor always sings after class is finished.

The discussion above focuses on the construction, meaning and syntactic function or syntactic position of adjectives of exocentric construction in Tibetan. However, in practical texts, the identification of this category of adjectives involves diversified complicated phenomena: (1) whether it can be recognized and tagged as a whole or not; (2) whether its variants can be discriminated or not. In this respect more complicated phenomena will be explored in Sect. 3, with an aim to provide much more references for the further establishment of machine automatic identification of this category of adjectives.

3 Complicated Variants of Exocentric Construction Adjectives

The key point for identifying exocentric construction adjectives is to give prior examination on their inner structure and syntactic distribution. Apart from basic construction mentioned above $[[N_R+ADJ_R]+po_{SUF}]$, inner structure involves other variants, mainly including (1) variants of adjective affix or syntactic particles, such as ཚོ – mo_{suffix}, པ $-pa_{suffix}$/ བ $-ba_{suffix}$ or syntactic particle in comparative degree, ཤོས $shos_{syntactic particle in}$ superlative degree, ལོས $los_{modal adverb meaning "sure, certainly"}$ etc. (2) omission of suffix པོ $-po$ etc. in particular conditions. For example:

16. བ་ཚང་   གི   ཟུར   ཞིག   ཏུ   ས་དོང   གཏིང་རིང་བ ཞིག   འདྲུས །
    ba-tshang gi   zur zhig tu   sa-dong gting-ring-ba zhig vdrus
    oxer   GEN side a LOC burrow deep   a   dig
    On one side of the oxer a deep burrow is dug. (གཏིང་ རིང་བ་ gting ring ba is the modifier of ས་དོང་ sa dong)

If the inner structure of $[[N_R+ADJ_R]+po_{SUF}]$ changes, an adverbial modifier will be inserted between the noun and the adjective. This is not constituting an exocentric construction adjective. For example:

17. ཆུ་   འདི   གཏིང   ཤིན་ཏུ   རིང   བས །
    chu vdi   gting shin-tu ring   bas.
    river here depth rather   deep/long ASP

This river is rather deep. (བས་ bas is the omitted form of བ་གིས་ ba gis. See Sent. 23)

18. ཁོ ནི   ཁ   འཇམ   གཏིང   གནག་གི   མི   ཅིག རེད །
    kho ni   kha vjam gting   gnag-gi   mi   cig red.
    3sg TOP mouth gentle (heart)buttom venomous-GEN person a   is
    He is a person stainless in words but foul in deeds.

In the sentence, ཁ་འཇམ་པོ་ kha vjam po and གཏིང་གནག་པོ་ gting gnag po have the corresponding meaning of "an iron hand in a velvet glove", omitting the suffix and constituting the phrase with a possessive case marker as the preposed modifier.

19. རྫོང་   དེ   གཞིས་ཀ་རྩེ   ནས   ཐག་རིང་ལོས   ཡོག་རེད །
    rdzong de   gzhis-ka-rtse nas   thag-ring-los yog-red.
    county that gzhis-ka-rtse ABL far   ASP
    It is too far from gzhis-ka-rtse to that county.

The modal adverbial ཚོས་ *los* "certainly" usually is followed after an adjective. And then
པོ་ –*po* in རིང་པོ་ *ring po* is omitted.

20. ཁྱེད་རང་   ནི་   མི་   ཆུང་   ཁ་བདེ་   རང་   རེད །
khyed-rang ni   mi   chung kha-bde   rang red.
you-self   TOP person small mouth-sharp rather is
You are a rather base person, eloquent but without truth.

When the adverb རང་ *rang* "rather" is added after *kha bde po* "eloquent", པོ་ *po* is omitted.

21. འབྲོག་ལས་   ཡིན་ན་ བོད་ལྗོངས་ཀྱི་   དཔལ་འབྱོར་ཁྱབ་ཁོངས་   ནང་གི་
vbrog-las   yin-na bod-ljongs-kyi dpal-vbyor-khyab-khongs nang-gi
husbandry TOP Tibet-GEN   economy-field   in-GEN
གལ་ཆེ་   ཤོས་   ཀྱི་   གྲས་   ཅིག་ རེད །
gal-che   shos kyi   gras cig red
important most GEN type a   is

Husbandry is an important type in economy field of Tibet. (གལ་ཆེ་ *gal che* is modified by the
particle ཤོས་ *shos* which indicates the superlative degree)

Syntactic distribution position is estimated according to its syntactic function, mainly
involving predicate context and modifier context. Exocentric construction adjectives as predicates can be identified in accordance with predicate aspect markers at the end, and pronouns,
nouns, topic markers and other identifiable units.

22. ཡིན་ནའི་   དེང་སང་   ཡིག་ཚད་   རན་ཚང་   བྲེལ་བ་ཆེན་པོ་   བྱུང་ །
yin-navi deng-sang yig-tshad ran-tsang brel-ba-chen-po byung.
but   recently exam   should-so busy   ASP

But recently we should have an exam, so I'm busy.

In such a case, disyllabic nouns བྲེལ་བ་ *brel ba* and ཆེན་པོ་ *chen po* constitute the adjective. བྱུང་
b*yung* at the end of the sentence, whose original meaning is "occur, happen", is also
frequently-used aspect marker and here as a realization aspect marker.

23. སུང་ཅང་   གིས་ " ཁྱོད་ཀྱི་   བུ་མོ་   ཧམ་པ་ཆེ་བས་   ང་ས་   བསད་ པ་ཡིན་ " ཞེས་ བཤད །
sung-cang gis " khyod gi bu-mo   ham-pa-che-ba-s nga-s bsad pa-yin" zhes bshad.
Song-Jiang AG 2sg-GEN daughter rude-V-ASP   1sg-AG kill ASP   say

Song Jiang said, "your daughter is too rude, so she has been killed by me."
ཧམ་པ་ཆེ་བས་ *ham-pa-che-bas* acts as adjective predicate of the sentence, in which -ས་-*s* bound to
བས་ *bas* is the spoken form of durative aspect གིས་ *gis*, equal to གི་འདུག *gi vdug*, so the preceding
context is the noun བུ་མོ་ *bu mo*.

24. ཁྱེད་རང་   གི་   སྤུ་གུ་   འདི་ ནི་   ངུ་བྱང་ལང་པོ་   འདུག་   ག །
khyed-rang gi   spu-gu vdi ni   ngu-byang-lang-po vdug   ga .
you-youself-GEN child   this TOP cry(always)   ASP MOOD
This child of yours are always crying.

According to the analysis of the preceding section, ང་བྱང་ལང་པོ *ngu byang lang po* "lachrymose" on the whole is considered as an adjective, which is followed by the resultative aspect marker *vdug*, and *ni* as its preceding topic marker.

25. ཇག་པ་   དེ་ཚོ་   དེ་འདྲའི་   ཧམ་པ་ཆེ་བ་   ལ།
jag-pa de-tsho de-vdravi ham-pa-che-ba la.
bandit that-PL so-GEN audacious ASP/MOOD
That gang of bandits are so audacious.

Adjective predicate sentences in Lhasa dialect occasionally allow ལ *la* as aspect marker and mood markers to bring themselves to end.

Exocentric construction adjectives, just like conventional adjectives, usually serve as post posited modifiers. If there are multiple postpositive modifiers, they are even placed rear, such as Sentence 20. The prepositive modifiers serving as nouns are in most cases followed by possessive case markers, while they acting as adverbials are usually followed by adverbial markers. See 6-10 for relevant examples. Here more complicated cases are examined.

26. ལྡེབས་རིས   ནི   པོ་བྲང་པོ་ཏ་ལའི་   གལ་ཆེའི་   གྲུབ་ཆ   རེད།
ldebs-ris ni pho-brang-po-taa-lavi gal chevi grub-cha red .
mural TOP the Potala Palace-GEN important-GEN component is
Murals are an important component of the Potala Palace.

Tibeto-Chinese Lhasa Vernacular Dictionary collects གལ་ཆེ་ *gal che*, without tagging its part of speech (it is excluded from other dictionaries). We speculate that the addition of a possessive marker, coordinated antithesis (Sent.18), and the demands of rhythmical syllables give rise to disyllabic adjectives which are the representation of trisyllabic adjectives. However, most of them can return to the original affixes. For example, སྟོབས་ཆེན *stobs chen* and སྟོབས་ཆེན་པོ *stobs chen po* "muscular", བློ་བདེ་ *blo bde* and བློ་བདེ་པོ *blo bde po* "reassuring", are taken as the omitted forms of གལ་ཆེ་ *gal che(n) po*.

21. འབྲོག་ལས   ཡིན་ན   བོད་ལྗོངས་ཀྱི་   དཔལ་འབྱོར་ཁྱབ་ཁོངས་   ནང་གི
vbrog-las yin-na bod-ljongs-kyi dpal-vbyor-khyab-khongs nang-gi
husbandry TOP Tibet-GEN economy-field in-GEN
གལ་ཆེ་   ཤོས་   ཀྱི་   གྲས་   ཅིག་ རེད།
gal-che shos kyi gras cig red
important most GEN type a is

The original meaning of རྩི *brtsi* in the sentence is "to calculate" (with a noun as its object). Later on, it is generalized and then derived the meaning of "to plan, to intend" (with a verb as its object). In the process, the grammatical meaning of "to be going to" is generated as a result of further reduction. It is inappropriate to regard གལ་ཆེན་པོ *gal chen po* as a nominal phrase denoting "crucial moment" for the reason that གལ *gal* cannot be used independently, and that *rtsi* should be followed by a verbal object. Therefore, it is assumed that གལ་ཆེན་པོ *gal chen po* serves as an adjective after the loss of its usage as a verb. Nevertheless, in the sight of identification, the construction རྩི *rtsi*+ an aspect marker can be treated as a common verb-object construction.

28. ཁྲེལ་བ་ཚ་པོ་   ཞེ་དྲགས་   མེད་པའི་   ཅ་ལག
brel-ba-tsha-po zhe-drags med pavi   ca lag
hasty   very   notBe-NMZ-GEN stuff
མོ་ཊའི་   ནང་ ལ་   བཏང་ གི་ཡོད།
mo-tavi   nang la   btang gi yod.
motor-GEN home-LOC place ASP
The stuff, as not strictly needed, should be transported by motor.

In the sentence, after being nominalized, the predicative sentence of the adjective ཁྲེལ་བ་ཚ་པོ་ *brel ba tsha po* serves as the modifier of ཅ་ལག *ca lag*. It is somewhat complicated that there are both adverb and a negative in the phrase.

29. ཁོ་ སེར་སྣ་ ཚ་   ཚོ་   ལོས་ གང་འདྲས་ གཅིག་ ཡོག་ རེད་།
kho ser-sna tsha los gang-vdras gcig yog-red.
he miserly too   how   a have
To what extent is he too miserly.

This is an existential sentence (possession). However, we can find other abstract things with their subjects having no case marker. The adverb གང་འདྲས་ *gang vdra* "how" is postpositioned to modify the adjective ཚ་ཚོས་ *tsha los*. Then the whole phrase modifies the noun སེར་སྣ་ *ser sna*. In other words, སེར་སྣ་ཚ་ཚོས་ *ser sna tsha los* does not a constitute exocentric construction adjective.

30. བུ་མོ་   རྒན་པ་   ནི་   ལོ་   བཅུ་བཞི་ར་   སླེབས་ ཙམ་   ཡིན་ ཡང་
bu-mo rgan-pa ni lo bcu-bzhi-r   slebs tsam yin yang
girl   older TOP year ten-four-LOC arrive about likewise
རྒན་བཟོ་དོད་པོ་   ཞིག་ ཆགས་   ཡོད།
rgan-bzo-dod-po zhig chags   yod.
old-age   a appear ASP
The older girls about fourteen years old appear to be old age likewise.

In the light of the revision of many dictionaries, རྒན་ *rgan* does not constitute a disyllabic word with བཟོ་ *bzo*, and therefore cannot be regarded as being modified by དོད་པོ་ *dod po* (in general cases, བཟོ་དོད་པོ་ *bzo dod po* is excluded from dictionaries). རྒན་བཟོ་དོད་པོ་ *rgan bzo dod po* "old age, senescence" is included as an adjective in both *Tibeto-Chinese* and *Lhasa* dictionaries. Thus, there is a paradox in such a sentence, for if the word རྒན་བཟོ་དོད་པོ་ *rgan bzo dod po* serves as a predicate, then ཆགས་ཡོད་ *chags yod* has to be taken as a form of special predicate sentence ending. Furthermore, it is imperfect if ཞིག་ *zhig* serves as an adverb or a numeral, and certainly complicated when it is spoken in practical expressions.

4 Conclusion

Exocentric construction adjectives, in practice, came out in Tibetan at earlier times. Because of the ambiguous existence of nominal phrases and adjectivization, they are discriminated from other constructions. The well-known Tibetan historical document *Ba Xie* (written in the 8th century or the 11th century) records such a construction in many places. Hereby is an example below:

31. ཚོད་ཀྱི་   བསོད་ནམས་ ཉམས་པ་ དང་ འདྲེ་སྲིན་ ཀུན་ མགོ་རྒོད་པ་ས།

bod kyi   bsod-nams nyams-pa dang vdre-srin kun mgo-rgod-pa-s,

Tibetan-GEN welfare   decay   and demon all   head undomesticated

མི་   ནག་པོ་ ཀུན་གྱི་ གློ་བ་ ར་   གསོལ་ནས།

mi   nag-po kun gyi glo-ba ra   gsol nas.

person black all-GEN hearts LOC accept

Tibetan's Buddhism decays and demons who are rampant recklessly perplex numerous persons fond of the wicked industry. (*Ba Xie*)

In the context of the sentence, མགོ་རྒོད་པ་ *mgo rgod pa(po)* should be clearly analyzed as an adjective predicate, parallel with the verb ཉམས་པ་ *nymas pa*, in which ⁻ས་ *–s* is the predicate ending, meaning "barbarous and unruly". If we analyze such a construction independently, the ambiguity is indeed in existence. For example, མགོ་གྲུང་པོ་ *mgo grung po* can be interpreted as a nominal phrase "brilliant brain" or as an exocentric construction adjective "intelligent". The latter, hence, can modify any other nouns: མི་མགོ་གྲུང་པོ་ *mi mgo grung po* "an intelligent person".

This paper discusses the machine automatic identification and the tagging of linguistic phenomena aiming to provide references for further studies. It will also practically enlighten the compiling of Tibetan dictionaries, language teaching and learning, and Tibetan translation. It is especially worthy of notice that exocentric construction adjectives can be taken as an independent unit and thus established as a standard of the identification of particles. By far, Guan Bai, in his discussion, has mentioned this phenomenon as a particle unit, which are called compounds of a noun + an adjective with transferred meanings [9]. For example, གནམ་སྔོན་པོ་ *gnam sngon po* "blue sky" is a phrase. However, when the meaning is as a metephor transferred, it is used as a folk oath "testimony by God" (simply included in *Tibeto-Chinese Dictionary* as "gnam dpan du vdzugs pavi mnav tshig cig" As God as my witness). Here, "blue sky" is transferred to "God", distinctly different from གནམ་དྭངས་པོ་ *gnam dwangs po* "sunny day". In this connection, we do hope that the discussion will draw the continuous exploration of this linguistic phenomenon in academic circle so as to deepen ontological studies on Tibetan grammar.

Acknowledgments. This work was supported by the National Natural Science Fundation of China(31271337, 61132009) and the National Social Science Foundation of China(12&ZD174). Many thanks to Dr. Long CJ, and Dr. Li ML, who take much time to discuss the data with me. And thanks to Prof. Dong XF for her help on linguistic theory.

References

1. Dong, X.F.: Lexicalization: the origin and evolution of Chinese disyllabic words(Revised Edition). The Commercial Press, Beijing (2011)
2. Song, Z.Y.: The latest developments of generative lexicon theory. J. Lang. **44**, 1–14 (2011). The Commercial Press, Beijing
3. Fabb, N.: Compounding. The Handbook of Morphology. In: Spencer, A., Zwicky, A. (eds.) Oxford, pp. 66–83 18 (1998)
4. Pustejovsky, J.: Pierrette Bouillon, Hitoshi Isahara, Kyoko Kanzaki, Chungmin Lee.: Advances in Generative Lexicon Theory. Springer, Heidelberg(2013)

5. Liu, DQ.: An approach framework of adjectives and adjective phrases. Minzuyuwen vol. 5, 28–38 (2005)
6. Jiang, D., Hu, H.Y.: The construction and identification approaches of adjectival predicate in modern Tibetan. Stud. Lang. Linguist. **2**, 115–122 (2005)
7. Jiang, D.: Aspect, evidentiality and egocentricity in Lhasa Tibetan. Linguist. Sci. **4**(1), 70–88 (2005)
8. Zhou, J.W., Xie, H.F.: A grammar of Lhasa Tibetan language. Minzu Press, Beijing (2003)
9. Guan, B. (དཀོན་རྗེ dkon bhe): Research on the segmentation unit of Tibetan word for information processing. J. Chin. Inf. Proces. **24**(3), 124–128 (2010)

Mongolian Speech Recognition Based on Deep Neural Networks

Hui Zhang, Feilong Bao$^{(\boxtimes)}$, and Guanglai Gao

College of Computer Science, Inner Mongolia University, Hohhot 010021, China
alzhu.san@163.com, {csfeilong,csggl}@imu.edu.cn

Abstract. Mongolian is an influential language. And better Mongolian Large Vocabulary Continuous Speech Recognition (LVCSR) systems are required. Recently, the research of speech recognition has achieved a big improvement by introducing the Deep Neural Networks (DNNs). In this study, a DNN-based Mongolian LVCSR system is built. Experimental results show that the DNN-based models outperform the conventional models which based on Gaussian Mixture Models (GMMs) for the Mongolian speech recognition, by a large margin. Compared with the best GMM-based model, the DNN-based one obtains a relative improvement over 50 %. And it becomes a new state-of-the-art system in this field.

Keywords: Mongolian · Deep Neural Networks (DNNs) · Gaussian Mixture Models (GMMs) · N-gram language model

1 Introduction

More than 7000 living languages are spoken in the world today [1]. However, Automatic Speech Recognition (ASR) systems have been built only for a small number of major languages, such as English, Chinese, Spanish and Arabic. Most other languages are virgin territory for the ASR research. Mongolian is one of the less studied languages for speech recognition.

Mongolian language is used mainly in Mongolia, parts of China (Inner Mongolia, Uugar), Russia (Buryat, Khalmyc) and their neighboring areas. Today, about 6 million people speak Mongolian [1]. There are two written systems in Mongolian language: (1) Traditional Mongolian scripts are used mainly in Inner Mongolia of China. (2) Cyrillic scripts are used mainly in Mongolia. A word can be written in both of the two scripts, and its pronunciation does not change. In this study, we focus on Traditional Mongolian. In Traditional Mongolian, the relationship between grapheme and phoneme is complex. Phonemes may insert, loss or vary during pronouncing. Furthermore, Mongolian has a very large vocabulary. Since it is an agglutinative language, new words can be formed by combining stem with a lot of optional suffixes. These make speech recognition for Mongolian difficult.

© Springer International Publishing Switzerland 2015
M. Sun et al. (Eds.): CCL and NLP-NABD 2015, LNAI 9427, pp. 180–188, 2015.
DOI: 10.1007/978-3-319-25816-4_15

The speech recognition research for Mongolian starts at 2003 in China [2–5], and it is just getting started in Mongolia [6]. All of these studies have achieved some success by employing the sophisticated speech recognition models which are the Gaussian Mixture Models and Hidden Markov Models (GMM-HMM). Recently, researchers have made a breakthrough on the ASR by introducing the Deep Neural Networks (DNNs) into this field. New DNN-HMM models are utilized in the ASR systems. The new models have been shown to outperform GMM-HMM models on a variety of speech recognition benchmarks, sometimes by a large margin [7]. In this study, we bring the success of DNN-HMM into the Mongolian ASR research, and build a Mongolian Large Vocabulary Continuous Speech Recognition (LVCSR) system. Experimental results show the DNN-HMM-based system outperforms the GMM-HMM-based one by a large margin.

The rest of the paper is organized as follows. In the next section, we present an overview of the Mongolian speech recognition framework. The experiments and results are presented in Sect. 3. And we conclude the paper in Sect. 4. In the last section, we list the future works.

2   Mongolian Speech Recognition Framework

In this study, we build a LVCSR system for Mongolian. The framework is shown in Fig. 1. Speech recognition is the translation of spoken words into text. We split the whole task into some steps. Each step recognizes some level of units in the speech. Specifically, we first recognize the phonemes, then use the recognized phonemes to make up words, finally output the recognized text.

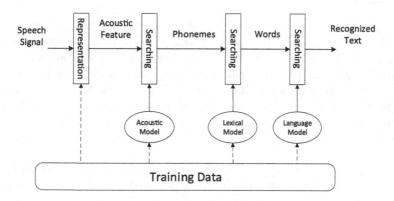

Fig. 1. Speech recognition framework

The entire processing can be split into two stages, the representation stage and the searching stage.

2.1 Representation

In the GMM-HMM-based ASR systems, the speech signal is typically represented by the Mel-Frequency Cepstral Coefficients (MFCCs) [8] computed from the raw waveform. And the MFCCs usually are concatenated with their first and second order temporal differences to get some dynamic properties [9]. MFCC is designed to discard the large amount of information in waveforms that is considered to be irrelevant for recognition and to express the remaining more useful information.

But in DNN-HMM-based ASR systems, the Fourier-transform-based log filter-bank (fbank) coefficients outperform the MFCCs [10], because fbank remains more information. Compared with the MFCCs, the fbank are strongly correlated. Modeling fbank with GMM is computationally expensive. Therefore conventional ASR systems use the MFCCs rather than the fbank.

Both the MFCCs and the fbank are nonadaptive. We can also employ some acoustic feature adaptations by utilizing the training data. Linear Discriminant Analysis (LDA) is one of such methods. LDA transform the raw feature into a new one which facilitates discrimination by supervised training. And $f$eature space Maximum Likelihood Linear Regression (fMLLR) [11] is another feature adaptation method but focuses on speaker adaptation, which aimed to eliminate the mismatch caused by the difference of speakers.

In this study, we use MFCCs for GMM-HMM-based system and fbank coefficients for the DNN-HMM-based system. The MFCCs contains 23 coefficients together with their first and second order temporal differences. The fbank feature contains 40 coefficients (and energy) distributed on a mel-scale. The LDA and fMLLR are also applied.

2.2 Searching

After getting the acoustic feature, the problem left to the ASR system is searching for the most optimal answer: the text which is most probable to generates the input acoustic feature. It can be implemented by dynamic programming, such as the Viterbi algorithm [12]. And pruning techniques are usually used to accelerate the searching. The most important task in this stage is modeling the probability of the text generates the input acoustic feature, $p(acoustic\_feature|text)$. To make the task easier, we decompose it into a series steps, and model the probability by a series individual models, which are acoustic models, lexical models and languages models.

The acoustic model models the relationship between the acoustic features and phonemes. Usually, a GMM-HMM or a DNN-HMM model is used here. The lexical model models the relationship between the phonemes and the words. It is a pronouncing dictionary or some grapheme-to-phoneme models. The language model assigns a probability to a sequence of words. High probability indicates the sequence is more likely to occur in the language. The language model provides context to distinguish between words and phrases that sound similar. The language model is usually implemented in a N-gram fashion which models the probability of a word occurs in a context of $N - 1$ words.

2.3   Acoustic Model Based on GMM-HMM

Acoustic model is the fundamental component of the ASR system. The GMM-HMM-based acoustic model achieves its great success in ASR, since the introduction of the expectation-maximization (EM) algorithm for joint training of GMMs and HMMs. The GMMs give acoustic feature a score which indicates the probability of the acoustic feature is generated by a HMM state. Then the scores are used in HMM to decode the input into phonemes. Despite the success of the GMM-HMM models, GMMs have some shortcomings, especially on the modeling efficiencies. While, a discriminative model, like DNN, can do better.

2.4   Acoustic Model Based on DNN-HMM

Deep Neural Network (DNN) is an artificial neural network with multiple hidden layers between the input and output layers. DNN is a powerful classifier, and has shown its strength in the speech recognition [7], object recognition [13], natural language understanding [14], and so forth.

In the ASR research, DNN is used as an alternative of the GMM. It assigns scores for each acoustic feature to HMM states. Those scores are then used for HMM decoding. A DNN-based acoustic model is shown in Fig. 2. The input of the DNN is a window of frames of real-valued acoustic coefficients. And the output layer is a softmax layer that contains one unit for each possible state of each HMM. The DNN is trained to predict the HMM state corresponding to the central frame of the input window. These targets are obtained by using a baseline GMM-HMM system to produce a forced alignment.

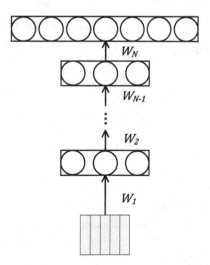

Fig. 2. DNN-based acoustic model.

3   Experiments and Results

We implement the Mongolian LVCSR system based on the Kaldi speech recognition toolkit [15] and use the SRI Language Modeling Toolkit (SRILM) [16] to train the language model.

3.1   Dataset

We build a Mongolian speech corpus which contains about 78 hours recordings. The material includes Mongolian dialogues, Mongolian news and articles from Mongolian text books of junior school. The corpus involves 193 speakers, in which there are 110 male speakers and 83 female speakers. The corpus is divided into training set and test set randomly, where the test set is about 10 % of the whole corpus. There are no overlap between the training and test set.

We also build a Mongolian text corpus for language model training. This corpus is a collection of Mongolian web pages, which contains about 85 million tokens.

A pronouncing dictionary is built based on widely used Mongolian dictionaries. It contains about 40,000 items which cover a variety of daily used Mongolian words. And the pronunciation is described with 63 phonemes which include 37 vowels and 26 consonants as listed in Table 1.

Table 1. Mongolian phonemes.

Vowels	Consonants
ɑ ə ɪ ɪ ɔ ʊ o u æ œ ɣ ɑː əː ɪː iː ɔː ʊː oː uː æː eː œː ă ĕ ĭ ĭ ŏ ŏ ʊɪ ui ʊæ ue ʊɑ y ʅ ʅ ɚ	b p w m s d t l r ʤ ʧ ʃ ʝ g x ŋ f k x ɬ ʥ ts dʐ tʂ ʂ ʐ

3.2   Models

We follow an iterative training scheme, and train a series of models. The latter models are trained based on the alignment of the former models. The dependence relationships among the models are illustrated in Fig. 3.

The name of models start with a description of model, then a level index, and end up with a letter to distinguish the models. The configurations of each model are introduced as follows.

mono1 is a mono-phone model based on GMM-HMM. The feature used here is MFCC with its first and second order temporal difference. Training starts with an equally spaced alignment.

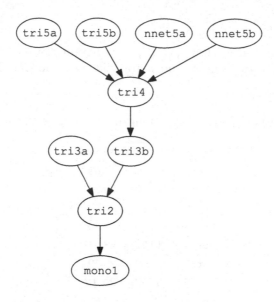

Fig. 3. Dependence relationships among the models. The arrows point to the model, which provides alignment results.

tri2 is a cross-word tri-phone model based on GMM-HMM. tri2 is trained based on the alignment of mono1. And the feature is same as the mono1.

tri3a is same as tri2, but is trained based on the alignment of tri2.
tri3b is same as tri3a, but apply a speaker adaptation using fMLLR.
tri4 is same as tri3b, but is trained based on the alignment of tri3b.
tri5a is same as tri4, but is trained based on the alignment of tri4.
tri5b is same as tri5a, but used 40-D LDA feature based on the MFCC.

nnet5a is a tri-phone model based on DNN-HMM. The model is trained based on the alignment of tri4. This model uses 40-D fbank feature with a context window of 9 frames (the preceding 4 frames and the following 4 frames). Then the features are converted into 360-D by LDA. The DNN is composed of 1 tanh hidden layer, which contains 1024 nodes. The output transformation is softmax. There are approximately 3.7 million trainable parameters in the DNN.

nnet5b is also a tri-phone model based on DNN-HMM. But the DNN in nnet5b is much larger than the one in nnet5a. This model uses 40-D fbank feature with a context window of 15 frames (the preceding 7 frames and the following 7 frames). Then the features are converted into 900-D by LDA. The DNN is composed of 6 tanh hidden layers, in which the former 3 layers contain 3762 nodes in each layer and the latter 3 layers contain 1536 nodes in each layer. There are about 50 million trainable parameters in the DNN.

3.3 Evaluation

We employ the Word Error Rate (WER) as the evaluation metric and generate decode results with the 2-gram and 3-gram language model. The results are listed in Table 2.

Table 2. Performances of different models: %WERs.

Model	2-gram	3-gram
mono1	69.71	57.65
tri2	41.69	29.22
tri3a	38.87	27.46
tri3b	36.10	25.40
tri4	40.22	28.24
tri5a	36.32	25.79
tri5b	**35.46**	**25.12**
nnet5a	19.01	13.82
nnet5b	**16.47**	**12.37**

From Table 2, as we expected, we see DNN-HMM-based models outperform the GMM-HMM-based ones. And the 3-gram language model is better than the 2-gram language model. For 2-gram language model, the best DNN-HMM-based model achieves a relative improvement of 53.55 % compared with the best GMM-HMM-based model. And for 3-gram language model, the relative improvement is 50.76 %.

The improvement comes from three factors. (1) The fbank is better than MFCC when modeling by DNN. (2) The input context of DNN is larger than that in GMM. (3) DNN is more powerful than GMM.

4 Conclusion

In this study, we introduce the DNN-HMM models into the Mongolian speech recognition. The new ASR system achieves significant performance gains as in other languages in previous works [7]. It obtains word correct recognition rate of 87.63 % in the test set. As far as we know, the DNN-HMM-based Mongolian ASR system becomes the state-of-the-art one in this field.

5 Future Works

We plan to build a practical Mongolian LVCSR system. This paper is just an initial report of this long term project. There are some works to do in the future.

(1) In this study, we only deal with Traditional Mongolian. And Cyrillic Mongolian should also be taken into consideration. Some conversion systems have been proposed [17,18] to convert Traditional to Cyrillic Mongolian and vice versa. With those conversion systems, the recognized results can be output in any written systems.

(2) Mongolian has a very large vocabulary. Although the pronouncing dictionary used in this study covers the frequently-used Mongolian, the vocabulary should be expanded for a wider range of application. And [5] proposes a segmentation-based method, which seems a promising way to combat the large vocabulary problem.

(3) Recurrent Neural Network (RNN) is used more frequently in ASR now [19–22]. We plan to explore its power both in the language model and the acoustic model.

Acknowledgements. This research was supported in part by the China national nature science foundation (No.61263037), Inner Mongolia nature science foundation (No. 2014BS0604) and the program of high-level talents of Inner Mongolia University.

References

1. Lewis, M.P., Simons, G.F., Fennig, C.D.: Ethnologue: Languages of the World, 18th edn. Sil International, Dallas, TX (2015). http://www.ethnologue.com
2. Gao, G., Biligetu, Nabuqing, Zhang, S.: A mongolian speech recognition system based on HMM. In: Huang, D.-S., Li, K., Irwin, G.W. (eds.) ICIC 2006. LNCS (LNAI), vol. 4114, pp. 667–676. Springer, Heidelberg (2006)
3. Qilao, H., Gao, G.: Researching of speech recognition oriented mongolian acoustic model. In: Chinese Conference on Pattern Recognition, CCPR 2008, pp. 406–411. IEEE (2008)
4. Bao, F., Gao, G.: Improving of acoustic model for the mongolian speech recognition system. In: Chinese Conference on Pattern Recognition, CCPR 2009, pp. 616–620. IEEE (2009)
5. Bao, F., Gao, G., Yan, X., Wang, W.: Segmentation-based mongolian LVCSR approach. In: 2013 IEEE International Conference on Acoustics, Speech and Signal Processing (ICASSP), pp. pp. 8136–8139. IEEE (2013)
6. Ayush, A., Damdinsuren, B.: A design and implementation of HMM based mongolian speech recognition system. In: 2013 8th International Forum on Strategic Technology (IFOST), vol. 2, pp. 341–344, June 2013
7. Hinton, G., Deng, L., Yu, D., Dahl, G.E., Mohamed, A.-R., Jaitly, N., Senior, A., Vanhoucke, V., Nguyen, P., Sainath, T.N., et al.: Deep neural networks for acoustic modeling in speech recognition: The shared views of four research groups. IEEE Signal Process. Mag. **29**(6), 82–97 (2012)
8. Davis, S., Mermelstein, P.: Comparison of parametric representations for monosyllabic word recognition in continuously spoken sentences. IEEE Trans. Acoust. Speech Signal Process. **28**(4), 357–366 (1980)
9. Furui, S.: Cepstral analysis technique for automatic speaker verification. IEEE Trans. Acoust. Speech Signal Process. **29**(2), 254–272 (1981)

10. Mohamed, A.-R., Hinton, G., Penn, G.: Understanding how deep belief networks perform acoustic modelling. In: 2012 IEEE International Conference on Acoustics, Speech and Signal Processing (ICASSP), pp. 4273–4276. IEEE (2012)
11. Gales, M.J.: Maximum likelihood linear transformations for HMM-based speech recognition. Comput. Speech Lang. **12**(2), 75–98 (1998)
12. Forney Jr., G.D.: The viterbi algorithm. Proc. IEEE **61**(3), 268–278 (1973)
13. Krizhevsky, A., Sutskever, I., Hinton, G.E.: Imagenet classification with deep convolutional neural networks. In: Advances in Neural Information Processing Systems, pp. 1097–1105 (2012)
14. Bengio, Y., Schwenk, H., Senécal, J.-S., Morin, F., Gauvain, J.-L.: Neural probabilistic language models. In: Holmes, D.E., Jain, L.C. (eds.) Innovations in Machine Learning, pp. 137–186. Springer, Heidelberg (2006)
15. Povey, D., Ghoshal, A., Boulianne, G., Burget, L., Glembek, O., Goel, N., Hannemann, M., Motlíček, P., Qian, Y., Schwarz, P., et al.: The Kaldi speech recognition toolkit (2011)
16. Stolcke, A., et al.: SRILM-an extensible language modeling toolkit. In: INTERSPEECH (2002)
17. Bao, F., Gao, G., Yan, X., Wang, H.: Language model for cyrillic mongolian to traditional mongolian conversion. In: Zhou, G., Li, J., Zhao, D., Feng, Y. (eds.) NLPCC 2013. CCIS, vol. 400, pp. 13–18. Springer, Heidelberg (2013)
18. Bao, F., Gao, G., Yan, X., Wei, H.: Research on conversion approach between traditional mongolian and cyrillic mongolian. Comput. Eng. Appl. **2014**(23), 206–211 (2014)
19. Mikolov, T., Karafiát, M., Burget, L., Cernocký, J., Khudanpur, S.: Recurrent neural network based language model. Annual Conference of the International Speech Communication Association (INTERSPEECH), pp. 1045–1048 (2010)
20. Sundermeyer, M., Oparin, I., Gauvain, J.L., Freiberg, B., Schlüter, R., Ney, H.: Comparison of feedforward and recurrent neural network language models. IEEE International Conference on Acoustics, Speech and Signal Processing (ICASSP), pp. 8430–8434 (2013)
21. Hannun, A., Case, C., Casper, J., Catanzaro, B., Diamos, G., Elsen, E., Prenger, R., Satheesh, S., Sengupta, S., Coates, A., et al.: Deepspeech: Scaling up end-to-end speech recognition (2014). arXiv preprint arXiv:1412.5567
22. Chan, W., Lane, I.: Deep recurrent neural networks for acoustic modelling (2015). arXiv preprint arXiv:1504.01482

Tibetan Word Segmentation as Sub-syllable Tagging with Syllable's Part-of-Speech Property

Huidan Liu[1]([⊠]), Congjun Long[1,2], Minghua Nuo[1], and Jian Wu[1]

[1] Institute of Software, Chinese Academy of Sciences, Beijing 100190, China
huidan@iscas.ac.cn
[2] Institute of Ethnology and Anthropology, Chinese Academy of Social Sciences, Beijing 100081, China

Abstract. When Tibetan word segmentation task is taken as a sequence labelling problem, machine learning models such as ME and CRFs can be used to train the segmenter. The performance of the segmenter is related to many factors. In the paper, three factors, namely strategy on abbreviated syllables, tag set, and the syllable's Part-Of-Speech property, are compared. Experiment data show that: first, if each abbreviate syllable is separated into two units for labelling rather than one, the F-measure improves 0.06 % and 0.10 % on 4-tag set and 6-tag set respectively. Second, if 6-tag set is used rather than 4-tag set, the F-measure improves 0.10 % and 0.14 % on the two strategies on abbreviated syllables respectively. Third, when the syllable's Part-Of-Speech property is take into account, F-measure improves 0.47 % and 0.41 % respectively than the other two methods without using it on 4-tag set, while it improves 0.45 % and 0.35 % on 6-tag set, which is much more higher than the former improvements. So it's a better choice to take advantage of the syllable's Part-Of-Speech property information while using the sub-syllable as the tag unit.

Keywords: Tibetan word segmentation · Tibetan · Sub-syllable tagging · CRFs · Syllable's POS property

1 Introduction

Tibetan text is written without natural word delimiters, so word segmentation is an essential, fundamental and foremost step in Tibetan language processing. In recent years, people take Tibetan word segmentation as a sequence labelling problem and use machine learning models to train a word position tagger for it. However, as there are many abbreviated syllables in Tibetan text, and abbreviation exists in nearly all Tibetan sentences. It's still a not thoroughly solved task to recognize whether a syllable is abbreviated in a certain sentence. Thus, it's a problem to find which tagging unit is the best for Tibetan when taking the word segmentation task as a sequence labelling problem.

In this paper, we compare the influence of different tagging methods to the performance of word segmenter. The paper is organized as follows: In Sect. 2 we

M. Sun et al. (Eds.): CCL and NLP-NABD 2015, LNAI 9427, pp. 189–201, 2015.
DOI: 10.1007/978-3-319-25816-4_16

recall related work on Tibetan word segmentation. In Sect. 3, we simply introduce the concept of Tibetan syllable and abbreviated syllable. We explain different approaches which take syllable and sub-syllable as the tagging unit respectively or with syllable's POS property in Sect. 4. Then, in Sect. 5 we make experiments to compare the performances of those approaches. Section 6 concludes the paper.

2   Related Work

In this section, we recall the research history and current situation on Tibetan word segmentation. As Tibetan script is also used to write Dzongkha language, Dzongkha word segmentation related work is also included.

Jiang analysed the problems existing in Tibetan word segmentation in last century, including which word should be included in the dictionary [14]. Zhaxiciren designed and implemented a machine assisted Tibetan word segmentation and new word registration system [40]. However, Jiang thinks it's not an applicable system [14]. Chen *et al.* proposed a method based on case auxiliary words and continuous features to segment Tibetan text [6–8]. As grammar rules are used, the method is very general and can be used in different domains [6–8]. Caizhijie designed and implemented the Banzhida Tibetan word segmentation system based on Chen's method, using reinstallation rules to identify the abbreviated words (syllables) [2,4,5]. Qi proposed a three level method to segment Tibetan text [26]. Sun *et al.* researched Tibetan Automatic Segmentation Scheme and disambiguation method of overlapping ambiguity in Tibetan word segmentation [30–33]. Dolha *et al.*, Zhaxijia *et al.*, Cairangjia, Gyal and Zhujie made researches on the word categories and annotation scheme for Tibetan corpus and the part-of-speech tagging set standards [1,10,12,41]. Liu proposed a rule based method to process identify Tibetan numbers [21], which is a post procedure of Tibetan word segmentation. Norbu *et al.* described the initial effort in segmenting the Dzongkha scripts [24]. They proposed an approach of Maximal Matching followed by bigram techniques. Experiment shows that it achieves an overall accuracy of 91.5 % on all 8 corpora in different domains [24]. Chungku *et al.* described the application of probabilistic part-of-speech taggers to the Dzongkha language, and proposed a tag set containing 66 tags which is applied to annotate their Dzongkha corpus [9].

Before 2010, people mainly use maximum matching method based on dictionary in Tibetan word segmentation [3,4,6,8,32,33] accompanying with some grammar rules sometimes. Meanwhile, machine learning models which are used in Chinese word segmentation, such as HMM, ME, CRFs, are widely used in Chinese word segmentation task.

Xue reformulated Chinese word segmentation as a tagging problem [35–37], which is a reform of Chinese word segmentation. The approach uses the maximum entropy tagger to label each Chinese character with a word-internal position tag, and then combines characters into word according to their tags. Ng and Low used the same method in their segmenter [22,23]. Peng *et al.* first used the CRFs for Chinese word segmentation by treating it as a binary decision task, such that each character is labeled either as the beginning of a word or the continuation of one [25]. Tseng *et al.* presented a Chinese word segmentation system submitted to the closed track of Sighan bakeoff 2005 [34]. This segmenter uses a conditional random field sequence model which provides a framework to use a large number of linguistic features such as character identity, morphological and character reduplication features [34]. In the two International Chinese Word Segmentation Bake-offs held in 2003 and 2005, character based tagging methods using machine learning models quickly rose in two Bakeoffs as a remarkable one with state-of-the-art performance [11,28]. Especially, two participants, Ng and Tseng gave the best results in almost all test corpora [22,23,34].

Tibetan researchers draw inspiration from the methods of Chinese word segmentation by character tagging after 2010, and begin to use machine learning models in Tibetan word segmentation.

Shi ported the Chinese word segmentation system named Segtag to Tibetan word segmentation task and got the Yangjin system in which the Hidden Markov Model (HMM) is used. They get 91 % precision on a test set including 25 KB text [27]. Jiang used the Conditional Random Fields (CRFs) model with 4 tags (BMES), 10 basic features and 2 additional features to train the word position tagger on a training set including 2500 sentences. He got a 93.5 % precision on a test set including 225 sentences. It also showed that the method is better than the maximum matching method [15]. Liu trained a word position tagger for Tibetan with CRFs on a training set including 131903 sentences which are generated by another rule based word segmenter [19,20] and got a 95.12 % F-measure precision. He also compared the influence of different tag sets to the performance the segmenter. In Liu's method, two additional tag are used to label abbreviated syllables. Li implemented a Tibetan word segmentation system with CRFs and compared the influence of tag sets (tagging units actually) and different processing strategies of the abbreviated syllable recognition [18]. Sun proposed a discriminative model based approach for Tibetan word segmentation. He compared the influence of different word-formation units to the performance, and found syllable is the best unit [29]. He compared different machine learning models, namely CRFs, Maximum Entropy (ME) and Max-Margin Markov Networks (M^3N), and found CRFs is the best one, which get a F1-measure of 94.33 % [13].

Generally speaking, when machine learning models such as ME and CRFs are used to train a Tibetan word segmenter. The performance of the segmenter is related to many factors. In the paper, we will compare the influence of three factors, namely strategy on abbreviated syllables, tag set, and the syllable's Part-Of-Speech property.

3   Tibetan Syllable and Abbreviated Syllable

3.1   Tibetan Syllable

The Tibetan alphabet is syllabic, like many of the alphabets of India and South East Asia. A syllable contains one or up to seven character(s). Syllables are separated by a marker known as "tsheg", which is simply a superscripted dot.

192   H. Liu et al.

Linguistic words are made up of one or more syllables and are also separated by the same symbol, "tsheg", thus there is a lack of word boundaries in the language. Consonant clusters are written with special conjunct letters. Figure 1 shows the structure of a Tibetan word which is made up of two syllables and means "show" or "exhibition".

Fig. 1. Structure of a Tibetan word.

Tibetan sentence contains one or more phrase(s), which contain one or more words. Another marker known as "shed" indicates the sentence boundary, which looks like a vertical pipe. (a) shows a Tibetan sentence and (b) is its translation.

(a) ང་ཚོས་སྤྱི་ཚོགས་རིང་ལུགས་ཀྱི་སྤྱི་ལ་དབང་བའི་ལས་ལུགས་དང་ཆོལ་ བསྟུན་ཐོབ་སྟོད་ཀྱི་རྩ་དོན་མཐའ་འཁྱོངས་ བྱས་ཡོད།

(b) We have always followed the principles of socialist public ownership and distribution according to work.

3.2   Abbreviated Syllables

In Tibetan text, some words, including " འི ", " ས ", " ར ", " འང ", " འམ ", " འོ " (We call them abbreviation marker (AM) in this paper), can glue to the previous word without a syllable delimiter "tsheg", which produce many abbreviated syllables.

For example, when the genitive case word " འི " follows the word " རྒྱལ་པོ " (king), we don't put a "tsheg" between them and get the fused form " རྒྱལ་པོའི " (king[+genitive], king's), in which " པོའི" is an abbreiated syllable. When the ergative case word " ས" follows the word " ང་ཚོ" (we), it forms " ང་ཚོས" (we[+ ergative]), in which " ཚོས" is an abbreviated syllable. In the above two examples, either abbreviated syllable should be broken into two parts while segmenting, and the left part has to be combined with the previous syllable(s) to form a word, while the right part is a 1-syllable word. In addition, the word before the AM can be 1-syllable word. For instance, if " འི " follows " ང " (I), it forms " ངའི་ " (I [+genitive], my), and the abbreviated syllable should be broken into two 1-syllable words. Table 1 shows more examples.

Table 1. Examples of Tibetan abbreviated syllables. When Tibetan words are followed by one of the abbreviation markers, the suffix letter /a/ (if any) and the tsheg may be omitted.

word	AM	result	explanation
ད་	ས་	དས་	Tsheg is omitted.
གལ་ཆེ་	འི་	གལ་ཆེའི་	Tsheg is omitted.
གོ་	འང་	གོའང་	Tsheg is omitted.
རྫ་བ་	འམ་	རྫ་བའམ་	Tsheg is omitted.
སུ་	འམ་	སུའམ་	Tsheg is omitted.
དབང་པོ་ལྷ་	འོ་	དབང་པོ་ལྷའོ་	Tsheg is omitted.
སུ་མཐའ་	འི་	སུ་མཐའི་	འ (/a/) and tsheg are omitted.
ནམ་མཁའ་	འི་	ནམ་མཁའི་	འ (/a/) and tsheg are omitted.
བཤད་པ་	ར་	བཤད་པར་	Tsheg is omitted.
རྒྱལ་པོ་	འི་	རྒྱལ་པོའི་	Tsheg is omitted.

4 Different Methods

4.1 Method 1: Syllable as the Tagging Unit

The idea of word segmentation as tagging assigns a tag to each unit, namely B (Begin), M (Middle), E (End) and S (Single), according to its position in the word in a certain context. The rules are as follow:

- It's tagged B if it's the left boundary of a word.
- It's tagged M if it's at middle of a word.
- It's tagged E if it's the right boundary of a word.
- It's tagged S if it's a word by itself.

Tags are used to combine the tag units into words in the subsequent procedures. As presented in Sect. 3.2, Abbreviated syllable should be broken into two parts, thus Liu [19] used another two tags ES (End and Single) and SS (Single and Single). Kang [16] used the same strategy. The rules to use the two additional tags are as follow:

- It's tagged ES if it comes from a multiple-syllable word and an AM.
- It's tagged SS if it comes from a single-syllable word and an AM.

Using the above tags, the Tibetan sentence in (a) can be tagged as (c), and the segmentation result is (d):

(c) ར་/B ཚོས་/ES སྐྱི་/B ཚོགས་/M རིང་/M ལུགས་/E ཀྱི་/S སྐྱི་/B ལ་/M དབང་/M བའི་/M
ལམ་/M ལུགས་/E དང་/S ཆོས་/S བརྩན་/S ཐོབ་/S སྲིད་/S ཀྱི་/S རུ་/B དོན་/E མཐར་/B
འཁྱེར་/E བྱས་/S ཡོད/S །/S

(d) དཀྱ/ ས་/ སྐྱི་ཚོགས་རིང་ལུགས་/ ཀྱི་/ སྐྱི་ལ་དབང་བའི་ལམ་ ལུགས་/ དང་/ ཆོས་/ བརྩན་/ ཐོབ་/ སྲིད་/ ཀྱི་/
རུ་དོན་/ མཐར་འཁྱེར་/ བྱས་/ ཡོད/ །/

Model Training Stage: When Tibetan word segmentation corpus is being converted into training format, abbreviation marks are combined with the former syllable to form an abbreviated syllable, and get the tag ES or SS. All other syllables, which have an abbreviated mark at the tail but aren't abbreviated syllables actually, will get the tag B, M, E or S. Thus, the model is able to make the disambiguation.

Model Applying Stage: In the method, as each unit will have a tsheg with it, when applying the model, Tibetan text are segmented into syllables by tshegs. Then, the model assigns each syllable a tag. Syllables are combined into words according to their tags and meanwhile abbreviated syllables are segmented into tow syllables.

4.2   Method 2: Sub-syllable as the Tagging Unit

As abbreviation marks plays an important role in Tibetan text, they provide much clearer informations to the tagger than those abbreviated syllables. Thus if abbreviation marks are taken as the tag units, more context information will be provided to the model. We call this method "sub-syllable as the tagging unit", because syllables which have an abbreviation mark as suffix will be segmented into two units. So the unit is smaller than a syllable actually. Using the method, the above mentioned Tibetan sentence will be tagged as follow:

(e) ར་/B ཚོ་/E ས་/S སྐྱི་/B ཚོགས་/M རིང་/M ལུགས་/E ཀྱི་/S སྐྱི་/B ལ་/M དབང་/M
 བའི་/M ལམ་/M ལུགས་/E དང་/S ཆོས་/S བརྩན་/S ཐོབ་/S སྲིད་/S ཀྱི་/S རུ་/B དོན་/E
མཐར་/B འཁྱེ་/E བ/B ས་/E ཡོད/S །/S

The differences between (e) and (c) are as follow:

– ཚོས་ is tagged as ཚོས་/ES in (c) but ཚོ་/E ས་/S in (e) because it's an abbreviated syllable.
– བའི is tagged as བའི་/M in (c) but བ་/M བི་/M in (e) because it's an abbreviated syllable but occurs at the middle of the word.
– བྱས་ is tagged as བྱས་/S in (c) but བྱ་/B ས་/E in (e) because it's not an abbreviated syllable but has an AM (ས) as the suffix.

– ཚིགས་ ,ལུགས་ ,ལུགས་ and འཆོར་ས་ are tagged as the same in (c) and (e) because the ས is at the secondary suffix position rather than suffix position in those syllables, so it can't be an AM by checking spelling rules and those syllables can't be abbreviated syllables. (See Fig. 1.)
– The two tags ES and SS used in (c) aren't used in (e) because abbreviated syllables are segmented into sub-syllables in (e).

Model Training Stage: When Tibetan word segmentation corpus is being converted into training format, abbreviation marks in abbreviated syllable get the tag S. Normal syllables which have a abbreviation mark in its suffix position will be segmented into two units, and the abbreviation mark in them gets a tag M or E. The model is able to make the disambiguation too.

Model Applying Stage: When applying the model, Tibetan text are segmented into syllables by tshegs and syllables with an AM as the suffix are segmented into sub-syllables further. Then, the model assigns each syllable a tag. Syllables are combined into words according to their tags.

4.3 Method 3: Sub-syllable Tagging with Syllable's POS Property

In many cases, a syllable is a word itself and has semantic meanings. All multi-syllable word can be taken as formed by several monosyllable words. As a syllable is a word, it also has the part-of-speech property. So we can assign a POS tag to each syllable denoting it's a noun, verb or others. The POS property may contribute to word segmentation.

So, based on Method 2, we assign each sub-syllable with a combined tag of the syllable's POS property tag and the in-word position tag. This is Method 3.

(f) [ད/rh ཚ/pl] [ས/ka] [ཐི/a ཚིགས/n རིང/n ལུགས/n] [ཀྱི/kg] [ཐི/a ལ/kp དབང/v ག/h ནི/kg ལས/n ལུགས/n] [དང/c] [ཅེས/n] [བསྟན/v] [ཐོབ/v] [སྟོད/v] [ཀྱི/kg] [ཇ/n རོན/n] [མཐར/n འཆོར་ས/v] [ཐས/v] [ཡོད/ve] [།/xp]

(g) ད/rh-B ཚ/pl-E ས/ka-S ཐི/a-B ཚིགས/n-M རིང/n-M ལུགས/n-E ཀྱི/kg-S ཐི/a-B ལ/kp-M དབང/v-M ག/h-M ནི/kg-M ལས/n-M ལུགས/n-E དང/c-S ཅེས/n-S བསྟན/v-S ཐོབ/v-S སྟོད/v-S ཀྱི/kg-S ཇ/n-B རོན/n-E མཐར/n-B འཆོར་ས/v-E ཐས/v-B ས/v-E ཡོད/ve-S །/xp-S

Model Training Stage: The corpus are prepared as (f), and converted to (g), which is used to train a tagger. As the POS property is on syllable level, but the tag unit is a sub-syllable, we have to split a certain syllable into two sub-syllables. It occurs when a normal syllable has an abbreviation mark as suffix. In the above sentence, ཐས/v is broken into two sub-syllables and tagged as ཐ/v-B ས/v-E. The first part of the combined tag denotes the POS property while the last part denotes the word boundary property.

Model Applying Stage: When applying the model, Tibetan text are segmented into syllables by tshegs and syllables with an AM as the suffix are segmented into sub-syllables further. Then, the model assigns each syllable a combined tag. Syllables are combined into words according to the last part of the combined tag.

5   Experiments and Results

5.1   Corpus

A corpus from some textbooks used in primary school and middle school is used in this work. Sentences are segmented into words and syllables and tagged with the POS property tag. Word boundaries are marked by special characters. About 1/5 of the corpus are randomly selected as the test set, 3,983 sentences (47,332 words) in total. The remaining 15,931 sentences (191,852 words) forms the training set. The OOV rate of the test set is 5.34 %.

5.2   Tag Set

Generally, tag set $\{B, M, E, S\}$ (4-tag set) and $\{B, B2, B3, M, E, S\}$ (6-tag set) [19,38,39] are used in the experiments to compare the influence of different tag sets on the performance. The difference is that two additional tags are used for units at the middle of a word. The first middle unit is tagged as B2, while the second middle unit is tagged as B3. Table 2 compares the tag results by the two tag sets. As needed another two additional tags ES and SS are used on Method 1 to tag the abbreviated syllables.

5.3   Machine Learning Model

Maximum Entropy (ME) tagger was used in early character-based tagging for Chinese word segmentation [22,23,35–37], In recent years, more and more people choose linear-chain CRFs as the machine learning model in their studies [25,34, 38,39].

CRFs model is firstly introduced into language processing by Lafferty [17]. Peng et al. [25] first used this framework for Chinese word segmentation by treating it as a binary decision task, such that each Chinese character is labelled either as the beginning of a word or not.

The probability assigned to a label sequence for a tagging unit sequence by a CRFs is:

$$p_\lambda(Y|W) = \frac{1}{Z(W)} exp \left(\sum_{t \in T} \sum_k \lambda_k f_k(y_{t-1}, y_t, W, t) \right). \tag{1}$$

where $Y = y_i$ is the label sequence for the sentence, W is the sequence of unsegmented units, $Z(W)$ is a normalization term, f_k is a feature function, and t indexes into units in the label sequence.

Table 2. Tag results by 4-tag set (4nt) and 6-tag set (6nt) on words with different lengths. The first, second and other middle units in a word are tagged as B2, B3 and M respectively by 6-tag set, while all of them are tagged M by 4-tag set.

word	tag set	tag sequence	sub-syllable/tag sequence
རེ	4nt	S	རེ /S
	6nt	S	རེ /S
ཅུའར	4nt	B-E	ཅུ /B འར /E
	6nt	B-E	ཅུ /B འར /E
སྐྱིད་ཕྱུག་ཅན་	4nt	B-M-E	སྐྱིད /B ཕྱུག /M ཅན /E
	6nt	B-B2-E	སྐྱིད /B ཕྱུག /B2 ཅན /E
བློ་ཙེ་གཅིག་སྐྱེས་	4nt	B-M-M-E	བློ /B ཙེ /M གཅིག /M སྐྱེས /E
	6nt	B-B2-B3-E	བློ /B ཙེ /B2 གཅིག /B3 སྐྱེས /E
གནས་རིག་ལབས་པ	4nt	B-M-M-M-E	གནས /B རིག /M ལབ /M ས /M པ /E
	6nt	B-B2-B3-M-E	གནས /B རིག /B2 ལབ /B3 ས /M པ /E
ཅེ་དགའི་རྣམ་འགྱུར	4nt	B-M-M-M-M-E	ཅེ /B དག /M འི /M རྣམ /M འགྱུ /M ར /E
	6nt	B-B2-B3-M-M-E	ཅེ /B དག /B2 འི /B3 རྣམ /M འགྱུ /M ར /E
ཕར་འགྲོ་ཀྱིར་འོར་བྱེད	4nt	B-M-M-M-M-M-E	ཕ /B ར /M འགྲོ /M ཀྱི /M ར /M འོར /M བྱེད /E
	6nt	B-B2-B3-M-M-M-E	ཕ /B ར /B2 འགྲོ /B3 ཀྱི /M ར /M འོར /M བྱེད /E

Table 3. Feature templates TMPT-10 used in this paper. A 5-unit context window is used. The unigrams and bigrams of the units are used to express the context of the current unit.

Feature	Explanation
C_n, $n = -1, 0, 1$	The previous, current and next unit
C_{-2}	The unit before the previous unit
C_2	The unit after the next unit
$C_n C_{n+1}$, $n = -1, 0$	The previous (next) unit and current unit
$C_{-1} C_1$	The previous unit and next unit
$C_1 C_2$	The next two units
$C_{-2} C_{-1}$	The previous two units

As theory and research practices on many sequence labelling tasks show that CRFs is better than ME, we use CRFs to train the taggers in this work. The CRF++ toolkit 0.58[1] by Taku Kudo is used.

5.4 Feature Template

A 5-unit context window and TMPT-10 defined in Table 3 are used in this work.

---

[1] http://taku910.github.io/crfpp.

Table 4. Performance comparison of the 3 methods. Method 2 (m2) improves the F-measure by 0.06 % and 0.10 % on 4-tag set (4nt) and 6-tag set (6nt) respectively over Method 1 (m1). Method 3 (m3) improves the F-measure by 0.47 % and 0.41 % over the other methods without using it on 4-tag set, while it improves 0.45 % and 0.35 % on 6-tag set.

	R(%)	P(%)	F1(%)	R(OOV)	R(IV)		R(%)	P(%)	F1(%)	R(OOV)	R(IV)
m1-4nt	93.99	93.78	93.88	70.84	95.29	m1-6nt	94.14	93.82	93.98	70.45	95.48
m2-4nt	94.12	93.77	93.94	69.70	95.51	m2-6nt	94.32	93.83	94.08	69.51	95.73
m3-4nt	94.63	94.07	**94.35**	68.08	96.13	m3-6nt	94.88	93.99	**94.43**	68.04	96.39

5.5   Comparison and Analysis

In the work, several experiments are made to compare factors that impact the performance.

Influence of Different Strategies on Abbreviated Syllables. Table 4 also shows that Method 2 gets an F-measure improvement of 0.06 % and 0.10 % on 4-tag set (4nt) and 6-tag set (6nt) respectively. The recall improvements are 0.13 % on 4-tag set and 0.18 % on 6-tag set, while the precisions almost keep the same. It seems that Method 2 leads to a more significant improvement on recall than on precision. Comparing with Method 1, the OOV recall rate declines 1.14 % on 4-tag set and 0.94 % on 6-tag set, while the IV recall rate improves 0.22 % and 0.25 %.

Influence of Different Tag Sets. Table 4 shows that 6-tag set (6nt) gets an F-measure improvement of 0.10 % on Method 1 and 0.14 % on Method 2 respectively compared with 4-tag set (4-nt). Meanwhile, the recall and precision are both improved when 6-tag set is used rather than 4-tag set, which shows that 6-tag set is slightly better than 4-tag set.

Influence of Syllable's POS Property. Table 4 lists the performance data of the three methods on 4-tag set. It shows that Method 3 outperforms the other two methods. Comparing with Method 1 and Method 2, the recall and precision improve both significantly, thus Method 3 gets an F measure improvement of 0.47 % and 0.41 % respectively over the other two methods without using it on 4-tag set, while it improves 0.45 % and 0.35 % on 6-tag set, which is much more higher than those former improvements. Consequently, the syllable's POS property is a more important factor to improve the overall performance than the strategy on abbreviated syllables and the tag set. However, comparing with the other two methods, Method 3 has a worse performance on the Out-Of-Vocabulary words.

6   Conclusion

The performance of Tibetan word segmenter is related to many factors. Three factors are compared in the paper, namely strategy on abbreviated syllables, tag set, and the syllable's Part-Of-Speech property. Experiment data show that: first, if each abbreviate syllable is separated into two units for labelling rather than one, the F-measure improves 0.06 % and 0.10 % on 4-tag set and 6-tag set respectively. Second, if 6-tag set is used rather than 4-tag set, the F-measure improves 0.10 % and 0.14 % on the two strategies on abbreviated syllables respectively. Third, when the syllable's Part-Of-Speech property is taken into account, F-measure improves 0.47 % and 0.41 % respectively over the other two methods without using it on 4-tag set, while it improves 0.45 % and 0.35 % on 6-tag set, which is much more higher than the former improvements. So it's a better choice to take advantage of the syllable's Part-Of-Speech property information while using the sub-syllable as the tag unit.

Acknowledgements. We thank the reviewers for their critical and constructive comments and suggestions that helped us improve the quality of the paper. The research is partially supported by National Science Foundation (No. 61202219, No. 61202220, No. 61303165) and Informationization Project of the Chinese Academy of Sciences (No. XXH12504-1-10).

References

1. Cai, R.J.: Research on the word categories and its annotation scheme for tibetan corpus. J. Chin. Inf. Process. **23**(04), 107–112 (2009)
2. Cai, Z.: The design of banzhida tibetan word segmentation system. In: Researches and Advancements of Information Processing for Chinese Minority Languages and Characters (2009)
3. Cai, Z.: The design of banzhida tibetan word segmentation system. In: 12th Symposium on Chinese Minority Information Processing (2009)
4. Cai, Z.: Identification of abbreviated word in tibetan word segmentation. J. Chin. Inf. Process. **23**(01), 35–37 (2009)
5. Cai, Z.: The design of banzhida tibetan word segmentation system. J. Ethic Normal Coll. Qinhai Normal Univ. **2**, 75–77 (2010)
6. Chen, Y., Li, B., Yu, S.: The design and implementation of a tibetan word segmentation system. J. Chin. Inf. Process. **17**(3), 15–20 (2003)
7. Chen, Y., Li, B., Yu, S., Lan, C.: An automatic tibetan segmentation scheme based on case auxiliary words and continuous features. Appl. Linguist. **1**, 75–82 (2003)
8. Chen, Y., Yu, S.: The present situation and prospect of the study of technological methods concerning handling the information in tibetan script. China Tibetol. **04**, 97–107 (2003)
9. Chungku, C., Rabgay, J., Faaß, G.: Building nlp resources for dzongkha: a tagset and a tagged corpus. In: Proceedings of the 8th Workshop on Asian Language Resources, pp. 103–110. Beijing, China (2010)
10. Dolha, Z., Losanglangjie, O.: The parts-of-speech and tagging set standards of tibetan information process. In: the 11th Symposium on Chinese Minority Information Processing (2007)

11. Emerson, T.: The second international chinese word segmentation bakeoff. In: Proceedings of the Fourth SIGHAN Workshop on Chinese Language Processing, pp. 123–133. Jeju Island, Korea (2005)
12. Gyal, T., Zhu, J.: Research on tibetan segmentation scheme for information processing. J. Chin. Inf. Process. **23**(04), 113–117 (2009)
13. He, X., Li, Y., Ma, N., Yu, H.: Study on tibetan automatic word segmentation as syllable tagging. Appl. Res. Comput. **32**(1), 61–65 (2015)
14. Jiang, D.: History and progress of tibetan text information processing. In: Frontiers of Chinese Information Processing Proceedings of the 25th Anniversary Conference of Chinese Information Processing Society, pp. 83–97. Press of Tsinghua university, Beijing (2006)
15. Jiang, T.: Tibetan word segmentation system based on conditional random fields. In: Software Engineering and Service Science (ICSESS), pp. 446–448 (2011)
16. Kang, C., Jiang, D., Long, C.: Tibetan word segmentation based on word-position tagging. In: 2013 International Conference on Asian Language Processing (IALP), pp. 239–242. IEEE (2013)
17. Lafferty, J., McCallum, A., Pereira, F.: Conditional random fields: probabilistic models for segmenting and labeling sequence data. In: Proceedings of the Eighteenth International Conference on Machine Learning, pp. 282–289 (2001)
18. Li, Y., Jam, Y., Zong, C., Yu, H.: Research and implementation of tibetan automatic word segmentation based on conditional random field. J. Chin. Inf. Process. **27**(4), 52–58 (2013)
19. Liu, H., Nuo, M., Ma, L., et al.: Tibetan word segmentation as syllable tagging using conditional random fields. In: Proceedings of the 25th Pacific Asia Conference on Language, Information and Computation (PACLIC 2011), pp. 168–177 (2011)
20. Liu, H., Nuo, M., Zhao, W., et al.: SegT: a practical tibetan word segmentation system. J. Chin. Inf. Process. **26**(1), 97–103 (2012)
21. Liu, H., Zhao, W., Nuo, M., Jiang, L., Wu, J., He, Y.: Tibetan number identification based on classification of number components in tibetan word segmentation. In: Proceedings of the 23rd International Conference on Computational Linguistics, pp. 719–724. Association for Computational Linguistics, Posters (2010)
22. Low, J.K., Ng, H.T., Guo, W.: A maximum entropy approach to chinese word segmentation. In: Proceedings of the Fourth SIGHAN Workshop on Chinese Language Processing, pp. 161–164. Jeju Island, Korea (2005)
23. Ng, H.T., Low, J.K.: Chinese part-of-speech tagging: one-at-a-time or all-at-once? word-based or character-based. In: Proceedings of 2004 Conference on Empirical Methods in Natural Language Processing, pp. 277–284 (2004)
24. Norbu, S., Choejey, P., Dendup, T., Hussain, S., Mauz, A.: Dzongkha word segmentation. In: Proceedings of the 8th Workshop on Asian Language Resources, pp. 95–102, Beijing (2010)
25. Peng, F., Feng, F., McCallum, A.: Chinese segmentation and new word detection using conditional random fields. In: Proceedings of the 20th International Conference on Computational Linguistics, pp. 562–568, Geneva (2004)
26. Qi, K.: Research on tibetan automatic word segmentation for information processing. J. Northwest Univ. National. Philos. Soc. Sci. **04**, 92–97 (2006)
27. Shi, X., Lu, Y., Yang, J.: A tibetan segmentation system. J. Chin. Inf. Process. **25**(4), 54–56 (2011)
28. Sproat, R., Emerson, T.: The first international chinese word segmentation bakeoff. In: Proceedings of the Second SIGHAN Workshop on Chinese Language Processing, pp. 133–143, Sapporo (2003)

29. Sun, M., Huaquecairang, C., Jiang, W., et al.: Tibetan word segmentation based on discriminative classification and reranking. J. Chin. Inf. Process. **28**(2), 61–66 (2014)

30. Sun, Y., Luosang, Q., Yang, R., Zhao, X.: Design of a tibetan automatic segmentation scheme. In: Researches and Advancements of Information Processing for Chinese Minority Languages and Characters - Proceedings of the 12th Symposium on Chinese Minority Information Processing, pp. 228–237 (2009)

31. Sun, Y., Luosang, Q., Yang, R., Zhao, X.: Study of segmentation strategy on tibetan crossing ambiguous words. In: Researches and Advancements of Information Processing for Chinese Minority Languages and Characters, pp. 238–243 (2009)

32. Sun, Y., Wang, Z., Zhao, X., et al.: Design of a tibetan automatic word segmentation scheme. In: Proceedings of 2009 1st IEEE International Conference on Information Engineering and Computer Science, pp. 1–6 (2009)

33. Sun, Y., Yan, X., Zhao, X., et al.: A resolution of overlapping ambiguity in tibetan word segmentation. In: Proceedings of 2010 3rd International Conference on Computer Science and Information Technology, pp. 222–225 (2010)

34. Tseng, H., Chang, P., Andrew, G., Jurafsky, D., Manning, C.: A conditional random field word segmenter for sighan bakeoff 2005. In: Proceedings of the Fourth SIGHAN Workshop on Chinese Language Processing, pp. 168–171, Jeju Island (2005)

35. Xue, N.: Chinese word segmentation as character tagging. Comput. Linguist. Chin. Lang. Process. **8**(1), 29–48 (2003)

36. Xue, N., Converse, S.P.: Combining classifiers for chinese word segmentation. In: Proceedings of the First SIGHAN Workshop on Chinese Language Processing, pp. 63–70, Taipei (2002)

37. Xue, N., Shen, L.: Chinese word segmentation as lmr tagging. In: Proceedings of the Second SIGHAN Workshop on Chinese Language Processing in conjunction with ACL03, pp. 176–179, Sapporo (2003)

38. Zhao, H., Huang, C.N., Li, M.: An improved chinese word segmentation system with conditional random field. In: Proceedings of the Fifth SIGHAN Workshop on Chinese Language Processing, pp. 108–117, Sidney (2006)

39. Zhao, H., Huang, C., Li, M., Lu, B.: Effective tag set selection in chinese word segmentation via conditional random field modeling. In: Proceedings of the 20th Pacific Asia Conference on Language. Information and Computation, pp. 87–94, Wuhan (2006)

40. Ciren, Z.: The design of a machine assisted tibetan word segmentation and new word registeration system. In: Proceedings of Modernization of Chinese Minority Nationality Languages (1999)

41. Zhaxijia, D., Losanglangjie, O., et al.: Theoretical explanation on the parts-of-speech and tagging set standards of tibetan information processing. In: Procedings of the 11th China National Conference on Minority Language Information Processing, pp. 441–452 (2007)

Learning Distributed Representations of Uyghur Words and Morphemes

Halidanmu Abudukelimu[1]([⊠]), Yang Liu[1,2], Xinxiong Chen[1], Maosong Sun[1,2], and Abudoukelimu Abulizi[3]

[1] State Key Laboratory of Intelligent Technology and Systems Tsinghua National Laboratory for Information Science and Technology, Department of Computer Science and Technology, Tsinghua University, Beijing, China
{abdklmhldm,cxx.thu}@gmail.com

[2] Jiangsu Collaborative Innovation Center for Language Competence, Nanjing, Jiangsu, China
{liuyang2011,sms}@tsinghua.edu.cn

[3] Lab of Computational Linguistics, Center for Psychology and Cognitive Science School of Humanities, Tsinghua University, Beijing, China
keram1106@163.com

Abstract. While distributed representations have proven to be very successful in a variety of NLP tasks, learning distributed representations for agglutinative languages such as Uyghur still faces a major challenge: most words are composed of many morphemes and occur only once on the training data. To address the data sparsity problem, we propose an approach to learn distributed representations of Uyghur words and morphemes from unlabeled data. The central idea is to treat morphemes rather than words as the basic unit of representation learning. We annotate a Uyghur word similarity dataset and show that our approach achieves significant improvements over CBOW, a state-of-the-art model for computing vector representations of words.

Keywords: Distributed representations · Uyghur · Word · Morpheme

1 Introduction

Developing natural language processing techniques for Uyghur is difficult, not only because of the unavailability of publicly accessible annotated corpora, but also due to its nature of agglutination. On one hand, the annotated corpora of Uyghur for morphological analysis, POS tagging, parsing, translation and sentiment analysis are far more limited in both quantity and coverage as compared with resource-rich languages such as English and Chinese. On the other hand, Uyghur words often consist of many morphemes and differ significantly from English and Chinese in terms of morphology and syntax, making it difficult to directly adopt state-of-the-art NLP models and algorithms.

© Springer International Publishing Switzerland 2015
M. Sun et al. (Eds.): CCL and NLP-NABD 2015, LNAI 9427, pp. 202–211, 2015.
DOI: 10.1007/978-3-319-25816-4_17

Fortunately, unsupervised learning of distributed representations brings hope to addressing the resource scarcity problem. In recent years, learning distributed representations of words from unlabeled data has received intensive attention [1,6,9]. Distributed representations, which are continuous dense real-valued vectors, are capable of capturing multiple degrees of syntactic and semantic similarities between words. These representations have proven to benefit many NLP tasks including language modeling [1,11], machine translation [2], and semantic analysis [7].

However, most existing methods treat words as the atomic units in distributed representation learning [1,6,9]. This is problematic for agglutinative languages such as Uyghur in which most words are composed of many morphemes. As most Uyghur words only occur once on the training data, it is hard for approaches treating words as the basic unit to learn vector representations accurately due to the data sparsity. To address this problem, a number of authors propose to learn word presentations by exploiting the minimum meaning bearing units such as characters in Chinese and morphemes in Russia [2,3,8,12].

In this work, we follow this line of research to learn distributed representations of Uyghur words and morphemes from unlabeled data. The basic idea is to treat Uyghur morphemes as the atomic unit to account for the internal structure of Uyghur words. We propose a morpheme-enhanced continuous bag-of-words (mCBOW) model that uses morpheme vectors to derive word vectors. We annotate a Uyghur word similarity dataset and show that our approach achieves significant improvements over CBOW [9], a state-of-the-art model for computing vector representations of words.

2   Background

Uyghur belongs to the Karluk branch of the Turkic language family and is spoken mainly by the Uyghur people in the Xinjiang Uyghur Autonomous Region of Western China. Similar to many other Turkic languages, Uyghur is agglutinative, lacks grammatical articles and noun classes. The basic word order of Uyghur is subject-object-verb.

Figure 1 shows some Uyghur words and their corresponding English translations. One single Uyghur word usually contains rich information by combining various morphemes including stems, prefixes, and affixes.

Due to the scarcity of resources for Uyghur processing, it is appealing to learn distributed representations of Uyghur words and morphemes from unlabeled data using the continuous bag-of-words (CBOW) model [9]. The intuition is that a good model should be able to predict a word given its surrounding context.

Figure 2(a) illustrates the idea of CBOW. Given a Uyghur sentence *ular mekteptin kaldi*, the model aims to predict *mekteptin* given the context words *ular* and *kaldi*, which are all represented as real-valued vectors. These distributed representations are surprisingly good at capturing syntactic and semantic regularities in language [9].

UYGHUR PRODUCTIVE DERIVATION	
يەر yer	land
يەرلىك yerlik	local
يەرلىكلەش yerliklex	to be localed
يەرلىكلەشتۈر yerliklextür	localized
يەرلىكشتۈروۈل yerliklextürül	to be localized
يەرلىكشتۈروۈلمە yerliklextürülme	to not be localized
يەرلىكشتۈروۈلمەيمز yerliklextürülmeymiz	We unable to be localized

Fig. 1. Example: Uyghur words and their corresponding English translations.

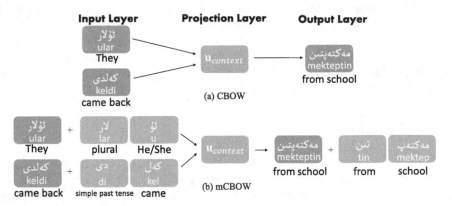

Fig. 2. (a) The continuous bag-of-words (CBOW) model and (b) the morpheme-enhanced continuous bag-of-words (mCBOW) model. Given a Uyghur sentence *ular mekteptin kaldi*, the mCBOW model predicts the word *mekteptin* by taking two context words *ular* and *kaldi* as input. mCBOW differs from CBOW in that it takes both word and morpheme vectors into account.

More formally, given a training corpus $D = \{w_1, \ldots, w_T\}$, the training objective of CBOW is to maximize the average log probability

$$\frac{1}{T} \sum_{t=1}^{T} \log P(w_t | w_{t-c}, \ldots, w_{t-1}, w_{t+1}, \ldots, w_{t+c}) \tag{1}$$

where c is the size of the training context around the center word w_t. The prediction probability can be defined using a softmax function

$$P(w_t|w_{t-c}, \ldots, w_{t-1}, w_{t+1}, \ldots, w_{t+c}) = \frac{\exp(\mathbf{u}_{context}^{\top} \cdot \mathbf{v}_{w_t})}{\sum_{w' \in W} \exp(\mathbf{u}_{context}^{\top} \cdot \mathbf{v}_{w'})} \qquad (2)$$

where W is the vocabulary, $\mathbf{v}_{w_t}$ is the input vector of w_t, and $\mathbf{u}_{context}^{\top}$ is the output vector of the surrounding context:

$$\mathbf{u}_{context}^{\top} = \frac{1}{2c} \sum_{t-c \leq i \leq t+c, i \neq t} \mathbf{u}_{w_i} \qquad (3)$$

Note that the output vector of the surrounding context is the average of all context word vectors.

Although the CBOW model works well for many languages such as English and Chinese, it faces a severe data sparsity problem when processing agglutinative languages such as Uyghur: most words only occur once on the training data. As a result, modeling at the word level is insufficient to capture the linguistic regularities in morphologically-rich languages.

3   Morpheme-Enhanced CBOW

A number of authors have proposed to exploit the internal structures of words to address the data sparsity problem [2,3,8,12]. The central idea is that the minimum meaning-bearing units, say morphemes in Uyghur or characters in Chinese, are also modeled as real-valued vectors of parameters to derive the vectors of words. While Luong et al. [8] leverage recursive neural networks to model the internal hierarchical structure, Botha and Blunsom [2] and Chen et al. [3] simply use addition as composition function. They show that modeling at the morpheme or character level outperforms modeling at the word level for a variety of languages.

In this work, we follow this line of research and propose a **morpheme-enhanced continuous bag-of-words (mCBOW)** model for Uyghur. As shown in Fig. 2(b), mCBOW extends CBOW to consider both word and morpheme vectors, highlighted in blue and yellow, respectively. The basic idea is to derive word vectors from morphme vectors:

$$\mathbf{v}_{unfortunately} = \mathbf{v}_{un} + \mathbf{v}_{fortunate} + \mathbf{v}_{ly}$$

We hope that the inclusion of morpheme vectors enables the model to be more robust to data sparsity.

More formally, suppose a Uyghur word w is composed of K morphemes: $w = m_1, \ldots, m_K$. We use m_k to denote the k-th morpheme in the word. Following Botha and Blunsom [2], the vector representation of w can be computed using the vectors of morphemes:

$$\tilde{\mathbf{u}}_w = \mathbf{u}_w + \sum_{k=1}^{K} \mathbf{u}_{m_k} \tag{4}$$

$$\tilde{\mathbf{v}}_w = \mathbf{v}_w + \sum_{k=1}^{K} \mathbf{v}_{m_k} \tag{5}$$

Note that the surface form of a word (i.e., $\mathbf{u}_w$ and $\mathbf{v}_w$) is also included as a factor to account for noncompositional constructions as suggested by Botha and Blunsom [2]. They indicate that this strategy also overcomes the order-invariance of additive composition.

Given a training corpus $D = \{w_1, \ldots, w_T\}$, the training objective of mCBOW is still to maximize the average log probability as shown in Eq. (1). The prediction probability can be defined using a softmax function

$$P(w_t|w_{t-c}, \ldots, w_{t-1}, w_{t+1}, \ldots, w_{t+c}) = \frac{\exp(\tilde{\mathbf{u}}_{context}^{\top} \cdot \tilde{\mathbf{v}}_{w_t})}{\sum_{w' \in W} \exp(\tilde{\mathbf{u}}_{context}^{\top} \cdot \tilde{\mathbf{v}}_{w'})} \tag{6}$$

where $\tilde{\mathbf{v}}_{w_t}$ is the input vector of w_t, and $\tilde{\mathbf{u}}_{context}^{\top}$ is the output vector of the surrounding context:

$$\tilde{\mathbf{u}}_{context}^{\top} = \frac{1}{2c} \sum_{t-c \leq i \leq t+c, i \neq t} \tilde{\mathbf{u}}_{w_i} \tag{7}$$

Following Mikolov et al. [9], we exploit stochastic gradient descent (SGD) and negative sampling to train the mCBOW model. The gradients are calculated using the back-propagation algorithm. The word and morpheme vectors are initialized randomly.

It is clear that the mCBOW model is a natural extension of CBOW that includes the vectors of morphemes. As we use addition as the composition function, it is still easy and efficient to train the model using negative sampling [9]. Our work is also in spirit close to Botha and Blunsom [2] and Chen et al. [3]. While both Botha and Blunsom [2] and mCBOW use addition as composition function at the morpheme level, Botha and Blunsom [2] exploit the log-bilingual model [10] at the word level but we leverage the CBOW model. The difference from Chen et al. [3] is that our model considers the morphemes of the word to be predicted, which is very useful for improving the accuracy.

4   Experiments

We evaluate our approach on a Uyghur word similarity task. We build a Uyghur word similarity dataset, which we refer to as *uyWordSim-353*, by manually translating the popular *WordSim-353* [5] into Uyghur. The training set contains news articles from the Tianshan website with 1.26M words[1]. We use Morfessor v0.9.2 [4] to segment Uyghur words into morphemes by setting the parameter

---

[1] http://uy.ts.cn.

"PPLTHRESH" to 200. The evaluation metric is Spearman's rank correlation coefficient ($\rho \times 100$) between similarity scores assigned by the model and by human annotators.

Table 1. The distribution of word frequencies. We find that 47.66 % of Uyghur words occur only once on the training data.

Freq.	# Words	Percent. (%)
1	32,457	47.66
2	9,524	13.98
3	4,691	6.89
4	3,045	4.47
5	2,199	3.23
6	1,617	2.37
7	1,223	1.80
8	974	1.43
9	843	1.24
10	717	1.05
> 10	10,812	15.88
Total	68,102	100.00

4.1 Data Sparsity in Uyghur

We find on the training data that the average lengths of words, stems, affixes, and suffixes are 17, 14, 5, and 4, respectively. The maximum length of a Uyghur word is 33 characters. 53 % of words contain at least two morphemes.

As shown in Table 1, over 80 % of words occur no greater than 10 times on the training data. In particular, about 47 % of words occur only once. This leads to severe data sparsity for learning distributed representations of Uyghur words.

4.2 Comparison with CBOW and Skip-Gram

We compare mCBOW with CBOW and Skip-Gram. The Skip-Gram model is a reverse variant of CBOW: predicting the surrounding context given a specific word [9]. We set the number of negative examples in negative sampling to 10 and run the training algorihm for 30 iterations.

We find that there are many words in *uyWordSim-353* do not occur on the training data. In addition, the Uyghur translation of an English word is sometimes a phrase. To handle these OOV words and phrases, the similarity scores of these OOV words are set to –1. After removing these OOV words and phrases, we obtain a subset called *uyWordSim-196*.

As shown in Table 2, mCBOW significantly improves over CBOW and Skip-Gram. Note that the correlation coefficients are very low due to the presence of

Table 2. Comparison with CBOW and Skip-Gram. "353 pairs" denotes the Uyghur translations of the original *WordSim-353* dataset. "196 pairs" denotes a subset of "353 pairs" that removes words that do not occur on the training data.

Method	uyWordSim	
	353 pairs	196 pairs
CBOW	8.21	43.12
Skip-Gram	9.22	45.34
mCBOW	**10.88**	**45.50**

OOV words and phrases as well as the severe data sparsity. Our approach also outperforms CBOW and Skip-Gram on the *uyWordSim-196* dataset, in which all words occur on the training data. mCBOW still achieves higher accuracy than CBOW, suggesting that modeling the internal structures of Uyghur words does benefit representation learning.

The improvement over Skip-Gram on the *uyWordSim-196* dataset is insignificant because Skip-Gram itself is better than CBOW on this task. It is possible to extend our approach to morpheme-enhanced Skip-Gram. We leave this for future work.

4.3 Effect of Word Frequencies

We find most words in the *uyWordSim-196* dataset occur more than 100 times on the training data. To investigate the effect of word frequencies on the accuracy, we compare CBOW and mCBOW on various subsets of *uyWordSim-196* in terms of word frequencies.

As shown in Table 3, CBOW achieves a higher accuracy than mCBOW on 137 word pairs that occur more than 100 times on the training data, indicating that it is unnecessary to consider internal structures of words if the training data is not sparse. However, the accuracy of CBOW drops dramatically with the decrease of word frequencies and even achieves a negative correlation coefficient. In contrast, our approach is more robust to data sparsity.

Table 3. Effect of word frequencies on accuracy. While CBOW works well for high-frequency words, mCBOW is more capable of handling infrequent words.

Freq.	Pairs	CBOW	mCBOW
> 100	137	46.96	44.01
< 100	59	34.76	51.98
< 50	50	35.17	48.62
< 30	29	19.70	24.14
< 20	18	−0.49	36.52
< 10	14	6.59	26.92

Table 4. Effect of morpheme count on accuracy. "# Morph." denotes the number of morphemes in a Uyghur word. While 53 % of words contain at least two morphemes on the training data, the percentage is 85 % on the *uyWordSim-196* dataset. mCBOW outperforms CBOW when dealing with multi-morpheme Uyghur words.

# Morph	Pairs	CBOW	mCBOW
1	167	48.12	47.83
> 1	30	5.52	26.23

4.4   Effect of Morpheme Count

On the training data, 53 % of words contain at least two morphemes and 47 % of words occur only once. However, this is not the case on the test set because 85 % of Uyghur words only contain stems.

Table 4 shows the effect of morpheme count on accuracy. If a Uyghur word only contains stem, CBOW slightly outperforms mCBOW but the difference is not significant. Dealing with multi-morpheme Uyghur words, however, mCBOW improves over CBOW by a large margin. This finding confirms the effectiveness of our approach.

Words	CBOW	mCBOW
ۋېيتنام Vietnam	ساغلاملىقىغا health ئۆكتەبىرنى October سەھنىلەرگە stage شەنزىن (person name) لوگكىسى (World) Cup	ئەرەبىستان Saudi Arabia بىرنىبى (place name) ۋېنگرىيە Hungary جۇڭگو China راللى (a kind of sport game)
يۇمۇر humor	ساۋاتلىرىمۇ common sense سۇنۇشنىلا present ئاتكىرتكا greeting card شېئىر poem سۆزلىيەلەيدۇ can speak	شېئىر peom ئەدەبى literature ئەتكەن make نادىر excellent يازالايدىغان can write
جىسىم entity	كونتورى contour فازىلىق phase مۇڭغۇلچە Mongolian ھىدروگېن hydrogen سانو (person name)	ئاقار meteor ئۆلترا infrared گۈلنى flower ئاكۇپ tunnel جىسمانىي materially

Fig. 3. Top 5 nearest neighbors of example Uyghur words.

4.5   Case Study

Figure 3 shows the top 5 closest words to some Uyghur infrequent words obtained from CBOW and mCBOW. It is clear that our approach is capable of capturing the semantic similarities between Uyghur words.

As shown in the figure, the results of the nearest neighbors of *Vietnam* returned by mCBOW are better than CBOW. In mCBOW, almost all the nearest words are semantically closely related to *Vietnam* except *(a kind of sport game)*. However, in CBOW, the results differ a great deal from the semantic meaning of Vietnam. The results for *humor* and *entity* are similar as well (In CBOW, *common sense, present, greeting card* and *can speak* are unrelated to *humor, contour, phase, Mongolian* and *personal name* have little correlation with *entity*).

5   Related Work

Distributed word representations, low dimension real-valued vectors for words, usually capturing both semantic and syntactic information of words. These representations have been successfully used in a variety of NLP tasks. Most word representation models exhibits high computational complexity, which makes them unable to work for large-scale text corpora efficiently. Recently, Mikolov et al. [9] proposed two efficient models, continuous bag-of-words mode (CBOW) and Skip-Gram model, to learn word embeddings from large-scale text corpora. The training objective of CBOW is to combine the embeddings of context words to predict the target word; while Skip-Gram is to use the embedding of each target word to predict its context words.

The unsupervised learning of distributed representations on large corpus brings hope to addressing the resource scarcity problem of Uyghur. However, most existing methods treat words as the atomic units in distributed representation learning [1,6,9]. This is problematic for agglutinative languages such as Uyghur in which most words are composed of many morphemes. To address this problem, a number of authors propose to learn word presentations by exploiting the minimum meaning bearing units.

To learn morpheme representations, Lazaridou et al. [7] had used compositional distributional semantic models, originally designed to learn meanings of phrases, to derive representations for complex words. Luong et al. [8] also choose to operate at the morpheme level and used a recursive neural network to explicitly model the morphological structures of words and learn morphologically-aware embeddings. Botha and Blunsom [2] used addition as composition function at the morpheme level and exploit the log-bilingual model. Chen et al. [3] decided to learn representations at the character level and proposed multiple-prototype character representations to deal with the ambiguity problem of characters.

In this paper, we focus on Uyghur and follow this line of work to learn both word and morpheme representations of Uyghur.

6   Conclusion

We have presented a morpheme-enhanced continuous bag-of-words (mCBOW) model for learning vector representations of Uyghur words and vectors. The model treats morphemes as the basic unit and uses addition as the composition function. Experiments on the Uyghur word similarity task show that our approach significantly outperforms the CBOW model. In particular, the mCBOW model is more capable of handling infrequent and multi-morpheme Uyghur words than CBOW.

Note that our model is an unsupervised model, thus it can also be applied to other agglunative languages, like: Turkish, Uzbek, Kazak, etc.

In the future, we plan to apply our idea to more models such as the log-bilingual model [10] and the Skip-Gram model [9]. It is also interesting to model the recursive structure of Uyghur words like Luong et al. [8].

Acknowledgments. This research is supported by National Key Basic Research Program of China (973 Program 2014CB340500), the National Natural Science Foundation of China (No. 61331013), the National Key Technology R & D Program (No. 2014BAK10B03), the Singapore National Research Foundation under its International Research Center @ Singapore Funding Initiative and administered by the IDM Programme. We are grateful to Meiping Dong, Lei Xu, Liner Yang, Yu Zhao, Yankai Lin, Chunyang Liu, Shiqi Shen, and Meng Zhang for their constructive feedback to the early draft of this paper.

References

1. Bengio, Y., Ducharme, R., Vincent, P., Jauvin, C.: A neural probabilistic language model. J. Mach. Learn. Res. **3**, 1137–1155 (2003)
2. Botha, J.A., Blunsom, P.: Compositional morphology for word representations and language modelling. In: Proceedings of ICML (2014)
3. Chen, X., Xu, L., Liu, Z., Sun, M., Luan, H.: Joint learning of character and word embeddings. In: Proceedings of IJCAI (2015)
4. Creutz, M., Lagus, K.: Unsupervised models for morpheme segmentation and morphology learning. ACM Trans. Speech Lang. Process. 4(1), article 3 (2007)
5. Finkelstein, L., Gabrilovich, E., Matias, Y., Rivlin, E., Sloan, Z., Wolfman, G., Ruppin, E.: Placing search in context: the concepted revisited. ACM Trans. Inf. Syst. **20**(1), 116–131 (2002)
6. Huang, E., Socher, R., Manning, C.D., Ng, A.Y.: Improving word representations via global context and multiple word prototypes. In: Proceedings of ACL (2012)
7. Lazaridou, A., Marelli, M., Zamparelli, R., Baroni, M.: Compositionally derived representations of morphologically complex words in distributional semantics. In: Proceedings of ACL (2013)
8. Luong, M.T., Socher, R., Manning, C.D.: Better word representations with recursive neural networks for morphology. In: Proceedings of CoNLL (2013)
9. Mikolov, T., Sutskever, I., Chen, K., Corrado, G., Dean, J.: Distributed representations of words and phrases and their compositionality. In: Proceedings of NIPS (2013)
10. Mnih, A., Hinton, G.: Three new graphical models for statistical language modelling. In: Proceedings of ICML (2007)
11. Mnih, A., Hinton, G.: A scalable hierarchical distributed language model. In: Proceedings of NIPS (2008)
12. Qiu, S., Cui, Q., Bian, J., Gao, B., Liu, T.Y.: Co-learning of word representations and morpheme representations. In: Proceedings of COLING (2014)

Machine Learning Method for NLP

EHLLDA: A Supervised Hierarchical Topic Model

Xian-Ling Mao[1]([✉]), Yixuan Xiao[1], Qiang Zhou[1], Jun Wang[2],
and Heyan Huang[1]

[1] Department of Computer Science and Technology,
Beijing Institute of Technology, Beijing, China
{maoxl,1120121905,qzhou,hhy63}@bit.edu.cn
[2] Institute of Biz Big Data, Sogou Inc., Beijing, China
wangjunbj7526@sogou-inc.com

Abstract. In this paper, we consider the problem of modeling hierarchical labeled data – such as Web pages and their placement in hierarchical directories. The state-of-the-art model, hierarchical Labeled LDA (hLLDA), assumes that each child of a non-leaf label has equal importance, and that a document in the corpus cannot locate in a non-leaf node. However, in most cases, these assumptions do not meet the actual situation. Thus, in this paper, we introduce a supervised hierarchical topic models: *Extended Hierarchical Labeled Latent Dirichlet Allocation* (EHLLDA), which aim to relax the assumptions of hLLDA by incorporating prior information of labels into hLLDA. The experimental results show that the perplexity performance of EHLLDA is always better than that of LLDA and hLLDA on all four datasets; and our proposed model is also superior to hLLDA in terms of p@n.

Keywords: Topic modeling · Supervised learning · Hierarchical topic modeling

1 Introduction

A number of topic models have been developed for the data without labels [11,26,28], and the data with non-hierarchical labels [3,23,24]. For the data with hierarchical labels, like webpages and their corresponding hierarchical directories, to the best of our knowledge, the *hierarchical Labeled Latent Dirichlet Allocation* (hLLDA) [19] is the only topic model proposed to model this kind of data. The generative process of hLLDA is: (1) choose a random path c_d for a document d among all the paths in the hierarchical labeled tree; (2) draw a proportion over the labels in path c_d; (3) each of the N words in d is selected from one of the topics (labels). Note that hLLDA takes each label as a topic, i.e. a distribution over vocabulary, thus hLLDA needs to learn a distribution for each label. In this paper, a "label" means a character string or a distribution over vocabulary, which can be distinguished in different context. From the

© Springer International Publishing Switzerland 2015
M. Sun et al. (Eds.): CCL and NLP-NABD 2015, LNAI 9427, pp. 215–226, 2015.
DOI: 10.1007/978-3-319-25816-4_18

generative process, hLLDA has two latent assumptions: (i) hLLDA treats each child of a non-leaf label equally (See step (1)); (ii) hLLDA also assumes that each document in the corpus must have a leaf label, i.e. each document cannot locate in the non-leaf node in the hierarchy of labels. However, in most cases, these assumptions do not meet the actual situation. For assumption (i), often each child has different importance. For example, in Yahoo! Answer, the number of questions is different for different sub-categories of a category, which shows the importance of labels is different. For assumption (ii), documents often locate in intermediate layers. For example, in Yahoo! Answer, the categories in inter-mediate layers often have questions, which shows that documents can locate in non-leaf nodes. In this paper, we extend hLLDA to a model named *Extended Hierarchical Labeled LDA* (EHLLDA) by taking advantage of prior information of labels and relaxing assumptions.

We demonstrate the effectiveness of the proposed model on large, real-world datasets in the question answering and website category domains. We also observe that prior information is very valuable when incorporated into topic learning.

2 Extended Hierarchical Labeled LDA

In this paper, we introduce a supervised hierarchical topic model, i.e., the *Extended Hierarchical Labeled LDA* (EHLLDA). EHLLDA is a probabilistic graphical model that describes a process for generating a hierarchical labeled document collection. Like the hLLDA, EHLLDA models each document as a mixture of underlying topics and generates each word from one topic; mean-while EHLLDA incorporates supervision by simply constraining the topic model to use only those topics that correspond to a document's (observed) hierarchical labels. Unlike hLLDA, EHLLDA incorporates prior information of labels by cap-turing the relation between a parent label and its child labels, i.e., the relation between a super-topic and its sub-topics.

The graphical model of EHLLDA is depicted in Fig. 1. Each label in EHLLDA has its corresponding topic. The model can be viewed in terms of a generative process that first generates c_d labels from the hierarchy of labels for a documnet d, and then draw a proportion over the c_d labels, and finally each of the N words in d is selected from one of the c_d topics (labels).

In the model, N is the number of words in a document, D is the total number of documents in a collection, K is the number of labels in the hierarchy, L is the height of hierarchy of labels, c_i is an observed node in the ith level in the hierarchical labeled tree for a document, $\boldsymbol{c_d} = \{c_1, c_2, ..., c_{|c_d|}\}$ be the labels for a document d, l_i be the set of labels in the ith level in the hierarchy of labels. η, α and μ_{c_i} are dirichlet prior parameters, β_k is a distribution over words, θ is a document-specific distribution over topics, δ_{c_i} is a multinomial distribution over observed sub-topics of topic c_i, w is an observed word, z is the topic assigned to w, $Dir_k(.)$ is a k-dimensional Dirichlet distribution, $Mult(.|.)$ is a multinomial distribution, γ is a Multi-nomial distribution over paths in the tree, and V is the size of vocabulary.

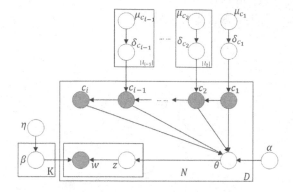

Fig. 1. The graphical model representation of the Extended Hierarchical Labeled LDA.

A EHLLDA model assumes the following generative process for a document and its hierarchical labels ($\boldsymbol{w_d}; \boldsymbol{c_d}$):

1. For each topic $k \in \{1, ..., K\}$.
   (a) Generate $\beta_k = (\beta_{k,1}, ..., \beta_{k,V})^T \sim Dir(.|\eta)$
2. For each level l_j, $j \in \{2, ..., L-1\}$:
   (a) For each node c_i in l_j, draw $\delta_{c_i} \sim Dir(.|\mu_{c_i})$
3. For each document d:
   (a) For each level l_i, $i \in \{2, ..., L\}$:
      i. Draw $c_i \sim Mult(.|\delta_{c_i})$
      ii. If c_i is an "exit" node, goto (b)
   (b) Draw a distribution over the nodes in the set $\boldsymbol{c_d}$, $\theta_d \sim Dir(.|\alpha, \boldsymbol{c_d})$
   (c) For each $i \in \{1, ..., N_d\}$:
      i. Generate $z_i \sim Mult(.|\theta_d)$
      ii. Generate $w_i \sim Mult(.|\beta_{z_i})$

Specifically, we associate with each label c in the hierarchy of labels a document-specific dirichlet distribution with dimensionality equal to $N_c + 1$, where N_c is the number of children of the label node c. This distribution allows us to traverse the hierarchy of labels and exit at any node in the hierarchy of labels — given that we are at a label node c_i, there are N_{c_i} child labels to choose from and an additional option to choose an "exit" child to exit the labeled tree at label node c_i. We start our walk through the hierarchy of labels at the root node and select a node from its children. We repeat this process until we reach an exit node. A word is generated from one of the topics from the root to the parent of the exit node. We illustrate an example of the hierarchical labeled tree in Fig. 2 for six documents. It shows the paths of six documents through the hierarchy of labels. The solid lines connect each node to the sub-nodes. The shaded circles stand for observed labels, and black circles stand for "exit" node. For example, the 5th document, it first chooses label $A1$ according to a probability distribution, then chooses $A3$, finally chooses $A5$. $A5$ is a "exit" node, thus the 5th document has labels: $A1$ and $A3$; meanwhile the 5th document is generated by topics: $A1$ and $A3$. Here, we can see that the 5th document has located in a

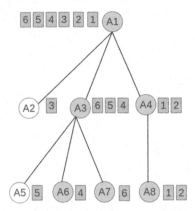

Fig. 2. An example of the hierarchical labeled tree for six documents. It shows the paths of six documents through the hierarchy of labels. The solid lines connect each node to the sub-nodes. The shaded circles stand for observed labels, and black circles stand for "exit" node.

non-leaf label, which has relaxed the assumption of hLLDA. In addition, from the generative process, each label has assigned a different choosing probability, which relaxes another assumption of hLLDA.

3   Parameter Estimation

3.1   Learning and Inference

In Fig. 1, the labels for a document are observed, so θ and δ_{c_i} are d-separated from the rest of the model given labels c_d. Therefore the learning and inference for EHLLDA are similar to traditional LDA, can be solved using collapsed Gibbs sampling.

For each document, the topics used for inference are those found in the set of labels from the root to the "exit" node in the hierarchy of labels. Once the target labels c_d is known, the model is reduced to LDA over the set of topics comprising c_d. Although the joint distribution $p(\theta, \mathbf{z}, \mathbf{w}|c_d)$ is intractable [5], individual word-level assignments can be obtained by collapsed Gibbs-sampling [11]. In collapsed Gibbs-sampling, a Markov chain is constructed to converge to the target distribution, and samples are then taken from that Markov chain. Each state of the chain is an assignment of values to the variables being sampled. To apply this algorithm we need the full conditional distribution $p(z_i = j|\mathbf{z}_{-i}, \mathbf{w}, c_d)$. Specifically, the probability of assigning w_i, the ith word in document d, to the jth topic in the set c_d, conditioned on all other word assignments $\mathbf{z}_{-i}$, is given by:

$$p(z_i = j|\mathbf{z}_{-i}, \mathbf{w}, c_d) \propto \frac{n_{-i,j}^{w_i} + \eta}{V(\eta + 1)} \times \frac{n_{-i,j}^d + \alpha}{|c_d|(\alpha + 1)} \tag{1}$$

where $n_{-i,j}^d$ is the frequency of words from document d assigned to topic j other than word i, $n_{-i,j}^{w_i}$ is the frequency of word w_i in topic j, that does not include the current assignment z_i, η and α are Dirichlet prior parameters for the topics and topic word multinomials respectively, and V is the size of vocabulary.

Having obtained the full conditional distribution, the Gibbs sampling algorithm is then straightforward. The z_i variables are initialized to determine the initial state of the Markov chain. The chain then runs for a number of iterations, each time finding a new state by sampling each z_i from the distribution specified by Eq. (1). After obtaining individual word assignments $\mathbf{z}$, we can estimate the topic multinomials and the per-document mixing proportions. Specifically, the topic multinomials are estimated as

$$\beta_{c_d[j],i} = p(w_i|z_{c_d[j]}) = \frac{\eta + n_{z_{c_d[j]}}^{w_i}}{V_\eta + \sum n_{z_{c_d[j]}}} \tag{2}$$

while the per-document mixing proportions can be estimated as:

$$\theta_{d,j} = \frac{\alpha + n_{.,j}^d}{|c_d|\alpha + n^d}, j \in 1, ..., |c_d| \tag{3}$$

where $c_d[j]$ means the jth topic in c_d. Although the equations above look exactly the same as those of LDA, there is an important distinction in that, the target topic j is restricted to belong to the set of labels in c_d.

Dirichlet-Multinomial Parameter Estimation. For EHLLDA model, except for z, θ, we have to estimate μ_{c_i}, which are the parameters of Dirichlet-multinomial distribution (Polya distribution). It is a compound distribution where δ_{c_i} is drawn from a Dirichlet $Dir(.|\mu_{c_i})$ and a sample of discrete outcomes $\mathbf{x}$ is drawn from the multinomial with the probability vector δ_{c_i}. Let n_k be the number of times, and the outcome is k. Then the resulting distribution over $\mathbf{x}$, a vector of outcomes, is given as:

$$p(\mathbf{x}|\mu_{c_i}) = \int_{\delta_{c_i}} p(\mathbf{x}|\delta_{c_i})p(\delta_{c_i}|\mu_{c_i})d\delta_{c_i} \tag{4}$$

$$= \frac{\Gamma(\sum_k \mu_{c_i k})}{\Gamma(\sum_k n_k + \mu_{c_i k})} \prod_k \frac{\Gamma(n_k + \mu_{c_i k})}{\Gamma(\mu_{c_i k})} \tag{5}$$

This distribution is also parameterized by $\mu_{c_i k}$, which can be estimated from a training set of count vectors: $D = \{x_1, ..., x_N\}$. The likelihood is

$$p(D|\mu_{c_i}) = \prod_j p(x_i|\mu_{c_i}) \tag{6}$$

$$= \prod_j \left(\frac{\Gamma(\sum_k \mu_{c_i k})}{\Gamma(\sum_k \mu_{c_i k} + n_j)} \prod_k \frac{\Gamma(n_{jk} + \mu_{c_i k})}{\Gamma(\mu_{c_i k})} \right) \tag{7}$$

We apply fixed-point iteration [17] to maximize the gradience of $\log p(D|\mu_{c_i})$ as follows:

$$\mu_{c_i k}^{new} = \mu_{c_i k} \frac{\sum_j \Psi(n_{jk} + \mu_{c_i k}) - \Psi(\mu_{c_i k})}{\sum_j \Psi(n_j + \sum_k \mu_{c_i k}) - \Psi(\sum_k \mu_{c_i k})} \tag{8}$$

where Ψ is the digamma function. Through Eq. (8), we can obtain the estimation of μ_{c_i}.

4   Experiment

4.1   Dataset

To construct comprehensive datasets for our experiments, we crawled data from two websites. First, we crawled question-answer pairs (QA pairs) of two top categories of Yahoo! Answers: *Computers & Internet* and *Health*. We refer to the data from the category *Computers & Internet* as *Y_Comp*, and the data from the category *Health* as *Y_Hlth*. In addition, we first crawled two categories of Open Directory Project (ODP)[1]: *Home* and *Health*. Then, we removed all categories whose numbers of Web sites are less than 3. Finally, for each Web site in the categories, we submitted its url to Google and used the words in the snippet and title of the first returned result to extend the summary of the Web site. We denote the data from the category *Home* dataset as *O_Home*, and the data from the category *Health* as *O_Hlth*. The statistics of all datasets are summarized in Table 1.

Because hLLDA cannot process the situation in which there are documents in non-leaf nodes, we treat the corresponding label of each document as its path in hLLDA to ensure fairness.

Table 1. The statistics of the datasets.

Datasets	#labels	#paths	Max level	#docs
Y_Comp	27	23	4	3,203,793
Y_Hlth	28	24	4	4,122,983
O_Hlth	6695	6505	10	54939
O_Home	2432	2364	9	24254

4.2   Performance of Proposed Topic Models

In the area of topic modeling, there are usually three methods to evaluate the proposed model: (i) Case study; (ii) Perplexity; (iii) Evaluated indirectly in the third-party application. Here, we will first observe a training result from the proposed model, and then evaluate how well the proposed model describes a dataset in terms of *perplexity*, and finally evaluate the ranking quality of the model, comparing with hLLDA.

Case Study. With topic modeling, the top associated words of topics can be used as good descriptors for labels in a hierarchy. In Fig. 3, we show an example of a path of categories "/Computers & Internet/Hardware/Laptops & Notebooks" from the *Y_Comp* dataset. The topics are the results of EHLLDA with 1500 Gibbs sampling iterations, and symmetric priors $\alpha = 0.01$, $\eta = 0.01$.

---

[1] http://dmoz.org/.

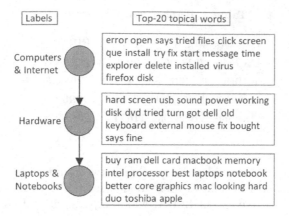

Fig. 3. A topical hierarchy learned with EHLLDA for the path "/Computers & Internet/Hardware/Laptops & Notebooks" in Yahoo! Answer dataset; the top 20 words are shown for each topic. Labels are shown on the left side, and the topical words of each label are shown on the right side.

We made two major observations from the example: (i) topic words for higher level categories are more general than lower level ones. For example, words like "open", "files", "click" and "installed" are associated with the top *"Computer & Internet"*, while more specific words like "screen", "usb" and "keyboard" are associated with lower category *"Hardware"*. This shows that EHLLDA is capable of capturing the hierarchical topic structure of the dataset. (ii) The parent-child relation is reflected by the phenomenon of inherence: some topic words appear in categories that are in a path. For example, "screen" and "disk" appear in both *"Computers & Internet"* and *"Hardware"* which are considered a pair of parent-child categories. Note that the two common words have different importance in the two categories, which further verifies that parent-child categories are related but different. These observations further confirm that EHLLDA is a hierarchy structure aware topic model.

Measure by Perplexity. A good supervised hierarchical topic model should be able to generalize to unseen data. To measure the prediction ability of our models, we computed the perplexity of the given categories under $p(c_d|d)$ for each document d in the test sets [5]. The perplexity of M test documents is calculated as:

$$perplexity(D_{test}) = exp\left\{ -\frac{\sum_{d=1}^{M} \sum_{m=1}^{N_d} \log p(w_{dm})}{\sum_{d=1}^{M} N_d} \right\} \qquad (9)$$

where D_{test} is the test collection of M documents, N_d is document length of document d and w_{dm} is the mth word in document d. We trained LLDA [21], hLLDA [19] and EHLLDA, on all four datasets to compare the prediction performance of these models. LLDA is a state-of-the-art supervised non-hierarchical topic

Table 2. Perplexity of the datasets.

Datasets	LLDA	hLLDA	EHLLDA
Y_Comp	33296.4	22952.3	**21848.3**
Y_Hlth	3017.8	2998.7	**2994.5**
O_Hlth	1667721.1	108640.0	**93954.9**
O_Home	1196459.3	116541.8	**95989.3**

model, which does not consider the relation between labels. hLLDA is a state-of-the-art supervised hierarchical topic model, intending to model the relation between labels. Our model, EHLLDA, will compare with LLDA and hLLDA. We keep 80 % of the data collection as the training set and use the remaining collection as the held-out test set. We build the models based on the training set with 1500 Gibbs sampling iterations, and symmetric priors $\alpha = 0.01$, $\eta = 0.01$, and compute the preplexity of the test set to evaluate the models. Thus, our goal is to achieve high likelihood on a held-out test set.

Table 2 shows the perplexity of each model. From the table, we can see that the perplexities of all supervised hierarchical topic models, i.e., hLLDA and EHLLDA, are lower than supervised non-hierarchical topic model – LLDA. It shows that the performance of models that consider the relation between labels is better than that without considering the relations between labels. Furthermore, we can also see that the perplexities of EHLLDA are lower than that of hLLDA over all four datasets. The results show that our proposed model can model the supervised hierarchical data better than the state-of-the-art model – hLLDA.

Measure by p@n. For each test document, we run the comparing systems to predict a ranking of all C possible paths and compare their performance in terms of precision at top n (p@n). hLLDA is used as our baseline algorithm again. For all the datasets and comparing models, we keep 80 % of the data in the collection as the training set and the remaining collection as the test set. All models are trained with 1500 Gibbs sampling iterations, and symmetric priors $\alpha = 0.01$, $\eta = 0.01$. The experimental results are shown in Table 3. From the table, we can see that EHLLDA outperforms the baseline method (hLLDA) significantly on all four datasets. The improvement is significant by t-test with 95 % significance. This suggests that EHLLDA is better at modeling the topics of the documents thus leads to better ranking results. From the table, the p@n values of hLLDA and EHLLDA over O_Home and O_Hlth are very low. This is because there are too many paths in these two datasets, thus it's hard to discriminate these paths for baseline and proposed algorithms. However, since our aim is to verify the proposed model is better than the baseline by the ranking problem, not to research the ranking problem itself, low p@n values don't change our conclusion.

Table 3. Ranking Predictions for each dataset.

Datasets	Models	Measures			
		P@1	P@2	P@5	P@10
Y_Comp	hLLDA	0.2106	0.2585	0.3688	0.4599
	EHLLDA	**0.2417**	**0.3181**	**0.4552**	**0.5261**
Y_Hlth	hLLDA	0.3655	0.4601	0.5595	0.6103
	EHLLDA	**0.4139**	**0.5027**	**0.5932**	**0.6426**
O_Home	hLLDA	0.0206	0.0289	0.0510	0.0669
	EHLLDA	**0.0283**	**0.0397**	**0.0546**	**0.0809**
O_Hlth	hLLDA	0.0350	0.0462	0.0730	0.0914
	EHLLDA	**0.0418**	**0.0560**	**0.0849**	**0.1113**

5   Related Works

Topic model has been widely and successfully applied to blog articles and other text collections to mine topic patterns [4,5]. There have been many variations of topic models (TM). The existing topic models can be divided into four categories: *Unsupervised non-hierarchical topic models, Unsupervised hierarchical topic models*, and their corresponding supervised counterparts.

Unsupervised non-hierarchical topic models are widely studied, such as LSA [9], pLSA [12], LDA [5], Hierarchical-concept TM [7,8], *d*-BTM [27], Correlated TM [2], TMIO [10] and Concept TM [6,7] etc. The most famous one is Latent Dirichlet Allocation (LDA). LDA is similar to pLSA, except that in LDA the topic distribution is assumed to have a Dirichlet prior. LDA is a completely unsupervised algorithm that models each document as a mixture of topics. Another famous model that does not only represents topic correlations, but also learns them, is the Correlated Topic Model (CTM). Topics in CTM are not independent; however it is noted that only pairwise correlations are modeled, and the number of parameters in the covariance matrix grows as the square of the number of topics.

However, the models above cannot capture the relation between super and sub topics. To address this problem, many models have been proposed to model the relations, such as Hierarchical LDA (HLDA) [1], Hierarchical Dirichlet processes (HDP) [26], Hierarchical PAM (HPAM) [16] and nHDP [13] etc. The relations are usually in the form of a hierarchy, such as the tree or Directed Acyclic Graph (DAG). HDP is proposed to model the groups of data that have a pre-defined hierarchical structure. HDP can capture topic correlations defined by this type of nested data structure; However, it does not automatically discover such correlations from unstructured data. To handle the large topic space, PAM, which uses a DAG structure, is developed to represent and learn the arbitrary, nested, and possibly sparse topic correlations. In PAM, the concept of topics is extended to be distributions not only over words, but also over other topics.

Although unsupervised topic models are sufficiently expressive to model multiple topics per document, they are inappropriate for labeled corpora because they are unable to incorporate the supervised label set into their learning procedure. Several modifications of LDA to incorporate supervision have been proposed in the literature. Two such models, Supervised LDA [3,4] and DiscLDA [14] are first proposed to model documents associated only with a single label. Recently, IRTM [20] is proposed to combine the strengths of MNIR and LDA. Another category of models, such as the MM-LDA [22], Author TM [24], TRTM [15], SNT [13], Prior-LDA [25], Dependency-LDA [25], MedLDA [29] and Partially LDA (PLDA) [23] etc., are not constrained to one label per document because they model each document as a bag of words with a bag of labels, with topics for each observation drawn from a shared topic distribution.

None of these models, however, leverage dependency structure, such as parent-child relation, in the label space. HSLDA [18] and hLLDA [19] are proposed to capture the structral relation. HSLDA still needs to decide manually how many topics in a collection, i.e. parameter K. hLLDA takes each label as a topic, i.e. a distribution over vocabulary, thus hLLDA assumes that the number of topics in a labeled collection is the one of labels. From the generative process, hLLDA has two latent assumptions: (i) hLLDA treats each child of a non-leaf label equally; (ii) hLLDA also assumes that each document in the corpus must have a leaf label, i.e. each document cannot locate in the non-leaf node in the hierarchy of labels. However, in most cases, these assumptions do not meet the actual situation. Thus, in this paper, we extend hLLDA to a model named *Extended Hierarchical Labeled LDA* (EHLLDA) by taking advantage of prior information of labels and relaxing assumptions.

6   Conclusion and Future Work

In this paper, we considered the problem of modeling hierarchical labeled data – such as web pages and their placement in hierarchical directories, and product descriptions and catalogs. We proposed a supervised hierarchical topic model, i.e. EHLLDA, which incorporated prior information of paths and relaxed the assumption of hLLDA. The experimental results show that our model is always better than baseline in terms of perplexity and p@n.

In the future, we will continue to explore novel topic models for supervised hierarchical data to further improve the performance; meanwhile we will also apply our supervised hierarchical topic models to other media forms, such as image, to test model's generalization ability and solve related problems in these area.

Acknowledgments. The work was supported by National Natural Science Foundation of China (No. 61402036), 863 Program of China (No. 2015AA015404) and 973 Program (No. 2013CB329605).

References

1. Blei, D., Griffiths, T., Jordan, M., Tenenbaum, J.: Hierarchical topic models and the nested chinese restaurant process. In: Advances in Neural Information Processing Systems, vol. 16, pp. 106 (2004)
2. Blei, D., Lafferty, J.: Correlated topic models. In: Advances in Neural Information Processing Systems, vol. 18, p. 147 (2006)
3. Blei, D., McAuliffe, J.: Supervised topic models. In: Proceeding of the Neural Information Processing Systems (NIPS) (2007)
4. Blei, D., McAuliffe, J.: Supervised topic models (2010). Arxiv preprint arXiv:1003.0783
5. Blei, D., Ng, A., Jordan, M.: Latent dirichlet allocation. J. Mach. Learn. Res. **3**, 993–1022 (2003)
6. Chemudugunta, C., Holloway, A., Smyth, P., Steyvers, M.: Modeling documents by combining semantic concepts with unsupervised statistical learning. In: Sheth, A.P., Staab, S., Dean, M., Paolucci, M., Maynard, D., Finin, T., Thirunarayan, K. (eds.) ISWC 2008. LNCS, vol. 5318, pp. 229–244. Springer, Heidelberg (2008)
7. Chemudugunta, C., Smyth, P., Steyvers, M.: Combining concept hierarchies and statistical topic models. In: Proceeding of the 17th ACM Conference on Information and Knowledge Management, pp. 1469–1470. ACM (2008)
8. Chemudugunta, C., Smyth, P., Steyvers, M.: Text modeling using unsupervised topic models and concept hierarchies (2008). Arxiv preprint arXiv:0808.0973
9. Deerwester, S., Dumais, S., Furnas, G., Landauer, T., Harshman, R.: Indexing by latent semantic analysis. J. Am. Soc. Inf. Sci. **41**(6), 391–407 (1990)
10. Du, L., Pate, J.K., Johnson, M.: Topic segmentation with an ordering-based topic model. In: Twenty-Ninth AAAI Conference on Artificial Intelligence (2015)
11. Griffiths, T., Steyvers, M.: Finding scientific topics. In: Proceedings of the National Academy of Sciences of the United States of America, vol. 101(Suppl 1), p. 5228 (2004)
12. Hofmann, T.: Probabilistic latent semantic analysis. In: Proceedings of Uncertainty in Artificial Intelligence, UAI1999, p. 21. Citeseer (1999)
13. Kawamae, N.: Supervised n-gram topic model. In: Proceedings of the 7th ACM International Conference on Web Search and Data Mining, pp. 473–482. ACM (2014)
14. Lacoste-Julien, S., Sha, F., Jordan, M.: ndisclda: Discriminative learning for dimensionality reduction and classification. In: Advances in Neural Information Processing Systems, vol. 21 (2008)
15. Ma, Z., Sun, A., Yuan, Q., Cong, G.: A tri-role topic model for domain-specific question answering. In: Proceedings of The Twenty-Ninth AAAI Conference on Artificial Intelligence (2015)
16. Mimno, D., Li, W., McCallum, A.: Mixtures of hierarchical topics with pachinko allocation. In: Proceedings of the 24th International Conference on Machine Learning, pp. 633–640. ACM (2007)
17. Minka, T.: Estimating a dirichlet distribution. Ann. Phys. **2000**(8), 1–13 (2003)
18. Perotte, A.J., Wood, F., Elhadad, N., Bartlett, N.: Hierarchically supervised latent dirichlet allocation. In: Advances in Neural Information Processing Systems, pp. 2609–2617 (2011)
19. Petinot, Y., McKeown, K., Thadani, K.: A hierarchical model of web summaries. In: Proceedings of the 49th Annual Meeting of the Association for Computational Linguistics: Human Language Technologies: short papers, vol. 2, pp. 670–675. Association for Computational Linguistics (2011)

20. Rabinovich, M., Blei, D.: The inverse regression topic model. In: Proceedings of the 31st International Conference on Machine Learning, pp. 199–207 (2014)
21. Ramage, D., Hall, D., Nallapati, R., Manning, C.: Labeled lda: a supervised topic model for credit attribution in multi-labeled corpora. In: Proceedings of the 2009 Conference on Empirical Methods in Natural Language Processing, vol. 1, pp. 248–256. Association for Computational Linguistics (2009)
22. Ramage, D., Heymann, P., Manning, C., Garcia-Molina, H.: Clustering the tagged web. In: Proceedings of the Second ACM International Conference on Web Search and Data Mining, pp. 54–63. ACM (2009)
23. Ramage, D., Manning, C., Dumais, S.: Partially labeled topic models for interpretable text mining. In: Proceedings of the 17th ACM SIGKDD International Conference on Knowledge Discovery and Data Mining, pp. 457–465. ACM (2011)
24. Rosen-Zvi, M., Griffiths, T., Steyvers, M., Smyth, P.: The author-topic model for authors and documents. In: Proceedings of the 20th Conference on Uncertainty in Artificial Intelligence, pp. 487–494. AUAI Press (2004)
25. Rubin, T., Chambers, A., Smyth, P., Steyvers, M.: Statistical topic models for multi-label document classification (2011). Arxiv preprint arXiv:1107.2462
26. Teh, Y., Jordan, M., Beal, M., Blei, D.: Hierarchical dirichlet processes. J. Am. Stat. Assoc. 101(476), 1566–1581 (2006)
27. Xia, Y., Tang, N., Hussain, A., Cambria, E.: Discriminative bi-term topic model for headline-based social news clustering. In: The Twenty-Eighth International Flairs Conference (2015)
28. Xiao, H., Wang, X., Du, C.: Injecting structured data to generative topic model in enterprise settings. In: Zhou, Z.-H., Washio, T. (eds.) ACML 2009. LNCS, vol. 5828, pp. 382–395. Springer, Heidelberg (2009)
29. Zhu, J., Ahmed, A., Xing, E.P.: Medlda: maximum margin supervised topic models. J. Mach. Learn. Res. 13(1), 2237–2278 (2012)

Graph-Based Dependency Parsing with Recursive Neural Network

Pingping Huang[1,2] and Baobao Chang[3,4]([✉])

[1] School of Electronics Engineering and Computer Science, Peking University,
Beijing 100871, China
[2] Collaborative Innovation Center for Language Ability, Xuzhou 221009, China
[3] Key Laboratory of Computational Linguistics, Ministry of Education,
School of Software and Microelectronics, Beijing 100871, China
[4] School of Electronics Engineering and Computer Science, Peking University,
Xuzhou 221009, China
{pinghpp,chbb}@pku.edu.cn

Abstract. Graph-based dependency parsing models have achieved
state-of-the-art performance, yet their defect in feature representation
is obvious: these models enforce strong independence assumptions upon
tree components, thus restricting themselves to local, shallow features
with limited context information. Besides, they rely heavily on hand-
crafted feature templates. In this paper, we extend recursive neural network into dependency parsing. This allows us to efficiently represent the
whole sub-tree context and rich structural information for each node. We
propose a heuristic search procedure for decoding. Our model can also
be used in the reranking framework. With words and pos-tags as the
only input features, it gains significant improvement over the baseline
models, and shows advantages in capturing long distance dependencies.

Keywords: Dependency parsing · Recursive neural network ·
Weighted-sum pooling

1   Instruction

Dependency parsing is a fundamental NLP task in which the syntactic structure
of a sentence is depicted by the dependency relations between words. It also
wildly used in other applications that rely on syntactic trees.

Current supervised models mainly fall into two fundamentally different categories: transition-based models (see Yamada and Matsumoto 2003; Nivre et al.
2006) and graph-based models (see Eisner 1996; McDonald et al. 2005). The
former resorts to a set of transition actions, thus turning the search for the best
tree structure into the search for the optimal choices of transition sequence. By
contrast, graph-based models explicitly parametrize the dependencies between
words, and search over all possible trees which span the whole sentence for the
optimal structure. With carefully designed features and proper search procedures, both of these models achieve state-of-the-art performance.

© Springer International Publishing Switzerland 2015
M. Sun et al. (Eds.): CCL and NLP-NABD 2015, LNAI 9427, pp. 227–239, 2015.
DOI: 10.1007/978-3-319-25816-4_19

In the two types of models, graph-based models usually decompose the whole tree structure into small sub-graphs and enforce strong independence assumption among them. When scoring an individual sub-graph, the features are constrained inside this small part. The drawbacks of these models are obvious:

1. The independence assumption is not justified linguistically, because the sentence is an organized whole item, and there are complicated interactions among different sub-graphs.
2. The parsing performance relies heavily on hand-crafted features, which demands much expertise knowledge. Besides, dealing with the enormous amount of features are time-consuming in parsing, and increases the risk of over-fitting.

In face of these drawbacks, we propose a recursive neural network model for graph-based dependency parsing. The main advantages of our model are as follows:

1. Much wider contexts are taken into account. In our model, each node in the dependency tree is represented with the whole sub-tree context into consideration.
2. Our model does not rely on complicated feature templates. Instead, it only needs words and pos-tags as input features, the representation and selection of features are automatically learned during the training.
3. Our model can also be used as a reranking model.

We evaluate our model on the English Penn Treebank. Experiment results show that our models gains significant improvement over the baseline system. Especially when used as a reranking model, the improvement is more exciting. Experiments also demonstrate that our model exhibits advantages in capturing long distance dependencies.

The remaining part of this paper is organized as follows. Section 2 describes the motivation behind our model. Section 3 elaborates on our recursive neural networking model for dependency trees. The parsing algorithm is described in Sect. 4. In Sect. 5, we describe how our model can be used as a reranking model. The training method is given in Sect. 6. Experiments, results and analysis are given in Sect. 7. Section 8 summarizes related work. Section 9 draws the conclusions.

2   Motivation

In graph-based models, the parsing process is the search for the highest scored tree structure that spans all the words of the sentence and roots at an artificial node "ROOT". A fundamental property of graph-based parsing systems is that, for input sentence x, the score of a structure y is assumed to factor through the scores of independent sub-graphs:

$$score(x, y) = \sum_{g \in y} h(g) = \sum_{g \in y} \boldsymbol{w} \cdot \boldsymbol{\psi}_g \qquad (1)$$

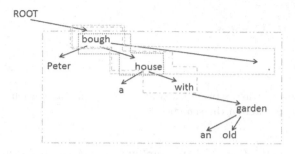

Fig. 1. Illustration of the context ranges for different order models when scoring the dependency between *bought* and *house*. The red block indicates the context for the first-order model, the yellow block the second-order model, and the blue block the third-order model. The green block is the sub-tree context in our model for node *bought* (Color figure online).

where g is the decomposed sub-graph in tree y, h is the score function, and is often a liner model as we use it here. ψ_g is the high dimensional feature vector defined on g, and w is the corresponding weight vector.

According to the number of edges each decomposed sub-graph contains, the order of a system is thus defined. The first-order model, which is also called edge-factored model (see Eisner 2000; McDonald et al. 2005), assumes that the score of a tree structure is the sum scores of independent edges. In second-order models, each sub-graph contains a pair of adjacent edges, like the same-side sibling edges (see McDonald and Pereira 2006), or head-modifier-grandchild edges (see Carreras 2007; Koo and Collins 2010). In third-order models, the size of sub-graph further expands to certain patterns of three edges, like grand-siblings or tri-siblings structures (see Koo and Collins 2010; Hayashi et al. 2011). A crucial limitation of these models is that the associated sub-graphs are typically small, losing much of the contextual information and interactions with other components, as is illustrated in Fig. 1. When scoring the dependencies for *bought*, even the third-order model can only reaches context in a very limited local region. For a similar sentence: *"Peter bought a house with an old friend."*, the above mentioned context information will be quite insufficient to decide whether the head of *with* should be *bought* or *house*.

Correspondingly, the features that the model can draw on is also limited inside each sub-graph. Commonly used features are like the words and pos-tags of parent and child, the arity of the parent, the distance between them, the sibling's words and pos-tag, and most importantly, the various conjunctions for two of three of these atomic features. The weights for these high dimensional sparse features will be poorly estimated in a linear model due to data sparsity. What's worse, those local and lexical features are incapable to catch various interactions in a wide context.

In this paper, we propose a model that scores the tree according to all its sub-tree structures rooted at each nodes, and this score function will move beyond

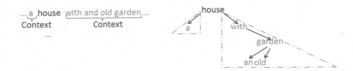

Fig. 2. Equivalence relation between the descendants for node *house* in the dependency tree and its context words in the sentence.

the limitation of previous models to employ more global and structure context. At the same time, our model learns to select useful features all by itself instead of hand-crafted feature templates.

Different from traditional graph-based models that score on edges, we score the tree as the sum over all the nodes:

$$score(x, y) = \sum_{n \in y} s(n) \tag{2}$$

where n is a node in y, yet this node is not scored in isolation. The score $s(n)$ given by our model judges how likely this whole sub-tree rooted at node n is the right structure for the corresponding spanned words.

Our assumption is that the syntactic role for a word is decided by two factors: the word's interior meaning and its surrounding context. In a sub-tree structure, the root node serves as the head word for the corresponding span and carries the most important information. Therefore, we need to consider the root node's input as the interior information.

We notice that in a projective dependency tree, descendant nodes for a root is equal to the context that surrounds this word in the sentence, as shown in Fig. 2. Therefore we also need to represent the information carried by the descendants nodes in the sub-tree for this root. We have further observed that dependency words before and after a head word usually play different roles. Therefore, we use two features, *leftContext* and *rightContext*, to represent descendant nodes from this two different directions.

In this way, each root node in the tree contains three parts: context from left descendants, the information carried by the node itself, and the context from right descendants. Compared to traditional models, we incorporates much larger context and more patterns of interactions. Then the question remains: how can we represent and score each node with all these information in consideration?

3   Recursive Neural Network for Dependency Trees

The idea of recursive neural networks (see Socheret al. 2010; Coller and Kuchler 1996) is to learn hierarchical feature representations by applying the same neural network recursively in a tree structure. But the standard network architecture can only be applied to a fixed-tree structure. We adapt this network for dependency trees and propose the *content-context* vectorial representation for each node, this node representation compresses rich context of the whole sub-tree information.

3.1   Node and Context Representation

One of the revolutionary changes coming with the rise of Deep Neural Network(DNN) is the idea of representation learning and automatic feature selection. The most convincing example is word and feature embedding learning that shows great superiority (see Bengio et al. 2003; Mikolov et al. 2010; Mikolov et al. 2013).

Inspired by these success, we use word and pos-tag as the only input information and leave it to the model to learn the vectorial representations, and feature selection and combination. For each node in the tree, its word and pos-tag are indexed through lookup tables into low-dimensional dense valued embeddings. Then we concatenate these two embeddings and get the *content* embedding for a node:

$$content_i = f[I_{word_i} \cdot L_{words}; I_{pos_i} \cdot L_{poses}] \tag{3}$$

where f is the nonlinear transformation function, I_{word} is the one-hot high dimensional vector for word w_i, and I_{pos} is the one-hot vector for the pos-tag p_i. L_{words} and L_{poses} are lookup tables of word and pos-tag embeddings, which are learned during the training. Each child's *content* embedding will be propagated forward into the parent node's *context* embedding. And there will be specific null embeddings to indicate the context for leaf nodes.

3.2   Weighted-Sum Pooling

The standard recursive neural networks requires a fixed local structure for each tree node. But for dependency trees, the number of children in each node varies. Thus we need a way to deal with this structural speciality so that all nodes can share the weights when propagating information in the tree.

We introduce weighted sum pooling strategy that assigns a weight to each child node. This weight indicates how important this child is among its siblings, and correlates to the sub-tree size spanned by this node. The more words this sub-structure spans, the more important role it will play in parent's context embedding. The weight w_j for node j is computed as follows:

$$cnt_i = \begin{cases} 1, & \text{if } i \text{ is a leaf} \\ 1 + \sum_{(i,j) \in y} cnt_j, & \text{otherwise} \end{cases} \tag{4}$$

$$w_j = Cnt_j/Cnt_i, \text{ for}(i,j) \in y \tag{5}$$

That is, the weight of a child node is the ratio of this node's number of spanned words in that of its parent's. With this pooling strategy, we can propagate all the information from arbitrary number of children into parent while sharing one set of parameter.

3.3   Network Architecture

When a tree structure y is given, we propagate the content of children into the context of parent node in a bottom-up direction as follows:

$$context_{left}(i) = f(W1 \cdot \sum_{(i,j) \in y, j < i} w_j \cdot content_j + b_l) \qquad (6)$$

$$context_{right}(i) = f(W2 \cdot \sum_{(i,j) \in y, j > i} w_j \cdot content_j + b_r) \qquad (7)$$

where w_j is the weight associated with each node, $W1$ and $W2$ are the weight matrix that combine incoming children from two different directions into the parent. f is the non-linear transformation function in the neural network.

Till now, we have filled the *content-contex* embeddings for each node. Then we concatenate these vectorial representations as features and directly score on it:

$$s(i) = W3 \cdot [context_{left}(i); content(i); context_{right}(i)] \qquad (8)$$

where $W3$ is the weight matrix that is used to score on these representations. The higher the score is, the more likely this given sub-tree structure rooted at the current node is the correct structure.

The network structure and the forward propagation process is shown in Fig. 3. As the tree is built in the bottom-up fashion, each node's content will appear in parent's context, and then the grand node and so on. In this way, even the far-most leaf's information will be propagated into the root's context, thus the context information for each node we can use is the whole sub-tree. Once the forward propagation is done we get the score for each node, and the score of a given tree is the sum score of them. In our model, the only feature we use is the word and pos-tag for each node. Instead of carefully designing the feature templates to capture certain kinds of interactions among nodes, the model learns to select useful information and interactions by tuning the weight matrix.

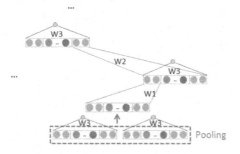

Fig. 3. Model architecture and the propagation process in a dependency tree

4 Parsing

Parsing is the search for the highest scored tree structure that spans all the words in a sentence. As recursive neural network scores each node in a bottom-up way, the Eisner algorithm for first order projective parsing launches the parsing in a similar direction (see Eisner 2000; McDonald et al. 2005). With the edge independence assumption, this algorithm employs dynamic programming for exact search.

But as we score each node with the whole sub-tree structure in consideration, which breaks the dynamic programming condition and thus the model can only use inexact search. We extends Esiner algorithm with beam search strategy, and use the same chart table and parsing structures as in the original algorithm. The only difference is that in each chart cell, we keep B highest scored candidates instead of just one, and call this list an *agenda*. When combing two chart cells to form a bigger structure, we try all the available combinations coming from this two agendas. When all the chart cells are filled, we get the highest scored tree structure in $E[0][n][1][0]$. This is the target structure coving all words with "ROOT" as the root node.

But when we take a further look into the chart cell combination process, each trial combination involves several matrix operations and a non-linear transformation to update the newly combined candidate structure's score. This will be time-consuming in practise. Therefore we use the prune heuristic to filter out unlikely combined candidates. We follow the similar strategy in (Socher et al. 2013): we use the k-best list from a baseline system, arcs that never appeared in any of the k-best is pruned directly. Note that though this prune strategy relies on a k-best list, it differs from re-ranking in two main aspects: first each node will just get access to the local information that whether another node is a possible child, instead of the whole tree or any other global information. Second, we can generate tree structures that is not in the k-best list. This prune allows the second pass to be very fast yet still keep the exploration space large enough.

5 Used as a Reranking Model

As our model can give scores of a whole tree structure, it can also be directly used in the reranking phase. The max margin training criterion expects the score of the correct tree to be higher than that for an incorrect tree by a margin, therefore it can discriminate good structure from bad ones. Besides, as the parsing algorithm is heuristic search, reranking eliminates the risk of search errors thus gives a more directly measure to the model's ability to discriminate good structures from bad ones. Therefore we also experiments in the reranking framework, without any extra training once we get the model trained for parsing.

6 Training

For model training, we use the Max-Margin criterion. Given a training instance (x_i, y_i), we search for the dependency tree with the highest score. The structured margin loss between the predicted structure and the given correct tree is defined on the discrepancy between trees. It is measured by counting the number of nodes $N(y_i)$ with incorrect head in the predicted tree:

$$(y_i, \hat{y}_i) = \sum_j^n \kappa 1\{h(y_i, x_i) \neq h(\hat{y}_i, x_i)\} \tag{9}$$

where n is the length for the sentence x_i. We set the parameter $\kappa = 0.1$ throughout the experiment. The loss increases the more incorrect the proposed parse tree is.

The object of Max-Margin training is that the highest scoring tree is the correct one $y_i^* = y_i$ and its score will be larger up to a margin to other possible tree $\hat{y}_i \in Y(x_i)$:

$$score(x_i, y_i; \theta) \geq score(x_i, \hat{y}_i; \theta) + \Delta(y_i, \hat{y}_i) \tag{10}$$

Then the regularized objective function for m training examples is thus defined:

$$\begin{aligned} J(\theta) &= \frac{1}{m} \sum_{i=1}^m (l_i(\theta) + \frac{\lambda}{2}||\theta||), \text{where} \\ l_i(\theta) &= max_{\hat{y} \in Y(x_i)} (score\,(x_i, \hat{y}; \theta) + \Delta\,(y_i, \hat{y}_i)) - score\,(x_i, y_i; \theta) \end{aligned} \tag{11}$$

We train the network with Back Propagation Through Structure(BPTS) (see Goller and Kuchler 1996). As the objective function is not differentiable due to the hinge loss, we follow Socher et al. (2013) to use generalized gradient descent via the sub-gradient method (see Ratliff et al. 2007) which computes a gradient-like direction.

$$\frac{\partial J}{\partial \theta} = \sum_i \frac{\partial s(x_i, \hat{y}_{max})}{\partial \theta} - \frac{\partial s(x_i, y_i)}{\partial \theta} + \lambda \theta \tag{12}$$

where $\hat{y}_i$ is the tree with highest score. We use the diagonal variant of AdaGrad (see Duchi et al. 2011) with minibatchs for optimization.

7   Experiment

7.1   Data and Setup

We experiment on the English Penn Treebank (PTB3.0) and use the head rules of (see Yamada and Matsumoto 2003) and Penn2malt[1] tool to extract dependency trees. We follow the standard splits of PTB3, using Sect. 2–21 for training, Sect. 22 as development set and 23 as test set. The pos-tag is labelled by The Stanford POS Tagger (see Toutanova et al. 2003). We first tag the development and test data trained on the whole training data. The training itself is tagged with the ten-way jackknifing strategy. The overall pos-tagging accuracy is around 97.2 %.

---

[1] http://stp.lingfil.uu.se/~nivre/research/Penn2Malt.html.

We use our implementation of beam search based arc-standard system to generate the k-best list for pruning and for reranking. The model is trained with the structured perceptron learning with early update strategy (see Collins and Roark 2004). Rich feature templates are used following (see Huang and Sagae 2010; Zhang and Nivre 2011; Huang et al. 2009).

7.2 Parameter Setting

The parameters of our neural network include:

$$\theta = \{W_1, W_2, W3, b_r, b_l, L_{words}, L_{pos}\}$$

We set the dimension of word and context embeddings to be 50, pos tag embedding of dimension 20. We initialize the word embeddings using wor2vec (see Mikolov et at. 2013) by pre-training on Gigaword corpus (see Graff et al. 2003). Pos tag embeddins are random initialized as $L_{pos} \sim U[-1, 1]$. We use $tanh$ as the non-linear transformation function throughout the experiments. Weight matrix takes Xavie initialization (see Glorot and Bengio 2010): $r = \sqrt{6/(fanIn + fanOut)}$, $W \sim U[-r, r]^2$. We fix the regularization parameter $\lambda = 10^{-3}$ for all parameters. The minibatch size was set as 20. We also cross-validated on AdaGrad's learning rate which was eventually set to 0.04.

7.3 Result

As our neural network scorer judges whether a bare tree structure is reasonable, we measure its performance in UAS without punctuation[3]. We examine it in both parsing and in a re-ranking framework. The result is shown in Table 1. We use our implementation, the Beam Arc-Standard as the comparing baseline. Early trial experiments show that the beam size in the training phase has a direct effect on the parsing performance and training speed. To trade off training time and accuracy, we chose a beam size of 60 for model training. But during the parsing, we cross-validated on the development data and used a larger beam size of 200 to explore more search space.

Table 1. Experiment result of UAS without punctuations.

Model	Dev	Test
OurModel-parsing	91.56	91.41
OurModel-rerank	**92.84**	**92.46**
Beam arc-standard	90.79	90.63

---

[2] $fanIn$ is the number of node from incoming layer and $fanout$ is the number for the next layer.
[3] UAS: Unlabelled Attachment Score. Following previous work, we excludes tokens with pos tags of { "" , ; .}.

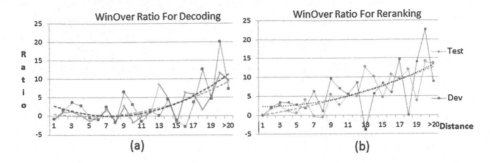

Fig. 4. The win-over ratio of our model versus baseline at different distances. (a) is the result of decoding, (b) is the result at re-ranking. The smoothed lines are binomial trend lines.

When used in parsing, we achieve the an UAS of 91.56 on the development data, and 91.41 on the test data. We then directly applies this trained model in a reranking framework. The top-60 candidate trees are generated by the our baseline, the Beam Arc-Standard system. Then our model scores each tree and chooses the highest scored candidate as the final output. This yields a more promising result: we get an UAS of 92.84 and 92.46 on development and test set, which is an improvement of 2.1 and 1.83 over the baseline.

7.4   Analysis

Ability to Capture Long Distance Dependencies: Our main motivation for introducing recursive neural network into dependency parsing is to make use of richer context and thus better capturing dependencies that lie beyond traditional models' reach. Therefore we compare our model with the baseline in view of the ability to discriminate dependency relations at different distances. We plot the comparison result in Fig. 4 for both decoding and reranking setup.[4] The smooth dash lines are polynomial trends for each comparison setup.

We can see that our model wins over the baseline in most cases, especially when the distance get larger than a certain threshold. What's more, there is an ascending trend for both decoding and reranking. Especially in the re-ranking setup, our model shows continuous superiority. This shows that our sub-tree based context does capture the long distance better as we expected.

Ability of Embedding Learning: To see what kind of information and interactions our model has learned, we probe into the learned embedding representations for pos-tags. Figure 5 is the visualization result.

We can see that, on one hand, our model captures the syntactic similarities among pos-tags quite well. As shown in Fig. 5(b)/(c), pos-tags for verbs/nous

---

[4] The win-over ratio is defined as: $r =$ (the number of dependencies our model gets right $-$ the number of dependencies the baseline gets right) / total number of dependencies at this distance. $r > 0$ indicates that our model performs better than baseline at this distance, the higher the ratio is, the bigger advantage we gains.

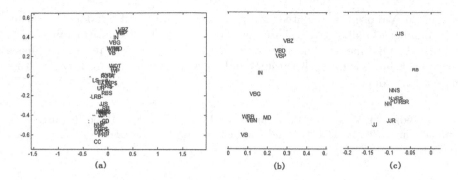

Fig. 5. Visualization of pos embeddings, (b) and (c) are the amplified local for (a).

are clustered closely. On the other hand, these embeddings also capture the relatedness among tags that usually form dependencies, as in Fig. 5(b) IN and MD are clustered with verbs. And in Fig. 5(c) adjective tags scatters closely among noun tags. This is quiet a desirable representation.

8   Related Work

Models for dependency parsing have been studied with considerable effort in the NLP community. Among them, we only focus on the graph-based models here. Traditional models decompose the tree into small sub-graphs and scores independently. McDonaldet.al (2005) proposed the first-order model which is also know as arc-factored model. Pereira (2006) further extend the first-order model to second-order model where sibling information is available during decoding. Carreras (2007) proposed a more powerful second-order model that can score both sibling and grandchild parts. To exploit more structure information, Koo and Collins (2010) proposed three third-order models that further include grand-siblings and tri-siblings structures into consideration. Compared with these models, our system considers richer more structural context information, and we do not rely on hand-crafted feature templates.

Recently, neural network models have been increasingly focused on. Chen and Manning (2014) uses a neural network to substitute the classifier in a transition-based models with a few atomic features. Recursive neural network for tree parsing was first introduced by Socher et al. (2010) into phrase structure parsing. And was extended for dependency trees in Le and Zuidema (2014), but this generative model can only be used during the reranking, while our model can be used in parsing.

9   Conclusion

In this paper, we adapts the recursive neural network for dependency trees to employ richer context and more structural information. Each node is represented by a content and two context embeddings so that the sub-tree structure is scored as a whole. We use the weighted sum pooling strategy so that nodes with arbitrary number of children can share one set of parameters to forward-propagate in the tree. Our model can be used both in parsing and in reranking phase. And both achieve competitive results and show an advantage in discriminating long-distance dependencies.

Acknowledgments. This work is supported by National Key Basic Research Program of China (2014CB340504) and National Natural Science Foundation of China (61273318).

References

Bengio, Y., Ducharme, R., Vincent, P., Janvin, C.: A neural probabilistic language model. J. Mach. Learn. Res. **3**, 1137–1155 (2003)

Carreras, X.: Experiments with a higher-order projective dependency parser. In: EMNLP-CoNLL, pp. 957–961 (2007)

Chen, D., Manning, C.D.: A fast and accurate dependency parser using neural networks. In: Proceedings of the 2014 Conference on Empirical Methods in Natural Language Processing (EMNLP), pp. 740–750 (2014)

Collins, M., Roark, B.: Incremental parsing with the perceptron algorithm. In: Proceedings of the 42nd Annual Meeting on Association for Computational Linguistics, p. 111 (2004)

Duchi, J., Hazan, E., Singer, Y.: Adaptive subgradient methods for online learning and stochastic optimization. J. Mach. Learn. Res. **12**, 2121–2159 (2011)

Eisner, J.M.: Three new probabilistic models for dependency parsing: an exploration. In: Proceedings of the 16th Conference on Computational Linguistics, vol. 1, pp. 340–345 (1996)

Eisner, J.: Bilexical grammars and their cubic-time parsing algorithms. In: Bunt, H., Nijholt, A. (eds.) Advances in Probabilistic and Other Parsing Technologies. Text, Speech and Language Technology, vol. 16, pp. 29–61. Springer, Netherlands (2000)

Glorot, X., Bengio, Y.: Understanding the difficulty of training deep feedforward neural networks. In: International Conference on Artificial Intelligence and Statistics, pp. 249–256 (2010)

Goller, C., Kuchler, A.: Learning task-dependent distributed representations by backpropagation through structure. In: IEEE International Conference on Neural Networks, vol. 1, pp. 347–352 (1996)

Hayashi, K., Watanabe, T., Asahara, M., Matsumoto, Y.: Third-order variational reranking on packed-shared dependency forests. In: Proceedings of the Conference on Empirical Methods in Natural Language Processing, pp. 1479–1488 (2011)

Huang, L., Sagae, K.: Dynamic programming for linear-time incremental parsing. In: Proceedings of the 48th Annual Meeting of the Association for Computational Linguistics, pp. 1077–1086 (2010)

Huang, L., Jiang, W., Liu, Q.: Bilingually-constrained (monolingual) shift-reduce parsing. In: Proceedings of the 2009 Conference on Empirical Methods in Natural Language Processing, vol. 3, pp. 1222–1231 (2009)

Koo, T., Collins, M.: Efficient third-order dependency parsers. In: Proceedings of the 48th Annual Meeting of the Association for Computational Linguistics, pp. 1–11 (2010)

Le, P., Zuidema, W.: The inside-outside recursive neural network model for dependency parsing. In: Proceedings of the 2014 Conference on Empirical Methods in Natural Language Processing (EMNLP), pp. 729–739 (2014)

McDonald, R.T., Pereira, F.C.N.: Online learning of approximate dependency parsing algorithms. In: EACL (2006)

McDonald, R., Crammer, K., Pereira, F.: Online large-margin training of dependency parsers. In: Proceedings of the 43rd Annual Meeting on Association for Computational Linguistics, pp. 91–98 (2005)

Mikolov, T., Karafiát, M., Burget, L., Cernockỳ, J., Khudanpur, S.: Recurrent neural network based language model. In: INTERSPEECH 2010, 11th Annual Conference of the International Speech Communication Association, Makuhari, Chiba, Japan, 26–30 September 2010, pp. 1045–1048 (2010)

Mikolov, T., Chen, K., Corrado, G., Dean, J.: Efficient estimation of word representations in vector space (2013). arXiv preprint http://arxiv.org/abs/1301.3781

Nivre, J., Hall, J., Nilsson, J., Eryigit, G., Marinov, S.: Labeled pseudo-projective dependency parsing with support vector machines. In: Proceedings of the Tenth Conference on Computational Natural Language Learning, pp. 221–225 (2006)

Socher, R., Manning, C.D., Ng, A.Y.: Learning continuous phrase representations and syntactic parsing with recursive neural networks. In: Proceedings of the NIPS-2010 Deep Learning and Unsupervised Feature Learning Workshop, pp. 1–9 (2010)

Socher, R., Bauer, J., Manning, C.D., Ng, A.Y.: Parsing with compositional vector grammars. In: Proceedings of the ACL conference (2013)

Toutanova, K., Klein, D., Manning, C.D., Singer, Y.: Feature-rich part-of-speech tagging with a cyclic dependency network. In: Proceedings of the 2003 Conference of the North American Chapter of the Association for Computational Linguistics on Human Language Technology, vol. 1, pp. 173–180 (2003)

Yamada, H., Yuji, M.: Statistical dependency analysis with support vector machines. In: Proceedings of IWPT, vol. 3, pp. 195–206 (2003)

Zhang, Y., Nivre, J.: Transition-based dependency parsing with rich non-local features. In: Proceedings of the 49th Annual Meeting of the Association for Computational Linguistics: Human Language Technologies. short papers, vol. 2, pp. 188–193 (2011)

A Neural Network Based Translation Constrained Reranking Model for Chinese Dependency Parsing

Miaohong Chen, Baobao Chang[(✉)], and Yang Liu

Key Laboratory of Computational Linguistics,
Ministry of Education School of Electronics Engineering and Computer Science,
Peking University Collaborative Innovation Center for Language Ability,
Xuzhou 221009, China
miaohong-chen@foxmail.com, {chbb,cs-ly}@pku.edu.cn

Abstract. Bilingual dependency parsing aims to improve parsing performance with the help of bilingual information. While previous work have shown improvements on either or both sides, most of them mainly focus on designing complicated features and rely on golden translations during training and testing. In this paper, we propose a simple yet effective translation constrained reranking model to improve Chinese dependency parsing. The reranking model is trained using a max-margin neural network without any manually designed features. Instead of using golden translations for training and testing, we relax the restrictions and use sentences generated by a machine translation system, which dramatically extends the scope of our model. Experiments on the translated portion of the Chinese Treebank show that our method outperforms the state-of-the-art monolingual Graph/Transition-based parsers by a large margin (UAS).

Keywords: Bilingual dependency parsing · Reranking · Neural network · Machine translation

1 Introduction

Dependency parsing is a crucial task of natural language processing (NLP) and has been intensively explored during the last decades. Dominant dependency parsing methods mainly falls into two categories: transition-based [1,2] and graph-based [3]. Both methods demonstrated relatively high accuracies on parsing English texts. However, the performance of existing Chinese dependency parsers is still considerably inferior compared to their English counterpart, due to the limited size of annotated Treebank and the morphology-poor characteristics of the language.

To improve the accuracy of Chinese dependency parsing and reduce the performance gap, we propose a neural network based translation constrained reranking model for Chinese dependency parsing in this paper. Our motivation

M. Sun et al. (Eds.): CCL and NLP-NABD 2015, LNAI 9427, pp. 240–249, 2015.
DOI: 10.1007/978-3-319-25816-4_20

for this model is twofold. (1) Using deep learning methods to avoid complicated and tricky feature engineering. Instead of manually designing various linguistics-motivated features, we simply use distributed representations as the input of the reranking model. Embeddings of words and pos tags as well as the interactions between them are automatically learning through the neural network. (2) Enhancing Chinese dependency parsing performance with the help of automatically generated English translations. This is motivated by the fact that Chinese and English are not always ambiguous in the same way. When a Chinese sentence is syntactically ambiguous, its English translation might not be the case. Specifically, we train the reranking model with dependency annotated Chinese sentences in the training set as well as their translations generated by a machine translation system. Since the English translations are automatically generated, the model does not rely on golden aligned sentences for training or testing any more, which makes our method much more applicable.

We conduct our experiments on the commonly used translated portion of Chinese Treebank. Experimental results show that the reranking model improves two state-of-the-art dependency parsing systems (transition-based and graph-based) by a large margin. To show the impact of the translation noise on the performance, we also train a model with golden translations. The comparison shows that only slight performance difference is observed and the reranking model is robust enough to work with the rather noisy translations.

The rest of this paper is organized as follows: Sect. 2 introduces some most related work. Then the model is detailed in Sect. 3. Section 4 shows the experimental results we conducted on the translated portion of Chinese Treebank. We conclude this paper in Sect. 5.

2   Related Work

Bilingual constraints have been mostly investigated by previous work to biparsing task. [4] combined three statistical models into a unified bilingual parser that jointly searches for the best English parse, Korean parse and word alignments. They showed that bilingual constraints can be leveraged to transfer parse quality from a resource-rich language to resource-impoverished one. [5] presented a log-linear model over triples of source trees, target trees and node-to-node tree alignments between them. They also showed that parsing with joint models on bilingual texts improves performance on either or both sides. However, since both [4,5] aimed to improve the parsing performance of source and target language jointly, they required not only bilingual texts but also syntactic trees on both sides, which are hard to obtain.

[6] proposed a bilingually constrained monolingual shift-reduce parsing model. They introduced several bilingual features based on word alignment information to resolve what they called shift-reduce conflicts. [7] proposed a dependency parsing method that uses bilingual subtree constraints. They used a subtree list collected from large scale automatically parsed data on the target side as additional features for the source side dependency parser. Although [6,7]'s work focus on improving the parsing performance of one language at a

time, they still need bilingually aligned sentences for both training and testing, which makes their methods not applicable in common cases where golden translations are not available. [7] proposed a method to improve the accuracy of parsing bilingual texts (bitexts) with the help of statistical machine translation (SMT) systems. But their method needs a monolingual parser on the target side and very large auto-parsed sentences are used.

There are mainly two differences between our work and most previous methods. Firstly, our model avoids complicated manually designed features since it is based on deep learning methods, while most previous work focus on designing complicated features. Secondly, most previous work rely heavily on bilingually aligned sentences, which is hard to obtain. Thus their application scenarios are limited to bilingual processing. We see this problem from the opposite point of view and use automatically translated sentences during training and testing. This makes our model much more applicable.

3   Reranking Model

3.1   Scoring Candidate Trees with Neural Network

Suppose we have a Chinese sentence c, its corresponding English translation e and a set of word-to-word alignments A where $a = (i, a_i) \in A$ means that the ith Chinese word in c (c_i) is aligned to the a_ith English word in e (e_{a_i}). Now we have a candidate dependency tree t of sentence c, what we want to do is scoring this tree with all the information we have. First, we score the entire tree t as follows:

$$s_t(t|c, e, A) = \sum_{i=1}^{|c|} s_a(Context(c_i)) \tag{1}$$

where $|c|$ denotes the length of sentence c. This means that we have a score at each position of c according to its contextual information $Context(c_i)$, and then sum them up to be the score of the tree.

Now we introduce how to obtain $Context(c_i)$ given c, e, t and A. We take the following information into consideration:

- $c[i - ws : i + ws]$: c_i's context words in c, ws is the parameter for window size which we set to 2.
- $pos[i - ws : i + ws]$: POS tags of c_i's context words in c.
- c_{p_i}, c_{lc_i}, c_{rc_i}: corresponds to c_i's parent, left-most child and right-most child in tree t separately.
- $e[a_i - ws : a_i + ws]$: c_i's aligned English word and its context words in e.

We use dense feature embeddings for words and POS tags [18] in $Context(c_i)$. Once we get $Context(c_i)$, we concatenate all the word and POS tag embeddings together to form a feature vector x_i. Then we take x_i as the input of a neural network which has one hidden layer:

$$f(x_i) = W_2[\sigma(W_1 x_i + b_1)] + b_2 \tag{2}$$

where σ is an element-wise activation function. $\theta = (W_1, b_1, W_2, b_2)$ is the parameters of the neural network.

As we can see, there are only unigrams of words and POS tags in $Context(c_i)$, no complicated features are designed at all. The feature embeddings and interactions of words and POS tags are automatically learned by the neural network. For simplicity, we let $s(t, \theta)$ denotes $s_t(t|c, e, A)$ as in Eq. 1. Then we have:

$$s(t, \theta) = \sum_{i=1}^{|c|} f(x_i) \tag{3}$$

decoding becomes the problem of finding highest scoring tree among all candidate trees. Since each candidate t is generated by a monolingual parser with corresponding score $s_m(t)$, we take this into consideration, find the best candidate tree t^* as follows:

$$t^* = \arg \max_{t \in T(c)} \lambda s(t, \beta) + (1 - \beta)s_m(t) \tag{4}$$

where $T(c)$ is a candidate set generated by monolingual parser and β is the weighting coefficient.

3.2   Max-margin Training with AdaGrad

Since the neural network model is reranking-oriented, our training goal is that the highest scoring tree will always be the golden tree $\hat{t}$. And its score will be larger up to a margin than any other candidate trees. Then the max-margin criteria requires that for each tree t in the candidate set $T(c)$, the following inequality holds:

$$s(\hat{t}, \theta) \geq s(t, \theta) + \Delta(\hat{t}, t) \tag{5}$$

where $\Delta(\hat{t}, t)$ is the margin loss denotes the discrepancy between trees. It is measured by counting the number of words whose parent is different:

$$\Delta(\hat{t}, t) = \kappa \sum_{i=1}^{|c|} I(p_{\hat{t}, i} \neq p_{t, i}) \tag{6}$$

where $\kappa = 0.1$ is a discount parameter, $I(\cdot)$ is an indicator function and $p_{t, i}$ is the parent of c_i in tree t. This leads to our final regularized objective function:

$$J(\theta) = \frac{1}{m} \sum_{i=1}^{m} r_i(\theta) + \frac{\lambda}{2} ||\theta||_2^2, \text{where}$$

$$r_i(\theta) = \max_{t \in T(c)} (s(t, \theta) + \Delta(\hat{t}_i, t)) - s(\hat{t}_i, \theta) \tag{7}$$

As this objective is minimized, the score of the golden tree $\hat{t}$ increases and the score of the highest scoring incorrect candidate tree decreases. Following [8,9], we use the subgradient method and diagonal variant of AdaGrad [10] with minibatches to optimize this function.

4   Experiments

4.1   Setup

Bilingual Data. Following [6,7], we conduct our experiments on the translated portion of Chinese Treebank (CTB) [11,12], articles 1–325, which have golden English translations. We use Penn2Malt[1] to convert the data into dependency trees. We also use the same split as in [6], which is shown in Table 1. Table 1 also shows the number of bilingual pairs we extracted from the bilingual articles. Note that not all sentence pairs can be included, since many of them are not one-to-one aligned at sentence level.

Monolingual Baselines. In order to generate candidate trees for the reranking model, we train two state-of-the-art baseline parsers using the rest articles of CTB: a second-order graph-based parser trained using MSTParser[2] [3], and a self implemented transition-based parser, whose features templates are used following [13] . The best k parse trees generated by the baseline parsers are treated as the candidate set $T(c)$.

Alignment and MT System. Since bilingual features are extracted through word alignment, we train a word alignment model with the GIZA++[3] implementation of IBM4 using approximately 0.8M bilingual sentence pairs, which do not include the CTB data. We also remove the notoriously bad links in {a, an, the} $\times$ { (DE), (LE)} following the work of [6]. To generate English translations for Chinese sentences, we use the same 0.8M sentence pairs to train a phrase-based translation model with Moses [14] and tune the parameter using minimum error rate training with other 3k sentence pairs.

Hyperparameters. We use the development set to select hyperparameters for the reranking model. Finally, the reranking models are trained for 15 iterations, the hidden layer's size $h = 200$, word and POS tag embedding size $n = 50$, candidate set size $k = 12$, regularization weight $\lambda = 0.0001$, and initial learning rate $= 0.05$. For the weighting coefficient in Eq. 4, we set $\beta = 0.2$ for graph-based parser and $\beta = 0.8$ for transition-based parser.

Initialization. We initialize Chinese/English word embeddings with embeddings pre-trained on Chinese/English Gigaword [15,16] using Word2Vec[4]. Chinese POS tag embeddings and the neural network's weight matrices (W_1, W_2) are randomly initialized using uniform distribution $[0.2, 0.2]$. The bias vectors b_1 and b_2 are initialized as zeros.

---

[1]   http://stp.lingfil.uu.se/~nivre/research/Penn2Malt.html.

[2]   http://sourceforge.net/projects/mstparser/.

[3]   http://www.statmt.org/moses/giza/GIZA++.html.

[4]   http://code.google.com/p/word2vec/.

Table 1. Training, testing and development data from the translated portion of Chinese Treebank as in [5]

	Training	Test	Dev
CTB articles	1–270	271–300	301–325
Bilingual pairs	2494	263	252

4.2   Results

We test the reranking model with three different settings:

- **Ours-MM:** In this setting we use English translations automatically generated by Moses for training and testing.
- **Ours-GM:** Different from "Ours-MM", "Ours-GM" uses golden English translations for training while translations for testing sentences are still generated by Moses.
- **Ours-GG:** Golden translations are used for both training and testing data.

As we can see, "Ours-MM" only depends on automatically generated translations during training and testing. Thus it will be applicable for resource-poor languages which have no translated treebank for training at all, which is often the case. In setting "Ours-GM", golden translations are only required for training. Hence it still works when golden translations of testing sentences is missing. "Ours-GG" is most similar to previous bilingual parsing models but it can only be applied to limited cases where golden translations of training and testing sentences are given.

We report unlabeled attachment score (UAS) and unlabeled exact match (UEM). Figure 1 shows the performance (UAS) of the reranking model on development set with different candidate set size k, the baseline here is graph-based. As we can see, the performance improves as k gets larger at first. When k is around 12, the performance reaches its maximum. Then it goes down along with the increase of k. Thus we finally set k to 12 for all the experiments.

The main results are shown in Table 2. As we can see from the table, the reranking model improves the baselines by a large margin on all three settings. Compared to the two state-of-the-art baselines, our translation constrained reranking model "Ours-MM" yields an improvement of $+2.06/+3.22$ on UAS over the graph-based/transition-based monolingual parsers and also an improvement of $+4.56/+3.42$ on UEM, while "Ours-GG" gets an improvement of $+2.27/+3.22$ on UAS and $+4.82/+3.55$ on UEM. Despite the fact that it is trained and tested on automatically generated translations, "Ours-MM" only performs slightly worse than "Ours-GG", which is trained and testing with golden translations. This indicates that the reranking model still works well even without any golden translations. Among all the three settings, "Ours-GM" performs the worst, which may caused by the inconsistency of the training (golden translation) and testing (Moses generated).

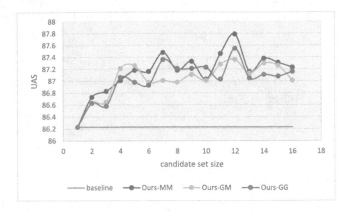

Fig. 1. Performance of the reranking model on development set with different candidate size when baseline is graph-based.

Table 2. Experimental results on test set. UAS: unlabeled attachment score, UEM: unlabeled exact match.

	Graph-based		Transition-based	
	UAS	UEM	UAS	UEM
Baseline	83.57	36.50	83.71	31.94
Ours-MM	85.63	41.06	**86.93**	35.36
Ours-GM	85.08	40.30	86.46	34.47
Ours-GG	**85.84**	**41.32**	**86.93**	**35.49**

4.3 Effect of Global and Bilingual Information

As described in Sect. 3.1, in our reranking model, we use two kinds of features that are not available to the baseline parses: (1) **bilingual features** extracted through word alignment, (2) **global features** such as left/right-most child in the dependency tree. In this section, we demonstrate their effects on our reranking models. Figure 2 shows the performance (UAS) of our reranking model when bilingual or global features are excluded separately. As we can see from the figure, the performances decline with the absence of bilingual or global features, but still outperform the baselines. The rerankers almost perform the best in all cases (except "MG-G") when both kinds of features are available. This indicates that, although bilingual and global features are both important to the reranking model, they provide different kinds of information and play different roles.

4.4 Effect of Word Embedding Initialization

All the experiments showed in the above sections use word embeddings pre-trained on Gigaword with Word2Vec. In this section we further analyze the influence of using pre-trained word embeddings as for initialization. In order

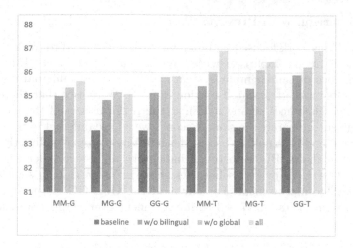

Fig. 2. The effects of global and bilingual information. "w/o bilingual" represents the reranking model without bilingual feature, "w/o global" represents the reranking model without global features. "all" means both kinds of features are used in the reranking model. "–G" means that the baseline is graph-based and "–T" means transition-based. For instance, "MM-G" represents the reranking model with setting "Ours-MM" and the baseline is graphs-based.

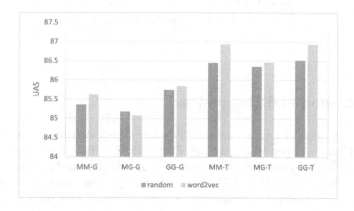

Fig. 3. Effect of word embedding initialization. Systems share the same meaning as in Fig. 2.

to show the comparison, we randomly initialize all word embedding using uniform distribution[0.2, 0.2]. From Fig. 3 we can see that, using pre-trained word embeddings tends to produces better results than using randomly initialized word embeddings. But the differences are barely obvious, and the rerankers still get comparable accuracies without the help of pre-trained word embeddings.

4.5   Comparison with Previous Work

As most previous work focused on biparsing task or assumed to work with bilingual texts, a direct comparison with them is hard to conduct. Table 3 shows the performance of some similar systems. [6,7] reported bilingual dependency parsing results on the translated portion of CTB. We notice that there are still some obvious differences among us. First, the performances of the monolingual baseline parsers are barely the same. Second, we all use different extra resources. Third, our method is reranking-based. Hence it is not proper to directly compare our work with theirs. But as a rough indicator, we just consider the absolute improvement of UAS over baseline. As show in Table 3, [6,7] separately get +0.6 and +2.93 improvement. For our models, "Ours-GG" is most similar to their settings and gets +2.27/+3.22 improvement over graph/transition based baselines.

Table 3. Comparison with similar work (UAS).

System	Baseline	Final	Improvement
Huang09	85.70	86.30	+0.60
Chen10	87.2	90.13	+2.93
Ours-GG-G	83.57	85.84	+2.27
Ours-GG-T	83.71	86.93	**+3.22**

5   Conclusion and Discussion

This paper presents a neural network based translation constrained reranking model for Chinese dependency parsing. Distributed feature representations free us from complicated and tricky feature designing. We use machine automatically generated rather than golden English translations for both training and testing. This makes our model be applicable in much broader scenarios and enables it to continuously benefit from the improvement of machine translation techniques. Experimental results show that the reranking model outperforms both the graph-based and transition-based monolingual models by a large margin. Due to its simplicity, our method can be easily applied to any other resource-poor languages.

Acknowledgments. This work is supported by National Key Basic Research Program of China (2014CB340504) and National Natural Science Foundation of China (61273318).

References

1. Yamada, H., Matsumoto, Y.: Statistical dependency parsing analysis with support vector machines. In: Proceedings of the Eighth International Workshop on Parsing Technologies (IWPT) (2003)
2. Nirve, J.: An efficient algorithm for projective dependency parsing. In: Proceedings of the Eighth International Workshop on Parsing Technologies (IWPT) (2003)
3. McDonald, R., Grammer, K., Peereira, F.: Online large-margin training of dependency parsers. In: Proceedings of the 43rd Annual Meeting on Association for Computational Linguistics, pp. 91–98. Association for Computational Linguistics (2005)
4. Smith, D.A., Smith, N.A.: Bilingual parsing with factored estimation: using english to parse Korean. In: Proceedings of EMNLP (2004)
5. Burkett, D., Klein, D.: Two languages are better than one (for syntactic paring). In: Proceedings of the Conference on Empirical Methods in Natural Language Processing, pp. 877–886. Association for Computational Linguistics (2008)
6. Huang, L., Jiang, W., Liu, Q.: Bilingually-constrained (monolingual) shift-reduce parsing. In: Proceedings of the 2009 Conference on Empirical Methods in Natural Language Processing, vol. 3. Association for Computational Linguistics, pp. 1222–1231 (2009)
7. Chen, W., Kazama, J., Torisawa, K.: Bitext dependency parsing with bilingual subtree constraints. In: Proceedings of the 48th Annual Meeting of the Association for Computational Linguistics, pp. 21–29. Association for Computational Linguistics (2010)
8. Socher, R., Bauer, J., Manning, C.D., Ng, A.Y.: Parsing with compositional vector grammars. In: Proceedings of ACL (2013)
9. Pei, W., Ge, T., Baobao, C.: Max-margin tensor neural network for Chinese word segmentation. In: proceedings of ACL (2014)
10. Duchi, J., Hazan, E., Singer, Y.: Adaptive subgradient methods for online learning and stochastic optimization. J. Mach. Learn. Res. 12, 2121–2159 (2011)
11. Nianwen, X., Chiou, F.D., Palmer, M.: Building a large-scale annotated Chinese coupus. In: Proceedings of the 19th International Conference on Computational Linguistics, vol. 1, pp. 1–8. Association for Computational Linguistics (2002)
12. Bies, A., Palmer, M., Mott, J., Warner, C.: English Chinese translation treebank v1.0. LDC2007T02 (2007)
13. Huang, L., Sagae, K.: Dynamic programming for linear-time incremental parsing. In: Proceedings of the 48th Annual Meeting of the Association for Computational Linguistics, pp. 1077–1086. Association for Computational Linguistics (2010)
14. Koehn, P., Hoang, H., Birch, A., Callison-Burch, C., Federico, M., Bertoldi, N., Cowan, B., Shen, W., Moran, C., Zens, R., Dyer, C., Bojar, O.: Alexandra constantin, and evan herbst. In: Moses: Open Source Toolkit for Statistical Machine Translation. Proceedings of the 45th Annual Meeting of the ACL on Interactive Poster and Demonstration Sessions, pp. 177–180. Association for Computational Linguistics (2007)
15. Graff, D., Chen, K.: Chinese Gigaword. LDC2003T09 (2003)
16. Graff, D., Cieri, C.: English Gigaword. LDC2003T05 (2003)
17. van der Maaten, L., Hinton, G.: Visualizing data using t-SNE. J. Mach. Learn. Res. 9, 85 (2008)
18. Chen, D., Manning, C.D.: A fast and accurate dependency parser using neural networks. In: Proceedings of the 2014 Conference on Empirical Methods in Natural Language Processing (EMNLP), pp. 740–750 (2014)

Knowledge Graph and Information Extraction

Distantly Supervised Neural Network Model for Relation Extraction

Zhen Wang[✉], Baobao Chang, and Zhifang Sui

Key Laboratory of Computational Linguistics,
Ministry of Education School of Electronics Engineering and Computer Science,
Peking University Collaborative Innovation Center for Language Ability,
Xuzhou 221009, China
wzpkuer@gmail.com, {chbb,szf}@pku.edu.cn

Abstract. For the task of relation extraction, distant supervision is an efficient approach to generate labeled data by aligning knowledge base (KB) with free texts. Albeit easy to scale to thousands of different relations, this procedure suffers from introducing wrong labels because the relations in knowledge base may not be expressed by aligned sentences (mentions). In this paper, we propose a novel approach to alleviate the problem of distant supervision with representation learning in the framework of deep neural network. Our model - Distantly Supervised Neural Network (**DSNN**) - constructs the more powerful mention level representation by tensor-based transformation and further learns the entity pair level representation which aggregates and denoises the features of associated mentions. With this denoised representation, all of the relation labels can be jointly learned. Experimental results show that with minimal feature engineering, our model generally outperforms state-of-the-art methods for distantly supervised relation extraction.

1 Introduction

Relation extraction was defined as the task of generating relational facts from unstructured natural language texts. Traditional approaches to relation extraction [9,17], using supervised learning with relation-specific examples on small hand-labeled corpora, can achieve high precision and recall. However, fully supervised paradigm is limited by the scalability of hand-labeled training data, and cannot satisfy the demand of large-scale web texts containing thousands of relations.

Distant supervision is an approach to alleviate the problem of traditional fully supervised paradigm for relation extraction. The intuition is that the training data of relations can be generated by heuristically aligning knowledge bases to free texts. Figure 1 shows the process of distant supervision to generate training examples. A *relation instance* is defined as the form $r(e_1, e_2)$, where r is the *relation name* and e_1 and e_2 are two *entity names*. An *entity mention* is a sequence of text tokens that matches the corresponding entity name in some text. A *relation mention* (*mention*) of relation instance $r(e_1, e_2)$ is a sequence of text (sentence), which contains a pair of entity mentions of e_1 and e_2. As shown

© Springer International Publishing Switzerland 2015
M. Sun et al. (Eds.): CCL and NLP-NABD 2015, LNAI 9427, pp. 253–266, 2015.
DOI: 10.1007/978-3-319-25816-4_21

in Fig. 1, the knowledge base provides two distinct relation names between an entity pair *(Barack Obama, U.S.)*. After alignment, four mentions from free texts are extracted and selected as training instances. Subsequently, previous methods often extract sophisticated lexical and syntactic features from these aligned mentions, combine them and produce extraction models which can predict new relation instances from texts.

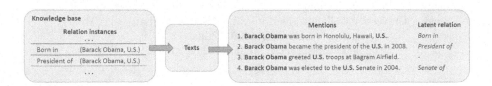

Fig. 1. Training examples generated by distant supervision with knowledge base and aligned mentions related to the entity pair *(Barack Obama, U.S.)*.

This paradigm is effective to generate large-scale training data for relation extraction. However, it suffers from three major problems.

- **Wrong Labels**. Not all mentions express the relation instances from knowledge base. As shown in Fig. 1, the last two sentences are not correct examples for any of the relations. Simply assuming every mention satisfies the relation instances may introduce a lot of wrong labels.
- **Multiple Labels**. As shown in Fig. 1, the same pair of entities may have multiple relation labels each instantiated in different scenarios, how to capture dependencies between these relations and learn them jointly is an important question.
- **Feature Engineering**. Without the knowledge of what kinds of features are important for relation extraction, a huge number of lexical and syntactic features are extracted from mentions, and the performance of previous work is heavily dependent on the designing of these sophisticated features.

Concerning these challenges, in this paper, we formulate distantly supervised relation extraction from a novel perspective of representation learning, which makes the following contributions:

- We propose a Distantly Supervised Neural Network model for relation extraction. In spite of the power of neural network both in supervised and unsupervised paradigm, our model is the first neural model trained in a manner of distant supervision. The test results on the benchmark dataset show that our model outperforms previous work under the same experimental environment.
- We construct more powerful mention level representation through tensor-based transformation, which models multiple interactions in the features extracted from the mention.

- We propose an approach to combine the information from each mention representation and result in the entity pair level representation. This process can be regarded as a way to aggregate evident features and discard noises introducing by wrong labels.
- We apply the joint learning schema in our model to solve the multi-label problem. With the entity pair level representation, correlations of relations can be captured and the labels can be jointly learned.
- Compared with previous work that relied on a huge number of handcrafted features, our model can achieve better performance with minimal feature engineering.

The remainder of this paper is organized as follows. Section 2 introduces our model from a detailed perspective. The experimental results are presented in Sect. 3. Section 4 reviews the related work. Section 5 concludes this paper.

2 Distantly Supervised Neural Network

In this paper, we apply representation learning in the framework of deep neural network for distantly supervised relation extraction. In the area of NLP, it is often the case that with the help of deep neural network, representations for different levels of units, such as words, phrases, sentences and paragraphs, can be learned. With these representations, classification can be easily processed for different tasks. Inspired by the idea of representation learning, our model - Distantly Supervised Neural Network (**DSNN**) - builds the mention level representation and further entity pair level representation. With the help of these representations, all of the relation labels can be jointly learned in an efficient way.

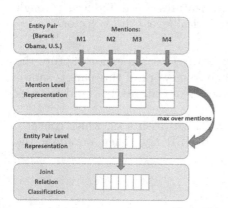

Fig. 2. The architecture of our Distantly Supervised Neural Network.

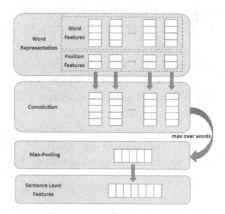

Fig. 3. The extraction framework of sentence level features.

2.1   The Neural Network Architecture

The architecture of our **DSNN** model is illustrated in Fig. 2. Given a pair of entities, we extract aligned sentences from free texts. Then each sentence (mention) is represented by its feature vector, i.e. the mention level representation. In succession, we combine the information from all of the mentions to form entity pair level representation. Finally, this representation is fed into a set of binary classifiers each represents a kind of relation label. The output value of each classifier is the confidence score of the entity pair having the corresponding relation.

2.2   Mention Level Representation

The first part of our network is to transform a mention into its feature vector representation. Many approaches can be adopted in this process. For example, in the work of [15], given a sentence with parsed tree, recursive neural nets can learn the sentence vector in a bottom-up procedure. [8] proposed dynamic convolutional neural network to capture short and long-range relations when modelling sentences. [10] showed paragraph vector can be learned in a similar way as word vector. In our work, given a mention and associated entity pair, we first generate a feature vector similar to the approach proposed by [22], which combines lexical level features and sentence level features. Then we correlate these features by tensor-based transformation to form more powerful mention level representation.

Lexical Level Features. Lexical level features for a mention convey the information locally embedded in the context of the given entity pair. In our work, lexical level features include the two entities, their NER tags, and the neighbor tokens of these two entities. All of these features are introduced through embeddings. After concatenation, we get the lexical level feature vector.

Sentence Level Features. Sentence level features for a mention capture the global information of the whole sentence. The framework of this part is shown in Fig. 3. Each word in the sentence has two kinds of features, i.e. word features and position features.

For word features, we initialize the i-th word with vector $\mathbf{c}_i$, which concatenates the embeddings for word, POS tag and NER tag. Then we adopt the window approach to generate word features:

$$\mathbf{w}_i = [\mathbf{c}_{i-d_{win}/2}^T, ..., \mathbf{c}_i^T, ..., \mathbf{c}_{i+d_{win}/2}^T]^T$$

d_{win} is the size of window, i is the current position.

For position features, we measure the distance of the current word to the two entities respectively. Then combining these two distance vector $\mathbf{d}_{i1}$ and $\mathbf{d}_{i2}$, position features are generated:

$$\mathbf{p}_i = [\mathbf{d}_{i1}^T, \mathbf{d}_{i2}^T]^T$$

Combining word features and position features, we get word representation:

$$\mathbf{x}_i = [\mathbf{w}_i^T, \mathbf{p}_i^T]^T$$

Word represented in this way only captures its local information. Inspired by [4], we adopt convolution approach to combine these local word representations of a mention into a global one. Specifically, we transform the above word representations by a linear map:

$$\mathbf{U} = \mathbf{W}_1 \mathbf{X}$$

$\mathbf{X}$ forms a matrix, standing for the ensemble of the word representations in a sentence, $\mathbf{W}_1 \in \mathbb{R}^{n_1 \times n_0}$ is a linear transformation, where n_0 is the length of word representation. To find out the most useful feature in each dimension of the feature vectors in $\mathbf{U}$, a max-pooling operation is followed:

$$h_i = max\mathbf{U}(i,.) \quad 1 \leq i \leq n_1$$

Now, we get a fixed length feature vector, which captures the global information within the sentence:

$$\mathbf{h} = [h_1, h_2, ..., h_{n_1}]^T$$

Then we adopt a nonlinear transformation to learn more complex features:

$$\mathbf{s} = f(\mathbf{W}_2 \mathbf{h})$$

$\mathbf{W}_2 \in \mathbb{R}^{n_2 \times n_1}$ is a linear transformation matrix, f is an activation function and we use *tanh* in our experiments. The sentence level feature vector is then defined as $\mathbf{s}$.

The final extracted feature vector $\mathbf{m}$ combines lexical level feature vector $\mathbf{l}$ and sentence level feature vector $\mathbf{s}$, formally, we adopt:

$$\mathbf{g} = [\mathbf{l}^T, \mathbf{s}^T]^T$$

$$\mathbf{m} = f(\mathbf{W}_3 \mathbf{g})$$

$\mathbf{W}_3 \in \mathbb{R}^{n_4 \times n_3}$, where n_3 equals the dimension of lexical features $\mathbf{l}$ plus the dimension of sentential features $\mathbf{s}$.

Tensor-Based Transformation. Tensor describes relatedness between scalars, vectors and other tensors, hence it has the advantage to explicitly model multiple interactions in data. For this benefit, tensor-based methods have been used in many tasks. For example, [12,16] applied neural tensor layer to relate input vectors in the problems of semantic analysis and word segmentation respectively.

In our work, we adopt neural tensor layer to model the interactions of above extracted features in a mention. Figure 4 indicates this process of tensor-based transformation. As a result, the correlations among different features can be captured and more powerful mention level representation can be formed.

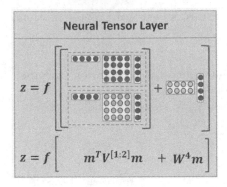

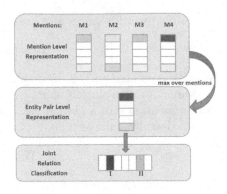

Fig. 4. The formulation of neural tensor layer. Each dashed box represents one tensor slice, which defines the bilinear form on vector **m**.

Fig. 5. The max-pooling operation to get entity pair representation. Assume the first dimension of mention representation corresponds to relation I, and the last to II. This process indicates a true relation I not relation II between the given entity pair.

Formally, a 3-way tensor $\mathbf{V}^{[1:n_5]} \in \mathbb{R}^{n_5 \times n_4 \times n_4}$ is defined to directly model the interactions. The output of a tensor product is a vector $\mathbf{a} \in \mathbb{R}^{n_5}$, whose each dimension a_i is the result of the bilinear form defined by each tensor slice $\mathbf{V}^{[i]} \in \mathbb{R}^{n_4 \times n_4}$:

$$\mathbf{a} = \mathbf{m}^T \mathbf{V}^{[1:n_5]} \mathbf{m}$$

$$a_i = \mathbf{m}^T \mathbf{V}^{[i]} \mathbf{m} = \sum_{j,k} V_{jk}^{[i]} m_j m_k$$

As indicated by equations above, in each tensor slice, the interactions are explicitly modeled by the bilinear form of the features in **m**. Intuitively, we can interpret each slice of the tensor as capturing a specific type of interaction.

In our work, we augment the above tensor product with linear transformation, resulting in the final form of neural tensor layer:

$$\mathbf{z} = f(\mathbf{m}^T \mathbf{V}^{[1:n_5]} \mathbf{m} + \mathbf{W}_4 \mathbf{m})$$

where $\mathbf{W}_4 \in \mathbb{R}^{n_5 \times n_4}$ is a linear transformation matrix.

The feature vector **z** models the interactions among different features extracted from a mention, and thus can be regarded as a more powerful representation at the mention level.

In our work, we adopt a tensor factorization approach inspired by [12]. In this way, the calculation of neural tensor layer is efficient and the risk of overfitting can be alleviated.

2.3   Entity Pair Level Representation

The distinction between distantly supervised relation extraction and traditional problem of relation classification is that although from knowledge base, we can figure out what relations the given entity pair has, we have no idea which mentions in texts truly convey these relations. Therefore, only depending on mention level representation to classify relations may introduce a lot of noises.

In our work, we combine the information embedded in all of the mentions associated with the given entity pair to form the entity pair level representation. Formally, we have the max-pooling operation along the same dimension of all the mention level representations:

$$t_i = max\mathbf{Z}(i,.)   1 \leq i \leq n_5$$

$\mathbf{Z}$ is a matrix composed of all the mention representations associated with the given entity pair.

Then, we get the entity pair level representation:

$$\mathbf{t} = [t_1, t_2, ..., t_{n_5}]^T$$

We use this representation to jointly learn all of the relation labels. This process is shown in Fig. 5.

The benefit of this max-pooling operation to get entity pair representation is multifold.

First, because distant supervision relation extraction is the entity pair level classification, we need to combine mention level representations all together to get global information.

Second, by max-pooling operation, each dimension of entity pair representation can hold the most important feature, which is determinant for the subsequent relation classification. Features not evident will be discarded, this can be seen as a way of feature denoising. As illustrated by Fig. 5, we expect some dimension of mention level representation is crucial for a certain relation. Then, if a mention truly conveys this relation, thus has evident value in the corresponding dimension, the max-pooling operation will preserve it, and use it to indicate a true relation between the pair of entities. Otherwise, if all the mentions do not express the relation, the feature after max-pooling will not be evident either to indicate this relation.

Third, operation in this way helps us get a fixed-length feature vector, no matter how many mentions the entity pair has in texts.

At last, this operation is fairly efficient, and entity pair represented in this way is easy to calculate.

2.4   Joint Learning of Relations

Relation extraction is actually a multi-label relation classification problem. Given a pair of entities, we have no idea how many relations can be expressed. Because relation types concerned are not exclusive, it is unsuitable to regard this problem as a simple multi-classification. In our work, we treat multi-label relation classification as a set of binary relation identification problems. Concerning a certain relation type, we construct a binary classifier to determine whether the entity pair has this relation. Formally, we adopt the logistic regression model, which has the form:

$$P(Y_i = 1|\mathbf{t}) = \frac{1}{1 + e^{-\mathbf{r}_i \cdot \mathbf{t}}}$$

where $\mathbf{t}$ is the feature vector of entity pair representation, $\mathbf{r}_i$ is the weight vector associated with the i-th relation name, $Y_i = 1$ indicates the entity pair expresses the i-th relation. This logistic function has an obvious explanation, that the higher the value of $P(Y_i = 1|\mathbf{t})$, the greater probability that the entity pair $\mathbf{t}$ indicates the i-th relation.

We can think of this procedure from a joint learning perspective. Instead of learning a specific entity pair representation for each distinct relation name, we share entity pair representation for all relations. In another word, the representation learned contains information from all of these relations, hence it can capture the correlations among different relations. Moreover, this joint learning procedure can both be efficient and avoid overfitting.

2.5 Training Criteria

Given a pair of entities x, the network with parameter θ outputs a N dimension vector $\mathbf{o}$ (N is the number of relation labels concerned in our work). The i-th component o_i corresponds to the probability that this entity pair has the i-th relation label, thus:

$$p(Y_i = 1|x, \theta) = o_i$$
$$p(Y_i = 0|x, \theta) = 1 - o_i$$

Given all our training examples:

$$T = (x^{(i)}, y^{(i)})$$

where $x^{(i)}$ denotes the i-th training entity pair, $y^{(i)}$ is the corresponding N dimension vector, and $y_k^{(i)} = 1$ indicates $x^{(i)}$ has the k-th relation.

The log likelihood with a single training sample is:

$$\sum_{k=1}^{N} logp(y_k^{(i)}|x^{(i)}; \theta)$$

And the full log likelihood of the whole training corpus is:

$$J(\theta) = \sum_{i=1}^{T} \sum_{k=1}^{N} logp(y_k^{(i)}|x^{(i)}; \theta)$$

To compute the network parameter θ, we maximize the log likelihood $J(\theta)$ using stochastic gradient ascent:

$$\theta \rightarrow \theta + \lambda \frac{\partial J(\theta)}{\partial \theta}$$

where λ is the learning rate controlling the step of gradient ascent.

Table 1. Hyper parameters of our model DSNN.

Remark	Choice
Window size	$d_{win} = 3$
Word embedding dimension	$n_{word} = 50$
POS tag dimension	$n_{pos} = 20$
NER tag dimension	$n_{ner} = 10$
Distance dimension	$n_{dis} = 20$
Hidden layer 1	$n_1 = 200$
Hidden layer 2	$n_2 = 100$
Hidden layer 3	$n_4 = 200$
Neural tensor layer	$n_5 = 100$
Learning rate	$\alpha = 10^{-3}$

Table 2. Results at the highest F1 point in the precision-recall curve.

Models	P	R	F1
Mintz et al., 2009	26.17	22.67	24.29
Hoffmann et al., 2011	32.05	24.05	27.48
Surdeanu et al., 2012	**32.92**	20.56	25.32
DSNN	29.81	**33.45**	**31.53**

3   Experiments

To evaluate the performance of our proposed approach, we conduct three experiments. The first one compares our **DSNN** with previous landmark methods on the public dataset. The second is carried out in our **DSNN** framework with or without the neural tensor layer, the experiment is designed to show the ability of tensor operation to get more powerful mention level representation. The last experiment displays the distribution of entity pair level representations after training, the result shows the effectiveness of this representation to capture relation information.

3.1   Dataset

We evaluate our algorithm on the widely-adopted dataset developed by [13]. In this dataset, Freebase was used as the distant supervision source and New York Times (NYT) was selected as the text corpus. The Freebase relation types concerned in this dataset focus on four categories of entities: "people", "business", "person" and "location", and NYT data contains over 1.8 million articles between January 1, 1987 and June 19, 2007, which are partitioned into training set and testing set. After alignment, we get 51 kinds of relation labels.

3.2   Experimental Results

The hyper parameter setting of our **DSNN** are reported in Table 1. The POS tags and NER tags are automatically generated by CoreNLP[1]. We initialize the word embeddings with pre-trained distributed vectors devoted by [4]. The embeddings of POS tags, NER tags and other weights in our model are randomly initialized.

---

[1] http://nlp.stanford.edu/software/corenlp.shtml.

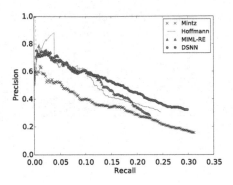

Fig. 6. Results comparison on the Riedel dataset.

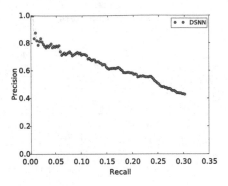

Fig. 7. Results on instances with more than 1 mention.

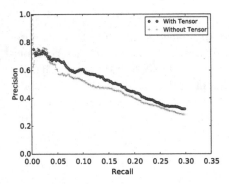

Fig. 8. The comparison of results with or without the neural tensor layer.

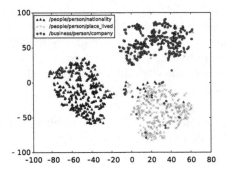

Fig. 9. The feature vectors of entity pair representation are visualized using t-SNE.

The first part of our experiments is to compare our work with previous landmark methods [7,11,18]. The results of previous work can be reproduced by the open source code[2] developed by [18].

Figure 6 indicates that our **DSNN** model generally outperforms the current state-of-the-art results on the Riedel dataset. As shown in the figure, in the area of low recall, our model performs competitively with previous methods, and as recall gets larger, the performance of **DSNN** is significantly better than all of the competitors. Therefore, our approach gets largest precision-recall area and highest F1 score, which is shown in Table 2.

As Fig. 6 indicates, our approach can maintain a fairly high precision even when recall is larger. Therefore, when it is the situation that we need to pick out a large number of candidate relation instances with relatively high precision, our **DSNN** model is the most suitable choice.

---

[2] http://nlp.stanford.edu/software/mimlre.shtml.

We can explain this performance improvement via the distinction between our model and previous ones. Previous approaches more relied on the sophisticated features extracted from mentions, and resulted in a large number of sparse features. As a consequence, if testing instances can reproduce the features in the training procedure, the probability of right prediction will be fairly high. However, because of the sparsity, when the features do not match between testing and training, the generalization ability of feature-based methods will be badly hurt. With the framework of neural network, our model discards the sophisticated features, learns the entity pair distributed representation. This can be regarded as the process of letting data decide what are important features for our problem. Because of this advantage, feature sparsity is alleviated and the generalization ability is enhanced.

To further clarify the ability of our entity pair representation to aggregate information from mentions, we conduct experiment on relation instances with more than 1 mention aligned in texts, with the result shown in Fig. 7. The precision-recall performance in this subset is highly improved compared to the initial dataset. Therefore, more mentions give more confidence on the prediction of relations with our approach. With this knowledge, if we are more concerned with the precision of relation instances extracted, we can resort to the number of mentions for further improvement.

The second part of our experiments is carried out in our **DSNN** framework with or without the neural tensor layer. The comparison of results is illustrated in Fig. 8. As shown in this figure, mention level representation learned by tensor-based transformation is more powerful and has a good influence on the performance of distant supervision relation extraction.

The third part of our experiments is to demonstrate the effectiveness of our entity pair representation. Using t-SNE[3], the feature vectors of entity pair representation can be well painted as indicated in Fig. 9. In this experiment, we take three kinds of relations into consideration, and each relation contains a large number of entity pairs holding this relation. As a result of Fig. 9, entity pair instances with the same relation will be gathered together, which shows the ability of our entity pair representation to convey relation information.

4   Related Work

4.1   Distant Supervision

Distant supervision is first introduced by [5], who focused on the field of bioinformatics. Since then, this approach scaled to many other fields [2,14,20]. As for relation extraction, [11] adopted Freebase to distantly supervise Wikipedia corpus. This work was dependent on the basic assumption that if an entity pair participates in a relation in the knowledge base, all sentences from texts that matched the facts are labeled by that relation name. As shown in Fig. 1, this procedure may introduce a lot of wrong labels. To avoid this problem, [13]

---

[3] http://lvdmaaten.github.io/tsne/.

relaxed the distant supervision assumption with multi-instance learning framework, which replaced all sentences with at least one sentence expressing the relation. Then [7] proposed multi-label circumstance to enrich previous work. [18] advanced with a novel approach to jointly model all the mentions in texts and all the relation labels in knowledge base, resulting in a multi-instance multi-label learning framework for relation extraction. [19] proposed a generative approach to model the heuristic labeling process in order to reduce wrong labels. [6] applied matrix completion with convex optimization to tackle the sparsity and noise challenges of distant supervision. [1] provided partial supervision using a small number of carefully selected examples. [21] resolved the noise features and exploited sparse representation to solve the problem.

4.2 Representation Learning

Representation learning is a paradigm to capture the underlying explanatory factors hidden in the observed data and make learning less dependent on feature engineering. In the area of NLP, with a powerful representation, classification can be easily processed. Therefore, the idea of representation learning has been scaled to many tasks [3,4,15].

[22] made use of lexical level features and sentence level features to form mention level representation, then with a softmax classifier the problem of relation classification was well solved. We get inspiration from their work to form the features extracted from mentions. However, relation classification is a totally supervised problem, which has no trouble of wrong labels and multi-label circumstance. With the entity pair representation and joint learning schema, our model can solve these challenges pretty well. Moreover, we enrich their mention features with tensor-based transformation, resulting in a more powerful mention level representation.

5   Conclusion

In this paper, we showed that distant supervision for relation extraction can be formulated with the framework of deep neural network. In our model **DSNN**, interactions of extracted features in a mention are captured to construct more powerful mention level representation. Then the pair of entities combines the information from all the aligned mentions, and forms the representation at the level of entity pair. This process can aggregate evident features from different mentions, as well as discard noises, which are introduced by the paradigm of distant supervision. The learned representation then is used to jointly learn all of the relation labels. Moreover, with the framework of deep neural network, the heavy job of feature engineering is much alleviated. Experiments show the effectiveness of the mention level tensor-based transformation and the ability of the entity pair level representation to capture relation information. Moreover, we compare our model with state-of-the-art results on the benchmark dataset, and demonstrate our approach achieves improvements on performance.

Acknowledgments. This research is supported by National Key Basic Research Program of China (No. 2014CB340504) and National Natural Science Foundation of China (No. 613-75074,61273318). The contact authors of this paper are Baobao Chang and Zhifang Sui.

References

1. Angeli, G., Tibshirani, J., Wu, J.Y., Manning, C.D.: Combining distant and partial supervision for relation extraction. In: Proceeding of The 2014 Conference on Empirical Methods on Natural Language Processing (2014)
2. Bellare, K., McCallum, A.: Learning extractors from unlabeled text using relevant databases. In: Sixth International Workshop on Information Integration on the Web (2007)
3. Bengio, Y., Ducharme, R., Vincent, P., Janvin, C.: A neural probabilistic language model. J. Mach. Learn. Res. **3**, 1137–1155 (2003)
4. Collobert, R., Weston, J.: A unified architecture for natural language processing: Deep neural networks with multitask learning. In: Proceedings of the 25th International Conference on Machine Learning, pp. 160–167. ACM (2008)
5. Craven, M., Kumlien, J.: Constructing biological knowledge bases by extracting information from text sources. In: ISMB, vol. 1999, pp. 77–86 (1999)
6. Fan, M., Zhao, D., Zhou, Q., Liu, Z., Zheng, T.F., Chang, E.Y.: Distant supervision for relation extraction with matrix completion. In: Proceedings of the 52nd Annual Meeting of the Association for Computational Linguistics, vol. 1, pp. 839–849 (2014)
7. Hoffmann, R., Zhang, C., Ling, X., Zettlemoyer, L., Weld, D.S.: Knowledge-based weak supervision for information extraction of overlapping relations. In: Proceedings of the 49th Annual Meeting of the Association for Computational Linguistics: Human Language Technologies, vol. 1, pp. 541–550. Association for Computational Linguistics (2011)
8. Kalchbrenner, N., Grefenstette, E., Blunsom, P.: A convolutional neural network for modelling sentences. In: Proceedings of the 52nd Annual Meeting of the Association for Computational Linguistics (2014)
9. Kambhatla, N.: Combining lexical, syntactic, and semantic features with maximum entropy models for extracting relations. In: Proceedings of the ACL 2004 on Interactive poster and demonstration sessions, p. 22. Association for Computational Linguistics (2004)
10. Le, Q.V., Mikolov, T.: Distributed representations of sentences and documents (2014). arXiv preprint arXiv:1405.4053
11. Mintz, M., Bills, S., Snow, R., Jurafsky, D.: Distant supervision for relation extraction without labeled data. In: Proceedings of the Joint Conference of the 47th Annual Meeting of the ACL and the 4th International Joint Conference on Natural Language Processing of the AFNLP, vol. 2, pp. 1003–1011. Association for Computational Linguistics (2009)
12. Pei, W., Ge, T., Baobao, C.: Maxmargin tensor neural network for chinese word segmentation. In: Proceedings of ACL (2014)
13. Riedel, S., Yao, L., McCallum, A.: Modeling relations and their mentions without labeled text. In: Balcázar, J.L., Bonchi, F., Gionis, A., Sebag, M. (eds.) ECML PKDD 2010, Part III. LNCS, vol. 6323, pp. 148–163. Springer, Heidelberg (2010)

14. Snow, R., Jurafsky, D., Ng, A.Y.: Learning syntactic patterns for automatic hypernym discovery. In: Advances in Neural Information Processing Systems, vol. 17 (2004)
15. Socher, R., Huval, B., Manning, C.D., Ng, A.Y.: Semantic compositionality through recursive matrix-vector spaces. In: Proceedings of the 2012 Conference on Empirical Methods in Natural Language Processing (EMNLP) (2012)
16. Socher, R., Perelygin, A., Wu, J.Y., Chuang, J., Manning, C.D., Ng, A.Y., Potts, C.: Recursive deep models for semantic compositionality over a sentiment treebank. In: Proceedings of the Conference on Empirical Methods in Natural Language Processing (EMNLP), vol. 1631, p. 1642. Citeseer (2013)
17. Suchanek, F.M., Ifrim, G., Weikum, G.: Combining linguistic and statistical analysis to extract relations from web documents. In: Proceedings of the 12th ACM SIGKDD International Conference on Knowledge Discovery and Data Mining, pp. 712–717. ACM (2006)
18. Surdeanu, M., Tibshirani, J., Nallapati, R., Manning, C.D.: Multi-instance multi-label learning for relation extraction. In: Proceedings of the 2012 Joint Conference on Empirical Methods in Natural Language Processing and Computational Natural Language Learning, pp. 455–465. Association for Computational Linguistics (2012)
19. Takamatsu, S., Sato, I., Nakagawa, H.: Reducing wrong labels in distant supervision for relation extraction. In: Proceedings of the 50th Annual Meeting of the Association for Computational Linguistics: Long Papers, vol. 1, pp. 721–729. Association for Computational Linguistics (2012)
20. Wu, F., Weld, D.S.: Autonomously semantifying wikipedia. In: Proceedings of the Sixteenth ACM Conference on Information and Knowledge Management, pp. 41–50. ACM (2007)
21. Zeng, D., Lai, S., Wang, X., Liu, K., Zhao, J., Lv, X.: Distant supervision for relation extraction via sparse representation. In: Sun, M., Liu, Y., Zhao, J. (eds.) NLP-NABD 2014 and CCL 2014. LNCS, vol. 8801, pp. 151–162. Springer, Heidelberg (2014)
22. Zeng, D., Liu, K., Lai, S., Zhou, G., Zhao, J.: Relation classification via convolutional deep neural network. In: Proceedings of COLING, pp. 2335–2344 (2014)

Learning Entity Representation for Named Entity Disambiguation

Rui Cai$^{(\boxtimes)}$, Houfeng Wang, and Junhao Zhang

Key Laboratory of Computational Linguistics, Ministry of Education,
Peking University, Beijing, China
{cairui,wanghf,zhang.junhao}@pku.edu.cn

Abstract. In this paper we present a novel disambiguation model, based on neural networks. Most existing studies focus on designing effective man-made features and complicated similarity measures to obtain better disambiguation performance. Instead, our method learns distributed representation of entity to measure similarity without man-made features. Entity representation consists of context document representation and category representation. Document representation of an entity is learned based on deep neural network (DNN), and is directly optimized for a given similarity measure. Convolutional neural network (CNN) is employed to obtain category representation, and shares deep layers with DNN. Both models are trained jointly using massive documents collected from Baike http://baike.baidu.com/. Experiment results show that our method achieves a good performance on two datasets without any manually designed features.

Keywords: Entity disambiguation · Entity representation · Deep neural network

1 Introduction

Named entity disambiguation (NED) is an important research task in information extraction (IE) and natural language processing (NLP). Given a set of documents and a knowledge base, it's needed to determine whether an identical mention occurring in different documents refers to the same thing in real world, and link them to knowledge base entries.

At the heart of NED is the notion of similarity. The majority of exiting approaches follow [2] and employ different ways to measure the similarity of mention and candidate entities. To obtain better disambiguation performance, most studies focus on designing more effective features and similarity measures. For example, [1] propose a learning to rank algorithm for entity linking which utilizes hand-crafted features.

To avoiding excessive task specific feature engineering, neural network architecture have been applied to various natural language processing tasks [10] and can learn representations useful to specific task. Existing neural networks for

© Springer International Publishing Switzerland 2015
M. Sun et al. (Eds.): CCL and NLP-NABD 2015, LNAI 9427, pp. 267–278, 2015.
DOI: 10.1007/978-3-319-25816-4_22

paragraph embedding [19] and sentence modelling [12] ignore the situation of ambiguous mention and performs well in many tasks, but they are not suitable for disambiguation task. In the present work, we propose a model learning document representation (**LDR**) of the context of ambiguous mention based on DNN. Context representation are optimized for a given similarity measure, and allow us to compare context and entity at some higher level. Features are learned leveraging large scale annotation of Baike, without any manual designed efforts.

Convolutional neural network (CNN) has been applied to solve sentence classification [11] and achieve a good performance. A CNN classifying entity is trained for learning category representation (**LCR**). The output of CNN is a vector of probabilities, each element of which corresponds to a specific category and can be regarded as a distributed representation of category. Inspired by multi-task learning [10], **LDR** and **LCR** share deep layers and achieve better performance when they are trained jointly. The final similarity score is the combination of document similarity and category similarity, utilizing document representation and category representation separately.

Compared with English NED, the Chinese NED is even more challenging. Many common words and geographic names can often be used as a person name in Chinese. The lack of morphology information (such as the capital word for named entity) in Chinese also increases the difficulty [22]. Our method is applied to the Chinese named entity recognition and disambiguation (NERD) Task in the CIPS-SIGHAN joint conference on Chinese language processing (CLP2012). This task focuses on NERD in Chinese language, and presents some challenges unique to Chinese introduced previously.

Experiment are conducted at two parts. We test our method on a Chinese dataset for personal name disambiguation. Then we apply our method on data of CLP-2012 Chinese Named Entity Recognition and Disambiguation task.

2   Learning Entity Representation

Given an ambiguous mention string m with its context document d, a list of candidate entities $e_i \in C(m)$ in knowledge base, for each candidate entity we compute a score $sim(d, e_i)$ indicating how likely m refers to e_i. The linking result is $e = argmax_{e_i} sim(d, e_i)$.

Our algorithm consists of two parts. Document representation learning (**LDR**) is based on DNN and the network weights are fined-tuned to optimize the document similarity score $sim_{doc}(d, e)$. Category representation learning (**LCR**) based on CNN is trained by maximizing a likelihood over the training data. The final similarity score $sim(d, e)$ combines document similarity $sim_{doc}(d, e)$ and category similarity $sim_{cat}(d, e)$.

2.1   Learning Representation of Document

The context document is a variable length sequence of words, and there are two common approaches to obtain fixed length input: a window approach, and a convolutional approach. Window approach assumes the meaning of a mention depends mainly on its neighboring words. Convolutional approach is a simple and effective methods for compositionality learning in vector based semantics (Mitchell and Lapata [14]). Entity disambiguation task requires the consideration of the whole context, the natural choice becomes convolutional approach.

Collobert [10] introduce a model to learning word embedding based on the syntactic contexts of words. Formally, in entity disambiguation task, we have a word dictionary D of size $|D|$. Each word w in D is represented as a d-dimensional vector $Embed(w)$. For a word $w \in D$, the corresponding word embedding $Embed(w) \in R^d$ is retrieved by lookup table layer shown in Fig. 1:

$$Embed(w) = LT_w.w \tag{1}$$

where $LT_w \in R^{d \times |D|}$ is a matrix of parameters to be learnt, $Embed(w) \in R^d$ is the wth column of LT_w. Given any sequence of n words $w_{1:n}$ in D, lookup table layer applies the same operation for each word in sequence, and the output is represented as:

$$Embed(w_{1:n}) = Embed(w_1) \oplus Embed(w_2) \oplus ... \oplus Embed(w_n) \tag{2}$$

where $\oplus$ is the concatenation operator. The concatenation of word embedding can be fed to further neural network layers.

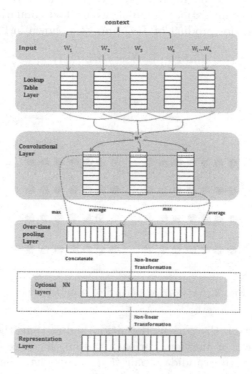

Fig. 1. Learning continuous representation of context

A convolution operation involves a filer $\mathbf{w} \in \mathbf{R}^{hd}$, which is applied to a window of h words to produce a new feature. For example, a feature x_i is generated from a windows of words $Embed(w_{i:i+h-1})$ by

$$x_i = f(\mathbf{w} \cdot Embed(w_{i:i+h-1}) + b) \tag{3}$$

Here $b \in \mathbf{R}$ is a bias term and f is a non-linear function such as the hyperbolic tangent. This filter is applied to each possible in the sequence to produce a feature map

$$\mathbf{x} = [x_1, x_2, ..., x_{n-h+1}] \tag{4}$$

with $\mathbf{x} \in \mathbf{R}^{n-h+1}$. Our model uses multiple filters to obtain multiple global features. We then apply an average and a max pooling operation over the feature map, and take the average value $\bar{x} = mean\{\mathbf{x}\}$ and the maximum value $\hat{x} = max\{\mathbf{x}\}$. Local feature vectors extracted by the convolutional layers are combined to obtain a global feature vector by pooling operation, with fixed-size independent of context length. Global feature vector are fed to stacked full connected hidden layers, and the number of hidden layers depends on specific disambiguation task. As shown in Fig. 1, a representation layer is stacked on hidden layers, the output of which is the continuous representation of context document.

We optimize the document representation towards the similarity score $sim(d, e)$, with large annotation as supervision. The similarity score of (d, e) pair is defined as the dot product of $f(d)$ and $f(e)$ shown in Fig. 2:

$$sim(d, e) = \text{Dot}(f(d), f(e)) \tag{5}$$

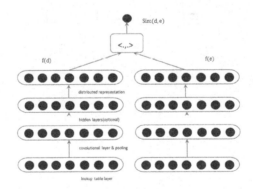

Fig. 2. Network structure of training stage

Our goal is to rank the correct definition higher than the rest candidates relative to the context of mention. For each training instance (t, d), we contrast it with one of its negative candidate pair (t, d'). This gives the pairwise ranking criterion:

$$\mathcal{L}(d, e) = \{0, 1 - sim(t, d) + sim(t, d')\} \tag{6}$$

Alternatively, we can contrast with all its candidate pairs (t, d_i). That is, we raise the similarity score of correct pair $sim(t, d)$ and penalize all the rest $sim(t, d_i)$. The loss function is defined as negative log of softmax function:

$$\mathcal{L}(t, d) = -\log \frac{\exp sim(t, d)}{\sum_{d_i \in C(m)} \exp sim(t, d_i)} \tag{7}$$

Finally, we seek to minimize the following training objective across all training instances. We find that penalizing more negative examples, convergence speed can be greatly accelerated. In our experiment, the *softmax* loss function consistently outperforms pairwise loss function, which is taken as a default setting.

For regularization, we employ dropout on the penultimate layer (Hinton et al. [18]). Dropout prevents co-adaptation of hidden units by randomly dropping out a proportion p of the hidden units during foward-backpropagation. That is, given the penultimate layer $\mathbf{z}$, for output unit y in forward propagation, dropout uses

$$y = \mathbf{w} \cdot (\mathbf{z} \circ \mathbf{r}) + b \tag{8}$$

where $\circ$ is the element-wise multiplication operator and $\mathbf{r} \in \mathbf{R}^m$ is a 'masking' vector of Bernoulli random variables with probability p of being 1. Gradients are backpropagated only through the unmasked units. At test time, the learned weight vectors are scaled by p such that $\hat{\mathbf{w}} = p\mathbf{w}$, and $\hat{\mathbf{w}}$ is used to score unseen context.

2.2 Learning Category Representation

The category informations of ambiguous mention m are helpful to disambiguation task. Take the personal name disambiguation for example, the document containing ambiguous name and the correct candidate entity are used to share a same category such as *politician*. Our approach for learning category representation (**LCR**) is inspired by the method for sentence classification. The model architecture is a slight variant of the CNN architecture of (Collobert et al. [10]). The output of softmax layer is a multi-dimensional category vector $\mathbf{c}$, and $\mathbf{c}_i$ is the probability of being the i-th category.

Training dataset is denoted as $\mathcal{D}$, and each training instance is a pair of context document and category denoted as (d, c). In the case of multi-class classification, it is very common to use the negative log-likelihood as the loss, which is equivalent to maximizing the likelihood of the dataset $\mathcal{D}$:

$$\mathcal{L} = -\log \prod_{i=0}^{|D|} P(C = c^{(i)}|d^{(i)}) \tag{9}$$

The CNN architecture automatically learns features for classification task in the deep layers of its architecture. Learning continuous representation of the context and its category are two highly related task, and it make sense that features useful for one task might be useful for another one. As shown in Fig. 3,

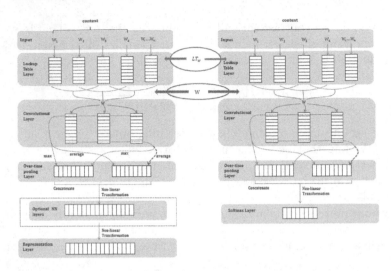

Fig. 3. LCR in the right section shares lookup table layer and convolutional layer with **LDR**

the lookup table layers and convolutional layers in two models share the same architecture. Our work is inspired by the multitask learning, which is a procedure of learning several tasks at the same time with the aim of mutual benefit (Collobert et al. [10]). Training is achieved in a stochastic manner by looping over two tasks.

The category similarity score of (d, e) pair is defined as the dot product of two category representations. The final similarity score $sim(d, e)$ becomes the combination of context similarity $sim_{doc}(d, e)$ and category similarity $sim_{cat}(d, e)$:

$$sim(d, e) = sim_{doc}(d, e) + \lambda sim_{cat}(d, e) \tag{10}$$

The value of λ is chosen depends on the performance of experiments.

3   Experiments

3.1   Disambiguation of Entities in Web Pages

Training Settings: For the lookup table layer, word vectors are initialized using the publicly available word2vec vectors that were trained on gigaword. The vectors have dimensionality of 200 and were trained using the continuous bag-of-words architecture. For the convolutional layer, We use filter window of 3 with 200 feature maps. Representation layer has 200 units with sigmoid activation. We use learning rate of 1e-3 and dropout rate of 0.5. The mini-batch size is set to 20.

Dataset: We constructed a dataset of web pages obtained from Baike, where every name string m corresponds to a describing page which lists multiple web pages in the reference. For each name, we create a collection of six web pages: given a describing page in Baike, only one page corresponds to the same entity with it, whereas the rest of pages are not. Totally 113,681 names are picked out and are split into three set: 80 % for training, 10 % for validation, and 10 % for testing.

We experiment with several variants of the model:

LDR: The model introduced in Sect. 3.1 with pre-trained vectors from word2vec and applies two pooling operations on convolutional layer. Rank candidate entities with document similarity.

LDR-rand: Same as above but word vectors are randomly initialized and then modified during training.

LDR-max-pooling: The model only applies max-pooling operation on convolution layer.

LDR-average-pooling: The model only applies average-pooling operation on convolution layer.

LDR+LCR-joint: The model introduced in Sect. 3.2. Learning representations of document and category of entities jointly. The final similarity score becomes the combination of document similarity and category similarity.

LDR+LCR: Similar with above but LDR and LCR model are trained separately.

Table 1. Comparison results of several variants of model

#	Methods	Precision	
		With dropout	Without dropout
1	LDR	0.865	0.873
2	LDR-rand	0.843	0.849
3	LDR-max-pooling	0.851	0.865
4	LDR-average-pooling	0.838	0.844
5	LDR+LCR-joint	0.887	**0.891**
6	LDR+LCR	0.885	0.889

Results of several variants of the model was shown in Table 1. Our model with all randomly initialized words(LDR-rand) does not perform well on its own. Different global features are extracted by max and average operation, and a better performance is achieved in LDR by combining both of them. Performance gains through the use of category representation for similarity score, and the result of LDR+LCR suggests that category information is helpful to disambiguation task, even though LCR is trained for entity classification individually. Joint training is employed in LDR+LCR-joint, and improves the performance of LDR+LCR to 89.1 %.

We compare our approach with following baseline methods:

Vector Averaging: This method computes the weighted average of all word vectors in the document. We use idf-weighting as the weighting function.

Bag-of-words: A document is represented as the bag of its words, disregarding grammar and word order but keeping multiplicity.

Bag-of-bigrams: Similar to bag-of words, a document is represented as the bag of its bigrams. Both methods are performed with TF-IDF weighting.

Topic model: A document is represented as a distribution on multiple topics utilizing the toolkit JGibbLDA[1]. The similarity of two documents is measured by the similarity of two topic distributions.

Paragraph Vector: Proposed by [19], an unsupervised algorithm that learns fixed-length feature representations from variable-length pieces of text. This algorithm represents each document by a dense vector which is trained to predict words in the document.

Table 2. Comparison results of models computing features for documents

#	Methods	Precision
1	Vector averaging	0.734
2	Bag-of-words	0.758
3	Bag-of-bigrams	0.767
4	Topic model	0.
5	Paragraph vector	0.
6	LDR+LCR	0.889
7	LDR+LCR-joint	0.891

The result of our method and other baselines are reported in Table 2. In this task, we find that TF-IDF weighting performs better than raw counts and therefore we only report the results of methods with TF-IDF weighting. Our method significantly outperforms bag-of-words and bag-of-bigrams methods, for they lose the ordering words and ignore semantics of the words. Topic model and paragraph vector achieved better performance than BoW model and that suggests that they are useful for capturing the semantics of the document. Both topic model and Paragraph Vector are trained unsupervisedly, while in our method the features for documents are optimized for specific disambiguation task.

3.2 Experiments on NERD Dataset

The named entity recognition and disambiguation (NERD) in CIPS-SIGHAN 2012 is the task detecting entity mentions from raw text and classifying each mention to its real world entity. There are 16 names in the sample data and

---

[1] http://jgibblda.sourceforge.net/.

32 names in the test data. For each name N, there is a document collection T and knowledge base (KB) which contains several persons, organizations or locations who share the same name N. For each document in T, the task is to find the target entity of the name N in KB; if the target entity of the name N in document is not contained in KB, then the system needs to determine whether N is a common word or not; if not, we need to cluster these documents into subsets, each of which refers to one single entity.

We defined two pseudo entities for each name using the same way as Han [22]. The *other* pseudo entity describes the situation that name is used as a common word and *out* pseudo entity represents the target entities which are not contained in KB. For each document D in test dataset, name N in D is linked to the entity E in KB with highest similarity score $sim(D, E)$. We compare our methods with top three systems participated NERD task in CIP-SIGHAN 2012. The result in Table 3 shows that our method outperforms the best team.

Table 3. Comparison with top three teams in NERD task

#	Methods	Precision (%)	Recall (%)	F (%)
1	LDR+LCR-joint	83.77	81.52	82.63
2	Han et al. [22]	79.48	80.98	80.22
3	Hao et al. [23]	72.56	79.23	75.75
4	Liu et al. [25]	67.18	85.62	75.39

[22] adopt a two-stage method which can incorporate classifying and clustering techniques. [23] proposed an extraction algorithm of keyword features based on the distribution of unlabeled data for this task. [25] extracted 19 kinds of attributes for personal named entity, and trained Support Vector Machine (SVM) to classify documents. All teams above extract attributes information from document using toolkit of named entity recognition (NER) and then design features for name N manually. Our method outperforms the best team by 2.41 % without any manual designed features.

4 Related Work

4.1 Named Entity Disambiguation

In recent years, many methods have been proposed for entity disambiguation or linking which dates back to Bunescu and Pasca [2]. Bunescu and Pasca [2] built a system to compare the context of mention to the Wikipedia categories of an candidate entity. (Cucerzan [3]) extended this framework with more carefully designed feature for similarity measure. Many similarity measures have been employed in previous work, such as cosine similarity, Kullback-Leibler divergence, Jaccard distance and so on (Hoffart et al. [5]; Bunescu and Pasca [2]; Cucerzan [3]) The straightforward solution that measures the relatedness between the context of mention and definitions of candidate entities in knowledge base is local and it lacks collective notion of coherence between Wikipedia pages. Moreover, these man-made features are often duplicate and over-specific.

The straightforward solution that measures the relatedness between the context of mention and definitions of candidate definitions in knowledge base is local and it lacks collective notion of coherence in knowledge base. To overcome the disadvantages of local disambiguation, some works focus on collective disambiguation (Han et al. [4]; Ratinov et al. [7]; Hoffat et al. [5]). Collective methods disambiguate all mentions in a text simultaneously based on the coherence among decisions. Graph-based methods has been proposed for collective disambiguation (Han [4]), and Page-Rank algorithm is applied to rank nodes in the graph (Alhelbawy [6]). Moro [9] presented Babelfly, a unified graph-based approach to name entity and word sense disambiguation. However, Ratinov [7] has shown that local methods based on similarity of context and entity definition achieve a good performance and are hard to beat, even though collective disambiguation can be improved slightly.

Many efficient methods have been proposed for CLP-2012 named entity recognition and disambiguation task. Han [22] adopt a two-stage method which can incorporate classifying and clustering techniques. Hao [23] proposed an extraction algorithm of keyword features based on the distribution of unlabeled data for this task. [25] extracted 19 kinds of attributes for personal named entity, and trained Support Vector Machine (SVM) to classify documents.

4.2   Representation Learning

To fight the curse of dimensionality, Bengio [8] learns simultaneously a distributed representations for words with the probability function for word sequences based on neural networks. Tang and Wei [13] develop three neural networks to learn sentiment specific word embedding, which encodes sentiment information in the continuous representation of words. However, most existing algorithms for learning continuous word representations typically only model the syntactic context of words but ignore the ambiguity of words.

Various neural models have been described to achieve phrase level or sentence level representation (Mitchell and Lapata [14]; Zanzotto et al. [16]; Mikolov et al. [17]). A simple approach of sentence models is that of Neural Bag-of-Words(NBoW) models. For instance, the weighted average of all words in document is used as input of following fully connected layers, which loses the word order information in context. Recursive Neural Network (RecNN) (Socher et al. [15]) combining the word vectors in an order given by parse tree, which has been shown work for only sentences because it relies on parsing. Paragragh Vector (Mikolov et al. [19]) has been proposed to construct representations of input sequences of variable length. It does not require task-specific tuning of the word weighting function or does it rely on the parse tree. The paragraph vector containing ambiguous mention is trained in an unsupervised way, which means that the representation of sentence or paragraph isn't suitable for disambiguation task.

To learn entity representations for entity disambiguation, (He et al. [20]) first employed Stacked Denoising Auto-encoders to learn an initial document representation and a supervised fine-tuning stage follows to optimize the representation towards the similarity measure. The input of each document is a binary bag-of-words vector which loses the word order information. The input layers has 100,000 units and it makes the training process more difficult and time-consuming.

5 Conclusion and Future Work

We propose a approach that automatically learns context-entity similarity for entity disambiguation based on deep neural networks. The intermediate representation are learned using large scale annotations in Baike, without any man-made feature. Experiment reveals the importance of context modeling in entity disambiguation task. In the following work, we are trying to extend our method to other disambiguation task such as word sense disambiguation (WSD) and personal name disambiguation. Representations of ambiguous word and personal name will be learned for a novel similarity measure.

Acknowledgements. Our work is supported by National High Technology Research and Development Program of China (863 Program) (No. 2015AA015402), National Natural Science Foundation of China (No. 61370117 & No. 61433015) and Major National Social Science Fund of China (No. 12 & ZD227).

References

1. Zheng, Z., Li, F., Huang, M., Zhu, X.: Learning to link entities with knowledge base. In: Human Language Technologies: The 2010 Annual Conference of the North American Chapter of the Association for Computational Linguistics, pp. 483–491. Association for Computational Linguistics, June 2010
2. Bunescu, R.C., Pasca, M.: Using encyclopedic knowledge for named entity disambiguation. In: EACL, vol. 6, pp. 9–16, April 2006
3. Cucerzan, S.: Large-scale named entity disambiguation based on wikipedia data. In: EMNLP-CoNLL, vol. 7, pp. 708–716, June 2007
4. Han, X., Sun, L., Zhao, J.: Collective entity linking in web text: a graph-based method. In: Proceedings of the 34th International ACM SIGIR Conference on Research and Development in Information Retrieval, pp. 765–774. ACM, July 2011
5. Hoffart, J., Yosef, M.A., Bordino, I., Frstenau, H., Pinkal, M., Spaniol, M., Weikum, G.: Robust disambiguation of named entities in text. In: Proceedings of the Conference on Empirical Methods in Natural Language Processing, pp. 782–792. Association for Computational Linguistics, July 2011
6. Alhelbawy, A., Gaizauskas, R.: Graph ranking for collective named entity disambiguation. In: Annual Meeting of the Association for Computational Linguistics, pp. 75–80 (2014)

7. Ratinov, L., Roth, D., Downey, D., Anderson, M.: Local and global algorithms for disambiguation to wikipedia. In: Proceedings of the 49th Annual Meeting of the Association for Computational Linguistics: Human Language Technologies, vol. 1, pp. 1375–1384. Association for Computational Linguistics, June 2011
8. Bengio, Y., Ducharme, R., Vincent, P., Janvin, C.: A neural probabilistic language model. J. Mach. Learn. Res. **3**, 1137–1155 (2003)
9. Moro, A., Raganato, A., Navigli, R.: Entity linking meets word sense disambiguation: a unified approach. Trans. Assoc. Comput. Linguist. **2**, 231–244 (2014)
10. Collobert, R., Weston, J., Bottou, L., Karlen, M., Kavukcuoglu, K., Kuksa, P.: Natural language processing (almost) from scratch. J. Mach. Learn. Res. **12**, 2493–2537 (2011)
11. Kim, Y.: Convolutional neural networks for sentence classification (2014). arXiv: arXiv:1408.5882
12. Kalchbrenner, N., Grefenstette, E., Blunsom, P.: A convolutional neural network for modelling sentences (2014). arXiv: arXiv:1404.2188
13. Tang, D., Wei, F., Yang, N., Zhou, M., Liu, T., Qin, B.: Learning sentiment-specific word embedding for twitter sentiment classification. In: Proceedings of the 52nd Annual Meeting of the Association for Computational Linguistics, pp. 1555–1565 (2014)
14. Mitchell, J., Lapata, M.: Composition in distributional models of semantics. Cognit. Sci. **34**(8), 1388–1429 (2010)
15. Socher, R., Lin, C.C., Manning, C., Ng, A.Y.: Parsing natural scenes and natural language with recursive neural networks. In: Proceedings of the 28th International Conference on Machine Learning (ICML-11), pp. 129–136 (2011)
16. Zanzotto, F.M., Korkontzelos, I., Fallucchi, F., Manandhar, S.: Estimating linear models for compositional distributional semantics. In Proceedings of the 23rd International Conference on Computational Linguistics, pp. 1263–1271. Association for Computational Linguistics, August 2010
17. Mikolov, T., Sutskever, I., Chen, K., Corrado, G.S., Dean, J.: Distributed representations of words and phrases and their compositionality. In: Advances in Neural Information Processing Systems, pp. 3111–3119 (2013)
18. Hinton, G.E., Srivastava, N., Krizhevsky, A., Sutskever, I., Salakhutdinov, R.R.: Improving neural networks by preventing co-adaptation of feature detectors (2012). arXiv: arXiv:1207.0580
19. Le, Q.V., Mikolov, T.: Distributed representations of sentences and documents (2014). arXiv: arXiv:1405.4053
20. He, Z., Liu, S., Li, M., Zhou, M., Zhang, L., Wang, H.: Learning entity representation for entity disambiguation. In: ACL vol. 2, pp. 30–34, August 2013
21. Song, Y., Huang, J., Councill, I.G., Li, J., Giles, C.L.: Efficient topic-based unsupervised name disambiguation. In: Proceedings of the 7th ACM/IEEE-CS Joint conference on Digital Libraries, pp. 342–351. ACM, June 2007
22. Han, Z.P.L.S.X.: SIR-NERD: a chinese named entity recognition and disambiguation system using a two-stage method. In: CLP 2012, p. 115 (2012)
23. Hao, Z., Wong, D.F., Chao, L.S.: A template based hybrid model for chinese personal name disambiguation. In: CLP 2012, p. 121 (2012)
24. Tian, W., Pan, X., Yu, Z., Xian, Y., Yang, X.: Chinese name disambiguation based on adaptive clustering with the attribute features. In: CLP 2012, p. 132 (2012)
25. Han, W., Liu, G., Mao, Y., Huang, Z.: Attribute based chinese named entity recognition and disambiguation. In: CLP 2012, p. 127 (2012)

Exploring Recurrent Neural Networks to Detect Named Entities from Biomedical Text

Lishuang Li[✉], Liuke Jin, and Degen Huang

School of Computer Science and Technology,
Dalian University of Technology, Dalian 116024, Liaoning, China
{lils,Huangdg}@dlut.edu.cn,
dllg_lkjin@mail.dlut.edu.cn

Abstract. Biomedical named entity recognition (bio-NER) is a crucial and basic step in many biomedical information extraction tasks. However, traditional NER systems are mainly based on complex hand-designed features which are derived from various linguistic analyses and maybe only adapted to specified area. In this paper, we construct Recurrent Neural Network to identify entity names with word embeddings input rather than hand-designed features. Our contributions mainly include three aspects: (1) we adapt a deep learning architecture Recurrent Neural Network (RNN) to entity names recognition; (2) based on the original RNNs such as Elman-type and Jordan-type model, an improved RNN model is proposed; (3) considering that both past and future dependencies are important information, we combine bidirectional recurrent neural networks based on information entropy at the top layer. The experiments conducted on the BioCreative II GM data set demonstrate RNN models outperform CRF and deep neural networks (DNN), furthermore, the improved RNN model performs better than two original RNN models and the combined method is effective.

Keywords: Bio-NER · Recurrent neural network · Word embeddings · Bidirectional · Information entropy

1 Introduction

Entity mention extraction is an important technology to provide structured information from raw text. In biomedical information extraction, named entities are defined as the names of existing objects, such as protein, genes, drugs and etc. Identifying these entities from explosive incremental biomedical texts can provide great convenience for medical researchers. Hence the biomedical named entity recognition is fundamental for a wide variety of natural language processing application in the biomedical field, such as coreference resolution, relation extraction and etc. [1].

Traditional research methods for bio-NER can be mainly classified into three categories which are dictionary-based methods, rule-based methods and statistical machine learning methods [2]. Because of the irregularities and ambiguities in bio-entities nomenclature and the difficulty in constructing proper and complete rule sets, the statistical machine learning method has become a better choice. In the camp of

M. Sun et al. (Eds.): CCL and NLP-NABD 2015, LNAI 9427, pp. 279–290, 2015.
DOI: 10.1007/978-3-319-25816-4_23

machine learning which mainly depends on a rich set of hand-designed features, many learning models, such as Support Vector Machine (SVM) [3], Maximum Entropy (ME) [4], Hidden Markov Model (HMM) [5] and Conditional Random Fields (CRF) [6], have been adopted in the NER task. However, their performance and promotion may be affected by some common drawbacks as followings:

- with the change of corpora and languages, the process to reconstruct feature set is difficult;
- some complex features with syntactic information rely on the performance of other NLP modules;
- the features with expert knowledge are expensive to acquire.

As the shallow machine learning methods described above have strong dependency on the artificial features and are hard to represent the complex models, deep learning has been applied on NER in recent years. Collobert et al. [7] proposed unified neural network architecture and learning algorithm for various natural languages processing tasks which also achieved a better result in the NER task. Chen et al. [8] adopted deep belief network (DBN) to extract entity mentions in Chinese documents which outperformed the traditional machine learning approach. Long short-term memory was applied for named entity recognition which had complex system architecture [9].

However, at the highest level of complexity for named entity recognition, one has to take into account the concept dependencies beyond the words surrounding the word of interest. To capture dependencies beyond the input window, Recurrent neural network (RNN) architecture can exploit the time-connection feedback. RNN is a neural network model developed under the deep learning architecture [10]. Different from other feed-forward neural network language models, RNN can maintain historical information with recurrent connections, which give RNN a potential to model long span dependencies [11]. Besides, RNNs have recently been shown to produce state-of-the-art results in the spoken language understanding (SUL). For example, Mesnil et al. [12] implemented and compared two important recurrent neural network architectures, the Elman-type network [13] which considered previous hidden layer and Jordan-type network [14] which considered previous output layer. In order to improved the performance on the Elman-type network, a context real-value input vector was provided in association with each word [15].

Leveraging RNN's recurrent property, in this paper we explore different RNN architectures and improve them adapted to named entity recognition. Firstly, we apply two simple types of RNN models Elman-type and Jordan-type networks on bio-NER. Then we integrate their strengths and propose a new RNN architecture. Finally, we combine the bidirectional recurrent neural networks based on information entropy. Experimental results show that the RNN architecture can achieve better performance than CRF and DNN with the same input.

The rest of this paper is organized as follows: Sect. 2 introduces recurrent neural network models. Application of improved RNN on bio-NER is described in Sect. 3. Section 4 shows the experiments and gives the comparison and analysis. Finally, conclusions are given in Sect. 5.

2   Recurrent Neural Network Model

2.1   Two Types of RNN Architectures

Two variants of RNNs for modeling sequential prediction was described [12]: the Elman-type RNN and the Jordan-type RNN as shown in Fig. 1. The two models consist of an input layer, a hidden layer with recurrent connections that propagate time-delayed signals, and an output layer, plus the corresponding weight matrices.

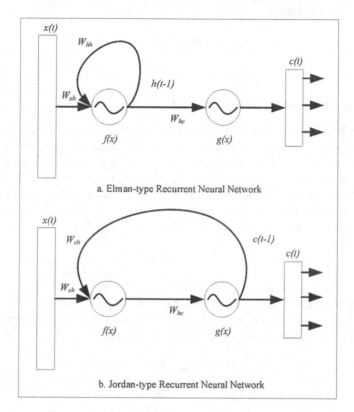

a. Elman-type Recurrent Neural Network

b. Jordan-type Recurrent Neural Network

Fig. 1.   Two original recurrent neural networks

In the Elman-type RNN, the output from the hidden layer at time t-1 is be kept and fed back to the hidden layer at time t, together with the raw input $x(t)$. At each time step, the input is propagated in a standard feed-forward neural network, and then stochastic gradient descent is applied to update the parameters, taking into account the influence of previous nodes through the recurrent connections. Thus previous information can be propagated to time t through the recurrent connections from time t-1. And the network can maintain and learn a sort of state summarizing past inputs, allowing it to perform sequence prediction. In Fig. 1, hidden layer of the Elman-type RNN can be represented mathematically with Eq. (1) and the output layer can be computed as Eq. (2).

$$h(t) = f(x(t) \cdot W_{xh} + h(t-1) \cdot W_{hh}) \tag{1}$$

$$c(t) = g(h(t) \cdot W_{hc}) \tag{2}$$

Besides, Jordan-type RNN is similar to Elman-type networks, except that the information of memory node is fed from the output layer instead of the hidden layer. The result of hidden layer can be obtained from the Eq. (3). W_{hc} is weight matrix connecting the result from output layer to the hidden layer. c(t-1) refers to values in the output layer from last node.

$$h(t) = f(x(t) \cdot W_{xh} + c(t-1) \cdot W_{ch}) \tag{3}$$

2.2   Improved Recurrent Neural Network

Two simple RNN models described above exhibit two different ways using historical information, both of which only consider one layer as memory node and input their values into next hidden layer. In order to fully utilizing all the information saved in previous nodes, we give an improved RNN architecture which can not only maintain a copy of hidden layer but also record the probability of output layer. When computing hidden neurons, we take the same action with Elman-type RNN and use sigmoid function as the activation function of the hidden layer with Eq. (4).

$$f(z) = 1/1 + e^{-z} \tag{4}$$

Different from Jordan-type RNN, the results of output layer from last node are inputted into the current output layer with Eq. (5). W_{cc} represents the parametric matrix connecting the output layers of two adjacent nodes. And at the output layer, we use a Softmax function to predict the probabilities, e.g. Eq. (6).

$$c(t) = g(h(t) \cdot W_{hc} + c(t-1) \cdot W_{cc}) \tag{5}$$

$$g(z_m) = e^{z_m} / \sum_k e^{z_k} \tag{6}$$

Figure 2 shows our improved RNN model. For each step t, we take the $x(t)$ and $h(t-1)$ as inputs of hidden layer, then the result of calculations and $c(t-1)$ are inputted into the output layer. Therefore, the hidden layer can maintain a representation of the sentence history; the output layer can maintain probabilities of previous labels which intuitively, would allow the model to perform a kind of disambiguation since no hard decision is made. Our RNN model blends the previous memories of hidden layer and output layer. Thus, the improved RNN not only receives different types of information representation from last node, but also retains consistency of information between layers.

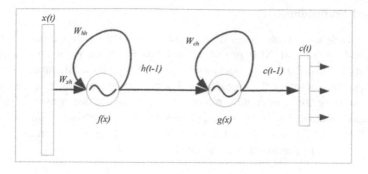

Fig. 2. Improved recurrent neural network

2.3   Combined Bidirectional Recurrent Neural Networks

For sequence labeling, it is beneficial to have access to future as well as past context. However, since regular RNNs process sequences in temporal order, they ignore future context [16]. To use all available input information, it is possible to use two separate networks (one for each time direction) and then somehow merge the results [17]. Therefore we build two different RNNs respectively, namely ordered model (predicting from the past to the future) and reversed model (predicting from the future to the past). Then two unidirectional recurrent neural network models are combined to bidirectional neural networks based on information entropy at the top layer.

According to Shannon's entropy, the entropy represents the uncertainty of information. The less the entropy of the model is, the more certain the prediction is. For each word, the two models with different directions are firstly used to output the probabilities of different labels. Then the information entropy can be computed as (7). We compute the information entropy respectively ($H(p)_{ordered}$ and $H(p)_{reversed}$) based on the probability distribution at the output layer, and select the label predicted by the model which has a lower value as the correct label.

$$H(p) = -\sum p(y) \log p(y) \tag{7}$$

3   Named Entity Recognition Based on RNN

The system architecture for named entity recognition can be summarized in Fig. 3. It accepts an input sentence and gives a label y for each word in the sentence. The first layer obtains word embeddings by a lookup table operation. Then the context information can be extracted by concatenating all the words in the context window. Thus the representation x of input layer is obtained. Finally each word vector x is inputted into the improved RNN and the output layer gives the label.

3.1   Word Embeddings

Word embeddings, also known as distributed representation, has recently been proposed to address several NLP problems and has achieved great success. A word expressed by the distributed representation is a dense, low-dimensional and real-valued vector, hopefully capturing the syntactic and semantic information in each dimension [18]. The word vectors can capture many linguistic regularities, which is superior to one-hot representation, e.g. the biomedical term *"gene"*, *"proteins"*, *"kinase"* are close to each other, and far from the other type of nouns "weeks", "months", while for one-hot encoding, all the words are equally distant.

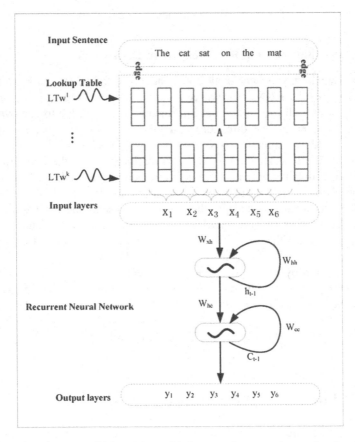

Fig. 3. Named entity recognition system with improved recurrent neural network language model

In our experiments, we use the distributed representations of words trained by Word2Vec tool developed by Mikolov [19], rather than hand-designed features. A real-valued embedding vector is associated with a word, and all the real-valued vectors are obtained by training a skip-gram model from 5.6 GB unlabeled text downloaded from PubMed. In our experiments, the vector dimension is set to 200.

After that, we can map each word in our corpora to an embedding and initialize the word lookup table with the embeddings. For all the words appearing in the corpus but not in the lookup table, we use *"unk"* as their unified representation, and give them a customized vector with the same dimension.

Given a sentence and a lookup table as shown in Fig. 3, we construct a matrix A in which we denote $[A]_{i,j}$ the coefficient at row i and column j. And in order to capture short-term temporal dependencies in a sentence, we use a word-context window. With each word mapped to an embedding vector, the word-context window is the ordered concatenation of word embedding vectors. We concatenate the d_{win} column vectors around the ith column vector in the matrix A to represent x_i:

$$([A]_{1,i-d_{win}/2} \cdots [A]_{k,i-d_{win}/2} \cdots [A]_{1,i+d_{win}/2} \cdots [A]_{k,i+d_{win}/2}) \tag{8}$$

In experiments, d_{win} is set to 5. Besides, to process the sentence boundaries, namely the first word and last word in the sentence, we set a customized vector with same dimension to represent the boundary vectors.

3.2 Chunk Representation

Entity mention extraction can be considered as a sequential token tagging task as in [20]. They demonstrated that choice of encoding scheme had a big impact on the system performance and the less used BILOU formalism significantly outperformed the widely adopted BIO tagging scheme. Therefore BILOU tagging scheme is selected to find the entity boundary in our experiment. **B** refers to the beginning word of a gene name, **I** and **L** respectively indicate inside tokens and the last token in a gene name if it contains more than one word, **O** refers to the words which are not included in a gene name, and finally **U** represents the unit-length chunks.

3.3 Named Entity Recognition Using RNN

In Fig. 4, we present the process about how to train ith word in the sentence. Before training, we first randomly initialize two parameters, one is in the hidden layer (e.g. h_0), and the other is in the output layer (e.g. c_0). The two parameters are constantly updated during the training. Then, with raw inputs $x(i-T + 1)$, h_0 and c_0, we calculate the neurons in the hidden layer and the probabilities in output layer about the first word in the sliding window consisting of T words. The outputs of hidden layer and output layer are saved and inputted into the next node. We repeat the process till the last word (e.g. i^{th} word) is computed. Finally, the label of ith word can be predicated.

In the Fig. 4, the process fragment with the dotted box is described in more detail in the Fig. 2. We can compute the hidden layer and output layer by (9) and (11), with parameters θ and λ. Any feed-forward recurrent neural network with T words in hidden layer and output layer can be seen as a composition of function $f_{\theta}^t(\cdot)$ and $g_{\lambda}^t(\cdot)$, corresponding to the ith word:

$$f_\theta(\,\cdot\,) = f_\theta^T(f_\theta^{T-1}(\cdots f_\theta^1(\,\cdot\,)\cdots)) \qquad (9)$$

$$f_\theta^1 = f(x(i - T + 1) \cdot W_{xh} + h_0 \cdot W_{hh}) \qquad (10)$$

$$g_\lambda(\cdot) = g_\lambda^T(g_\lambda^{T-1}(\cdots g_\lambda^1(\cdot)\cdots)) \qquad (11)$$

$$g_\lambda^1 = g(h(i - T + 1) \cdot W_{hc} + c_0 \cdot W_{cc}) \qquad (12)$$

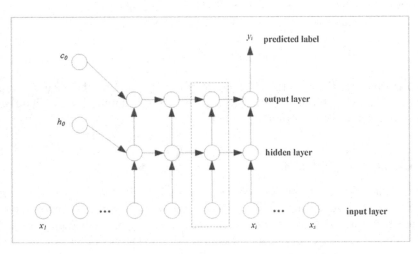

Fig. 4. The process to train the ith word in the sentence

4 Experiments and Results

Our experiments are carried out on the BioCreative II GM corpus which consists of 15,000 training sentences and 5,000 testing sentences. Bio-NERs in those sentences were manually annotated. Note that boundaries of gene names in text can be fuzzy even for human annotators and therefore alternative annotations were also provided with the corpus. In the experiment, we think an entity is correctly recognized if it matches the correct annotations or alternative annotations.

The results from different models will be shown in this section. All of them apply no post-processing so that the impact of post-processing is excluded. We measure the precision, recall and F-score of the improved RNN and compare with CRF baseline, deep neural network (DNN) and original RNNs. In experiments, all the deep networks are based on the common Theano neural network toolkit[1] and all the RNN models are trained with the same hyper-parameters. Besides, during the process, we set word-context window to 5, and fix the sliding window T to 5. To keep the consistent depth with RNN, we also set DNN to one hidden layer.

---

[1] http://deeplearning.net/tutorial/rnnslu.html.

4.1 Evaluation Methodology

We use F-score as our assessing criteria to evaluate our method. The definition of Precision (P), Recall (R) and F-score (F) are shown as (13, 14, 15). TP is short for true positives, FP represents false positives, and FN stands for false negatives.

$$P = TP/(TP + FP) \tag{13}$$

$$R = TP/(TP + FN) \tag{14}$$

$$F - score = 2 * P * R/(P + R) \tag{15}$$

4.2 Results and Analysis

Results with Different Models. We experiment using three different types of models, namely CRF, DNN and RNN. From Table 1, the results show that both CRF and RNN have better performance than DNN. And all the RNN models can achieve significant improvements by about 10 % F-scores than DNN. It is shown that maintained historical information in RNN can play an important role in the sequence prediction. Furthermore, compared with CRF, the RNN models can also obtain higher F-scores by over 5 %. The results demonstrate that RNN models have a distinct advantage in named entity recognition.

Table 1. Comparison among different models.

Model	P (%)	R (%)	F (%)
CRF(baseline)	79.79	69.65	74.38
DNN	75.00	63.78	68.93
Jordan	82.38	76.54	79.35
Elman	82.23	76.40	79.21
Ordered improved RNN	82.06	78.56	**80.27**
Reversed improved RNN	80.36	81.59	**80.97**
Combined *bidirectional* RNN	82.61	81.21	**81.91**

Compared with two original RNN models, the ordered improved RNN can obtain higher F-scores than Jordan-type by 0.92 %, than Elman-type RNN by 1.06 %, and the reversed improved RNN achieves 80.97 % F-score, which is higher than Jordan by 1.62 % and higher than Elman by 1.76 %. The results show that both improved RNN models outperform original RNNs. Finally, the combined bidirectional improved RNN achieves the best performance of 81.91 % F-score which is higher than the ordered improved RNN by 1.64 % and higher than the reversed improved RNN by 0.94 %. It is obviously shown that the proposed combined method is effective.

Comparison Between the Improved and Two Original Models. Figure 5 shows the compared results among three kinds of RNNs with ordered model and reversed model respectively. We can see that even though both Jordan-type and Elman-type RNNs have similar shifting trend within specified number of iterations in both models, the improved RNN can always achieve better performance. This mainly because that the improved model not only takes into account the history messages in the hidden layer, but also considers the probabilities in the output layer.

Comparison Between Bidirectional and Unidirectional Models. Figure 6 describes the comparison between unidirectional and combined bidirectional models of our improved RNN. It is can be observed that the combined bidirectional model can obtain better performance. The main reason for the significant improvement lies in the

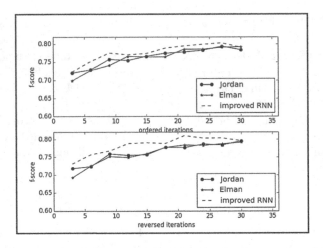

Fig. 5. Results of different RNNs with ordered and reversed models

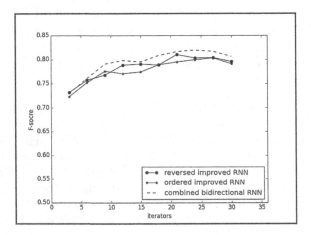

Fig. 6. Results of improved RNNs with different models

combined approach which can fully weigh bidirectional historical information by computing the information entropy and choose the appropriate model as the temporary decisive model.

More interestingly, we also observe that the RNNs' reversed model performs very well while its ordered model gives worse results, even though mathematically these two kinds of model are symmetric to each other. According to the similar analysis of [12], this maybe mainly because most of the named entities to be predicted in the BioCreative II are located in the first half of sentences, which makes the ordered model perform prediction with very little historical information.

5 Conclusion

In this paper, we apply different RNN models on the named entity recognition with word embeddings, and achieve better performance than CRF and DNN. Then, based on two simple original RNNs, we propose an improved RNN model which can maintain a copy of previous information at hidden layer and output layer. The experimental results show that our model is effective in NER task. Simultaneously, considering the context information from past and future has an important impact on the prediction, we present combined bidirectional recurrent neural networks based on information entropy whose performance is much higher than those of both unidirectional models.

Acknowledgment. The authors gratefully acknowledge the financial support provided by the National Natural Science Foundation of China under No. 61173101, 61173100.

References

1. Chen, Y., Ouyang, Y., Li, W., Zheng, D., Zhao, T.: Using deep belief nets for chinese named entity categorization. In: Proceedings of the 2010 Named Entities Workshop, pp. 102–109 (2010)
2. Li, L., Fan, W., Huang, D., Dang, Y., Sun, J.: Boosting performance of gene mention tagging system by hybrid methods. J. Biomed. Inform. **45**, 156–164 (2012)
3. Lee, K.J., Hwang, Y.S., Kim, S., Rim, H.C.: Biomedical named entity recognition using two-phase model based on SVMs. J. Biomed. Inform. **37**, 436–447 (2004)
4. Saha, S.K., Sarkar, S., Mitra, P.: Feature selection techniques for maximum entropy based biomedical named entity recognition. J. Biomed. Inform. **45**, 2673–2681 (2009)
5. Shen, D., Zhang, J., Zhou, G., Su, J., Tan, C.L.: Effective adaptation of a hidden markov model-based named entity recognizer for biomedical domain. In: Proceedings of the ACL 2003 Workshop on Natural Language Processing in Biomedicine, vol. 13, pp. 49–56 (2003)
6. Sun, C., Guan, Y., Wang, X., Lin, L.: Rich features based conditional random fields for biological named entities recognition. Comput. Biol. Med. **37**, 1327–1333 (2007)
7. Collobert, R., Weston, J., Bottou, L., Karlen, M., Kavukcuoglu, K., Kuksa, P.: Natural language processing (almost) from scratch. J. Mach. Learn. Res. **12**, 2493–2537 (2011)
8. Chen, Y., Zheng, D., Zhao, T.: Exploring deep belief nets to detect and categorize chinese entities. In: Motoda, H., Wu, Z., Cao, L., Zaiane, O., Yao, M., Wang, W. (eds.) ADMA 2013, Part I. LNCS, vol. 8346, pp. 468–480. Springer, Heidelberg (2013)

9. Hammerton, J.: Named entity recognition with long short-term memory. In: Proceedings of the Seventh Conference on Natural Language Learning at HLT-NAACL 2003, vol. 4, pp. 172–175 (2003)

10. Mikolov, T., Karafiat, M., Burget, L., Cernoky, J., Khudanpur, S.: Recurrent neural network based language model. In: 11th Annual Conference of the International Speech Communication Association, INTERSPEECH 2010, Makuhari, Chiba, Japan, pp. 1045–1048 (2010)

11. Mikolov, T., Kombrink, S., Burget, L., Cernocky, J., Khudanpur, S.: Extensions of recurrent neural network language model. In: Acoustics, Speech and Signal Processing (ICASSP), pp. 5528–5531 (2011)

12. Mesnil, G., He, X., Deng., Bengio Y.: Investigation of recurrent neural network architectures and learning methods for spoken language understanding. In: INTERSPEECH, pp. 3771–3775 (2013)

13. Elman, J.L.: Finding structure in time. Cogn. Sci. **14**, 179–211 (1990)

14. Jordan, M.I.: Serial order: A parallel distributed processing approach. Adv. Psychol. **121**, 471–495 (1997)

15. Mikolov, T., Zweig, G.: Context dependent recurrent neural network language model. In: SLT, pp. 234–239 (2012)

16. Graves, A.: Supervised sequence labelling. In: Graves, A. (ed.) Supervised Sequence Labelling with Recurrent Neural Networks. SCI, vol. 385, pp. 5–13. Springer, Heidelberg (2012)

17. Schuster, M., Paliwal, K.K.: Bidirectional recurrent neural networks. IEEE Trans. Signal Process. **45**, 2673–2681 (1997)

18. Turian, J., Ratinov, L., Bengio, Y.: Word representations : a simple and general method for semi-supervised learning. In: Proceedings of the 48th Annual Meeting of the Association for Computational Linguistics, pp. 384–394 (2010)

19. Mikolov, T., Chen, K., Corrado, G., Dean, J.: Efficient Estimation of Word Representations in Vector Space. arXiv preprint arXiv:1301.3781(2013)

20. Ratinov, L., Roth, D.: Design challenges and misconceptions in named entity recognition. In: Proceedings of the Thirteenth Conference on Computational Natural Language Learning, pp. 147–155 (2009)

Discourse, Coreference and Pragmatics

Predicting Implicit Discourse Relations with Purely Distributed Representations

Haoran Li[(✉)], Jiajun Zhang, and Chengqing Zong

National Laboratory of Pattern Recognition, CASIA,
Beijing, People's Republic of China
{haoran.li,jjzhang,cqzong}@nlpr.ia.ac.cn

Abstract. Discourse relations between two consecutive segments play an important role in many natural language processing (NLP) tasks. However, a large portion of the discourse relations are implicit and difficult to detect due to the absence of connectives. Traditional detection approaches utilize discrete features, such as words, clusters and syntactic production rules, which not only depend strongly on the linguistic resources, but also lead to severe data sparseness. In this paper, we instead propose a novel method to predict the implicit discourse relations based on the purely distributed representations of words, sentences and syntactic features. Furthermore, we learn distributed representations for different kinds of features. The experiments show that our proposed method can achieve the best performance in most cases on the standard data sets.

Keywords: Implicit discourse relation · Distributed · Word level representation · Sentence level representation

1 Introduction

Automatic discourse relation recognition is an important task of discourse analysis, and it is beneficial to many NLP applications such as question answering, sentiment analysis and information retrieval. For instance, contingency relation detection can improve question answering systems and event relation extraction. Contrast relation recognition can eliminate intra-sentence polarity ambiguities.

Discourse relations can be grouped into explicit and implicit relations according to whether there are relation connectives. Connectives play a crucial role in inference of explicit discourse relations. For example, "but" is a strong indicative for COMPARISON relation while "and" for EXPANSION. In fact, previous studies [1] show that just using discourse connectives can achieve 94 % accuracy for explicit relation classification. In contrast, implicit discourse relations are much more difficult to be determined due to the absence of evident relation cues. In the natural texts, sentences without connectives account for a large proportion. For instance, about 39.54 % of the total discourse relations are annotated as implicit in Penn Discourse Treebank (PDTB). Consequently, researchers mainly focus on implicit relation recognition.

© Springer International Publishing Switzerland 2015
M. Sun et al. (Eds.): CCL and NLP-NABD 2015, LNAI 9427, pp. 293–305, 2015.
DOI: 10.1007/978-3-319-25816-4_24

To solve this issue, prior work resorted to explore diverse linguistically informed features, which started with lexical features introduced by [2], and then syntactic features were proved more effective [3, 4]. Subsequent work focused on introducing more features [5, 6] or selecting an optimal feature set [7]. These features are usually acquired by the help of external linguistic resources. For instance, word's polarity features are assigned according to its attribution in the Multi-perspective Question Answering Opinion Corpus, and inquirer tags are extracted from General Inquirer lexicon. WordNet features, verb class, affect features are leveraged as well.

The traditional methods introduced above for implicit relation classification face two major challenges. Firstly, they strongly depend on the external linguistic lexicons, which lack the generalization of the approaches for different languages. Taking the Inquirer tags feature as an example, the number of words which can't find the corresponding semantic categories in General Inquirer lexicon is more than 10,000, accounting for around 40 % of the whole words in PDTB.

Secondly, all of the traditional methods adopt discrete features which lead to severe data sparsity and cannot explore the similarities between discrete features. More than 10,000 production rules and 100,000 word pairs can be extracted from the PDTB even though a frequency threshold 5 has been used. [6, 8, 9] attempted to make the features less sparse. For example, [9] employed the Brown word clusters. These approaches can alleviate the data sparse problem to some extent, but they are still based on discrete features and cannot take full advantage of the similarities between discrete features.

In this paper, we propose a novel method based on the purely distributed representations. Our goal is to learn the low-dimensional dense vector representations for the discrete features from words, sub-sentence to syntactic production rules. Furthermore, we explore different algorithms for representation learning, such as deep neural networks (DNN) and principle component analysis (PCA).

With the learnt distributed representations, we then design an ensemble model to investigate different kinds of incorporation of the features in different levels.

We make the following contributions in this paper.

- Instead of discrete features, we propose a novel method of implicit discourse relation classification using only the purely distributed representations.
- We have explored the representation learning for different level features, from words, part-of-speech (POS), sentences to syntactic production rules. In addition, we apply different algorithms to learn different presentations for different kinds of discrete features.
- We have designed an ensemble model to explore various combinations of the distributed representations in different levels. The experiments show that we can obtain the best performance in most cases on the standard test sets. Figure 1 shows the framework of our method.

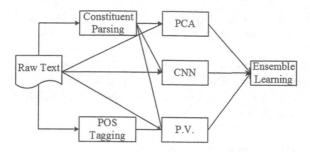

Fig. 1. Framework of our method, P.V. denotes paragraph vector model (can perform word2vec and sent2vec)

2   Related Work

2.1   Implicit Discourse Relation Recognition

Marcu and Echihabi [10] presented an unsupervised approach to identify discourse relations trained on a huge artificial corpus with the word pair features. Their training data was generated manually from raw corpora by detecting certain patterns based on cue phrases. For example, if there is a word "but" between two successive sentences, the sentence pairs are extracted as CONTRAST instance after removing the discourse connectives. They showed lexical features are effective for identifying discourse relations.

This work was followed by [11]. They performed an experiment to recognize discourse relations in Japanese by combining word pairs and phrasal patterns. A phrasal pattern explores the information existing in longer context beyond two sentence pairs. For instance, the pattern "...should have done ..." immediately following "...did ..." can intensely imply the discourse relation is CONTRAST.

Pitler et al. [2] is the first study to infer implicit discourse relations on natural data. They compared the performance of various types of word pair features, and explored the utility of several linguistically informed features including polarity tags, inquirer tags, verb classes and modality, showing lexical features are useful for recognizing implicit discourse relations. Lin et al. [3] is the first to introduce syntactic features, specifically, constituent parse features and dependency parse features. They presented an implicit discourse relation classifier on Level 2 types in the PDTB using syntactic and lexical features. [12] extended this work by applying tree kernel method to the syntactic features. [4] proposed a method that uses the language models to automatically predict implicit connectives. [13] extended this work by integrating various linguistically informed features. Park et al. [7] optimized the combination of lexical and syntactic features and achieved a solid performance.

Subsequence works focused on settling the data sparsity problem. [6] aggregated lexical feature by re-weighting word pairs. [8] introduced the simplification of the parse tree to relieve the sparsity of syntactic features. [9] employed Brown cluster to generate more compact word pair features, reducing the feature size from quadratic in the vocabulary to 3200^2. To date, [14] manifested the best results by training the model with elaborately collected explicit discourse relation data.

Compared to the previous work, we resort to the purely distributed representations of these discrete features. In this way, we can not only alleviate the data sparsity problem to a large extent, but also fully explore the similarities between the discrete features.

2.2 Distributed Representations

Word embeddings as a kind of distributed representations for words have shown successful applications in many NLP tasks including statistical language modeling, machine translation, named entity recognition, semantic role labeling, syntactical parsing and word sense disambiguation By projecting words from one-hot representation onto a much lower dimensional vector space, we can obtain the denser representations of words which have been proved contains more semantic information: vectors that are close to each other are shown to be semantically related.

Phrase and sentence distributed representations attracted much attention in recent years [15,16] applied convolutional neural networks with shallow architectures to learn sentence distributed representations for classification. This model consists of a local convolution layer and a global max-pooling layer over sentence.

Inspired by the above methods, we propose to learn appropriate distributed representations of the discrete features in different levels. Besides the surface level words and sentences, we also try to present the POS and syntactic production rules in the dense continuous vector space. In addition to the neural network based approaches, we also apply other algorithms, such as PCA, to learn the distributed representations.

3 Overview of the Penn Discourse Treebank

The Penn Discourse Treebank (PDTB) is the largest available discourse corpus annotated on 2,312 Wall Street Journal (WSJ) articles, where there are 40,600 instances with five main types of discourse relation labels: Explicit, Implicit, AltLex, EntRel and NoRel. The senses of discourse relations are organized into a hierarchical structure in which the top level contains four major classes: "COMPARISON", "CONTINGENCY", "EXPANSION" and "TEMPORAL". The next two levels consist of more fine-grained relation types. PDTB provides an available resource for analyzing discourse structure and detecting discourse relations.

A discourse relation instance has two components: the substring bounded by the connective is called Arg2, the remainder is Arg1. There are natural connectives such as "but", "because", "and" in explicit discourse relations, while for implicit relations, the connectives are manually inserted. Here we give an example of implicit discourse relation in PDTB style: Implicit connectives are in small caps. For the arguments, Arg1 is presented in italics, and Arg2 in bold.

Comparison: *A figure above 50 indicates the economy is likely to expand,*
Implicit = WHILE **one below 50 indicates a contraction may be ahead.**

4   Distributed Representation Learning

The focus of our method is to learn the better representation of the semantic and syntactic features of the argument pairs for implicit discourse relation recognition without any external lexicons. The previous methods exploring discrete features (words, clusters and syntactic production rules) suffer from data sparsity problem and cannot fully use the similarity between words. We attempt to learn distributed representations for each kind of discrete features from words, sentence to deep syntactic features. We will explain our feature learning methods in detail below.

4.1   Representation Learning for Words/Word-Pairs

Lexical words are usually the most important features for NLP classification tasks. In implicit discourse relation recognition, almost all of the previous approaches have employed the lexical features which were proved to be effective since the work of [1]. All of the lexical feature templates are combinations of surface words, such as bigrams and skip-bigrams. Following the previous work, we focus on the most popular two types of lexical feature templates: word-pair and first-last-first3, which are explained below.

Word-Pair: any skip-bigram in which the first word is located in Arg1 and the second word appears in Arg2. For the sentence of Comparison relation given in Sect. 3, we can extract "A" and "one" from Arg1 and Arg2 respectively, therefore, (A, one) is a word pair feature of this sentence.

First-Last-First3: the first, the last and the first trigram in Arg1 and Arg2 along with the pair of the first words in Arg1 and Arg2, the pair of the last words in Arg1 and Arg2. We use an example to clarify this kind of feature. Regarding the sentence in Comparison relation given in Sect. 3, the first-last-first3 feature can be expressed as: (A, one, expand, ahead, A_figure_above, one_below_50, A_one, expand_ahead).

In spite of the validity of word pairs and first-last-first3, this kind of discrete lexical features heavily suffered from sparsity problem. For example, when we set a cutoff number of 5 to remove the infrequent word pairs, we can still extracted 123,472 word pairs in total. We aim to learn dense continuous representations to alleviate the data sparsity and explore the similarities between words, instead of regarding them as independent tokens. We investigate two directions: one is matrix factorization based methods such as Singular Value Decomposition (SVD) and Principal Component Analysis (PCA), and the other is neural network based approaches such as word2vec.

Word2vec first randomly initialize each word with a fixed low-dimensional real-valued vector. Then, in the continuous vector space, it uses the context vectors to predict the central word or utilizes the central word vector to predict the context words. The word embeddings are optimized to maximize the likelihood of the large-scale monolingual data. As the training data PDTB is very limited, we employ other unlabeled monolingual data to enrich the training set so that we can obtain the accurate word embeddings.

With the learnt word embeddings, we concatenate them to form the representation of trigrams and other combination of lexical words. However, it is difficult to represent the word pair feature. Since sentences in different length contain different number of word pairs, concatenation of word embeddings cannot lead to a fixed-length vector representation. We thus resort to PCA.

PCA is a simple unsupervised linear algebra algorithm which can reduce a sophisticated feature matrix to a low-dimensional representation. PCA is widely used for optimal feature extraction and data compression because of the ability to uncover simplified structures that often underlie it. Therefore, we employ PCA to transform traditional one-hot vectors used in the prior work to a low-dimensional real-valued vector representation. Through a linear transformation matrix P, PCA can project an original data set X into a new set Y:

$$PX = Y \tag{1}$$

Here, X denotes discrete surface features such as word pairs (as well as first-last-first3) in binary vector whose dimension is the vocabulary size of word pairs, and Y denotes dense distributed representations whose dimension can be adjusted.

4.2   Representation Learning for Sentences

To determine the implicit relation between Arg1 and Arg2, the ideal method is to acquire the semantic meaning of these two sub-sentences respectively. However, it is impossible to represent the meaning of (sub-) sentences using discrete variables due to the severe data sparsity. Previous methods did not consider the sub-sentence or sentence level features. In this work, we plan to explore the effectiveness of distributed representations of (sub-) sentences.

There are several neural network based approaches to perform sentence embedding. In this work, we try two simple but effective methods: Paragraph Vector (sent2vec) [17] and convolutional neural network (CNN) [18].

Paragraph Vector is the augmentation of word2vec. Based on word2vec, the sentence embedding is also employed to predict the target word. After the optimization of the same objective as word2vec, we can get the final sentence embeddings. In order to obtain the distributed representation of Arg1 and Arg2, we also regard them as single sentences during Paragraph Vector training.

Consisting of the convolution and pooling layers, CNN provides a standard architecture which maps variable-length sentences into fixed-size distributed vectors. The CNN model takes as input the sequence of word embeddings, summarizes the sentence meaning by convolving the sliding window and pooling the saliency through the sentence, and yields the fixed-length distributed vector with other layers, such as dropout layer and fully-connected layers.

Given a sentence $w_1, w_2, \ldots, w_t, \ldots, w_T$, each word w_t is first projected into a vector x_t. Then, we concatenate all the vectors to form the input $X = [x_1, x_2, \ldots, x_t, \ldots, x_T]$.

Convolution Layer involves a number of filters $W \in R^{h \times k}$ which summarize the information of h-word window and produce a new feature. For the window of h words $X_{t:t+h-1}$ a filter F_l $(1 \leq l \leq L)$ generates the feature y_t^l as follows:

$$y_t^l = f(W X_{t:t+h-1} + b) \tag{2}$$

When a filter traverses each window from $X_{1:h-1}$ to $X_{T-h+1:T}$, we get the output of the feature map: $y^l = [y_1^l, y_1^2, ..., y_1^{T-t+1}]$, $(y^l \in R^{T-h+1})$. Note that the sentences differ from each other in length T, and then y^l has different dimensions for different sentences. It becomes a key question how to transform the variable-length vector y^l into a fixed-size vector.

Pooling Layer is designed to perform this task. In most cases, we apply a standard max-over-time pooling operation over y^l and choose the maximum value $\hat{y}^l = \max\{y^l\}$. With L filters, the dimension of the pooling layer output will be L. Using two layers of fully-connected linear layers, we obtain a fixed-length output representation.

The final fixed-length sentence representation is used to classify the implicit discourse relations in PDTB. Since the labeled training data in PDTB is not adequate, the leant sentence embedding with CNN may be not good enough. We will combine this sentence representation with the distributed representations of other kinds of features, such as word-level and syntactic-level features.

4.3 Representation Learning for Syntactic Features

To infer the implicit relation between Arg1 and Arg2, the structure difference between them may provide some clues. We thus consider two types of syntactic features and learn their distributed representations respectively. The first type is POS tags and the second one is syntactic production rules extracted from the constituent parse tree such as S → NP VP, VB → "have".

For POS tags, we learn their distributed representations in the same way as we have done in word embedding. After POS tagging of the training data, we just retain the POS sequence for each sentence and adopt word2vec/ Paragraph Vector to obtain their low-dimensional real-valued vectors.

For syntactic production rules, we first simplify the rules by splitting a rule with more than one child into unary rules following [19]. For example, S → NP VP becomes S → NP and S → VP. [19] showed that this heuristic can get an average of 1.04 % F-score improvement. For these production rules, we apply both PCA and word2vec to learn their distributed representations. When applying PCA, we collect all the production rules appearing in Arg1, Arg2 and the whole sentence, and then form a binary vector whose dimension is the vocabulary size of production rules. PCA will transform this high-dimensional binary vector into a low-dimensional real-valued vector. When applying word2vec, we should first transform the set of production rules in a sentence into a unique sequence. To achieve this goal, we use breadth-first traversal to transform a constituent parse tree into a unique sequence of production rules (e.g. S → NP). Each production rule is considered as a single token and the sequence is fed to word2vec.

5   Ensemble Learning for Implicit Discourse Relation Classification

In the previous section, we investigate the distributed representation learning for words, sentences and syntactic features with different methods (e.g. PCA, word2vec and CNN). Each kind of distributed representation can be regarded as a different view of the sentence (Arg1 and Arg2) considered. We attempt to integrate all the distributed features by ensemble learning. The ensemble learning methods can be categorized into two types based on fixed rules and trained methods. Fixed rules, such as voting rule, combine the individual outputs in a fixed manner. On the other hand, trained methods, such as weighted combination, combine outputs via training on a development dataset.

In weighted combination, the final score for class j can be expressed as follow:

$$O_j = \sum_{k=1}^{K} w_k o_{kj} \tag{3}$$

where O_j denote the final score for class j, w_k denote the weight of feature k, o_{kj} denote the score of feature k for class j. We intuitively assign the F1 score of feature k on development dataset to w_k.

6   Experiment

6.1   Experimental Settings

Following the previous work [2,4,14] on implicit relation inference, we use sections 2–20 of PDTB as training data, sections 0–1 as development set and sections 21–22 as test set.

It should be noted that the data preparation for EXPANSION relations follows the work of [4,14]. It is different from the work of [2] in which they regarded EntRel relation as a part of EXPANSION.

The distribution of implicit discourse relations in PDTB is highly skewed, especially for COMPARISON and TEMPORAL, which only occupy 15.06 % and 5.72 % of the total. [2] randomly chose the negative instances to balance the number of positive, but this down-sampling approach was proved throwing away useful information. [19] presented several strategies to address this problem by including down-sampling, up-sampling and weight-cost. The experiments showed that weight-cost is better than re-sampling. [9] employed a similar method as weight-cost by re-weighting the instance in each class so that the positive and negative classes acquire the same weights in total. We adopt this method in our experiments to achieve balance between positive and negative instances.

For evaluating effect of syntactic feature in real-world data, we didn't use the gold standard parse results provided by the Penn Treebank. Our constituent parse results are obtained by Stanford Parser, and POS tags are generated by nltk package. We also employ lowercasing, stemming and tokenization. Additionally, when we are training with discrete features, we follow the previous methods and remove the discrete features whose occurrence number lower than a cut-off, which is 3, 5, and 5 for first-last-first3, words pairs and production rules respectively.

When we learn distributed representations with word2vec and sent2vec models, we remove the words and production rules which only appear once in the dataset. To enlarge the data scale for word/sent2vec training, we employ a large-scale unlabeled monolingual data from Reuters. From the raw Reuters data, we choose only the sentences in which all the words should appear in PDTB so as to avoid noise. The chosen Reuters corpus contains 1.7 billion tokens and 67.2 million sentences.

We have studied the effects of parameter set in word/sent2vec including the dimension of vectors, the size of context windows, the number of negative sample tokens and the learning rate. We found that the dimension of vector has a significant influence on the final performance, and 25 is a satisfactory size. To make a fair comparison, the dimension of the vectors acquired via PCA is set the same as word/sent2vec.

For CNN, we use one convolution layer, one max-pooling layer, one dropout layer and two fully-connected linear layers. We adopt sigmoid function for non-linear projection. In the convolution layer, we set the window h=3 and employ F=100 filters. We set the dropout ratio 0.5 in the dropout layer. The dimension of two fully-connected layers is set 50 and the output length is set 25.

Given the distributed representations, we compare the performance between SVM from libsvm and MaxEnt from MALLET. We found that these two classifiers perform similarly. Our experimental results that we reported in this paper are obtained by linear model in SVM with the parameters set to default values.

6.2   Experimental Results

In this section, we try to answer four questions: (1) whether distributed representation is better than discrete features in implicit relation recognition; (2) which kinds of features are more effective; (3) which method for distributed representation learning performs better; and (4) whether can our method surpass the best reported results. The detailed experimental results listed in Table 1 can answer the first three questions. We can see from Table 1 that distributed representations can substantially outperform the discrete features in most cases. The largest improvement can be up to 16.43 F1-score for CONTINGENCY relation inference using syntactic production rules.

When we focus on the rows in Table 1, we can find that different kinds of features con-tribute very differently to the final performance. Overall, the syntactic features perform stably over the four relations and achieve the best performance in most cases. The sentence-level features can obtain good performance as well, indicating that representations of Arg1, Arg2 and the whole sentence are helpful in implicit relation recognition.

When we look at the columns in Table 1, we will see that word/sent2vec wins 3 out of 4 relation recognition tasks. The exception is the EXPANSION relation task, in which CNN performs best.

Table 1. The performance (F1-score) of discrete and distributed feature on recognition four classes of implicit discourse relations. Disc. denotes discrete features, P.V. denotes the distributed featured acquired by Paragraph vector model (can perform word2vec and sent2vec). Scores marked by "*" are significantly better (p < 0.05; t-test) than counterpart discrete features.

COMPARISON					CONTINGENCY				
Features	Disc	PCA	P.V	CNN	Features	Disc	PCA	P.V	CNN
Word Pair	26.71	29.24	-	-	Word Pair	34.48	47.92	-	-
First-Last-First3	25.55	30.37	-	-	First-Last-First3	34.67	45.64	-	-
Word-sentence	27.75	30.79*	37.81*	23.81	Word-sentence	36.36	47.96*	48.58*	33.91
Production Rules	27.81	34.68*	37.57*	18.83	Production Rules	35.09	49.32*	51.52*	32.67
POS	-	-	35.37	-	POS	-	-	51.52	-
EXPANSION					TEMPORAL				
Features	Disc	PCA	P.V	CNN	Features	Disc	PCA	P.V	CNN
Word Pair	60.18	64.22	-	-	Word Pair	20.93	15.75	-	-
First-Last-First3	56.22	61.71	-	-	First-Last-First3	12.50	13.90	-	-
Word-sentence	59.75	64.7*	65.44*	69.79*	Word-sentence	24.32	17.18	26.19*	9.71
Production Rules	60.82	66.00*	65.21*	69.28*	Production Rules	17.98	28.97*	29.72*	10.77
POS	-	-	67.13	-	POS	-	-	25.48	-

The final ensemble results shown in Table 2 answers the last question. In ensemble learning, we apply the weighted combination approach. We investigate three-level ensemble models: we first ensemble features learnt by word/sent2vec models because they perform best in Table 1. Then we add PCA method. Finally, we combine all the distributed features learnt by word/sent2vec, PCA and CNN. The experimental results in Table 2 tell us that our method can achieve the best performance in three out of three relation recognition tasks when compared to the state-of-the-art approaches using discrete features. It gets the improvement over the state-of-the-art by 1.34, 1.31 and 1.7 F-score respectively. In the COMPARISON task, we also obtain a competitive result. These results demonstrate that our ensemble method with distributed representations is very promising for implicit discourse relation inference.

6.3   Discussion

Distributed representations learned by word/sent2vec and CNN model outperform the discrete features by a larger margin, and achieve the best results against the state-of-the-art except the relation of Expansion. We analyze the gap of F1 score in Expansion relation and find that the majority of performance comes from the polarity tag features used in the prior work. It is verified by [2,6] that polarity tags have a remarkable effect for inferring Expansion relations, while our model seems insensitive to polarity. For example, by calculating the cosine distance between the word vectors trained by word2vec, "good" is most similar to "bad". Similarly, others include "better" to "worse", "positive" to "negative"

Table 2. Experimental results of our system.

		Com. vs Not	Con. vs Not	Exp. vs Not	Tem. vs Not
Pitler et al. (2009)		21.96	47.13	-	16.76
Zhou et al. (2010)		31.79	47.16	65.95	20.30
Rutherford and Xue (2014)		39.70	54.42	70.23	28.69
Rutherford and Xue (2015)		**41.00**	53.80	69.41	33.30
prospose	P.V.	40.55	53.52	67.67	**35.00**
	P.V.+PCA	39.10	**55.14**	69.46	28.91
	P.V.+PCA+CNN	38.52	54.15	**70.71**	31.51

and "can" to "cannot". The reason is that we use context-based models and these words share the similar contexts.

Table 1 shows that principal component analysis (PCA), acquire substantially improvement over discrete counterpart. And the distributed representations learned by PCA achieve a similar performance to word/sent2vec model except for TEMPORAL relation, verifying the finding of [20] that word2vec is proved actually implicitly factorization of word-context matrix. F1 score decline for TEMPORAL relation may be due to the smallest proportion of TEMORAL instances in the whole dataset.

7   Conclusion and Future Work

In this paper, we have proposed a novel method for implicit discourse relation recognition using purely distributed representations without relying on any external linguistic resources, such as WordNet. We presented different approaches (e.g. word2vec, CNN and PCA) to learn distributed vectors for discrete features in different levels from words, sentences to syntactic features. Finally, we adopted the ensemble learning algorithm to integrate all of the distributed representations in various linguistic levels.

The experimental results show that dense low-dimensional representations have advantage over sparse discrete counterparts. Our final system obtain the best performance for CONTINGENCY, EXPANSION and TEMPORAL relations, while keeps competitive in COMPARISON relation compared to the state-of-the-art methods. In the future, we will devote ourselves to encode more linguistically features into distributed representation and explore more effective method to learn long-distance dependency of the syntax and semantics.

Acknowledgments. The research work has been partially funded by the Natural Science Foundation of China under Grant No. 61333018 and No. 61402478.

References

1. Pitler, E., Raghupathy, M., Mehta, H., Nenkova, A., Lee, A., Joshi, A.K.: Easily identifiable discourse relations. In: COLING (2008)
2. Pitler, E., Louis, A., Nenkova, A.: Automatic sense prediction for implicit discourse relations in text. In: Proceedings of the Joint Conference of the 47th Annual Meeting of the ACL and the 4th International Joint Conference on Natural Language Processing of the AFNLP, vol. 2, pp. 683–691. Association for Computational Linguistics (2009)
3. Lin, Z., Kan, M.-Y., Ng, H.T.: Recognizing implicit discourse relations in the penn discourse treebank. In: Proceedings of the 2009 Conference on Empirical Methods in Natural Language Processing, vol. 1, pp. 343–351. Association for Computational Linguistics (2009)
4. Zhou, Z.-M., Xu, Y., Niu, Z.-Y., Lan, M., Su, J., Tan, C.L.: Predicting discourse connectives for implicit discourse relation recognition. In: Proceedings of the 23rd International Conference on Computational Linguistics: Posters. Association for Computational Linguistics, pp. 1507–1514 (2010)
5. Louis, A., Joshi, A., Prasad, R., Nenkova, A.: Using entity features to classify implicit discourse relations. In: Proceedings of the 11th Annual Meeting of the Special Interest Group on Discourse and Dialogue, pp. 59–62. Association for Computational Linguistics (2010)
6. Biran, O., McKeown, K.: Aggregated word pair features for implicit discourse relation disambiguation. In: Proceedings of the Conference ACL, p. 69 (2013)
7. Park, J., Cardie, C.: Improving implicit discourse relation recognition through feature set optimization. In: Proceedings of the 13th Annual Meeting of the Special Interest Group on Discourse and Dialogue, pp. 108–112. Association for Computational Linguistics (2012)
8. Li, J.J., Nenkova, A.: Reducing sparsity improves the recognition of implicit discourse relations. In: 15th Annual Meeting of the Special Interest Group on Discourse and Dialogue, p. 199 (2014)
9. Rutherford, A.T., Xue, N.: Discovering implicit discourse relations through brown cluster pair representation and coreference patterns. EACL 2014, 645 (2014)
10. Marcu, D., Echihabi, A.: An unsupervised approach to recognizing discourse relations. In: Proceedings of the 40th Annual Meeting on Association for Computational Linguistics, pp. 368–375. Association for Computational Linguistics (2002)
11. Saito, M., Yamamoto, K., Sekine, S.: Using phrasal patterns to identify discourse relations. In: Proceedings of the Human Language Technology Conference of the NAACL, Companion Volume: Short Papers, pp. 133–136. Association for Computational Linguistics (2006)
12. Wang, W., Su, J., Tan, C.L.: Kernel based discourse relation recognition with temporal ordering information. In: Proceedings of the 48th Annual Meeting of the Association for Computational Linguistics, pp. 710–719. Association for Computational Linguistics (2010)
13. Xu, Y., Lan, M., Lu, Y., Niu, Z.Y., Tan, C.L.: Connective prediction using machine learning for implicit discourse relation classification. In: The 2012 International Joint Conference on Neural Networks (IJCNN), pp. 1–8. IEEE (2012)

14. Rutherford, A., Xue, N.: Improving the inference of implicit discourse relations via classifying explicit discourse connectives. In: Proceedings of the 2015 Conference of the North American Chapter of the Association for Computational Linguistics: Human Language Technologies. Denver, Colorado: Association for Computational Linguistics, pp. 799–808, May-June 2015. http://www.aclweb.org/anthology/N15-1081

15. Mikolov, T., Sutskever, I., Chen, K., Corrado, G.S., Dean, J.: Distributed representations of words and phrases and their compositionality. In: Advances in Neural Information Processing Systems, pp. 3111–3119 (2013)

16. Kim, Y.: Convolutional neural networks for sentence classification (2014). arXiv preprint arXiv:1408.5882

17. Le, Q.V., Mikolov, T.: Distributed representations of sentences and documents (2014) arXiv preprint. arXiv:1405.4053

18. Kalchbrenner, N., Grefenstette, E., Blunsom, P.: A convolutional neural network for modelling sentences (2014) arXiv preprint. arXiv:1404.2188

19. Li, J.J., Nenkova, A.: Addressing class imbalance for improved recognition of implicit discourse relations. In: 15th Annual Meeting of the Special Interest Group on Discourse and Dialogue, p. 142 (2014)

20. Levy, O., Goldberg, Y., Dagan, I.: Improving distributional similarity with lessons learned from word embeddings. Trans. Assoc. Comput. Linguist. 3, 211–225 (2015)

Information Retrieval and Question Answering

Answer Quality Assessment in CQA Based on Similar Support Sets

Zongsheng Xie[1]([⊠]), Yuanping Nie[1], Songchang Jin[1], Shudong Li[1,2], and Aiping Li[1]

[1] School of Computer Science, National University of Defense Technology, Changsha 410073, China
{xiezongsheng,yuanpingnie}@nudt.edu.cn, {jsc04,lishudong}@126.com
apli1974@gmail.com
[2] College of Mathematics and Information Science, Shandong Institute of Business and Technology, Yantai 264005, Shandong, China

Abstract. Community question answering portal (CQA) has become one of the most important sources for people to seek information from the Internet. With great quantity of online users ready to help, askers are willing to post questions in CQA and are likely to obtain desirable answers. However, the answer quality in CQA varies widely, from helpful answers to abusive spam. Answer quality assessment is therefore of great significance. Most of the existing approaches evaluate answer quality based on the relevance between questions and answers. Due to the lexical gap between questions and answers, these approaches are not quite satisfactory. In this paper, a novel approach is proposed to rank the candidate answers, which utilizes the support sets to reduce the impact of lexical gap between questions and answers. Firstly, similar questions are retrieved and support sets are produced with their high quality answers. Based on the assumption that high quality answers of similar questions would also have intrinsic similarity, the quality of candidate answers are then evaluated through their distance from the support sets in both aspects of content and structure. Unlike most of the existing approaches, previous knowledge from similar question-answer pairs are used to bridged the straight lexical and semantic gaps between questions and answers. Experiments are implemented on approximately 2.15 million real-world question-answer pairs from Yahoo! Answers to verify the effectiveness of our approach. The results on metrics of MAP@K and MRR show that the proposed approach can rank the candidate answers precisely.

1 Introduction

In the age of web 2.0, people can easily publish on the World Wide Web in all kinds of systems and modes, such as twitter, facebook, blogs, online discussion forums, wikis and question answering sites. In most of these platforms, the information is represented in natural language form rather than more structured formats, and most people involved are in equal positions to share experience and

© Springer International Publishing Switzerland 2015
M. Sun et al. (Eds.): CCL and NLP-NABD 2015, LNAI 9427, pp. 309–325, 2015.
DOI: 10.1007/978-3-319-25816-4_25

express opinions. Consequently, the amount of user-generated content (UGC) available on the Web is conspicuously increasing which constitutes an important source of information. However, it is the lack of editorial control that makes the information quality on the Web vary dramatically from professional to abusive.

Community question answering services, such as Yahoo! Answers (Y!A)[1], Baidu Knows[2] and Quora[3], are typical UGC portals that have become very popular in recent years. In CQA services, people post problems they encountered at work and in daily life and seek for help. Fellow users who know the answers or have similar experiences would reply their opinions, sometimes under the incentive mechanism of the site. Usually, the content in the site is organized as questions and lists of answers associated with metadata such as user votes and askersawards to the best answers. Attracted a great number of users, these web sites have become hot platforms for people to seek help, share knowledge, and learn from each other. What is more, with the accumulation of question-answer pairs over time, this data in CQA archives becomes valuable repositories of information and knowledge.

Although CQA service has brought significant benefits for us to solve daily problems and seek information, there are still some drawbacks in most of the CQA systems. As a type of UGC portal, one of the most important problems is the quality of the answers. An example of question with answers of various quality is given below:

- **question:** What are the best techniques to deal with stress?
- **answers 1:** When dealing with stressful situations, consider the four points below.
    1. Nothing and no one can make you feel anything. How you feel and the way you deal with a situation is a choice. Im reminded of a counselor who would often state no one can drive your car unless you give them the keys. You cannot control others actions, but you can be responsible for your reactions.
    2. Exchange attitude for gratitude. Our attitude has a profound effect on how we deal with situations. Negative attitudes affect our physical, spiritual, and mental well being.
    3. Relax, relax, relax. Amidst the hustle and bustle of everyday life, sometimes we forget to take care of ourselves. If we do not help ourselves, how can we effectively help others? Relaxation rejuvenates the body, mind, and spirit and leaves us better equipped to handle stressful situations when they come.
    4. Look at the big picture. Evaluate your stressful situation from a big picture point of view. Ask yourself how important is this? and will this matter in the long run? If the answer is no, its likely not worth your time and energy. OR you can get online consultation at helpingdoc.com

---

[1] http://answers.yahoo.com.

[2] http://zhidao.baidu.com.

[3] http://www.quora.com.

- **answers 2:** When i am so stressed out, i usually do exercise, go for walks and meditate and listen to music. Thats how i manage stress!
- **answers 3:** dont refuse help from friends

As can be seen from the above, the quality of the answers range from very high to low, or even abusive. As previously noted [1], the quality of answers in CQA portals is good on average, but the quality of specific answers varies significantly. According to the author's study on the answers of a set of questions in Yahoo! Answers, the fraction of correct answers to specific questions varied from 17 % to 45 %, while the fraction of questions with at least one good answer was much higher, varying from 65 % to 90 %. This study suggests that most of the questions are expected to obtain a good answer, but are also likely to get low quality ones. Methods to find high quality answers therefore can have a significant impact on the users satisfaction of the system. Besides, the efficiency of solving new problems is often not quite commendable in CQA. As shown in the study [2], more than 80 % new questions cannot be solved within 48 hours. Recommending similar questions with satisfactory answers would be an advisable solution to remedy the situation. In this case, the answer quality assessment is also very meaningful. Though CQA sites have provided many mechanisms to find high quality answers, such as thumb up and thumb down voted by viewers and the best answer award voted by askers, this shortcoming still exists since such feedback requires some time to accumulate, and often remains sparse for obscure or unpopular topics [3].

It is common to analyze answer quality in CQA through superficial features, such as user voting, user or editor recommendations, and the metadata of users who provide the answers. There are several common problems with the approaches utilizing these popularity and social interaction measures to predict the answer quality. Firstly, this information is not always available in real world applications. For instance, there is no voting or recommendation available for new posted answers, and no metadata available for new users or visitors without login. Secondly, there is no necessarily causal relationship between user metadata and answers the he posts, since an expert user associated with lots of good answer voting and recommendations may not be good at answering all questions, while many good answers are provided by common users whose metadata may not be indicative of the quality of their answers. It is also a familiar way to measure answer quality by calculating textual features, such as the length of answers, overlapped words between questions and their answers, length ratio between questions and answers [4,5]. However, the lexical gap between questions and answers is usually very large, which makes these approaches powerless.

In this paper we propose two hypotheses: the the lexical gap between similar questions and that between their answers are much smaller than the gap between questions and their answers; high quality answers of similar questions should also share some common intrinsic features. Based on these two hypotheses we propose a novel approach to evaluate the answer quality. Unlike most of the existing approaches, we do not calculate relevance between questions and answers directly, instead we use previous knowledge from similar question-answer pairs to bridge the lexical gap. Utilizing the support sets, the impact of the straight lexical gap between questions and answers is reduced effectively. The results of experiments on approximately 2.15 million real-world question-answer pairs from Yahoo! Answers suggest that our hypotheses are meaningful indeed, and our approach can rank the candidate answers precisely.

2   Related Work

Providing popular platforms for people to seek solutions to problems and share opinions, CQA portals have drawn a great number of users in the last decade. A great deal of attentions from researchers are also attracted in related fields, such as investigating information seeking behaviours [6], user motivations [7], expert recommendation [8,9], question retrieval [3,8] and answer quality assessment [4,10,11]. In this section, we will discuss the latter two, which are relevant to our study.

2.1   Question Retrieval

Content from community-built question-answer sites can be retrieved by searching for similar question already answered, and the task of question retrieval is to find relevant question-answer pairs for new questions posed by users in the QA archive [12]. The issue of question retrieval was first raised in the field of frequently asked questions (FAQs). Burke et al. [13] produced a FAQ finder which combined statistical similarities and semantic similarities between questions to rank FAQs. With the flourishing of CQA, more attention is paid to question searching in this field recently. The major challenge for question retrieval in CQA is the word mismatch between new question and the question-answer pairs in the archive, which is similar to most information retrieval tasks. To solve this problem, many different approaches have been proposed. Based on the assumption that the relationship between words can be modeled through word-to-word translation probabilities, many researchers adopted translation-based approaches [14] to solve the word mismatch problem. Jeon et al. [12] proposed a word-based translation model to fix the lexical gap problem. Xue et al. [15] combined the query likelihood language model with the classic IBM translation model 1. Cai et al. [16] assembled the semantic similarity based latent topics with the translation-based language model. Besides, some other methods improved the traditional language models by leveraging metadata in CQA. The language model by Cao et al. [17,18] estimated new smoothing item with leaf category smoothing. Zhang et al. [8] proposed a topic-based approach to match questions on both term level and topic level.

Unlike the normal question retrieval, we are not aiming at finding relevant question-answer pairs for new questions to improve user experience, but finding questions similar in content and in structure which is a preparation for our model. We simply find similar questions through the overlap of words with different weights.

2.2   Answer Quality Evaluating

A range of approaches have emerged for evaluating answer quality in CQA, which can mainly be divided into two categories. The first kind of method is based on content analysis. These methods mainly assess the answer quality through the relevance between answers and questions. Toba et al. [4] classified questions into several types, and implemented a type-based quality classifier to predict answer quality of different types of questions with different groups of content features. Surdeanu et al. [19,20] built a answer ranking engine for non-factoid questions combining several strategies into a single model, such as question-to-answer transformations, frequency and density of content. They also expanded them with large amounts of available Web data. The second kind of methods mainly utilized user information to estimate the quality of the answers they posted. There are generally two kinds of user information that are usually used: the user log information and the linked graphs of users. User log analysis approaches use past performance of users to measure the popular and expert degree of the user [21,22], such as the number of best answers they posted, user voting and recommendations. These methods supposed that the reputed users are more likely to give high quality answers. Methods analyzing linked graphs of users, which consist of users as vertices and the interactions of ask-answer as edges, usually employ link-based ranking algorithms such as HITs [23] and PageRank [24]. Exploiting the interactions between users, these methods assign active users who have posted more high quality answers with higher probabilities of giving good answers, such as ExpertiseRank by Zhang et al. [25] and CQARank by Yang et al. [11].

Despite the success of these approaches in many situations, there are some shortages in them. For example, the lexical gaps in some question-answer pairs may be very large where the content analysis approaches will be incapable to evaluate their relevance precisely, and the approaches utilizing user information tend to recommend expert users and may fail when facing new users or visitors without login whose user information is not available. In our approach, different from the above approaches, the impact of large lexical gap between questions and answers is reduced by utilizing previous knowledge from the similar question-answer pairs, and we also don't need to analyze user profiles. The method most close to ours is [26]. However, they used the vector of textual and non-textural features to represent question-answer pairs, and mainly trained a bayesian logistic regression to predict answer quality, which are different from our method.

3   The Approach

3.1   Process Overview

Our approach is based on two hypotheses:

The lexical gap between similar questions and that between their answers are much smaller than that between questions and answers.

Most of state-of-the-art methods evaluate the answer quality in CQA through the relevance between questions an answers. Unfortunately, through a large number of observations we found that, in most instances the lexical and semantic distances between questions and their answers were very considerable. On the other hand, given a new question, we could find some similar questions in the CQA archive having the gap between them much smaller, with their answers quite close to the candidate answers too. There are two samples of questions and corresponding answers extracted from Yahoo! Answers:

- **question 1:**
  I'm 13 how can I keep fit ?
- **answers 1:**
    - Any and all exercise helps, ideally a mix of resistance and cardiovascular exercise. Jogging is excellent.
    - Walking/jogging Weight lifting Kettle bell (one kettle bell can allow for many exercises). My opinion is any weight lifting exercise is good for a young person. It builds strength, balance, and bone strength. It also forms a very nice body for when you get to the point to show it off–believe me.
    - exercises like pull ups or sit ups work for U and push ups
    - Swimming, Walking and riding a bike.

- **question 2:**
  How can I keep fit at a young age?
- **answers 2:**
    - Getting back into running can be very good for you physically and emotionally.
    - Running in place- self explanatory.
    - just regular basic cardio exercises like going for a run or cycling can keep you in pretty good shape

As we can see in that two samples, few meaningful words are shared by the questions and their answers. It is obviously inadvisable to evaluate the quality of answers through the relevance between question and answer in this case. However, if we take question 2 as the similar question to question 1, we could find that the lexical gap between them is much smaller, while the answers of them also share lots of common features in semantics and structure. Based on this discovery, we suppose that it would be more effective to evaluate answer quality utilizing previous knowledge from similar questions and their answers than through the relevance between questions and answers directly.

Similar questions will have similar answers, and high quality answers of similar questions will also share some common traits. As demonstrated by previous studies [27,28], there are some common intrinsic features that are shared by high quality answers. Intuitively, questions asking about similar content should have answers similar in content, and questions similar in structure should have answers similar in structure, too. For example, high quality answers of factid questions asking for same thing should also talk about same object,

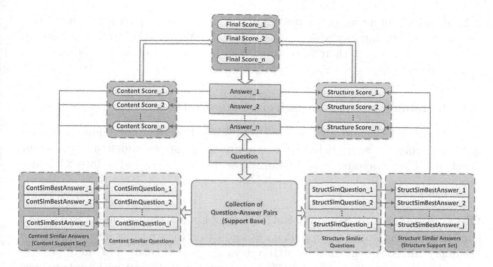

Fig. 1. Sketch of the our approach: (a) Given a question as a query, get content similar questions and structure similar questions from the support base (yellow blocks in the figure); (b) Get the corresponding best answers as the CSS and SSS, and count the content score and structure score of every candidate answers through the similarity with CSS and SSS (green blocks and blue blocks); (c) Integrate the content score and structure score into the final score (orange block) ; (d) Rank the candidate answers according to the final score (Color figure online).

and good answers of why-type questions may share same syntax of adverbial clause of cause. As the questions above, answers of them are usually talking about going on a diet or doing some exercise, and high quality ones should tell how to do that in detail.

Base on these two hypotheses, we propose a novel model to rank the candidate answers. The sketch of our model is shown in Fig. 1. The processes of our approach are mainly as follow:

In the offline stage, we build a support base which is made up of a large number of question-high quality answer pairs. The best answers are used as the high quality answers in our method, because they are voted by askers which means that they are satisfactory, therefore supposed to be of high quality. The support base is built on the search platform of Solr[4], which is powerful in indexing and searching. The question-best answer pairs of the support base are stored and indexed, and can be queried through the search engine of Solr.

In the online stage, a new question is treated as a query, and two sets of similar questions and corresponding best answers (similar in content and similar in structure, which will be described in detail in Sect. 3.2) will be returned from support base. These two parts of best answers will be used as our content support set (referred to as CSS) and structure support set (referred to as SSS) in our model. For every candidate answer of the question we are considering, we score

---

[4] http://lucene.apache.org/solr.

it base on its content and structure similarity with the support sets. Then these two scores will be integrated into a final score. Finally, All the candidate answers will be ranked through their final scores, and the top-ranked answer is supposed to be the best one.

3.2   Obtaining Support Sets from Support Base

To obtain the CSS and SSS, we will search for two different kinds of similar questions from the support base: content similar questions and structure similar questions. Their corresponding best answers are then extracted to form CSS and SSS.

Obtaining Content Support Set. The key issue when searching for content similar questions from the support base is how to measure the relevance between the query and the documents. TF-IDF relevancy model is chosen in our approach, which combines boolean model (BM) of information retrieval with vector space model (VSM) of information retrieval. The formula of TF-IDF relevance scoring model is:

$$Score_{tf/idf}(q, d) = coord(q, d) * \sum_{t \in q} (tf(t \in d) * idf(t)^2 * boost(t)) \qquad (1)$$

where q is the query; d is the the document to be scored; t is the terms appear in the query; $coord(q, d)$ is a score factor based on how many the query terms are found in the specified document. $tf(t \in d)$ is the frequency of terms; $idf(t)$ stands for inverse document frequency; $boost(t)$ is a search time boost of term t in the query q, which is specified by user in the query text. The formula of $idf(t)$ in our model is:

$$idf(t) = 1 + \log \frac{numDocs}{docFreq + 1} \qquad (2)$$

where $docFreq$ means the number of documents containing the term t, and $numDocs$ is the number of documents to be scored.

The points of the TF-IDF relevance model is that:

– The more terms a document contains, the higher the score;
– The more times a term appears in a document, the higher the score;
– Rarer terms, which is supposed to be more discriminating, give higher contribution to the score;
– The higher weight a term is specified, the higher it contribute to the score.

Before querying, the sentence of the question will be parsed with the Stanford POS Tagger [29], which generates a syntactic parse tree of the sentence. Then the real words, i.e. nouns and adjectives in our model, are extracted and specified with a higher weight in the query text, which makes the content contribute higher in the query. Finally, we search the support base with the query text, and get a set of questions with similar content and a set of corresponding best answers, i.e. the CSS.

Obtaining Structure Support Set. Similar to the way the CSS is obtained, the SSS is extracted from the support base with the same score model and the same syntactic parse tool. The difference is that, after the syntactic parse tree is generated, the real words are removed from the query with the skeleton frame of the question left. An example of the skeleton frame extracted from the question is as below:

- **Question:** What is more important, love or money, why?
- **Tagged sentence:** What_WP is_VBZ more_RBR important_JJ ,_, love_NN or_CC money_NN ,_, why_WRB ?_.
- **Skeleton frame:** What is more , or, why?

With the query of skeleton frame, we will get a set of questions similar in structure, and their responding best answers, i.e. the SSS.

3.3 Scoring the Candidate Answers

In this part, we will score the candidate answers leveraging the similarity between them and the support sets. Corresponding to the two parts of support sets, the candidate answers will also be scored in two different angles.

Scoring in Content. Firstly, the candidate answers will be scored in the aspect of content based on the similarity between them and the CSS. We tried several different scoring methods: Cosine similarity, DRF similarity, TF-IDF model, and BM25 model, and the last one which performed the best in our experiment was finally chosen. The main idea of the BM25 model is to analyze the similarity of every term in the query, and count their weighted sum:

$$Score_{bm}(q, d) = \sum_i^n W_i * R(t_i, d) \tag{3}$$

where q is the query and t_i is a term in the query; W_i is the weight of t_i. The IDF of the term is used as weight in our model; d is the document; $R(t_i, d)$ is the similarity between the term t_i and the document d:

$$R(t_i, d) = \frac{f_i * (k + 1)}{f_i + k * (1 - b + b * \frac{dl}{avgdl})} \tag{4}$$

where k and b are the regulative factors, which are generally specified according to experience and is set as $k = 2$ and $b = 0.75$ in our model; f_i is the frequency of t_i in d; dl is the length of d, and $avgdl$ is the average length of all documents. Consequently, the formula of score in the BM25 model is:

$$Score_{bm}(q, d) = \sum_i^n IDF(t_i) * \frac{f_i * (k + 1)}{f_i + k * (1 - b + b * \frac{dl}{avgdl})} \tag{5}$$

Notice that, to every candidate answer A_i and similar best answer d_i^j pair, there will be a score calculated to measure the similarity between them. Unlike the normal query systems, we do not rank the documents according to the score, but calculate the average score of every candidate answer, which is supposed to be the similarity of the candidate answer A_i and its whole CSS:

$$Score_{css}(A_i) = \frac{1}{|CSS_i|} \sum_{d_i^j \in CSS_i} Score_{bm}(A_i, d_i^j) \qquad (6)$$

where CSS_i is the CSS corresponding the candidate answer A_i; $|CSS_i|$ is the size of the CSS_i.

Scoring in Structure. In the process of scoring in structure, we follow the approach used in many previous studies [4,19,27] that to quantify the properties of the answers by extracting and calculating representative features from the question-answer pairs. The features used in our method can be generally divided into two categories:

– **Numeric features:** It is supposed that the answers of questions similar in structure will share some common numeric features, such as the number of sentences, the number of nouns, verbs and adjectives and so on.
– **Ratio features:** As the answers of similar questions may have different length, the ratio features are taken into consideration, such as the ratio of the length of answer and question, and the ratio of nouns, verbs, adjectives in the answer.

All the features and their explanations are listed in Table 1.

These features are extracted from the best answers in the SSS, and their average value is counted as the representative. On the other hand, the features from the candidate answers are also extracted, and their distance with the representative one are calculated. Notice that, a smaller distance means the feature

Table 1. Features used to score in structure

Features	Explanation
aLength	Length of answer
aNumNoun	Number of nouns in answer
aNumVerb	Number of verbs in answer
aNumAdj	Number of adjectives in answer
aNumSent	Number of sentences in answer
aRatioNoun	Ratio of nouns in answer
aRatioVerb	Ratio of verbs in answer
aRatioAdj	Ratio of adjectives in answer
qaRatioSent	Ratio of sentences in question and answer
qaRatioLen	Ratio of question length and answer length

of the candidate answer is more close with the representative. Then the candidate answers are ranked base on the distance where the smaller the distance, the closer it is to the top. A matrix of the ranks is generated as the result:

$$\begin{bmatrix} R11 & R12 & ... & R1m \\ R21 & R22 & ... & R2m \\ ... & ... & ... & ... \\ Rn1 & Rn2 & ... & Rnm \end{bmatrix} \tag{7}$$

where the element of Rif means the rank of candidate answer i on the feature f. In order to integrate all the features and get rid of the difference between dimensions, the sum of the inversion rank is used as the integrated score:

$$Score_{sss}(A_i) = \sum_{f=1}^{m} \frac{1}{Rif} \tag{8}$$

where m is the number of features we extracted.

Getting Final Score. After getting both the scores in content and in structure, we combine them to get the final score with the same method mention in the above section:

$$Score_{final}(A_i) = \frac{1}{Rank(CSS)} + \frac{1}{Rank(SSS)} \tag{9}$$

where $Rank(CSS)$ is the rank based on the content score, and $Rank(SSS)$ based on the structure score.

Finally, the candidate answers are ranked depending on this final score, and it is supposed that the closer a answer is to the top, the higher its quality is.

4   Experiment

4.1   Dataset

In the WebScope Program of Yahoo! Research[5], there are several datasets available to researchers. The dataset of Yahoo! Answers Comprehensive Question and Answers is one of them, which is collected from the website of Yahoo! Answers, and covers all categories in Yahoo! Answers. Our dataset used in this experiment is extracted from the above corpus, containing full text of 2,258,383 questions and their answers, including the best answers voted by the askers to each question.

From our dataset, we randomly extracted 1,787,975 questions and their best answers to build the support base. We stored them into database, and created full text indexes of their questions, with the search platform of Solr. When creating the indexes and searching in the support base, we implemented the TF-IDF similarity model described in Sect. 3.2 to rank the correlation of the questions. The other 497,408 questions left with their all candidate answers were used as the testing set. Statistics about our dataset are synthesized in Table 2

---

[5] http://webscope.sandbox.yahoo.com.

Table 2. Statistics about dataset

Dataset	Number of questions	Number of answers	Average number of answers
Support base	1,787,975	1,787,975(best answers)	-
Testing set	497,408	2,148,802	4.32

4.2   Evaluation Metrics

In our experiment, best answer tagged by the askers in Yahoo! Answers was used as the ground truth, i.e. if our approach found the best answer from all the answers, it was supposed to be correct, otherwise incorrect. In order to measure the performance of our approach, two metrics were used for the evaluation: Mean Average Precision at K (MAP@K) and Mean Reciprocal Rank (MRR). These metrics are commonly used to measure the accuracy of ranked retrieval results.

For a given query, the metrics of Average Precision at K is the mean fraction of relevant answers ranked in the top K results:

$$AP@K = \sum_{i=1}^{K} P(i)/min(m, K) \tag{10}$$

where P(i) means the precision at cut-off i in the item list, m is the number of relevant results returned by the rank system. The MAP@K is the mean value of the average precision:

$$MAP@K = \frac{1}{n} \sum_{i=1}^{n} AP_i@K \tag{11}$$

where n is the number of the questions in our testing set.

The Mean Reciprocal Rank (MRR) metric take the exact rank of a correct answer into account and the score is counted as the mean of the reciprocal rank:

$$MRR = \frac{1}{|Q|} \sum_{q \in Q} \frac{1}{r_q} \tag{12}$$

where Q is the set of the testing queries; r_q is the rank of correct answer for the query q.

As mentioned in the Sect. 2.2, most of state-of-the-art approaches assess the answer quality though the relevance between questions and answers. We therefore compared our model with methods calculating these features. Two baselines were used as comparisons: the method based on Cosine Distance Metric (COS), and the method based on Linear Regression Prediction(LR). The method of COS measured the answer quality though the cosine distance between questions and answers. The approach of LR extracted textual features from questions and answers, and used the method of linear regression to predict the quality of answers. As is commonly used in many state-of-the-art approaches [4,19], we extracted 15 textual features to represent a question-answer pair. In addition to

Table 3. Portion of the textual features used in LR

Features	Explanation
qaTF	Term frequency of question answer pair
comStrLen	Length of common string
resemblance	Proportion of the set of overlapping n-grams, and the set of all n-grams for the question and its answer
containment	Proportion of n-grams from the answer that also appear in the question
cosDist	Cosine distance between a question and its answer

the 10 features listed in Table 1, the other 5 are shown in Table 3. The linear regression model was trained and tested with our dataset in the proportion of approximately 70 % : 30 % of training : testing.

4.3 Performance

Overall Results. The performance of our model and the baselines on the MAP@K metric when K is set as 1, 5 and 10 are illustrated in Fig. 2, while Table 4 shows the performance on the metrics of MRR. As is illustrated in the figure and the table, the method of LR worked better than COS, and our method significantly outperforms the baselines on the metric of MAP@K in all cases when K is 1, 5 and 10, as well as on the metric of MRR. The performance of COS which is the worst in the result, tells that the lexical gap between questions and answers is usually very large, and it's not advisable to assess the answer quality through the word overlap between questions and answers directly. The better performance of LR suggests that high quality answers do share some common traits. The outperformance of our method on both MAP@K and MRR proves that our hypotheses are significative indeed, and our approach can rank the candidate answers more precisely.

Table 4. MRR for baselines and our model

	COS	LR	Our Method
MRR	57.2 %	66.4 %	72.8 %

Contribution of CSS and SSS. In order to investigate the effectiveness of CSS and SSS, we conducted experiments assembling scores of CSS and SSS with different proportion. As mentioned in Sect. 3.3, we used reciprocal rank of CSS and SSS to count overall score:

$$Score_{final}(A_i) = \frac{\lambda}{Rank(CSS)} + \frac{1 - \lambda}{Rank(SSS)} \tag{13}$$

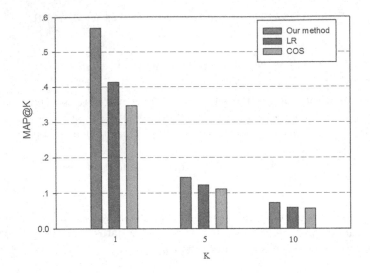

Fig. 2. MAP@K when K = 1, 5, 10

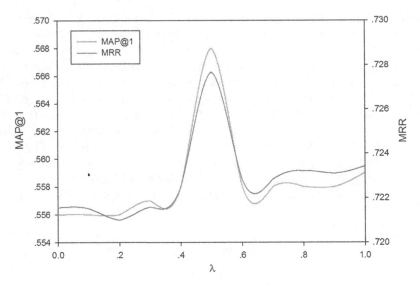

Fig. 3. MAP@1 and MRR with different λ

where λ is the parameter to control proportion. Notice that when $\lambda = 0$, only the the score of SSS is valid, and when $\lambda = 1$ CSS only. When λ ranges from 0 to 1, the results are shown in Fig. 3, which illustrates that we get the best result at both the metrics of MAP@1 and MRR when $\lambda = 0.5$.

5   Conclusion

In this paper, we proposed a novel approach to evaluate the answer quality in CQA. We assumed that: the lexical gap between similar questions and that between their answers is much smaller than that between questions and answers; and high quality answers of similar questions will also share some common traits. We built a support base which was made up of a large number of question-high quality answer pairs in the offline stage. In the online stage we obtained content support set and structure support set for every candidate answer and measured their quality utilizing the similarity between them and the high quality answers in the support sets. Unlike most of state-of-the-art methods, we did not analyze the relevance between questions and answers directly, but used previous knowledge from the similar question-answer pairs to bridge the lexical gap. The experiment on dataset from real-world question-answer pairs from Yahoo! Answers showed that, our model ranked the candidate answers more precisely on both metrics of MAP@K and MRR. The comparison with the baselines suggested that taking previous knowledge into account is advisable when assessing the quality of noisy user-generated content in CQA.

This work can be extended in several directions. First, rather than treated equally, the similar answers in the support sets could be of different weights when counting the the candidate answer scores, according to the similarity between their corresponding questions and the original question. In addition, the value of λ, which regulates the score weights of two different support sets, could be dynamically adjusted based on the reliability of different support sets. Another interesting and meaningful problem is the methods to measure the similarity between questions and that between answers, both in content and structure. It could be beneficial to develop some more accurate method in this domain.

Acknowledgement. The work described in this paper was supported by National Natural Science Foundation of China (No. 61202362), National Key Basic Research Program of China (NO. 2013CB329606) and Project funded by China Postdoctoral Science Foundation (NO. 2013M542560).

References

1. Su, Q., Pavlov, D., Chow, J.-H., Baker, W.C.: Internet-scale collection of human-reviewed data. In: Proceedings of the 16th International Conference on World Wide Web, pp. 231–240. ACM (2007)
2. Li, B., King, I.: Routing questions to appropriate answerers in community question answering services. In: Proceedings of the 19th ACM International Conference on Information and Knowledge Management, pp. 1585–1588. ACM (2010)
3. Zhou, G., Liu, K., Zhao, J.: Joint relevance and answer quality learning for question routing in community qa. In: Proceedings of the 21st ACM International Conference on Information and Knowledge Management, pp. 1492–1496. ACM (2012)
4. Toba, H., Ming, Z.-Y., Adriani, M., Chua, T.-S.: Discovering high quality answers in community question answering archives using a hierarchy of classifiers. Inf. Sci. **261**, 101–115 (2014)

5. Bian, J., Liu, Y., Agichtein, E., Zha, H.: Finding the right facts in the crowd: factoid question answering over social media. In: Proceedings of the 17th International Conference on World Wide Web, pp. 467–476. ACM (2008)

6. Kim, S., Oh, J.S., Oh, S.: Best answer selection criteria in a social qa site from the user oriented relevance perspective. Proc. Am. Soc. Inf. Sci. Technol. **44**(1), 1–15 (2007)

7. Shah, C., Oh, J.S., Oh, S.: Exploring characteristics and effects of user participation in online social Q&A sites. First Monday **13**(9), 18 (2008)

8. Zhang, K., Wu, W., Wu, H., Li, Z., Zhou, M.: Question retrieval with high quality answers in community question answering. In: Proceedings of the 23rd ACM International Conference on Conference on Information and Knowledge Management, pp. 371–380. ACM (2014)

9. Bouguessa, M., Dumoulin, B., Wang, S.: Identifying authoritative actors in question-answering forums: the case of Yahoo! answers. In: Proceedings of the 14th ACM SIGKDD International Conference on Knowledge Discovery and Data Mining, pp. 866–874. ACM (2008)

10. Zhou, Z.M., Lan, M., Niu, Z.Y., Lu, Y.: Exploiting user profile information for answer ranking in cqa. In: Proceedings of the 21st International Conference Companion on World Wide Web, pp. 767–774. ACM (2012)

11. Yang, L., Qiu, M., Gottipati, S., Zhu, F., Jiang, J., Sun, H., Chen, Z.: Cqarank: jointly model topics and expertise in community question answering. In: Research Collection School of Information Systems (2013)

12. Jeon, J., Croft, W.B., Lee, J.H.: Finding similar questions in large question and answer archives. In: Proceedings of the 14th ACM International Conference on Information and Knowledge Management, pp. 84–90. ACM (2005)

13. Burke, R.D., Hammond, K.J., Kulyukin, V., Lytinen, S.L., Tomuro, N., Schoenberg, S.: Articles question answering from frequently asked question files experiences with the FAQ finder system. AI Mag. **18**(2), 57–66 (1997)

14. Berger, A., Caruana, R., Cohn, D., Freitag, D., Mittal, V.: Bridging the lexical chasm: statistical approaches to answer-finding. In: Proceedings of the 23rd Annual International ACM SIGIR Conference on Research and Development in Information Retrieval, pp. 192–199. ACM (2000)

15. Xue, X., Jeon, J., Croft, W.B.: Retrieval models for question and answer archives. In: Proceedings of the 31st Annual International ACM SIGIR Conference on Research and Development in Information Retrieval, pp. 475–482. ACM (2008)

16. Cai, L., Zhou, G., Liu, K., Zhao, J.: Learning the latent topics for question retrieval in community QA. IJCNLP **11**, 273–281 (2011)

17. Cao, X., Cong, G., Cui, B., Jensen, C.S., Zhang, C.: The use of categorization information in language models for question retrieval. In: Association for Computing Machinery (2009)

18. Cao, X., Cong, G., Cui, B., Jensen, C.S.: A generalized framework of exploring category information for question retrieval in community question answer archives. In: WWW (2010)

19. Surdeanu, M., Ciaramita, M., Zaragoza, H.: Learning to rank answers on large online QA collections. In: Proceedings of the 46th Annual Meeting for the Association for Computational Linguistics: Human Language Technologies, ACL-2008: HLT, pp. 719–727 (2008)

20. Surdeanu, M., Ciaramita, M., Inc, G., Zaragoza, H.: Learning to rank answers to non-factoid questions from web collections. Comput. Linguist. **37**(2), 351–383 (2011)

21. Shah, C., Pomerantz, J.: Evaluating and predicting answer quality in community QA. In: Proceedings of International Conference on Research & Development in Information Retrieval SIGIR, pp. 411–418 (2010)
22. Lou, J., Fang, Y., Lim, K.H., Peng, J.Z.: Contributing high quantity and quality knowledge to online Q&A communities. J. Am. Soc. Inf. Sci. Technol. **64**(2), 356–371 (2013)
23. Kleinberg, J.M.: Authoritative sources in a hyperlinked environment. J. ACM **46**(5), 604–632 (1999)
24. Page, L., Brin, S., Motwani, R., Winograd, T.: The pagerank citation ranking: bringing order to the web. Stanford Infolab (1999)
25. Zhang, J., Ackerman, M.S., Adamic, L.: Expertise networks in online communities: structure and algorithms. In: Proceedings of the 16th International Conference on World Wide Web, pp. 221–230. ACM (2007)
26. Wang, X.J., Tu, X., Feng, D., et al.: Ranking community answers by modeling question-answer relationships via analogical reasoning. In: SIGIR Proceedings of International ACM SIGIR Conference on Research & Development in (2009)
27. Shah, C., Pomerantz, J.: Evaluating and predicting answer quality in community QA. In: Proceedings of the 33rd International ACM SIGIR Conference on Research and Development in Information Retrieval, pp. 411–418. ACM (2010)
28. Ishikawa, D., Kando, N., Sakai, T.: What makes a good answer in community question answering? an analysis of assessors criteria. In: Proceedings of the 4th International Workshop on Evaluating Information Access (EVIA), Tokyo, Japan. Citeseer (2011)
29. Toutanova, K., Manning, C.D.: Enriching the knowledge sources used in a maximum entropy part-of-speech tagger. In: Proceedings of the 2000 Joint SIGDAT Conference on Empirical Methods in Natural Language Processing and Very Large Corpora: Held in Conjunction with the 38th Annual Meeting of the Association for Computational Linguistics, vol. 13, pp. 63–70. Association for Computational Linguistics (2000)

Learning to Rank Answers for Definitional Question Answering

Shiyu Wu[1], Xipeng Qiu[1(✉)], Xuanjing Huang[1], and Junkuo Cao[2]

[1] Shanghai Key Laboratory of Intelligent Information Processing School of Computer Science, Fudan University, Shanghai, China
{sywu13,xpqiu,xjhuang}@fudan.edu.cn
[2] Department of Computer Science, Hainan Normal University, Haikou, China
jkcao@qq.com

Abstract. In definitional question answering (QA), it is essential to rank the candidate answers. In this paper, we propose an online learning algorithm, which dynamically construct the supervisor to reduce the adverse effects of the large number of bad answers and noisy data. We compare our method with two state-of-the-art definitional QA systems and two ranking algorithms, and the experimental results show our method outperforms the others.

1 Introduction

Definitional question answering (QA), as an important form of complex QA, has attracted more and more attention recently. Definitional QA looks for extended answers that are composed of pieces of relevant information spread over many documents in a corpus, such as a biography of a person (e.g. "Who is George Bush?"), and the definition of a generic term (e.g. "What is naproxen?") [9].

The development of definitional QA has been boosted by the Text Retrieval Conference (TREC). For a definitional question such as "Who is X" or "What is X", we call "X" **target**. Most definitional QA systems have the following pipeline structure:

1. Use target as query to retrieve the related sentences;
2. Rank the returned candidate sentences;
3. Remove redundant sentences and return top k sentences as answers.

In definitional QA, most works focus on the second step, such as pattern based methods [3,5,10] and centroid vector based methods [1,7]. Xu et al. [10] ranked candidate sentences by RankSVM [6]. Han et al. [4] ranked the candidate sentences from the two points of view: topic and definition.

However, most of these rank methods have two weaknesses: firstly, it is difficult to sample bad answers because the number of bad answers is usually far larger than good answers; secondly, it is hard to judge whether an answer is good or not in an objective way, so the training data is often noisy.

In this paper, we propose an online learning algorithm, which dynamically construct the supervisor on each iteration and assure the quality of the top k

© Springer International Publishing Switzerland 2015
M. Sun et al. (Eds.): CCL and NLP-NABD 2015, LNAI 9427, pp. 326–332, 2015.
DOI: 10.1007/978-3-319-25816-4_26

returned answers, instead of optimizing rank of the whole candidate list. Our learning algorithm is based on Passive-Aggressive algorithm [2], which passively accepts a solution whose loss is zero, while it aggressively forces the new prototype vector to stay as close as possible to the one previously learned.

The rest of the paper is organized as following. We present our algorithm to rank the candidate sentences in Sect. 2 and describe the features in Sect. 3. Then we give our experiments in Sect. 4. Section 5 concludes the paper.

2   Rank Answers with Variant Passive-Aggressive Algorithm

In this section, we propose an online learning algorithm to rank the answers. Given a target x and the set of its associated candidate answers C, we find a subset of $\hat{Y} \subset C$ with size k as the returned answers by

$$\hat{Y} = \arg \max_{Y \subset C} \mathbf{w}^T \Phi(x, Y), \tag{1}$$

where $\Phi(x, Y)$ is a feature vector.

We define the distance between two sets A and B by inverse Jaccard Similarity,

$$\Delta(A, B) = |A \cup B| / |A \cap B|. \tag{2}$$

Assuming that the subset $Y^* \subset C$ concludes all good answers. We wish to learn $\mathbf{w}$ so that $\Delta(\hat{Y}, Y^*)$ is as small as possible.

We use Passive Aggressive (PA) algorithm [2] to find the new weight vector w_{t+1} to be the solution to the following constrained optimization problem in round t.

$$\mathbf{w}_{t+1} = \arg \min_{\mathbf{w}} \frac{1}{2} ||\mathbf{w} - \mathbf{w}_t||^2 + \mathcal{C}\xi \tag{3}$$

$$\text{s.t. } \ell(\mathbf{w}; x_t) <= \xi \text{ and } \xi >= 0. \tag{4}$$

where $\ell(\mathbf{w}; x_t)$ is the hinge-loss function, ξ is a slack variable, and $\mathcal{C}$ is a positive parameter which controls the influence of the slack term on the objective function.

Different from standard PA algorithm, we define the loss as,

$$\ell(\mathbf{w}; x) = \begin{cases} 0, & \gamma(\mathbf{w}; x) > \Delta(Y^*, \hat{Y}) \\ \Delta(Y^*, \hat{Y}) - \gamma(\mathbf{w}; x), & \text{otherwise} \end{cases} \tag{5}$$

where

$$\gamma(\mathbf{w}; x) = \mathbf{w}^T \Phi(x, Y^*) - \mathbf{w}^T \Phi(x, \hat{Y}), \tag{6}$$

We abbreviate $\ell(\mathbf{w}; x)$ to ℓ. If $\ell = 0$ then $\mathbf{w}_t$ itself satisfies the constraint in Eq. (3) and is clearly the optimal solution. We therefore concentrate on the case where $\ell > 0$.

Since it is hard to judge whether an answer is good or not in an objective way, we do not use directly the manual answer set Y^* in our learning process. We dynamically construct the supervisor on each iteration.

We define $\theta = \min\{|\hat{Y} - Y^*|, |(C - \hat{Y}) \cap Y^*|\}$ is the minimal number of bad answers in top-k and good answers out of top-k. In each iteration, we build Y^{**} by inserting θ good answers, denoted as P, from out of top-k into top-k, and excluding the same number of bad answers, denoted as Q.

$$Y^{**} = (\hat{Y} - Q) \cup P. \tag{7}$$

Now, we will show how we decide P and Q.

Assuming in the round i, the rank of the s^t is $r_i(s^t)$. After the update of w, the rank of the s^t is $r_{i+1}(s^t)$. We defined the distance of two rankings, $d(r_i, r_{i+1})$ as the sum of un-concordant pairs.

Theorem 1. *Given two rankings r_1, r_2, over $s_1, s_2, \ldots, s_m$, w.l.g. we let $r_1(s_i) = i$, if $r_2(s_i) > r_2(s_j), i < j$, then $d(r_1, r_2) \geq j - i$*

Proof. Consider the rank r_2^0 : $s_1 \ldots s_{i-1}, s_j$, $s_i, s_{i+1} \ldots s_{j-1}$, $s_{j+1} \ldots s_m$. Obliviously, $d(r_1, r_2^0) = j - i$ and the set of the un-concordant pairs of r_2^0 is NC^0 : $\{(s_j, s_i), (s_j, s_{i+1}), \ldots, (s_j, s_{j-1})\}$. Assuming that there is a rank r_2^1 : $r_2^1(s_i) > r_2^1(s_j)$, set of the un-concordant pairs of which is denoted as NC^1 and $d(r_1, r_2^1) < j - i$. Then there must be some $K \subseteq [i+1, j-1]$: $\forall k \in K, (s_j, s_k) \in NC^0 \vee (s_j, s_k) \notin NC^1$. However, $\forall k \in K, (s_i, s_k) \in NC^1$, so $|NC^1| \leq |NC^0|$, which is contrast with the assumption.

Theorem 1 can easily be extended to the following case.

Theorem 2. *Given two rankings r_1, r_2, over $s_1, s_2, \ldots, s_m$, w.l.g. we let $r_1(s_i) = i$, if $I, J \subseteq [1, m], \forall i \in I, \forall \in J, i < j$ and $r_2(s_i) > r_2(s_j)$, then $d(r_1, r_2) \geq \sum_{j \in J} j - \sum_{i \in I} i$*

Let the positions of elements of P in $r_i(s^t)$ are $r_i(P_1) < r_i(P_2) < \cdots < r_i(P_\theta)$, and positions of elements of Q are $r_i(Q_1) < r_i(Q_2) < \cdots < r_i(Q_\theta)$, then according to our constraints and the Theorem 2

$$d(r_i(s^t), r_{i+1}(s^t)) \geq \sum_{j=1}^{\theta} (r_i(P_j) - r_i(Q_j)) \tag{8}$$

The lower bound of the distance of two rankings is $\sum_{j=1}^{\theta} (r_i(P_j) - r_i(Q_j))$. We assume $\|w_{i+1} - w_i\|$ will be increased with the increase of the lower bound. The intuition interpretation is if it is asked to change the positions of two adjacent sentences in $r_i(s^t)$, the change of w will be small, and instead, if it is asked to change the positions of two sentences which are the begin and the end of the ranked list, w will change more largely. In order to minimize $\|w_{i+1} - w_i\|$, $\sum_{j=1}^{\theta} (r_i(P_j) - r_i(Q_j))$ should be minimized by minimizing each $r_i(P_j)$ and maximizing each $r_i(Q_j)$. So we get:

P : the top-θ good answers in $C - Y^*$;
Q : the bottom-θ non-answers in $\hat{Y}$.

Similar to [2], we get the update step,

$$\alpha_t = \min \left(C, \frac{\Delta(Y^{**}, \hat{Y}) - \mathbf{w}_t^T \left(\Phi(\mathbf{x}, Y^{**}) - \Phi(\mathbf{x}, \hat{Y}) \right)}{||\Phi(\mathbf{x}, Y^{**}) - \Phi(\mathbf{x}, \hat{Y})||^2} \right). \tag{9}$$

Our final algorithm is shown in **Algorithm** (1).

---

input : training data set: $(x_n, C_n, Y_n^*), n = 1, \cdots, N$, and parameters: C, k
output: w

Initialize: $\mathbf{w} \leftarrow 0,$;
for $t = 0 \cdots T - 1$ **do**
    pick a sample (x_t, C_t, Y_t^*) from data set;
    calculate $\hat{Y}_t$ and Y^{**}; calculate $\gamma(\mathbf{w}; x_t)$,and$\Delta(Y_t^{**}, \hat{Y}_t)$;
    if $\gamma(\mathbf{w}; x) \leq \Delta(Y_t^{**}, \hat{Y}_t)$ **then**
        calculate α_t by Eq. (9);
        update $\mathbf{w} \leftarrow \mathbf{w} + \alpha_t(\Phi(x_t, Y_t^{**}) - \Phi(x_t, \hat{Y}_t))$;
    end
end

Algorithm 1: Passive-Aggressive Algorithm for Answering Raning

---

3 Features

For simplicity, we assume that each sentence is independent with others and remove the redundance later, the feature vector can be decomposed by $\Phi(x, Y) = \sum_{s \in Y} \phi(x, s)$.

3.1 Features Based on Language Models

For a candidate sentence s, we can calculate $\log P(s|Corpus)$ using language models trained on different corpora. Here we use four corpora: AQUAINT, modified AQUAINT (AQUAINT*), target corpus (TC) and definition corpus (DC).

Aquaint Aquaint consists of newswire text data in English, drawn from three sources and contains roughly 375 million words correlating to about 3GB of data. $P(s|Aquaint)$ is used to estimate the complexity of the sentence.

Aquaint* Aquaint* is the modified version of Aquaint, which replace the named entities and number word with their entity types(PERSON, LOCATION, ORGANIZATION, BASICNAME) and POS tag (CD). $P(s|Aquaint*)$ is used to measure the complexity of sentence after eliminating the effect of different number words and named entity of same type.

Target Corpus(TC) To each target, we build a TC correspondingly. We get top ranked 100 snippets by Google with the target as the query. Parameters are smoothed on Aquaint by Dirichlet smoothing [11].

Definition Corpus(DC) We build a corpus composed of definitional sentence by collection Wikipedia article on the train targets. Because some words like named entity phrase and number word may be high related with the specific target, we rewrite them in the same way as Aquaint*.

We use unigram model to get the four features of the sentence s, $\log P(s|TC)$, $\log P(s|DC)$, $\log P(s|Aquaint)$, $\log P(s|Aquaint*)$, where the models train by TC and DC are Dirichlet smoothed with the general corpus of Aquaint and Aquaint*, respectively.

3.2 Features Based on Dependency Relation Patterns

The syntax of a sentence is also important. For example, appositive structure often appears in the definition sentences. We use Minipar [8] to get a set of dependency relations patterns. First, to each sentence s as training sample, we get a set of triples: ⟨word, relation, word⟩. Then, we use two wildcard IN_TARGET, OUT_TARGET to indicate whether the content word is the target. Thus, we can get 20 most frequent patterns in the form of <IN_TARGET, relation, OUT_TARGET>.

Redundancy Features. Redundancy features are in the form of $\psi(x^t, s^t_{i_j}, s^t_{i_1 \ldots i_{j-1}})$ to the sentence $s^t_{i_j}$ for the target x^t. For each content word tw in target, we test a range $[a, b]$ centered by tw, denoted as r_{tw}, in $s^t_{i_j}$ for it. The word w is in the range r_{tw} if and only if there are at least $a - 1$ and at most $b - 1$ words between w and tw. We calculate how many content words have been appeared in the previous sentences as following.

$$\frac{|\{w : \exists tw, w \in r_{tw} \vee \exists s^t_{i_{j'}}, 1 \leq j' \leq j - 1, w \in s^t_{i_{j'}}\}|}{|\{w : \exists s^t_{i_{j'}}, 1 \leq j' \leq j - 1, w \in s^t_{i_{j'}}\}|}$$

We used 3 different range $[1, 5], [6, 10], [10, +\infty]$ to catch features (Tables 2 and 3).

Table 1. Results on TREC 2005 ($k = 12$)

System	F-3 Score
Soft-Pattern (SP)	0.29
Human Interest Model (HIM)	0.30
RankPA	**0.35**

Table 2. F-3 score on the TREC 2006

k	RankPA	RankSVM	Han
10	**0.25**	0.18	0.23
15	**0.29**	0.23	0.24
20	**0.28**	0.24	0.26
25	**0.28**	0.244	0.26
30	**0.26**	0.234	0.26
35	**0.23**	0.194	0.23

Table 3. Recall on the TREC 2006

k	RankPA	RankSVM	Han
10	**0.31**	0.23	0.29
15	**0.39**	0.32	0.33
20	**0.45**	0.37	0.38
25	**0.45**	0.40	0.40
30	**0.46**	0.40	0.42
35	**0.47**	0.42	0.44

4 Experiments

We use three datasets from TREC 2004 ~ 2006, which include 65, 75, 75 definitional questions respectively.

We firstly use Lucene[1] to get at most 200 sentences from Aquaint related to the target, and the query is just the target.

We adopt F-3 score, which used in the TREC definitional question answering task [9].

$$NR = \frac{r}{R} \tag{10}$$

$$NP = \begin{cases} 1, & l < 100 \times (r + a) \\ 1 - \frac{l - 100 \times (r+a)}{1}, & \text{otherwise} \end{cases} \tag{11}$$

$$F\text{-}3 = \frac{10 \times NR \times NP}{9 \times NP + NR} \tag{12}$$

where r is number of vital nuggets in the system response, R is number of vital nuggets in the gold standard, a is number of okay nuggets in the system response and l is length of the system response. Vital nuggets represent the most important facts about the target and should be included. Okay nuggets contribute to relevant information but are not essential.

4.1 Comparison with Other Systems

Kor and Chua [7] gave the results of Soft Pattern model (SP) and Human Interests Model (HIM), which both used questions in TREC 2004 as training data and questions in TREC 2005 as test data. Table 1 shows our method clearly outperforms SP and HIM.

---

[1] Apache Lucene, http://lucene.apache.org.

4.2   Comparison with Other Ranking Algorithms

To demonstrate the effectiveness of our ranking method, we also compare it with RankSVM [10] and Han [4]. We use the questions in TREC 2005 as training data and TREC 2006 as test data. The targets include PERSON, ORGANIZATION, THING, EVENT.

5   Conclusion

In this paper, we propose an online learning algorithm, which dynamically construct the supervisor on each iteration and assure the quality of the top k returned answers, instead of optimizing rank of the whole candidate list. In the future, we will seek the applications of our method on the ranking problems in other tasks such as summarization.

Acknowledgments. We would like to thank the anonymous reviewers for their valuable comments. This work was partially funded by the National Natural Science Foundation of China (61472088, 61363032), the National High Technology Research and Development Program of China (2015AA015408), Shanghai Science and Technology Development Funds (14ZR1403200).

References

1. Chen, Y., Zhou, M., Wang, S.: Reranking answers for definitional qa using language modeling. In: Proceedings of ACL (2006)
2. Crammer, K., Dekel, O., Keshet, J., Shalev-Shwartz, S., Singer, Y.: Online passive-aggressive algorithms. J. Mach. Learn. Res. **7**, 551–585 (2006)
3. Cui, H., Kan, M.: Generic soft pattern models for definitional question answering. In: Proceedings of ACL (2005)
4. Han, K., Song, Y., Rim, H.: Probabilistic model for definitional question answering. In: Proceedings of SIGIR (2006)
5. Hildebrandt, W., Katz, B., Lin, J.: Answering definition questions using multiple knowledge sources. In: Proceedings of HLT-NAACL (2004)
6. Joachims, T.: Optimizing search engines using clickthrough data. In: Proceedings of SIGKDD (2002)
7. Kor, K., Chua, T.: Interesting nuggets and their impact on definitional question answering. In: Proceedings of SIGIR (2007)
8. Lin, D.: Minipar: a minimalist parser. In: Maryland Linguistics Colloquium (1999)
9. Voorhees, E.: Overview of the trec 2004 question answering track. In: Proceedings of TREC (2004)
10. Xu, J., Cao, Y., Li, H., Zhao, M.: Ranking definitions with supervised learning methods. In: Proceedings of WWW (2005)
11. Zhai, C., Lafferty, J.: A study of smoothing methods for language models applied to information retrieval. ACM Trans. Inf. Syst. **22**, 179–214 (2004)

A WordNet Expansion-Based Approach for Question Targets Identification and Classification

Tianyong Hao[1,2(✉)], Wenxiu Xie[2], and Feifei Xu[3]

[1] Key Lab of Language Engineering and Computing of Guangdong Province,
Guangdong University of Foreign Studies, Guangzhou, China
haoty@126.com
[2] Cisco School of Informatics,
Guangdong University of Foreign Studies, Guangzhou, China
981555724@qq.com
[3] College of Computer Science and Technology,
Shanghai University of Electric Power, Shanghai, China
xufeifei1983@hotmail.com

Abstract. Question target identification and classification is a fundamental and essential research for finding suitable target answer type in a question answering system, aiming for improving question answering performance by filtering out irrelevant candidate answers. This paper presents a new automated approach for question target classification based on WordNet expansion. Our approach identifies question target words using dependency relations and answer type rules through the investigation of sample questions. Leveraging semantic relations, e.g., hyponymy, we expanse the question target words as features and apply a widely used classifier LibSVM to achieve question target classification. Our experiment datasets are the standard UIUC 5500 annotated questions and TREC 10 question dataset. The performance presents that our approach can achieve an accuracy of 87.9 % with fine gained classification on UIUC dataset and 86.8 % on TREC 10 dataset, demonstrating its effectiveness.

Keywords: Question target classification · Question target words · WordNet

1 Introduction

Question Answering (QA) has become a hot research area in recent years targeting for providing concise answers rather than a long list of documents [1]. Generally, Question Target Classification (QTC) is the first step in a QA system. A correct and meaningful classification of the question target can benefit the system on efficient and accurate answer extraction. From existing research, incorrect QTC has been addressed as one of the major factors for the poor performance of the Question Answering Systems [2]. Moldovan et al. [3] reported that 36.4 % of answering failures caused by incorrect question analysis.

The correct identification of question target is the vital task. Different from question topic, question target (QT) is a representation of users' intention of desirable answer

M. Sun et al. (Eds.): CCL and NLP-NABD 2015, LNAI 9427, pp. 333–344, 2015.
DOI: 10.1007/978-3-319-25816-4_27

type thus it directly helps in detecting answer relevance. For instance, as for the question *"Who is the largest producer of laptop computers in the world?"*, the question target (answer type) is *"organization"* rather than *"person"*. It helps to classify the question to the correct target category, which directly enhances the answer filtering performance, as filtering out answers in *"person"* category in the example.

In this paper, we propose an automated approach based on dependency relation analysis to identify question target words and extract target semantic features by WordNet expansion. These semantic features are further calculated with QTC taxonomy for acquiring best category labels. Parts of features are used to train LibSVM classifier to obtain correct question target categories. Our datasets are two standard publicly available datasets: UIUC 5500 annotated QA dataset and TREC 10 QA dataset. Applying on a two-layered classification taxonomy proposed by Li and Roth [4], our approach achieved an accuracy of 87.9 % with fine gained classification on UIUC dataset and 86.8 % on TREC 10 dataset, significantly improved the baseline SVM classifier, demonstrating the effectiveness in improving question target categorization.

The organization of this paper is as follows: Sect. 2 describes the related work and Sect. 3 presents the detailed information of our approach, particularly the QTW extraction. Section 4 shows our experiments and results on two open datasets. Finally, Sect. 5 summarizes the paper.

2 Related Work

Regardless of the characteristics of question target (answer type), question target classification can be treated as a question classification problem. There are many different methods to resolve the question classification problem. Most of the approaches can be divided into two categories: pattern-based classifiers using patterns and heuristic rules [5] and supervised classifiers using machine learning methods.

Representative researches include Li and Roth [4]. They developed a machine learning approach utilizing SNoW (Sparse Network of Winnows) learning architecture for question classification. They also built a UIUC question target category taxonomy, which has been extensively used around the world. In their approach, a set of syntactic features as well as semantic features using WordNet[1] [6] were used to identify class-specific related words. Using the features, they reported question classification accuracy as high as 98.8 % for coarse gained classification. Huang et al. [7] presented two methods to obtain augment semantic features of defined head words based on WordNet. The results demonstrated that the WordNet-based approach significantly increased the accuracy. Their linear SVM (Support Vector Machine) and ME (Maximum Entropy) models achieved accuracy of 89.2 % and 89.0 %, respectively. Bakhtyar et al. [8] proposed a new hierarchy for processing questions that belong to the class "Other" and presented an automatic hierarchy creation method to add new class nodes using WordNet and noun-phrase parsing.

---

[1] http://wordnet.princeton.edu/.

Particularly, we investigated a number of recent question classification techniques mainly about two aspects: the machine learning-based method SVM (Support Vector Machine) and WordNet-based question classification techniques during 2013–2015 as follows:

Machine learning-based methods [9–13] have been applied to various domains and languages [14] and have achieved results comparable to previous rule-based QA systems. The SVM is one of the most successful classification algorithms from them. An advantage of the SVM is that, once non-support vectors (non-SVs) that do not have any influence on classifier are identified, the vectors can be thrown away in the next test phase [15]. Recently, Yen et al. [16] employed TREC-QA tracks and question classification benchmarks to evaluate the machine learning-based method. Their experimental results showed that the question classifier achieved 85.60 % accuracy without any additional semantic or syntactic taggers, and reached 88.60 % after they employed a term expansion technique and a predefined related-word set. Hardy et al. [17] used Extreme Learning Machine (ELM) for question classification based on semantic features to improve both training and testing speeds compared with benchmark Support Vector Machine (SVM) classifier. Improvements have also been presented on the head word extraction and word sense disambiguation processes. Their results reached a higher accuracy (an increase of 0.2 %) for the classification of coarse gained classes compared to the benchmark.

WordNet corpus is also popular in leveraging semantic in question feature identification. In 2013, Jeong et al. [18] applied WordNet and demonstrated that unit feature dependency information and deep-level WordNet hypernyms are useful for event recognition and type classification. Their experimental results showed that the method outperformed an accuracy of 83.8 %. Later, Gao et al. [19] presented a new approach for semantic similarity measuring based on edge-counting and information content theory and resulted in a better distribution characteristics of the coefficient. Eduard et al. [20] used three widely used linguistic resources for taxonomic and non-taxonomic relation extraction: WordNet, general corpora acquired from the Web, and Wikipedia.

These work motivated us to conduct research on question target classification by refereeing the existing ideas of WordNet usage and machine learning methods from question classification area even though they have significant differences task by task.

3 The WordNet-Based Expansion Approach

As defined by Li and Roth [4], question target classification is a task, given a question, to map its question target to one of the predefined k classes, which indicates a semantic constraint on the sought-after answer. To identify the question target, we need to obtain question target representations and prune out irrelevant information which may mislead the classification process. Therefore we propose to use Question Target Words (QTWs) which is a group of words (existing or not existing in the question) as the target representations for specifying the answer type that the question seeks.

Our method contains three main steps: the QTW Extraction, WordNet expansion, and SVM classification. The processing workflow is shown in Fig. 1. The first step is to obtain QTWs utilizing a principle-based English parser MiniPar[2] [21]. Afterwards, the QTWs are expanded with hyponymy features using WordNet to acquire their categories according to depth and distance-based semantic relevance calculation. Finally, the features are sent to a trained LibSVM classifier to obtain their question target (answer type) categories.

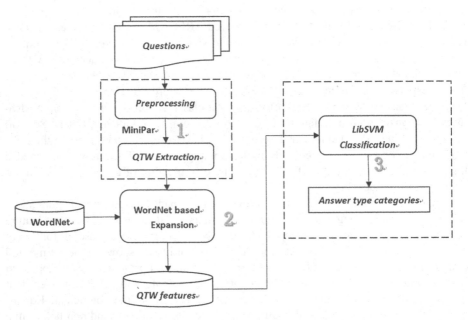

Fig. 1. The workflow of our question target classification approach using WordNet-based expansion and LibSVM classifier

3.1   Question Target Word Extraction

As the accuracy of QTW Extraction directly affects the overall classification performance, we concern a lot on this step and have tried several strategies to ensure the extraction quality. In this process, we apply a principle-based English parser MiniPar to generate a dependency tree for a given question. A dependency relation is a binary relation between two words with one marked as a head word and another marked as a dependent using pos : relation : pos between them. For instance, the dependency relations of the question *"where can I buy a Guitar in Guangzhou?"* analyzed by MiniPar are shown as Fig. 2. According to the dependency tree, we can extract the main verb-relation: buy ←V:obj:N→ guitar ← N:mod:Prep → in ← N:pcomp-n:N →

---

2 Available at http://www.cs.ualberta.ca/~lindek/minipar.htm.

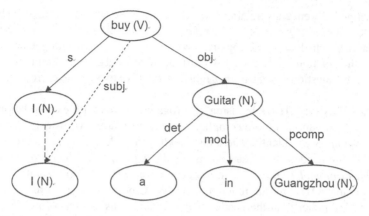

Fig. 2. The dependency relations of the question *"where can I buy a Guitar in Guangzhou?"* analyzed using MiniPar

Guangzhou. Therefore, we can extract needed information from it, e.g., *"buy a guitar"* in the example as main event.

Therefore, the essential work is to detect useful relations to extract needed QTWs. Due to the manner of question asking and the variety of interrogative words, the syntactic structures of different questions may be much different. After analyzing hundreds both questions dependency relations and syntactic structures between the manually identified QTWs and other (irrelevant) parts of the questions, three situations are identified and analyzed with each of them having a specific processing strategy. Please note the strategies are applied sequentially starting from *Strategy 1*.

Strategy 1: extract QTWs by locating interrogative words

The first strategy is to extract QTWs by directly referring the interrogative words of a question when the question is in formal representation. It is the most common situation for question target word extraction.

For instance, as for the question *"What's the abbreviation for trinitrotoluene?"*, the dependency relation of the question by MiniPar is shown below. The relation between *abbreviation* and *trinitrotoluene* is therefore represented as: *what* ←N:subj:N→ *abbreviation* ←N:mod:Prep→ *for* ←Prep:pcomp-n:N→ *trinitrotoluene*. Through the representation, we can extract the target of the question as *abbreviation* which leads to the answer type "ABBR:abbreviation".

fin	C:whn:N	what
fin	C:i:VBE	be
be	VBE:pred:N	abbreviation
abbreviation	N:subj:N	what
abbreviation	N:det:Det	the
abbreviation	N:mod:Prep	for
for	Prep:pcomp-n:N	trinitrotoluene

The defined dependency relations with interrogative words as rules include "C: whn:N", "C:wha:A", "Q:whn:N", "N:det:Det", "N:subj:N", "N:nn:N", and "N:gen:N". These relations help locate interrogative words and the question target being asked. Moreover, the relation rules can also be applied to questions without interrogative words, e.g., the question *"Name a tiger that is extinct"* to extract the correct target word *"tiger"*.

Strategy 2: extract QTWs by using interrogative words with extra relations

The second situation is more complicated as interrogative words cannot ensure the correct question target identification thus additional rules of relations, e.g., "Prep: pcomp-n:N", are needed. For example, as for the dependency relation of the question *"What kind of animal is Babar?"*, the interrogative words *"What"* cannot be simply used to identify QT through relation analysis. Otherwise, the word of *"kind"* is extracted as QT rather than the needed word *"animal"*, as shown below.

fin	C:whn:N	*kind*
kind	N:det:Det	*what*
kind	N:comp1:Prep	*of*
of	Prep:pcomp-n:N	*animal*
fin	C:i:VBE	*be*
be	VBE:pred:N	*Babar*
Babar	N:subj:N	*kind*

In the dependency relation of the question example, a new relation link: *what* ← N:det:Det → *kind* ← N:comp1:Prep → *of* ← Prep:pcomp-n:N → *animal* can be identified to solve this kind of problems. According our investigation, a list of relation rules are summarized as as "C:whn:N", "Q:whn:N", "N:det:Det", "N:subj:N", "N:nn: N", "Prep:pcomp-n:N", "N:gen:N" for solving the situation.

Strategy 3: extract QTWs by using verb-centered relations

The third situation is the most complex one. The interrogative word and above relations as well as related rules sometimes could not extract correct target words. The reason is that these questions contain at least one verb and generated dependency tree is verb-rooted, causing incorrect relation link analysis. For instance, the question *"What garment was named for Bradley, Voorhees and Day"*. The dependency relation is as below:

fin	C:whn:N	*what*
fin	C:i:V	*name*
name	V:s:N	*garment*
name	V:be:be	*be*
name	V:obj2:N	*what*
name	V:obj1:N	*garment*
name	V:mod:Prep	*for*
for	Prep:pcomp-n:N	*Bradley*

A new relation link is observed as *fin* ← C:i:V → *name* ← V:s:N → *garment* without interrogative words and pcomp relations. The main relation is linked by a verb "*name*". Looking inside the relations, we define a list of relation rules as "C:whn:N", "C:i:V", "YNQ:head:V", "V:subj:N", "V:obj:N", "V:obj1:N", "V:obj2:N", and "V:s: N" as the strategy to deal with such kind of questions.

3.2   WordNet-Based Feature Expansion

With regarding to the weakness of WordNet in dealing with verbs and interrogative words, the previous step is to identify QT words with obvious relations. The obtained QTWs can be further expanded by WordNet to acquire expected answer types. In WordNet, senses are organized into hierarchies with hyponyms relationships, i.e., *A* is a kind of *B*, providing a way to augment hyponyms feature for the QTWs. For instance, the QTW of the question "*What kind of flowers does detective Nero Wolfe raise*" is "*flower*". The hierarchy for the noun sense of "*flower*" is as: "*flower → flowering plant → seed plant → vascular plant → plant → organism → living thing → object → physical entity → entity*", where "*A → B*" representing that *B* is the hyponyms of *A*.

With the hyponym hierarchy, the hyponym labels as the super semantic layers can be calculated with our QTC taxonomy to obtain best category labels. To achieve that, we firstly design a QTC taxonomy, as shown in Table 1, by following Li & Roth in the research of UIUC QA category [4].

Table 1. The QTC taxonomy defining two-level categories following Li & Roth [4]

Coarse	Fine grained	Count
ABBR	abbreviation, expansion	2
DESC	definition, description, manner, reason	4
ENTY	animal, body, color, creation, currency, disease/medical, event, food, instrument, language, letter, other, plant, product, religion, sport, substance, symbol, technique, term, vehicle, word	22
HUM	description, group, individual, title	4
LOC	city, country, mountain, other, state	5
NUM	code, count, date, distance, money, order, other, percent, period, speed, temperature, size, weight	13

Though the hyponym hierarchy in WordNet is commonly used, e.g. [7], we calculate the conceptual similarity differently, as relevance, between each hyponym label of a QTW and each category label defined in the taxonomy. By referring the similarity matrix proposed in [22], we define a new relevance calculation measure utilizing both depth and distance information in WordNet, as shown in Eq. (1). The higher the relevance, the higher possibility of a category label is chosen as the candidate QTC.

$$Relevance_{QTC} = \frac{(Depth_{label_i} + Depth_{label_j})}{2 \times Max(Depth_{label_i}, Depth_{label_j})} \times \frac{1}{Log(Distance(label_i, label_j)) + 1}$$
(1)

Relevance$_{QTC}$ denotes the relevance of a hyponym label *label*$_i$ of a QTC word with a category label *label*$_j$. *Depth*$_{label}$ denotes the number of levels of the label *label*$_i$ from the root node in WordNet; *Max* is to obtain the maximum depth for normalization; *Distance* is the minimum length of all ancestral paths between the two labels. Thus the minimum length between any two labels is 1. The relevance value is finally normalized into [0, 1].

The WordNet-based expansion is able to identify QTC alone. However, according to our observation on a large number of questions, certain types of questions are difficult for the method to achieve high performance, e.g., "Entity/other", as shown in Table 2 in next section. We therefore employ both WordNet-based expansion and a standard LibSVM classifier for improving classification performance. The used features are all the words in a question. As LibSVM is a widely used classification tool, it will not be described repeatedly in the paper.

4   Experiments and Results

Two publicly available standard datasets are used to test the effectiveness of our approach: (1) Dataset A: 5500 questions with manually annotated question target labels from University of Illinois at Urbana-champaign (UIUC)[3]; (2) Dataset B: 500 TREC 10 (Text Retrieval Conference) questions with manually annotated question target labels from UIUC [4]. Both the two dataset were mapped to 6 coarse grained classes and 50 fine grained classes, where the classess are shown in Table 1. Based on them, we split dataset A and B into training and testing datasets for three experiments. Our measurement is the commonly used accuracy defined as the total number of questions with correctly labeled QTC divided by the total number of questions in experiment dataset.

The first experiment evaluated the effects of different size training datasets and testing datasets to question target classification performance. The purpose was to view the stablibility of our apporach by using different sizes of datasets. We firstly randomly selected 1000 questions from Dataset A as testing dataset UIUC 1000 and randomly selected 1000 to 3500 questions from the same Dataset A as training datasets. For each training dataset, accuracy was calculated. Similarly, 2000 questions from Dataset A were randomly selected from Dataset A as UIUC 2000 and the training datasets were also the data from 1000 to 35000. The accurracy calculation results are shown as Fig. 3. From the result, the size of training dataset contributes accuracy much when the training dataset size is below 1500. After that, the accuracies on both UIUC 1000 and 2000 tend to be stable and the accuracies are very close when the training dataset size ranges from 3000 to 3500. The experiment results indicate that the performance of our approach is not affected by training dataset size much. This is meaningful since our approach enables achieving stable performance using a relatively small training dataset, which is helpful in large dataset processing.

---

[3] http://cogcomp.cs.illinois.edu/Data/QA/QC/train_5500.label.

[4] http://cogcomp.cs.illinois.edu/Data/QA/QC/TREC_10.label.

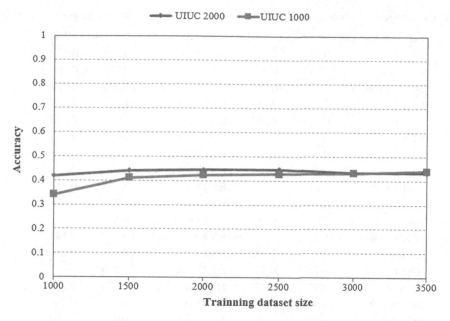

Fig. 3. Number of training dataset vs. classification accuracy on UIUC 1000 and 2000 testing questions

The second experiment conducted a comparison between the contribution of WordNet-based expansion (as WordNet) and SVM-based classification (as LibSVM) on every detailed fine grained category. The purpose was to view the strength and weakness of the two approaches on different categories. The training dataset was randomly selected 3500 questions from Dataset A and the other 2000 were used as testing dataset. The result, as shown in Table 2, presented that these two classifiers were complementary to each other on certain categories. WordNet achieved much higher accuracy on "ENTY:religion", "ENTY:letter", "ENTY:plant", "ENTY:veh", and "NUM:volsize" while LibSVM achieved much higher accuracy on "DESC:def", "ENTY:symbol", "NUM:temp", etc. For "ENTY:color", "ENTY:currency", "NUM: ord", and "NUM:period", both the two methods obtained excellent performance. However, both the methods obtained bad performance on "NUM:code" and "ENTY: techmeth", indicating big space for improvement on these categories.

The third experiment evaluated the performance improvement of our approach (as WordNet + LibSVM) compared with WordNet-based expansion and LibSVM classi-fication. In the WordNet-based expansion, we further separated it into WordNet-based expansion on identified categories by removing categories that WordNet-based expansion preformed 0 accuracy according to the analysis of the second experiment as WordNet-concise and WordNet-based expansion on all categories as WordNet. The first testing dataset was 2000 questions randomly selected from Dataset A (other 3500 questions are used as training dataset) as UIUC(2000). The second dataset was all the

Table 2. Accuracy comparison using WordNet and LibSVM on 50 fine grained categories

Category/accuracy	WordNet	LibSVM	Category/accuracy	WordNet	LibSVM
ABBR:abb	0.688	1	ABBR:exp	0.774	0.667
DESC:def	0.042	0.911	DESC:desc	0.696	0.704
DESC:manner	0.99	0.959	DESC:reason	0.906	0.923
ENTY:animal	0.848	0.484	ENTY:currency	1	1
ENTY:body	0.222	0.333	ENTY:dismed	0.854	0.833
ENTY:color	1	1	ENTY:event	0.68	0.333
ENTY:cremat	0	0.589	ENTY:food	0.67	0.471
ENTY:instru	0.7	1	ENTY:religion	0.75	0
ENTY:lang	0.875	0.78	ENTY:sport	0.706	0.75
ENTY:letter	0.78	0	ENTY:substance	0.75	0.571
ENTY:other	0	0.442	ENTY:symbol	0.25	1
ENTY:plant	0.77	0	ENTY:techmeth	0	0.143
ENTY:product	0.738	0.222	ENTY:termeq	0.111	0.786
ENTY:word	0.77	0.60	ENTY:veh	0.929	0
HUM:desc	0.979	0.857	HUM:ind	0.874	0.88
HUM:gr	0.406	0.485	HUM:title	0	0.20
LOC:city	0.845	0.962	LOC:country	0.9	0.964
LOC:mount	0.905	0.625	LOC:other	0	0.848
LOC:state	1	0.929	NUM:code	0	0
NUM:count	0.967	0.984	NUM:date	0.156	0.958
NUM:dist	0.571	0.50	NUM:money	0.765	0.90
NUM:ord	1	1	NUM:other	0	1
NUM:perc	0.857	0.25	NUM:period	1	1
NUM:speed	1	0.667	NUM:temp	0	1
NUM:volsize	0.923	0	NUM:weight	0	0.25

500 questions from Dataset B (the same training dataset as the first one) as TREC_10 (500). Table 3 shows the results of the comparison. WordNet-concise has a relatively high accuracy compared with WordNet, indicating our WordNet-based expansion is effective to some extent regardless of the QTC categories that the method cannot process. WordNet achieved 74.2 % accuracy on UIUC(2000) but only 33 % on TREC_10(500). This is reasonable as the training questions are from UIUC rather than TREC_10. LibSVM obtained better results than WordNet. However, as analyzed in the previous experiment, WordNet has obvious advantages in processing of certain categories. Our method WordNet + LibSVM achieved the best performance with an accuracy of 87.9 % on UIUC(2000) and 86.8 % on TREC_10(500), presenting significant improvement compared with both LibSVM and WordNet.

Table 3. Accuracy comparison among our approach WordNet + LibSVM and other classification strategies on the two datasets

	UIUC(2000)	TREC_10(500)
WordNet-concise	91 %	77 %
WordNet	74.2 %	33 %
LibSVM	78 %	79 %
WordNet + LibSVM	87.9 %	86.8 %

5 Conclusions

Targeting at question target identification and classification for answer type filtering, this paper proposed a method based on dependency tree analysis for question target word identification. Afterwards, a compact but effective WordNet-based hyponymy expansion strategy was proposed to classify the identification question target words into question target categories. Based on two standard fully annotated datasets: UIUC dataset and TREC 10 dataset, we conducted three experiments to evaluate the effectiveness of our approach through the comparison with other methods. The results presented that our approach achieved the best performance from the comparison, demonstrating its capability in question target classification task.

Acknowledgements. This work was supported by National Natural Science Foundation of China (grant No. 61403088 and No.61305094).

References

1. Le-Hong, P., Phan, X.-H., Nguyen, T.-D.: Using dependency analysis to improve question classification. In: Nguyen, V.-H., Le, A.-C., Huynh, V.N. (eds.). AISC, vol. 326, pp. 673–686Springer, Heidelberg (2015)
2. Ray, S.K., Shailendra, S., Bhagwati, P.J.: A semantic approach for question classification using WordNet and Wikipedia. Pattern Recogn. Lett. **31**(13), 1935–1943 (2010)
3. Moldovan, D., Paşca, M., Harabagiu, S., Surdeanu, M.: Performance issues and error analysis in an open-domain question answering system. ACM Trans. Inf. Syst. (TOIS) **21**(2), 133–154 (2003)
4. Li, X., Roth, D.: Learning question classifiers. In: Proceedings of COLING (2002)
5. Voorhees, E.M.: Overview of the TREC 2003 Question Answering Track. TREC (2003)
6. Miller, G., Christiane, F.: WorldNet: An electronic lexical database. MIT Press, Cambridge (1998)
7. Huang, Z.H., Thint, M., Qin, Z.C: Question classification using head words and their hypernyms. In: Proceedings of the Conference on Empirical Methods in Natural Language Processing (EMNLP) (2008)
8. Bakhtyar, M., Kawtrakul, A., Baber, J., Doudpota, S.M.: Creating multi-level class hierarchy for question classification with NP analysis and WordNet. J. Digit. Inf. Manage. **10**(6), 379 (2012)

9. Martin, A.I., Franz, M., Roukos, S.: IBM's statistical question answering system-TREC-10. In: Proceedings of the Tenth Text REtrieval Conference (TREC) (2001)
10. Moschitti, A., Quarteroni, S.: Kernels on linguistic structures for answer extraction. In: Proceedings of ACL (2008)
11. Quarteroni, S., Moschitti, R., Man, S., Basili, R.: Advanced structural representations for question classification and answer re-ranking. LNCS, pp. 234–245 (2007)
12. Ray, S.K., Singh, S., Joshi, B.P.: A semantic approach for question classification using WordNet and Wikipedia. Pattern Recogn. Lett. **31**(13), 1935–1943 (2010)
13. Wu, Y.Z., Zhang, R.Q., Hu, X.H., Kashioka, H.: Learning unsupervised SVM classifier for answer selection in web question answering. In: Proceedings of EMNLP-CoNLL, pp. 33–41 (2007)
14. Sasaki, Y.: Question answering as question-biased term extraction: a new approach toward multilingual. In: Proceedings of ACL, pp. 215–222 (2005)
15. Ogawa, K., Takeuchi, I.: Safe screening of non-support vectors in pathwise SVM computation. In: Proceedings of International Conference on Machine Learning (ICML) (2013)
16. Yen, S.J., Wu, Y.C., Yang, J.C., Lee, Y.S., Lee, C.J., Liu, J.J.: A support vector machine-based context-ranking model for question answering. Inf. Sci. **224**(2), 77–87 (2013)
17. Hardy, H., Cheah, Y.N.: Question classification using extreme learning machine on semantic features. J. ICT Res. Appl. **7**(1), 36–58 (2013)
18. Jeong, Y., Myaeng, S.-H.: Using wordnet hypernyms and dependency features for phrasal-level event recognition and type classification. In: Serdyukov, P., Braslavski, P., Kuznetsov, S.O., Kamps, J., Rüger, S., Agichtein, E., Segalovich, I., Yilmaz, E. (eds.) ECIR 2013. LNCS, vol. 7814, pp. 267–278. Springer, Heidelberg (2013)
19. Gao, J.B., Zhang, B.W., Chen, X.H.: A WordNet-based semantic similarity measurement combining edge-counting and information content theory. Eng. Appl. Artif. Intell. 80–88 (2015)
20. Barbu, E.: Property type distribution in WordNet, corpora and Wikipedia. Expert Syst. Appl. **42**(7), 3501–3507 (2015)
21. Berwick, R.C.: Principles of principle-based parsing, pp. 1–37. Principle-Based Parsing. Springer, Netherlands (1992)
22. Hao, T.Y., Xu, F.F., Lei, J.S., Liu, W.Y., Li, Q.: Toward automatic answers in user-interactive question answering systems. Int. J. Softw. Sci. Comput. Intell. **3**(4), 52–66 (2011)

Social Computing

Clustering Chinese Product Features with Multilevel Similarity

Yu He, Jiaying Song, Yuzhuang Nan, and Guohong Fu[✉]

School of Computer Science and Technology, Heilongjiang University, Harbin
150080, China
heyucs@yahoo.com, jy_song@outlook.com,
yuzhuangnan@gmail.com, ghfu@hotmail.com

Abstract. This paper presents an unsupervised hierarchical clustering approach for grouping co-referred features in Chinese product reviews. To handle different levels of connections between co-referred product features, we consider three similarity measures, namely the literal similarity, the word embedding-based semantic similarity and the explanatory evaluation based contextual similarity. We apply our approach to two corpora of product reviews in car and mobilephone domains. We demonstrate that combining multilevel similarity is of great value to feature normalization.

Keywords: Opinion mining · Product reviews · Aspect normalization · Clustering

1 Introduction

Feature normalization, also referred to as feature grouping or feature co-reference resolution, aims to recognize co-referred feature expressions in product reviews and normalize them with a standard name. Obviously, feature normalization benefits many opinion mining applications, such as opinion summarization and aggregation (Liu 2010, Zhai et al. 2010, Zhai et al. 2011).

While much work has been done to date on feature normalization, studies are still needed to explore more informative clues for feature normalization. Firstly, most current study has focused on exploiting different semantic similarity measurements such as the WordNet similarity (Carenini et al. 2005) or the topic model (Guo et al. 2009) for feature grouping, few studies use word embeddings from big data. Unlike traditional semantic representations, word embeddings employ low-dimensional and real valued vectors to preserve the semantic relationship between words Mikolov et al. (2013c). As such, we believe that word embeddings would provide a more convenient and effective way for exploring potential semantic clues for product feature normalization. More importantly, word embeddings can be learned from large corpora in an unsupervised manner. Secondly, the evaluation expressions collocated with product features has proven to be of great value to feature grouping (Yang et al. 2012). However, previous studies usually ignore evaluation information or do not distinguish explanatory evaluations from non-explanatory evaluations (Yang et al. 2012). Actually, non-explanatory evaluations

M. Sun et al. (Eds.): CCL and NLP-NABD 2015, LNAI 9427, pp. 347–355, 2015.
DOI: 10.1007/978-3-319-25816-4_28

like 好 'good' provide less-informative indicators than explanatory evaluations for normalizing the features they are modifying (Kim et al. 2013).

In this work we present an unsupervised clustering method for normalizing features in online Chinese product reviews. To approach this, we explore three levels of similarities, namely the literal similarity, the semantic similarity based on word embeddings and the contextual similarity based on explanatory evaluations, to handle different connections between co-referred product features in product reviews. These similarity measures are further combined with a linear interpolation strategy under a framework of hierarchical clustering to determine whether a given set of feature expressions should be clustered into a suitable feature group. We apply our approach to two corpora of product reviews in car and mobilephone domains. We demonstrate that combining multilevel similarity is of great value to feature clustering.

2 Feature Expressions in Chinese

To investigate how product features are expressed in Chinese product reviews, we built two corpora of product reviews in car and mobilephone domains, respectively. The two corpora are manually annotated with multiple linguistic information, including word segmentation, part-of-speech tags and opinion elements (viz. opinion objects, product features, evaluations and sentiment polarity). In addition, all co-referred feature expressions within the corpora are manually recognized and paired with their corresponding explanatory evaluations.

As can be seen from Table 1, a product feature can be expressed in many ways. For example, there are more than 20 different expressions on average for a feature in car reviews. This shows that co-referred feature expressions are very common in product reviews, illustrating in a sense the importance of feature normalization to review mining.

Table 1. Distributions of features expressions

	Car[1]	Mobilephone[2]
#Reviews	2340	5670
#Feature expressions	408	169
# feature groups	20	15
# co-referred expressions per feature	20.40	11.27

[1]http://www.autohome.com.cn/.
[2]http://www.jd.com/.

3 Our Method

Let S = {$<f_1,e_1>,<f_2,e_2>,\ldots,<f_n,e_n>$} be a set of collocated feature-evaluation pairs from product reviews, our goal is to discover all co-referred feature expressions within S and further cluster them into a suitable group.

As shown in Fig. 1, in order to handle the above-mentioned three levels of similarities, viz. literal similarity (LS), semantic similarity (SS) and contextual similarity

(*CS*), between co-referred feature expressions, we explore multilevel similarity criteria and further combine them in a hierarchical clustering algorithm for feature grouping.

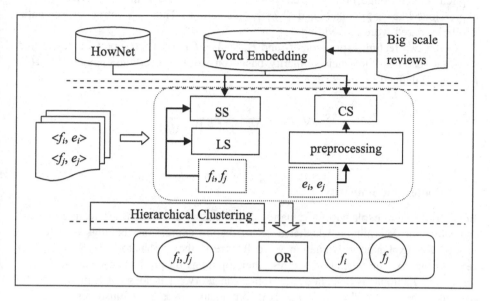

Fig. 1. Overview of our method

3.1 Literal Similarity

Co-referred feature expressions in Chinese usually contain identical characters or words. Take two pairs of feature expressions (外表, 外形) and (油耗, 耗油) as examples. 外表 and 外形 contain the same Chinese character 外 'outer' and thus have the same meaning 'appearance', while 油耗 and 耗油 are formed with identical Chinese characters in different orders, and therefore share the same meaning 'fuel consumption'.

Considering that edit distance cannot objectively reflect the real similarity for some co-referred feature expressions like 油耗 and 耗油, for the reason that their edit distance similarity is only 0.3 and it is inconsistent with the actual similarity. We exploit Jaccard coefficient to calculate the literal similarity of two feature expressions f_1 and f_2. As shown in Eq. (1), Jaccard coefficient measures the similarity of feature expression pairs by counting the number of common characters within them, ignoring the influence of character location.

$$LS_{JC}(f_i, f_j) = \frac{|SET(f_i) \cap SET(f_j)|}{|SET(f_i) \cup SET(f_j)|} \tag{1}$$

Where, SET(f_i) denotes the set of characters within f_i (i = 1,2).

3.2   Semantic Similarity

Literal similarity relies on literal matching and works only for feature expressions with explicit literal connections, which does not always exist in co-referred feature expressions like 像素 'pixel' and 分辨率 'resolution'. Thus, we introduce semantic similarity based word embeddings.

Given two feature expressions f_1 and f_2, let $Vec(f_1)$ and $Vec(f_2)$ be their respective word embeddings, then their similarity based on word embeddings, namely $SS_{WE}(f_1, f_2)$, can be defined by Eq. (2).

$$SS_{WE}(f_i, f_j) = \frac{Vec(f_i) \cdot Vec(f_j)}{|Vec(f_i)| \times |Vec(f_j)|} \tag{2}$$

3.3   Contextual Similarity

In contrast to non-explanatory evaluations, explanatory evaluations are feature-specific indicators for determining whether a set of feature expressions belongs to a feature group. The explanatory evaluation we call here is the explanatory parts in product reviews that explain why users express their opinions on product features, such Sentence B in Example 1. Sentence A is non-explanatory for it does not explain why the user likes the screen while Sentence B is explanatory because it illustrates the reason (viz. "screen resolution is very high").

Example 1:

A. 这部手机太棒了！我最喜欢它的屏幕！(This phone is so great! And its screen is my favorite!)

B. 这个手机的屏幕分辨率很高，我非常喜欢！(The screen resolution of this mobilephone is very high. I like it very much!)

Let e_1 and e_2 be the respective explanatory evaluations for two product features f_1 and f_2, we take the following three steps to compute their contextual similarity (denoted by $CS_{EE}(f_1, f_2)$).

(1) **Explanatory Keyword Extraction**. For an explanatory evaluation e with n words $\{w_1, w_2, ..., w_n\}$, only parts of them are actually helpful cues for feature grouping. We refer these cue words for feature clustering to as explanatory keywords. Thus, we employ the *tf-idf* technique to extract a set of explanatory keywords (denoted by $S_{EK}(e)$).

(2) **Explanatory Synset Generation.** In this step, we employ the semantic paraphrasing method (Bhagat and Hovy 2013) to generate a synset (denoted by Set (e) for explanatory keywords in $S_{EK}(e)$.

(3) **Contextual Similarity Computing.** Let $Set(e_1)$ and $Set(e_2)$ be the explanatory synsets generated in the second step for e_1 and e_2, respectively, we can then employ Jaccard coefficient in Eq. (1) to compute their explanatory evaluation based contextual similarity, namely $CS_{EE}(f_1, f_2) = |Set(e_1) \cap Set(e_2)|/|Set(e_1) \cup Set(e_2)|$.

It should be noted that in this work we also exploit the Jaccard coefficient between common evaluation pairs to compute the contextual similarity between the relevant feature pairs, denoted by CS_{CE}, which is used as the baseline in our experiment to examine the effectiveness of the explanatory evaluation similarity (viz. CS_{EE}).

4   The Clustering Algorithm

Considering the fact that some flat clustering algorithms like k-means do not satisfy the consistency constraint for different granularity clusters (Pavlopoulos et al. 2014), in this work we employ the hierarchical clustering algorithm to perform feature grouping.

Furthermore, different co-referred feature expressions may involve multiple connections. As such, each separate similarity measurement may have its own shortcomings while offering its advantages in dealing with various connections between different feature expressions. To compensate for this, we employ the linear interpolation strategy to combine the above three levels of similarity measures, as shown in Eq. (3).

$$Sim(f_i, f_j) = \alpha * LS + \beta * SS + \gamma * CS \tag{3}$$

Where, α, β and γ denote the relevant interpolation coefficients and $\alpha + \beta + \gamma = 1$.

Figure 2 presents the hierarchical clustering algorithm with multilevel similarities for feature normalization. Where, θ is for the threshold for feature clustering. ClusterSim(c_i, c_j) is the average similarity between each pair of features (f_i, f_j) from the two clusters c_i and c_j, as shown in Eq. (4).

$$ClusterSim(c_i, c_j) = \frac{\sum_{f_i \in c_i} \sum_{f_j \in c_j} Sim(f_i, f_j)}{|c_i| \times |c_j|} \tag{4}$$

Input: The input set of features $F=\{f_1, f_2, ..., f_n\}$ for normalization, and their explanatory evaluations

Output: A set of feature groups $G=\{c_1, c_2, ..., c_k\}$.

(1) Initialization: Let each feature $f_i \in F$ be a cluster c_i $(1 \leq i \leq n)$, then $G=\{c_1, c_2, ..., c_n\}$
(2) For each $c_i \in \{c_1, c_2, ..., c_n\}$,
(3)   if $\exists c_j$ that makes *ClusterSim*(c_i, c_j) be the maximum, and *ClusterSim*(c_i, c_j) > θ,
(4)   then merge clusters c_i and c_j, and update G.
(5) Repeat 2-4 until the number of the groups in G remains unchanged.
(6) Output G as the feature clusters.

Fig. 2. The algorithm for feature clustering

5   Experiments

5.1   Experimental Setup

In our experiments, the two corpora in Table 1 are used as the test sets. To learn word embeddings for feature grouping, two larger corpora of car reviews and mobilephone reviews are also collected from the Web. Furthermore, the Google open source tool[1], viz. word2vec, is used here to learn word embeddings.

To evaluate feature clustering performance, we employ entropy and purity (Zhai et al. 2010). In fact, entropy measures the average uncertainty after feature clustering. Generally, feature clustering with smaller entropy has less uncertainty, indicating the result is better. On the contrary, the purity metric is for describing average purity after clustering. Higher purity indicates that a good clustering result is achieved.

As baselines, we consider methods below.

- **k-means**. k-means is a classical clustering method based on distributional similarity.
- **The Latent Dirichlet Allocation (LDA).** LDA is a kind of topic model and is widely used in text classification and clustering. Here we use explanatory evaluations as documents for learning LDA in that there are more representative terms.
- **SC-EM.** SC-EM is a state-of-the-art semi-supervised method for grouping product features in English product reviews (Zhai et al. 2010).
- **SC-EM + WNS.** SC-EM + WNS is modified version of the SC-EM algorithm by considering both product features and their evaluation information (Yang et al. 2012).

Table 2 presents the results of baselines over the test data.

Table 2. Feature grouping results for baselines

Methods	Car		Mobilephone	
	Purity	Entropy	Purity	Entropy
k-means	0.352	2.837	0.545	1.980
LDA	0.352	2.768	0.373	2.357
SC-EM	0.572	1.909	0.672	1.634
SC-EM + WNS	0.585	1.959	0.700	1.589

5.2   Experimental Results

(1) Results for Separate Similarity.

Our first experiment is conducted to test the effectiveness of separate similarity measurements. The results are summarized in Table 3. It should be notated that with a consideration to the great differences between different similarity measures, we use

---

[1] http://code.google.com/p/word2vec/

different threshold θ for clustering. In addition, our guidelines are trying to achieve a set of clusters that is identical to the pre-defined feature groups in number.

LS_{ED} is the literal similarity of edit distance and SS_{HN} is the semantic similarity based on HowNet. From Table 3, we have a number of observations. First, among the six measurements, Jaccard coefficient yields the best performance in terms of purity and entropy. This might be due to the fact that most co-referred feature expressions have common parts and are similar with regard to word forms. But on the contrary, some co-referred feature expressions are completely dissimilar with regard to their forms. Second, the cluster number produced by word embeddings is closest to the real number, but the relevant purity and entropy are not satisfactory. This may result from the characteristic of word embeddings. Word embeddings prove to be good tool for discovering implicit linguistic regularities. Actually, each pair of words has a certain similarity when mapping them into a vector space. However, it is very difficult to highlight the interaction between two words with the same semantics. Such interference exits in the case of explanatory evaluations with dynamic polar words. For example, the polar word 高 'high' can modify both 像素 'resolution' and 价格 'price'. Finally, the HowNet similarity produces the worst results. This may be due to the poor coverage of the HowNet lexicon to domain-specific features in online product reviews. In addition, the results for different similarity measurements also provide us with a good suggestion for choosing suitable interpolation coefficients.

Table 3. Results for separate similarity

Methods	Car		Mobilephone	
	P	**E**	**P**	**E**
LS_{ED}	0.690	1.557	0.727	1.137
LS_{JC}	**0.750**	**1.218**	**0.763**	**0.945**
SS_{HN}	0.245	3.137	0.302	2.626
SS_{WE}	0.310	2.777	0.547	1.164
CS_{CE}	0.301	2.674	0.359	2.244
CS_{EE}	0.335	2.661	0.388	2.220

(2) Results for Multilevel Similarity.

Our second experiment is to examine the effectiveness of multilevel similarity for feature clustering. In particular, we consider four kinds of similarity combinations, namely $LS_{JC} + SS_{WE}$, $LS_{JC} + CS_{EE}$, $SS_{WE} + CS_{EE}$ and $LS_{JC} + SS_{WE} + CS_{EE}$.

It should be noted that multilevel similarity measurements are combined via linear interpolation. Considering the effectiveness of literal similarity in feature clustering and the normalization of probability distribution as well, we employ the following two heuristic rules to determine the interpolation coefficients: (1) $\alpha + \beta + \gamma = 1$; and (2) $\alpha \geq \beta \geq \gamma$. Here, we explored Hill-Climbing algorithm (Skalak 1994) to search the optimal coefficient iteratively. Thus, we set α, β and γ to be 0.62, 0.24 and 0.14, respectively, after iterate optimization.

Table 4 presents the results for multilevel similarities. It can be seen that the multi-similarities fusion technique with all three layers of measurements yield the best results. By comparing Tables 2 and 3, our system consistently outperforms all the baseline systems in two product reviews. The result proved that the fusion of multilevel similarity can access semantic information of features roundly and indicated in a sense the effectiveness of our approach (Table 4).

Table 4. Results for separate similarity

Methods	Car		Mobilephone	
	P	E	P	E
$LS_{JC} + SS_{WE}$	0.66	1.555	0.723	0.981
$LS_{JC} + CS_{EE}$	0.655	1.453	0.719	1.086
$SS_{WE} + CS_{EE}$	0.325	2.742	0.475	1.835
$LS_{JC} + SS_{WE} + CS_{EE}$	**0.675**	**1.373**	**0.788**	**0.786**

6 Conclusions and Future Work

In this paper we have explored three layers of clues, namely literal connections, semantic similarity and explanatory evaluations, and further combine them in a hierarchical clustering algorithm for product feature expressions in online product reviews. Our experimental results demonstrate that combining different levels of clues is beneficial to feature clustering.

The encouraging results of the present study suggest several possibilities for future research. First, word embeddings has shown their great value in handling semantic similarity. However, we only employed log-linear models by Mikolov et al. (2013) to learn word embeddings. Future research might usefully extend the present method to explore systematically word embedding learning techniques to achieve more precise semantic similarity measures. Second, explanatory evaluations have proven to be informative clues for feature clustering. However, explanatory evaluation recognition is still at its earlier stage. So further exploration is still needed on explanatory evaluation recognition to acquire more desirable explanatory clues for feature grouping.

Acknowledgments. This study was supported by National Natural Science Foundation of China under Grant No. 61170148 and the Returned Scholar Foundation of Heilongjiang Province.

References

Bhagat, R., Hovy, E.: What is a paraphrase? Computat. Linguist. **39**(3), 463–472 (2013)

Carenini, G., Ng, R.T., Zwart, E.: Extracting knowledge from evaluative text. In: Proceedings of the 3rd International Conference on Knowledge Capture, pp. 11–18 (2005)

Guo, H., Zhu, H., Guo, Z., Zhang, X.X., Su, Z.: Product feature categorization with multilevel latent semantic association. In: Proceedings of CIKM 2009, pp. 1087–1096 (2009)

Kim, H.D., Castellanos, M.G., Hsu, M., Zhai, C.X., Dayal, U., Ghosh, R.: Ranking explanatory sentences for opinion summarization. In: Proceedings of SIGIR 2013, pp. 1069–1072 (2013)

Liu, V.: Sentiment analysis and subjectivity. In: Handbook of Natural Language Processing, vol. 2, pp. 627–666 (2010)

Mikolov, T., Chen, K., Corrado, G., Dean, J.: Efficient estimation of word representations in vector space. arXiv preprint arXiv:1301.3781 (2013a)

Mikolov, T., Sutskever, I., Chen, K., Corrado, G.S., Dean, J.: Distributed representations of words and phrases and their compositionality. In: Advances in Neural Information Processing Systems, pp. 3111–3119 (2013b)

Mikolov, T., Yih, W., Zweig, G.: Linguistic regularities in continuous space word representations. In: Proceedings of HLT-NAACL 2013, pp. 746–751 (2013c)

Pavlopoulos, J., Androutsopoulos, I.: Multi-granular aspect aggregation in aspect-based sentiment analysis. In: Proceedings of EACL 2014, pp. 78–87 (2014)

Zhai, Z., Liu, B., Xu, H., Jia, P.: Grouping product features using semi-supervised learning with soft-constraints. In: Proceedings of COLING 2010, pp. 1272–1280 (2010)

Zhai, Z., Liu, B., Xu, H., Jia, P.: Clustering product features for opinion mining. In: Proceedings of WSDM 2011, pp. 347–354 (2011)

Yang, Y., Ma, Y., Lin, H.: Clustering product features in opinion mining. J. Chin. Inf. Process. 26(3), 104–108 (2012)

He, Y., Pan, D., Fu, G.: Chinese explanatory opinionated sentence recognition based on auto-encoding features. Acta Scientiarum Naturalium Universitatis Pekinensis, 1–7 (2015)

Skalak, D.: Prototype and Feature Selection by Sampling and Random Mutation Hill Climbing Algorithm. In: Proceedings of ICML 1994, pp. 293–301 (1994)

Improving Link Prediction in Social Networks by User Comments and Sentiment Lexicon

Feng Liu[✉], Bingquan Liu, Chengjie Sun, Ming Liu, and Xiaolong Wang

School of Computer Science and Technology,
Harbin Institute of Technology, Harbin, China
{fengliu,liubq,cjsun,mliu,wangxl}@insun.hit.edu.cn

Abstract. In some online Social Network Services, users are allowed to label their relationship with others, which can be represented as links with signed values. The link prediction problem is to estimate the values of unknown links by the information from the social network. A lot of similarity based metrics and machine learning based methods are proposed. Most of these methods are based on the network topological and node states. In this paper, by considering the information from user comment and sentiment lexicon, our methods improved the performances of link prediction for both similarity based metrics and machine learning based methods.

Keywords: Link prediction · Social networks · Link network structure · User comments · Sentiment lexicon

1 Introduction

With the explosive growth of SNS(Social Network Services) websites, there are large scale data of social media. The mass data includes the interactions among social members, such as comments and links. The comment is always a short paragraph with only one or a few sentences, which are sent from one user to another. The link is usually a label with sign value that represent one user's certain kind of opinion to another, such as expressing support or oppose.

Taking social members as vertexes and links as directed edges, the link network can be modeled as graph. The classical link prediction, as shown in Fig. 1(a), is to predict the relation of one user toward another from the evidence provided by their relations with other members from the surrounding social network [10,15]. The survey [24] introduced that the state-of-art link prediction methods can be roughly divided into two classes: user similarity based metrics and machine learning based methods.

The user similarity based metrics are usually used for recommending tasks, such as co-authorship prediction problem [1,5,9], and friendship prediction problem [2,7,12]. Their metrics are mainly based on collaborative filtering of users and articles, or analyzing the topology of link network. showed The similarity based metrics is low computing cost and can predict top k recommendations

© Springer International Publishing Switzerland 2015
M. Sun et al. (Eds.): CCL and NLP-NABD 2015, LNAI 9427, pp. 356–365, 2015.
DOI: 10.1007/978-3-319-25816-4_29

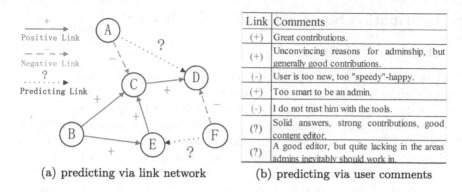

Link	Comments
(+)	Great contributions.
(+)	Unconvincing reasons for adminship, but generally good contributions.
(-)	User is too new, too "speedy"-happy.
(+)	Too smart to be an admin.
(-)	I do not trust him with the tools.
(?)	Solid answers, strong contributions, good content editor.
(?)	A good editor, but quite lacking in the areas admins inevitably should work in.

(a) predicting via link network   (b) predicting via user comments

Fig. 1. The link prediction problem.

with good performance [21]. But when the k value becomes large, its performance drops sharply.

The machine learning based methods treated the link prediction problem as a classification task. Logistic regression model is used to predict links' values based on features extracted from link network in [13]. Support vector machine is used to analyze how link network structure features effect link's values in [20]. Deep belief network based approaches for link prediction is introduced in [18,19]. These methods need the detail structure of link network to train a high performance model. As a result, in the condition that only a small part of the link network is observed, these methods would not works well. This problem is named as 'Cold Start'.

The sentiment analysis or opinion mining is the computational study of people's opinions, appraisals, attitudes, and emotions toward entities, individuals, issues, events, topics and their attributes [16,17]. Taking the 'link' as one user's opinion to another user, the link prediction task is some kind like the sentiment analysis or opinion mining task, as shown in Fig. 1(b). The whole document is modeled as a vector of words, and the support vector machine classifier is learned on word vectors to determine whether a review is positive or negative in [22]. The combination of lexical and syntactic features are used to predict the twitter's sentiment properly [4]. User comments are used in [25] to improve the performance of state theory introduced in [14]. It shows that the link prediction problem can also be solved by using user comments with opinion mining methods, which do not need to know the structure of link network.

The main contributions of this paper are summarized as following:

1. In order to improve the performance for similarity based metrics with large k value, we considered both the topology of link network and information from sentiment lexicon, and proposed the method SentiTNS;
2. To solve the cold start problem, we added features from user comments and sentiment lexicon when learning a model. The experiment results show that our method works well and the performance of link prediction is improved.

2   Information Sources for Link Prediction

2.1   Link Network Structure

The link network could be represented as a directed graph $G = (V, E)$, where V is the set of users and E is the set of edges. The edge directly linking from user u to v is denoted as $e(u, v)$, and the set containing all the paths from u to v is denoted as $Path(u, v)$. And denote $Ne(u)$ as the set of u's neighbour nodes and $CNe(u, v)$ as the common neighbours shared with u and v.

The topology information contains the shortest path $p(u, v)$ calculated from $Path(u, v)$. The node features include the in-degrees and out-degrees with sign values. Denote $d_{in}^+(u)$ for positive in-degree, $d_{in}^-(u)$ for negative in-degree, $d_{out}^+(u)$ for positive out-degrees and $d_{out}^-(u)$ for negative out-degrees. There are totally 8 kinds of node features from node u and v.

The neighbour features includes statistical information from $CNe(u, v)$, such as $c_{Ne}^N(u, v)$ is the number of nodes w in $CNe(u, v)$ and $c_{Ne}^E(u, v)$ is the number of edges between w and u, v. Then select any node w from $CNe(u, v)$, whose edges could have any direction with any sign value connected with u and v, denote $c(u_-^+ w_-^+ v)$ as the number of nodes who get positive links from both u and v. There are 2 directions and 2 kinds of sign values, so the relationships of u, v and w can be divided into 16 kinds. There are totally 18 kinds of neighbour features from node u and v.

2.2   User Comments and Sentiment Lexicon

The text, such as comment, could be represented by the Bag of Words model(BOW). It treats each comment as the bag of its words, and represents text as a vector of words via the word dictionary. The word dictionary Dic contains all the appeared words, and the dictionary size is $lenDic$. The set of words appeared in comment from u to v is denoted as $W(u, v)$. Then build a word vector $w(u, v)$ with dimension $lenDic$, and set the ith position to '1' if the Dic 's ith $word \in W(u, v)$, while all other positions are set to '0'.

Sentiment lexicon is a kind of dictionary that contains sentiment scores for words. The scores reflects the degrees of positivity, negativity, or neutrality for the sentiment or opinion which held by words. We extend $w(u, v)$ with sentiment scores. We build a sentiment vector $senti(u, v)$ with dimension $2 \times lenDic$. If the ith position w_i is '1' in $w(u, v)$, we set $senti(u, v)$'s ith position to the w_i's positive sentiment score and set its $(lenDic + ith)$ position to the w_i's negative sentiment score. So $senti(u, v) = (s_1, ... s_{lenDic}, s_{lenDic+1}, ... s_{2 \times lenDic})$. It maybe that not all words in Dic appear in the sentiment lexicon, and we use '0' as their sentiment scores.

The details of how to get user dictionary words' positive and negative polarity scores is shown in Algorithm 1. The example uses the sentiment lexicon Senti-WordNet, which is based on WordNet. The synset is basic unit in WordNet, so SentiWordNet is also structured by $SynsetTerms$. One word can belongs to many synsets, and each synset has its own positive polarity score and negative polarity score. We use the average score of all synsets, named as $SynsetTerms$ in SentiWordNet, that a word belongs to as the word's scores.

Input: User word dictionary $WordList$; Sentiment lexicon $SentiWordNet$
Output: Scores of words' positive polarity $PosScoreList$; Scores of words'
         negative polarity $NegScoreList$

for *each record in SentiWordNet* **do**
    for *each word in record.SynsetTerms* **do**
        if *(wordIndex = wordList.index(tempWord))* **then**
            $PosScoreList[wordIndex]$ += $record.PosScore$;
            $NegScoreList[wordIndex]$ += $record.NegScore$;
            $WordSynsetCount[wordIndex]$ += 1;
        end
    end
end
for *i in range (0,len(WordList))* **do**
    if *(WordSynsetCount[wordIndex] != 0)* **then**
        $PosScoreList[i] = PosScoreList[i]/WordSynsetCount[wordIndex]$;
        $NegScoreList[i] = NegScoreList[i]/WordSynsetCount[wordIndex]$;
    end
end

Algorithm 1: Processing sentiment lexicon

---

3 Improving Similarity Based Metrics

3.1 SentiSUB

In some conditions, it is difficult to get the structure of link network, even none link could be observed. The similarity based metrics based on link network structure become unavailable at that time. In order to estimate a link's value in such condition, we design a naive method, SentiSUB by calculating the sentiment polarity of the link starting user's comment as:

$$SentiSUB(u,v) = \sum_{i=1}^{l} s_i - \sum_{j=l+1}^{2\times l} s_j \tag{1}$$

where $l = lenDic$ and $s_i \in senti(u,v)$ as defined in Sect. 2.2.

3.2 SentiTNS

In the condition that the link network structure is observable, the similarity based metrics become available. We also improve its metric by taking the sentiment of comment into account. [23] introduced FriendTNS which takes both positive and negative links into account when calculating user similarity.

The FriendTNS is based on transitive node similarity, which calculates the similarity of two indirectly connected users by using their shortest path, $p(u, v) = (u, w_2, ..., w_i, ..., w_{l-1}, v)$. The $FriendTNS(u, v)$ is calculated as:

$$FriendTNS(u, v) = \begin{cases} 0 & \text{disconnected} \\ sim(u, v) & \text{neighbors} \\ \prod_{i=1}^{l-1} sim(w_i, w_{i+1}) & \text{otherwise} \end{cases} \quad (2)$$

and

$$sim(u, v) = \frac{1}{\partial(u) + \partial(v) - 1} \quad (3)$$

where $\partial(u) = d_{in}^+(u) + d_{out}^-(u) - d_{out}^+(u) - d_{in}^-(u)$ is defined by the state theory introduced by [14].

We propose the method SentiTNS that considers both kinds of information from link network structure and user comments sentiment. We extent the node's link degrees $d_{out}^+(u), d_{in}^+(u), d_{out}^-(u), d_{in}^-(u)$ to sentiment degrees as:

$$\begin{aligned} sd_{(out)}^+(u) &= \sum_v \sum_{i=1}^l s_i & (v : v \text{ belongs to } Ne(u)) \\ sd_{(in)}^+(u) &= \sum_u \sum_{i=1}^l s_i & (u : u \text{ belongs to } Ne(v)) \\ sd_{(out)}^-(u) &= \sum_v \sum_{i=l+1}^{2 \times l} s_i & (v : v \text{ belongs to } Ne(u)) \\ sd_{(in)}^-(u) &= \sum_u \sum_{i=l+1}^{2 \times l} s_i & (u : u \text{ belongs to } Ne(v)) \end{aligned} \quad (4)$$

where $l = lenDic$ and $s_i \in senti(u, v)$.

The state theory assumes that one node's link degrees can reflect the node social state in that social network, and its metric works well. Depending on similar assumption, we assume that the node's sentiment degrees could reflects the node 'sentiment state' in the network. Then we extent SentiSUB by changing the Eq. (3) as:

$$sentiment\_sim(u, v) = \partial(u) - \partial(v) \quad (5)$$

where $\partial(u) = sd_{in}^+(u) + sd_{out}^-(u) - sd_{out}^+(u) - sd_{in}^-(u)$ calculated by Eq. (4).

Then we could calculate the user similarity $SentiTNS(u, v)$ by Eq. (2) with $sentiment\_sim(u, v)$, and make recommendation by the rank of similarities between users.

4   Improving Machine Learning Based Methods

The machine learning based methods for link prediction are mainly based on training a statistics model over the link network structure features. There are two directions to improve them, one is using more powerful models, the other is taking more features into account. More powerful models could improve the performance over the original feature set, but it is not so suitable for solving the cold start problem. That is because in the condition of cold start, when most part of the link network is unobservable, the representation ability of link structure features becomes weak.

From above analysis, taking more features into account could be an effective method for cold start problem. We added the word vector and sentiment vector as features for training a model. As some other sentiment classification and opinion mining methods, the model Support Vector based Classifier(SVC) is used [6, 22]. For testing the effectiveness of word vector and sentiment vector, we learned models over each source of features individually and tried all possible combinations.

5 Experiments and Analysis

5.1 Experiments Setup

In our experiments, the social media data of Wikipedia RfA [25] is used. Before build the comment word vector, we removed all the words such as 'support', 'supporting', 'supported' and similar words for 'oppose'.

As a sentiment lexicon is needed for our method, the SENTIWORDNET 3.0 [3] is used. When calculate the prior polarities for words, we used similar method $mean_m$ introduced in [11]. It calculates the mean of the positive and negative scores for all the senses over synsets, so the part of speech tagging is not needed.

We extracted features and implemented the similarity based metrics by programming in Python, and the toolkit 'LIBLINEAR'[8] is used for learning SVC. In experiments of machine learning based methods, we balanced the data by randomly dropping positive links to avoid the samples imbalance effects, and totally 79660 balanced samples is used. The 5 fold cross-validation is performed to avoid the performance metric variance caused by sample distribution.

5.2 Similarity Based Metrics

The experiment results of similarity based metrics is shown in Fig. 2. We recommend top k links as positive and bottom k links as negative for a user at the same time. If a user does not have more than k positive or negative links, the k value is set to the number of how many links does that user has. We use FriendTNS, inteoduced in [23], as the baseline method. All metrics perform well with small k values, and their accuracies drop when k becomes larger. That is because when k becomes large, the difference between positive link similarity and negative link similarity becomes little, and the metric makes wrong recommendation.

When k is less than 10, the performance of SentiSUB is best. It shows that comments with strong sentiment polarity could represent the link's value properly. When the value of k becomes larger than 20, SentiTNS performs better than the other two. Even when k = 500, nearly all links are recommended as positive or negative, SentiTNS still has accuracy over 65 %. It means the sentiment state

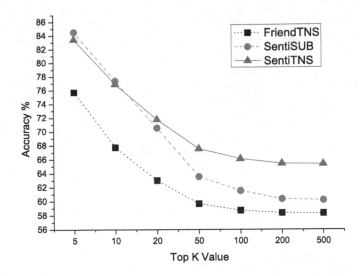

Fig. 2. Similarity based metrics

theory is suitable for recommending most links in the network. FriendTNS also has good performance when k is little, and it only uses the information from link network.

5.3   Machine Learning Based Methods

The experiment results of machine learning based metrics is shown in Fig. 3. 'LNS' is link network structure feature, 'BOW' is comment word feature, and 'SEN' is the sentiment score feature. The '+' means using the two sources of features together, and 'All' is using all the three sources of features. The X axis is the observed scale of link network by randomly lost none, 10%, and up to 90% links in the network when collecting LNS.

The performance of model learned over LNS drops with the decrease of observed scale. This phenomenon is caused by the cold start problem. The performances of models learned over BOW, SEN and BOW+SEN are 3 parallel lines with X axis, Because they do not effect by the link network structure. When add other features with LNS, the curves do not drop fast with the observed scale. It means that the cold start problem could be solved properly by this method. We get the best accuracy with model learned over all features. It means that the performance of link prediction is improved than only using LNS.

The cure of BOW+SEN is nearly the same as BOW, and cure of ALL(LNS+BOW+SEN) is nearly the same as LNS+BOW. And the curve of LNS+SEN shakes the most over all curves. It shows that the sentiment vector features are not so suitable for combination with other features, when training a SVC.

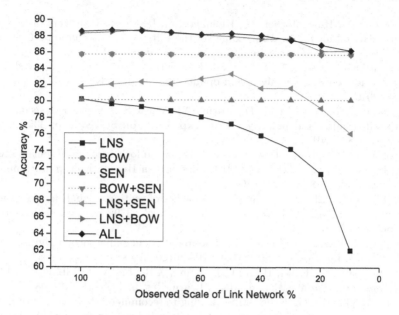

Fig. 3. Machine learning based methods

6 Conclusion

In this paper, by taking information from user comment and sentiment lexicon into account, methods for link prediction based on similarity metrics and machine learning models are proposed. The method SentiTNS considers both the topology of link network and user comment's sentiment polarity, and it has good performance for recommending links with large top k value. The feature combination method can solve the cold start problem properly and it also improves the link prediction performance in conditions that most part of the link network is observable.

Acknowledgement. This work is supported by the National Natural Science Foundation of China (61272383 and 61300114), Specialized Research Fund for the Doctoral Program of Higher Education (No. 20132302120047), the Special Financial Grant from the China Postdoctoral Science Foundation (No. 2014T70340), China Postdoctoral Science Foundation (No. 2013M530156), and Natural Science Foundation of Heilongjiang Province(F201132).

References

1. Hasan, Al: M., Chaoji, V., Salem, S., Zaki, M.: Link prediction using supervised learning. In: SDM 2006: Workshop on Link Analysis. Counter-terrorism and Security, pp. 1–10. SIAM, Philadelphia, PA, USA (2006)

2. Anderson, A., Huttenlocher, D., Kleinberg, J., Leskovec, J.: Effects of user similarity in social media. In: Proceedings of the Fifth ACM International Conference on Web Search and Data Mining, pp. 703–712. ACM (2012)
3. Baccianella, S., Esuli, A., Sebastiani, F.: Sentiwordnet 3.0: an enhanced lexical resource for sentiment analysis and opinion mining. In: LREC, vol. 10, pp. 2200–2204 (2010)
4. Becker, L., Erhart, G., Skiba, D., Matula, V.: Avaya: Sentiment analysis on twitter with self-training and polarity lexicon expansion. In: SemEval, p. 333, Atlanta, Georgia, USA (2013)
5. Brzozowski, M.J., Hogg, T., Szabo, G.: Friends and foes: ideological social networking. In: Proceedings of the SIGCHI Conference on Human Factors in Computing Systems, pp. 817–820. ACM (2008)
6. Chalothom, T., Ellman, J.: Simple approaches of sentiment analysis via ensemble learning. In: Kim, K.J. (ed.) ISA. LNEE, vol. 339, pp. 631–639. Springer, Heidelberg (2015)
7. Chelmis, C., Prasanna, V.K.: Social link prediction in online social tagging systems. ACM Trans. Inf. Syst. (TOIS) 31(4), 20–46 (2013)
8. Fan, R.E., Chang, K.W., Hsieh, C.J., Wang, X.R., Lin, C.J.: Liblinear: a library for large linear classification. J. Mach. Learn. Res. 9, 1871–1874 (2008)
9. Freno, A., Garriga, G., Keller, M.: Learning to recommend links using graph structure and node content. In: Neural Information Processing Systems Workshop on Choice Models and Preference Learning, NIPS, pp. 1–7 (2011)
10. Getoor, L., Diehl, C.P.: Link mining: a survey. ACM SIGKDD Explor. Newsl. 7(2), 3–12 (2005)
11. Guerini, M., Gatti, L., Turchi, M.: Sentiment analysis: how to derive prior polarities from sentiwordnet. In: Proceedings of the Conference on Empirical Methods in Natural Language Processing, pp. 1259–1269. Association for Computational Linguistics (2013)
12. Kunegis, J., Lommatzsch, A., Bauckhage, C.: The slashdot zoo: mining a social network with negative edges. In: Proceedings of the 18th International Conference on World Wide Web, pp. 741–750. ACM (2009)
13. Leskovec, J., Huttenlocher, D., Kleinberg, J.: Predicting positive and negative links in online social networks. In: Proceedings of the 19th International Conference on World Wide Web, pp. 641–650. ACM (2010)
14. Leskovec, J., Huttenlocher, D., Kleinberg, J.: Signed networks in social media. In: Proceedings of the SIGCHI Conference on Human Factors in Computing Systems, pp. 1361–1370. ACM (2010)
15. Liben-Nowell, D., Kleinberg, J.: The link-prediction problem for social networks. J. Am. Soc. Inf. Sci. Technol. 58(7), 1019–1031 (2007)
16. Liu, B.: Sentiment analysis and subjectivity. Handb. Nat. Lang. Process. 2, 627–666 (2010)
17. Liu, B., Zhang, L.: A survey of opinion mining and sentiment analysis. In: Aggarwal, C.C., Zhai, C.X. (eds.) Mining Text Data, pp. 415–463. Springer, New York (2012)
18. Liu, F., Liu, B., Sun, C., Liu, M., Wang, X.: Deep learning approaches for link prediction in social network services. In: Lee, M., Hirose, A., Hou, Z.-G., Kil, R.M. (eds.) ICONIP 2013, Part II. LNCS, vol. 8227, pp. 425–432. Springer, Heidelberg (2013)
19. Liu, F., Liu, B., Sun, C., Liu, M., Wang, X.: Deep belief network-based approaches for link prediction in signed social networks. Entropy 17(4), 2140–2169 (2015)

20. Liu, F., Liu, B., Wang, X., Liu, M., Wang, B.: Features for link prediction in social networks: a comprehensive study. In: 2012 IEEE International Conference on. Systems, Man, and Cybernetics (SMC), pp. 1706–1711. IEEE (2012)
21. Lü, L., Zhou, T.: Link prediction in complex networks: a survey. Phys. A: Stat. Mech. Appl. **390**(6), 1150–1170 (2011)
22. Pang, B., Lee, L.: Seeing stars: Exploiting class relationships for sentiment categorization with respect to rating scales. In: Proceedings of the 43rd Annual Meeting on Association for Computational Linguistics. pp. 115–124. Association for Computational Linguistics (2005)
23. Symeonidis, P., Tiakas, E.: Transitive node similarity: predicting and recommending links in signed social networks. World Wide Web **17**(4), 743–776 (2014)
24. Wang, P., Xu, B., Wu, Y., Zhou, X.: Link prediction in social networks: the state-of-the-art. Sci. China Inf. Sci. **58**, 1–38 (2014)
25. West, R., Paskov, S.H., Leskovec, J., Potts, C.: Exploiting social network structure for person-to-person sentiment analysis. Trans. Assoc. Comput. Linguist. **2**(1), 297–310 (2014). http://aclweb.org/anthology/Q14-1024

NLP Applications

Finite-to-Infinite N-Best POMDP for Spoken Dialogue Management

Guohua Wu$^{(\boxtimes)}$, Caixia Yuan, Bing Leng, and Xiaojie Wang

School of Computer,
Beijing University of Posts and Telecommunications, Beijing, China
{wugh,yuancx,lb19900314,xjwang}@bupt.edu.cn

Abstract. Partially Observable Markov Decision Process (POMDP) has been widely used as dialogue management in slot-filling Spoken Dialogue System (SDS). But there are still lots of open problems. The contribution of this paper lies in two aspects. Firstly, the observation probability of POMDP is estimated from the N-Best list of Automatic Speech Recognition (ASR) rather than the top one. This modification gives SDS a chance to address the uncertainty of ASR. Secondly, a dynamic binding technique is proposed for slots with infinite values so as to deal with uncertainty of talking object. The proposed methods have been implemented on a teach-and-learn spoken dialogue system. Experimental results show that performance of system improves significantly by introducing the proposed methods.

Keywords: Partially Observable Markov Decision Process (POMDP) · Spoken Dialogue System (SDS) · Dynamic binding · N-best

1 Introduction

Spoken dialogue system (SDS) is to provide an interface for human to access and manage information. Since the 1990s, many SDSs have been developed. For example, flight reservation system (Mercury) [8], weather information system (JUPITER) [14]. More recently developed systems are used as virtual assistants. For example, SDS for interactive search (PARLANCE) [2], Apple's intelligent personal assistant and knowledge navigator (Siri) and in-car voice assistant of Nuance (Dragon Drive).

Among all these dialogue systems, there is a kind of dialogue systems designed for retrieving specific important information. For instance, flight reservation system is such kind of dialogue system whose objective is to obtain all the information essential for flight-ticket ordering such as date, flight number and destination. Generally such kind of essential information is called slot and such kind of dialogue system is known as slots-filling based dialogue system.

Generally spoken dialog systems have a common logical architecture of three modules: spoken language understanding (SLU), dialogue management (DM) and natural language generation (NLG). Of all three modules, dialogue management is the core module, which controls the dialog flow.

© Springer International Publishing Switzerland 2015
M. Sun et al. (Eds.): CCL and NLP-NABD 2015, LNAI 9427, pp. 369–380, 2015.
DOI: 10.1007/978-3-319-25816-4_30

According to the method employed, DMs can be divided into finite state-based, frame-based, agent-based and statistical based. In finite state-based DMs [3,7], the user is taken through a dialogue consisting of a sequence of predetermined steps or states. This approach is suitable for well-structured tasks, but it can't deal with the uncertainty introduced by SLU. In frame-based DMs [3,7], user can communicate with dialogue system in a more flexible way and uncertainty introduced by SLU can be disposed to some extent at the cost of more elaborate control in algorithm. In agent-based DMs [3,7], communication is viewed as interaction between two agents, each of which is capable of reasoning about its own actions and beliefs, and sometimes also about the actions and beliefs of the other agent. Construction of such system requires lots of expert knowledge. Statistical DMs describe a dialogue as a probability decision procedure of which POMDP [4,9] is one of the most representative models. POMDP-based DMs [6,10–13] model dialogue as a decision procedure under uncertainty due to errors in speech recognition and SLU. Parameters and policy of POMDP-based DMs is estimated from data. Thus, it can reduce the development cycle and improve domain portability.

POMDP-based DMs suffer from two principal problems. On the one hand, due to errors of speech recognition and semantic understanding, the observation attained by dialogue management is unreliable. Thus, how we estimate probability distribution of observation in POMDP will severely affect POMDP's performance. Williams et al. [10,11] proposed SDS-POMDP model factorized hidden state of dialog into three quantities, which include user's goal, user action and dialogue history. However, SDS-POMDP doesn't make use of the entire N-Best output of the automatic speech recognition (ASR).

On the other hand, POMDP-based DMs have the limitation that the number of slot value should be finite. For example, it can be applied to the ticket-ordering task where the possible values for date, flight number and destination are all finite. However, many tasks in real world can't meet this limitation. Taking the teach-and-learn task for example, even if objects mentioned in this task have fix-sized slots, the possible values of slots are infinite because of infinity of objects.

In this paper, we propose dynamic object binding method which can be applied to tasks whose fixed-size slots have infinite possible values. In addition, a method to estimate observation probability of POMDP by making use of entire N-Best list of ASR is presented. We conduct a series of experiments on a teach-and-learn dialogue system. Results of experiments indicate that the proposed model can help dialogue system accomplish teach-and-learn tasks with infinite objects with better performance.

The paper is organized as follows. In Sect. 2, we discuss how to make use of N-Best list of ASR to improve POMDP's observation function and propose a dynamic object binding method to solve certain case of infinite slot values problem. Furthermore, we introduce our improved POMDP-based DM model with its algorithm based on improvements mentioned above. Section 3 presents experimental setup and results. Section 4 concludes.

2   Model

The proposed model is based on SDS-POMDP, thus, we will first introduce original POMDP model and its application in DM known as SDS-POMDP model before introducing our model.

2.1   SDS-POMDP Model

A POMDP can be formally defined as a tuple $\{S, A, T, R, O, Z\}$. S is a set of world states. A is a set of actions the agent may take. T is a state transfer function $P(s'|s, a)$, which indicates the probability that the agent takes action a in state s the world ends in state s'. R is a reward function $R(s, a) \in \mathbb{R}$, which is the reward that the agent obtains when it takes action a in state s. O is a set of observation the agent may obtain from outer world. Z is an observation function $P(o'|s', a)$ which indicates the probability of obtaining observation o when the agent takes action a and lands in state s'.

The POMDP operates as follows. At each time-step, the world is at some state $s \in S$. Since s is not known exactly, the agent is maintaining a belief state b which is a distribution over states, with initial belief state b_0. $b(s)$ indicates the probability of being in a particular state s. Based on b and POMDP policy π (policy indicates a map from belief state space to action space $\pi(b) \in A$), the agent selects an action a, receives a reward $R(s, a)$, and makes the world transmit to state s'. The agent then receives an observation o' depending on s' and a, and updates its belief state b as follows:

$$b'(s') = p(s'|o', a, b) = \frac{p(o'|s', a, b)p(s'|a, b)}{p(o'|a, b)} = k \cdot p(o'|s', a) \sum_{s \in S} p(s'|a, s)b(s) \quad (1)$$

Williams et al. [10,11] cast spoken dialog as a POMDP. The system's dialogue act is formulated as the POMDP's action a and the output of ASR/SLU is regarded as POMDP observation o. Hidden state of dialogue is referred to information that system can't observe directly and can be cast as hidden POMDP state s. In the SDS-POMDP model, the hidden state contains three quantities $s = (s_u, a_u, s_d)$. s_u indicates user's long-term goal in dialogue. a_u indicates true, unobserved user action. s_d indicates history of dialogue which records aspects of hidden state which the dialog designer considers important.

We substitute $s = (s_u, a_u, s_d)$ into the POMDP belief update in Eq. (1) and make some reasonable independence assumptions in [11], the SDS-POMDP belief update equation becomes

$$b'(s'_u, s'_d, a'_u) = k \cdot \underbrace{p(o'|a'_u)}_{\text{observation model}} \cdot \underbrace{p(a'_u|s'_u, a_m)}_{\text{user action model}} \cdot \underbrace{\sum_{s_u \in S_u} p(s'_u|s_u, a_m)}_{\text{user goal model}}$$

$$\cdot \underbrace{\sum_{s_d \in S_d} p(s'_d|a'_u, s'_u, s_d, a_m)}_{\text{dialog history model}} \cdot \sum_{a_u \in A_u} b(s_u, s_d, a_u) \quad (2)$$

Equation (2) can be composited into observation model, user action model, user goal model and dialog history model.

2.2   The Improved SDS-POMDP Model

In this section, we will describe our improvement to SDS-POMDP. The improved model is superior to SDS-POMDP in two aspects. First, the observation probability of POMDP is estimated from entire N-Best list of ASR rather than the top one. Secondly, the improved model can be applied to slots with infinite values so as to deal with uncertainty of object. In the following sections, we will first discuss these two improvements and then outline a principled framework for model solution.

Observation Model Based on ASR N-Best List. Considering that 1-best output of speech recognition isn't accurate enough, N-Best result of ASR is employed by DM instead. In this way, DM obtains more information with which it can guide the dialogue in a more appropriate direction when 1-best result of speech recognition is inaccurate. This method is somewhat similar to the way people make ambiguous information explicit as dialogue proceeds.

Assume that the N-Best list of ASR is:

$$[< hyp_1, conf_1 >, < hyp_2, conf_2 >, \cdots, < hyp_N, conf_N >]$$

where hyp_i is i^{th} entry of N-Best list and $conf_i$ is corresponding confidence. A probability distribution over possible user actions is generated by SLU as follows:

$$[< \tilde{a}_u^1, p_1 >, < \tilde{a}_u^2, p_2 >, \ldots, < \tilde{a}_u^M, p_M >]$$

where $p_m = P(a_u = \tilde{a}_u^m | hyp_i)$. Every one of these probabilities corresponds to a certain entry in N-Best list. The weighted sum of these N probability distributions is calculated according to corresponding confidence:

$$P(a_u = \tilde{a}_u^m | o) = \sum_{i \in N} P(a_u = \tilde{a}_u^m | hyp_i) \cdot conf_i$$

After normalization of the sum of N distributions, observation of DM is finally obtained:

$$o = \left[< \tilde{a}_u^1, p_1 >, < \tilde{a}_u^2, p_2 >, \ldots, < \tilde{a}_u^M, p_M > \right] \tag{3}$$

Here p_i is $P(a_u = \tilde{a}_u^i | o)$, but it's $P(o|a_u)$ required in belief update Eq. (2). Thus, probability provided in this list can't be applied to updating the belief state directly. A transformation based on Bayes' rule is applied to these to probabilities [10] as follows:

$$P(o|a_u) = \frac{P(a_u|o)P(o)}{P(a_u)} = k_1 \cdot \frac{P(a_u|o)}{P(a_u)} \approx k_2 \cdot P(a_u|o) \tag{4}$$

During belief update, $P(o)$ is constant, which means it can be absorbed into the normalization constant k_1. In addition, we assume $P(a_u)$ is uniform over all user actions, which make it can also be absorbed into the normalization constant k_2 in (4).

Dynamic Object Binding. In slot-filling tasks based on SDS-POMDP, set of user goals S_u is Cartesian product of all slots, which needs to be defined in advance. Supposing that we need to fill N slots in a dialogue, $SLOT = \{slot_1, slot_2, \ldots, slot_n\}$ represents the finite set of slots, where the set of value for $slot_i$ is $V_i = \{v_{i,1}, v_{i,2}, \ldots, v_{i,n_i}\}$,which is a finite set for $i = 1, 2, \cdots n$. In the case mentioned above, S_u is a finite set, thus this dialogue can be well modeled by SDS-POMDP. However, SDS-POMDP can't be employed to tasks where $SLOT$ or any V_i is infinite. Therefore, some improvement is made to SDS-POMDP to extend it to tasks where $SLOT$ is finite and value set of V_j is infinite for some exact j. A typical example for this situation is the teach-and-learn task. For instance, in a dialogue concerning teach-and-learn , our goal is to teach the robot some object's class, color and shape. At this point, the goal of our task is to fill four slots of what (object), class, color and shape. We can assume that slots of class, color and shape are with finite possible values. For example, the slot of class may take four possible values from fruit, vegetable, meat and other. However, slot of what may have infinite values because the goal of the task is to teach these three attributes of any object to robot. What deserves attention is that here we can't avoid the demand for listing all the objects even if we have a simple assumption that slots have a value of other, because it's ridiculous that an object known as "other" appears in dialogue with attributes of class, color and shape. However, it's reasonable to assign value of "other" to the other slots, such as the class of the desk is "other".

First of all, a generalized assumption is made that if j^{th} slot with infinite values is given a certain value, values of other slots can be obtained with a similar POMDP policy. Take the teach-and-learn task for example. If slot of "what" has been obtained, system may obtain values for other three slots using a similar policy. In this way, system can learn other three slots for different teaching objects like apple, watermelon, tomato, basketball or pencil-box. Let set of values for slots with infinite values be $V_j = \{target, other\}$. Here $target$ is a variable to be bind to some value during dialogue when values of other slots remain unchanged. Take the Cartesian product of all possible values of four attributes, we'll get the whole user goal space.

Secondly, when the DM finds out user's current action is to tell system the value of V_j in a dialogue, system needs to confirm value of V_j extracted from ASR results with user. After value of V_j is confirmed, we bind this value to variable $target$. Then an observation is constructed to update belief state. The rest of slots are obtained completely by similar POMDP policy.

We take the teach-and-learn task as an example to explain dynamic object binding. System performs language understanding when user inputs an utterance, which includes intention recognition and slot value extraction. Intention recognition is the process of being aware of the intentions of user. In the teach-and-learn task, intentions of user include teaching slot of what, slot of class, slot of color, slot of shape and other (refer to them as *teach-what, teach-class, teach-color, teach-shape* and *other*). Slot value extraction is the process of extracting teaching object, class, color and shape. For example, when user inputs

"这是一个柿子 (this is a persimmon.)"", this utterance is processed by intention recognition and a distribution over intentions is obtained as follows:

$$[< teach\text{-}what, 0.74 >, < teach\text{-}class, 0.12 >, \ldots, < other, 0.01 >]$$

From the distribution above, we can find out user's current action is to tell system the value of what, and system will extract slot values from user's utterance. In this example, slot value extraction gives the value of what is "柿子 (persimmon)". Due to current value of *target* is empty, the probability of *teach-what* will be assigned to *teach-what-other*, we finally get the observation for DM:

$$o = [< teach\text{-}what\text{-}other, 0.74 >, < teach\text{-}what\text{-}target, 0.00 >, \ldots, < other, 0.01 >]$$

Because *target* is empty, DM will confirm "柿子 (persimmon)" as value of "what" with user. After value of what is confirmed by user, we bind this value to variable *target*, and then an observation is constructed to update belief state:

$$o = [< teach\text{-}what\text{-}target, 0.9 >, < teach\text{-}what\text{-}other, 0.01 >, \cdots, < other, 0.01 >] \qquad (5)$$

The rest of three slots is obtained completely by POMDP policy.

Algorithm. In Algorithm 1, we give out algorithm for the improved SDS-POMDP, which is consistent to algorithm for SDS-POMDP. First, we need to initialize the belief state. Then system figures out what action should take at present according to POMDP policy π. After that, DM obtains observation from SLU. At last, dialogue system updates belief state according to current belief state and observation, and figures out what action should be taken in next round. Dialogue system will be executing above procedures until it takes the *submit* action.

Our modification to observation model is mainly reflected in line 6 and line 17 to 20. Line 6 mainly reflects how we get observation probability according to (3). Line 17 to 20 is mainly about how to update belief state using observation probability according to (2).

The procedure of dynamic binding is shown between lines 7 to 16. When POMDP-based DM observes *teach-what-other* with the highest probability in all the user actions, it'll extract the object that user's talking about and bind this object's name to the *target* variable. At the same time, POMDP will confirm whether the object user talking about in this round is exactly the value of target variable. If user gives the answer of yes, algorithm will construct observation in (5) and use it to update belief state. Or algorithm will empty variable of *target* and go into the next round without updating belief state.

Combining these two improvements, our algorithm for the improved SDS-POMDP is obtained. The improved model can make full use of information of N-Best list of ASR to produce more accurate belief state updates, and expands the application range of SDS-POMDP to situation where *SLOT* is finite and value set of V_j is infinite for some exact j.

Algorithm 1. Algorithm for the improved SDS-POMDP

Require: Solving POMDP to find policy π

1: *Initialize belief state b*
2: *target $\leftarrow$ None*   ▷ Doesn't know what slot currently
3: $a \leftarrow \pi(b)$
4: **while** $a \neq$ *submit* **do**
5:     *Execute action a*
6:     *Observe $o' \leftarrow [< \tilde{a}_u^1, p_1 >, < \tilde{a}_u^2, p_2 >, \cdots, < \tilde{a}_u^M, p_M >]$*
             where $p_m = P(a_u = \tilde{a}_u^m | o')$ and $p_1 \geq p_2 \cdots \geq p_M$
             from SLU module
7:     **if** $(\tilde{a}_u^1 = teach\text{-}what\text{-}other)$ *and* $(target = None)$ **then**
8:         ▷ Bind object
9:         *target $\leftarrow$ teaching object extracted from user utterance*
10:        *result $\leftarrow$ confirm target value with user*
11:        **if** *result $= yes$* **then**   ▷ Positive confirm
12:            $o' \quad \leftarrow \quad [< \quad$ teach-what-target$, 0.9 \quad >, <$
                 teach-what-other$, 0.01 >, \cdots, <$ other$, 0.01 >]$
13:        **else**
14:            *target $\leftarrow$ None*   ▷ Reset target to unknown
15:            *continue* ▷ Skip follow statements, jump to next loop
16:        **end if**
17:    **end if**
18:    **for all** (s'_u, s'_d, a'_u) in $S_u \times S_d \times A_u$ **do**   ▷ Belief update
19:        ▷ Adopt approximation $P(o|a_u) \approx k_2 \cdot P(a_u|o)$
20:        *Update $b'(s'_u, s'_d, a'_u)$ according to equation (2).*
21:    **end for**
22:    $b \leftarrow b'$
23:    $a \leftarrow \pi(b)$
24: **end while**

---

3   Experiments and Results

3.1   Experimental Setup

In this paper, a teach-and-learn dialogue system based on the improved model is implemented. Where the ASR and text to speech (TTS) are implemented by calling Google API, NLG is implemented by simple template filling. The SLU module consists of intention recognition based on Maximum Entropy Model and slot value extraction based on Conditional random field.

In experiments, user attempts to teach a robot some object's type, color and shape. As shown in Table 1, let set of objects be *WhatSet*, set of class be *ClassSet*, set of color be *ColorSet* and set of shape be *ShapeSet*. The user's goal is given as $s_u = (x, y, z, w)$, where $x \in$ *WhatSet*, $y \in$ *ClassSet*, $z \in$ *ColorSet* and $w \in$ *ShapeSet*. The total number of user goals $|S_u|$, which is size of Cartesian product of four sets shown in Table 1, is 128. And the initial distribution over user goals is uniform. The user's action a_u is drawn from the set *teach-what-x, teach-class-y,*

Table 1. Set of value for each slot

What collection	Class collection	Color collection	Shape collection
target	fruit	red	circular
	vegetable	green	square
other	stationery	yellow	triangle
	other	other	other

teach-color-z, teach-shape-w and *other*, where in all cases $x \in$ *WhatSet*, $y \in$ *ClassSet*, $z \in$ *ColorSet* and $w \in$ *ShapeSet*. The dialogue history $s_d = (x) : x \in \{0,1\}$ indicates whether the current turn is the first turn (1) or not (0). These state components yield a total of 3841 states with an absorbed state according to $s = (s_u, a_u, s_d)$. The POMDP agent has 134 actions available, including *greet*, *ask-what*, *ask-class*, *ask-color*, *submit-x-y-z-w* and *fail*, where in all cases $x \in$ *WhatSet*, $y \in$ *ClassSet*, $z \in$ *ColorSet* and $w \in$ *ShapeSet*.

It is assumed that the user's goal is fixed throughout the dialogue (i.e. $p(s'_u|s_u, a_m) = 1$ when $s'_u = s_u$). User action model indicates the probability of different responses user may take to some system's action under new user's goal. A portion of user action model is given in Table 2, the probabilities were handcrafted based on experience of slot-filling dialogue system. Probabilities in Table 2 describe the probability of every response user may take to different system's actions under the premise of that s'_u is *(targe,fruit,red,circular)*.

Table 2. Portion of user action model employed in experiments

a_m	s'_u	a'_u	$p(a'_u|s'_u, a_m)$
greet	*(targe,fruit,red,circular)*	*teach-what-target*	0.3
		teach-class-fruit	0.2
		teach-color-red	0.2
		teach-shape-circular	0.2
		other	0.2
ask-what	*(targe,fruit,red,circular)*	*teach-what-target*	0.6
		teach-class-fruit	0.15
		teach-color-red	0.09
		teach-shape-circular	0.09
		other	0.07

We define the observation function as

$$p(o'|s', a) = p(\tilde{a}'_u|a'_u) = \begin{cases} 1 - p_{err} & \text{if } \tilde{a}'_u = a'_u, \\ \frac{p_{err}}{|A_u|-1} & \text{if } \tilde{a}'_u \neq a'_u. \end{cases} \tag{6}$$

When solving POMDP policy we set p_{err} to 0.3. Observation received from SLU module will be utilized directly to update belief state in the improved SDS-POMDP when we are interacting with user.

Because of s_d contains only information about whether the current turn is the first turn (1) or not (0), the dialog history model $p(s'_d|a'_u, s'_u, s_d, a_m) = 1$ only when $s'_d = 0$ (i.e. next turn of dialogue must not be the first turn).

The reward measure reflects both task completion and dialog "appropriateness". The reward assigns -1 or -100 for taking the *greet* at beginning of the dialog or not, respectively; -10 for taking the *fail* action; $+20$ or -20 for taking the *submit-x-y-z-w* action when the user's goal is (x, y, z, w) or not, respectively; and -1 otherwise.

POMDP optimization was performed with an efficient point-based value iteration algorithm called *SARSOP* [5].

The MDP-based dialogue system is constructed to compare the improved SDS-POMDP in their ability to make decision under uncertainty of ASR/SLU. We define 81 MDP states as

$$S = \{what\text{-}class\text{-}color\text{-}shape, start, end\}, where$$
$$what \in \{u, o, c\}, class \in \{u, o, c\}, color \in \{u, o, c\}, shape \in \{u, o, c\} \quad (7)$$

The four components of *what-class-color-shape* refer to the *what* slot, *class* slot, *color* slot and *shape* slot respectively. u indicates unknown; o indicates observed but not confirmed; c indicates confirmed.

Action set of MDP-based DM is similar to that of POMDP-based DM. They both have *greet*, *ask-what*, *ask-class*, *ask-color*, *ask-shape* and *submit*. But dialogue system based on MDP needs four extra actions of *confirm-what*, *confirm-class*, *confirm-color* and *confirm-shape*. They are used to confirm teaching object, class of object, color of object and shape of object. In MDP, states are assumed to be observed completely. However, the value of attribute MDP obtains from SLU may be wrong, so every slot need to be confirmed with user once. Differently, POMDP uses observation function to model uncertainty of observation. When POMDP believe some slot is not certain enough, it will take the responding action of ask. For instance, when POMDP think color is not believable enough, it will continue taking action of *ask-color*. Thus, spoken dialogue system based on POMDP doesn't need action of confirm. The MDP is optimized using Q-Learning [1].

3.2   Results

In experiments, user will teach a robot four attributes of some objects includes object's name, class, color and shape. We have two measurements to evaluate our system. One is the length of dialogue denoted by D in which user has accomplished teaching an object. The other is Knowledge Acquisition Rate denoted by K, which is used to measure the level at which knowledge learned by system can meet user's requirement. The Knowledge Acquisition Rate is defined as

$$K = \frac{Number\ of\ slots\ obtained\ correctly}{Number\ of\ slots\ obtained} \quad (8)$$

Due to the characteristic of teaching task, we're paying more attention to knowledge acquisition rate. In the following experiments, three users are guided to teach these 12 groups of objects separately, and average knowledge acquisition rate $\bar{K}$ and average length of dialogue $\bar{D}$ are computed based on the data collected.

To evaluate whether the method of dynamic object binding can deal with uncertainty of teaching object, we have carried out a series of comparative experiments. Knowledge usability rate denoted by U is defined to show the necessity of introducing the method of dynamic object binding.

$$U = \frac{Number\ of\ objects\ whose\ all\ slots\ are\ taught\ correctly}{Number\ of\ objects\ obtained} \qquad (9)$$

Average of U is denoted by $\bar{U}$. For instance, when user teaches system cherry, robot learns that name of teaching object is *other*, that class is fruit, that color is red and that shape is circular. Although type, color and shape in this case are all learned correctly, knowledge obtained from this dialogue is still useless for teaching object is not obtained correctly. The result of our experiment is show in Table 3. The value of N for N-Best in our experiment is 5. We can see that adopting dynamic object binding method makes the length of dialogue increase by 2.67 rounds as well as knowledge acquisition increase to 0.993 from 0.75. System without dynamic object binding can only achieve a knowledge acquisition rate of 0.75 because it can't obtain the slot of teaching object. Moreover, knowledge usability rate of system without dynamic object binding is poorly 0, because none of objects is taught completely correctly. That is, knowledge obtained by that kind of system can't be assigned to an appropriate object, which means it's of little use. Thus, we come to the conclusion that dynamic object binding can deal with the problem of infinite teaching objects.

In Table 4, we give out how average knowledge acquisition rate and average length of dialogue change as N for N-best changes. As N increases, system's average knowledge acquisition rate increases and the length of dialogue decreases.

Table 3. The impact of adapting dynamic object binding

Dynamic object binding is employed?	$\bar{K}$	$\bar{D}$	$\bar{U}$
No	0.75	5.75	0.0
Yes	0.993	8.42	0.972

Table 4. System performance with different size of N-Best in noise environment

N	$\bar{K}$	$\bar{D}$
1-Best	0.979	10.89
3-Best	0.993	9.28
5-Best	0.993	8.47

Table 5. The robustness of MDP-based and POMDP-based SDS in environment with and without noise

Dialogue system	In noisy environment or not	$\bar{K}$	$\bar{D}$
MDP	No	0.987	8.67
	Yes	0.882	10.17
POMDP	No	0.993	7.81
	Yes	0.979	10.89

It can be concluded that a proper larger N can make use of more information, improve the accuracy of belief update and reliability of system and reduce the length of dialogue.

The robustness of MDP-based and POMDP-based SDS to ASR error are compared in Table 5. Because of the limitation of MDP-based SDS, Only the top 1 hypothesis of N-Best is employed in both these systems for fairness. With the introduce of noise, the average knowledge acquisition rate of POMDP decreases by 0.014, but the average knowledge acquisition rate of MDP decreases by 0.105. It can be concluded that POMDP-based system is more capable of overcoming ASR errors. However, the average dialog length of POMDP increases by 3 rounds while that of MDP increases by 1.5 rounds. Length of POMDP increases because action "other" obtains a fairly high probability when noise exists and it won't help to determine user's goal. The reason why MDP increases less than POMDP is that MDP frequently confirm an incorrect value by a double error when noise exists. For example, an input of "它是个篮球 (It's a basketball)" may be recognized as "他是 一个男囚 (He is male prisoner)". "男囚 (male prisoner)" is extracted as the value of what. Then it's confirmed with user. Unfortunately, user's response of "不是 (No)" is mistakenly recognized as "是 (Yes)". These two mistakes made by MDP may have itself regard the incorrect value as the correct. This kind of double error doesn't increase dialog length but do decrease knowledge acquisition rate.

4   Conclusion

The improved SDS-POMDP model proposed in this paper can be employed to situation where the number of possible objects is infinite and every object has finite slots. Also, we come up with an approach to improve reliability of observation probability by making full use of N-Best list of ASR. We implement a teach-and-learn SDS based on the improved model and conduct a series of experiments on this system. Results of experiments indicate that our method can effectively overcome the infinite teaching objects problem in the teach-and-learn task. Moreover, estimating observation based on N-Best list of ASR can improve system robustness and the overall performance especially for dialogues with high ASR/SLU uncertainties. We solve the certain case of infinite slot values in this paper, and we will seek to model more general case of infinite slot values in future work.

Acknowledgments. This work was partially supported by National Natural Science Foundation of China (No.61273365, No.61202248), discipline building plan in 111 base (No.B08004) and Engineering Research Center of Information Networks, Ministry of Education.

References

1. Barto, A.G.: Reinforcement Learning: An Introduction. MIT press, Cambridge (1998)
2. Hastie, H., Aufaure, M.a., Alexopoulos, P., Cuayáhuitl, H., Dethlefs, N., Gasic, M., Henderson, J., Lemon, O., Liu, X., Mika, P., Mustapha, N.B., Rieser, V., Thomson, B., Tsiakoulis, P., Vanrompay, Y., Villazon-terrazas, B., Young, S.: Demonstration of the Parlance system: a data-driven, incremental, spoken dialogue system for interactive search. In: Proceedings of the SIGDIAL 2013 Conference, pp. 154–156 (2013). http://www.aclweb.org/anthology/W/W13/W13-4026
3. Jokinen, K., McTear, M.: Spoken dialogue systems. Synth. Lect. Hum. Lang. Technol. **2**(1), 1–151 (2009)
4. Kaelbling, L.P., Littman, M.L., Cassandra, A.R.: Planning and acting in partially observable stochastic domains. Artif. Intell. **101**(1), 99–134 (1998)
5. Kurniawati, H., Hsu, D., Lee, W.S.: SARSOP: efficient point-based POMDP planning by approximating optimally reachable belief spaces. In: Robotics: Science and Systems (2008)
6. Levin, E., Pieraccini, R., Eckert, W.: A stochastic model of human-machine interaction for learning dialog strategies. IEEE Trans. Speech Audio Process. **8**(1), 11–23 (2000)
7. McTear, M.: Spoken dialogue technology: enabling the conversational user interface. ACM Comput. Surv. (CSUR) **34**(1), 90–169 (2002)
8. Seneff, S., Polifroni, J.: Dialogue management in the Mercury flight reservation system. In: Proceedings of the 2000 ANLP/NAACL Workshop on Conversational Systems, vol. 3. pp. 11–16. Association for Computational Linguistics (2000)
9. Shani, G., Pineau, J., Kaplow, R.: A survey of point-based POMDP solvers. Auton. Agent. Multi-Agent Syst. **27**(1), 1–51 (2012). http://link.springer.com/10.1007/s10458-012-9200-2
10. Williams, J.D.: A case study of applying decision theory in the real world: POMDPs and spoken dialog systems. In: Decision Theory Models for Applications in Artificial Intelligence: Concepts and Solutions, pp. 315–342 (2010)
11. Williams, J.D., Young, S.: Partially observable Markov decision processes for spoken dialog systems. Comput. Speech Lang. **21**(2), 393–422 (2007)
12. Young, S., Gasic, M., Thomson, B., Williams, J.D.: Pomdp-based statistical spoken dialog systems: A review. Proc. IEEE **101**(5), 1160–1179 (2013)
13. Young, S., Gašić, M., Keizer, S., Mairesse, F., Schatzmann, J., Thomson, B., Yu, K.: The hidden information state model: A practical framework for POMDP-based spoken dialogue management. Comput. Speech Lang. **24**(2), 150–174 (2010). http://linkinghub.elsevier.com/retrieve/pii/S0885230809000230
14. Zue, V., Seneff, S., Glass, J.R., Polifroni, J., Pao, C., Hazen, T.J., Hetherington, L.: JUPITER: A telephone-based conversational interface for weather information. IEEE Trans. Speech Audio Process. **8**(1), 85–96 (2000)

Academic Paper Recommendation Based on Heterogeneous Graph

Linlin Pan, Xinyu Dai$^{(\boxtimes)}$, Shujian Huang, and Jiajun Chen

National Key Laboratory for Novel Software Technology,
Nanjing University, Nanjing 210023, China
{panll,dxy,huangsj,chenj}@nlp.nju.edu.cn

Abstract. Digital libraries suffer from the overload problem, which makes the researchers have to spend much time to find relevant papers. Fortunately, recommender system can help to find some relevant papers for researchers automatically according to their browsed papers. Previous paper recommendation methods are either citation-based or content-based. In this paper, we propose a novel recommendation method with a heterogeneous graph in which both citation and content knowledge are included. In detail, a heterogeneous graph is constructed to represent both citation and content information within papers. Then, we apply a graph-based similarity learning algorithm to perform our paper recommendation task. Finally, we evaluate our proposed approach on the ACL Anthology Network data set and conduct an extensive comparison with other recommender approaches. The experimental results demonstrate that our approach outperforms traditional methods.

Keywords: Academic paper recommendation · Heterogeneous graph · Citation information · Content information · Similarity learning

1 Introduction

Recommender system is a hot research topic in the age of big data, and has a wild range of applications. For instance, Amazon recommender system recommends some similar products that you may be interested in according to your browsing record and your registration information. As for the academic area, more and more academic papers are coming out from a lot of conferences and journals [1]. As the number of papers increased dramatically, the existing academic papers retrieval tools cannot satisfy researcher's needs. As a consequence, researchers would like to have other tools which can help to find out relevant papers to their current work. So, in order to help researchers find relevant papers quickly and precisely, paper recommender system arises at this time.

For paper recommendation, there are a variety of forms. The definition of academic paper recommendation in our work can be described as: given a paper

This work was supported by the National Natural Science Foundation of China (No. 61472183, 61333014).

M. Sun et al. (Eds.): CCL and NLP-NABD 2015, LNAI 9427, pp. 381–392, 2015.
DOI: 10.1007/978-3-319-25816-4_31

(target paper), the recommendation system finds out some papers related to target papers. For this task, most of the existing related works recommend papers by calculating the smilarities between papers with certain information, such as citation, content, and so on. So the approaches for paper recommendation include citation-based methods [2–5], content-based methods [6] and hybrid methods [7].

In this paper, to make use of both citation information and content knowledge, we propose a new approach to perform paper recommendations. The main idea of our approach is to design a similarity learning method based on a heterogeneous graph that contains different kinds of features. We firstly present how to construct a heterogeneous graph with citation and content features in papers. Then we introduce a heterogeneous graph-based similarity learning algorithm. The similarities between target paper and candidate papers can help perform the paper recommendation task.

This paper is organized as follows: In Sect. 2, we briefly review three approaches of paper recommendation. In Sect. 3, we introduce the structure of a heterogeneous graph to represent papers and their relations. And then we present a heterogeneous graph-based similarity learning algorithm which is further applied for recommendation. In Sect. 4, the experimental results are shown to evaluate our method. We conclude the paper and give the future work in Sect. 5.

2   Related Work

Co-coupling was the first citation-based method proposed by Kessler for paper recommendation [3]. Citations were analyzed to establish the similarities between papers. Co-coupling occurred when two papers referred a common third paper, then that two papers were Co-coupling. It was an indication to say that the two papers were related to the same topic. The Co-coupling strength of two given papers was higher if they referred more common papers. Kessler [3] considered that the larger the value of Co-coupling strength of the two papers, the larger the probability of the two paper shared a common topic.

Co-citation, like Co-coupling, was also a paper recommendation approach that makes use of the citation information [5]. Co-citation was defined as the frequency with which two papers were cited together by other papers. If two given papers were both cited by many other papers, that two given papers must be highly relevant.

Lawrence proposed an approach called CCIDF (Common Citation Inverse Document Frequency) [4]. The algorithm calculated the CCIDF value of all papers in the database to a given paper A. The CCIDF was calculated according to the following three steps:

1. Use the Identical Citation Group algorithm to get a count (c_i) of how frequently each cited paper i occurs in the database. Take the inverse of these frequencies as a weight for that citation ($w_i = \frac{1}{c_i}$).
2. Find the set of n papers B_j which share at least one common citation with A.

3. Compute the CCIDF score between paper A and $B_j(j = 1, ..., n)$, the function is defined as follow:

$$CCIDF_j = \sum_{(i \in A) \bigcap (i \in B_j)} w_i \tag{1}$$

Finally, choose the N-best papers with high CCIDF values for researchers as recommendation.

Another citation-based method was proposed by Yicong Liang [2], Which performed recommendation from an citation network. Firstly, they used a new metric called Local Relation Strength to measure the relatedness between cited and citing papers. Secondly, they used a Global Relation Strength model to compute the relatedness between two papers in the entire citation network. Nevertheless, these citation-based methods disregarded other useful information.

Almost all citation-based methods have the risk of that if a candidate paper has no citation relation to the target paper, the candidate paper will never be recommended even they share many common contents, like keywords or topic words. So, citation-based methods obviously disregarded some other useful information, such as content of papers.

Ohta et al. [1] proposed a content-based method to recommend relevant papers to support online-browsing of research papers. They generated a bipartite graph which consists of two kinds of nodes to represent the papers and the terms respectively. Then, they applied the HITS algorithm to assign each candidate paper a hub score, And finally according to the hub scores, the top-N papers would be recommended.

Hassan and Radev [7] firstly used both citations information and content knowledge to compute the similarity between two papers. They used the cosine measure to compute the content similarity. And if one paper had citation relation to another paper, the two papers were also considered similar. And they simply define a linear combination of the two similarities as follow:

$$s(x, y) = \omega * content(x, y) + (1 - \omega) * citation(x, y) \tag{2}$$

where $\omega \leq 1, s(x, y)$ is the mixture similarity between paper x and paper y, $context(x, y)$ is the content similarity, and $citation(x, y)$ is the citation similarity. This formulation clearly did not take into account any dependency between content and citation.

3   Our Approach: Paper Recommendation with Heterogeneous Graph

In this section, we will introduce our approach which can jointly make use of both citation and content knowledge for paper recommendation with a heterogeneous graph. In Sect. 3.1, we propose the construction of a heterogeneous graph to represent the citation information and the text content knowledge simultaneously. In Sect. 3.2, we introduce a heterogeneous graph-based similarity learning algorithm which is further applied to recommend papers. Finally, we present a simple introduction of the solution of the similarity learning algorithm.

3.1 Construction of the Heterogeneous Graphs

Both citation information and content knowledge are valuable for papers recommendation. In detail, the references and citations between papers and the
words in papers are key clues for papers recommendation. And there are also
dependencies between the words in papers. The heterogeneous graph is a natural representation for the data with different kinds of features. A heterogeneous
graph also can be called as a multi-layer graph for more clearly presented.

As for our paper recommendation task, we can construct a multi-layer graph
with nodes of papers and nodes of words. We now formally present the definitions
of the multi-layer graph as follows.

Definition 1: Papers Citation Graph. The paper citation graph describes
the relationship between the citation papers. For simplicity, the citation graph
is an undirected graph, which can be represented by a two tuple, $G_p = \{V_p, E_p\}$.
Each node represents a paper, and each edge represents citation or reference
between two papers. If paper p_i cites paper p_j, the initial weight of edge w_{ij}
equals to $context(p_i, p_j)$. The context function is as follow:

$$context(p_i, p_j) = cosine(p_i, p_j) = \frac{||p_i \cdot p_j||}{||p_i|| \times ||p_j||} \tag{3}$$

where p_i and p_j are vectors, which represent the content of paper p_i and p_j
respectively. The key-terms are extracted based on the $tfidf$ score, the weights
of these key-terms are computed by wordnet, and if key-terms t_j appears in
paper p_i.

Definition 2: Key-Terms Graph. Contents, like words or terms, are another
kind of key features. So, we will construct a words graph, $G_t = \{V_t, E_t\}$. Considering the scale of the graph, we extract some key-terms as nodes with the
following three main steps:

1. We remove the stop words from these papers.
2. We use TF-IDF [8] to score all the candidate key terms, and all the candidate
   key-terms are ranked according to the TF-IDF score, then we select the K
   top ranked terms from each paper as the nodes in the key-terms graph. The
   $tfidf_i$ of the term t_i is defined as follow:

$$tfidf_i = tf_i \times \log\left(\frac{N}{m}\right) \tag{4}$$

   where tf_i is the frequent count of the term t_i in a document, N is the total
   number of the documents, and m is the number of documents which contain
   the term t_i. At the same time, we regularize the $tfidf$ score for each word in
   the same paper, then, the $tfidf$ score is regarded as the initial score of the
   importance the key-term to the paper.
3. We compute the initial similarity between the key-terms.

Now, each node represents a key-term and each edge represents the similarity score of two terms. In this paper, we use a knowledge-based approach to compute the similarity between two terms. WordNet is a lexical database for English. This database links English nouns, verbs, adjectives, and adverbs to sets of synonyms that are in turn linked through semantic relations that determine word definitions. We use the Leacock-Chodorow which relies on the shortest path between two terms in WordNet [9,10]. First, the method finds the Least Common Subsumer (LCS) [11], and gets the shortest path between the two terms. The Leacock-Chodorow method is defined as follow:

$$sim_{LC} = -\log\left(\frac{shortest\_path(t_i, t_j)}{2W}\right) \tag{5}$$

where $W = 16$ and $shortest\_path$ represents the distance of term t_i to term t_j through the LCS of term t_i and t_j.

Definition 3: Connectivity between Paper Citation Graph and Key-Terms Graph. The two graphs, G_p and G_t, are connected as follows. There exists an edge between paper p_i and key-term t_j if t_j appears in paper p_i.

The layer connectivity function is as below:

$$Z_{p_i t_j} = \begin{cases} 1 \text{ or } tfidf_j, & \text{if } t_j \in p_i \\ 0, & \text{otherwise} \end{cases} \tag{6}$$

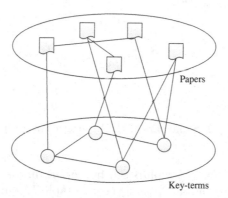

Fig. 1. An example of heterogeneous graph

Figure 1 shows the construction of a heterogeneous graph to represent the citation information and the text content knowledge simultaneously.

3.2 Similarity Learning on Graph for Paper Recommendation

The approach for incorporating information from different heterogeneous features is inspired by the graph-based framework in a semi-supervised manner [12].

Given a dataset $\{(x_1, y_1), ..., (x_L, y_L), x_{(L+1)}, ..., x_n\}$, which contained n instances, and L instances whose labels were given by $y(x)$. The method defined a single graph $G(V, E, w)$. The set of nodes was represented as $V = \{(x_1, x_2, ..., x_n)\}$. The edge weights w_{ij} represented similarity between instance x_i and x_j. The problem was to classify all other nodes using a discriminant function f. The main idea of graph-based semi-supervised classification was that similar instances tended to have similar categories. The definition of the objective function was as follow:

$$F = u \sum_{x \in L} (f(x) - y(x))^2 + \frac{1}{2} \sum_{i,j=1}^{n} w_{ij}(f(x_i) - f(x_j))^2 \qquad (7)$$

where u is a hyperparameter, and $0 \leq u \leq 1$. The objective function contains two terms. The former term aims at minimizing the difference between the ground truth labels and the predicted ones while the latter one attempts to regularize the node labeling over the network such that similar instances share similar labels.

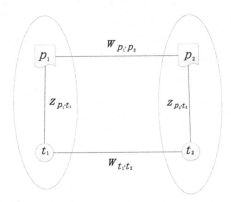

Fig. 2. Some part of the heterogeneous graph

According to the idea of graph-based framework in a semi-supervised manner, we apply the idea on our heterogeneous graph. In our method, according to the citation relationship between papers, we could compute the content similarity between papers which are the labeled instances. Figure 2 shows the main structure of the heterogeneous graph. We consider node p_1 and node t_1 as a whole, and simultaneously we consider node p_2 and node t_2 as another whole, then we consider $w_{p_1,p_2} * w_{t_1,t_2}$ as the similarity of the two parts. Similarly, we also could consider node p_1 and node p_2 as a whole, and consider node t_1 and node t_2 as another whole, then consider $z_{p_1,t_1} * z_{p_2,t_2}$ as the similarity of the two parts. So far, we transform the heterogeneous graph into a single graph, so that we extend the idea of graph-based framework in a semi-supervised manner into our task paper recommendation.

The algorithm is called heterogeneous graph-based learning algorithm which was firstly introduced by Pradeep [13]. According to the definition of paper recommendation, given a node of paper, we could recommend the top N papers according to the ranking of similarities between the target paper and the candidate papers. We can transfer our paper recommendation task to similarity learning problem.

We defined an objective function to learn the edges weight iteratively. The edges include the edges in the same layer and the connective edges between the different layers. The objective function is defined as follow:

$$F(W, Z) = \alpha_0 * \sum_{p_1, p_2 \in G_p} (w_{p_1, p_2} - w_{p_1, p_2}^*)^2 + \alpha_1 * \sum_{p \in G_p, t \in G_t} (z_{p,t} - z_{p,t}^*)^2$$

$$+ \alpha_2 * \sum_{p_1, p_2 \in G_p} \sum_{t_1, t_2 \in G_t} z_{p_1, t_1} z_{p_2, t_2} (w_{p_1, p_2} - w_{t_1, t_2})^2$$

$$+ \alpha_3 * \sum_{p_1, p_2 \in G_p} \sum_{t_1, t_2 \in G_t} w_{p_1, p_2} w_{t_1, t_2} (z_{p_1, t_1} - z_{p_2, t_2})^2 \qquad (8)$$

where $\alpha_0 + \alpha_1 + \alpha_2 + \alpha_3 = 1$. w_{p_1, p_2}^* represents the initial similarity between papers, and $z_{p,t}^*$ represents the initial importance of key-terms to the papers, w_{p_1, p_2} and $z_{p,t}$ are the updated values.

The objective function contains four terms. The first and the second terms try to minimize the difference between the updated similarity and the initial similarity. And the third and the fourth terms try to regularize the similarity between nodes such that similar parts achieve similar weights. Given a heterogeneous graph, we will apply a graph-based similarity learning algorithm to update the similarities between two nodes iteratively.

3.3   The Solution of Objective Function

We minimize the objective function in Sect. 3.2 using Alternating Optimization, an approximate optimization method. The partial derivative of the objective function is given as follows:

$$\frac{\partial F(W, Z)}{\partial w_{p_1, p_2}} = 2\alpha_0 * (w_{p_1, p_2} - w_{p_1, p_2}^*)$$

$$+ 2\alpha_2 * \sum_{t_1, t_2 \in G_t} z_{p_1, t_1} z_{p_2, t_2} (w_{p_1, p_2} - w_{t_1, t_2})$$

$$+ \alpha_3 * \sum_{t_1, t_2 \in G_t} w_{p_1, p_2} w_{t_1, t_2} (z_{p_1, t_1} - z_{p_2, t_2})^2 \qquad (9)$$

To minimize the above function, we set the function to zero, then the solution is achieved as follows:

$$w_{p_1, p_2} = \frac{1}{C_1} (\alpha_0 w_{p_1, p_2}^* + \alpha_2 \sum_{t_1, t_2 \in G_t} z_{p_1, t_1} w_{t_1, t_2} z_{p_2, t_2}) \qquad (10)$$

where

$$C_1 = \alpha_0 + \alpha_2 \sum_{t_1,t_2 \in G_t} z_{p_1,t_1} z_{p_2,t_2} + \frac{\alpha_3}{2} \sum_{t_1,t_2 \in G_t} w_{t_1,t_2} (z_{p_1,t_1} - z_{p_2,t_2})^2 \qquad (11)$$

Similarly, we can also update the importance score, z_{p_1,t_1}. Since objective function needs to update multiple iterations, here we stop iterating when,

$$|w_{p_1,p_2}^t - w_{p_1,p_2}^{t-1}| \leq \tau, \forall (p_1, p_2 \in G_p) \qquad (12)$$

Finally, we would achieve the final similarity score between two papers according to the final graph, and according to the rank of similarities between candidate papers and target paper, we would recommend the top n papers.

4 Experiments

4.1 Dataset

We use an open dataset to evaluate our proposed approach. The dataset is a subset of ACL Anthology Network (ANN) [2]. ANN is a collection of journal, conference and workshop papers. The ANN dataset consists of 18572 papers and 70756 citation links where these papers are published between 1965 and 2011. The subset consists of two parts, one part contains 15 target papers published in 2008 or 2009 from 15 junior researchers, and the other part contains 597 full papers published from 2000 to 2006 as the candidate papers. Each target paper has a list of related papers which is manually labelled.

4.2 Evaluation Measures

For the information retrieval (IR), the results which are more relevant with the query will be at the top. Our paper recommendation is similar to IR. In order to properly evaluate the effect of paper recommendation approach, we apply IR evaluation measures: (1) Normalized Discounted Cumulative Gain (NDCG) (2) Mean Reciprocal Rank (MRR) (3) F1-Score [14,15].

Normalized Discounted Cumulative Gain (NDCG). Discounted Cumulative Gain gives more weight to highly relevant documents , while the highly relevant documents appearing lower in a search result list should be penalized as the graded relevance value is reduced logarithmically proportional to the position of the result. The DCG is defined as:

$$DCG_p = rel_1 + \sum_{i=2}^{p} \frac{rel_i}{log_2 i} \qquad (13)$$

where p is document rank position, i denotes the ith ranked position, and rel_i is the weight of the document which in the ith ranked position. In our work, if the document is relevant to the query document, then $rel = 1$ and $rel = 0$ for the irrelevant document.

$$nDCG_p = \frac{DCG_p}{IDCG_p} \tag{14}$$

where $IDCG_p$ is called Ideal DCG till position p, which represents the best result score.

The average normalized DCG over all target set is selected to show the accuracy of recommendation. General recommendation system will recommend some items for the user. In our work, we use $NDCG@N(N = 5, 10)$ for evaluation where N is the number of top-N papers recommended by our approach.

Mean Reciprocal Rank (MRR). Mean Reciprocal Rank is only concerned about the ranking of the first relevant term which is returned by the system, average over all target papers. The MRR is defined as:

$$MRR = \frac{1}{|Q|} \sum_{i=1}^{|Q|} \frac{1}{rank_i} \tag{15}$$

where $|Q|$ represents the number of the target papers, and the $rank_i$ represents the rank of the ith target paper.

F1-Score. F1-Score is an oft-used measure in the information retrieval and natural language processing communities. This measure was first introduced by C. J. van Rijsbergen. F1-Score combines recall (r) and precision (p) with an equal weight in the following form:

$$F_1(r, p) = \frac{2rp}{r + p} \tag{16}$$

4.3   Results

We evaluate the performance of the our method compared with citation-based methods, Co-citation [5], Co-coupling [3], CCIDF [4], GRS [2], content-based method, HITS [6], and the citation and content linear combination method called Linear Combination [7]. In the following experiments, $K = 50$ which means we select the top 50 ranked terms from each paper as the nodes in the key-terms graph, and the method parameters are solely tuned based on the test set, among them $\alpha_0 = 0.35, \alpha_1 = 0.35, \alpha_2 = 0.15$ and $\alpha_3 = 0.15$.

The result of our methods and other related work are shown in Table 1. From Table 1, we can see that Linear Combination and Multi-layer graph methods which use citation information and content knowledge perform better than most of the methods which just use one type of information. Compared with other methods, the our heterogeneous graph method improves the results significantly.

We further validate our method on the evaluation criterion of NDCG. Figure 3 shows the results of NDCG@N (N = 5, 10, 20, 30) from all the methods. The figure shows that our method gets the best performance.

Table 1. Top-10 Results of NDCG and MRR

Approach	NDCG@10	MRR	F@10
Co-coupling	0.070	0.084	0.023
Co-citaiton	0.085	0.120	0.028
CCIDF	0.087	0.098	0.027
GRS	0.257	0.193	0.101
HITS	0.106	0.093	0.030
Linear Combination	0.223	0.174	0.087
Multi-layer Graph	**0.324**	**0.267**	**0.185**

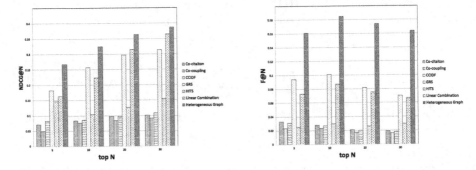

Fig. 3. NDCG@NResults

According to the definitions of heterogeneous graph, the weights of edges have multiple initialization methods. In the paper citation graph, the weights of edges can be computed by three methods: (a1) Citation-based. If p_i and p_j exist citation relationship, then $w_{ij} = 1$. (a2) Content-based. $w_{ij} = Context(i, j)$. (a3) Citation, Content-based. If p_i and p_j exist citation relationship, then $w_{ij} = Context(i, j)$. Likewise, the weights of edges have three methods in the key-terms graph: (b1) Knowledge-based. the weight can be calculated using the above method WordNet. (b2) Co occurrence-based. If two terms appeared in the same paper, the weight equals to 1. (b3) Co occurrence, WordNet-based. If two terms appeared in the same paper, then the weight can be calculated using the above method WordNet.

In order to examine the sensitive of the initial weights of the edges, we do the other experiment. Table 2 is the results of five different weights of edges combinations in the heterogeneous graph. From Table 2, we can find that no matter what settings, our method is better than the Linear Combination method, and the graph-3 which combine citation, content-based and knowledge-based together performs better than other graph settings. Therefore, for the paper citation graph need to combine citation information and content knowledge together, and for the key-terms graph, the similarity between them only need to consider their actual similarity, don't have to consider their relationships in the data set.

Table 2. The results of different initial weights of edges combination graph

Settings	Combinations	NDCG@10	MRR
Linear Combination		0.223	0.174
Graph-1	a1+b1	0.223	0.174
graph-2	a2+b1	0.287	0.236
graph-3	a3+b1	**0.324**	**0.267**
graph-4	a3+b2	0.253	0.215
graph-5	a3+b3	0.272	0.226

5   Conclusion and the Future Work

Finding papers related to the target paper is becoming increasingly important especially when information overload. In this paper, we introduce a heterogeneous graph-based approach to find some papers related to the target paper which the researcher has browsed. Firstly, we use a multi-layer graph to represent the citation information and the text content knowledge of these papers. In the first layer, each node represents a paper, and in the second layer, each node represents a key-term. Secondly, we use a multi-layer graph-based similarity learning algorithm to compute the similarity score between papers. The relevance between the target papers and the candidate papers could be affected by the relationships of features with the same type and the importance of features to the paper. Finally, we do some experiments on the real database, and the experimental results showed that this method performs more effective than the state-of-the-art methods for recommending relevant papers for the researchers.

But there are still some disadvantages of our method. For example, due to the large number of key-terms, the number of nodes in the multi-layer graph is also large so that the speed of convergence is slow.

References

1. Ohta, M., Hachiki, T., Takasu, A.: Related paper recommendation to support online-browsing of research papers. In: 2011 Fourth International Conference on the Applications of Digital Information and Web Technologies (ICADIWT), pp. 130–136. IEEE (2011)
2. Liang, Y., Li, Q., Qian, T.: Finding relevant papers based on citation relations. In: Wang, H., Li, S., Oyama, S., Hu, X., Qian, T. (eds.) WAIM 2011. LNCS, vol. 6897, pp. 403–414. Springer, Heidelberg (2011)
3. Kessler, M.M.: Bibliographic coupling between scientific papers. Am. Documentation **14**(1), 10–25 (1963)
4. Lawrence, S., Lee Giles, C., Bollacker, K.: Digital libraries and autonomous citation indexing. Computer **32**(6), 67–71 (1999)
5. Small, H.: Co-citation in the scientific literature: A new measure of the relationship between two documents. J. Am. Soc. Inf. Sci. **24**(4), 265–269 (1973)

6. Lu, W., Janssen, J., Milios, E., Japkowicz, N., Zhang, Y.: Node similarity in the citation graph. Knowl. Inf. Syst. **11**(1), 105–129 (2007)
7. Basu, C., Hirsh, H., Cohen, W., et al.: Recommendation as classification: Using social and content-based information in recommendation. In: AAAI/IAAI, pp. 714–720 (1998)
8. Sparck Jones, K.: A statistical interpretation of term specificity and its application in retrieval. J. Documentation **28**(1), 11–21 (1972)
9. Miller, G.A.: Wordnet: a lexical database for english. Commun. ACM **38**(11), 39–41 (1995)
10. Leacock, C., Chodorow, M.: Combining local context and wordnet similarity for word sense identification. WordNet: Electron. Lexical Database **49**(2), 265–283 (1998)
11. Küsters, R., Molitor, R.: Computing least common subsumers in ä æ. In: Proceedings of the 17th International Joint Conference on Artificial Intelligence (IJCAI01). Morgan Kaufmann. Citeseer (2001)
12. Zhu, X., Ghahramani, Z., Lafferty, J., et al.: Semi-supervised learning using gaussian fields and harmonic functions. In: ICML, vol. 3, pp. 912–919 (2003)
13. Muthukrishnan, P.: Unsupervised graph-based similarity learning using heterogeneous features. Ph.D. dissertation, The University of Michigan (2011)
14. Järvelin, K., Kekäläinen, J.: Ir evaluation methods for retrieving highly relevant documents. In: Proceedings of the 23rd Annual International ACM SIGIR Conference on Research and Development in Information Retrieval, pp. 41–48. ACM (2000)
15. Voorhees, E.M., et al.: The trec-8 question answering track report. In: TREC, vol. 99, pp. 77–82 (1999)

Learning Document Representation
for Deceptive Opinion Spam Detection

Luyang Li, Wenjing Ren, Bing Qin[✉], and Ting Liu

Research Center for Social Computing and Information Retrieval,
Harbin Institute of Technology, Harbin, China
{lyli,wjren,qinb,tliu}@ir.hit.edu.cn

Abstract. Deceptive opinion spam in reviews of products or service is
very harmful for customers in decision making. Existing approaches to
detect deceptive spam are concern on feature designing. Hand-crafted
features can show some linguistic phenomenon, but is time-consuming
and can not reveal the connotative semantic meaning of the review. We
present a neural network to learn document-level representation. In our
model, we not only learn to represent each sentence but also represent the
whole document of the review. We apply traditional convolutional neural
network to represent the semantic meaning of sentences. We present
two variant convolutional neural-network models to learn the document
representation. The model taking sentence importance into consideration shows the better performance in deceptive spam detection which
enhances the value of F1 by 5 %.

Keywords: Deceptive spam detection · Convolutional neural network ·
Representation learning

1 Introduction

Deceptive opinion spam detection is an urgent and meaningful task in the field
of natural language processing. By continuous growth of the user-generated
reviews, the appearance of deceptive opinion spam arouses people's attention [24,25,40,42]. Deceptive opinion spam is the review with fictitious opinions
which is deliberately written to sound authentic [34]. For commercial motive,
some businesses hire people to write undeserving positive reviews to promote
the products or giving unjust negative reviews to damage the reputations of
the objects [14]. It is very difficult to distinguish deceptive spam by people. In
the test of Ott et al. [34], the average accuracy of three human judges is only
57.33 %. Hence, the research in detecting deceptive opinion spam automatically
by machine is necessary.

The review is always a short document consisting of a few sentences. The
objective of the task is to distinguish the document whether a spam or a truth.
The task can be transformed into a spam classification problem. The majority

© Springer International Publishing Switzerland 2015
M. Sun et al. (Eds.): CCL and NLP-NABD 2015, LNAI 9427, pp. 393–404, 2015.
DOI: 10.1007/978-3-319-25816-4_32

of existing approaches follow Ott et al. [34] and employ machine learning algorithms to build classifiers. Under this direction, most studies focus on designing effective features to better classification performance. Feature engineering is important but labor-intensive. It also can not reveal inherent law from the semantic perspective in data. For the task of deceptive opinion spam detection, an effective feature learning method is to compose the representation of the document. Learning the representation of the document can capture the global feature and take word order and sentence order into consideration. That has more advantages than common features like n-grams, POS, etc.

We aim to learn the representation of the document for deceptive opinion spam detection. The learning model is consisting of two stages which are sentence representation learning and document representation learning. At the stage of sentence representing, we apply sliding window to capture sequential words and transform to a vector. We exploit two variant models of convolution neural network to learn document representation which are different at the second stage. In consideration of the effect of sentence order to semantic representing, our first model, sentence convolutional neural network (SCNN), apply sliding window to capture sequential sentences and transform to a vector. Namely, a multilayer convolutional neural network is applied to learn the representation of the document. In a review, which is a document, a few sentences may include the more important concepts, and thus should be more heavily weighted. Based on the consideration, we utilize information gain to evaluate the importance of sentences, and develop a sentence weighted neural network (SWNN) by assigning a different weight according to the importance of the sentence to each term.

We use a basic method to represent document and apply as features in a supervised learning framework for deceptive opinion spam detection on the public data sets [21] and gain an comparable result with state-of-the art method. We also find that our document representation perform more robust on cross-domain data. We also apply the two variant models of convolution neural network on the mixture-domain data sets, and SWNN model gains better performance than baseline methods. The major contributions of the work presented in this paper are as follows.

- We show that the document representation based on the word embedding performs more robust than traditional common feature on cross-domain data in the task.
- We exploit two convolutional neural-network based models to learn the document representation and the results show the effectiveness on the public data sets.

2   Methodology

In the section, we present the details of learning document representation for deceptive opinion spam detection. We extend the existing text representation learning algorithm [4] and develop two convolutional neural network models to learn document representation for deceptive opinion spam detection.

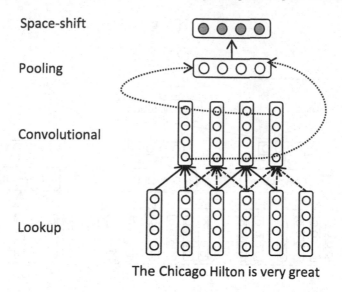

Space-shift

Pooling

Convolutional

Lookup

The Chicago Hilton is very great

Fig. 1. The traditional neural network for learning sentence representation.

In the following subsections, we first introduce the traditional method and then present the detail of two document representation learning models.

2.1 Basic Convolutional Neural Network

Collobert et al. [4] introduce a sentence approach network to learn the representation of a sentence. The architecture is given in Fig. 1. It is a multilayer neural network which consists of four types of layers. Giver a sentence "*The Chicago Hilton is very great*", the model apply the lookup layer to map these words into corresponding word embeddings which are continuous real-valued vectors. The convolutional layer extracts local features around each window of the given sequence by representing the semantic meaning of the words in the window. The size of the output of convolutional layer depends on the number of words in the sentence fed to the network. Pooling layer obtain a global feature vector by combining the local feature vectors through previous layer. Common operations are doing max or average over the corresponding position of the sequence. The average operation captures the influence of all words to the certain task. The max operation captures the most useful local features produced by convolutional layer. The space-shift layer include linear layer and non-linear layer, and maybe include another linear layer if the output is scores of corresponding categories in certain task. Non-linear layer is necessary to extract high level features.

2.2 The Document Representation Learning Model

Basic Model. We apply the traditional convolutional neural network model to represent sentences. To make a composition for the document, we use average

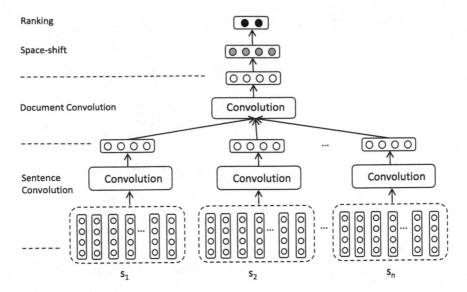

Fig. 2. The our SCNN model for learning sentence representation.

operation to capture all of the sentences features on the pooling layer. This is a basic model, which is modified below to suit the deceptive opinion spam detection task.

SCNN Model. As the architecture is given in the Fig. 2, SCNN model consists of two convolutional layers to do the composition. The sentence convolution is to make a composition of each sentence by a fix-length window. The document convolution transforms sentence vectors into a document vector. The ranking layer produces the scores according to each category. We use hinge loss as the ranking objective function in Eq. 1.

$$Loss(r) = max(0, m_\delta - f(r_t) + f(r_{t^*})) \tag{1}$$

where t is the gold label of the review r, t^* stands for the another label, m_δ is the margin in the experiment.

SWNN Model. The sentence-weighted neural network model is a modified model of the basic document representation learning model. As a matter of fact, the words in a review play different roles in the semantic representation. Some words must be more important in distinguishing spam from the truth reviews. Hence, each sentence also owns its importance weight according to the words in it. We compute the importance weight of the sentence based on the importance weights of words in the sentence. We apply KL-divergence as the importance weight of the word. The value of KL-divergence stands for the capacity of a feature in dividing documents which is a feature selection approach. In fact, we also try $tf - idf$ as a candidate of weight computing method, however, it does not perform as well as KL-divergence in the experiment. We assume that

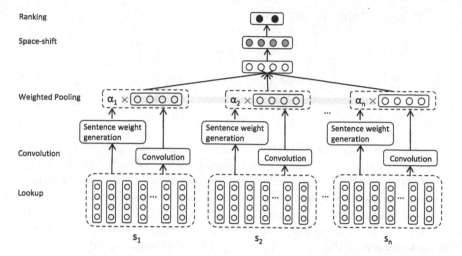

Fig. 3. The our SWNN model for learning sentence representation.

$U = \{U_1, ..., U_i, ..., U_n\}$ is the universal set of words in the review which U_i is the word set of the ith sentence, and W_j stand for the weight of the jth word. The sentence weight is a normalization value like in the following formula.

$$\alpha_i = \frac{\sum_{j \in U_i} W_j}{\sum_{k \in U} W_k} \tag{2}$$

In the Fig. 3, the architecture of SWNN model is given. Each sentence of the input document review transforms into the fixed-length vector through convolutional layer. The process of generating sentence weights produce normalized weight α_i corresponding to the ith sentence. Through the pooling layer, the sentence vectors transform into a document vector by a weighted-average operation. More important sentences have more influences during producing the document vector. The vector transforms through space-shift layer to extract high level features. The ranking layer produce the scores of the categories.

3   Experiment

We conduct experiments to empirically evaluate our document representation learning model by applying the it to do the deceptive opinion spam detection task. We do two comparison experiments to show the effectiveness our model.

3.1   Experiment Setup

We apply the public data sets released by Jiwei Li [21]. The data sets contain three domains which are hotel, restaurant, and doctor. The distribution of the dataset is shown in Table 1. In Li's public dataset, there are three types of data

Table 1. Statistics of the three domain dataset.

	Turker	Customer
Hotel(P/N)	400/400	400/400
Restaurant(P/N)	200/0	200/200
Doctor(P/N)	356/0	200/0

in each domain which are "Turker", "Expert", and "Customer". They stand for various different data sources. The spam reviews are edited by Turkers and experts who have domain knowledge. The truth reviews are from customers who really have consumption experience. However, Li do not apply "Expert" data in his experiment. According to Li's paper, he only apply 200 spam reviews from 356 spam reviews in Doctor domain. Hence, we do our best to use data with the same distribution in the cross-domain experiment comparing with Li.

Our target is to exploit domain-independent method to resolve deceptive opinion spam detection. Hence, we construct a mixture domain dataset. The samples in the dataset are divided into two categories, i.e. spam (Turker) and truth (Customer). The proportion among training set, development set and test set is 6 : 1 : 3. Each category data in each domain is assigned by the proportion.

3.2   Cross-Domain Classification

To frame the problem as a domain adaptation task, we want to find a more robust feature on cross-domain dataset. On the latest public data, only Li show the experiment results. Hence, we do the comparison with his method. We apply basic document representation as features which is the average vector of all word embedding in the paragraph.

Baseline Method. Li respectively apply Unigram, LIWC and POS features in SVM and SAGE classifiers to explore a more general classifier of the task. SAGE is sparse additive generative model which can be viewed as an combination of topic models and generalized additive models. However SAGE do not outperform SVM, we apply SVM as the classifier in the comparison experiment. In Li's experiment, the method gains best results by using Unigram an POS features in test datasets (restaurant and doctor domains) by training hotel domain data. Hence, we just list the best results from his paper.

Results and Analysis. Table 2 show the results from baseline method as well as our method. We can see the our basic document representation perform comparable respectively with the best results of baseline on two domain. Additionally, the document representation perform more robust on the cross-domain dataset.

3.3   Domain-Independent Classification

We apply various document representations learnt by our variant neural network models as features to do the deceptive spam classification. As we introduce above,

Table 2. Classifier performance in cross-domain test data.

Features	Restaurant				Doctor			
	A	P	R	F1	A	P	R	F1
Unigram	0.785	0.813	0.742	0.778	0.550	0.573	0.725	0.617
POS	0.735	0.697	0.815	0.751	0.540	0.521	0.975	0.679
Paragraph-average	0.733	0.684	0.865	0.764	0.588	0.555	0.885	0.682

we randomly construct domain-independent datasets by the uniform distribution from three domain data. For each variant model, we train on the training set, adjust parameters on the development set and predict on the test set.

The Basic CNN is the basic convolutional neural network model which sentences are representing through convolutional layer and transform into a document vector by the average operation. SCNN apply convolutional layer to replace the average operation. SWNN is the modification of the Basic CNN model by using sentence weights.

Table 3. Deceptive opinion spam classification.

Model	A	P	R	F1
Paragraph-average	0.676	0.673	0.903	0.771
Basic CNN	0.709	0.739	0.813	0.774
SCNN	0.699	0.670	0.859	0.753
SWNN	0.795	0.761	0.898	0.823

Results and Analysis. We do the comparison among various document representations. Table 3 show the results that our SWNN model learn the best representation and gain the best result in deceptive spam classification. The scores of accuracy and F1 are all far above the other neural-network based methods. The results show the effectiveness of incorporating sentence weight in representing document. We also find more complex model like SCNN do not perform as well as simple model like Paragraph-average model and Basic CNN model.

Parameter Settings. The parameters of SWNN model used in the deceptive opinion spam detection experiment is listing followed. The embedding length and the vector length in two hidden layers are all 50. The learning rate is 0.1. The window size is set as 2. We experimentally study the effect of window size in our presented convolutional neural network method. We tune the parameter on trial dataset. In Fig. 4, we vary the value of window size and compute the accuracy and F1. It shows the accuracy scores have one top (0.795) when the value of window size equals to 2 which we applies in the test. The F1 also has the best result at the same point.

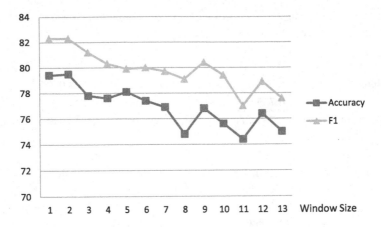

Fig. 4. Effect of window size.

4   Related Work

We present a brief review of the related work from two perspectives. One is deceptive opinion spam detection, and another is deep learning for specific task representation learning.

4.1   Deceptive Opinion Spam Detection

On the Internet, various kinds of spam brings troubles to people. Over the years, many studies focus on spam detection. Web spam has been extensively studied [2,8,10,11,23,30,45] The objective of the web spam is to gain high page rank and attract people to click by fooling search engines. Email spam is another related research, which is pushing unsolicited advertisements to users [3,5]. The web spam and mail spam have a common character that they have irrelevant words. Opinion spam is quite different and more crafty. By the explosive growth of user-generated content, the number of opinion spam in the reviews, which contain opinions of users about products and services, increased continuously. This phenomenon attracted researchers attention. Opinion spam was firstly investigated by Liu et al. [14] that also summarized the opinion spam into different types. In terms of the different damage to users, we can further conclude the opinion spam into two types which are deceptive opinion spam and product-irrelevant spam. In the former spam, the spammers give undeserving positive reviews or unjust negative reviews to the object for misleading costumers. The latter spam contain no comments about the object. Obviously, the deceptive opinion spam is more difficult to detect.

The approaches of detecting deceptive opinion spam can be divided into unsupervised methods and supervised methods. Liu et al. [27] take a Bayesian approach and formulate opinion spam detection as a clustering problem. There are also many unsupervised methods researching on detecting spammers [22,28,29,44] or mining reviewing patterns [15]. Due to the lack of gold standard data, most methods take the research on pseudo labeled data. Liu et al. [14] assumed duplicate and near duplicate reviews to be deceptive spam. They also applied features of review texts, reviewers and products. Yoo et al. [47] first collected a small amount of deceptive spam and truth reviews and do a linguistic analysis on them. By applying Amazon Mechanical Turk, Ott et al. [31–34] gathered a gold standard labeled data. A few follow-up researches have been done on the data set. Ott et al. estimated prevalence of deceptive opinion spam in reviews [32], and identified negative spam [33]. Li et al. [20] identified manipulated offerings on review portals. Feng et al. [6] applied context free grammar parse trees to extract syntactic features to improve the performance of the model. Vanessa Feng et al. [7] take the group of reference reviews into account according to the same product. Although there are deceptive opinion spam in the Ott's data sets, it still can not reflect the real condition with the lack of cross-domain data, and the Turkers also lack of professional knowledge. Li et al. [21] created a cross-domain data sets (i.e. hotel, restaurant, and doctor) with part of reviews from domain experts. On this labeled data set, they use n-gram features as well as POS and LIWC features in classification and show that POS perform more robust on cross-domain data.

4.2   Deep Learning for Representation Learning

Representation learning by deep learning methods has been proven to be effective in avoiding task-specific engineering. Hence, the processing does not need much prior knowledge. As a continuous real-valued vector, representation can be incorporated as features in a variety of natural language processing tasks [4,16,19], such as POS tagging, chunking, named entity recognition [4,43], semantic role labeling, parsing [36], language modeling [1,26], and sentiment analysis tasks [39,41]. Representation learning is to learn continuous representations of text with different grains, like word, phrase, sentence and document. For representing a document, the existing deep learning methods consist of two processing stages. Firstly, word embedding should be learnt by massive text corpus. Some work utilizes global context of document and multiple word prototypes [13], or global word-word co-occurrence to improve word embedding [35]. There are also some work for task-specific word-embedding [41]. After obtaining word representation, many research works focus on composing for coarse-grained semantic unit by composition models. For learning semantic composition,

Yessenalina et al. use matrixes to model each word and applying iterated matrix multiplication to combine words [46]. Glorot et al. develop Stacked Denoising Autoencoders for domain adaptation [9]. Socher et al. propose Recursive Neural Network (RNN) [38], matrixvector RNN [37] and Recursive Neural Tensor Network (RNTN) [39] to learn the compositionality of unfixed-length phrases. Hermann et al. (2013) learn the compositionality of sentence by Combinatory Categorial Autoencoders, which is the combination of Combinatory Categorial Grammar and Recursive Autoencoder [12]. Li et al. [18] use feature weight tuning to control the effect one specific unit makes to the higher-level representation in a Recursive Neural Network. Le et al. [17] learn the representation of paragraph.

5 Conclusion

We introduce a novel convolutional neural network to learn document representation for deceptive opinion spam detection. Sentences play different important role in the document. We model the semantic meaning of document-level reviews by incorporating sentence important weights into document representation learning. We construct experiments on the latest public data set and compare with multiple baseline methods. We show that sentence-weighted neural network is more effective than other two convolutional neural-network based models in document representation and spam classification. The results of the experiments also show that the basic document representation perform more robust than the hand-crafted features on cross-domain data set.

Acknowledgments. This work was supported by the National High Technology Development 863 Program of China (NSFC) via grant 2015 AA015407, NSFC via grant 61133012 and NSFC via grant 61273321.

References

1. Bengio, Y., Ducharme, R., Vincent, P., Janvin, C.: A neural probabilistic language model. J. Mach. Learn. Res. **3**, 1137–1155 (2003)
2. Castillo, C., Donato, D., Gionis, A., Murdock, V., Silvestri, F.: Know your neighbors: Web spam detection using the web topology. In: Proceedings of the 30th Annual International ACM SIGIR Conference on Research and Development in Information Retrieval, pp. 423–430. ACM (2007)
3. Chirita, P.A., Diederich, J., Nejdl, W.: Mailrank: using ranking for spam detection. In: Proceedings of the 14th ACM International Conference on Information and Knowledge Management, pp. 373–380. ACM (2005)
4. Collobert, R., Weston, J., Bottou, L., Karlen, M., Kavukcuoglu, K., Kuksa, P.: Natural language processing (almost) from scratch. J. Mach. Learn. Res. **12**, 2493–2537 (2011)
5. Drucker, H., Wu, D., Vapnik, V.N.: Support vector machines for spam categorization. IEEE Trans. Neural Netw. **10**(5), 1048–1054 (1999)
6. Feng, S., Banerjee, R., Choi, Y.: Syntactic stylometry for deception detection. In: Proceedings of the 50th Annual Meeting of the Association for Computational Linguistics: Short Papers, vol. 2, pp. 171–175. Association for Computational Linguistics (2012)
7. Feng, V.W., Hirst, G.: Detecting deceptive opinions with profile compatibility. In: Proceedings of the 6th International Joint Conference on Natural Language Processing, Nagoya, Japan, pp. 14–18 (2013)
8. Fetterly, D., Manasse, M., Najork, M.: Detecting phrase-level duplication on the world wide web. In: Proceedings of the 28th Annual International ACM SIGIR Conference on Research and Development in Information Retrieval, pp. 170–177. ACM (2005)
9. Glorot, X., Bordes, A., Bengio, Y.: Domain adaptation for large-scale sentiment classification: A deep learning approach. In: Proceedings of the 28th International Conference on Machine Learning (ICML-2011), pp. 513–520 (2011)

10. Gyöngyi, Z., Garcia-Molina, H.: Link spam alliances. In: Proceedings of the 31st International Conference on Very Large Data Bases, pp. 517–528. VLDB Endowment (2005)
11. Gyöngyi, Z., Garcia-Molina, H., Pedersen, J.: Combating web spam with trustrank. In: Proceedings of the Thirtieth International Conference on Very Large Data Bases, vol. 30, pp. 576–587. VLDB Endowment (2004)
12. Hermann, K.M., Blunsom, P.: The role of syntax in vector space models of compositional semantics. In: ACL, vol. 1, pp. 894–904 (2013)
13. Huang, E.H., Socher, R., Manning, C.D., Ng, A.Y.: Improving word representations via global context and multiple word prototypes. In: Proceedings of the 50th Annual Meeting of the Association for Computational Linguistics: Long Papers, vol. 1, pp. 873–882. Association for Computational Linguistics (2012)
14. Jindal, N., Liu, B.: Opinion spam and analysis. In: Proceedings of the 2008 International Conference on Web Search and Data Mining, pp. 219–230. ACM (2008)
15. Jindal, N., Liu, B., Lim, E.P.: Finding unusual review patterns using unexpected rules. In: Proceedings of the 19th ACM International Conference on Information and Knowledge Management, pp. 1549–1552. ACM (2010)
16. Kalchbrenner, N., Grefenstette, E., Blunsom, P.: A convolutional neural network for modelling sentences. arXiv preprint arXiv:1404.2188 (2014)
17. Le, Q.V., Mikolov, T.: Distributed representations of sentences and documents. arXiv preprint arXiv:1405.4053 (2014)
18. Li, J.: Feature weight tuning for recursive neural networks. arXiv preprint arXiv:1412.3714 (2014)
19. Li, J., Jurafsky, D., Hovy, E.: When are tree structures necessary for deep learning of representations? arXiv preprint arXiv:1503.00185 (2015)
20. Li, J., Ott, M., Cardie, C.: Identifying manipulated offerings on review portals. In: EMNLP, pp. 1933–1942 (2013)
21. Li, J., Ott, M., Cardie, C., Hovy, E.: Towards a general rule for identifying deceptive opinion spam
22. Lim, E.P., Nguyen, V.A., Jindal, N., Liu, B., Lauw, H.W.: Detecting product review spammers using rating behaviors. In: Proceedings of the 19th ACM International Conference on Information and Knowledge Management, pp. 939–948. ACM (2010)
23. Metaxas, P.T., DeStefano, J.: Web spam, propaganda and trust. In: AIRWeb, pp. 70–78 (2005)
24. Meyer, D.: Fake reviews prompt belkin apology. CNet News (2009)
25. Miller, C.: Company settles case of reviews it faked. New York Times (2009)
26. Mnih, A., Hinton, G.E.: A scalable hierarchical distributed language model. In: Advances in Neural Information Processing Systems, pp. 1081–1088 (2009)
27. Mukherjee, A., Kumar, A., Liu, B., Wang, J., Hsu, M., Castellanos, M., Ghosh, R.: Spotting opinion spammers using behavioral footprints. In: Proceedings of the 19th ACM SIGKDD International Conference on Knowledge Discovery and Data Mining, pp. 632–640. ACM (2013)
28. Mukherjee, A., Liu, B., Glance, N.: Spotting fake reviewer groups in consumer reviews. In: Proceedings of the 21st International Conference on World Wide Web, pp. 191–200. ACM (2012)
29. Mukherjee, A., Liu, B., Wang, J., Glance, N., Jindal, N.: Detecting group review spam. In: Proceedings of the 20th International Conference Companion on World Wide Web, pp. 93–94. ACM (2011)
30. Ntoulas, A., Najork, M., Manasse, M., Fetterly, D.: Detecting spam web pages through content analysis. In: Proceedings of the 15th International Conference on World Wide Web, pp. 83–92. ACM (2006)

31. Ott, M.: Computational linguistic models of deceptive opinion spam (2013)
32. Ott, M., Cardie, C., Hancock, J.: Estimating the prevalence of deception in online review communities. In: Proceedings of the 21st International Conference on World Wide Web, pp. 201–210. ACM (2012)
33. Ott, M., Cardie, C., Hancock, J.T.: Negative deceptive opinion spam. In: HLT-NAACL, pp. 497–501 (2013)
34. Ott, M., Choi, Y., Cardie, C., Hancock, J.T.: Finding deceptive opinion spam by any stretch of the imagination. In: Proceedings of the 49th Annual Meeting of the Association for Computational Linguistics: Human Language Technologies, vol. 1, pp. 309–319. Association for Computational Linguistics (2011)
35. Pennington, J., Socher, R., Manning, C.D.: Glove: Global vectors for word representation. In: Proceedings of the Empiricial Methods in Natural Language Processing (EMNLP 2014) vol. 12, pp. 1532–1543 (2014)
36. Socher, R., Bauer, J., Manning, C.D., Ng, A.Y.: Parsing with compositional vector grammars. In: Proceedings of the ACL Conference. Citeseer (2013)
37. Socher, R., Huval, B., Manning, C.D., Ng, A.Y.: Semantic compositionality through recursive matrix-vector spaces. In: Proceedings of the 2012 Joint Conference on Empirical Methods in Natural Language Processing and Computational Natural Language Learning, pp. 1201–1211. Association for Computational Linguistics (2012)
38. Socher, R., Lin, C.C., Manning, C., Ng, A.Y.: Parsing natural scenes and natural language with recursive neural networks. In: Proceedings of the 28th International Conference on Machine Learning (ICML-2011), pp. 129–136 (2011)
39. Socher, R., Perelygin, A., Wu, J.Y., Chuang, J., Manning, C.D., Ng, A.Y., Potts, C.: Recursive deep models for semantic compositionality over a sentiment treebank. In: Proceedings of the Conference on Empirical Methods in Natural Language Processing (EMNLP), vol. 1631, p. 1642. Citeseer (2013)
40. Streitfeld, D.: For 2 a star, an online retailer gets 5 star product reviews. New York Times, 26 January 2012
41. Tang, D., Wei, F., Yang, N., Zhou, M., Liu, T., Qin, B.: Learning sentiment-specific word embedding for twitter sentiment classification. In: Proceedings of the 52nd Annual Meeting of the Association for Computational Linguistics, vol. 1, pp. 1555–1565 (2014)
42. Topping, A.: Historian orlando figes agrees to pay damages for fake reviews. The Guardian, 16 July 2010
43. Turian, J., Ratinov, L., Bengio, Y.: Word representations: a simple and general method for semi-supervised learning. In: Proceedings of the 48th Annual Meeting of the Association for Computational Linguistics, pp. 384–394. Association for Computational Linguistics (2010)
44. Wang, G., Xie, S., Liu, B., Yu, P.S.: Review graph based online store review spammer detection. In: 2011 IEEE 11th International Conference on Data Mining (ICDM), pp. 1242–1247. IEEE (2011)
45. Wu, B., Davison, B.D.: Identifying link farm spam pages. In: Special Interest Tracks and Posters of the 14th International Conference on World Wide Web, pp. 820–829. ACM (2005)
46. Yessenalina, A., Cardie, C.: Compositional matrix-space models for sentiment analysis. In: Proceedings of the Conference on Empirical Methods in Natural Language Processing, pp. 172–182. Association for Computational Linguistics (2011)
47. Yoo, K.H., Gretzel, U.: Comparison of deceptive and truthful travel reviews. In: Höpken, W., Gretzel, U., Law, R. (eds.) Information and Communication Technologies in Tourism, pp. 37–47. Springer, Heidelberg (2009)

A Practical Keyword Recommendation Method Based on Probability in Digital Publication Domain

Yuejun Li[1,2(✉)], Xiao Feng[1], and Shuwu Zhang[1]

[1] Institute of Automation, Chinese Academy of Sciences, Beijing 100190, China
273253612@qq.com, {xiao.feng,shuwu.zhang}@ia.ac.cn
[2] Department of Computer Science and Technology,
Shandong Jianzhu University, Jinan 250101, China

Abstract. The increase of information and knowledge has brought great challenge in knowledge management which includes knowledge storage, information retrieval and knowledge sharing. In digital publication domain, books are segmented into items that focus on target topic for dynamic digital publication. The management of items has great need to annotate items automatically instead of annotating by editor manually. This paper proposed probability based and hybrid method to recommend meaningful keywords for items. Experiment shows that the methods we proposed get more than 90 % precision, recall and f1 value on the digital publication dataset which outperforms the traditional extraction based and tfidf similarity based method in keyword recommendation.

Keywords: Keywords recommendation · Probability based keywords recommendation · Digital library

1 Introduction

Keywords summarize a document concisely and give a high-level description of the document content [1]. Keyword has been used in various domains which include document summarization [2], document classification, document clustering [3], document retrieval, topic search, and document analysis [1]. As the development of digital libraries and publication, there is a need to assemble new books or resources by taking advantage of books which having been published and stored in digital libraries. Editors of the press segment the book into hundreds of items which is subject to one's own topic. As each item is to some extent semantically independent from each other and correspond to one topic or more topics, previously, editors need to assign several keywords to the item manually according to its meaning which is a time-consuming process. When more new books come, the workload of editors to designate new keywords becomes heavier. So an automatic keyword recommendation mechanism is needed to faster the process of making items of books.

Numerous methods have been proposed to automatically extract keywords from a text. Keyword extraction technique tries to extract words that can summarize the text mostly which means the keyword must come from the text content.

© Springer International Publishing Switzerland 2015
M. Sun et al. (Eds.): CCL and NLP-NABD 2015, LNAI 9427, pp. 405–416, 2015.
DOI: 10.1007/978-3-319-25816-4_33

In digital libraries and publication domain, there are huge amount of books accumulated that can be used as corpus of developing automatic keyword recommendation system. The problem is when a new item comes, what keywords should be recommended. Traditional keyword extraction method like the TextRank [4] can extract important words from item, but in many cases, the keyword may even not appear in the content of the item. Under such circumstances, traditional keyword extraction can't solve the problem independently and it needs a supervised method to conduct the keyword recommendation process. The focus of this paper is to solve the item keyword recommendation problem using supervised keyword recommendation algorithm.

2   Keyword Extraction Methods

Earlier techniques mainly focus on the word frequencies of the text or the TFIDF values to determine the weight of the candidate words [5]. Although the frequency of word can imply the importance of the word in some cases, there are still some cases that the important words appear only few times. To overcome the problem of frequency-based keyword extraction method, graph-based method is proposed which is inspired by the PageRank [6] via building network of words/phrases and ranking the node using some kind of centrality measure, variants of the graph based method include [2] and HITS [7]. Semantic method is supposed to bring meaningful information to keyword extraction. Semantic relation of words can be found with help of WordNet or Wikipedia and HowNet to recommend semantically similar words of original words in the text. Topic modeling methods which include LSA, PLSA, and LDA are used to mind hidden topic to improve accuracy and coverage ability of keywords.

Keyword extraction can be formulated as a supervised classification problem. The word or phrase to be classified is represented as a vector of features which may include tf-idf [1] values, length or occurrence position [8]. A training set which is annotated as positive and negative should be provided, and during the testing phase, the candidate keywords should be formulated as a feature vector to be classified. Variants of machine learning method are used which include SVM [1], decision trees, conditional random fields [9]. The shortcoming of the supervised method is that it needs a manually constructed training set which is time-consuming and hard to get.

3   TFIDF-Similarity Based Keyword Recommendation

Traditional extraction method can extract keywords from the content itself. But when the content of the document is not long enough it will be difficult to extract useful keywords from the document directly. Recommending existed keywords to new documents can be implemented with the help of tfidf similarity based keyword recommendation technology which is described in [10].

Given a document set $D\{d_1, d_2, \ldots, d_n\}$, every document is annotated with several keywords: $d_i = \{text, tagset\}$, where the tagset comprised of several keywords and all the keywords form a keyword library T. Once there comes a new document q, we need to recommend proper existed keywords based on its content. The process can be described in two steps:

Step1. Compute $P(t|q,T,D)$, which is the probability of every keyword in keyword library T, comparing the new document q with document in D.

Step2. Sort $P(t|q,T,D)$ in descending order and select the top k keywords as the final recommendation.

$P(t|q,T,D)$ can be formulated as follows:

$$P(t|q,T,D) = \frac{keyWeight(t,q,D)}{\sum_{t \in T} keyWeight(t,q,D)} \tag{1}$$

Where $keyWeight(t,q,D)$ is the weight of keyword t according to the similarity of document t with all document in D.

$$keyWeight(t,q,D) = \sum_{d \in D} DocSim(q,d) \times isTag(t,d) \tag{2}$$

$DocSim(q,d)$ is the similarity of new document q and document d of corpus D and we select the cosine similarity measure to compute similarity.

$$DocSim(q,d) = \frac{q \cdot d}{\|q\| \times \|d\|} = \frac{\sum_{i=1}^{n} q_i \times d_i}{\sqrt{\sum_{j=1}^{n} q_i^2} \times \sqrt{\sum_{j=1}^{n} d_i^2}} \tag{3}$$

$$isTag(t,d) = \begin{cases} 1 & t \in d \\ 0 & t \notin d \end{cases} \tag{4}$$

When d is annotated with keyword t, then isTag(t,d) is given the value 1, otherwise is given to 0.

The q and d vector is the TF-IDF value of each word in document q and d.

$$q = (tfidf(w_1), tfidf(w_2), \ldots .tfidf(w_n)) \tag{5}$$

4 Probability-Based Keyword Recommendation

4.1 Problem Definition

Our keyword recommendation method of items in dynamic publication domain can be formulated as follows. The training set is composed of items annotated with keywords by editors.

TraininSet = {[Tags(1),Item(1),ClassId(1)],[Tags(2),Item(2),ClassId(2)],…,[Tags(i), Item(i),ClassId(i)),…, [Tags(n), Item(n), ClassId(n)]}, where Tags(i) is the keyword set assigned to item i by editors. Tags(i) = (key(1), key (2), ..., key(m)) where key(i) is the keyword and the keyword number m varies from one to ten or more. In digital publication areas, the keyword number for each item often varies from 3 to 5. ClassId(i) is the category id of item i which suggests that the item belongs to the class i. We utilize the text classify technology to classify the item first in order to narrow the range of recommending keywords because the training set is usually very large, direct keyword recommendation would face the problem that there are thousands of keywords to be evaluated and to find the best keywords in them is a difficult thing. Due to fact that the items of the training set have the information of classification, when a new item comes, through the process of classification, an item first can be classified to proper category, and then the keywords in the category can be recommended to the new item base on its content.

The process can be described as follows: First we run the classification algorithm to find the category of item with the result category k; Given a new item, our aim is to compute the probability of every keyword in category k and it can be described as follows: we compute the probability $p(k_i|item)$, where k_i is the keyword from category k. Then we sort the list of $p(k_i|item)$ and select the top k as the candidate keywords of item.

4.2   Probabilistic Modeling

The Bayes probability theory is used in modeling the probability of keywords k_i that mostly delegate the item. Given a new item we need to compute the probability $p(k_i|item)$:

$$p(k_i|item) = \frac{p(item|k_i) \times p(k_i)}{p(item)} \tag{6}$$

The probability of every new item is no different from each other, so we can ignore the probability $p(item)$, and the probability

$$p(k_i|item) \propto p(item|k_i) \times p(k_i) \tag{7}$$

Every item is a fragment of text composed of words/phrases, and we make a hypothesis that every word/phrases is independent from each other which we called bag of words model. The probability of item given the keyword k_i can be calculated as follows:

$$p(item|k_i) = \prod_{j=1}^{m} p(w_j|k_i) \tag{8}$$

where w_j is the term of item, and $p(w_j|k_i)$ is the probability of every term w_j of item when annotated keyword k_i occurs.

We models the probability $p(w_j|k_i)$ below which is different from that in [11] and more efficient in experiment result.

$$p(w_j|k_i) \propto \frac{tfidf(w_j) \times tf(w_j, k_i)}{p(k_i) \times \sqrt{\sum_{j=1}^{m} tf^2(w_j, k_i)}} \quad (9)$$

$tfidf(w_j)$ is the weight of term w_j which can be computed by the typical tfidf formulae.

$$tfidf(w_j) = tf(w_j) \times idf(w_j) \quad (10)$$

Where $tf(w_j)$ is term frequency of term w_j in item and $idf(w_j)$ is the inverse document frequency of term w_j.

$tf(w_j, k_i)$ is the term frequency of w_j in keywords k_i annotated items. $p(k_i)$ is the probability of keyword k_i in all the training set TR of category j and it can be computed as follows:

$$p(k_i) = \frac{tf(k_i, TR_j)}{\sum_{i} tf(k_i, TR_j)} \quad (11)$$

Where $tf(k_i, TR_j)$ is the term frequency of keywords k_i in the training set TR_j of category j.

In the training period, we first calculate the probability of $p(k_i), p(w_j|k_i)$, and stored the result to compute every $p(k_i|item)$ of each candidate keyword. Finally we sort $p(k_i|item)$ in descending order and select the top N keywords as the final recommendation.

5   A Hybrid Approach of Keyword Recommendation

The tfidf similarity based method and probability based method can utilize previous annotated keywords to precisely recommend meaningful keywords which keyword extraction techniques can't deal with. Keywords extraction method can find the relative words/phrases in the text content of items. In the scenarios of digital publication, some of the time, keywords that describe items do not come from the content directly but are some comprehensive words that describe the domain and character of the item, and some other time, if the item is quite different from existed training data, keywords extraction method would be useful in recommending new keywords to the editor. The editors audit and check the recommended keywords and give feedback to the system that whether the keywords are appropriate or not and give the right keywords to update the training model.

Our proposed algorithm selects a hybrid approach of keyword recommendation which considers both the probability based method and traditional extraction based method mentioned above. The reason we select extraction based method as the partner of probability based method is that we hope it can extract some useful words from the item directly where probability based method may not cover (Fig. 1).

Hybrid Approach of Keyword Recommendation

Input: item training set TR with annotated tags, new item to be annotated
Output: recommended N keywords of new item.
step1: for each annotated item in TR
        segment item into words(for Chinese words especially), delete stop words and xml tags.
step2: for each category j in TR
      for each annotated keyword k_i

$$\text{calculate } p(k_i) = \frac{tf(k_i, TR_j)}{\sum_{i=1}^{n} tf(k_i, TR_j)}$$

    serialize all $p(k_i)$
step3: for each category x in TR
      for each annotated keyword k_i
      for each word w_j in item of TR_k

$$\text{calculate } p(w_j \mid k_i) \propto \frac{tfidf(w_j) \times tf(w_j \mid k_i)}{p(k_i) \times \sqrt{\sum_{j=1}^{m} tf^2(w_j \mid k_i)}}$$

    serialize all $p(w_j \mid k_i)$
step4: classify new item into category x;
step5: for each annotated keyword k_i in category x

$$p(item \mid k_i) = \prod_{j=1}^{m} p(w_j \mid k_i)$$

$$p(k_i \mid item) \propto p(item \mid k_i) p(k_i)$$

step6: sort $p(k_i \mid item)$ and select the top N*(1-p) as key_probability.
step7: run TextRank keyword extraction algorithm, select top N*p keywords as key_extraction.
    p is the proportion of keywords which extraction based method generated in the final result.
step8: combine key_probability with key_ extraction result.

Fig. 1. Algorithm of hybrid keyword recommendation

Step1 to step3 is the training process of probability-based keyword recommendation. Step4 to step6 first classify the new item to category i, and then calculate the probability of every keyword in category i with respect to the new item. Step7 to step8 select part of the keywords from probability-based keyword recommendation and part of the keywords from the extraction based keyword recommendation method.

6   Experiments and Evaluation

6.1   Dataset

In digital publication domain, we have accumulated huge amounts of items collected from books published by the press. These items are xml texts which mainly contain Chinese words together with some English terminology. The annotated keywords are assigned to items by editors manually with each keyword consisting of one or more words. Items have been classified to a constrained category tree which will be used in the classification process. The dataset has 40147 annotated items in xml format with different category and number of keywords. We split the dataset into two parts: the training set and the test set and use the 10-fold cross-validation to test and validate our method. We evaluate our hybrid and probability based method against the traditional keyword extraction method (like TextRank [4]) and tfidf -similarity based method. We did not use the user study valuation method for that we have enough annotated items to test and the annotated items were annotated by expert editors who have enough authority in tagging work, and it also saves lots of time. The statistics of the corpus for training and testing is listed in Table 1.

Table 1. Statistics of the corpus for training and testing

Category	Number of docs	Number of keywords	Average doc length	Average number of keywords per doc
network security	2199	561	220	5.1
AutoCAD	1931	79	118	5.2
Java	1820	845	178	5.2
Electricity	884	162	52	4.1
photoshop	714	71	173	5.1
SCM	249	32	107	3.2
vehicle maintenance	169	9	123	6
graphics	134	489	129	5.3
...	...	...	...	...
Overall 98 categories	40147	21684	182	5

6.2   Evaluation Metrics

This section presents the evaluation metrics in our experiments which include precision, recall, F1. These metrics, when used in combination, have shown to be effective for evaluation of the effect of our method. Precision, recall, and F1 (F-measure) are well-known evaluation metrics in information retrieval literature [12]. T_r denotes the number of keywords returned by the algorithm when new item comes. We use the original set of keywords as the ground truth T_g.

In out experiment, Precision, recall and F1 measures are defined as follows:

$$precision = \frac{T_g \wedge T_r}{T_r}, recall = \frac{T_g \wedge T_r}{T_g}, F1 = \frac{2 \times precision \times recall}{precision + recall}$$

6.3 Results

We test the number of keywords recommended to the testing item from 1 to 15 using four different keyword recommendation algorithms which include the hybrid and probability based method we proposed. In the digital publication domain, editors often annotate 3 to 5 keywords/phrases per item, so we pay more attention to the result of keywords recommendation that recommend 3 to 5 keywords.

Figures 2, 3 and 4 plots the precision, recall and f1 value of the four different keywords recommendation method. We can see that the hybrid and probability based keywords recommendation methods we proposed outperform other methods like the tfidf-similarity based method and traditional keyword extraction method. The probability based method performs better than hybrid method when 3 to 5 keywords are recommended because the hybrid result contains keywords from the result of the traditional extraction method which result in the loss of precision. When one to five keywords are recommended, the probability based method can achieve precision more than 90 % which is much higher than the tfidf similarity and extraction based method.

Extraction based method performs worst since previous keyword annotation work of items is done by editors and the keywords annotated mostly are not from the content of the items directly but from a comprehensive understanding of the item. Another

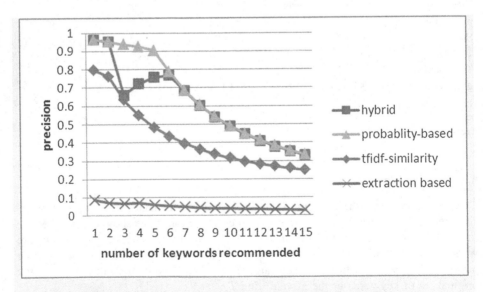

Fig. 2. Precision of four keywords recommendation method

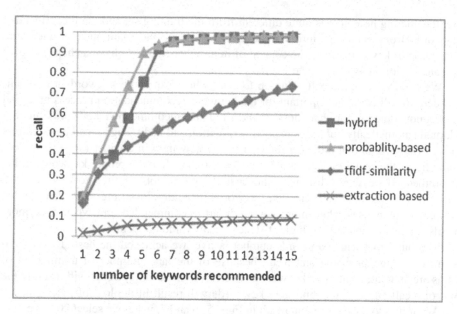

Fig. 3. Recall of four keywords recommendation method

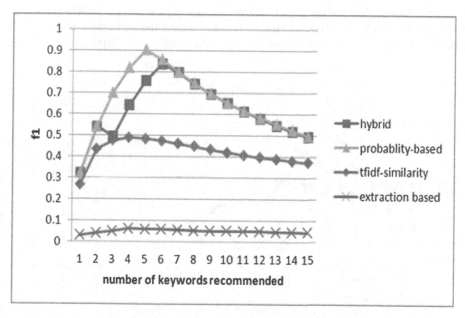

Fig. 4. F1 value of four keywords recommendation method

reason is that the average length of the items is only 182, and finding appropriate keywords in short item is not very easy for traditional keyword extraction method. But it does not means that we would abandon the extraction method because there are cases that the coming new item is quite different from the training set and the recommended keywords from statistical information may not cover the main idea of the item. Extraction of keywords from the content of item helps editors to have a chance to give personalization keywords to the item.

We achieve a high recall value up to 0.98 when 5 or more keywords are recommended. Recall is rather important for the keyword recommendation process in digital publication domain for that most of the time the recommended keywords are not adopted automatically but needs manual verification and audit. High recall helps editors to select keywords that are most relevant to the new item in a wider range while low recall limits the scope the editor and if the editor can't find the proper keywords in the recommended keywords list, it would cost the editor lots of time to look through the content of the item and select the keywords manually. From Fig. 3 we can see that the recall value rises when more keywords are recommended and when 5 or more words are recommended the highest steady recall value are achieved.

We found that when keywords number is five, we achieved the best f1 value(0.9) with pretty high precision and recall because of the large number of training set of items are annotated with five keywords. Less recommended keywords will result in the loss of recall and f1 value but more keywords will result in the loss of precision.

According to the experiment result in Figs. 5, 6 and 7, when we select 20 % percent of the result of extraction based method combining with 80 % percent of the result of probability based method, the relatively better precision, recall and f1 value are achieved. So we select the parameter ep20(0.2) as the p parameter in hybrid algorithm. The series ep0, ep20 to ep100 in Figs. 5, 6 and 7 means the percentage of extraction based method used in the final keyword recommendation process. ep0 equals with the

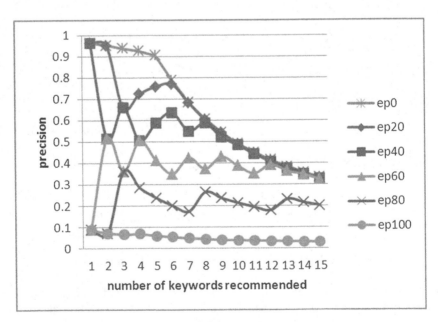

Fig. 5. Precision of Hybrid method with different proportion of extraction based method

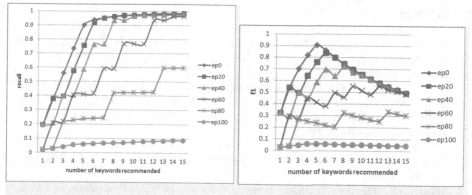

Fig. 6. Recall of Hybrid method with different proportion of extraction based method

Fig. 7. F1 value of Hybrid method with different proportion of extraction based method

probability based method and ep100 corresponds to the extraction based method. When editors hope recommend new keywords from the content of the item directly we can use the hybrid approach, otherwise, the probability approach are recommended.

7   Conclusions and Future Work

This paper presents probability based and hybrid keyword recommendation algorithm which get at most more than 90 % precision, recall and f1 value on the digital publication dataset which outperforms the traditional extraction based and tfidf similarity based method in keyword recommendation. The algorithm is motivated by the keyword annotation problem in digital publication. When there is a new item that is not annotated, the algorithm automatically recommends relative keywords to the editor.

The probability based method utilizes statistical information of annotated training sets to recommend existed annotated keywords to coming items. The hybrid method combines the traditional extraction based method and the probability based method to take advantage of the two methods. Experiments are done on the dataset of items of books provided by the press and show that probability based and hybrid method outperforms the traditional keyword extraction method and tfidf similarity based method. Future work includes experiment on other annotated datasets, improvement on topic model based algorithm and other extraction based algorithms.

Acknowledgments.   The paper is supported and completed under the financial aid of the National Science-Technology Support Plan Projects "Research and Development of Key Support Technology and Application Demonstration on Dynamic Digital Publishing" (2012BAH88F00, 2012BAH88F02).

References

1. Zhang, K., Xu, H., Tang, J., Li, J.: Keyword extraction using support vector machine. In: Yu, J.X., Kitsuregawa, M., Leong, H.-V. (eds.) WAIM 2006. LNCS, vol. 4016, pp. 85–96. Springer, Heidelberg (2006)
2. Litvak, M., Last, M.: Graph-based keyword extraction for single-document summarization. In: MMIES 2008 Proceedings of the Workshop on Multi-source Multilingual Information Extraction and Summarization, pp. 17–24. Association for Computational Linguistics, Stroudsburg, PA, USA (2008)
3. Tonella, P., Ricca, F., Pianta, E., Girardi, C.: Using keyword extraction for web site clustering. In: Fifth International Workshop on Web Site Evolution, pp. 41–48. IEEE Press, New York (2003)
4. Mihalcea, R., Tarau, P.: TextRank: bringing order into texts. In: Proceedings of EMNLP 2004, pp 404–411. Association for Computational Linguistics, Barcelona, Spain (2004)
5. Salton, G., Buckley, C.: Term-weighting approaches in automatic text retrieval. Inf. Proces. Manage. J. **24**(5), 513–523 (1988)
6. Page, L., Brin, S., Motwani, R., Winograd, T.: The pagerank citation ranking: bringing order to the web. In: Proceedings of the 7th International World Wide Web Conference, pp. 161–172, Brisbane, Australia (1998)
7. Wan, X.J., Xiao, J.G.: Single document keyphrase extraction using neighborhood knowledge. In: Proceedings of the 23rd national conference on Artificial intelligence (AAAI 2008), vol. 2, pp. 855–860. AAAI Press (2008)
8. Poibeau, T., Saggion, H., Piskorski J.: Multi-source multilingual information extraction and summarization. In: MMIES 2008, pp 17–24. Association for Computational Linguistics, Stroudsburg, PA, USA (2008)
9. Zhang, C.Z., Wang, H.L., Liu, Y., Wu, D., Liao, Y., Wang, B.: Automatic keyword extraction from documents using conditional random fields. J. Comput. Inf. Syst. **4**, 1169–1180 (2008)
10. Tuarob, S., Pouchard, L.C., Giles, C.L.: Automatic tag recommendation for metadata annotation using probabilistic topic modeling. In: Proceedings of the 13th ACM/IEEE-CS Joint Conference on Digital Libraries, vol. 15, pp. 239–248. ACM (2013)
11. Ni, N., Liu, K., Li, Y.D.: Study of automatic keywords labeling for scientific literature. J. Comput. Sci. **39**(9), 175–179 (2012)
12. Manning, C.D., Raghavan, P., Schtze, H.: Introduction to Information Retrieval. Cambridge University Press, NewYork (2008)

Automatic Knowledge Extraction and Data Mining from Echo Reports of Pediatric Heart Disease: Application on Clinical Decision Support

Yahui Shi[1], Zuofeng Li[2], Zheng Jia[3], Binyang Hu[1], Meizhi Ju[3], Xiaoyan Zhang[1(✉)], and Haomin Li[4,5(✉)]

[1] School of Life Science and Technology, Tongji University, Shanghai, China
xyzhang@tongji.edu.cn
[2] HealthCare, Philips Research China, Shanghai, China
[3] College of Biomedical Engineering and Instrument Science,
Zhejiang University, Zhejiang, China
[4] The Children's Hospital of Zhejiang University, Zhejiang, China
hmli@zju.edu.cn
[5] The Institute of Translational Medicine, Zhejiang University, Zhejiang, China

Abstract. Echocardiography (Echo) reports of the patients with pediatric heart disease contain many disease related information, which provide great support to physicians for clinical decision. Such as treatment customization based on the risk level of the specific patient. With the help of natural language processing (NLP), information can be automatically extracted from free-text reports. Those structured data is much easier to analyze with the existing data mining approaches. In this study, we extract the entity/anatomic site-feature-value (EFV) triples in the Echo reports and predict the risk level on this basis. The prediction accuracy of machine learning and rule-based method are compared based on a manual prepared ideal data, to explore the application of automatic knowledge extraction on clinical decision support.

Keywords: Echo reports · Natural language processing · Knowledge extraction · Machine learning · Clinical decision support

1 Introduction

Echocardiography (Echo) is one of the most widely used diagnostic tests in cardiology [1]. After examination, an Echo report recording the findings and conclusions is generated by the physician, which is regarded as an important evidence to support the clinical practice. Most electrocardiographic left ventricular hypertrophy (ECG-LVH) studies have used echocardiographic left ventricular mass (Echo-LVM) as the gold standard for evaluating ECG-LVH criteria [2]. Focused cardiopulmonary ultrasonography disclosed unexpected pathology in patients undergoing urgent surgical procedures [3]. When the patient is discharged, those reports are deposited in the database. As time goes on, there are more and more Echo reports being accumulated. In this

© Springer International Publishing Switzerland 2015
M. Sun et al. (Eds.): CCL and NLP-NABD 2015, LNAI 9427, pp. 417–424, 2015.
DOI: 10.1007/978-3-319-25816-4_34

situation, natural language processing (NLP) technique has been popularly used in medical domain to facilitate the conversion from free-text clinical records to structured data for analysis/mining [4]. Many studies have focused on such data sources to discover interesting pattern, to find a way to transform current clinical workflow and to improve the clinical quality [5–7]. Moreover, integrating NLP tool into decision support system also makes it possible to alert the physician to ambiguities and omissions when a report is generated [8].

We adopt a hybrid approach to extract and organize the anatomic site-related description in the Echo reports. Mining on these converted data is expected to provide evidence support and novel knowledge for clinical practice. In this study, a risk level is predicted for the patient based on the Echo report processed by the NLP module. Machine learning and rule-based methods are compared for their prediction performance.

2 Data and Methods

2.1 Data Collection

Currently, more and more patients would like to put their data online for consultant. Some patients voluntarily post their reports to ask the physician for medical advice. In some cases, the consultant information is freely available online (www.haodf.com, http://dxy.com/faq, etc.). At the same time, many hospitals have opened forums for the communication between physicians and patients such as Fuwai hospital, Shanghai Children's Medical Center (SCMC) and Fudan tumor hospital. Some physicians are actively involved in the online consultant. In this study, we use the data from SCMC. For each post, the physician ranks the risk level based on the Echo report contents and the patient's condition. This evaluation ranges from level one to level five as the risk increasing. (For detailed guideline refer to http://www.ibabyheart.com/hazard.html). In this study, those Echo report contents and the risk evaluation results are collected and analyzed.

A home-made python script is used to collect the posts from the Neonatal Congenital Heart Disease Forum, which filters the web pages with the keywords of "color Doppler ultrasound reports" ("彩超报告"). As labeled by xml tags, Echo report contents and the corresponding risk level evaluations are automatically recognized and extracted from the target web pages. The contents are organized in a flat file containing several sections (as shown in Fig. 1).

7062 posts posted before 2015 March were collected from the forum. 3464 posts among them contain both the Echo report contents and risk level evaluation, on which we try to explore our knowledge extraction and data mining approaches.

2.2 Free Text to Structured Data

Information Extraction and Normalization. A hybrid approach was adopted to extract all data from free text of Chinese Echo reports. The output of each step is the input of the next one. Firstly, we use the software CRF++ (version 0.58) to train a CRF

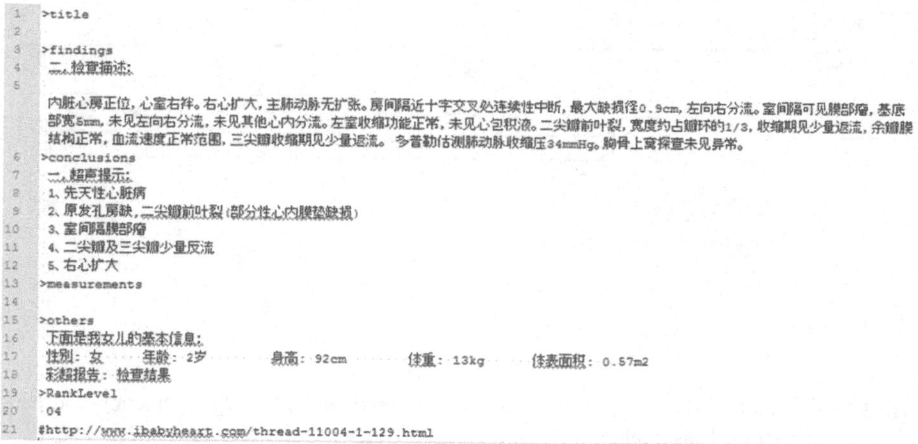

```
1   >title
2
3   >findings
4    一、检查描述：
5
    内脏心房正位，心室右袢。右心扩大，主肺动脉无扩张。房间隔近十字交叉处连续性中断，最大缺损径0.9cm。左向右分流。室间隔可见膜部瘤，基底部5mm。未见左向右分流，未见其他心内分流。左室收缩功能正常。未见心包积液。二尖瓣前叶裂，宽度约占瓣环的1/3，收缩期见少量返流，余瓣膜结构正常，血流速度正常范围，三尖瓣收缩期见少量返流。 多普勒估测肺动脉收缩压34mmHg。胸骨上窝探查未见异常。
6   >conclusions
7    二、超声提示：
8    1、先天性心脏病
9    2、原发孔房缺，二尖瓣前叶裂(部分性心内膜垫缺损)
10   3、室间隔膜部瘤
11   4、二尖瓣及三尖瓣少量反流
12   5、右心扩大
13   >measurements
14
15   >others
16   下面是我女儿的基本信息：
17   性别：女      年龄：2岁        身高：92cm        体重：13kg      体表面积：0.57m2
18   彩超报告：检查结果
19   >RankLevel
20   04
21   #http://www.ibabyheart.com/thread-11004-1-129.html
```

Fig. 1. An example showing file format. Each section is labeled by a title initiating with a right angle bracket (>).

model, which labels the free text reports with three classes: entity (anatomic site), feature and value. Secondly, a series of rules are applied to build the semantic relationships among the text spans. Then the pathological description about the anatomic sites in the raw text is converted to several Entity-Feature-Value (EFV) entries. Each entry consists of semantically related entity, feature and value. Thirdly, the labeled text spans are normalized and coded with the pre-defined ontology for entity and the dictionaries for each class. A dynamic programming-based algorithm is designed to implement the dictionary-look-up approach. The context information is used for the disambiguation of general words. After all the concepts are normalized, each EFV triple can be represented by a set of codes. Those codes are alphabetically sorted and jointed to form a string, which is called EFVCode. Lastly, the EFVCodes that we're interested in are collected to form a standard set of attributes for further analysis. Those attributes can be either Boolean or quantitative (Fig. 2). In this way, each report can be represented by a vector containing values of each attributes. The whole set of reports can be converted into a matrix for data mining, where every record represents a report and every column represents an attribute.

IdealData. For the sake of performance evaluation, 50 Echo reports (10 for each risk level) are randomly selected for manual annotation, generating the ground truth, which is called "IdealData". The details about annotation are described in Sect. 2.3.

Since it can be regarded as the perfect result of knowledge extraction, the IdealData can be used to compare the accuracy of machine learning and rule-based risk prediction. We feed it to the knowledge module to explore its application in clinical decision support.

2.3 Manual Annotation

Knowtator plug-in for Protégé is used as the annotation tool for tagging and semantic link. For normalization procedure and target entry selection, manual annotations are

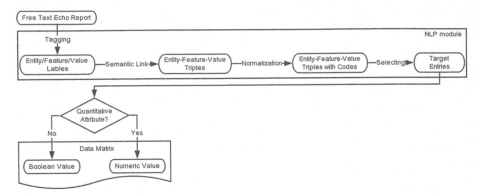

Fig. 2. Flow chart to show the NLP module (upper box) for knowledge extraction and data matrix for further analysis/mining.

organized in flat files. In a former work, two annotators have double annotated 420 templates of adult echo report for training the CRF model, which extracts EFV entries from free-text echo reports. After several rounds of discussion on the difficult cases and differences between two annotators' decisions, the final Inter-Annotator Agreement (IAA) has achieved 95.96% on average. The agreed annotation strategies were taken as the annotation guidelines.

In this study, as time and resources are limited, 5 trained annotators (including the two annotators mentioned before) prepared the IdealData collaboratively. Then the annotations were reviewed and refined by the most experienced annotator, to be consistent with the annotation guidelines.

2.4   Knowledge Module

Rule-Based Model. Based on the detailed guideline about risk level evaluation, we have built up a rule-based module as the baseline system. This module takes the data matrix (described in Sect. 2.2) as input and output the risk level evaluation. To build the module, the keywords in the definition of each risk level are picked out to be the criteria, like "complete transposition of great arteries, without pulmonary stenosis" for level five, "double outlet right ventricle" for level four, "atrial septal defect" for level three, "ventricular septal defect" for level two and "diameter of oval foramen less than 4 mm, and age not more than 3 months" for level one, and so on. For each patient, we firstly decide whether he/she belongs to the highest risk level. If the document is classified into this level, the work is done. If not, the patient will be evaluated with the criteria for the next level. If no risk level has been classified, the document will be labeled as 'unclassified' (as shown in Fig. 3).

Machine Learning Model. After machine learning, we get an EFV-based classifier, which takes the extraction results from NLP module as the input (data matrix

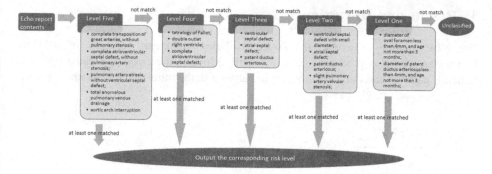

Fig. 3. The workflow to show the rule-based module for risk level evaluation.

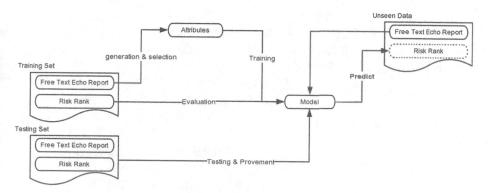

Fig. 4. The workflow of building the machine learning model for risk level prediction.

introduced in Sect. 2.2) to predict the risk level. Figure 4. shows the workflow of building the machine learning model.

We use the software Weka (version 3.6) as the tool to train a decision tree for prediction. The algorithm returns readable rules, making it possible for us to compare those rules to the physician's definition, conduct further improvement on both modules, and find some interesting results from the model.

2.5   Evaluation

For the performance of NLP part, the system output is evaluated against the IdealData. The risk level that physician provided in the online replies are used as ground truth, which are also extracted from the web pages during the data collection. By comparing the model prediction with the ground truth, we can calculate the accuracy of the prediction. The rule-based prediction is directly compared with the ground truth to get the performance. While the classifier trained by machine learning is validated through a 10-fold cross-validation approach.

3   Results and Discussion

The NLP module to extract the target attributes yields an accuracy of 0.44 in
F1-measure (0.51 in precision; 0.43 in recall). Most of the errors are caused by the
semantic patterns and clinical terms that are unseen in the training data, which is mainly

```
J48 pruned tree
------------------

三尖瓣收缩期反流 = 未提及
|   房水平分流 = 向右: 四级 (3.0/1.0)
|   房水平分流 = 未提及
|   |   房室瓣开放 = 未提及
|   |   |   二尖瓣位机械瓣功能正常 = 未提及
|   |   |   |   心包胸腔积液 = 未提及
|   |   |   |   |   室间隔回声 = 未提及
|   |   |   |   |   |   室间隔膜周部回声中断 = 未提及
|   |   |   |   |   |   |   肺动脉瓣血流速度 = 未提及
|   |   |   |   |   |   |   |   室间隔延续 = 完整: 二级 (2.0)
|   |   |   |   |   |   |   |   室间隔延续 = 未提及: 五级 (13.0/5.0)
|   |   |   |   |   |   |   |   室间隔延续 = 无中断: 二级 (1.0)
|   |   |   |   |   |   |   |   室间隔延续 = 中断: 五级 (0.0)
|   |   |   |   |   |   |   肺动脉瓣血流速度 = 未见增快: 五级 (0.0)
|   |   |   |   |   |   |   肺动脉瓣血流速度 = 正常: 五级 (0.0)
|   |   |   |   |   |   |   肺动脉瓣血流速度 = 增快: 二级 (2.0)
|   |   |   |   |   |   室间隔膜周部回声中断 = 中断: 三级 (2.0)
|   |   |   |   |   室间隔回声 = 完整: 三级 (1.0)
|   |   |   |   |   室间隔回声 = 中断: 三级 (4.0)
|   |   |   |   |   室间隔回声 = 无明显缺失: 二级 (5.0/1.0)
|   |   |   |   心包胸腔积液 = TRUE: 三级 (0.0)
|   |   |   |   心包胸腔积液 = 未见: 四级 (3.0/1.0)
|   |   |   二尖瓣位机械瓣功能正常 = 正常: 一级 (2.0)
|   |   房室瓣开放 = 可: 一级 (4.0/1.0)
|   |   房室瓣开放 = 正常: 四级 (1.0)
|   房水平分流 = 未见: 一级 (1.0)
|   房水平分流 = 双向: 四级 (2.0)
|   房水平分流 = 双向|向右: 四级 (1.0)
三尖瓣收缩期反流 = 少量: 四级 (2.0)
三尖瓣收缩期反流 = 可见: 五级 (1.0)
```

Fig. 5. The decision tree generated from IdealData using J48 algorithm provided by Weka. The
values in the parentheses represent the number of training instances reaching the leaf and that of
the misclassified (if any) respectively.

from the adult Echo reports. This indicates that further optimization is needed for the adaptation of the NLP tool to a new domain.

To explore whether the machine learning method can be used to automatic knowledge extraction, we trained a decision tree based on the IdealData (Fig. 5), whose prediction performance is provided in Table 1.

From the decision tree above, we can find it covers some criteria mentioned in the risk level evaluation guideline while referring to some other information. On one hand, this result indicates that the machine learning method is able to find the key information for clinical decision support. On the other hand, with further investigation, the newly found attributes may provide some novel knowledge for clinical practice.

Table 1. Accuracy of the machine learning system

Class	Precision	Recall	F-Measure	ROC Area
Level One	0.7	0.7	0.7	0.794
Level Two	0.429	0.3	0.353	0.519
Level Three	0.714	0.5	0.588	0.716
Level Four	0.286	0.2	0.235	0.575
Level Five	0.211	0.4	0.276	0.439
Weighted Avg.	0.468	0.42	0.43	0.609

The same data is also fed into the rule-based system. However, some definitions about the risk level are still vague, like "slightly defect" and "small diameter". Moreover, as there are many variations in the expression pattern, many criteria for risk level evaluation mentioned by the guideline can't be exactly found in the real-life reports. Thus 44 records in the IdealData can't be classified with the rule-based system. Among the others, 2 patients are correctly assigned to level three, 1 patient is correctly assigned to level two and 3 patients belonging to level four are misclassified as level three.

4 Conclusions and Future Work

Machine learning is a promising method for clinical decision support compared with the rule-based approach especially when there is no completed knowledge ready. The result indicates that our approach is powerful to facilitate the data mining on clinical free text. The key features and the rules extracted by our method are reasonable and conducive for clinical decision supporting.

For the next step, we will further improve the knowledge extraction and risk prediction accuracy and make the both modules more generalizable and extendable. In the future, the NLP module can be integrated into the report generating system, which alerts the physician when any critical information is omitted in the Echo reports. On the data matrix, other data mining approaches will be explored to utilize its clinical application.

Acknowledgment. The project is supported by the National Natural Science Foundation of China (81573023).

References

1. Maleki, M., Esmaeilzadeh, M.: The evolutionary development of echocardiography. Iran. J. Med. Sci. **37**, 222–232 (2012)
2. Rautaharju, P.M., Soliman, E.Z.: Electrocardiographic left ventricular hypertrophy and the risk of adverse cardiovascular events: A critical appraisal. J. Electrocardiol. **47**, 649–654 (2014)
3. Botker, M.T., Vang, M.L., Grofte, T., Sloth, E., Frederiksen, C.A.: Routine pre-operative focused ultrasonography by anesthesiologists in patients undergoing urgent surgical procedures. Acta Anaesthesiol. Scand. **58**, 807–814 (2014)
4. Hughes, K., et al.: The feasibility of using natural language processing to extract clinical information from breast pathology reports. J. Pathol. Inform. **3**, 23 (2012)
5. Krysiak-Baltyn, K., et al.: Compass: a hybrid method for clinical and biobank data mining. J. Biomed. Inform. **47**, 160–170 (2014)
6. Reiner, B.: Uncovering and improving upon the inherent deficiencies of radiology reporting through data mining. J. Digit. Imaging **23**, 109–118 (2010)
7. Mani, S., et al.: Medical decision support using machine learning for early detection of late-onset neonatal sepsis. J. Am. Med. Inform. Assoc. **21**, 326–336 (2014)
8. Bozkurt, S., Rubin, D.: Automated detection of ambiguity in BI-RADS assessment categories in mammography reports. Stud. Health Technol. Inform. **197**, 35–39 (2014)

Author Index

Printed in the USA, IS img.

By Bookmasters

Printed in the United States
By Bookmasters